WET ICE 2000

Proceedings

IEEE 9th International Workshops on Enabling Technologies: Infrastructure for Collaborative Enterprises

(WET ICE 2000)

June 14–16, 2000
National Institute of Standards and Technology, Gaithersburg, Maryland, USA

Sponsored by

IEEE Computer Society
Concurrent Engineering Research Center (CERC), West Virginia University
National Institute of Standards and Technology, USA
Linköping University, Sweden

Hosted by

National Institute of Standards and Technology, USA

IEEE COMPUTER SOCIETY

Los Alamitos, California
Washington · Brussels · Tokyo

IEEE Computer Society Order Number PR00798
ISBN 0-7695-0798-0
ISBN 0-7695-0800-6 (microfiche)
ISSN 1080-1383

Additional copies may be ordered from:

IEEE Computer Society
Customer Service Center
10662 Los Vaqueros Circle
P.O. Box 3014
Los Alamitos, CA 90720-1314
Tel: + 1 714 821 8380
Fax: + 1 714 821 4641
http://computer.org/
csbooks@computer.org

IEEE Service Center
445 Hoes Lane
P.O. Box 1331
Piscataway, NJ 08855-1331
Tel: + 1 732 981 0060
Fax: + 1 732 981 9667
http://shop.ieee.org/store/
customer-service@ieee.org

IEEE Computer Society
Asia/Pacific Office
Watanabe Bldg., 1-4-2
Minami-Aoyama
Minato-ku, Tokyo 107-0062
JAPAN
Tel: + 81 3 3408 3118
Fax: + 81 3 3408 3553
tokyo.ofc@computer.org

Editorial production by Lorretta Palagi

Cover art design and production by Alex Torres

Printed in the United States of America by The Printing House

IEEE
COMPUTER
SOCIETY

Table of Contents

IEEE 9th International Workshops on Enabling Technologies: Infrastructure for Collaborative Enterprises—WET ICE 2000

Workshop: Evaluating Collaborative Enterprises

Session 1: Evaluating Collaborative Enterprises

Session 2: Collaboration System Evaluation Methods and Tools

Session 3: Application-Specific Collaborative Enterprises

Workshop: Enterprise Security

Session 1: Secure Computing

Session 2: Intrusion Detection

Session 3: Internet Protocol

Session 4: Malicious Code

Session 5: Access Control

Session 6: Workflow Security

Workshop: Web-Based Infrastructures and Coordination Architectures for Collaborative Enterprises

♦ Voted Best Paper in individual workshop.

Preface

WET ICE 2000 (the Ninth WET ICE) was successfully held at the National Institute of Standards and Technology, Gaithersburg, Maryland, June 14-16, 2000. This year there were four parallel workshops: Enterprise Security, Web-Based Infrastructures and Coordination Architectures for Collaborative Enterprises, Knowledge Media Networking, and Evaluating Collaborative Enterprises. The last one is a new workshop. Sixty-seven papers were submitted of which 42 full papers (63% acceptance) and six short papers were accepted for publication. The workshop participants came from 11 different countries thus maintaining the international character of WET ICE.

The three plenary speakers—Drs. William O. Mehuron (Director of Information Technology Laboratory, National Institute of Standards and Technology), Pradeep K. Khosla (Philip and Marsha Dowd Professor of Engineering, Carnegie Mellon University), and Jack Corley (Senior Vice President and Chief Technical Officer, Advance Technology Institute) enlightened the audience with their presentations on collaboration technologies from the perspectives of government, academia and industry, respectively.

I would like to thank the following organizations for supporting WET ICE 2000: National Institute of Standards and Technology, The Institute of Electrical and Electronics Engineers, Inc., Concurrent Engineering Research Center of West Virginia University, and Linköping University, Sweden. Many thanks to the organizers and the program committee members of the workshops for their sincere and diligent work. Special thanks go to the Program Chair Dr. Nahid Shahmehri of Linköping University. Following her suggestion, the best paper from each workshop was presented by the authors at the final joint session. I also want to extend my deep appreciation to Bonnie Kasten, William Hunt, Kasandra Kasten of West Virginia University, Yelena Turetskaya of Linköping University, and Beverly Kephart of NIST. My heartfelt thanks go to Dr. Sumitra Reddy, who with her relentless work and dedication ensured the success of the workshop.

I am pleased to announce that Dr. Robert Tolksdorf of Technical University of Berlin, Germany, agreed to be the General Chair, and Drs. Kirstie L. Bellman of Aerospace Integration Science Center, California, USA, and Gabriele Kotsis of University of Vienna, Austria, will be the Program Chairs of WET ICE 2001.

Ram D. Sriram

General Chair

WET ICE Organizing Committees

General Chair

Ram D. Sriram
Manufacturing Engineering Laboratory
National Institute of Standards and Technology, USA

Program Chair

Nahid Shahmehri
Department of Computer and Information Science
Linköping University, Sweden

Steering Committee

Yahya Al-Salqan
Sun Microsystems, USA

Miroslav Benda
Amazon.com, USA

V. Juggy Jagannathan
Concurrent Engineering Research Center, West Virginia University, USA

Srinivas Kankanahalli
Hewlett-Packard Company, USA

Jintae Lee
Department of Decision Science
University of Hawaii, USA

Charles Petrie
Center for Design Research
Stanford University, USA

Ramana Reddy
Concurrent Engineering Research Center, West Virginia University, USA

Sumitra Reddy
Concurrent Engineering Research Center, West Virginia University, USA

Alexander Schill
Faculty of Computer Science
Technical University of Dresden, Germany

Nahid Shahmehri
Department of Computer and Information Science
Linköping University, Sweden

Ram D. Sriram (ex-officio)
Manufacturing Engineering Laboratory, National Institute of Standards and Technology, USA

Plenary Speakers

William O. Mehuron
Information Technology Laboratory, National Institute of Standards and Technology, USA

Pradeep K. Khosla
Philip and Marsha Dowd Professor of Engineering
Carnegie Mellon University, USA

Jack Corley
Advance Technology Institute, USA

Workshop Coordinator

Sumitra Reddy
Concurrent Engineering Research Center
West Virginia University, USA

Business Management

Bonnie Kasten
Concurrent Engineering Research Center, West Virginia University, USA

William L. Hunt
Concurrent Engineering Research Center, West Virginia University, USA

Kasandra D. Kasten
Concurrent Engineering Research Center, West Virginia University, USA

Workshop Organizing Committees

Knowledge Media Networking

Chair

Fawzi Daoud, *GMD–German National Research Center on Information Technology, Germany*

Program Committee

Angi Voss, *GMD, Germany*
Annika Waern, *SICS, Sweden*
Celestin Sedogbo, *Thomson CSF/LCR, France*
Christoph Ramshorn, *Schlumberger Research, UK*
Daniel Thalmann, *EPFL, Switzerland*
Elisabeth Andre, *DFKI GmbH, Germany*
Fumio Hattori, *NTT Labs, Japan*
Hiroshi Yajima, *Hitachi Labs, Japan*
Ingrid Carlbom, *Bell Labs, USA*
John Davies, *British Telecom Labs, UK*
Keiichi Nakata, *GMD, Germany*
Kenji Takahashi, *NTT Labs, USA*
Larry Korba, *NRC, Canada*
Liempd E.P.M. Van, *KPN Labs, Netherlands*
Michael Muller, *Lotus Research, USA*
Mike Daily, *HRL Labs, USA*
Natalie Glance, *Xerox Labs, France*
Peter Kellock, *Kent Ridge Digital Labs, Singapore*
Peter G. Selfridge, *AT&T Labs,USA*
Rodger Lea, *Sony Labs, Japan*
Sharon Laskowski, *NIST, USA*
Stefan Noll, *FhG-IGD, Germany*
Takahiko Nomura, *Fuji-Xerox, Japan*
Thomas Kirk, *AT&T Labs, USA*
Tom Erickson, *IBM Research Labs, USA*
Toshiro Minam, *Kyushu University and Fujitsu, Japan*

Evaluating Collaborative Enterprises

Co-Chairs

Robert Allen, *University of Maryland, USA*
Michelle Steves, *National Institue of Standards and Technology (NIST), USA*

Program Committee

Jill Drury, *The Mitre Corporation, USA*
Tom Finholt, *University of Michigan,USA*
Saul Greenberg, *University of Calgary, Canada*
Carl Gutwin, *University of Saskatchewan, Canada*
Doug Johnson, *Hewlett Packard, USA*
Amy Knutilla, *Knutilla Technologies, USA*
Srinivas Nidamarthi, *Cambridge University, UK*
Leysia Palen, *University of Colorado, USA*
Jennifer Preece, *University of Maryland, USA*
Jean Scholtz, *DARPA, USA*
Eswaran Subrahmanian, *Carnegie Mellon University, USA*
Marian Williams, *University of Massachusetts Lowell, USA*

Enterprise Security

Chair

Yahya Al-Salqan, *Sun Microsystems, USA*

Co-Chairs

Wu Wen, *Science University of Tokyo, Japan*
Mourad Debbabi, *Laval University, Canada*

Program Committee

Robert Charpentier, *Dept. of National Defence, Canada*
Michael Geva, *Java Security Group, USA*
Dima Hamad, *Birzeit University, West Bank*
Karl Leung, *IVE, Hong Kong, China*
Steve Lloyd, *Entrust, Canada*
Douglas Maughan, *DARPA, USA*
Gary McGraw, *Reliable Software Technology Inc., USA*
Fumio Mizoguchi, *Science University of Tokyo, Japan*
Tim Polk, *NIST, USA*
Aravindan Ranganathan, *Sun Microsystems, USA*
Sumitra Reddy, *CERC, West Virginia University, USA*
Vipin Samar, *Oracle, USA*
Ryoichi Sasaki, *Hitachi, Japan*
Kyo-ho Shin, *Fuji-Xerox, Japan*
Bill Soley, *Sun Microsystems, USA*
Nadia Tawbi, *Laval University, Canada*
Robert Thomys, *BSI, Germany*
Mark Vandenwauver, *IBM, USA*
Tatu Ylen, *SSH Communications Security, Finland*
Nick Zhang, *XETI, USA*

Web-Based Infrastructures and Coordination Architectures for Collaborative Enterprises

Organizers

Kirstie L. Bellman, *Aerospace Integration Science Ctr., USA*
Gabriele Kostis, *University of Vienna, Austria*
Christopher Landauer, *Aerospace Integration Science Ctr., USA*
Gustaf Neumann, *University of Essen, Germany*
Robert Tolksdorf, *Technische Universität Berlin, Germany*
Franco Zambonelli, *Università di Modena e Reggio Emilia, Italy*

Program Committee

Giacomo Cabri, *Univ. of Modena and Reggio Emilia, Italy*
Marco Cremonini, *Università di Bologna, Italy*
Alois Ferscha, *University of Vienna, Austria*
Christian Huemer, *University of Vienna, Austria*
Karin Hummel, *University of Vienna, Austria*
Gal Kaminka, *Univ. of Southern California, USA*
Letizia Leonardi, *University of Modena and Reggio Emilia, Italy*
Markus Seidl, *University of Vienna, Austria*
Paolo Torroni, *Università di Bologna, Italy*
Rainer Telesko, *University of Vienna, Austria*
V. Jagannathan, *West Virginia University & CareFlow Net, Inc., USA*

Workshop Participants

Knowledge Media Networking

Margaret Corbit — *Cornell Theory Center, USA*
Fawzi Daoud — *GMD FOKUS, Germany*
Ralf Dörner — *Fraunhofer-AGC, Germany*
Daphne Economou — *Department of Computing and Mathematics, Manchester Metropolitan University, UK*
Marie-Pierre Gleizes — *IRIT – University Paul Sabatier, France*
Yoshihisa Gonno — *Information Broadcasting Laboratories, Inc. (IBLabs), Japan*
Paul Grimm — *Fraunhofer-AGC, Germany*
Claire Knight — *University of Durham, Department of Computer Science, UK*
Cristina Maria Russo Dos Santos — *Institut Eurecom, France*
Shervin Shirmohammadi — *SITE, University of Ottawa, Canada*
Rachuri Sudarsan — *NIST – Design and Process Group, USA*
Dawit Yimam-Seid — *GMD – German National Research Center for IT, Germany*

Evaluating Collaborative Enterprises

Ad Aerts — *Eindhoven University of Technology, Netherlands*
Janet Allen — *The G.W. Woodruff School of Mechanical Engineering, USA*
Robert Allen — *NIST – Design and Process Group, USA*
Evan Atkinson — *Johns Hopkins University Applied Physics Laboratory, USA*
Mark Brown — *ERIM (Environmental Research Institute of Michigan), USA*
Prasun Dewan — *University of North Carolina, USA*
Cheryl Victoria Foster — *Geometric and Intelligent Computing Laboratory, USA*
Carl Gutwin — *University of Saskatchewan, Canada*
David Thomas — *Hallenbeck Concurrent Technologies, USA*
Erik Edward Hayes — *Geometric and Intelligent Computer Laboratory; Drexel University, USA*
Amy J. Knutilla — *Knutilla Technologies, USA*
Emile L. Morse — *NIST, USA*
David Louis Pinelle — *University of Saskatchewan, Department of Computer Science, Canada*
Catherine Plaisant — *Human-Computer Interaction Laboratory – University of Maryland, USA*
Sumitra Reddy — *West Virginia University, USA*
Jean C. Scholtz — *Defense Advanced Research Projects Agency (DARPA), USA*
Monica Schraefel — *Knowledge Media Design Institute, University of Toronto, Canada*
Jonathan Carl Sevy — *Geometric and Intelligent Computer Laboratory, USA*
Michelle Steves — *NIST, USA*
Eswaran Subrahmanian — *Carnegie Mellon University, USA*
Angran Xiao — *Systems Realizations Lab, Georgia Institute of Technology, USA*
Vera Zaychik — *Geometric and Intelligent Computing Laboratory, USA*

Enterprise Security

Yahya Alsalqan — *Sun Microsystems Laboratories, USA*
Gookwhan Ahn — *Information and Communications University (ICU), Korea*
Gail-Joon Ahn — *George Mason University, USA*
Deborah Blanchard — *Digital Signature Trust Company, USA*
Germano Caronni — *Sun Microsystems Laboratories, USA*
Claudiu Gabriel Duma — *Linköping University, Sweden*
Warwick Ford — *VeriSign, Inc., USA*
Sheila Frankel — *NIST, USA*
Åsa Hagström — *Linköping University, Sweden*

Lin Han — *Linköping University, Sweden*
Hyung Woo Kang — *ETRI, Korea*
David Gilliam — *Jet Propulsion Laboratory, USA*
Béchir Ktari — *Laval University, Canada*
Stephen Macgregor — *University of Strathclyde, UK*
Fumio Mizoguchi — *Science University of Tokyo, Japan*
Kang Myong — *NRL, USA*
Nahid Shahmehri — *Linköping University, Sweden*
Ali Aydin Selcuk — *University of Maryland Baltimore County, USA*
Takamichi Saito — *Science University of Tokyo, Japan*
Wu Wen — *Science University of Tokyo, Japan*
Torbjorn Wiberg — *Umea University, Sweden*
Thomas J. Wu — *Arcot Systems, USA*

Web-Based Infrastructures and Coordination Architectures for Collaborative Enterprises

Lukasz Michal Beca — *Syracuse University, USA*
Kristie Bellman — *Aerospace Integration Science Ctr., USA*
Wolfram Conen — *Universität Essen, Germany*
Enrico Denti — *DEIS (Dipartimento di Elettronica, Informatica e Sistemistica) – Università di Bologna, Italy*
Peter Dew — *University of Leeds, UK*
Alois Ferscha — *Institute for Computer Science and Business Informatics, Austria*
Eckhart Köppen — *University of Essen, Germany*
Gabriele Kotsis — *University of Vienna, Austria*
Christopher Landauer — *Aerospace Integration Science Ctr., USA*
Kristina A. Olanders — *Logistics Management Institute, USA*
Ramana Reddy — *West Virginia University, USA*
Vassil Roussev — *University of North Carolina, USA*
Yea-Jou Shiau — *University of Nottingham, UK*
Ram D. Sriram — *NIST – Design and Process Group, USA*
Simon Szykman — *NIST – Design and Process Group, USA*
Robert Tolksdorf — *Technische Universität Berlin, Germany*
Susan Volk — *Jet Propulsion Laboratory, USA*
Yong Wang — *NIST – Design and Process Group, USA*
Pinar Yolum — *North Carolina State University, USA*
Franco Zambonelli — *Università di Modena e Reggio Emilia, Italy*

Workshop

Knowledge Media Networking

Chair

Fawzi Daoud, GMD–German National Research Center on Information Technology, Germany

Workshop Report: Knowledge Media Networking

Chair: Fawzi Daoud

GMD- German National Research Center on Information Technology
Email:f.daoud@ieee.org

Introduction

Historically, systems for linking and supporting robust social connections between people, whether they are in close proximity or distributed over longer distances, have included point to point solutions (letters, the automobile, telephone), task-focused or work-modeling solutions (memos, forms, manuals), and one-to-many broadcast solutions (radio, TV, newspapers). More recently, computationally-based systems have been designed to support various aspects of collaboration, coordination and community: email, newsgroups, bulletin boards, and shared task tools and other examples.

New media technologies are emerging to design interactive virtual environments in which humans can interact with one another. People as well as virtual entities would "inhabit" such local/networked spaces within a mixed reality. In order to make these environments really useful, rich, interesting and engaging places, users should not be imposed a heavy load of manipulating, interpreting, and integrating information.

Knowledge media channels would allow coupling media with appropriate processing and integration of knowledge from different sources, domains, media and to support activities and arrangements for teams, organizations, communities, working together over distance and time.

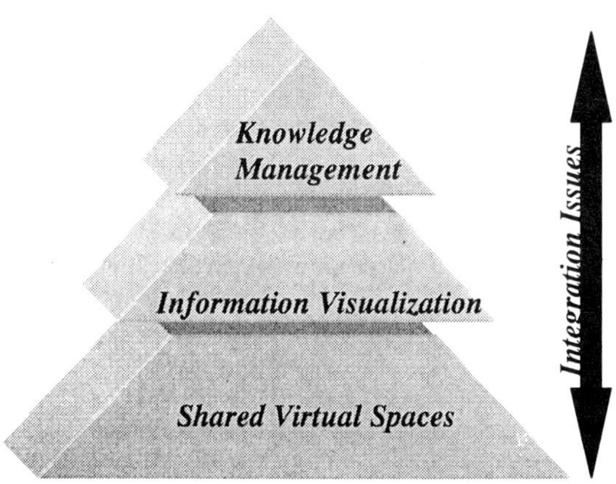

Technical Issues

The workshop on knowledge media networking has been concerned this year by three main topics: shared virtual environments, information visualization and knowledge management. Integration issues have been addressed in some cases.

The main focus of the ***Shared Virtual Environments*** has been on specific applications: mainly learning environments.

Learning types can be strongly related to different kinds of task behaviors: Searching for/receiving information (detects, observes, inspects, identifies, reads, surveys), Processing information (categorizes, calculates, codes, itemizes, tabulates, translates), Problem-solving (analyzes, formulates, estimates, plans), Decision-making (examines, chooses, compares, evaluates), Communication (advises, answers, directs, informs, instructs, requests, transmits), Sensory-motor processes (activates, adjusts, connects, regulates, tracks)

The behaviourist and programmed instruction model, where students learn by receiving pieces of information by the teachers reflects the traditional approach to education. Instructional design takes a very formal and precise approach to the design of learning environments. This approach is oriented to providing prescriptions of procedural sequences that should be applied to achieve the goal to help learners acquire structure.

In modern psychology learning is viewed as a dynamic process where a student through interacting with the world construct, tests and refines a cognitive representation to make sense of the world. Constructivist model is then concerned with a student's creation, management and linkage of new ideas to prior knowledge. An extended Constructivist model involves a large degree of student autonomy and initiative coupled with interaction between peers, teachers and other learning resources that are important factors in the cooperative, socio-cultural, and cognitive theories for learning. New approaches used to learning are grounded in and derived from constructivist epistemology: problem-based learning, generative

0-7695-0798-9/00 $10.00 © 2000 IEEE

learning, exploratory learning, situated cognition, anchored instruction, apprenticeship learning.

3D shared learning environments is well suited for constructivist based approach for learning. Some examples include training where these environments are used to simulate emergency conditions, to help you learn how to ski, to play the guitar or to dance. Another example may be architectural design to walk through the buildings and to test: alternative materials, colors, lighting and ergonomic factors. Recent studies on the affect of using 3D immersive environments in curriculum-based education suggest that virtual reality can enhance the learner's experience and help them understand such complex problems. Experience with these systems showed that these systems gain efficiency if the learner is not left on his own but receives some assistance. It is very helpful to be able to whisper back and forth with someone who is lost or confused, taking them out of the disrupting session. This assistance may be provided by a human tutor or by some avatars or agents. This technical support may relate to the manipulation and control of the interface, creation of custom content, and then introduction to the task at hand/ rules of the learning program. Knowledge based capabilities provide the means to 'rationalize' the behavior of a system from the standpoint of an external observer to fulfill the requirements of learning systems for example. The observer treats the system as a "black box" but maintains that it acts ,as if it possesses certain knowledge about the world and uses this knowledge in a perfectly rational way.

The focus of the ***Information Visualization*** has been based on 3D models: mainly the mapping between computer representation to perceived representation. Visual perceived representation has been considered. Generally such representation could be also auditory, tactile, etc. or a combination of these.

The main aspects of information visualization are: exploration/exploitation of information, enhancing understanding of concepts and processes, gaining new (unexpected, profound) insights, effective presentation of significant features, visualizing abstractions, quality control of simulations, measurements, increasing scientific productivity, medium of communication/collaboration.

Familiar visualization examples include histograms, plots, graphs, maps, images, surfaces, and volumes. By harnessing the perceptual abilities of the human vision system we are often able to rapidly obtain insights into the data characteristics (e.g. relationships, patterns, anomalies, trends, clusters). Some examples of visualization include: Network performance, stock market performance, cartography, molecular modeling, manufacturing scheduling..,

Visualization techniques could be categorized by the kind of data displayed ("attributes"): [scalar, nominal, direction, direction field, shape, position, spatially extended region or object, structure], visual attributes: (color, size, saturation..), as well by the operations acting on these attributes ("operations/judgments"): [identify, locate, distinguish, categorize, cluster, distribution, rank, compare within and between relations, associate, correlate].

The visualization is attempting to present some sort of "reality". If an inadequate scientific (mapping) model to represent the "reality" is chosen the resulting visualization will be inadequate. As real world data usually has noise, this may be reflected in a fuzzy place masking potential phenomena from being noticed. This is very relevant to the level of knowledge generated from the visualization. When a human looks at an object, researchers have identified different levels of cognition they go through to identify the object. The simplest level, the pre-attentive level, involves simple lines and simple objects. This level requires little to no cognitive work. As the object viewed grows more complex by adding shading, color and a three dimension, more and more cognitive effort is required. Thus as the complexity of the visualization grows, the possibility of cognitive stress increases. It is important that the planned visualization focus on allowing the viewer to put their cognitive effort on learning from the visualization not trying to decipher it. The related topics of interest in knowledge media research is how to build a mental model of the visual representation attributes? How visual, auditory, tactile, etc. or a combination of these representations can provide the key to critical and comprehensive appreciation of the data, thus benefiting subsequent analysis, processing, or decision making? How can we most effectively induce chosen mental models in the mind of an viewer ? How can we provide guidance on choosing appropriate models and their attributes to a human or automated display designer ?

The main focus of the ***Knowledge Management*** aspects has been on designing tools and solutions for the open information marketplace: mainly information brokerage and recommenders.

The main challenges investigated in Information Brokerage concern: 1) Knowledge Capture and Representation: dynamic capture and representation of subjects, concepts and relations between them in the particular domain, dynamic capture and representation content provider and their coverage of the subjects and concepts. 2) Request Processing: using the knowledge of the user and provider domain in order, the system has to process the users request by identify the appropriate subjects and concepts and content provider related to the query, access the content provides, retrieve the actual offers, prepare, compute and present the results in an appropriate manner. 3) Offer Processing/Propagation: using the knowledge of the provider domain, the system has to enable content providers to register or update their offers efficiently, associate the offer with the brokers categories, subjects and concepts. A self-organizing multi-agent system has been adopted, where the agents composing a system must pursue an individual goal (being cooperative with others) while adapting themselves to possible external perturbations through learning.

The objective of Expert finders (recommenders) systems is to help in tracing people with needed expertise. Making the knowledge held by people visible (and quickly traceable) in the organization motivates its optimal utilization through sharing and collaboration. Such tacit knowledge held by employees is as important as the information an organization explicitly processes and documents in the course of its day to day business. Within a knowledge space, it may be possible that people hold some electronic devices that store references to their expertise (i.e. as indicated in their CV..). As people walk and move around, these devices could react/interact when they meet other people with similar or desired expertise. This would help initiating interesting human contacts that would enrich/augment these spaces to create new special communities.

The ***integration*** issue have been investigated to implement some automated guidance in shared virtual environments for learning, or in visualizing an emergency phenomenon within a virtual environment, then trying to implement a mental model/behavior of the agent/actor that would react to such situation within a certain context. Other integration issues concern augmenting mixed-reality spaces with automated processing sothat computation becomes part of the environment. Computational devices and agents become part of furniture, walls, and clothing, physical space provides a sense of place that would be augmented towards knowledge space. Some research issues concern how devices coordinate their activities, considering that individuals and devices may change, either because devices enter or leave the space, or because devices within the space go in and out of operational readiness. To resolve heterogeneity issues, adopting new related standards would help speeding up solutions. Another issue is how the space presents itself to people, and how the space deals with multi-person interaction. Within a collaborative design, the space would take a proactive role, providing adequate information visualization model using some shared mental models for mapping reality to representations, suggesting relevant information from outside the session, including other designs it knows and consistency checking. The result is an enhanced design experience, guided by the space's understanding of the current and previous sessions.

Some ideas were partially discussed and would be investigated more in next years. The space must precisely understand its devices and their situation, in particular the computations they are performing, in order to understand what individuals in the space are doing. Existing attempts to catch this information rely on expressive factors, via faces, gestures, and other behaviors. However, expression is only one part of real interaction. In fact, the space needs to interpret not only your facial expression, but perhaps also other physical changes corresponding to your emotional feelings such as heart-rate, breathing, blood-pressure, muscular tightness, and posture. This would help the space identify your emotional state: distress, interest, and pleasure.. Experience shows that professional speakers and entertainers need to detect the emotional state of the audience to be effective to reach the goal of teaching, collaborating, informing, or entertaining..

Wearable devices, when equipped with special sensors with signal processing and pattern recognition capabilities, can potentially learn to recognize physical and physiological patterns—especially those that correspond to affective states—such as when you are fearful, stressed, or happily engaged in a task. Wearable computers, can be in physical contact with you in a long-term intimate way. A wearable may not just hang on your belt, but it may also reside in your hat, gloves, jewelry, shoes, or other clothing, providing a variety of kinds of physical contact beyond the traditional kind of contact, viz., fingertips touching the keyboard and mouse. However, we assume that these sensors would be activated only when needed (high performance tasks, professional collaborations..) as people may prefer natural interactions (with their families, during vacations..).

The integration issues involve generally multidisciplinary technologies, making them hard to resolve. One way to reduce this complexity is to address very specific applications, limiting eventual possibilities. This workshop has been interested in such applications in education and entertainment. it has attracted people from university, research centers, and industry. The best paper has been allocated to the paper "Collaborating in 3D Virtual Environments: A Synchronous Architecture", for the efforts to improve technology for synchronous collaborative environments.

NIST Smart Space: Pervasive Computing Initiative

Lynne Rosenthal and Vincent Stanford
National Institute of Standards and Technology
Information Technology Laboratory
(lrosenthal@nist.gov, vstanford@nist.gov)

1. Introduction

The next great computing paradigm shift, to pervasive computing, is already well under way and will have no less of an impact on industry, government, and daily life than the personal computing revolution. ***Pervasive computing*** refers to the emerging trend toward numerous, easily accessible computing devices connected to each other and to an increasingly ubiquitous network infrastructure. This trend will likely create new opportunities and challenges for Information Technology (IT) companies to place computers and sensors in virtually every device, appliance, and piece of equipment in buildings, homes, workplaces, factories, and even clothing. Within five years vendors will offer portable and embedded devices containing low-cost systems-on-a-chip (SOC) with enough CPU, memory, and input/output logic to execute complex software applications, and use pico-cellular wireless communications. Effective pervasive computing must present user interfaces distributed across numerous, often small, and even invisible devices. This requires new techniques in measurement, software testing, management of the frequency space, and human-computer interactions. Failure to develop and exploit these pervasive computing technologies and techniques may be very costly to U.S. IT companies.

The field of pervasive computing is in its infancy and many of the technologies required to make it a reality are immature and high risk. ITL has launched a pervasive computing initiative to investigate the technical and standards roadblocks impeding integration of the emerging and existing technologies. Consistent with ITL's strategic plan, the initiative involves working with industry to develop and demonstrate test methods, reference data, tests, proof of concept implementations, and standards to help pull the underlying technologies forward and thus help the field mature and grow. The initiative is multi-disciplinary and takes advantage of the expertise of several Divisions within ITL and creates new expertise. Areas addressed by the initiative include: information access and user interfaces, networking, software, and security. The pervasive computing effort is proceeding in two phases.

In phase 1, we are prototyping experimental smart spaces. The prototypes focus on advanced forms of human-computer-interaction, integrating pico-cellular wireless networks with dynamic service discovery, automatic device configuration, and software infrastructures required to successfully program pervasive computing applications. The objectives of phase 1 are to:

- Identify key areas which would benefit from standardization, e.g., service discovery, APIs, and interoperability,
- Provide 'hands-on' experience in identifying applicable measurements, e.g., conformance tests, interoperability tests, diagnostic tools, and benchmarks, to promote the technology,
- Identify security mechanisms needed to ensure privacy, integrity, and accessibility of implementations.

In phase 2, they are:

- Develop metrics, test methods, and standard reference data sets to 'pull' the technology forward,
- Provide reference implementations to serve as models for possible commercial implementations,
- Collaborate with industry standards groups to develop unambiguous, testable specifications,
- Establish partnerships with industry and academic organizations,
- Interconnect the phase 1 prototypes to explore key issues associated with distributed smart spaces.

2. Background

Smart Spaces are work environments with embedded computers, information appliances, and multi-modal sensors allowing people to perform tasks efficiently by offering unprecedented levels of access to information and assistance from computers. Smart Spaces support

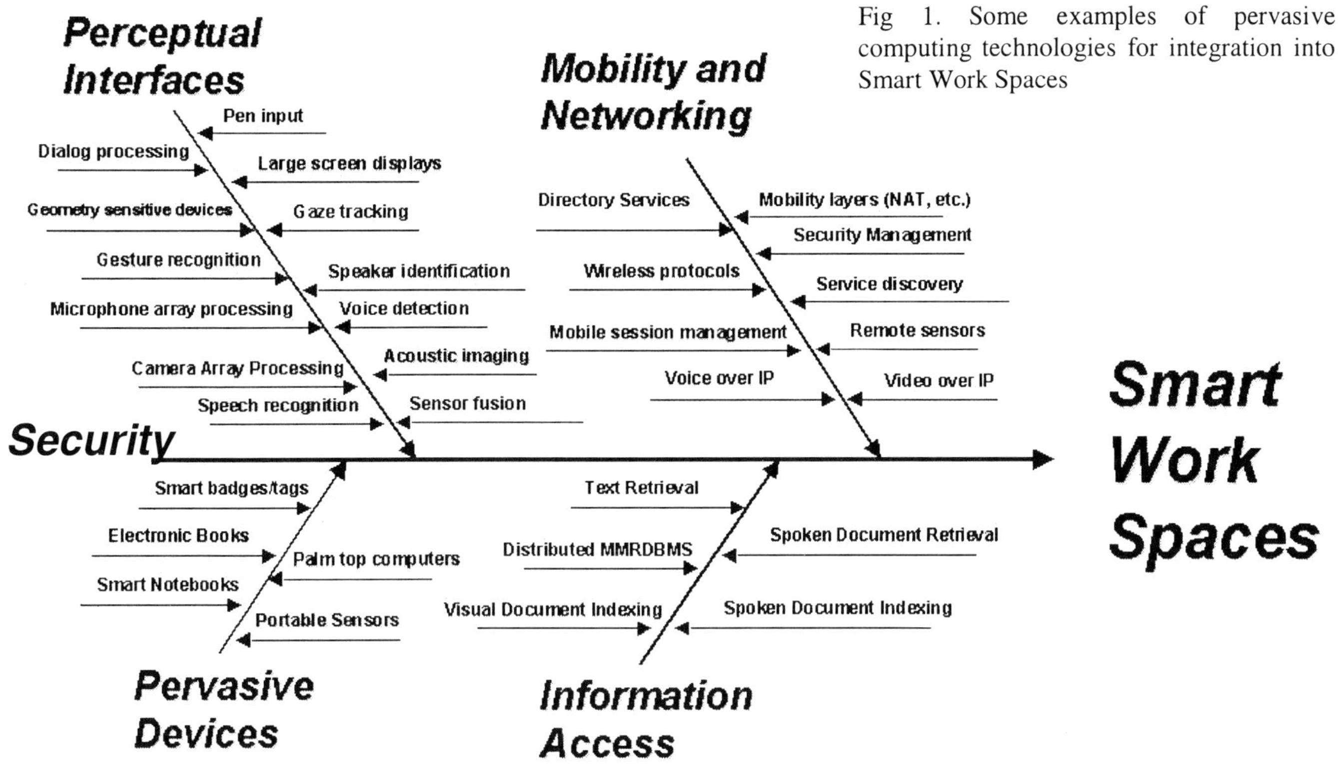

Fig 1. Some examples of pervasive computing technologies for integration into Smart Work Spaces

stationary and mobile information environments that may be connected to the Internet. Companies are Figure producing various portable and embedded information devices, e.g., PDAs, cellular telephones, and active badges, for mobile information environments. Concurrently, wireless technologies, including Bluetooth, IrDA, and HomeRF, will outfit these devices with high bandwidth, localized wireless communication capabilities to each other, and the globally wired Internet. The emerging network of the future includes small, specialized devices roaming among islands of wireless connectivity within a global ocean of wired networks. The islands are Smart Spaces, where services and embedded devices are discovered, accessed, and interconnected with portable devices carried into the spaces. Then the combination of imported and native devices can be exploited to support the information needs of the current island inhabitants. Mobile and stationary Smart Spaces may identify and perceive users, their actions, and even goals; facilitate interaction with information rich sources; provide extensive presentation capabilities; anticipate user needs during task performance; increase information interchange rates; provide improved records and summaries for later use; and support distributed and local collaboration. This picture is no longer fiction, but an imminent reality; once a number of challenges have been mastered.

3. Challenges Facing Industry

Companies, ranging from small innovative startups to larger traditional IT organizations, are embracing pervasive computing and producing a myriad of new products. The majority are focused on near-term needs, i.e., on development and use of information appliances – devices with computational capabilities used for specific applications – and the issues of getting them connected to the Internet through wireless and wired links. A large number of constituent technologies, too many for any single company to address, must be integrated in Smart Spaces. Issues of integration, interoperability, performance, and security are concerns; but for many companies, not yet primary objectives. Due to resource limitations and pressure to be first to market, many companies narrowly focus on a few pervasive computing technologies, rather than the boarder issues of integration, interoperability, and performance. Figure 1 illustrates some of the technologies needed to create smart workspaces, and their interdependencies.

To foster integration, interoperability, and the development of emerging technologies, standardization and measurements are critical, but for economic reasons, often are not addressed by individual companies. The lack of common software infrastructure, tools to create, manage, measure, test, and debug pervasive services, standards in key areas such as service discovery, APIs, pico-cellular wireless networks, automatic configuration, and ad hoc transactional security, all currently impede widespread adoption of pervasive computing. Also, measurements and tests developed and performed in a public forum allow competing research systems to be compared, and improved systems to be built on the best features of previous iterations.

4. Requests from Industry

At the October 1999 Jini[1] Technology Community Meeting, attended by over 200 stakeholders in pervasive computing, a survey of projects, including a technology Wish List, was conducted. Companies including Sun Mircrosystems, Xerox, Motorola, cOcO Technologies, Oki Data Americas, and Amiga, asked for:

- Standardization of testing and diagnostic tools,
- Security assessments and capability-based security,
- Interoperability among diverse applications, services and devices,
- Standardization of APIs,
- Reference implementations and standard reference materials,
- Improvements in robustness and software quality.

Industry and academic experts have indicated that ITL would be most effective by playing its traditional role in measurements, testing, and standards. In interviews R&D engineers suggested that ITL should aid the pervasive computing community by developing appropriate tasks and benchmarks for smart spaces, as well as reference data sets, measurement tools with generalized interfaces to experimental databases and a web site with pervasive computing information. Additional requests for ITL assistance in developing measurements, tests, and standards were also received, including:

- The Biometrics Consortium requested ITL to help develop APIs for biometrics-based systems,
- The Bluetooth Consortium requested ITL to help develop abstract test suites for the Bluetooth system (i.e., RF communications standard) and formal models of Bluetooth protocols to verify that the specifications are complete, unambiguous and free from deadlocks and livelocks,
- IEEE 802.15 Working Group on Wireless Personal Area Networks requested ITL to study the coexistence of IEEE 802.15 devices (e.g., Bluetooth and HomeRF) with each other and with devices in the unlicensed 2.4 GHz ISM band (e.g., wireless LAN systems and microwave ovens),
- GTE-BBN, IBM, HP, and Kaiser Permanente requested ITL to help develop performance evaluations of technologies, measurement tools, and to help define what data should be collected, annotated, and used to measure performance,
- Over 60 companies, including AT&T, GTE/BBN, GE, Harris, IBM, Lexis-Nexis, and TextWise, requested ITL to continue efforts to evaluate text retrieval technologies.

5. ITL's Role

Although many companies understand the value of working together on generic, pre-competitive technologies, it is not economical for them individually to develop standards, metrics and tests. Also, most universities engage in research and education, rather than develop metrics and tests. Even if industry or academia develop metrics and tests for their own products and systems, they would not push the technology in the way large-scale evaluations do, since they would not compare a wide range of systems. Furthermore such metrics and tests might be biased toward the products of the companies involved, and would not be trusted. NIST/ITL has earned a reputation for objective, impartial measurements, tests, and for high quality technical competence that instills trust in ITL's products. ITL measurement tools and techniques have achieved wide recognition and use in the United States and internationally.

To better understand the technical, standardization and measurement issues involved, ITL has taken a four-pronged approach:

1/ Interacting with Industry. ITL is sponsoring an ongoing series of conferences on pervasive computing. These bring together companies, academics, and non-profit organizations engaged in research, planning, and development of pervasive computing products, services and applications to provide a forum for discussions, demonstrations, projects, and issues. The Pervasive Computing 2000 Conference, held January 25-26, 2000, attracted major industry experts, (e.g., Bill Joy, Sun Microsystems, Craig Mundie, Microsoft, David Nahamoo, IBM, Tobin J. Lehman, IBM) and was very productive and well attended, despite the blizzard weather conditions. Additionally, ITL staff participates in conferences by presenting papers and demonstrations, e.g., Usenix and JavaOne Conferences, as well as

[1] Jini™ from Sun Microsystems, is a software infrastructure based on Java™ technology that enables all types of devices to simply connect into impromptu networks, making access to and delivery of new network services as simple as plugging in a telephone.

meeting with industry experts to discuss potential collaborations, e.g., Kaiser Permanente, DARPA.

2/ Developing Prototypes. ITL has established two projects focused on the development of prototype implementations (test beds) to gain competence, industry recognition, and identify the standardization and measurement issues in pervasive computing. The Software Diagnostic and Conformance Testing (SDCT) Division and the Advanced Network Technologies Division (ANTD) have joined together to develop the AirJava/Aroma prototype. This project focuses on the software infrastructure and networking aspects of pervasive computing. The Information Access and User Interfaces (IAUI) Division is developing a Smart Space Modular Test Bed which is focused on advancing human-computer interfaces and information access in environments embedded with computers and sensors. Appendix A contains brief descriptions of these prototypes. Although they are separate projects, there is a great deal of synergy between them and efforts are under way to coordinate goals, reuse software, solutions, and share expertise. As these projects mature, it is likely that a hybrid, combining features of both will be developed and expertise from other ITL Divisions, e.g., Computer Security, will be incorporated. They also provide measurement platforms for industrial technologies. Future prototypes will serve as reference implementations and be done in collaboration with other NIST Laboratories as well as with industry partners.

Topics	Technologies	ITL Role	Companies
Wireless Communications	Wireless telephony systems: W-CDMA & cdma2000	Performance evaluation and development of software testbeds	Int'l Telecom. Union, Qualcomm, Ericsson, European Telecom. Standards Institute
Pico-cell Wireless Systems	Bluetooth, MANET	Conformance and Interoperability testing; Protocol modeling & verification; Performance and coexistence evaluation	IBM, Intel, Ericsson, Nokia, Toshiba, SAIC, Raytheon, Mitre, SRI
Real-time System & Communications Protocol	Java/Jini	Help develop requirements for real-time Java; Performance metrics & tools	IBM, Microsoft, HP, Honeywell, Motorola, Nokia, Sun, SoftPLC, Siemens, etc.
Speech Understanding	Transcription, information extraction, topic detection & tracking, spoken document retrieval	Benchmark tests; Common test sets; Uniform scoring	AT&T, GTE/BBN, Dragon Systems, IBM, Claritech, GE, SRI, Philips
Interactive Dialogue	Speech-based dialogue	Develop metrics; Develop tests	MITRE, AT&T, GTE/BBN, CNRI, Hughes, IBM, Intel, Lockheed Martin, Lucent, Microsoft, Philips, etc.
Person Recognition	Speaker recognition, face recognition	Benchmark tests; Common test sets; Uniform scoring	GTE/BBN, Dragon Systems, ITT, SRI, Aegir, Excalibur, TASC
Multi-media Information Extraction	Text retrieval, web searching, question answering, interactive retrieval	Develop metrics; Develop test data; Uniform scoring	AT&T, GTE/BBN, Claritech, Lexis-Nexis, TextWise, IBM, Microsoft, GE, Harris, Fujitsu, etc.
Security	Cryptographic testing	Testing/Validating cryptographic modules	IBM, Entrust, Netscape, Motorola, nCipher, IButton, GTE, Cylink, SPYRUS, etc.
Biometrics	Biometric authentication, biometric system interoperability	Standards development & testing	Compaq, IBM, Microsoft, Novell, Miros, Identicator, Veridicom, etc.
Electronic Book	E-Book content, interoperability	Standards development & testing; Interoperability standards	Softbook, Nuvomedia, Librius, EveryBook, Microsoft, IBM, Adobe

Table 1. ITL Projects related to pervasive computing

3/ Participation in Standardization efforts. Working with industry, ITL participates in open, consensus-based standards forums such as Consortia, IEEE, and ISO/ANSI organizations to develop testable standards/specifications for emerging technologies. ITL is participating in several activities for pervasive computing: IEEE 802.15 Wireless Personal Area Networks, Bluetooth Consortium, HomeRF Consortium, NCITS R1 Real Time Systems, Jini Community Development Process, and IETF Zero Configuration Working Group. ITL continues to explore opportunities to participate in the development of new pervasive computing standards. ITL will take a leadership role in helping to identify and develop standards and specifications in areas where standards facilitate the acceptance of pervasive computing, e.g., service discovery, APIs, automatic configuration, and ad hoc transactional security.

4/ Participation in Measurement and Testing Efforts. The activities and outcome from industry interactions, prototypes, and standardization efforts will drive ITL efforts in developing measurements and testing approaches (e.g., metrics, reference data sets, diagnostic tools, abstract test suites, and conformance tests) to advance pervasive computing. For example, ITL is working with industry to define test scenarios, tasks, and to develop an integrated architecture for human-computer interaction in Smart Spaces.

Some of the initial ITL accomplishments and products produced as a result of our approach include:

- **Software quality** – develop software tools and tests to help ensure the quality and 'correctness' of pervasive software infrastructures and applications; e.g., Jini Services Scripting is a tool that makes it easier to install and deploy Jini services, by insulating the programmer from the necessary low-level software manipulations, and thus maximizing consistency and minimizing chances for errors,
- **Networking of Smart Spaces** – integrate various aspects of network communications and services to provide a networking environment that is easy to use and intelligent; e.g., AirJava, a reference implementation, that provides network discovery, self-configuration, and service discovery for a device in a dynamic-hybrid network environment and thus, provides industry with both 'proof-of-concept' model they can mimic or build upon,
- **User interfaces** – design of standard test materials and systematic metrics for areas like spoken language and biometric person identification to achieve intuitive user interactions; e.g., Multi-channel spontaneous speech data synchronized with video data will provide industry with reference data in a conference room scenario, such as an intelligent medical examination room.

In support of this four-pronged approach, other projects within ITL Divisions are also relevant to pervasive computing. Table 1 shows topics on which the ITL is currently working. Specific names of companies and other organizations involved in this area are also provided.

APPENDIX: Prototype Descriptions

AirJava [1]/Aroma[2]

The AirJava/Aroma project focuses on creating and studying the network and software aspects of a wireless, Jini-based smart space. The aim of this project is fourfold – to discover technical, measurement, and standards issues related to: (1) connecting portable wireless devices to traditional networks, (2) service discovery, self-configuration and dynamic resource sharing, (3) mobile code and data, and (4) software infrastructure needed to create and manage pervasive services and applications.

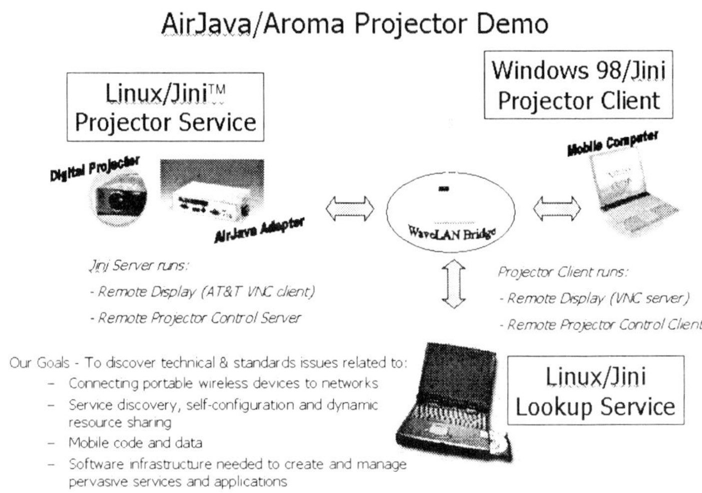

The initial research challenge was to design an ***AirJava*** adapter that can convert existing computer-controllable devices into prototype Smart Space devices. Such a device has been designed and constructed and is capable of running a Java Virtual Machine and Java-based distributed computing software such as Jini and JavaSpaces, communicating wirelessly to a Jini server and to peer devices, and connecting to a range of computer-controllable devices. The AirJava adapter will be used to implement a simple research information appliance using a digital projector to create a wireless, discoverable projector service.

The nature of pervasive computing will require that we research and develop the needed software prototypes, infrastructure, and tools to allow us to experiment with, debug, test, measure and manage the pervasive clients and services. We plan to explore the following areas:

- Various means of implementing pervasive services and clients including Java-based, non-Java-based and hybrid architectures,
- Java and native-based service browsing, diagnostic, debugging and testing tools,

- Pervasive service metrology,
- Pervasive service software infrastructure and "bootstrapping" code,
- The use of low computational-power devices as clients and servers,
- Lightweight OS and OS-less services using tools such as the Flux project's OSKit.

We plan to collaborate with other NIST, industry and academic groups to leverage resources, ideas and results from each group's efforts. Our software will be in the public domain for use by others and will be used to guide our participation in the standards process. As we tackle some of the research objectives related to pervasive computing, we will begin to identify requirements that will ultimately drive longer-term software and networking research and standards work at ITL. We will make the design for *AirJava* adapters available to other researchers outside NIST, so that those researchers can use or improve them. In addition, lessons learned in designing and constructing the adapters might also be of use to industrial designers.

SMART SPACE Modular Test Bed [3]

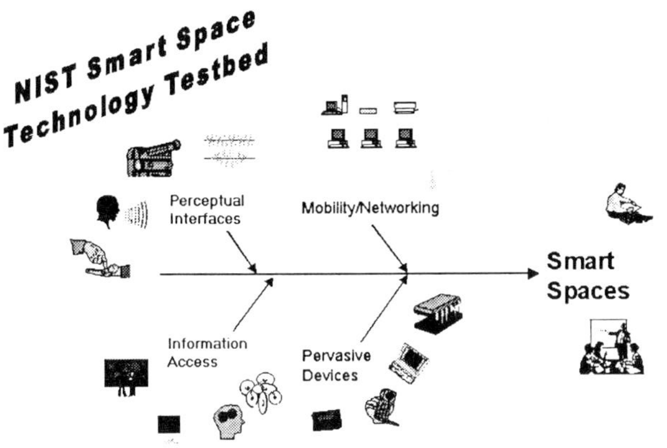

Working with numerous industrial and academic R&D institutions, ITL has played a leading role in metrics research in speech recognition, information retrieval, and natural language query generation. The aims of this project include: (1) Establish an integrated multi-sensor perceptual interface test bed for smart work spaces. (2) Support integration of the AirJava/Aroma components. (3) Deploy perceptual interface components from our industrial advisors to investigate system level performance and metrics issues. (4) Provide a multi-sensor data recording environment for the production of standard test materials.

We are developing the Smart Space Modular Test bed, which consists of a defined middleware API for real-time data transport, a connection broker server for sensor data sources, and processing data sinks. For example, a microphone array acquires a speech signal, reduces it to a single channel, and offers it as a data-flow. Then a speaker identification system subscribes to the signal flow, while a speaker-dependent speech recognition system subscribes as well. The speaker ID system then offers a real-time flow, to which the speech recognition system also subscribes. This layer makes it possible to integrate components that were not intentionally designed to work together, such as speaker identification and speech recognition systems. Many constituent technologies are under separate development in industry, so the issues of interoperability and integration are paramount. This project will develop metrics and reference material based on real implementations for industrial use. Important technologies include sensor-based collaborative interfaces using:

- Speech recognition
- Speaker identification
- Face recognition
- Source localization/separation
- Channel normalization
- Immersive video and acoustic displays
- Personal information appliances
- Pervasive networking
- Information storage and retrieval
  - multimedia data types
  - object-encapsulated
  - active data
  - Multiple Interconnected Spaces.

Impacts

- Increased ability to interact easily with computers, especially collaboratively.
- Ability to help set standards and metrics in sight and sound based information intensive interfaces.

More facile information retrieval and integration of greater information content, with integration into interfaces of the future.

References

[1]AirJava: //w3.antd.nist.gov/~mills/projects/AirJava/
[2]Aroma: http://www.itl.nist.gov/div897/ctg/aroma.html
[3] Smart Space Test Bed: http://www.itl.nist.gov/iaui/iaui/presentations/Smtspaces-darpa1/index.htm

CVE Technology Development Based on Real World Application and User Needs

Economou Daphne [1], Mitchell L. William [1], Pettifer R. Steve [2], West J. Adrian [2]
[1] *Department of Computing and Mathematics, The Manchester Metropolitan University*
Chester Street, M1 5GD, Manchester, England
{d.economou, b.mitchell}@doc.mmu.ac.uk
[2] *Advanced Interfaces Group, The University of Manchester,*
Oxford Road, M13 9PL, Manchester, England
{srp, ajw}@cs.man.ac.uk

Abstract

This paper argues that the development of Collaborative Virtual Environment (CVE) technology must be guided by application and end user needs. A collaboration is described between human factors and technological researchers based on observations of prototypes in use in a real world educational situation. The aim of the research is to develop a framework of design factors for the use of virtual actors in CVEs and to inform the development of underlying CVE technology.

The methodological approach followed involves the development of prototype virtual learning environments in a series of distinct phases of increasing sophistication. The environments are based on an ancient Egyptian game (senet) and are aimed at children at Key Stage Level 2 of the National Curriculum for education in England.

The paper shows how established two-dimensional multi-media technologies were used to develop robust prototypes which were then observed in use by children. Results from these phases have been used to guide the current phase of work. This involves the construction of a three-dimensional shared VE using the experimental Deva Virtual Reality system.

Index terms-- collaborative virtual environments, education, virtual actors, human factors

1. Introduction

Virtual Environment (VE) technology has provided a valuable new form of human computer interaction. However, the current understanding about VE design is poor [1] and there is still a long way to go until this level of supporting applications meets the users' needs. This is due to the fact that the development of the technology has been driven mainly by the challenge of developing the systems themselves and solving architectural problems rather than being based on applications development and users' needs.

DIVE [2, 3], MASSIVE [3, 4] and Diamond Park [5] are examples of social virtual environment systems in which distributed users can speak to each other and participate in joint activities. Currently these systems have been used mainly to investigate technical issues such as the system level mechanisms for supporting crowds in CVEs [6]. Technology development has also been driven by the need to improve rendering techniques, in order to maintain performance, and support photorealistic VEs and virtual human representations [7]. There has been a considerable amount of research on supporting issues like facial expressions and body language [8] to improve human communication.

MAVERIK [9] and Deva [10] are new VR systems under development in the Advanced Interfaces Group at the University of Manchester. Experience from developing the AVIARY VR system [11] a prototype multi-user Virtual Reality system for dealing with large-scale virtual environments, directed the design of MAVERIK and Deva. It highlighted the need for a different approach to spatial management and rendering in VEs (which are addressed by MAVERIK) as well as for techniques and tools for describing, managing and distributing behaviour in shared environments (which is the role of the companion system, Deva). Both systems have been developed from a primarily "architectural" perspective, attempting to overcome technological challenges in novel ways. However, the purpose of developing a technology is to serve the end user, rather than being an elegant piece of programming [12]. The human factors and user needs are important areas to be addressed in VE development in order for this technology to fulfil its potential [13, 14].

0-7695-0798-9/00 $10.00

This research aims to develop a framework of design factors relating to the use of virtual actors [15] in CVEs for learning. Virtual actors model human figures that move and function in VEs. They can represent software agents [16, 17] or humans (in which case they are known as avatars) [17, 18].

The role of virtual actors has been recognised in educational systems [19, 20]. The framework complements existing work by identifying interaction and communication factors relating to the use of virtual actors in CVEs used for learning. It also informs the development of the underlying technology according to user needs.

This paper focuses on the development of CVE technology based on observations of prototypes in use in a real world educational situation. The methodological approach followed involves the development of prototype learning environments in a series of distinct phases of increasing sophistication. It gives a brief description of the first two phases of work and shows how this has been used to shape the development of the third phase based on the Deva system. It describes the development of the current prototype, the issues to be investigated and the ways in which the work will be evaluated.

2. Methodology

2.1 Exploratory nature of the approach

The research approach has exploratory nature. Steed [21] distinguishes evaluation as belonging to either a scientific enquiry framework (concerned with the study of specific phenomena) or a usability engineering framework (concerned with measuring the effectiveness of a system). The studies being carried out are not evaluations but observations of what is going on. The work can thus be seen as belonging to the scientific enquiry framework.

Roussos [22] supports the need for such exploratory work which involves building novel learning applications and carrying out informal evaluations of them. Past studies have dealt with users with ready access to the technology. However, it is necessary to recognise the situated nature of the processes in collaborative learning. It is necessary to study a "real world" situation to determine the CVE requirements. Problems that determine the success or failure of a system can only arise in such a situation.

2.2 A "real world" application – Senet

The research uses a real world application based around Manchester Museum's Education Service [23]. The CVE is based on *senet*, an ancient Egyptian board game, from The Manchester Museum. The game allows both co-operation (in learning) and competition (in trying to win) to be studied. The social dimension of this game supports sociocultural theories of learning such as constructivism (learning by playing) [24, 25] and cognitive apprenticeship [26] as well as instructional methods of learning (some information is given to the players at the beginning of the activity in order to initiate the interaction). The impetus for collaborative learning comes from two main sources in the UK: the National Curriculum for education that places great emphasis on such learning and the National Grid for Learning (NGfL) [27, 28] proposed by the UK Government. The CVE is aimed at Key Stage Level 2 (~9-11 years old) of the National Curriculum for education in England.

A general description of the type of Collaborative Virtual Learning Environment (CVLE) to be studied can be created by synthesising models of VEs [1] and CVEs [6, 21] with models of classroom interaction [29]. A CVLE can be seen as consisting of three main elements:

1. ***entities***,
   the environment, objects within it, participants, groups of participants
2. ***actions*** between those entities,
   interactions with the environment and interactions with objects
3. the ***situation*** of the collaboration,
   the activity that is the subject of collaboration and pedagogy (the style of teaching/learning being used).

2.3 Iterative phased approach

One problem faced in this research is the vast number of factors involved in the construction of CVEs for learning. [1] has identified 46 design properties to be considered when designing VEs for usability. The number of factors increases dramatically when considering communication and collaboration issues in CVEs [20]. This makes it difficult to isolate which design decisions are responsible for the overall effectiveness of the environment. It is also difficult to identify the inter-play between various factors (e.g. the effects that usability issues have on pedagogic issues).

To simplify the study of design factors a phased iterative approach was adopted [30, 31]. Each phase structures the study of the CVE into a series of smaller studies. The research is divided into 3 main phases that differ in 3 main ways:

1. ***population***, the degree to which the environment is populated: semi- populated (the user sees other virtual actors present); fully-populated (the user can represent themselves via a virtual actor)
2. ***2D/3D***, use of a 2-dimensional environment simplifies issues relating to navigation and the way in which objects are manipulated
3. ***external/internal interaction***, whether users interactions take place outside or via the computer (Figure 1, 2).

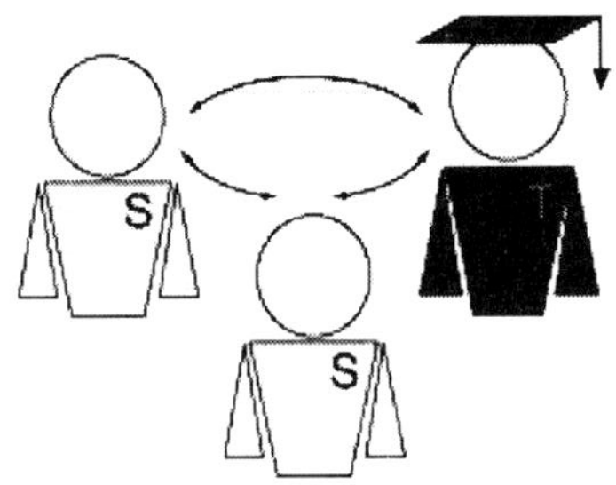

Figure1. Interactions external to the system ('S' student, 'T' teacher)

Figure 2. Interactions internal to the system ('S' student, 'T' teacher)

Each study represents a particular situation consisting of a subset of the range of factors in the CVE. Different prototypes are constructed for each study and observations made of them in use. The prototypes are based around the senet game. The phased approach provides several benefits. It provides the means of managing the complexity of factors by dealing with a manageable set of factors in each phase (e.g. 2D/3D and population). It allows the results of each phase to inform subsequent phases. In this way it allows requirements to be progressively identified. The use of more robust technologies allows the essential features of the situation (interactivity and social communication) to be studied with real users in a way not possible with more immature and inaccessible CVE technology.

The studies in the first two phases are aimed at deriving a rich set of qualitative information. From this a set of requirements can be identified and then used to inform the design of the third phase application. The work in the first two phases can be seen to be of a more exploratory nature, more like formative evaluation in contrast to the work in the third phase which will involve evaluation of a more summative nature.

3. First two phases

3.1 First Phase

Established two-dimensional multi-media technology has been used for the development of the first two phases of the research. The first phase prototypes (Figure 3), were examples of single display groupware [32], where interactions take place face-to-face in the real world external to the virtual environment (Figure 1). The prototypes were observed in use by the general public during an open week at Manchester Museum. Observations of school children were also conducted under more controlled conditions. Due to the nature of both activities and the environment that occurred note taking used for data collection.

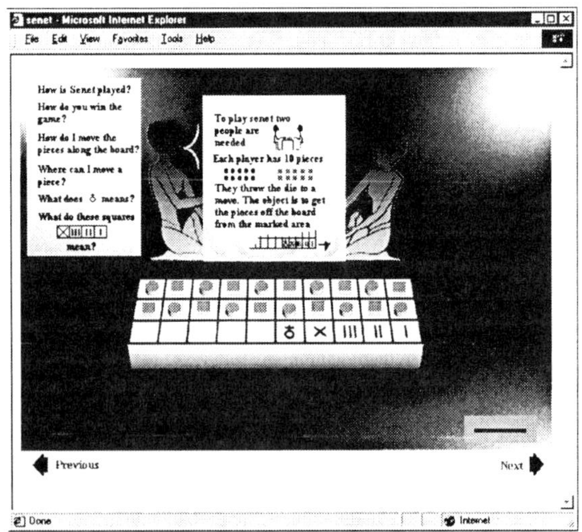

Figure 3. First phase prototype, single display groupware

The purpose of the first phase was primarily exploratory in nature. It gathered information about events in the real world game-playing situation and identified usability issues surrounding the prototype in order to inform the design of environments developed in subsequent phases. What stood out was mainly:

1. the rich range of interactivity and social communication that needs to be supported in CVLEs
2. the importance of the expert to be aware of and able to control even such a seemingly well structured activity as game playing.

3.2 Second Phase

In the second phase of work, prototypes were developed which took the form of conventional groupware systems (Figure 3, 4, 5). Participants were remotely located so interactions between them were internal to the computer (Figure 2). The prototypes were developed using 2D multimedia tools coupled with groupware technology typical of that used in education. The prototypes also introduced the concept of population to the environment. One prototype was semi-populated (the child could see a virtual actor representing the expert) (Figure 4) and the other two prototypes were fully populated (the child could also see their own virtual actor) (Figure 5, 6). Users communicated by typing text in chat boxes associated with their own (Figure 5, 6) actor or using a hand for pointing (Figure 4, 5, 6). Studies took place at a local school.

Data collection occurs by videotaping users, capture of text typed in chat boxes, and note taking. The Interactional Analysis[1] method [33] and Druin's[2] work [34] provided the foundation for the data analysis. The analysis results in a mixture of quantitative and qualitative findings. It deals with transforming vast amount of rich qualitative data in a quantitative form, that can be used to draw design principles for constructing CVEs for learning [35].

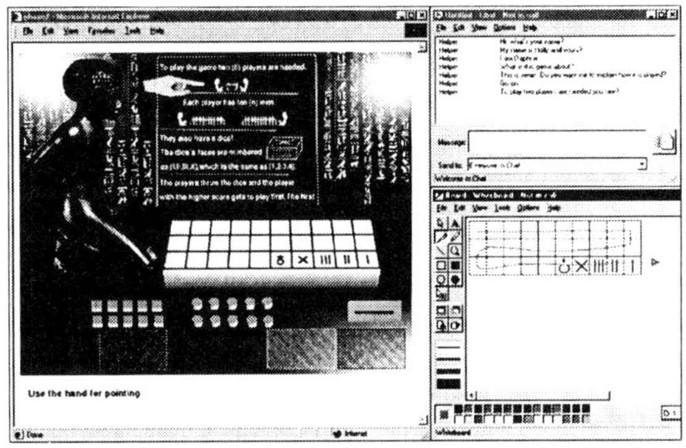

Figure 4. 2-D semi-populated, dialogue external to the game environment

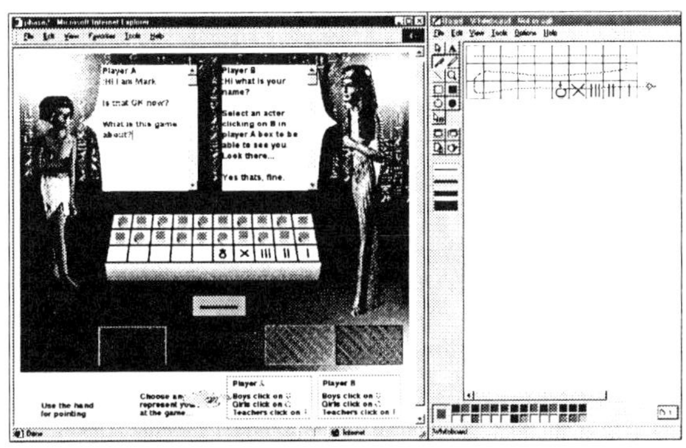

Figure 5. 2-D fully-populated, dialogue internal to the game environment

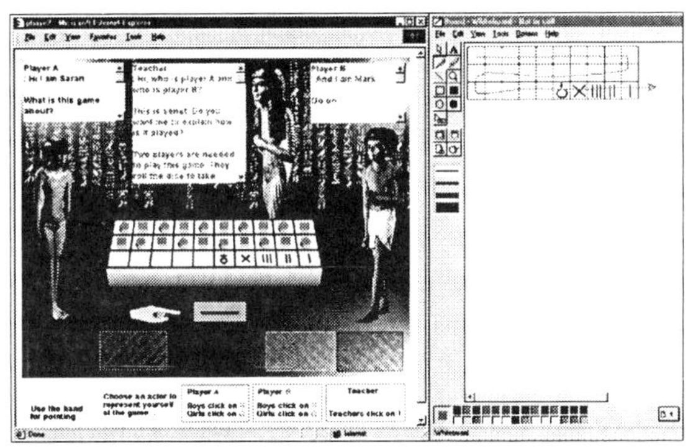

Figure 6. 2-D fully-populated, dialogue internal to the game environment, increased population

[1] Interaction Analysis is an interdisciplinary method for the empirical investigation of the interaction of human beings with each other and with object in the environment trying to identify routine practices and problems and their resources for their solution. The method is based on audio-visual recording for its primary records and on playback capability for their analysis. This provides a crucial ability to replay a sequence of interactions repeatedly for multiple viewers and for multiple occasions. This research borrows the Interaction Analysis pattern for the segmentation of the data to be analysed.

[2] Druin uses a framework for analysing qualitative data from observations of children and experts interacting with electronic educational applications, formed by the following criteria: time, quotes, activities, activity pattern, roles and design ideas.

The purpose of this phase was to explore issues surrounding the interaction being internal to the environment (communication via the tools in the prototypes) and the effects on the behaviour of participants. It indicated that problems arise because the established 2D collaborative technology limits the access of the expert to information about the situation. A comparison of the video of the expert and a video of the remotely located child showed such discrepancies.

Turn taking was particularly difficult. The expert was often unsure whether the child had completed their turn or was thinking over their actions. Technical problems (such as system lag) made this problem worse. To overcome these problems an informal turn taking protocol arose whereby a participant would place the mouse pointer in a particular area of the screen to signify turn completion. Another issue identified was the need to keep track of previous actions and dialogues.

The results from the first two phases have been mainly qualitative and served to elicit a set of requirements for the CVLE to be developed in the third phase. These requirements are currently being formulated into a framework of design factors concerning when using the CVLE in the third phase. The framework will include factors such as:

1. ***appearance*** (e.g. user's representation)
2. ***awareness***, what the actor perceives about the VE and situation
3. ***object manipulation***, ways in which the virtual actors uses objects (e.g. moving a piece in the senet game)
4. ***communication content***, the content of the communicative exchanges
5. ***communication modes***, the ways the virtual actors communicate (e.g. as text or as speech)
6. ***turn-taking***, i.e. communicating by taking turns (e.g. interrupting) or manipulating objects
7. ***role in situation***, this depends on the particular pedagogical style being followed.

4. Third Phase

The third phase studies focus on internal communication, interaction and collaboration processes in a 3D CVE. The studies in the third phase will be of a more evaluative nature. User studies of this environment will allow the design factors identified previously to be tested. Thus the development of the underlying technology is guided by user and real educational situations needs.

4.1 A brief description of Deva system

The Deva system aims to address a number of "large scale" issues VEs. These include management of large number of objects within an environment, large numbers of environments and applications co-existing, graphical complexity, and large numbers of geographically distributed users. Deva is architecturally a client/server system, with a cluster of servers forming a single virtual "world engine" that maintains the objective contents of all environments and their objects. Client viewer processes then connect to the world engine across the Internet in order to participate in the VEs. The MAVERIK kernel provides local graphics and input device handling for the clients, whilst Deva itself deals with the distribution and management of the behaviours of objects. Two novel features of Deva are:

1. its split between "objective reality" (managed in the server) and "perceived effect" (as presented by the viewers), and
2. its use of a high-level object orientated language for concise description of the nature of its environments and their contents.

Together, these features allow the system to explicitly manage the objects as they behave within and move between environments, and also to reduce network requirements by capitalising on aspects of human perception in order to "cull out" events in the VE that are never experienced (or are not important to) the users.

4.2 Conceptual design of the third phase

The main differences in this phase are:

1. it is a 3D environment
2. the environment is shared
3. the users can have control of individual input devices simultaneously
4. the virtual actors are fully functional (explained bellow)
5. the prototype that is being developed is fully-populated (Section 2.3).

The technology that is used is the DEVA 3D CVE system. Users have individual displays (a monitor, or a head-mounted display) and input devices (e.g. mouse or a 3D mouse) and the interactions between the users are internal to the environment. The environment contains artefacts related to the game like: the board, the pieces (that move in all (x, y) directions on a horizontal surface), the dice (that spins and gives random numbers from 1-4 when rolled) and the virtual actors' figures representing the participating users (Figure 7).

The users are represented by articulated virtual actors, allowing them to:

1. walk in the CVE, indicating the users' position in the space
2. select an object (if the virtual actor "within arm's reach" of the object then the avatar positions its hand correctly to "touch" it) or to pick a distant object by pointing (in which case a "laser pointer" from the hand indicates selection).

Current actors implemented in Deva support only static texture maps as faces, thus limiting the possibilities for facial expressions or "body language."

The communication is text based and external to the CVE prototype (similar to prototype 1 in the second phase). Although the second phase results showed a positive impact of the internalisation of the users dialogue it is difficult to implement such a system in a *fully* 3D environment. This is primarily due to limitations in screen resolution used to display CVEs, the effects of "anti-aliasing" which are more significant in 3D than in 2D, and also to the low-resolution depth or "Z" buffering provided by most 3D platforms. Although in principle there is nothing complex about managing text in a 3D environment, limitations of display technology mean that presentation of large quantities of readable text in CVEs is currently unrealistic.

The participant can obtain information about the game by using the dialogue box to ask the expert questions, or by reading the rules that appear on one of the walls of the environment. The expert can respond by typing text in the dialogue box or by pointing to rules on the wall or demonstrating something in the environment.

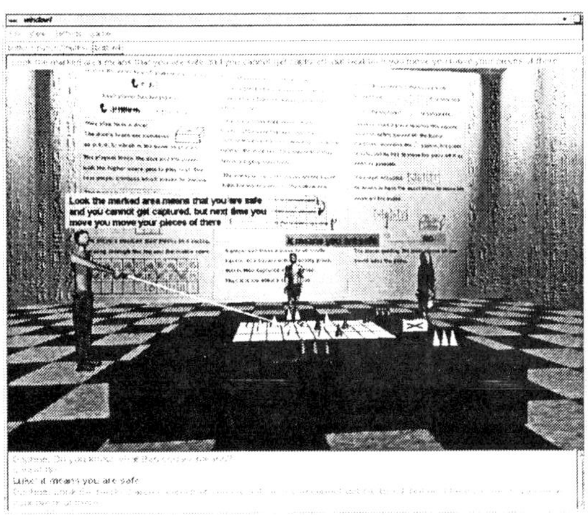

Figure 7. The senet prototype in Deva

4.3 Issues to be investigated

In the first two phases different means of communication (such as text, drawing and pointing) were used. Feedback from the second phase indicated that text worked satisfactorily apart from the system lag. The children commented that speech would provide a more direct way of communication and that they wouldn't have to worry about spelling. However, text is very important for the specific application, because a large set of rules has to be presented to the players. Additionally, skills such as reading and writing are of a significant importance in a learning environment and are strongly supported in the National Curriculum. It was also found that the chat boxes were useful because they provided a "transcript" of the dialogue that was used both by the expert and the children (e.g. scrolling back over an explanation) to kept track of previous actions and dialogues.

However, presenting text in VEs has not been developed to a sufficient level. Systems like MASSIVE support text that appears in a board inside the environment and some browsers (e.g. Active Worlds) support text that appears above the users' heads. These solutions are satisfactory only for a short text. It is almost impossible when a combination of text and illustrations has to be presented something very common for a learning environment. Observations of prototype 1 from the second phase (Section 3.2), indicated that an adequate solution can be provided by displaying the rules of the game on the wall. In the third phase rules will also appear on the wall (Figure 7).

Results from the first phase (Section 3.1), indicated the lack of use of the Egyptian virtual actor due to its inability to exhibit the behaviours shown by human experts. Previous work in the field has shown that actors with human like behaviours enhance the learning activity and increase children's motivation. Lester [36] describes a 2D educational environment in which two fully functional animated pedagogical agents (Herman and Bug) fly around, point out things of interest and provide children with problem-solving advice. In the second phase (Section 3.2), the virtual actors were provided with a hand to point with. This did aid the users' communication but it was treated mainly as a tool for communication separate from the virtual actor. It is expected that this will be improved in the third phase as the hands are parts of the limbs of the virtual actors, that communicate the user's actions (e.g. picking, moving and pointing objects).

Interactions in the CVE such as turn taking and control are of a great importance at this phase. The fact that the expert is remotely located from the child means that awareness cannot be achieved simply by looking at them. A comparison of the video of the expert (in which the expert voices the situation as they perceive it) and the video of the child, in the second phase, showed discrepancies in the expert's reading of the situation. The only cues available were the text appearing in the child's chat box or the movement of the hand pointer. The position of the mouse pointer gives some clue as to the other participant's focus of activity (e.g. if the other participant has moved the pointer to their chat box then it could be assumed that they are about to type in some dialogue). This is expected to be improved in the third phase as the virtual actors are capable of giving more visual clues of the actual interaction. However, giving visual clues about the users' intention to act is a subject of investigation for the third phase.

Turn taking became more difficult in the second phase. The NetMeeting tool only allowed one user to have control at a time, achieved by controlling the mouse pointer. However, an additional complicating factor was the lag in the system. One participant, seeing no apparent activity would take control of the pointer unaware (because of lag) that the other participant was in fact doing something. To overcome these problems an informal turn taking protocol arose during the studies whereby a participant would place the mouse pointer in a particular area of the screen to signify that their turn was completed. The Deva system supports simultaneous use of the input devices by any number of users. The problem that arises in this case is monitoring the individual user's activities. This is of significant importance in a learning environment, as the users need to be aware of the each other's actions in order to proceed and particularly for the expert who needs to know all the stages of the learner's activities. This is comparatively easy when face-to-face interaction occurs, but when the interactions are taking place remotely this is a difficult issue to deal with.

The biggest problem faced by the expert in the second phase was the number of times she was literally not in control in the environment. Whether it was due to lag or the child's lack of awareness of the expert's intended action it is not a situation that a teacher would want to see arise. This is an indication that one vital feature will be the ability to "freeze" the situation and take control. This is an issue supported by Deva system by virtue of its explicit management of the "Time" in an environment, allowing such notions as freezing, or even rewinding of "virtual time". Whether or not such apparently "unnatural" interventions in a teaching environment are appropriate, and exactly when such effects might be required in a 3D CVE is a matter for future investigation.

Another issue that needs further investigation is the effectiveness of the teaching techniques used. Thus different teaching styles are used, such as the reflection method (part of cognitive apprenticeship theory). For example, instead of giving direct feedback to children about their actions the expert ask one of the children to confirm that the other child's action was correct, e.g. "is this move correct", "what would you do if you were asked the same question". Such methods were used in the second phase and what stood out was that if system lag is involved it is very difficult to proceed and leads to frustration.

These application level issues all have implications that feed back into the architecture of the underlying CVE system.

4.4 Studies to take place

If possible the studies will be conducted by taking equipment into the school environment. This might be difficult due to the fact that the VE technology may not be easily portable. Two sets of studies will take place where the population will differ:

1. one child and an expert (played by a researcher)
2. two children and an expert. (played by a researcher)

At the start of the session the children will be shown how to use the system in order to start the activity. Different teaching styles will be used. Two ways of monitoring the activity will be used. The users will be video taped individually and all the activities and dialogues within the system itself will be recorded. This method of monitoring the activities has been decided upon after the second phase experience that indicated that the users had different perceptions of the actual situation. An after session discussion between the participants will follow.

As a starting point standard facilities (desktop monitor and mouse) will be used for the experiments. In future work it is planned to use other tools such as head mounted displays and a 3D mouse in order to examine the impact that these have on interaction and communication issues.

5. Conclusion

The paper has outlined a methodological approach to allow technology requirements to be studied from the point of view of users and the application. The previous phases of work have identified factors concerning the application and the problems of remotely located users. The studies planned for the current phase of work will allow these factors to be explored in more detail by using actual 3D CVE technology. The studies have more evaluative nature. The results of this phase will be used to refine the framework and determine how generic a set of CVLEs it will be applicable to. The findings will be of benefit not only in terms of human factors but also in shaping the direction in which the underlying technology itself develops.

6. Acknowledgement

Thanks to the State Scholarships Foundation of Greece for funding Daphne Economou's Ph.D.; the MMU Manchester Multimedia Centre for use of their facilities; the Advanced Interfaces Group at the University of Manchester Department of Computer Science for help with the third phase and Claremont Road Primary School and Knutsford High School for their co-operation.

7. References

Work from the Kahun project can be found at: http://www.doc.mmu.ac.uk/RESEARCH/virtual-museum/Kahun

[1] Kaur, K.: Designing virtual environments for usability, PhD thesis. Centre for HCI Design, City University, London, 1998.

[2] Carlsoon, C. & Hagsand, O.: DIVE- A Platform for Multiuser Virtual Environments, *Computer and Graphics*, Vol.17, No.6, pp.663-669, 1993.

[3] Benford, S., Bowers, J., Fahèn, L., Greenhalgh, C. & Snowdon, D.: User Embodiment in Collaborative Virtual Environments, Proceedings of ACM CHI'95 Conference on Human Factors in Computing Systems, ACM Press, pp.242-249, 1995.

[4] Greenhalgh, C. & Benford, S.: MASSIVE: a Collaborative Virtual Environment for Tele-conferencing, *ACM Transactions on Computer Human Interfaces (TOCHI), ACM Press,* Vol.2, No.3, pp.239-261, 1995.

[5] Waters, R., C., Anderson, D., B., Barrus, J., W., Brogan, D., C., Casey, M., A., McKeown, S., G., Nitta, T., Sterns, I., B. & Yerazunis, W., S.: Diamond Park and Spine: Social Virtual Reality with 3D Animation, Spoken Interactions, and Runtime Extendability, *Presence*, Vol.6, No.4, pp.461-481, 1997.

[6] Benford, S., Greenhalgh, C. & Lloyd, D.: Crowded Collaborative Virtual Environments, Proceedings of CHI'97, Conference on Human factors in computing systems, ACM Press, pp.58-66, 1997.

[7] Capin, T. K., Pandzic, I. S., Thalmann, N. M. & Thalmann, D.: Realistic Avatars and Autonomous Virtual Humans in: VLNET Networked Virtual Environments, in J.A. Vince & R.A. Earnshaw, *Virtual Worlds on the Internet, IEEE Computer Society Press,* 1998.

[8] Guye-Vuilleme, A., Capin, T. K., Pandzic, I. S., Thalmann, N. M. & Thalmann, D.: Nonverbal Communication Interface for Collaborative Virtual Environments, *Proceedings of CVE'98, Conference of Collaborative Virtual Environments*, pp.105-112, 1998.

[9] Hubbold, R., Cook, J., Keates, M., Gibson, S., Howard, T., Murta, A., West, A. & Pettifer, S.: GNU/MAVERIK: A micro-kernel for large-scale virtual environments, to appear *in proceedings of VRST'99*, London December, 1999.

[10] Pettifer, S.: An operating environment for large scale virtual reality, PhD Thesis, The University of Manchester, 1999.

[11] West, A. J., Howard, T. L. J., Hubbold, R. J., Murta, A. D., Snowdon D. N. & Butler, D. A.: A Generic Virtual Reality Interface for Real Applications, Earnshaw, R.A. & Gigante, M.A. & Jones, H., *Virtual Reality Systems, Academic Press,* pp.213-236, 1993.

[12] Norman, D. A.: Cognitive engineering, in D.A. Norman & S.W. Draper, Hillsdale, User centered system design: new perspectives on human-computer interaction, Lawrence Erlbaum Associates:NJ, 1986.

[13] Macredie, R.: Human factors issues in virtual reality, paper presented at *Virtuality-Human factors Issues Conference,* Cheltenham, 1995.

[14] Stanney, K., M., Mourant, R., R. & Kennedy, R., S.: Human Factors Issues in Virtual Environments: A Review of the Literature, *Presence*, Vol.1, No.7, pp.327-351, 1998.

[15] Zeltzer, D. & Johnson, M. B.: Virtual Actors and Virtual Environments, in MacDonald, L. & Vince, J., *Interacting with Virtual Environments, John Wiley & Sons,* pp.229-255, 1994.

[16] Laurel, B.: Computers as Theatre, Addison-Wesley, 1993.

[17] Granieri, J. P. & Badler, N. I.: Simulating Humans in Virtual Reality, R.A. Earnshaw, J.A. Vince & H.

Jones, Virtual Reality Applications, Academic Press, pp.253-269, 1995.

[18] Slater, M. & Usoh, M.: Body Centered Interaction in Immersive Virtual Environments, N. Thalmann & D. Thalmann, *Artificial life and Virtual Reality, John Wiley and Sons,* pp.123-147, 1994.

[19] Hughes, C. E. and Moshell, J. M.: Shared Virtual Worlds for Education: The Explore Net Experiments, *ACM Multimedia,* Vol.5, No.2, pp. 145-154, 1997.

[20] Johnson, W.L., Stiles, R. & Munro, A.: Integrating Pedagogical Agents into Virtual Environments. *Presence,* Vol.7, No.6, pp.523-546, 1998.

[21] Steed, A., & Tromp, J.: Experiences with the Evaluation of CVE Applications, *Proceedings of Collaborative Virtual Environments CVE'98, University of Manchester, U.K.*, pp.123-130, 1998.

[22] Roussos, M., Johnson, A., Moher, T., Leigh, J., Vasilakis, C. & Barnes, C.: Learning and Building Together in an Immersive Virtual World, *Presence,* Vol.8, No.3, 247-263.

[23] Mitchell, W.L.: Moving the museum onto the Internet: the use of virtual environments in education about ancient Egypt, J.A. Vince and R.A. Earnshaw, *Virtual Worlds on the Internet, IEEE Computer Society Press*, pp.263-278, 1999.

[24] Vygotsky, L. S.: Mind in Society: The Development of Higher Psychological Processes, Cambridge: Harvard University Press, 1978.

[25] Papert, S.: Situating Constructivism, in I. Harel, & S. Papert, *Constructionism, Norwood, Ablex Publishing Corporation:NJ,* pp.1-11, 1993.

[26] Collins, A., Brown, J.S. & Newman, S.E.: Cognitive apprenticeship: teaching the crafts of reading, writing and mathematics, L. B. Resnick, *Cognition and instruction: issues and agendas. Lawrence Erlbaum Associates*, 1989.

[27] DfEE97, Connecting the Learning Society: The Government's Consultation Paper on the National Grid for Learning, *U.K. Department of Education and Employment,* 1997.

[28] DfEE98, Open for Learning, Open for Business: The Government's National Grid for Learning Challenge, *U.K. Department of Education and Employment,* 1998.

[29] Bigge, M.L. & Shermis, S.S.: Learning Theories for Teachers, Harper Collins, 1992.

[30] Economou, D., Mitchell, W.L., and Boyle, T.: A Phased Approach to Developing a Set of Requirements for the Use of Virtual Actors in Shared Virtual Learning Environments, *Proceedings of ED-MEDIA 98: 10th World Conference on Educational Multimedia and Hypermedia.* Association for the Advancement of Computing in Education, pp.1620-1621, 1998.

[31] Economou, D., Mitchell, W. L., Boyle, T.: Requirements Elicitation for Virtual Actors in Collaborative Learning Environments, *Computers & Education*, Heller, R. S. & Underwood, J. (eds.), Elsevier Science Ltd., Oxford, to appear.

[32] Stewart, J., Bederson, B.B. & Druin, A.: Single Display Groupware: A Model for Co-operative Collaboration, *Proceedings of ACM CHI'99, Conference on Human Factors in Computing Systems, ACM Press,* 1999.

[33] Jordan, B. & Henderson, A.: Interaction Analysis,: Foundations and Practice, *The Journal of Learning Sciences, Lawrence Erlbaum Associates, Inc.*, Vol.4, No.1, pp.39-103, 1995.

[34] Druin, A., Stewart, J., Proft, D., Bederson, B. & Hollan, J.: KidPad: A Design Collaboration Between Children, Technologists and Educators, *Proceedings of ACM CHI'97, Conference on Human Factors in Computing Systems, ACM Press,* pp.463-470, 1997.

[35] Economou, D., Mitchell, W.L., and Boyle, T.: Towards a user-centred method for studying CVLEs, Proceedings of the one-day ERCIM WG UI4ALL joint Workshop with i3 Spring Das 2000 on "Interactive Learning Environments for Children, Athens, 2000.

[36] Lester, J.C., Converse, S.A., Kahler, S.E., Barlow, S.T, Stone, B.A. & Bhoga, R.S.: The Persona Effect: Affective Impact of Animated Pedagogical Agents, *Proceedings of ACM CHI'97, Conference on Human Factors in Computing Systems, ACM Press,* pp.359-366, 1997.

Building Virtual Worlds for Informal Science Learning (SciCentr and SciFair) in the Active Worlds Educational Universe (AWEDU)

Margaret Corbit
Cornell Theory Center
533 Rhodes Hall, Cornell Univ.
Ithaca, NY 14853 USA
+1 607 254 8716
corbitm@tc.cornell.edu

Abstract

As a focus of its exploration of desktop 3D environments for science outreach, the Cornell Theory Center (CTC), Cornell University's high-performance computing center, has been exploring the use of the Active Worlds client/server technology for implementation of a 3D multi-user virtual science museum, SciCentr, that incorporates interactive simulation-based exhibits. We present here early lessons in accommodating the needs of several, interconnected user groups as we move forward with establishing the SciCentr community within the greater educational community of AWEDU and the Contact Consortium's V-Learn3D initiative. We have realized that we must provide the user communities with both social and spatial frameworks within which to work and play. Social support ranges from one-on-one over-the-shoulder help, to guidance and training within the environment, to coordination of "inworld" activities. Spatial design requirements depend on the activities of the user group and benefit from study of real and virtual world examples.

1. SciCentr Concept

In contrast to most virtual science centers on the Internet, primarily Web sites for traditional science centers, SciCentr stands alone in cyberspace. The mission of SciCentr is to engage and educate all of its community members—in ways appropriate to their own levels of interest and commitment—to the excitement, humanity, and complexity of computational science.

SciCentr and its daughter world, SciFair, are loosely based on the social model of a bricks and mortar institution. The traditional museum community includes curators and exhibit designers, advisors, educators, docents, members, and visitors. Each of these groups has its own analog in the virtual environment and its own set of expectations, needs, and potential contributions. Thus the analogous SciCentr/SciFair "user community" is comprised of advisors and technical experts at its core, surrounded by clusters of content and exhibit developers along with educators and volunteers, and finally the target audience, primarily youth between the ages of 11 and 21. This community will build a body of knowledge incorporated into SciCentr in an engaging environment. It should be pointed out here that "upward mobility" is a goal of this project also, and that members of the target audience are encouraged to acquire the skills required to enable them to move closer to the core of expertise.

The spatial design model for SciCentr is a hybrid of a conventional museum and a World's Fair. SciFair is roughly analogous to the classroom/clubhouse of a museum. It serves as a place where youth can experiment with the MUVE technology and use it to construct and share their knowledge about the areas of science featured in SciCentr. Outstanding efforts in SciFair can be rewarded with "places" in the public exhibitions.

CTC's virtual worlds, including SciCentr and SciFair, are based on the Active Worlds client/server environment. In contrast to worlds created in VRML—see Damer, 1998 [1] for an overview of the different environments, these virtual places incorporate several kinds of 3D rendering formats and link to Web technologies but are wedded to a proprietary browser, which can be downloaded for free and is very efficient. All developers (student, professional, and high school world builders) have citizenships (user ids and passwords) that allow them to visit all of the worlds in AWEDU and that enable them to acquire building and more advanced privileges in individual worlds. In addition to the Active Worlds servers, we have incorporated IIS, SQLServer, MATLAB, and RealServer into the world server complex.

2. Early Development

Construction/creation of SciCentr began during the academic year 1998-9. To date, development of

0-7695-0798-9/00 $10.00

SciCenter has focused on interactive exhibits analogous to those of a traditional hands-on science center, but presented solely within the virtual space. These include: the Fourier Fountain, a multi-user musical crystal modeled after the Singing Fountains of the 1939 World's Fair; the Plant Breeding Beds of our Genehouse that allow avatars to selectively breed tomatoes and post and share their results; and the Fantastic Flask, currently serving as an interface to interactive VRML molecular modeling modules presented in the browser's WWW window. They represent nodes in terms of both content and space.

As a high-performance computing center, CTC has been involved in online science outreach since the Web came into being. We have developed many sites that focus on explaining the use of computer modeling and simulation to study a wide variety of problems ranging from molecular modeling to tokamak design and disaster management. We have a special interest in technologies that will allow us to share 3D research results, giving the audience insight into the scientists' experience. Recent studies on the affect of using immersive environments in curriculum-based education suggest that virtual reality can enhance the learner's experience and help them understand such complex problems [2]. With this in mind, SciCentr exhibits will feature 3D data files as annotated landscapes (for example the solution space of a financial model) and as objects within an exhibit.

SciCentr exhibits also will offer constructivist learning opportunities through game-like simulations. In particular, the Plant Breeding Beds represent an inquiry-based digital laboratory for plant breeding simulations. They are based on custom software that generates new generations of virtual plants (tomatoes in the first implementation) using quantitative genetics algorithms. Selective breeding takes place through a repetitive process. Individual users can document their results in 2D with text and images within the space for sharing and presentation.

In the area of wave science, SciCentr is developing an interactive feature that incorporates sound and graphics to present a virtual "singing fountain" inspired by a major feature in the 1939 World's Fair. This feature, the Fourier Fountain (Figure 1), is effectively an online, multi-user musical instrument that resembles a pipe organ. Designed in collaboration with digital artists at the Art Center College of Design (ACCD) in Pasadena, CA, the fountain is made up of a group of crystal-like objects: a central core structure and smaller "key" crystals floating in space around it. Users play the keys by clicking, hear a sound on their desktops and wait for a set number of keys to be played. At the end of a cycle, a message is sent to all avatars in the space and a combined chord is also sent to their desktop audio plugins. Thus users from around the planet can make chords together and hear them played back in "realtime", i.e., as quickly as the network can deliver them. In addition, the chords are visualized using MATLAB and the images are sent to files that can be viewed in the environment's Web window. The Web pages and documentation for this feature will encourage visitors to compile their own sets of sounds and submit them to be played on the fountain. As both of these features come into use, we expect to have to deal with scaling issues that are both technical and spatial (see Space and Place below).

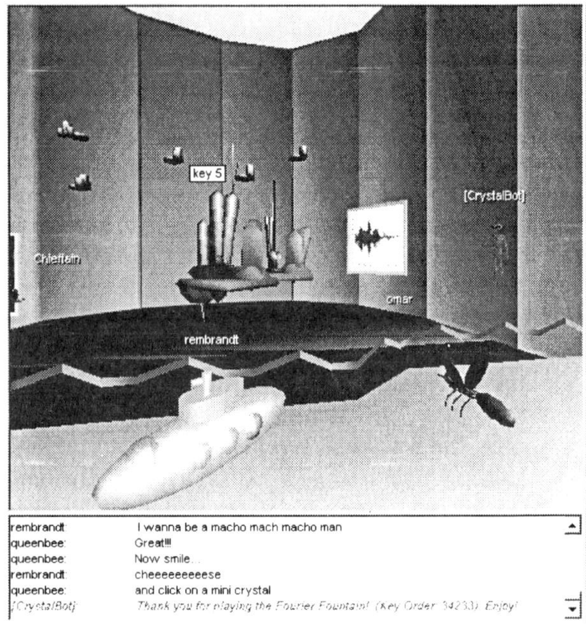

Figure 1. Avatars (omar, rembrandt, and Chieftain) play the small crystal keys of the Fourier Fountain. Corresponding sections of the central crystal structure flash yellow as the sound is played on the desktop. The CrystalBot tells them the order in which signals from the first five keys played were received and then plays back a "chord" based on sounds from the keys: 2, 3, and 4. Visualization of a sound generated by MATLAB is posted on a sign object in the space.

Technical development of our worlds involves server management, creation of 3D objects, animation of avatars, and programming of interactive bots and related programs. We opted to serve our worlds from a computer that is also serving the related Web pages, multimedia files, and running MATLAB. This system was set up for ease of access, and will no doubt need to be reconfigured as the project scales. 3D objects, generally created in the Renderware format, download compressed from the server to the desktop. Avatars are complex, animated, and fully 3D. They are assigned animation sequences, which provide them with use initiated behaviors (dance, wave, angry, etc.). Bots, while treated as avatars by the world system, can be assigned to any object or location in a world. In order to run independently, however, they must run as services. Further technical details are available at the ActiveWorlds help pages (http://www.activeworlds.com/help/). We found it straightforward to use the objects, avatars, and simple bots provided with the worlds (for example in SciFair), however, it is much more of a challenge to create the custom features needed for SciCentr.

3. Social Considerations

As an online community, SciCentr and SciFair users require a social structure that is extensible and tailored to their needs [3]. Although the developers, the audience, and the science fair youth each represent subgroups of this community, it will be important to establish and maintain movement and communications among them.

3.1 Developers

The developer community for SciCentr and SciFair is comprised primarily of undergraduate students at Cornell University. In addition, there are several high school student programmers who work in the lab on specific challenges (for example a flexible interface for creating chat trivia games that will be used by SciFair builders and avatar design). Developers' skills encompass graphic design, content development, avatar design, Web and multimedia design, C, C++, and JAVA programming, and systems management. Consequently, they must master 2- and 3D graphics software, texture mapping and changing tools, format translation tools, programming environments, multimedia tools and related servers, mathematical analysis and visualization tools, etc.

Students rely on each other, CTC staff, and the greater community of hobby and professional developers as they come up to speed. A significant amount of the program leader's time is devoted to supporting the developers. Facilitating communications among this group, literally spread out across 3 continents, has been difficult. As developers begin to master skills, their participation in the community also increases as long as the community is flexible enough to accommodate changing roles [4].

3.2 Early Users

Early users of SciCentr and SciFair fall into three categories: peers and the development team meeting for demonstrations and tour of works in progress; groups of students coming inworld for the first time and thus being exposed to both the medium and the content at the same time; and a pilot group of SciFair builders coming inworld remotely from a rural high school as an extracurricular activity. Each type of early user has important input to contribute to the formative evaluation of the project.

Peer visitors include design student, members of round table discussions/demonstrations coordinated by AWEDU, and informal groups of professional developers offering their insights/feedback on new features. These range from detailed suggestions for adding functionality to objects in the space to philosophical perspectives on "virtuality." The contributions of these "outside experts" are focused, useful, and important in terms of sustaining interest in the medium. These experienced users are eager to try new features and to play in new places.

We have hosted visits for more than 100 teens, mostly young women between the ages of 12 and 18, in lab environments for approximately 1.5 hours per session. This allows time to learn how to navigate, communicate, and be exposed to the building process, but leaves little time to explore content. Interviews suggest that these young users become immersed within minutes of logging in. Initial responses based on exit surveys have been overwhelmingly positive and appear to be correlated with prior interest in the Internet. Girls are excited about the medium, interested in contributing, but daunted by the perceived challenge of developing content. In contrast, adults coming inworld remotely for the first time (including academics that are sophisticated computer users) have been less comfortable with and less enthusiastic about the environment and appropriately more concerned about the content.

Members of the pilot group of teens for SciFair are learning how to use the medium in stages within a constructivist framework [5]. This group of up to six students comes online from their computer lab twice a week for about one hour per session. We have taken advantage of the online introductory documentation hosted by AW and training offered to the lab coordinator by the corps of volunteer educators. By the end of their first month, the SciFair students had taken possession of a corner of the world for homesteading, this includes establishment and construction of a conferencing facility, and were prepared to begin planning content around the concept of breeding tomatoes for different purposes.

4. Space and Place

There are at least two distinctly different approaches to the use of space in 3D virtual worlds. One is related to the text chat world model where space is divided into places according to theme. In this case, it doesn't matter where the places are because you access them by passing through portals. This mode of organizing space can be used effectively in 3D virtual worlds, especially in mazes and conferencing worlds, such as the AVATARS meeting worlds (AV98 and av99). It applies to world designs that ar intended to present a predetermined path or tour [6] through space. A second approach is to lay out the space in such a way that people explore the space and can create their own personal image of the places within the world. This approach benefits from landscape, interior, and urban design concepts.

The spatial layout of the virtual worlds SciCentr and SciFair differ because of their functions. SciCentr is modeled after a futuristic discovery space, a science center at the scale of a World's Fair. Exhibits requiring bots can be interwoven with spaces focused on other uses such as communication and display and are staged at different elevations. Overlooks and plazas are provided as landmarks and gathering points. This is an ambitious vision at the landscape scale. In contrast, SciFair is being laid out to facilitate novice developers and their efforts.

For SciCentr, we are drawing on design concepts from graphic, interior, museum, and landscape design, and in particular studying principles of urban planning [7] suggested by William Mitchell during an online forum (http://www.mheim.com/cyberforum/) hosted by ACCD. Our hope is to preserve a coherent whole while making it easy to tell when you have moved from one node to another. The visual scale and flavor of SciCentr was originally inspired by images of the 1939 World's Fair. As the world grows, we are encouraging annotation of the exhibits with references to the Fair through the use of 3D icons. These will link to Web pages that make connections between historic information and the exhibit in which they have been placed.

While the use of urban design concepts such as paths and nodes for navigation and support of the users' personal images of SciCentr as a place are very important, we have learned from expert designers that there are constraints built into the 3D environment that also affect layout. For example, experts have learned from experience that the Ground Zero area of a world and its immediate surroundings are best left open and used as a lobby rather than a center of activity. This is done primarily to minimize the initial download demand on the desktop when entering a new world with custom, and therefore new, objects and avatars.

Another constraint relates to point of view. Users are able to switch between looking through the eyes of your avatar and watching over its shoulder at a fair distance. If a room is too small, then you end up feeling as if you have been thrown out of it when you change your point of view and are left confused, i.e., outside looking in.

These issues serve as reminders that this is a digital space. And as such, the term "space" relates to file space, another concern in world design. In general, the compressed objects take up a small amount of space on the desktop. However, heavy use of custom objects and textures and multimedia features can put a severe demand on the latest of desktops and drive away potential visitors. Therefore, it is important to spread out content rich areas and to optimize compression.

SciCentr is a place to explore, while SciFair is more of a clubhouse, modeled after open building worlds. Kim [3] suggests that initial community spaces should be modest and their growth constrained by the needs of the community. This is certainly our approach to SciFair. Because of the spatial constraints for straightforward implementation of bots, SciFair is divided into 9 regions on the XY plane planned to support 8 working groups, each with its own isolated working area. In addition, we are encouraging citizens of SciFair to work together to layout an object yard, the virtual equivalent of a building supply yard, where they can view and select objects to incorporate into their designs. Object yards are tedious to create and difficult to maintain, however they serve an important role in supporting open building.

The space in virtual places cannot yet simulate real world physics and need not fall under its constraints. For example, some worlds make effective use of collision and gravity, while other ignore one or both. SciCentr and SciFair do not impose the AW interpretation of gravity and attempt to use collision selectively. ACCD world demonstrates an effective design that leaves behind gravity, including providing many bird and insect avatars. SciCentr follows this model with submarines, spaceships, and mosquitoes.

Sense of place in ActiveWorlds can be enhanced by ambient sound. While SciCentr and SciFair do not yet take advantage of this feature, several worlds offer sounds at Ground Zero that immediately give the visitor a flavor for the world. For example, a virtual representation of the eight residential campuses at the University of California, Santa Cruz, V-UCSC presents a recording of the natural background sounds on campus, birds and breexes. In contrast, evocative sounds usher you into the various nodes in ACCD world.

Finally, world designs span a continuum from the fantastic to the super real [8] depending on their purpose and the philosophies of their builders. Designers have just begun to explore the potential of this medium for designing digital places.

5. SUPPORT

All SciCentr developers encounter a significant learning curve in terms of the technology as our interests are focused on customizing the environment and content development. Working with limited resources and time, developers need to communicate among themselves in order to avoid redundancy of effort and to foster creativity. Creating new listserves, bulletin boards, etc. has not been effective. Rather, individuals participate in existing SIGs and lists supported by AWEDU and CCON. Members of these groups have also donated one-on-one support to student developers. Individuals generate Web resources for the group and then edit that content in response to feedback from new users coming online. In this way, they are able to contribute back to the larger community. (It should be noted that there are real concerns about copyrights and ownership of custom content that have not yet been addressed.)

Periodic presentations for new audiences, quasi-regular online meetings, and conferences sponsored by AW and CCON help to focus the work, ground the effort by providing insights into the experience of the target users, and offer the opportunity for the developers to think about the project from a broader perspective. In addition, V-Learn3D is establishing a world in AWEDU that will serve as a reference library for the community. Interestingly, interactions among these users are consistently playful and the culture appears to be strongly influenced by the medium. Developers gravitate to spaces where they can meet with minimum interruption from curious casual visitors and to especially designed conferencing spaces out of curiosity about new developments.

First time users appear to require personal support. Over-the-shoulder contact is ideal, supplemented by chat support from an online guide. Regardless of age or level of sophistication, first time users will play for an extended time period, exploring avatars, chat features, and navigation. Thus exposure to content at the first encounter is superficial. It is most important to engage the users and encourage them to plan to return for a deeper exploration, and consequently to establish a framework that will facilitate return visits and opportunities for contributing to the environment at a novice level. Each of the initial exhibits has at least one approach to enabling contribution incorporated into its conceptual design. The layout of SciCentr focuses on providing an engaging environment for this audience.

Participants in the pilot SciFair project are supported on site by the school's technology coordinator, René Carver, and online by students and staff at Cornell. This group has been assigned an isolated location in the grid layout of SciFair in which to experiment with designing virtual places. In addition, Carver has received online training from the AWEDU training corps. This is a group of adolescents working after school in a social environment. They need time to explore and play on their own. Interestingly, they immediately appointed a "real estate agent" to oversee allocation of space for home building.

Within the limitations of approximately one-hour sessions, we have moved forward quickly with technology training and in one month have begun to introduce the science concepts on which they will focus content development into the "conversation" that takes place as they work. Because content development will entail multimedia skills and writing/research, this team may seek new members, including girls, to fill out its skills roster. The initial team may shift the focus to training new members and to design issues. At this point, team responsibilities and goals can be established.

6. Conclusion

In the context of establishing a knowledge media environment, our early experience working in a 3D environment with avatars has been positive. We are confident that it is possible to present data within the virtual world dynamically and to allow visitors to contribute content to the space. We have experienced a steep learning curve and have established preliminary methods for supporting a very diverse user community. We rely heavily on the greater community of AW and AWEDU developers and designers for advice and mentoring. Because our project is evolving over time and is affected by ever-changing technologies, CTC focuses a great deal of energy on supporting the developers and plans to expand alliances with youth educators at regional and national institutions and with other educational world developers, for example student game developers, as the museum opens to the online public.

7. References

[1] Damer, Bruce. 1998. Avatars! Exploring and Building Virtual Worlds on the Internet, Berkeley, CA. Peach Pit Press.

[2] Dede, Chris, Marylin Salzman, R. Bowen Loftin, Debra Sprague. 1999. Multisensory Immersion as a Modeling Environment for Learning Complex Scientific Concepts, in Computer Modeling and Simulation in Science Education; Roberts et al [editors], Springer-Verlag.

[3] Kim, Amy Jo. 2000. Community Building on the Web. Berkeley, CA. Peach Pit Press.

[4] Kuuti, Kari. 1996. Activity Theory as a Potential Framework for Human-Computer Interaction Research, in Context and Consciousness, Bonnie A. Nardi [ed], The MIT Press, Camdridge, MA, USA.

[5] Kafai, Yasmin B. 1995. Minds in Play: Computer Game Design as a Context for Children's Learning. Lawrence Erlbaum Asociates, Mahwah, New Jersey, USA.

[6] Jensen, Jens. 1999. From "Flatland" to "Spaceland", Spatial Representation, Enunciation and Interaction in 3D-Virtual Worlds. WebNet Journal Vol.1, No. 1, pp 44-57.

[7] Lynch, Kevin, 1960. The Image of the City, The MIT Press, Camdridge, MA, USA.

[8] Corbit, Margaret D. 1999. Virtual Worlds: Literal vs Fantastic, http://www.tc.cornell.edu/Exhibits/Worlds/slides/litvsfan/index.html.

ETOILE – An Environment for Team, Organizational and Individual Learning in Emergencies

Ralf Dörner, Paul Grimm
Fraunhofer Applications Center for Computer Graphics
Frankfurt / Main, Germany
{doerner, grimm}@agc.fhg.de

Abstract

This paper discusses several aspects of the ETOILE system, an environment for team, organizational and individual learning in emergencies that may be considered as a knowledge networked environment. These aspects are authoring, combination of agents and integration of knowledge sources (databases or external simulators), visualization of behavior in a 3D virtual environment, design of the human – agent interface as well as modeling, describing and assessing human behavior. Based on the experiences in the ETOILE project conclusions are drawn for the design of a knowledge networked environment for learning purposes.

1 Introduction

The ETOILE (*E*nvironment for *T*eam, *O*rganizational and *I*ndividual *L*earning in *E*mergencies) system provides a knowledge networked environment for people who train how to communicate and act as a team. As an application example the training how to cope with emergency situations has been chosen. In ETOILE the following strategies are pursued in order to create an innovative training environment:

- Usage of intelligent agents. With agents we denote software units that are autonomous as well as reactive (perceive their environment and may react on events in its environment), pro-active (are able to make actions without external trigger) and that have a social ability (are able to communicate with other agents or human beings) [Wool97]. Intelligent agents are used for simulating humans in a training scenario and act analogously to "computer players" in a computer game. In this sense the agents represent the knowledge how humans behave in emergency situations. In this context, agents have been already successfully used [Rain00, Yin00]
- Usage of computer networks. Computer networks realize the distribution of the training scenario simulation and allow a location independent training.
- Usage of virtual reality. Virtual reality is used to enable a training participant to act with other participants and the agents in a virtual world. The virtual environment also provides means to interact and influence the simulation of the training scenario. It solves the problem associated with the usage of real equipment or the possibly dangerous simulation of emergency situations in a real environment.
- Usage of psychological models for human communication, interaction and team behavior. The psychological models are used to model, describe and assess the high-level semantic interaction of a human trainee with other training participants.

The topic of this paper is to discuss various aspects of the ETOILE system which we consider to be important for a successful application of a knowledge networked environment in the application area of emergency training. These aspects are

1. Authoring
2. Modeling, describing and assessing human behavior
3. Combination of agents and integration of knowledge sources (databases or external simulators)
4. Visualization of behavior in a 3D virtual environment
5. Design of the human – agent interface

The paper is organized as follows. Each of the aspect listed above is discussed in an own section relating to the reasons of its importance, the requirements for the knowledge networked environment and the approach taken in the ETOILE system. After this discussion conclusions are drawn for a general usage of knowledge networked environments for training purposes. But let us start in the next section with a brief description of the application background of ETOILE (in order to

0-7695-0798-9/00 $10.00 © 2000 IEEE

understand the application goals) as well as the context of its realization.

2 Application Background and Realization

First, let us consider which problems are associated with communication and decision team training for dealing with emergency situations. As an example, let us think of a Metro train that is on fire and stuck in a tunnel where the passengers need to be evacuated safely or an incident in a nuclear power plant where the environment is to be protected. The first problem is that in contrast to operational training many individuals and teams from different organizations are involved (e.g. operators, supervisors, management and owners, authorities, firemen and rescue). It is difficult to agree upon a common date and location for performing a training session. If one individual that has a certain role in a training scenario is missing the whole training cannot take place. And training is very costly (e.g. in a Metro training there are more than 400 people involved). This results in a low training frequency. Furthermore, it is not possible to train in the real location (e.g. in the nuclear power plant) or only at restricted times (e.g. in the night where there is no Metro service). Thus, the date of training is known and trainees are able to prepare themselves beforehand. Last but not least, a didactical training concept is needed that shows how to improve team performance and decision taking. In order to solve these problems the methodologies already addressed in the introduction have been used and implemented in the context of the ETOILE project [ETOI00]. Here the two training examples described above are developed, one for the Metro in Bilbao, the other for a nuclear power plant in Confrentes, Spain. A prototype system has been implemented in the object-oriented language Java [Java00] on a standard PC platform. In the implementation use has been made of the Java Beans framework. This existing component concept offers the advantage that already existing Bean development kits and authoring tools can be used. The VR part is implemented in a C++ graphics library [Open00] and connected with the Java native interface to the rest of the application. For performance reasons a special communication link exists between the VR parts in order to synchronize the shared virtual worlds using multicast. Criteria for the selection of the agent system have been the degree of support for an author in specifying the behavior, performance issues and the ease of integrating actions. The implementation has been done with Blaze Advisor [Blaz00], a rule-based system that was mainly designed for business applications. It is possible to directly invoke Java methods of arbitrary Java classes in the rules. Therefore the actions are organized as a Java class library. Figure 1 shows the graphical user interface of the learner and the trainer application. The same interfaces are used for the two different training scenarios. The trainer application provides administrative features like managing the training participants (e.g. definition which roles are played by an agent and which by a human) or starting and stopping a training session. Additionally it is possible for the trainer to mark certain training situations in that way, that alternative training sequences can be tested by setting back the training status to the marked situation. The review part of the trainer application allows the analysis of a training cycle by providing a "replay" of the training session based on logged information.

For interacting with the training system, the trainee is provided with two user interfaces that are shown in parallel: a 2D GUI and a 3D virtual environment. In the 2D GUI the trainee may take a look at the overall training scenario structure (e.g. which roles are involved in training, which role is played by a human, which communication devices do exist, what is the training status, etc.) and use assistance and help functions. In addition, the learner may interact with the virtual environment navigating with the mouse or cooperating with his colleagues (e.g. to talk to a colleague by selecting his avatar) and with the environment (e.g. using telephones or look at computer monitors).

In general, a training takes place with the following steps. First, the trainees connect to the trainer who selects a training scenario and distribute the roles of the scenario to the trainees and the agents. Second, the scenario starts by simulating the environment and provoke communication actions of the agents and the trainees. The trainees interact with the virtual environment. Third, the training scenario execution is stopped and the results are discussed among the training participants in a review phase.

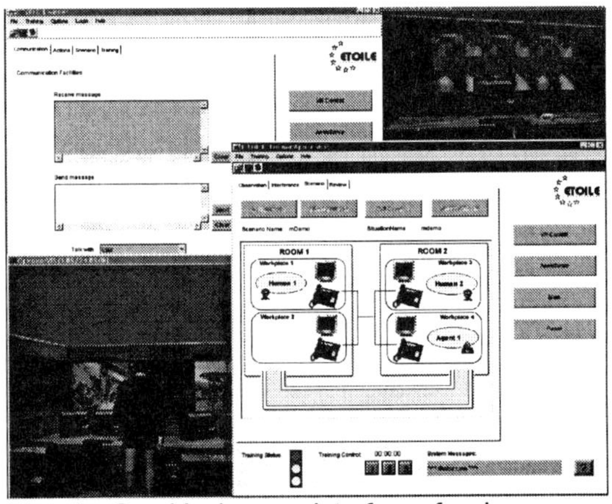

Fig. 1: Graphical user interface for learner and trainer of the ETOILE prototype

3 Concepts and Architecture of ETOILE

3.1 Authoring

Why is authoring so important? The acceptance of a knowledge networked environment depends mainly on its content. Especially for learning environments it is important, that an agent based training scenario will be persuasive. This means that the knowledge of the author has to be transferred to an agent description. Providing a realistic and practical content is only possible, if the author knows the application background very well. Additionally, an adaptation of the training scenario by the trainer (he controls a training) is necessary to run an adequate training session. Furthermore, the possibility to modify a training scenario by a trainer or trainees after the training in a review phase will lead to an improved scenario behavior description and is a strategy to realize organizational learning.

How can we enable the end-users (trainer and trainees) to perform authoring tasks mentioned above? First, the aim is to shift the programming skills to underlying libraries and basic components, which are used in higher abstraction levels. To reach the required training complexity several authoring layers have to be involved in the development of an effective and cost reducing system. Second, it is aimed to separate different author roles where a single author should have as few special skills (like skills in defining agents, application specific skills, pedagogical skills, geometric modeling skills) as possible. The overall goal is to build a pyramid of author roles (see Fig. 2) where on top is an end user. Third, specific editors supports a single author by accessing underlying authoring layers.

How have these theoretical rules been put into practice in ETOILE? Let us take the example that an end user wants to describe the behavior of an agent. Other authors with more knowledge in agent specifications, 3D animation and programming have written components that this author may use. On the one hand there is a library of actions, e.g. actions like "moving from one place to an other" or "telephoning". The author does not have to take care about implementation details, for example how the telephone is actually addressed or how a movement behavior is animated. The actions may have side effects like altering the status of the shared mental model of an agent or the writing of logs. Using these pre-defined actions an author writes rules that describe which action an agent takes when certain conditions are met. Beside the actions, the author is provided with rulesets and behavior patterns that he can add to the rules he writes. Or the author can modify existing rulesets by substituting actions. For example, a ruleset may describe the behavior of trying to reach someone via telephone. To support the author, tools are provided that allow him to browse the provided components, write the rules, organize behavior descriptions at different level of abstraction and view the results of his authoring efforts. An author needs different views (rule bases, ruleflows, petri networks, realistic presentation as 3D animation) on an agent description in order to control the complexity. The goal is that the users perception of an agent is already available during authoring. Therefore, it is difficult to write a whole training scenario with a common agent system such as Soar [Soar00] that provides a rather complex scripting language for expressing the rules. The lack of control between defining a small agent and writing a whole training scenario is a problem of most agent frameworks. This is the reason why a specific behavior editor has been developed (it is described in more detail in section 3.2). In order to write a complete training scenario the author from the end user side has to provide a description of the scenario geometry beside the agent behavior description. The according tool is described in section 3.4.

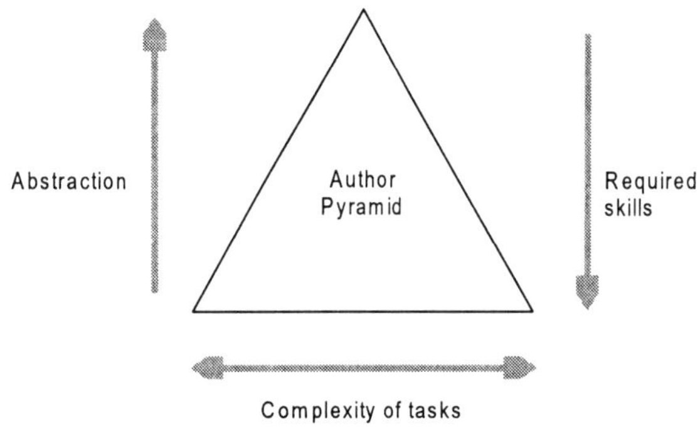

Fig. 2: Pyramid of authoring roles

Finally, let us take a look at some implementation issues that arise when we want to implement the authoring process described above. Separating the authoring process into several levels and tasks results in some implications. First it is necessary to store agent descriptions in behavior libraries as autonomous and encapsulated components, so that they can be reused to build different agents and training scenarios. Second these behavior libraries are organized in a hierarchy in order to implement the idea of an authoring pyramid. Third the agents are embedded in an object-oriented framework. Accordingly, a skeleton application is conceived that represents a working but generic "empty" training application. The application has to be filled, adapted and customized by an author in order to instantiate a specific training scenario. Components are provided for the filling of the skeleton application. Components can represent different entities used in the training application, for instance software classes, geometries, animation, rules or user interface elements. Each type of component has to obey standards in order to be able to collaborate. As the components are designed to be reusable they can be collected in a library. This is one advantage of this concept. Another advantage is that the inversion of control achieved with the usage of the skeleton application frees the author from the task of assembling components and make them work together.

3.2 Modeling, Describing and Assessing Human Behavior

For the application context of team and communicative training the intelligent agents have to know how to behave as a team member together with other humans and agents. This has to be true in general when the knowledge represented in the agents should be made available to humans in a persuasive and natural way.

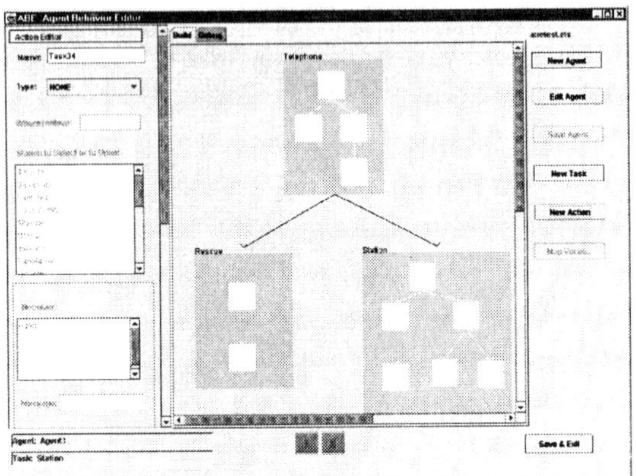

Fig. 3: Abstract view of a training scenario

Agents are well suited for modeling human behavior because often mentalistic notions like desire, belief or intention are used in order to describe agent behavior. Moreover, agent systems have been successfully used for implementing psychological models in a software environment, e.g. models of human team behavior like the joint intentions theory for aircraft combat trainings [Tamb97]. In ETOILE the theory of shared mental models [Gent83] is used in order to describe and assess human behavior. One way of implementing is to associate a simulation model with each agent that allows him to predict the actions of the humans. This comparison may also be logged and compared with the behavior of the human trainee in a review phase after a training session in order to assess the performance of the human.

The ETOILE system includes an agent behavior editor (ABE, see Fig. 3), which allows a graphical authoring of a training scenario. A scenario consists out of many tasks that compete with each other and are chosen due to their priority. To solve a task an agent carries out actions which itself describe atomic activities (e.g. calling somebody or going to an other room) or tries to solve sub-tasks. To write the behavior description of an agent the author has to arrange the tasks and the actions by selecting them from a library and by defining pre and post condition when they will be executed and when they will be finished. The resulting dependencies will be shown as arrows. Grouping actions in tasks allows reusability of recurring action patterns. This is a first step to reduce the given complexity. In addition, the editor offers the author means to specify parameters that are associated with each action.

3.3 Combination of Agents and Integration of Knowledge Sources

A collaborative knowledge system implies that agents are interoperable. Naturally, for a widespread usage reusability and exchangeability are necessary. Agents written by different authors should be able to cooperate and to share their knowledge. Addressing this goal it is common to define the communication layer between agents instead of defining an implementation interface. Today, there exist several agent communication languages and knowledge representations, for example KIF [Gene92], KQML [Fini94] and ACL [FIPA00]. Two kinds of access to existing knowledge bases are required. First of all this includes access to databases that store information to be used by the trainee and the scenario simulation, i.e. emergency plans. Interoperation between agents and databases are not a trivial problem, since the semantic structure of a database conflicts to an agent structure. Second, integration of external simulators can be necessary, e.g. a wind simulator has to be integrated in the nuclear incident training example.

In the ETOILE project we use message passing as communication layer. Since all communication in our system is based on message passing, the agent is connected to the system and thus to his environment by a message system. This means all sensory input as well as all actions of the agent are encapsulated in messages, which are sent through the communication platform. As an example, if the lights are turned off in the agent's room the agent will receive a message accordingly. If he wants to switch it on again he will send another message describing the action he is about to take.

Agents can only understand a message when there is a rule that interprets that message. This means that the set of meaningful messages is limited for any agent. We call this set "vocabulary" or specifically "passive vocabulary" since this is the vocabulary that the agent uses passively, i.e. that the agent understands. Additionally there is an "active vocabulary" which defines all messages that an agent will actively send out. These vocabularies are made explicit in the description of an ETOILE agent using a specific message format. Communication between two participants is always possible when the intersection between the active vocabulary of the sender and the passive vocabulary of the receiver is not empty.

The agents have to be embedded in the skeleton application as components. The task of the skeleton application is to provide a framework for the agent at syntax and implementation level. In order to avoid inconsistencies in the state of the environment, no agent or human may take decisions concerning the results or even the success of his actions (If the agent wants to "extinguish the fire" he can not decide if or when the fire is extinguished, but of course he can stop trying it if he decides that it takes too long). This evaluation of any action is done by a specialized agent, which is named *ScenarioAgent*. He has no graphical representation in the training scenario but is responsible for the behavior of everything, which is not represented by an agent or a human participant. There is only one ScenarioAgent in a single training. Changes in the state of the training environment occur in the ScenarioAgent and are propagated to all participants by messages.

3.4 Visualization of Behavior in a 3D Virtual Environment

A visualization of the training scenario as a virtual world enables a human trainee to interact with autonomous agents or with a remote trainee. Even for non computer scientists, like most of the trainees, it is an intuitive way to control and influence a training simulation, i.e. to look at somebody (or its avatar) if he wants to talk to him (see Fig. 4). Recognizing emotions is another example for visualization of information. Important to the visualization is that the training participant does not feel constricted. This affects in particular the interaction freedom and the level of detail. For example if a trainee finds communication facilities within the visualization, he should be able to use them. The visualization ensures that timely restrictions are obeyed as it takes the same time in reality to perceive information about the training scenario status (opposed to reading it as a text). It is possible to give many visual clues (like the movement of other training participants) and many communication requests at once, especially as in ETOILE real communication devices like telephone and fax are integrated in the training system. As a consequence a stressful training situation can be build that is needed for emergency trainings even if the training focuses only on the communication aspects.

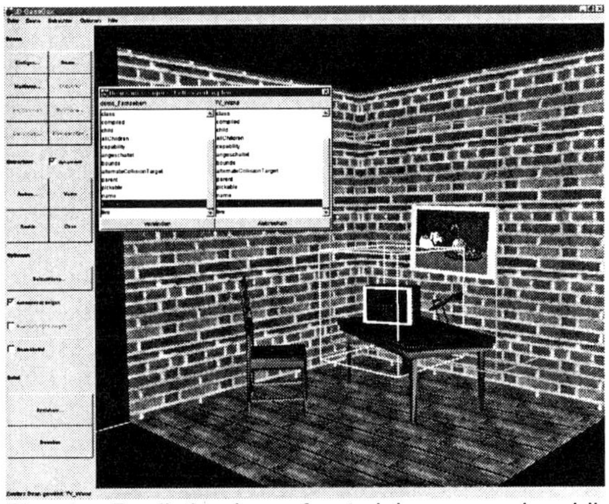

Fig. 4a: Realistic view of a training scenario while inserting the component "monitor" in the virtual environment using a 3D BeanBox

Fig. 4b: Virtual environment depicting a control room of a Metro station during training runtime

There are two possible solutions to integrate a visualization part into the ETOILE system. The first solution uses a monolithic application with one interface; the second one is to use a component-based approach, which divides the visualization into separated autonomous units. Each of these components is responsible for its own visualization in order to provide an own interface. Due to performance reasons the monolithic way is the most common. But the second alternative fits much better to the postulated authoring concept (see section 3.1), which is based on several individual authors. The concept of 3D Beans [Doer00], a component-based three-dimensional extension of JavaBeans, provides an adequate solution for the runtime environment as well as for the authoring. Here pre-defined geometric components with associated animations are provided that may be steered by the actions used by the agents behavior author or by mouse events. The authoring environment allows that the components are inserted in a virtual environment by a drag-and-drop metaphor. A geometrical component may be associated with a behavior description. Once this has been done the functionality of a component is directly available. Especially, the components can directly visualize the behavior specified by the author. The concept enables us to divide geometry related authoring tasks in the same way as it is done by the agent definitions.

The visualization of a distributed system requires an extension in the communication layer. The reason is that synchronization of distributed individual visualizations is bandwidth consuming. But in contrast to communication on a semantic level, which requires a reliable connection, it does not matter if some information is lost. For performance reasons often a multicast based layer is used in such a case. In the ETOILE project the communication layer consists of two separated communication channels, one reliable for semantic message exchange and one multicast based but non reliable for visualization synchronization.

3.5 Design of the Human – Agent Interface

There are two types of human agent interaction possible. The first one is based on the vocabulary. This means that a vocabulary is also written for the human. In this way agents can react on human action. Additionally exchanging a human with an agent during a training session is possible. A second type is a free interaction, where the human communication is not restricted. As it is not possible to automatically interpret a non restricted communication of a human it is not possible that an agent reacts on this communication (which is often not necessary at all). In fact, the communication is just recorded and is analyzed by the trainer and the trainees in the review phase after the training. As a result the behavior description of an agent (the one that is able to play the same role as the human did whose behavior has been evaluated) can be adapted according to the findings in the training review. This may be done by the trainer or the trainees as the system allows end users to make this adaptation.

Finally, in order to provide a more universal communication architecture a uniformly communication component, called communication entity, is included in the concept. It is assigned to a trainee or an agent and it will translate different dialects into each other.

4 Conclusions

Which lessons can we learn reflecting about the experiences in the ETOILE project? First of all the usage of virtual environments has proven to be essential although mostly considered only as a nice add-on by end users. Only the virtual environment allows to interact with agents and other knowledge sources (like data on computer programmes) as well as to perceive information about the status of the world in a suitable and timely correct way.

Although there a many possible pitfalls in using agent technology [Wool98] we consider the usage of agents essential in order to have "computer players" in the training scenario and in order to formalize the shared mental models as a set of status variables, rules and actions that directly or indirectly modify the status variables. In our opinion making authoring of agents behavior possible is the key to enable the creation of a realistic and high-quality knowledge networked environment that is accepted by users. In addition, for the application background of ETOILE it is important to allow organizational learning through defining and modifying the behavior of agents by the training participants. In literature there exist only few approaches, which take the authoring also into consideration in an integrated way. One good example is the agent sheets system [Agen00] with its approach of tactile programming [Repe96]. We found that component-based methodologies combined with frameworks are the most promising methodology in order to split the authoring tasks for different author roles while ensuring that their products fit together. However, the skills required from authors of the application domain are still extensive. While VR and animation related issues can be hidden from this type of author using the ETOILE approach and also dealing with rules may be made transparent using graphical metaphors there is still the need for the author to transfer his knowledge into some kind of formal representation and make it explicit. Here the authoring tools should use metaphors from the application domain, for example emergency plans are often represented as a flow diagram and thus authors are used to deal with this kind of knowledge representation. Another experience we made is that even agents with simple knowledge can be very beneficial so that positive effects of networked virtual environments can be reached in an early stage. For example, replacing the Metro passengers in our example application by agents leads to tremendous cost savings and also offers a new freedom in the design of the training as multiple alternatives may be tried by a trainee while the trainer can control the passengers behavior easily.

To solve the problem of using different tools that do not fit together or make the use of converters or adapters necessary we propose the usage of a skeleton application that is the same for all training scenarios. It has the generic architecture depicted in Fig. 5.

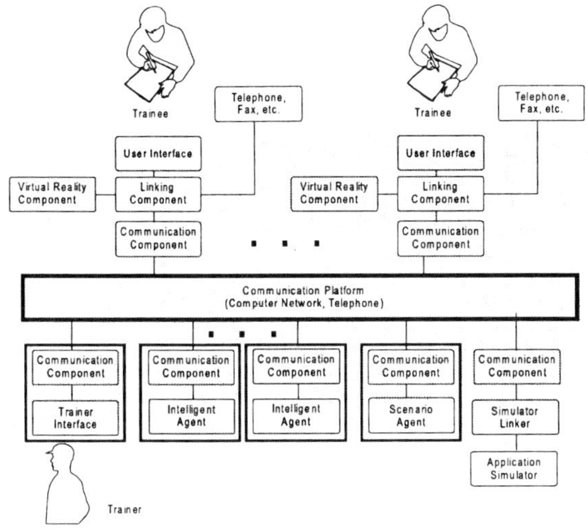

Fig. 5: Generic architecture of a skeleton application

How does this architecture correlate with current standards? On the one hand current standards may be used for implementing the architecture, for instance the ACL as a standard for the agents' communication or Java Beans for standardizing the components' interfaces. However, no standard comprises the whole skeleton application, building this application means therefore specifying a standard for a limited application domain. Having a standard there would allow a greater interoperability of components between different applications domains. On the other hand, current standards are too complex and to broad as they are meant for more generic use cases and do not take advantage of the constraints imposed by the usage of a skeleton application. For example, a HLA based runtime infrastructures [HLA00] may be used to implement the communication layer of the skeleton application where features of HLA are not used and result in an unnecessary overhead. To summarize, there is still the need for efforts in defining a suitable integrated standard which takes components, frameworks, agent communication and simulator linkage into consideration.

5 Acknowledgements

The work described in this paper has been undertaken in the context of the ETOILE project that consists of the following partners: Tecnatom, Iberdrola, Metro Bilbao, Labein, Fraunhofer-AGC, STN Atlas and the Centre for Studies in Advanced Learning Technology of the Lancaster University. The authors wish to thank all of the members of the project team and acknowledge their contributions. ETOILE is partly supported by the European Commission under the ESPRIT programme (project 29086).

6 References

[Agen00] http://www.agentsheets.com

[Blaz00] http://www.blazesoft.com

[Doer00] R. Doerner, P. Grimm: Three-dimensional Beans – Creating Web Content Using 3D Components In A 3D Authoring Environment, Proceeding of the Web3D – VRML 2000, pp. 69-74, ACM Press 2000

[ETOI00] http://etoile.tecnatom.es

[Fini94] T. Finin, R. Fritzson, D. McKay, R. McEntire: KQML as an Agent Communication Language, Proceedings of the Third International Conference on Information and Knowledge Management (CIKM'94), pp. 456ff, ACM Press, 1994

[FIPA00] http://www.fipa.org

[Gent83] D. Genter, A.L. Stevens (Eds.): Mental Models. Lawrence Erlbaum Associates, Hillsdale, New Jersey, 1983

[Gene92] M. Genesereth, R Fikes (Eds): Knowledge Interchange Format, Version 3.0 Manual, Technical Report Logic-92-1, Stanfort University, 1992

[HLA00] http://hla.dmso.mil

[Java00] http://java.sun.com

[Open00] http://www.openGVS.com

[Rain00] T. Raines, M. Tambe, S. Marsella: Automated Assistance to Aid Humans in Understanding Team Behaviors, Proceedings of the Fourth International Conference on Autonomous Agents, p. 419-426, Barcelona, ACM Press, 2000

[Repe96] A. Repenning, J. Ambach: Tactile Programming: A Unified Manipulation Paradigm Supporting Program Comprehension, Composition and Sharing. Proceedings of the IEEE Symposium on Visual Languages, pp. 102-109, 1996

[SOAR00] http://bigfoot.eecs.umich.edu/~soar/

[Tamb97] M. Tambe: Towards Flexible Teamwork. Journal of Artificial Intelligence Research 7 (1997), pp. 83 – 124, 1997

[Wool97] M. Woolridge, N.R. Jennings: Agent Theories, Architectures, Languages: A Survey. Intelligent Agents, Lecture Notes in Artificial Intelligence Research (7), pp. 84-124, Morgan Kaufmann Publishers, 1997

[Wool98] M. Wooldridge, and N. R. Jennings: Pitfalls of agent-oriented development, Proceedings of the second international conference on Autonomous agents, Minneapolis, ACM Press 1998

[Yin00] J. Yin, M. S. Miller, T. Ioerger, J. Yen, R.A.Volz: A Knowledge-Based Approach for Designing Intelligent Team Training Systems, Proceedings of the Fourth International Conference on Autonomous Agents, p. 427-434, Barcelona, ACM Press, 2000

Collaborating in 3D Virtual Environments: A Synchronous Architecture

Shervin Shirmohammadi and Nicolas D. Georganas
School of Information Technology and Engineering, University of Ottawa, Canada
[shervin|georgana]@mcrlab.uottawa.ca

Abstract

To collaborate in a 3D environment, update messages corresponding to the change in the state of a shared object must be communicated among users. While a lot of research has been done in terms of transmission of update messages representing the motion of avatars and objects, very few works focus on collaboration itself. In this paper, we present an architecture that enables tightly-coupled collaborative tasks to be performed efficiently in virtual environments.

Keywords: 3D Virtual Presence, Collaborative Virtual Environments, Networked Multiuser Shared 3D Spaces.

1. Introduction

Like other distributed simulations, Collaborative Virtual Environments (CVE) are shared virtual reality spaces where remote users participate in a simulation. In addition, CVEs also allow the participants to collaborate in closely coupled and highly synchronized tasks. These tasks require very close coordination between two or more users, such as two remote surgeons operating on a remote virtual patient. The applications of such environments are in military training, telepresence, collaborative design and engineering, distance training, entertainment, and many other personal and industrial applications [8].

One of the main research topics for such environments is how to efficiently transmit update messages in such a way as to provide scalability, minimized delay, and reliability. An update message is generated as a result of an entity's change of state. For example, when one user moves a shared object, update messages containing the new coordinates of that object are sent to all users in the system. The object representation in the other users' environments is then adjusted according to the update message received (Figure 1).

Recent research in the transmission of update messages includes using distributed synchronization and dead-reckoning to support multiplayer avatar-based games [11], using selectively reliable protocols to drastically reduce network traffic [13], and focusing on the reliability of only the last update message [5]. Although most of these techniques yield very good performance for generic virtual environments, they don't specifically support collaborative tasks. This paper is the result of our investigation about the issue of "synchronous collaboration" in virtual environments. In this article we introduce two concepts: an "Interaction Stream" model which translates a user's high-level collaborative actions into an application-level model; and a transport protocol for efficient transmission of this stream among a large number of participants. We start our discussion by examining different CVE data types.

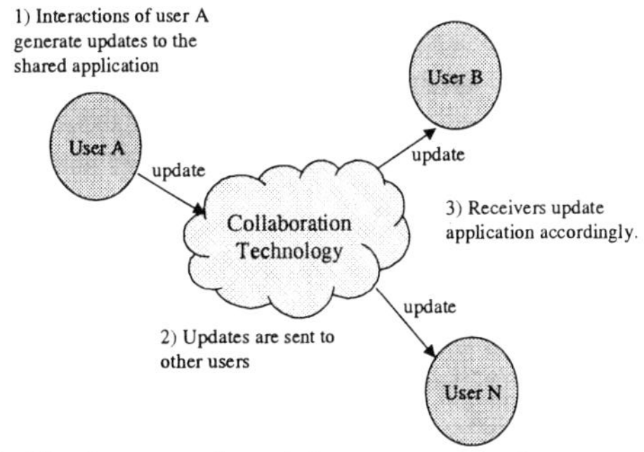

Figure 1. Exchange of update messages in collaboration systems.

1.1 CVE Data Types

There are many types of data exchanged in CVEs, each having different needs and service requirements. These can roughly be categorized as follows:

- real-time audio and video data;
- object/scene description data: data describing an object and its attributes; e.g., description of an avatar;
- CSCW data: this represents traditional 2D collaborative data such as whiteboards;
- control data: used by the system to perform tasks such as consistency control, management, and so on;
- update messages: as explained previously.

Each of these data types has a preferred transport mechanism: audio and video is usually sent by RTP or similar protocols, Object/scene data are usually loaded through TCP by using HTTP for example, CSCW data and control messages are usually transmitted by Reliable Multicast (RM) protocols, or client-server based architectures. Thorough discussion about these data types is beyond the scope of this paper.

The main subject of this paper is "collaborative" update messages. We make a distinction between collaborative update messages and regular ones. A collaborative update message is one that signifies a tightly-coupled action, such as update messages corresponding to the position of an object which is being carried by two remote users simultaneously, each holding one end of the object. A regular update message is, for example, the motion of a by-passer's avatar which, although important, is not critical for collaborative purposes. One contribution of this paper is the demonstration of the fact that collaborative update messages are somewhat different from regular update messages and require a class of their own.

Also notice that there are two modes of collaboration: synchronous mode and asynchronous mode. Unlike asynchronous collaboration which doesn't require very tight thresholds in terms of networking issues, latency and reliability heavily affect synchronous collaboration. Each of these modes of collaboration has its own set of applications and they are not competing technologies in most cases, rather complementary. Our work focuses on synchronous collaboration and the term "update messages" refers to the *synchronous collaborative update messages*, unless otherwise indicated.

2. Collaboration Requirements

Like regular update messages, collaborative update messages have strong delay requirements. It has been suggested that good collaboration environments must have an end-to-end delay of no more than 100 msec for update messages [12]. Other studies have loosened this requirement to 200 msec as acceptable delay [10]. The reason for such strict requirement is the fact that collaboration is a real-time and highly reactive multi-user process where users interact based on the each other's actions and reactions; therefore requiring very low transmission delay of updates.

Also, collaborative update messages are severely affected by jitter. It has been shown that a CVE session with a low 10 msec delay that has jitter, results in a collaboration environment which is almost as bad as one with 200 msec delay but no jitter [10]. Nevertheless, no clear thresholds have yet been found to indicate what is acceptable jitter and what is not. At this point, the goal is to minimize jitter as much as possible.

Finally, collaborative update messages have strict reliability requirements. It is obviously pertinent that all users receive update messages or they won't be able to collaborate. The question is: do we need to send all update messages in a reliable manner or just some of the update messages? This question can be answered by realizing that the last state of a shared object is the most crucial data in a CVE. For example, assume a user moves an object on a table, generating 10 update messages each 50 msec apart. Further assume that update messages 1, 7 and 9 are lost. In this scenario, it is clear that we do not need to retransmit the lost messages since the last state of the object is received correctly.

Figure 2 illustrates a "virtual theater", a research project at the Multimedia Communications Research Laboratory at the University of Ottawa which is an effort to create a virtual environment for rehearsals of theatrical plays, as well as actual performances in front of a large number of remote audiences. In this scenario, remote actors and directors gather in a virtual room where they rehearse and eventually perform their play. During a rehearsal, the director might ask an actress to pick up a hat from the floor and put it on the table, in reaction to which another actor should turn over a chair and read a specific phrase from the play. Also, There might be tasks more closely synchronized such as 2 people lifting the table and putting it at the opposite side of the room. During the actual play, 100s or 1000s of remote people might watch the play all of whom should receive the update messages correctly.

Figure 2. A virtual theater.

In such scenario, the following typical update messages can be generated:

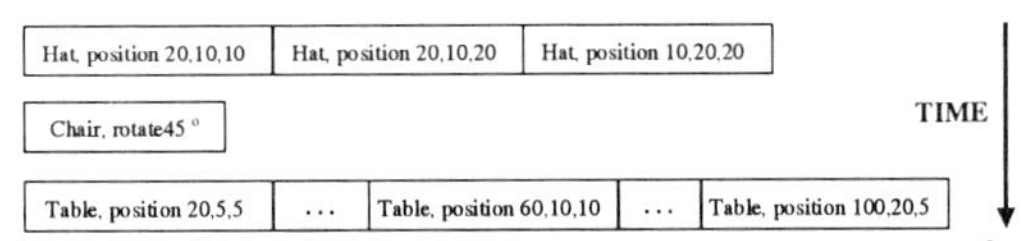

Figure 3. Typical update messages generated.

The exact number of messages depends on the application itself and the graphics system, but we can make the following general observations:

- Each interaction creates a rather short stream of update messages, some of which can be only one update message long.
- Some interactions can be longer, such as the action of carrying a table across the room which generates more update messages than turning over a chair.
- The most important message is the last message, if it is lost a potential collaboration failure occurs since the last position of the object will be perceived differently by different participants.

In the case of the streams with longer duration, we need

reliability not only for the last update message but also for some of the interim update messages.. It is still acceptable to loose some of the update messages, but certainly not all. Exactly what percentage and how often these losses are acceptable depends on the actual application.

3. Interaction Stream

Based on the above observations, we propose to group a sequence of update messages related to one sequence of interaction of a user with a shared object into one *stream*. To illustrate this notion, let us look at a generic *interaction stream* shown in figure 4.

Update 1	Update 2	. . .	Update N-1	Last Update

Figure 4. A generic stream resulting from a user's interaction with a shared object.

This stream will have some critical messages, such as the last update message, which must be sent reliably, and some regular messages which can be sent by best effort transport. Hence, we propose grouping of update messages into 2 types: *key* update messages, and regular update messages. An interaction stream will then consist of a series of key update messages and regular update messages, as shown in figure 5.

Key Update	Update	Update	. . .	Key Update	Update	. . .	Key Update

Figure 5. An *Interaction Stream*.

The last update message will be a key message for reasons explained above. In this scheme, key update messages will be delivered reliably and other update messages in between can be sent by best effort transport.

Determining the last message in the stream is an application dependent procedure. Generally however, one can determine the last message by monitoring graphics events in the environment in order to intercept the event of a user releasing an object. These graphics events can be intercepted through the API provided by both the operating system and graphics platform such as VRML and Java3D.

Another interesting issue is that of "differential messages". A differential message is an update message that instead of carrying information about an entity's current state, carries the difference between the current state and the previous state(s). For example, assume an object moves from location (12245, 156, -1233) to (12243, 155, -1230) and then to (12241, 153, -1229). Figure 6 shows two types of interaction streams; one is the regular one and another one uses differential messages.

As we can see, differential messages save a lot of bandwidth because instead of transmitting the entire object state, only the difference from the last state(s) is transmitted. Differential messages usually depend on a previously transmitted "reference" update message. In such cases the issue of reliability for those reference updates becomes even more important. Loosing one of those reference updates causes the differential updates to create inconsistencies.

Regular update messages

(12245, 156, -1233)	(12243, 155, -1230)	(12241, 153, -1229)

Differential update messages

(12245, 156, -1233)	(-2, -1, 3)	(-4, -3, 4)

Figure 6. Regular update messages (top) and differential update messages (bottom).

Figure 7 shows how differential messages can be sent using our architecture. The arrows indicate on which reference message a differential message depends on. Reference updates are sent as key messages while differential updates are sent by best-effort transport. Since the key messages are sent reliably, differential messages will result in the correct sequence of state changes.

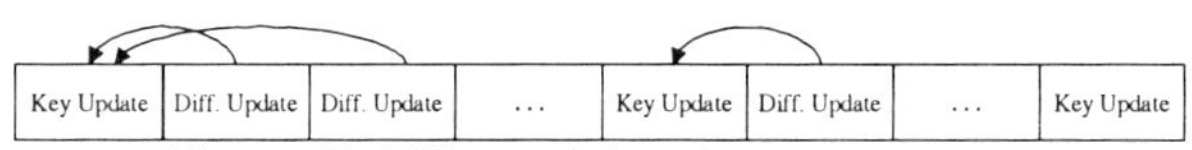

Figure 7. Differential update messages.

This scheme might look familiar to those who are exposed to multimedia encoding standards; more specifically the above scheme looks similar to an MPEG video stream with I, P and B frames. I frames are full frame descriptions that are bulky, whereas P and B frames use differential coding based on previous frames and are therefore much smaller in size. From multimedia communications perspective, it is important that I frames be received reliably because they are the basis for many other frames, whereas the loss of a P or B frame is not as important. A similar situation applies for CVEs: key update messages must be transmitted reliably because their loss might result in major errors, whereas the loss of a differential message is not as critical.

4. Communication

Up to this point we analyzed collaborative update messages and proposed the interaction stream model based on their characteristics. We will now discuss how to actually transmit these messages across the network.

TCP, UDP, and UDP multicast are considered generic protocols in that each has been designed for a specific type of service, not a specific type of data. It is assumed that most data will fall within some category of service requirement, such as reliable, connection-less, best effort, and other types of services. However, this assumption does not hold for many types of data. Multimedia communications, for example, requires its own protocols. A good example of this is the Real-Time Transport Protocol (RTP) which was designed for real-time transport of audio and video streams because the above generic protocols alone did not meet the needs of real-time streaming data. Similarly, CVE update messages need a transport protocol that provides scalability, low latency, and a special type of reliability. In the following section we examine some of the available architectures to determine if they meet such requirements.

4.1 Available Architectures

How update messages are exchanged among entities depends on the implementation of the system. We can roughly categorize existing systems into the following groups:

- **one-to-one communication:** An entity sends update messages to each of the other hosts in a peer-to-peer fashion. This approach becomes inefficient with increasing number of entities and hosts and does not scale.
- **client-server:** Clients send update messages to a server which forwards them to other clients. Although the server reduces the number of connections, it also becomes a bottleneck; furthermore there is an additional delay created since each update message must first go to the server first, and then be sent to other participants.
- **broadcast:** An entity broadcasts its update message which is received by everyone on the subnetwork. In practice broadcast turned out to be a nightmare because every host on the subnetwork, even those not participating in the simulation, receive and process the broadcast message. As a result, these types of systems have been used only with powerful computing and networking resources.
- **UDP multicast:** The most successful implementation of this approach is the Distributed Interactive Simulation (DIS). But there are certain problems with DIS when it comes to collaboration. There is no guaranty that the last state of a shared object is received by all participants due to unreliable nature of UDP multicast. Keep-alive messages, which are transmitted every 5 to 10 seconds, recover the last state of an object, but this falls far short from the 100 to 200 msec latency requirement for collaborative updates, not to mention the undesired bandwidth generated by these keep-alive messages since an object must send them even when it is not changing.
- **reliable multicast:** RM protocols use multicast while at the same time they assure reliability for all messages. But this very fact makes them inefficient for CVEs: RM achieves reliability for all transmitted packets, something that is not required and creates undesired bandwidth and delay for the interaction stream.

In general, the focus in virtual environments and simulations today is on update messages corresponding to motions of vehicles and avatars, not on collaboration. The general assumption is that objects transmit update messages often, and that the latest state of things can be determined by predictive techniques such as "dead-reckoning" algorithm. These assumptions work very well for scenarios such as simulation of battlefields or shoot-em up games where players move around quite often. But they fail for collaboration scenarios. In fact for collaboration the conditions are the opposite: objects often do not send continuous update messages, and when they do they are not necessarily in a predictable manner. It is a well-known fact that dead-reckoning and similar predictive algorithms loose efficiency in situations when precision and consistency are vital [17].

Existing systems fail to fulfill collaboration needs mainly because they do not consider the properties of collaboration data itself. This is evident from the vast amount of literature which spell out the requirements for shared and distributed virtual environments without looking specifically at collaboration data [1][14][15][16][18].

4.2 SCTP: The Synchronous Collaboration Transport Protocol

SCTP takes into account collaboration requirements and is designed based on the characteristics of the interaction stream described above. From an Internet protocol stack perspective, SCTP is a host-to-host layer protocol, comparable to the transport layer in the ISO protocol stack. SCTP is encapsulated into UDP packets and assumes that the underlying physical network supports IP multicasting. By using IP multicast it becomes scalable and fast due to the utilization of the low-overhead UDP packets.

In terms of packet format, SCTP-layer PDU carries enough information in its header to facilitate collaboration-specific update messages. Figure 8 illustrates an SCTP packet and its header fields.

control bit	key update	object ID	Stream number	sequence number	application payload (update message)

Figure 8. SCTP packet format.

The packet's header carries information that identifies which shared object is being interacted with and whether the specific packet is a key update or not. It also provides *stream ID* and *sequence number* information. *streamID* indicates the ID of the current interaction stream for this object, and *sequence number* indicates the position of this specific update message in the current stream. Together they can be used to discard messages that arrive late due to networking delay and congestion conditions. Notice that there are no clock or time-stamping information in the header. The reason for this is the highly time-sensitive characteristic of collaborative updates: upon receiving an update, it is immediately sent to the higher level where it is implemented at the graphics level. Therefore there is no need for clock or time-stamping information.

4.2.1 Reliability for Key Updates

The next design issue is how to achieve reliability for key updates. There are two main approaches for achieving reliability: ACK-based (sender-initiated) and NACK-based (receiver-initiated). Although not in the framework of CVEs, extensive studies have been done regarding these two approaches for Reliable Multicast protocols (RM). We refer the readers to the literature [9] and refrain from detailed discussion of this topic.

From the above two approaches, NACK-based approaches have gained wider popularity since they have been proven to out-perform ACK-based approaches in terms of network bandwidth and other parameters. NACK-based approaches use Automatic Repeat Request (ARQ), Forward Error Correction (FEC), or combinations of both. Most these techniques achieve very high performances for reliable multicast applications, but they are generally not efficient for the interaction stream scheme presented here.

A host in an ARQ-based scheme only detects a loss when it receives a newer update message with a larger time stamp/sequence number. This creates a problem because in CVEs the transmission of a newer message might happen very late leading to delay, or even worse, never happen at all (nothing is sent after the last update message) leading to a collaboration failure.

FEC-based techniques group many adjacent packets into a block and generate repair packets based on the contents of the packets in the block and transmit the repair packets at the end of the block. This way if an error occurs in the block, a receiver can repair it using the repair packets. This technique works quite well for reliable multicast situations, but again it's not suitable for the interaction stream. The problem is that in an interaction stream, adjacent packets don't require reliability. Hence the main purpose behind the design of FEC is defeated.

We therefore require a reliability architecture that is ACK-based; i.e., a sender explicitly requests that key update messages be immediately acknowledged. This way a sender automatically re-transmits the key update message in case it is lost. However, ACK-based approaches inherently lead to the infamous "ACK implosion" phenomenon. Even though in our design only key updates are acknowledged and not all the updates, the fact that there might be a huge number of users in the session creates a potential ACK implosion problem. This problem can be solved using a representative-based technique as suggested by [3], such as the following technique:

The first time a key update message is received, all receivers send their acknowledgments. The sender selects the recipient whose acknowledgement is received last as the representative of the group. Next the sender multicasts a control message indicating its choice for a representative. Other recipients will then refrain from sending ACK messages unless the representative fails to do so. For a given packet, if the representative does not send an acknowledgement, all recipients who have received the packet will send an ACK message based on a suppression algorithm similar to those used for NACK-based approaches, and the sender re-selects a representative from those recipients. When a host receives an ACK for an update message that it has not received, it sends a NACK. This NACK can be used both for the re-transmission of the lost packet and for congestion-control purposes. However, based on the n and t parameters discussed earlier, the receiver should not ask for a retransmission if it estimates that a newer update message will arrive faster than one requested by retransmission, and should send the NACK for congestion-control purposes only. The sender can then utilize the ACK and NACK messages in multicast congestion control mechanisms such as [3] to control its transmission rate.

The above approach uses both ACK and NACK messages to support the timliness and reliability requirements of updates, but it is mainly ACK-based. Notice that we do not use an RM-based protocol; we only use ACK-based and NACK-based techniques for key updates only.

4.2.2 Why A New Protocol?

There aren't many protocols that allow one to send reliably only specific packets and unreliably all other packets. One exception is the Selectively Reliable Transport Protocol (SRTP) [13]. SRTP is a very efficient protocol for generic distributed simulations, but it doesn't quite address the synchronous collaboration issues that were discussed in this article, mainly due to its NACK-based approach.

One could argue that a hybrid approach, which uses UDP multicast in conjunction with an already available RM protocol, could take care of this problem. In other words, send the regular messages with UDP multicast and send the key messages with an already available RM protocol. However, such hybrid protocols are not efficient enough for our purposes: in addition to the compatibility and implementation problems, the variety of available RM protocols out there don't precisely meet our requirements. In fact that's the reason that similar architectures, such as the SRTP protocol, use their own custom-made RM protocol instead of using hybrid designs. For example we simply cannot use purely NACK-based RM protocols, either utilizing FEC or ARQ techniques, due to reasons explained in 4.2.1. We can't use ACK-based RM protocols either because in our case we need to drop an old key update which is being replaced by a newer key update, even if the old one has not been received reliably yet. But RM protocols re-transmit that old packet until all participants successfully receive it, a feature which is very useful for most RM applications, but is problematic for our interaction stream. Hence the design of SCTP is justified by the lack of other protocol's providing functional requirements for highly-synchronous update messages based on the proposed interaction stream.

5. Simulation

We used the OPNET modeling and simulation tool [19] to study the behavior of SCTP. SCTP was fully modeled, except for the dynamic representative feature. A static multicast network was created with 54 hosts and a 200 msec diameter. 10 fixed hosts were strategically chosen as fixed representatives. 20 shared objects were randomly placed, each on one host. Shared objects were set to randomly produce update messages, at 10 frames per second, based on an "idle time" indicating for how long an object is idle before producing the next interaction stream, and a "stream length" indicating the number of update messages per stream. The idle time was uniformly distributed between 0 and a maximum adjustable upper bound, the stream length followed a positive Gaussian distribution centered around 20 packets. Gaussian distribution was chosen to make the occurrence of very short streams as unlikely as very long streams. Based on the above traffic, the router buffer sizes were experimentally adjusted in such a way as to produce a given network *loss rate*. The experiment was done for *idle time* with upper bound of 5 and 10 seconds, and *loss rate* of 15% and 30%. The retransmission timeout was set at 400 msec. In addition, the ACK-based mechanism of SCTP was replaced by a NACK-based mechanism, simulating a protocol similar to SRTP.

Since all our work is centered around "synchronous collaboration among users", we are particularly interested in measuring "collaboration failures". We define **Out-Of-Synch Time (OST)** as "the time that the representation of a shared object starts to become inconsistent with respect to its original, due to a lost message, until it gets back into synch by receiving the next update message". OST goes beyond delay, jitter, packet loss, and the usual network simulation parameters: it actually focuses specifically on collaboration. The results of the simulations are shown in the appendix at the end of the paper.

Each figure shows the OST value on the vertical axis, both as average and maximum, for each host (horizontal access). In addition, each figure shows the OST values for both ACK-based (left sub-figure) and NACK-based (right sub-figure) techniques.

5.1 Analysis

Analyzing the results, we can see that the NACK approach performs poorly with respect to "collaboration" requirements, resulting in longer OST durations. On the other hand, as expected, the ACK-based approach achieves much better results. In fact, careful examination of the results indicates that the ACK-based approach seems to be almost immune to variations in object *idle time*, and that it performs much better than the NACK-based approach under higher loss rates. This is consistent with our theory since the ACK-based approach will retransmit the key update until it is sure that all representatives have received it. On the negative side, the ACK-based approach did create an average of 30% more traffic than the NACK-based approach due to ACK packets. This additional traffic is the price we pay for better synchronous collaboration.

It is no coincidence that the average and maximum OST values for the NACK-based approach are very close to those of the *idle time* distribution. As explained previously, when the last update message is lost, an object can potentially be out of synch until the first update of the next stream arrives: a duration equal to the amount of time the object is not sending updates and hence is idle. This means that the average duration of each failure is very close to average amount of time an object is idle (offset by network delays). Similarly the maximum OST is close to the maximum idle time.

Hence, we can see from the results that in terms of collaboration requirements the performance of NACK-based approach is not as efficient as the ACK-based approach.

6. Implementation

We have implemented the architecture as a middleware component. This middleware can be used either as a plug-in in higher-level architectures such as CAVERNSoft [8], HLA [2], and The Virtual Reality Transfer Protocol (VRTP) [4], or it can be used as stand-alone. The middleware includes an "adapter" that can be used by higher-level systems and applications to connect to it and utilize its synchronous collaboration services.

For most efficient collaboration, it is preferred that higher-level system inform our middleware (through the adapter's API) about which messages are key updates, specially the last update message. At least, the high-level application should set the n and t parameters discussed earlier. However, for collaboration-unaware applications, the middleware also provides a fully transparent solution: every time an update is received from the upper layer, a *regulatory timer* is started. Initially, the duration of this timer is very short, typically about 50 to 100 msec. As more and more update messages are sent, the timer adjusts itself based on the framerate of the application, which it estimates from the frequency of update messages. If no update message is received from the upper layer when the timer expires, the last update message is re-sent as a key one; a new *stream ID* is also started and the sequence count is reset.

7. Conclusion

Several concepts with respect to collaboration in virtual environments were introduced in this paper. One was a new perspective that considers collaboration data as Interaction Streams, each consisting of a burst of update messages with a final and critical update message. No other work has addresses the issue of collaboration at such level and in such a way. We also showed that since interaction stream can be very short and shared objects often might not send update messages on a frequent basis, receiving the last update at the end of a stream is very crucial. Furthermore, reliability is not required for all messages, only a certain percentage of them, and low latency is also important as in all other virtual environments. All of the above factors and requirements gave rise to the design of SCTP which was presented in this paper. We argued the need for an ACK-based approach, specifically to better support synchronous collaboration, and we demonstrated this efficiency compared to NACK-based techniques.

We have tested our middleware subjectively in a fictional tele-surgery application with two remote surgeons and a remote patient, and it was revealed that collaboration with our architecture achieves a much higher degree of efficiency. We are now in the process of using this architecture with our CVE prototypes, such as our industrial training application [7].

References

[1] B. Blau et al, "Networked Virtual Environments", Proc. ACM SGGRAPH, 1992, pp. 157-164.

[2] Calvin, J. and Weatherly, R. "An Introduction to the High Level Architecture (HLA) Runtime Infrastructure (RTI)," Proc. DIS Workshop on Standards for the Interoperability of Defense Simulations. Orlando, Florida, March 1996.

[3] D. DeLucia, "A Multicast Congestion Control Mechanism for Reliable Multicast", 3rd IEEE Symposium on Computers & Communications, Athens, Greece, 1998.

[4] Don Brutzman et al, "Virtual Reality Transfer Protocol (vrtp) Design Rationale", Proc. Workshop on Enabling Technologies: Infrastructure for Collaborative Enterprises (WET-ICE): Sharing A Distributed Virtual Reality, IEEE Computer Society, Massachusetts, June 1997, pp. 179-186.

[5] G. Kessler, and L. Hodges, "A Network Communication Protocol for Distributed Virtual Environment Systems", Proc. IEEE Virtual Reality Annual International Symposium, 1996, pp. 214-221.

[6] J. C. Oliveira et al, "Collaborative Virtual Environment Standards: A Performance Evaluation", Proc. IEEE Workshop on Distributed Interactive Simulations and Real-Time Applications, 1999 (DIS-RT '99), pp. 14-21.

[7] J.C. Oliveira et al, "Virtual Theater for Industrial Training: A Collaborative Virtual Environment", Proc. 4th World Multiconference on Circuits, Systems, Communications & Computers (CSCC 2000), Athens, Greece, July 2000.

[8] Jason Leigh, "A Review of Tele-Immersive Applications in the CAVE Research Network", Proc IEEE International Conference on Virtual Reality (VR '99), Texas, March 1999.

[9] K. Obraczka, "Multicast Transport Protocols: A Survey and Taxonomy", IEEE Communications, Vol. 36, No. 1, 1998, pp. 94-102.

[10] K.S. Park and Robert V. Kenyon, "Effects of Network Characteristics on Human Performance in a Collaborative Virtual Environment", IEEE International Conference on Virtual Reality (VR '99), Houston, Texas, March 1999.

[11] L. Gautier et al, "End-to-End Transmission Control Mechanisms for Multiparty Interactive Applications on the Internet", Proc. IEEE Infocom '99, New York, U.S.A.

[12] M.M. Wloka, "Lag in Multiprocessor VR", Presence: Teleoperators and Virtual Environments (MIT Press), Vol. 4, No. 1, Spring 1995.

[13] M Pullen, "Reliable Multicast Network Transport for Distributed Virtual Simulation", Proc. IEEE Workshop on Distributed Interactive Simulations and Real-Time Applications, 1999 (DIS-RT '99), pp. 59-66.

[14] M. Pullen et al, "Limitations of Internet Protocol Suite for Distributed Simulation in the Large Multicast Environment", RFC 2502, February 1999.

[15] M.R. Macedonia, and M.J. Zyda, "A Taxonomy for Networked Virtual Environments", IEEE Multimedia Magazine, January-March 1997, pp. 48-56.

[16] S. Seidensticker et al, "Scenarios and Appropriate Protocols for Distributed Interactive Simulation", Internet draft, draft-myjak-lsma-scenarios-02, march 1997.

[17] Sandeep Singhal, and Michael Zyda, Networked Virtual Environments, ACM Press, NY, NY, 1999, p. 143.

[18] T. Funkhouser, "Network Topologies for Scalable Multi-User Virtual Environments", Proc. IEEE Virtual Reality Annual International Symposium, 1996, pp. 222-228.

[19] OPNET simulation tool, MIL3 Inc., http://www.mil3.com.

APPENDIX. Simulation Results

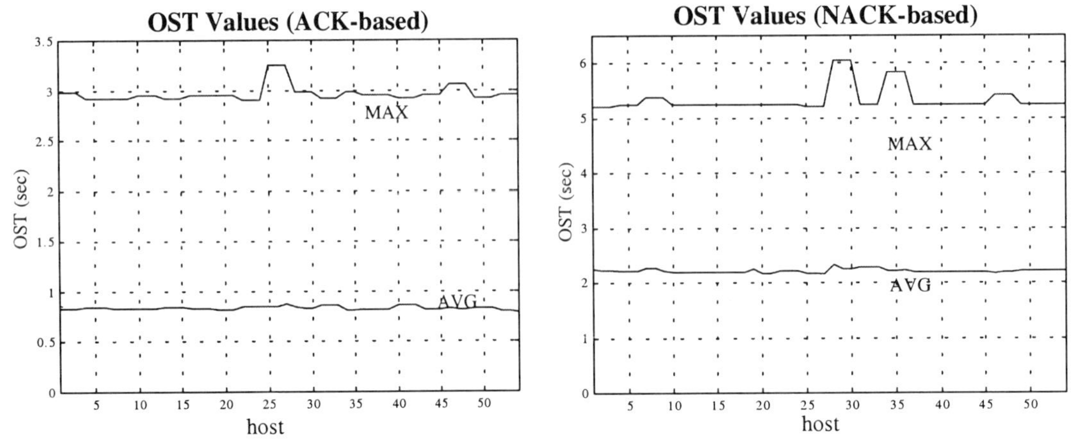

Figure 9. Object out-of-Synch Time loss=10% and idle time =5 sec.

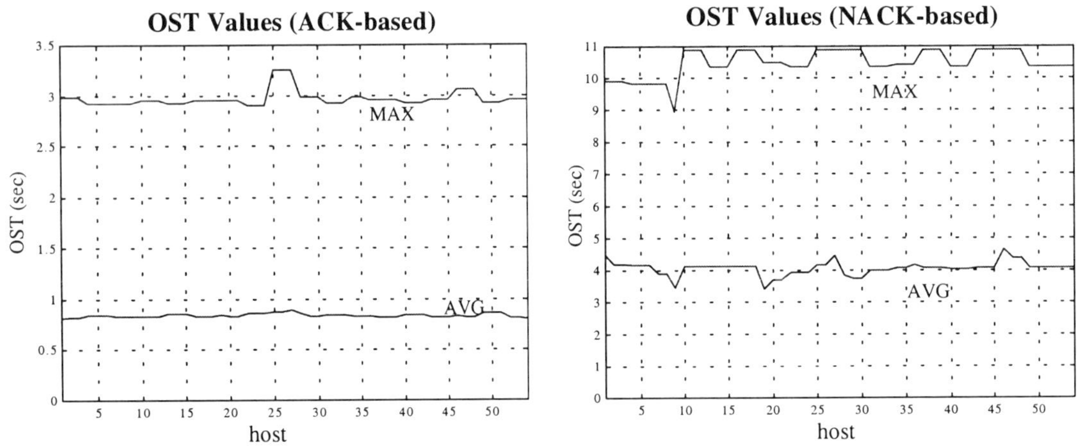

Figure 10. Object out-of-Synch Time loss=10% and idle time =10 sec.

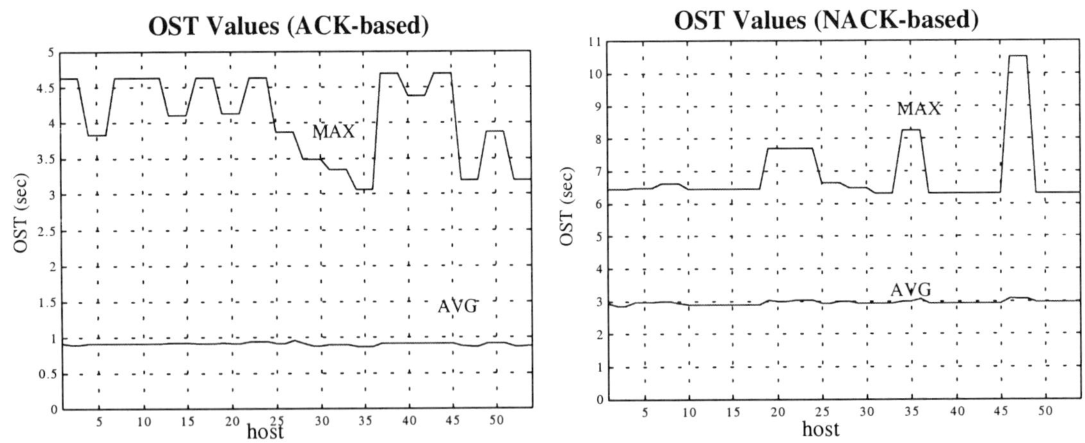

Figure 11. Object out-of-Synch Time loss=30% and idle time =5 sec.

Should Users Inhabit Visualisations?

Claire Knight and Malcolm Munro
Visualisation Research Group,
Research Institute in Software Evolution.
Department of Computer Science,
University of Durham,
Durham, DH1 3LE, UK.
{C.R.Knight, Malcolm.Munro}@durham.ac.uk

Keywords: Software Visualisation, System Visualisation, Multi-User Visualisation Environments, Information Visualisation

Abstract

The use of three-dimensions for visualisation is a lot newer than the technology required to achieve such visual representations. A further extension of this work is to add multiple users to one visualisation environment to create visualisations that go beyond individual intelligence amplification and become knowledge repositories, shared workspaces and integral parts of the management of the data which they represent. The issues surrounding such uses of visualisations are presented in this paper, with an extension of a three-dimensional visualisation to encompass these ideas.

1. Introduction

Visualisation is a powerful way of representing large and complex data sets. It is important that such techniques exist because of the amount of data that today's electronic society produces. Visualisation can be associated with many other areas, such as information foraging, to be able to cope with certain problems but the success of a visualisation relies on the representations and mappings used to visually display the underlying information.

The representations and mappings are usually specific to the task and data being represented, and to an extent, their success is judged by a user's appreciation of them. This appreciation stems from many things; exposure to that style of visual display, degree of spatial awareness, ability and desire to work with graphical forms, and the experience base of the user. These factors are themselves open to influence from the everyday experiences of the user and in industry, the organisational factors that are often not seen or appreciated by those outside that company. Since a visualisation relies so heavily on the representations and mappings used, any move towards creating multi-user visualisation environments needs to consider the same factors. The visualisation created needs to be navigable and represent the data in such a way so as to create understandable visualisations **and** environments that can be virtually inhabited.

The benefits of doing this can be numerous, but as with any visualisation, are not guaranteed unless suitable thought is given to uses and users of the visualisation. This paper presents some of the many areas in which three-dimensional visualisations can be enhanced through the addition of multi-user environmental capabilities. It then discusses in detail the areas that are most pertinent at this stage to visualisation designers and shows how this could be achieved with current software and software visualisations. An example of how a visualisation design does not intuitively map to a multi-user environment is also presented to demonstrate the point that multi-user is yet another criteria that must be considered at design time for three-dimensional visualisations.

2. Visualisation

There are many factors that are important for visualisation. The main ones in the context of software visualisation [6], and indeed for all information visualisation, are:

- Navigation, Interaction, and Orientation
- Scalability
- Evolution
- Automation

Navigation, interaction, and orientation are presented together because they are often highly interconnected. Orientation features are also very often useful for navigation and vice-versa. Interaction mechanisms are also affected by the navigation available to users. The final three bullet points cover issues that should be considered vital for all visualisations, including those that create virtual environments. Obviously there may have to be trade-offs for a particular system with respect to some of these features but striving to achieve all of these goes some way towards reliable creating useful and usable visualisations.

There are also several terms important when discussing visualisations and the component parts of that visualisation. As defined in [6] these are:

Abstraction – Any graphical representation is an abstraction because it is not the original data. The abstraction level of any visualisation can also be related to the level of the metaphor used, for example, atlas type maps being used to represent the entire system ranging down to buildings representing methods and their attributes. Abstractions are more common than is often appreciated; formal symbol systems right through to graphical user interface editors are all abstractions in their own way.

Metaphor – A logical framework that provides a constrained way of thinking about the graphical subject matter, whereby assumptions made within the metaphor are still valid for the data that it abstracts from. The metaphor provides a high level, understandable and identifiable, description of the possible representation set. An example metaphor is the urbanised development concepts that are used in cityscape style visualisations.

Representation – Detail of how the various constituents of the software system are shown graphically. The set of possible representations for any visualisation depends on the metaphor basis of that visualisation and the number of dimensions available for visual display. The metaphor guides the representations chosen, for example in a cityscape choosing buildings to represent methods rather than using a sphere resting on an upturned pyramid. The representations have to be embodiments of something that occurs normally within the metaphor description.

Mapping – This describes the relationship between the software constituents to be visualised and their representation. The logical framework of the metaphor provides the boundaries in which this mapping relationship needs to operate. If this restriction is not adhered to, it may well be the case that the visualisation is no longer considered useful because of the high cognitive overhead that the broken mapping and/or metaphor impose on the user. An example mapping is the use of *Software World* descriptions to describe the visual environment in which the software is being viewed.

Visualisation – The complete view of the data being visualised; the implementation of the metaphor, mapping and representations into an entire graphical system regardless of the abstraction level currently being used to view the data. An example of this is an entire visualisation application that is run to facilitate working with the representations and abstractions created of the software under consideration.

Some of these distinctions may seem obvious, but it is important that some clarification is made in order to be able to describe, use, and argue about visualisations.

2.1 Need for Multi-User Visualisations

The previous section provided some general visualisation information, which is necessary when considering how to make more use of those visualisations by expanding them into virtual spaces that can be inhabited by users. This section provides a brief rationale as to why this would be a desirable thing for three-dimensional visualisations.

Multi-user visualisations could prove very valuable to many industrial companies; a primary source of system information is contained within the minds of those who maintain that system. This information is rarely documented and when the maintainer leaves, the information is lost. By providing inhabitable virtual spaces directly representative of the system which is being maintained, in which fellow maintainers can communicate, provides one way for this information to at least be passed between colleagues.

Such organisational knowledge may exist about any information source in any organisation. The ability to explore not only the data, but any additional information relating to it is a powerful way of managing that data. The sharing of knowledge is also a very powerful motivator for providing representations for working with the data that facilitate communication, collaboration, and the dissemination of proprietary information [9].

2.2 Multi-User Suitability

Just as the success of a visualisation cannot at this time be guaranteed because of the multitude of factors upon which that judgement rests, the same applies to whether a visualisation is suitable for virtual habitation.

Some examples of this can be seen in recent software visualisations (historically which rely solely on nodes and arcs) such as SeeSoft and SeeSys [1, 2]. These are two-dimensional displays, and whilst such systems could be made multi-user (such as with shared whiteboards) there would be very little reason to do this with these visualisations. This limitation should not be seen as a criticism of these visualisations; they succeed in the tasks and uses for which they were designed. It just illustrates clearly that if a visualisation is to be made into a multi-user virtual space due consideration of the effects of this must be made.

2.3 Requirements for Three-Dimensions

The previous two sections should make it clear that such exploitation of visualisations requires that they be implemented in three-dimensions to successfully support user inhabitation [8]. This is to provide a suitable virtual space for users. Of course, not all three-dimensional represenations will translate well to inhabited spaces. An example of this can be seen in the work in [5] where a node and arc style structure is created. This provides very little frame of reference for navigation and orientation; two very important factors for multi-user spaces.

2.4 Navigation and Orientation Revisited

As identified at the start of this section, navigation is important because it affects the usability of the visualisation. The visualisation should be designed and structured with navigation in mind. If navigational features are added as an afterthought it will then be hard to add the necessary paths and beacons. As Young and Munro [3] write

> *"Well structured data terrain should also result in a more understandable layout and easier navigation".*

There are also guidelines for navigation and orientation that can be taken from city planning textbooks which indicate ways in which humans orient themselves in three-dimensional space.

Tied into navigation issues is the way in which any user of the visualisation is able to interact with it; to move around the virtual space and to find the information they require must be as intuitive as possible to make people view visualisations as useful tools. Unfortunately for designers of visualisations all users have different wants and needs where interaction with computers is concerned. For this reason the more flexibility the system offers, the better. The ability for the user to have a degree of configuration is also likely to lead to the acceptance and use of the visualisation system.

This area becomes much more vital when considering the visualisation as a virtual place. Not only is it important to be able to navigate and orientate oneself in the context of the data, but it is also necessary for the purposes of exploration and interaction with other users.

3. Areas for Expansion

Two primary areas of expansion identified by Knight in [6] are (a) Collaborative and knowledge sharing environments and (b) information location and visualisation, and using the visualisations to facilitate automated information retrieval. An extra issue would be the combination of these two aims to create an environment that is virtually inhabited by both human users and agent technologies.

3.1 Collaboration

Moving away from the advancement of the three-dimensional (software visualisation) techniques, there are also many issues relating to virtual environments. The concept of collaboration in real and virtual places with computer systems is one that has wide application. There is an entire research area concerned solely with the concept of multi-user Collaborative Virtual Environments (CVE) where the issues of representation of users, communication mechanisms, awareness of environment, self and others and the means of interaction with all elements of the environment (including users) are under investigation.

3.2 Information Foraging

Several data mining techniques have been suggested for integration with virtual environments in order to alleviate some of the problems associated with information location and comprehension (information foraging) [7]. There is already a body of visualisation literature that deals with the visual representation and display of the results of mining large data sources, such as visual query environments. The use of virtual environments to represent the data and then having some part of that system guide the user based on information foraging algorithms is an alternative area that could prove fruitful. The use of data visualisation based environments provides the user with a consistent environment each time the system is used, provides them with an awareness of the data set and provides them with a frame of reference for the data they are currently investigating. This cognitive familiarity should then be an aid to the user, in conjunction with the mining algorithms, when the underlying data needs to be understood in a variety of situations for possibly differing tasks.

A particular technology to achieve this guidance through the virtual world is the use of an agent that is able to "inhabit" the virtual space and learn about it as it moves through it. By knowing the environment, the agent can then aid the use in locating the information they require. There is also the alternative use of agent technology whereby it is used to search the environment for the information and to present it to the user who is in a different location in the environment. Both of these mechanisms can help to create a visualisation environment that is capable of being an intelligence amplifying tool.

3.3 Multi-User Foraging

An area of future research that affects users is the use of agents for information foraging as well as for collaboration. The difference is that such search and retrieval tools would also populate the virtual environment! These agents can (theoretically) reduce information overload, for example by locating of pieces of code, and then bookmarking or leading the user to it. These activities can also be carried out by other users in the system whose area of expertise and knowledge covers the iterm of interest. In this respect, information foraging agents and virtual users are not different. All of these agents would then appear in the world as other users.

4. Multi-User Visualisations; Examples

To illustrate that a visualisation needs to be designed as a three-dimensional space that considers the data **and** the multi-usability of the system an existing software visualisation will be presented, and then examples of how this could be enhanced with multi-user support provided.

4.1 Software World

This section provides an overview of the visualisation system *Software World* [4, 6] along with a basic breakdown of the metaphor and hence representations used. *Software World* is based on a real world metaphor that encompasses city objects and urban development ideas. The main reason for this choice of metaphor was the power it afforded in scaling so that software systems of varying sizes could still be accommodated coherently by the one metaphor and related group of representations.

Figure 1 – Various sizes of building in a district which represents methods of varying lengths in lines of source code

At a detailed level code artefacts are shown as buildings and districts in a city environment, whilst higher level detail is shown in a cartographic style globe, making use of visual overview and amalgamation techniques to fit the desired information into a finite space.

Figure 2 – Central garden; context for and extra data about the class underlying the visualisation

Software World is targeted at the visualisation of Java code and the levels of metaphor mapping are tailored to suit the language. The language definition of Java allows certain assumptions to be made and these have influenced the mapping decisions. The high level (in terms of detail) mapping from visualisation to code can be summarised as:

World: The software system as a whole.
Country: Directory structure, which maps to the packages in Java.
City: A file from the software system.
District: Class (contained within the specific file and hence city in the visualisation).
Building: Method.
Monument: Class variable.

Figure 3 – Different types of building; public methods are light buildings whilst private methods are darker

In order to show some of the method level views that can be created with this visualisation over 17,000 lines of Java code (which together composed a package) written by others was parsed, and district visualisations automatically generated. The code was split across 70 classes, which provided different district views. Some of the images that came out of this can be seen in Figure 1 through to Figure 3.

Software World provides a visualisation in a (potentially) inhabitable virtual environment in which the information foraging process can take place. Some aspects of this foraging can be seen in the various figures. The first of these figures (Figure 1) shows various building sizes across a city district. The height of the buildings is a normalised representation of the number of lines of code in the method that the building represents. The colour indicates whether the method is private or not (for an example of this see Figure 3); the darker buildings are private and hence subject to the various access restrictions that Java imposes. Figure 2 shows the central garden with a central structure that provides context by displaying the class name and providing ways of finding out the hierarchy position of the current class.

4.2 Software World for Multiple Users

This section considers the extension of the above three-dimensional visualisation to create a multi-user virtual environment. In addition to world generated by the visualisation for each data-set there are several aspects that exist in all worlds. These are based around user and co-operative issues. These items are located in a standard element (shown from the world view) so that they are consistently placed in all software worlds.

The first of these is a personal working space. This is effectively the users own desktop/workspace, and they can refer items found in the visualisation to the office for later investigation – acting very much like a bookmark. Ideally this would also allow the user's status (in the visualisation or not, area of work, ...) to be set to provide information for other users, and also allow the user to connect to outside applications such as a code editor, mailer and wordprocessor. Each user of the visualisation would see offices for all users but only be able to access their own. Messages to other users via their "office door" would enhance the co-operative capabilities of the visualisation environment.

There are several standard visualisation elements that are independent of the software actually being visualised, all of which can be described in more detail than the overview above provides. These elements are incorporated to enhance the co-operative aspects of the visualisation.

4.2.1 Status

It is important to consider the status of a user before those elements of the visualisation that make use of such information. The status of a user can provide information to other users as to the current work activity, whether they mind being disturbed and even basic information as to whether they currently inhabit the *Software World*. The provision of such information can lead to greater awareness of other users, and hence greater co-operative opportunities and avenues.

Before the status values available in the visualisation are discussed it is important to consider some issues regarding the misuse of these values. Obviously a user can use this information to "lie" as to his current task or whereabouts if the setting of them is done by hand rather than automatically to match the task they are using the computer for. Unfortunately this is a trait of human nature, and so such a system will have to work on a user to user trust basis. Without a visualisation environment it is easy not to answer the 'phone (or screen calls with an answer machine), not return e-mails, not answer the door, etc. The computer system provides another way of doing this, and so social issues for the sake of this visualisation are being accepted as is. If a user chooses to be economical with the truth in setting the status information then it is their concern. The different status messages are:

- In Visualisation, at the Office
- In Visualisation, "investigating"
- Admin, mail
- Admin, phone
- Coding – comprehension
- Coding – "hacking"
- Documentation – looking for information
- Documentation – adding and annotating
- Away

There is some overlap here, because in advanced versions of the visualisation then the coding and documentation (for example) can be carried out whilst the user is in their visualisation office. It is up to the user to choose the message they think the most appropriate.

There is a *In Do Not Disturb Mode* option on all status messages, and space for a line of free text. The first of these causes all sent messages to be queued until the user chooses to look at any sent messages. The latter allows for some personalisation and/or extra information to be provided by the user.

This status information can be displayed to other users of the visualisation system in several ways. The first is if they query the user's status. The second is that it is shown on the virtual office door, in the visualisation system. The final way is when the user sends a message (covered in §4.2.3) to another user, a sent receipt is generated which contains the user's status.

4.2.2 Office

The virtual office is really an extension of the user's desktop (as the windowing systems on computer systems are). Graphically it represents an office with a desk, chair, PC, filing cabinet(s), shelves and an office door. Some degree of user customisation such as desktop objects, arrangement of objects in the room and the placement of pictures on the walls is possible. This allows the user to place items spatially so that they are familiar with them and can easily work with them without having to drastically change their working habits. An example of such an office can be seen in Figure 4.

Figure 4 - The Virtual Office

The office door is used for two purposes. The first is to provide a gateway between the main visualisation system and the user's own workspace. In terms of virtual reality it acts as a portal between two areas, but with a degree of awareness and interaction between those two areas. The second use of the door is to display the current status of the user to other users of the visualisation who happen to be in the office block area of the visualisation.

Within the office, the furniture is used not only to create a realistic environment, but also to provide functionality for the user. The filing cabinets and shelves provide reference points to other pieces of information. The shelves can be links to documentation or code (shown as folders or books), whilst the filing cabinet contains notes and "bookmarks". These bookmarks act in the same way as pieces of paper in a printed book; they allow the user direct access to a certain point of the visualisation without needing to go through the preceding information each time. The PC provides a link to the standard computer desktop of the user (for temporarily leaving the visualisation environment) and also to search facilities used within the visualisation. Two such search mechanisms are to query the status of an individual user and to list all users currently connected to the visualisation system. Comprehension searching may take place at this level but it is more than likely that it will take place in the visualisation environment so that graphically the results can be indicated to the user.

The final main use of the office is to provide the user with access to previously stored information about the visualisation (gathered during user exploration) without connecting to the main visualisation system. Because the user makes no connection to the main visualisation system other users see them as being away. It also provides a more convenient way of retrieving information than waiting for the connection to be made and configured and the rest of the visualisation system to be loaded.

4.2.3 Messaging

Messaging within the visualisation allows users to communicate and co-operate without leaving the visualisation environment. Whilst sending standard mail messages can be carried out from the virtual office or by leaving the visualisation it is not always the most appropriate form of communication.

All users are able to see the names of all other currently connected users and their status. This can allow users to make informed decisions about who they send messages or chat requests to (messages can be left for offline users, whilst can requests can only be sent to users online). Messages and chat are the primary forms of communication in the visualisation environment.

Chat (through typed text rather than audio stream) can realistically only be carried out from a user's office. If a user receives a chat request whilst he is in the middle of the visualisation and wishes to accept the request there is a facility that can save his virtual world location (bookmark) and return him to his office. Once finished, he can return to the appropriate point in the visualisation by "jumping" directly back to that point in the visualisation without needing to walk around the visualisation as he may have done to get to that point in the first place. The main reason for this is that to remain consistent with the metaphor the user needs to use their virtual PC for this form of communication.

Static free text is a more free-roaming method of messaging. A user can both send and receive messages on the move (in the visualisation) through the user of a "pager". There is a size limit on such messages (a) to fit with the paging analogy and (b) so that the method is not misused, and entire documents sent to users in this way.

A common problem in 3D environments is the display of information that has no meaningful form in 3D such as text or 2D imagery. The visualisation system gets around this through the use of a piece of paper that the user carries with them. This piece of paper has the ability to display many pieces of information based on context and/or the users' requests. It solves the display problem because the paper surface is used to display the necessary information, rather than leave it "hanging" in space.

4.2.4 Annotation

Messages boards can be used to allow user annotation without the need for formal review of the messages (at least in the short term). These notice boards act much like notice boards in the real world and provide a place for information to be posted for all to view. Annotation is also possible through the use of sticky notes. The distinction in the visualisation is that sticky notes are not permanent. After a period of time the information on these notes will either be made more permanent and displayed as a piece of paper on the board or else discarded. Boards can be placed for each building and district. For the buildings this would entail having a notice board in the foyer, whilst for the district the garden area (which contains other district information) indicates the centre area of the district and messaging facilities can be made available here. This facility allows for informal transfer of system knowledge between the maintainers.

4.2.5 Users

The user is represented in the visualisation as a human form, and sees the world through the "eyes" of their avatar. Colour of garments etc. can be set by the user to provide a degree of customisation and in a small way to reflect their personality into the virtual world. "Out of body" experiences are not to be allowed.

The detective tasks of assimilation of evidence and hypothesising are very similar to the process of program comprehension. This can be mapped into the virtual environment of the visualisation. Leaving cards with "people" (for example at message boards or with other users) in case someone else comes up with a "clue" is one way to mirror the detective process. Integration of this concept with the visualisation office can also be done. The office could be enhanced with sub-rooms, one for each continuing "investigation" (or comprehension and maintenance task in Software Engineering terms), to a specified maximum number of rooms. Or investigation rooms could be used, where all users working on the same project could store collective information. These users would then have access to both this room and their own office, but not all users could enter the investigation room. Also users could "own" the information placed in the room to prevent others on the same project removing it! This use of notes and information rooms aligns well with ideas from the Clean Room Concept since the implementation of such features can be done in a way to support audit trails and review processes.

The assimilation of evidence from the code also relates to the forensic process of discovery from facts using only experience based knowledge (in this case programming knowledge) and the evidence available. Studying a corpse provides a good forensic scientist with many clues as to that person's death (and even facets of their life). In the same way, a program comprehension expert can, when "examining" the source code and related artifacts draw conclusions as to what that code does and how to make it do something different.

5. Conclusions

As has been pointed out in the paper, not all visualisations are suitable for being inhabited. Traditional two-dimensional node and arc displays are limited in their visualisation usefulness in respect of scale and complexity never mind having to deal with inhabitation. More advanced two-dimensional displays can become multi-user through whiteboard techniques but again are not really suitable for inhabitation. Essentially, to make the most of the visualisation and the inhabitation, the virtual environment needs to be depicted in three dimensions with suitable orientation and navigation aids.

Visualisations can benefit greatly from becoming shared spaces, but there needs to be consideration given to the multi-user aspects of the visualisation when designing it. The creation of visualisations that are considered suitable is already a hard and ultimately creative task. Much depends on the task for which the visualisation is to be used and the underlying data. There is also the issue of the users whose preferences will often affect whether they consider a visualisation to be useful and usable. Therefore the extension of three-dimensional visualisation guidelines (still very much a research issue in their own right) to consider multi-user environments is not that much of an extra burden and something which should be considered a vital part of future research.

Further work should also consider the implementation of such extensions to visualisations to be able to make more informed decisions about their practicality, such as with scaling and automation. Implementation would also allow the relevant techniques to be tested and refined so that information foraging techniques and visualisation can work well together for the purposes of intelligence amplification.

Acknowledgements

This work is financed by an EPSRC ROPA grant: VVSRE; **V**isualising **S**oftware in **V**irtual **R**eality **E**nvironments.

References

[1] **M. J. Baker** and **S. G. Eick**, *Space Filling Software Visualization*, Journal of Visual Languages and Computing, Vol. 6, pp 119-133, 1995.

[2] **S. G. Eick**, *Engineering Perceptually Effective Visualizations for Abstract Data*, In Scientific Visualization Overviews, Methodologies and Techniques, IEEE Computer Science Press, pp191-210, February 1997.

[3] **P. Young** and **M. Munro**, *Visualising Software in Virtual Reality*. Proceedings of the IEEE 6th International Workshop on Program Comprehension, June 24-26, 1998, pp19-26.

[4] **C. Knight** and **M. Munro**, *Comprehension with[in] Virtual Environment Visualisations*, Proceedings of the IEEE 7th International Workshop on Program Comprehension, pp4-11, May 5-7, 1999.

[5] **L. Feijs** and **R. de Jong**, *3D Visualization of Software Architectures*, Communications of the ACM, Vol. 41, No. 12, pp72-78, December 1998.

[6] **C. Knight**, *Virtual Software in Reality*, Ph.D. Thesis, Department of Computer Science, University of Durham, June 2000.

[7] **J. Leigh** and **S. Bailey**, *A Tele-Immersive Environment for Collaborative Exploratory Analysis of Massive Data Sets*, ASCI '99, June 1999.

[8] **M. Crossley, N. J. Davies, R. J. Taylor-Hendry,** and **A. J. McGrath**, *Three-Dimensional Internet Developments*, BT Technology Journal, Vol. 15, No. 2, April 1997.

[9] **J. Leigh, A. E. Johnson, M. Brown, D. J. Sandin,** and **T. A. DeFanti**, *Visualization in Teleimmersive Environments*, IEEE Computer, December 1999.

Experiments in Information Visualization Using 3D Metaphoric Worlds

C. Russo Dos Santos, P. Gros, P. Abel,
D. Loisel, N. Trichaud
Eurecom Institute, B.P. 193
Sophia Antipolis, France
{russo,gros,abel,loisel,trichaud}@eurecom.fr

J. P. Paris
CNET France Telecom
Sophia Antipolis
France
jeanpierre.paris@cnet.francetelecom.fr

Abstract

In this paper we present experiments concerning the use of three-dimensional (3D) visualization for representing information. These experiments were conducted in the context of the CyberNet research project. The CyberNet project is oriented toward the enhancement of the user interface of network management tools. Its aim is to study how metaphoric 3D visualization may help the user in the process of monitoring large amounts of dynamic information. Although the project focuses on a specific application domain, network management, the core framework is designed so that it can be applied to other domains, and the system may be accessed from a web browser, thus allowing for information and knowledge sharing.

1. Introduction

The objective of the CyberNet project is to study the usability and effectiveness of 3D techniques and virtual reality interfaces for system and network management. Some prior work has already been done in the field of using virtual worlds for network management and visualization, as in [5] and [3]. However this work focused mainly on visualizing static topological information and did not address the problem of visualizing high dynamic network service information. We intend to prove that the visualization of distributed dynamic data can be made more efficient with 3D technology.

For this purpose, we have designed a general framework that makes the development of specific visualization tools easy. This framework is designed to dynamically build and update 3D worlds according to the real world data. It also features some specific support for user interaction and navigation. We consider that the CyberNet framework is specific in its approach because of the following features:

- The processed data are dynamic. The visualizations are designed to cope with this dynamic nature so that the 3D worlds are permanently updated. New objects are added to the 3D scene, existing objects disappear, and the visual appearance of the displayed objects is continuously modified in order to reflect the state of the network data.
- The translation between the real world data and their visual counterparts is handled automatically by the system. We call this translation the mapping process. This feature allows for the automatic construction of the virtual worlds and for updating the visualizations on the fly.
- The visualization is based on 3D metaphors. The traditional way to represent network information in 3D is to extend the usual two-dimensional (2D) graphical business representations such as 3D bar charts, 3D graphs, and so on. These representations are well suited for displaying small amounts of information but they generally fall short when large amounts of information are involved and when it is important to show relationships between different data subsets.

  In order to represent information CyberNet uses metaphors based on real world structured systems such as towns, solar systems, and buildings, for instance. The idea behind the use of metaphors is to take advantage of the natural hierarchical structure found in most of these metaphors (cities are made of districts, each district is made of buildings and streets, each building has floors, rooms, windows, etc.). CyberNet uses this hierarchical structure in order to encode structured information related to a network service.

  The use of metaphors has also the advantage of producing worlds that are familiar to the user. Visual metaphors make appeal to analogies with real world objects that the user is already familiarized with, to introduce new concepts to the user [8]. This way, the end user can relate to a given metaphor, which facili-

0-7695-0798-9/00 $10.00 © 2000 IEEE

tates data representation comprehension. Using carefully designed visualizations, the CyberNet system can benefit from the user previous knowledge and thus enhance the user understanding of the world, as well as ease the navigation and interaction.

The CyberNet project framework is described in detail in [1]. In this paper, we focus in the different visual representations that were developed to deal with specific network monitoring needs. We also present our approach regarding user navigation and interaction with the virtual worlds.

The paper is organized as follows: Section 2 describes the automatic construction of the 3D metaphoric worlds. Section 3 presents the navigation in the virtual worlds. In Section 4 we describe the interaction with the metaphoric worlds. Finally, Section 5 presents the conclusions and outlines some perspectives for further work.

2. Building 3D worlds automatically

In this section we describe how we construct the metaphoric worlds. We begin by presenting the design of a service model example and then we describe the design of a 3D metaphor. Afterwards, we describe the process of mapping the service onto the metaphor. We also present an example of using different metaphors to visualize the same service, according to the user's interests.

2.1. Designing a service model: the NFS example

In order to be efficient, the representation of information requires the data to be logically structured into a network service model. Each data set has its own structure. This structure is dependent on the application domain and requires expertise knowledge. Basically, structuring the data requires to group data according to common properties and to identify relationships. In our structuring process the final service model is represented by a tree. It is the tree data structure that will be directly translated into visual elements.

The data model we have developed is based on the concept of entities. In the context of network management, an entity can represent a physical device (e.g., hubs, routers, computers, etc.) or conceptual items (e.g., connections, processes, etc.). Each entity groups all the values necessary to describe the current state of the data element it represents. An entity has a type (e.g., the hub type) and a defined set of typed values (e.g., for a hub its IP address, its number of ports, etc.). The entities are created by an entity collecting process described in [1]. Entities are stored in a repository that acts as a Database Managing System (DBMS).

The data model tree is composed of service nodes. A service node is an object that knows how to interpret a small part of the data model. The way a service node works is the following: the service node searches, using SQL(Structured Query Language)-like queries, for the entities that have some specific properties and analyzes the retrieved entities in order to create the children service nodes.

The service model together with the CyberNet framework are designed to be able to handle data dynamics: the repository updates the service nodes each time an entity that matches the query is created. This paper will not address the problems and solutions for managing the dynamic nature of the data and it will not address the mechanisms involved in the data collecting process either. Further information about these topics is given in [1].

Client/Server applications (like mail, DBMS, etc) are typical services for which we believe 3D metaphoric worlds can help. An example of such a service is the NFS (Network File System) client/server application. This application allows for computer disks to be shared in a user transparent way. NFS servers export their file systems to other computers and NFS clients import file systems from servers. Using NFS a remote disk is viewed in the same way as a local disk.

Nonetheless, from a network administrator and system manager's point of view, each access to a remote disk generates network traffic. A typical NFS site configuration involves a high number of computers on a typical Unix/NT workstation network. We chose NFS as an example of the administration of a complex networked client/server service. For this purpose, we developed data collecting agents that are able to get the NFS information from all over the Local Area Network (LAN) at Eurecom Institute.

The NFS service model designed by us is hierarchical as it is shown in the left part of Figure 1. The root service node of the hierarchy is the LAN, the second level comprises the different workgroups of the institute (split according to subnets). Each subnet service node groups a set of computers, each computer service node features a set of local disks and a set of remote disks (accessed through NFS). The local disk may be shared using NFS. In that case, the computers that remotely access the local disk are added as children of the local disk service node. Each client computer service node also groups all the filehandles opened on that file system.

The NFS service model is composed of the previously described service nodes hierarchy. In addition to the service nodes, the hierarchy includes as leaf nodes the references to the entities retrieved from the repository. For instance, a computer service node has the following children: one reference to the actual entity that describes all the characteristics of the computer (as retrieved by the collecting agents) plus a storage service node. This storage service node has two children service nodes: one for managing local disks and one for managing remotely accessed disks. The former has as many children service nodes as actual local disks; the latter has leaf nodes that are direct references to the entities that represent each remotely mounted disk on that computer.

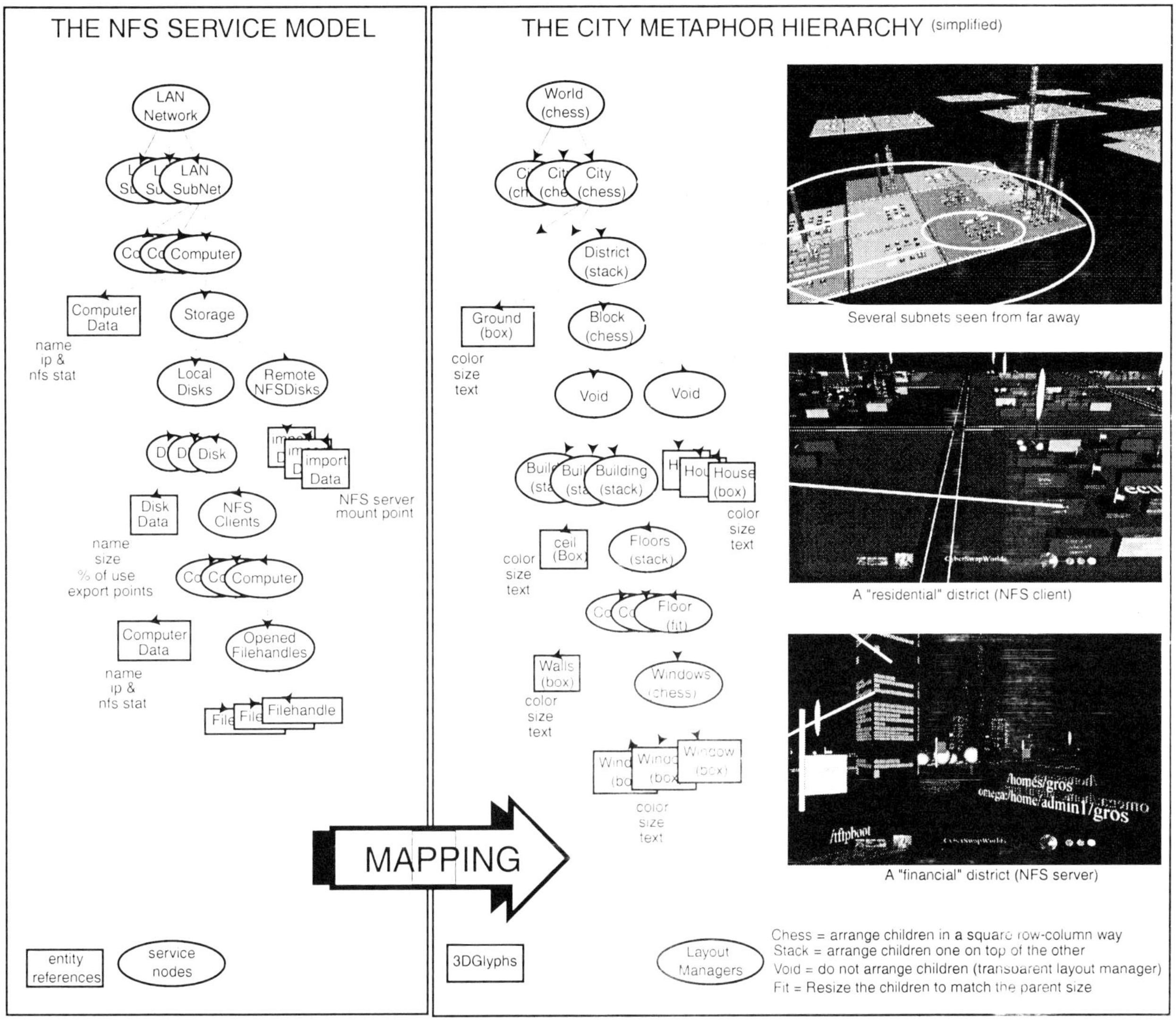

Figure 1. The NFS service model and its mapping onto the city metaphor.

One interesting characteristic of this example is that each local disk service node has descendents that reference the computer entities that are its NFS clients. Thus, the computer entity may be referenced several times in the same hierarchy. This characteristic will be exploited by the interaction mechanisms described in Section 4.

2.2. Designing 3D metaphors: the city example

Our visualization model is based upon the concept of 3D metaphors. There is previous work done in the field of information visualization using 3D metaphors, either real-based, such as a cityscape [7], a solar system [4] or a garden [4], or more abstract, such as a cone-tree [9]. Metaphors are used because their underlying structure is familiar to the user and therefore the user is able to relate to the relationships existing between different objects of the metaphoric world [8]. For example, in a city metaphor it is straightforward that houses in the same district share some common properties. We have designed real world based metaphors such as a building, a solar system or a city. It is important to note that a given metaphor is not designed for a specific service model. In fact, a service model can be visualized using any metaphor, provided the metaphor offers sufficient capabilities for viewing the service information.

A metaphor may be viewed as a world construction pattern. The metaphor is a hierarchical structure that will drive the world construction. Each node of this hierarchy is called

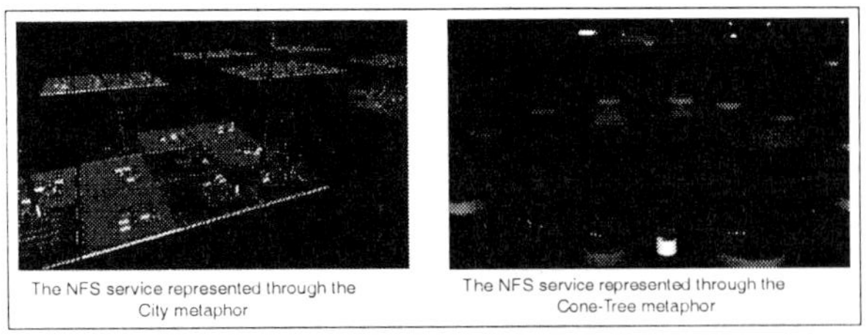

Figure 2. Representing the same service model using different metaphors.

a graphical component (GC). Intermediate nodes are called layout managers (LMs). The presentation of large volumes of information needs to be organized in space in order to make its interpretation easier [6]. Layout managers are a step towards organizing information spatially: the primary function of the layout managers is to arrange their children in space. They also have additional functions concerning navigation and interaction and may also generate some visual appearance such as semi-transparent bounding boxes, to enhance visual representation effectiveness, as suggested in [11]. Leaf nodes are 3D glyphs (3DGs).

3D glyphs are 3D graphical objects that represent data through visual parameters [2]. The level of complexity of a 3D glyph can be measured from the number of visual parameters it offers for modification and hence to the dimension of data that can be displayed. Some examples of complex 3D glyphs can be found in [2] and [10].

In the city example, visible on the right of Figure 1, the root of the metaphor hierarchy is the world LM. This layout manager arranges its children in 2D in a row/column way (like a chess plate). The children of the world LM are cities LMs. Cities are also LMs that arrange their children in a chess plate way. The children of cities layout managers are districts LMs, which stack a block LM on a ground 3DG. The block LM is a chess-like layout manager, whose children are buildings LMs and houses 3DGs. Buildings LMs are stacks of floors LMs, that are made of walls 3DGs and windows LMs. The window LM just arranges its children windows 3DGs.

This metaphor is used as a pattern for constructing a 3D world, examples of which can be seen on the far right part of Figure 1. This pattern is exploited by the mapping process described in the following section.

2.3. Mapping the service model onto the metaphor

Mapping is the process that automatically constructs a 3D metaphoric world from the information contained in a service model. It results in a graphical hierarchy where internal nodes are layout managers and leaves are 3D glyphs.

In the CyberNet system, special objects called *adaptors* handle the mapping. Adaptors are dependent on the type of metaphor used for displaying the information and provide the necessary mechanism to automatically construct the virtual worlds. An example of a mapping is given on Figure 1.

In our current implementation, each metaphor is defined as a hierarchy of graphical components (i.e, a city metaphor is based on GCs called city, districts, streets, buildings, floors, etc.). We name *hierarchical mapping* the process of defining which service element (entity or service node) will be visualized using which metaphoric component.

The main idea behind the mapping process is to define a set of association rules for each service based on the type of each service element and its position in the service tree. In particular, since an entity may be a part of several relations (thus being located at more than one position in the service model tree), it may have several visual counterparts in the presentation domain. The adaptors implement the mapping association rules.

For instance, in the previous NFS example, the model mapping rules state that computers=districts, local disks=buildings, remote disks=houses, NFSimportpoints=floors of the building, FileHandles=windows, and so on. So far, the mapping process is hard-coded but we are currently developing an automatic mapping process based on information and visual properties characterization.

The attributes of each entity must also be translated into visual information. This is the purpose of the *visual parameters mapping*. Each GC has a number of visual parameters that may be dynamically modified in order to display information (e.g., position, orientation, size, color, etc.).

A simple example is the mapping of a disk entity on a box glyph. In this example, the size of the disk could be mapped on the size of the box while the percentage of use of the disk could be mapped on the color of the box (green corresponds to 0%, yellow to 50% and red to 100%; the values in-between are mapped to the color transition between the limits). When defining the mapping rules, care must be taken to preserve metaphor coherency. For example, if one rule uses color for identification purposes, other rules can not use this visual parameter to represent a quantitative value.

In the previous NFS example, several mappings have been tested. Basically, one mapping is oriented toward NFS configuration while another is oriented toward NFS real-time monitoring. In the former, color and size are used to represent the type (e.g., system, user, etc.) the properties (e.g., backup strategy, speed, etc.) and the access rights (e.g., the rules for NFS exportation, etc.). The latter mainly shows NFS network statistics: mounted points, disks size and percentage of use, and so on. Both mappings are useful, depending on the operator task.

Figure 3. The metaphor-aware navigation path from one office to another.

The result of such mappings is the following: all the NFS information is available in one virtual world (Figure 1 on the right). In the virtual world, there are several cities (one city per subnet). Each city comprises several districts (a district is a computer) and it is easy to identify servers (districts with buildings) and server loads (tall buildings). NFS clients are residential districts made of houses.

2.4. Changing the current metaphor

Whenever a mapping between a service model and more than one metaphor is feasible, it is possible to swap from one representation to another. This is very useful to experiment different metaphoric representations and determine the one that is most suited to the current service model or to the user's task. Figure 2 shows an example of different metaphoric representations of the same service.

3. Navigating in 3D metaphoric worlds

In this section we present an example of metaphor based navigation. We also give an example of different types of navigation in the same metaphor.

3.1. Metaphor based navigation

Anyone who has ever experienced 3D interfaces will agree that navigating in a 3D world is not a trivial task. The user interface of traditional 3D browsers provides navigation mechanisms that allow the user to modify the virtual camera parameters. Using these tools, it is common that, after some movements, the user gets lost in space and tries to restart from the beginning. We feel that the navigation schemes provided by traditional 3D browsers are too generic for our specific navigation needs. It is evident that when the user navigates from office to office in a virtual

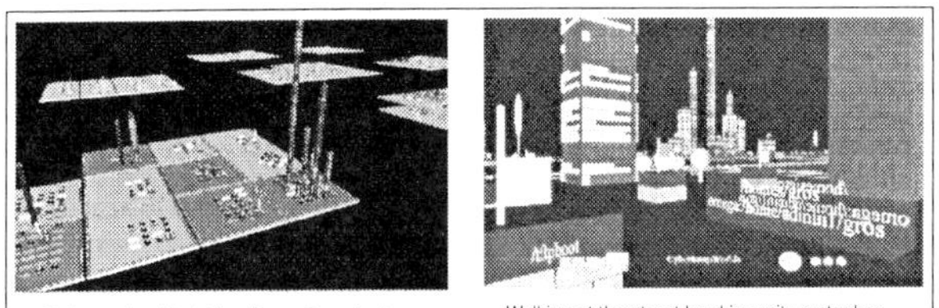

Flying at the district level in a city metaphor — Walking at the street level in a city metaphor

Figure 4. Navigating at different levels of the metaphor.

building he does not use the same navigation mechanisms that when he is exploring a landscape of data or studying the topological structure of a cone tree.

In the CyberNet visualization framework, all the metaphoric worlds are constructed using standard well-defined graphical components: layout managers are used to arrange 3D glyphs in space. For example, the same stack layout manager is used to align offices along a corridor and to stack floors on top of each other, in order to construct a building. However, the navigation along a corridor is not the same as the navigation from one floor to another. Our belief is that the navigation mechanisms should be associated to the graphical components. The objective is that the user navigates in the world with the mechanism most suited to the metaphor. We call this principle *metaphor-aware navigation.*

In order to be able to assist the user navigating, we have implemented this metaphor aware navigation mechanism in the context of the building metaphor (Figure 8). The building metaphor is used to present information about Eurecom Institute offices, staff and internal computer network. The offices and network devices location in the virtual world follow the real world location of these elements, but the virtual building is not an actual copy of the real life existing building.

The basic idea of our navigation system is to track the user current position in order to always be able to associate the user's current position with a node in the hierarchy. In addition, the system provides the user with a tool that allows him to select a destination node. This selection can be done, either by using a 3D embedded interface (e.g., by clicking on an object), or using an external menu. This menu is hierarchical and context sensitive.

The system determines the set of movements that must be done within the context of the current metaphor in order to go from the user's current node of interest to the new node of interest. These movements are dependent upon several user navigation modes but, basically, the user follows a logical path from his current position to his desired destination. The notion of path-based navigation is central to

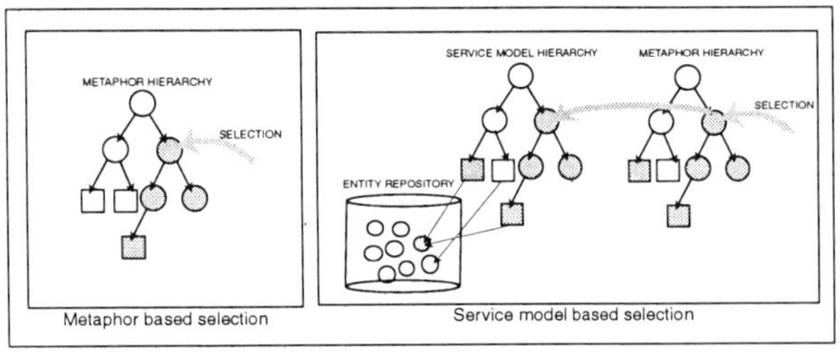

Figure 5. The selection mechanisms.

our navigation. The main interest of the path-based navigation is to give the user knowledge of the relative locations of objects in the virtual world. We already referred that it is of prime importance for the paths to be metaphor-aware. Navigating in a building is a good example of such a metaphor-aware navigation mechanism. When a user is in an office and wants to go to another office, the system automatically computes the logical path and animates the user position along that path (through the corridors and the stairs). Figure 3 shows an example of a metaphor-aware navigation mechanism.

3.2. Navigating at different levels of the hierarchy

In order to ease the navigation, the metaphor aware mechanism takes into account the actual level of the metaphor hierarchy the user is currently in. Different navigation schemes may be used for navigating at different levels of the metaphoric world hierarchy. This kind of navigation is helpful for easily acquiring survey knowledge, when navigating at a higher level. For instance, in a city, the user may navigate at the street level (Figure 4 on the right), walking in the streets in order to go from one building to another, or he may navigate at the district level, like a bird flying over the town (Figure 4 on the left). The user will have a global view (seen from far away) when he is navigating at the district level and a narrowed, more local view when navigating at the street level.

4. Interacting with 3D metaphoric worlds

This section presents some interaction mechanisms already implemented in the CyberNet project, namely the selection mechanism. We describe how the user can select objects inside a virtual world and across different worlds. We also briefly present other interaction mechanisms.

4.1. Selecting objects inside a world

Selection is one of the most important interaction mechanisms. The user should be able to select a node in the

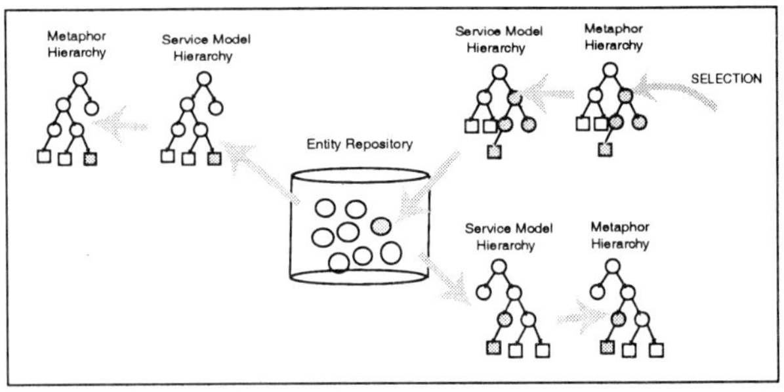

Figure 6. Propagating selection between views.

metaphor hierarchy using either direct manipulation or external menus. The user should also have the possibility to extend the selection to all the descendant nodes of the selected nodes.

In the building metaphor (Figure 8), these kinds of mechanisms can be used, for instance, to select all the computers that are located at a given floor. This kind of selection only allows to select groups of objects that belong to the same metaphor hierarchy sub-tree. For instance, selecting a building in the city metaphor (Figures 1 and 4) automatically propagates the selection to all the floors, walls and windows of that building. We call this selection mechanism a *metaphor based selection* (Figure 5 on the left) since the selection criteria are based on the metaphor structure.

However, the user often wants to select objects according to service model criteria, which may not be directly available from the hierarchical structure of the 3D world. In the city metaphor (Figures 1 and 4), when the user selects a building he may want to visualize which elements are related to that building. This is dependent upon the service model. We name this mechanism *service model based selection* (Figure 5 on the right).

In our previous NFS example (Figure 1), each floor of the building represents a client computer. NFS client computers are also represented as districts (generally, clients are residential districts). When selecting a building (which is related to a disk) the user may want to select all the districts/computers in all the towns/subnets that are related to that building/disk.

For that selection to be effective, the selection must be propagated from the metaphor to the service model down to the entity level. When a building is selected, the selection is transmitted to the corresponding local disk service node and all its descendant service nodes and related entities are also selected. When an entity is selected, the selection is retro-propagated to the service nodes that reference that entity and from these service nodes up to their graphical representation in the metaphoric world.

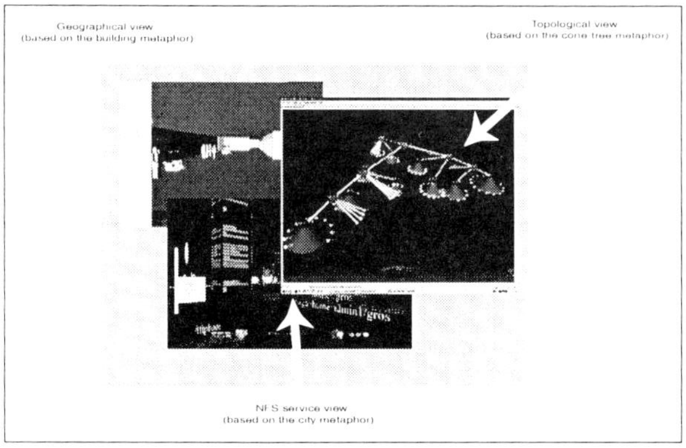

Figure 7. Working with several metaphoric worlds.

This mechanism can be used to help the user identifying the clients of a NFS server and, specially, the clients that are not located in the same subnet of the server. This is useful for performance tuning or for security purposes.

4.2. Selecting objects across different worlds

Being able to propagate the selection down to the service model and entities is a very powerful mechanism that can be exploited to extend the scope of the selection mechanism to several metaphoric worlds. The main idea is to allow the user to interact with several metaphors that represent different service models connected simultaneously to the same entity repository. We believe that one of the strengths of 3D metaphoric representation will come from the combined used of several interacting tools.

The multi-world selection mechanism (Figure 6) can be used to allow for specifying free selection criteria; i.e., selection criteria that are neither metaphor based nor service model based. The user may view the same network according to several views, each view being based on the metaphor that is most suited to represent each service model (Figure 7). In one view he may visualize the building and geographic location of computers and network devices. In another view, he can visualize the topology of the network (using for example the cone-tree metaphor). In a third view, the user can monitor the NFS service using the city metaphor.

With the multi-world selection mechanism, it is possible to select a network device (e.g., a hub) in the cone-tree view where they are more easily identified, and all the computers connected to that hub will be selected in all the three views. The user can also select the clients of the a NFS server in the city view and locate them in the building and in the topology views. The selection mechanism can be further extended in order to allow the user to combine several criteria (by ANDing or ORing successive selection actions).

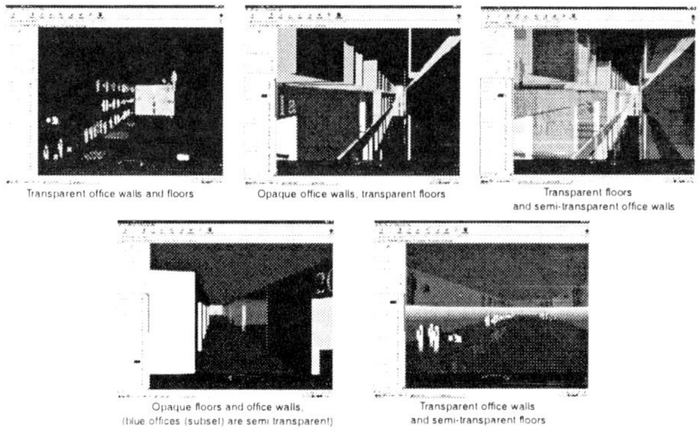

Figure 8. Modifying the appearance of the virtual representation of the Eurecom Institute building.

4.3. Other interaction mechanisms

We found that being able to interact with the world in order to modify its appearance was important. An example of such a study has been done within the context of the building metaphor. We felt that having a model of the building and being able to navigate and interact with the objects according to the actual building is important but sometimes restrictive. Virtual worlds should bring more possibilities than just mimic the real world. For this purpose, we have developed mechanisms that allow the user to have control over the world appearance itself.

For instance, in the building metaphor, the user may modify the transparency of walls and grounds. The user may render all the ground and office walls transparent in order to easily observe the contents of all the building. He may also render some offices partially transparent according to criteria such as the department they belong to, etc. Further stretching the interaction, the user may even decide to "rebuild" the building by placing a department per floor (in real life, the departments at Eurecom Institute are spread over the different floors). Figure 8 shows some examples of the above interactions.

5. Conclusions and perspectives

We have presented experiments done in the context of network management in order to study the advantages of 3D metaphoric virtual worlds for monitoring large volumes of multidimensional information. We have described how the system automatically builds virtual worlds for information display. We have also shown how the navigation and interaction are dealt with in order to ease user's tasks.

Preliminary feedback from users showed that 3D

metaphoric visualization seems promising. It eases problem detection and understanding. However, we are still looking for new visualizations that make the most of the opportunities of virtual environments. We are developing new metaphors and associated 3D glyphs and layout managers with special focus on their adaptive representation and navigation capabilities. New interaction mechanisms also need to be studied further.

Although this work has been done within the context of network management, every application that involves the user to interact with huge amounts of dynamically structured information may be targeted (such as stock exchange, bank trading or web administration). We must also refer that the end user may access the system from anywhere since it only requires a VRML (Virtual Reality Modeling Language) enabled WWW browser.

Several topics are currently under study. Data characterization is one of them. At current implementation, data values mappings onto visual parameters are hard-coded. We are developing a visual parameters taxonomy and a data characterization. These classifications will allow us to implement generic adaptors, and thus automatically map real world data values onto visual parameters, according to the current metaphor.

Further work also has to be done in the field of user interaction and combined use of different tools. We also have to study how to add persistence to the system in order to be able to playback and analyze some crucial sequence of events off-line. We also want to provide ways to interact with the real world (e.g. kill a process on a workstation).

The CyberNet project is supported by France Telecom and the Eurecom Institute. The CyberNet project web site is: http://www.eurecom.fr/~abel/cybernet. The authors would like to thank: B. Lugeon, P. Miauton and J. Pasini for their work on the building metaphor; M. Girardot and L. Oria for their work on the cone-tree metaphor; and P. Garcia, S. Monterde and R. Vincent for their work on the city metaphor.

References

[1] P. Abel, P. Gros, C. R. D. Santos, D. Loisel, and J.-P. Paris. Automatic construction of dynamic 3d metaphoric worlds: An application to network management. In J. R. Robert Erbacher, Philip Chen and C. Wittenbink, editors, *Visual Data Exploration and Analysis VII*, volume 3960, pages 312–323. SPIE - The International Society for Optical Engineering, Jan. 2000.

[2] M. C. Chuah and S. G. Eick. Information rich glyphs for software management data. *IEEE Computer Graphics & Applications*, 18(4), July – Aug. 1998. ISSN 0272-1716.

[3] K. C. Cox, S. G. Eick, and T. He. 3D geographic network displays. *SIGMOD Record (ACM Special Interest Group on Management of Data)*, 25(4):50–??, Dec. 1996.

[4] M. Crossley, N. J. Davies, R. J. Taylor-Hendry, and A. J. McGrath. Three-dimensional internet developments. *BT Technology Journal*, 15(2):179–193, Apr. 1997.

[5] L. A. Crutcher, A. A. Lazar, S. K. Feiner, and M. X. Zhou. Managing networks through a virtual world. *IEEE parallel and distributed technology: systems and applications*, 3(2):4–13, Summer 1995.

[6] K. M. Fairchild, S. E. Poltrock, and G. W. Furnas. SemNet: Three-dimensional graphic representation of large knowledge bases. In R. Guindon, editor, *Cognitive Science and its Applications for Human-Computer Interaction*, pages 201–233. Lawrence Erlbaum Associates, Hillsdale, New Jeresy, U.S.A., May 1988.

[7] N. Gershon and S. G. Eick. Visualization's new tack: Making sense of information. *IEEE Spectrum*, pages 38–56, Nov. 1995.

[8] W. M. Newman and M. G. Lamming. *Interactive System Design*. Addison-Wesley Publishing, Wokingham, England, 1995.

[9] G. G. Robertson, J. D. Mackinlay, and S. K. Card. Cone trees: Animated 3D visualizations of hierarchical information. In S. P. Robertson, G. M. Olson, and J. S. Olson, editors, *Proc. ACM Conf. Human Factors in Computing Systems, CHI*, pages 189–194. ACM Press, 28 Apr.–2 May 1991.

[10] R. M. Rohrer and E. Swing. Web-based information visualization. *IEEE Computer Graphics and Applications*, 17(4):52–59, July/Aug. 1997.

[11] S. Zhai, W. Buxton, and P. Milgram. The partial-occlusion effect: utilizing semitransparency in 3D human-computer interaction. *ACM Transactions on Computer-Human Interaction*, 3(3):254–284, Sept. 1996.

An Adaptive Multi-Agent Tool for Electronic Commerce

Marie-Pierre Gleizes
IRIT
University Paul Sabatier
118 route de Narbonne,
31062 Toulouse Cédex 4
France
Marie-Pierre.Gleizes@irit.fr

Jo Link-Pezet
IRIT
University Paul Sabatier
118 route de Narbonne
31062 Toulouse Cédex 4
France
pezet@cict.fr

Pierre Glize
IRIT
University Paul Sabatier
118 route de Narbonne
31062 Toulouse Cédex 4
France
Pierre.Glize@irit.fr

Abstract

The concept of Electronic Service Brokerage is based on the use of new information technologies to provide a service capable of facilitating and organizing the relationship between customers and offers providers. In this paper, a framework for Electronic Brokerage Service based on the emerging agent technology is presented. The first part of this article presents the requirements for electronic brokerage and the basic principles of the multi-agent used in Abrose. In the second part, we show the functionality of the Transaction Agents which represent the users inside the broker domain of Abrose. In the last part, we evaluate the dynamic properties of the user profile and belief network managed by each Transaction Agent.

This electronic brokerage service will be applied in three business domains (Tourism, Trading and Teleworking). It covers the following features : the collaborative agents for self-organizing multi-agent systems, the multi-agent system for knowledge representation of the market place domain, the dynamic knowledge capture for a domain knowledge evolution.

1. Concept and architecture of Abrose[1]

1.1. The general goal of brokerage

The electronic Commerce is based on the exchange of information between the involved stakeholders, using the underlying telecommunication infrastructure. Business-to-Consumer applications enable the providers to propagate their offers, they allow the customers to find an offer matching their demands. A huge collection of frequently updated offers and customers, the electronic marketplace, reveals the task of matching the demand and supply processes in a commercial mediation environment.

An Information Brokerage Service, in the context of the electronic commerce, facilitates this symmetrical matching process, as both parties are able to get in touch with each other [1], [2], [3], [4], [5], [6] [7] Brokerage has to be regarded as embedded in a commercial mediation platform. Services like billing, payment, delivery and accounting are supported by the underlying platform, they do not concern the brokerage process itself.

Ideally, an electronic brokerage tool is based upon the following essential features:

- *Matching the demand and supply*: improving the performance and the quality of mediation.
- *Remembering the success and quality of the past transactions*: for the benefit of the end users, the content providers and the market place service operator.
- *The propagation of offers and demands:* using the knowledge about the end-users and content providers

Abrose main goal is to improve the brokerage functions in using multi-agent technology. Abrose originality comes from multiple distributed dynamic knowledge concerning the customers and content providers. The new knowledge learnt about the customers allows the offer propagation to all relevant customers. The new knowledge learnt about the content providers guarantees a better matching of the demands and offers. The learning process, based on the previous transactions, is realized automatically during the life of the system. Before describing the adaptation and learning processes, we will present the system's general architecture.

1.2. The Abrose Architecture

Abrose [8], [9] is composed of two main parts: the broker domain (realizing the functions of brokerage and system management) and the user domain assuming the access to information and the displaying abilities for a user.

[1] The full Abrose consortium comprises : DT-Berkom, FT-CNET, Univ. of Toulouse, Univ. of Athens, Univ. of Madrid, Univ. of Berlin, Infomures from Romania, Tradezone International Ltd England, Dégriftour sa France.

0-7695-0798-9/00 $10.00 © 2000 IEEE

1.2.1. The adaptive multi-agent systems of ABROSE. The part of the system realizes the brokerage in Abrose: it is constituted by several adaptive multi-agent systems. At the most general level, there is the mediation agent (MA) representing the site where Abrose is. A mediation agent knows all the transaction agents (TA) present on the site.

At the middle level, the system is composed of an adaptive multi-agent system of the transaction agents present on the site. The transaction agent represents a customer or a content provider. It knows other transaction agents that are on its site.

At the lowest level, the beliefs that an agent possesses on other agents of a type similar to its type are implemented in an adaptive multi-agent system called belief network (BN). There is a belief network by transaction agent [EIN,99].

1.2.2. The user domain and the management tools. The user domain consists of several modules written in Java loaded from a server http executed with Netscape. These modules are in charge of the communication aspects between the user and the agent representing him in the system. They are formed of :

- A tool for the connection (CA),
- Graphical interfaces (AMA),
- A tool to aid the navigation in the agent beliefs network representing the user (NA) or in the belief network of the mediation agent,
- A tool in charge of the observation and memorization of a transaction contents between a user and a service provider (Spy).

The management of the multi-agent system of transactions agents and of the users is realized by modules in charge of the registration and checking of the users data (UAM) and the broker manager (BM). This last module

configurates the broker system (start, stop and save functions), allows the vizualisation of the agents (as we will see in the figures 3, 4 and 5), receives information about the system states and sends notifications to the operator terminal.

Abrose platform V1 is implemented in Java with JWS1.1.3, the communication between the Broker and the User domains is developed with OrbixWeb3.1. The broker runs under Solaris 2.6. All the specifications have been made in UML under Rational™ Rose98™. The client is a standard PC equipped with a standard browser.

The dynamic of the information brokerage domain implies important adaptive capabilities, and this is the main reason for Abrose technical choices. The agent technology allows the creation, the deletion and the autonomy in a simple way.

This architecture is not domain dependent as the following examples will show: pens as products proposed to customers or cars, and it can also be used to tourism, teleworking and training. The following parts of the paper will present the adaptive capabilities of the agents in Abrose.

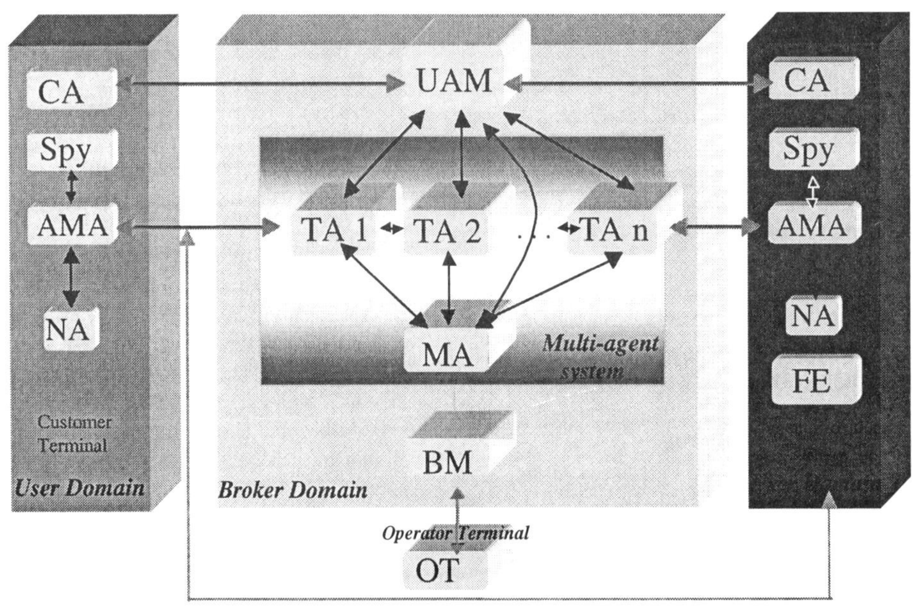

Figure 1. Abrose global architecture

1.3. Adaptive multi-agent system principles

Because of the increasing performance of the machines and networks, computer scientists are nowadays confronted with the development of complex artificial systems more and more difficult to understand. The degree of tractability of such systems is generally described by the intuitive notion of computational complexity many definitions of which can be found in the literature [10]. Here, we are concerned only with the applicability of this concept. A good way to reduce the complexity of artificial systems at their conception level is to avoid high global programming, which can be achieved by building it up from the microscopic level in a bottom-up fashion. The macroscopic structure then emerges from the microscopic computation [11]. In this case however, the difficulty arises from the fact that the emergent behavior of a large number of interacting entities is difficult to predict.

Abrose, as a multi-agent system consists of several agents able to interact with each other and with their environment. Each agent has a local view of the environment, has generally specific goals and is unable to solve by itself the global task[2] devoted to the system. The global characteristics of this system thus arise from the cooperation of its elements. The result of the cooperation, in turn, has consequences on the interactions between the agents and modifies the properties of the system in an intricate manner. Designing a cooperative multi-agent system consists in defining for each component -the agents- every possible uncooperative state at a local level and the actions associated to these states in order to eliminate them. When the system is running in a dynamic environment, an internal process is observed in which the relations between the agents are modified. Thus, the reorganization of the partial functions achieved by each agent leads to a modification of the global system functions. The non cooperative states due to unexpected events are progressively eliminated. With this approach when applied to Abrose, the goal of each autonomous agent is to find the right place inside the organization in order to interact with the other agents in a cooperative way. The behavior of an agent at each step, is determined by the fact that, from its point of view, only cooperative interactions are achieved.

2. The adaptation of the TAs to dynamic requests and offers

The global computation system is distributed into separated smaller functions : the transaction agents (TA). A TA is a thread written in Java inside a computer, without central administration. Each user is linked to an agent. TAs are built when a new service is created or when a customer registers. The TA is in charge of the autonomous exchange of requests or answers with the other TAs. The TA should also communicate with the customer or content provider to which it is associated via General User Interface (GUI).

2.1. Structure of TAs

Each TA consists in beliefs, skills, interaction language and social attitudes:

- The skills of a TA are the skills of the user it represents. It communicates by exchanging information about the knowledge domain of the whole Abrose system. When a TA receives a message, it interprets it and acts. The MA has the capability to help one of its TA unable to act by getting in touch with a local TA able to overcome the blockage.
- Beliefs. This term is related to the description that an agent possesses about the others' and its own skills. The following chapter is devoted to this presentation.

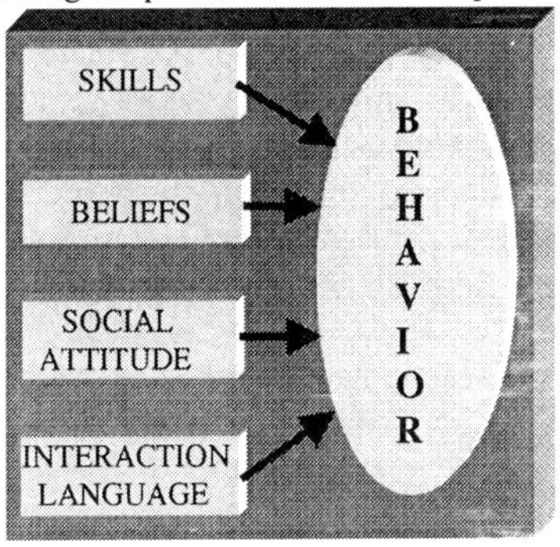

Figure 2. TA components

- Social attitude. In order to be coherent with the principles presented in 1.3, we will say that the social attitude of all the TAs is cooperation.
- Interaction language. An agent interacts with the other agents in using protocols and speech acts, as a subset according to Fipa [12] definition. A language act is neither an invocation method nor a procedure call. This approach for interacting software is useful in an open system where some unknown or unexpected events can occur. The main role of ACL is to give the system the ability to adjust its activities autonomously.
- Behavior. The autonomous agent behavior results from the beliefs, skills, goals and social attitude it possesses at a time. In short, it is willing to help another agent when it possesses the right skills; otherwise, it tries to find other relevant agents to perform the requested task.

2.2. The Transaction Agent behavior

Each cooperative agent is endowed with a cooperative social attitude. This implies three main properties:

Sincerity: If an agent knows that a proposition p is true, it cannot say anything different to others. This is also a main requirement in ACL of FIPA.

Willingness: All agents try to satisfy a received request if it is coherent with their own skills and the current state of the world.

Reciprocity: All the agents of a same society know that themselves and the others verify the two former conditions.

These requirements have some consequences :

1. A cooperative agent cannot act without beliefs about others.
2. An agent sends spontaneously information, without any previous demand, if it believes it is useful to the receiver.
3. If an agent is unable to satisfy a given request, it recruits automatically other agents that have relevant knowledge on the subject.

2.3. An example of a request/offer propagation between the TAs

[2] Many researchers consider that a global task is not needed in a MAS. On the opposite we think that this is a main characteristic which differentiate MAS from software as heaps of interacting agents. For example in information system the global task could be to give efficiently all the relevant information needed.

When a customer makes a request to Abrose, several situations can occur.

- In the first case, the customer's beliefs TA possesses knowledge about relevant content providers (previously used with Abrose). The brokerage is complete ended and the list of relevant content providers is sent to the end-user.
- In a second case, the customer's TA does not know any relevant content provider: therefore the TA asks the MA for help. The MA sends the request to the relevant content providers' TA and these TAs inform the customer's TA if they are relevant or not. The brokerage stops and the list of relevant content providers is given to the end-user.
- In the two previous cases, a relevant content provider's TA which receives a request, finds using its beliefs that other content providers' TA can be useful to answer a part of the request. As a consequence, it sends this part of the request to them. This situation is a composition of services.

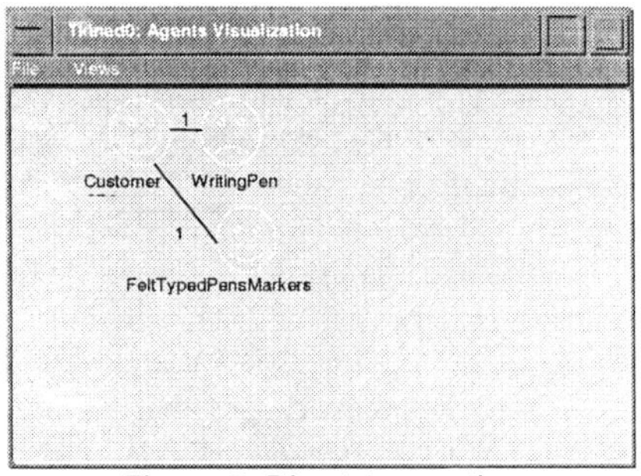

Figure 3. Direct transaction

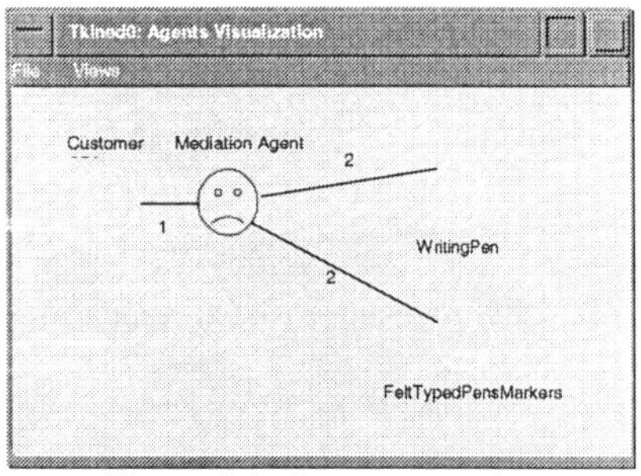

Figure 4. Indirect transaction

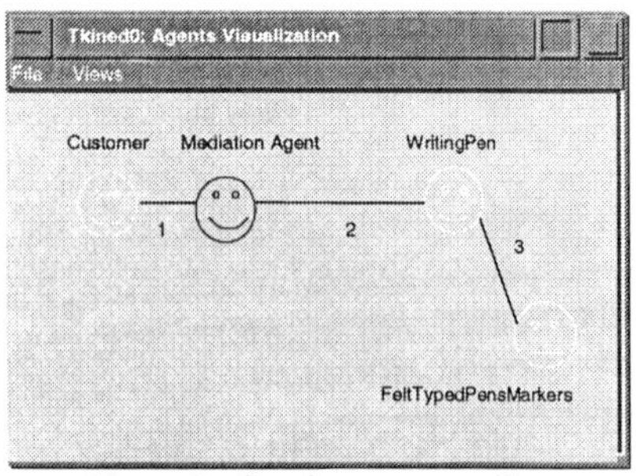

Figure 5. Services composition

By the way of the multi-agent management tool, we could follow these interactions processes, in which a face is associated to each agent (TAs or MA), as we can see in the three previous windows. The figure 3 represents the first case where the customer's TA knows (in its beliefs) already two relevant content providers. In the Figure 4, the customer's TA is helped by the MA. The figure 5 shows the MA sending the request to TA WritingPen, which considers that the TA FeltTypedPensMarkers has complementary skills.

In the following example, we are interested in three content providers of Abrose : the end-user's TA and the two TAs representing the two content providers "WritingPen" and "FeltTypedPensMarkers". These content providers propose similar kind of products : pens. The customer 's TA has no belief about others TAs when the end-user registers in Abrose, this is the example showed in the figure 4. On the other hand, the MA has belief concerning the offers of WritingPen and FeltTypedPensMarkers content providers.

The customer has an associated GUI to propose his request to his TA in Abrose. He has to select the button "make a request" and to fill up the subject of the request (with the label Subject in the figure 6) and the content of the request (with the label " Give your request or your offer " in the figure 6). The customer writes : "I want a pen with a brand artline and a metal barrel". The request could be written in a free format. In the right part of the window, a list sorted by relevance of content providers found is displayed. The role of the MA is not viewed by the customer. Then, the customer could select one or several content providers in the proposed list (the content provider "WritingPen" in the figure 6 has been selected).

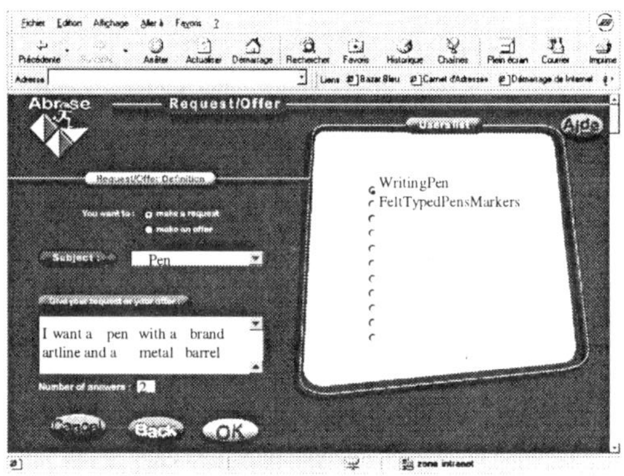

Figure 6. Abrose Request/Offer GUI

The transaction between the customer and the content provider takes place: the pen is bought. Afterwards, the customer can evaluate the transaction using three values: '*good*' if he is satisfied by the transaction, '*bad*' if he is not satisfied or '*don't care*' if he does not want to evaluate it (Figure 7). These values allow the customer's TA to learn about the content provider's skill. The knowledge learnt is composed by all the terms used during the transaction by the customer and which are given by the spy component of Abrose. The knowledge and the evaluation are sent to the content provider's TA. So it can learn about itself. All the time, the knowledge learnt can be stored in the beliefs of the TA or forgotten.

Previously, we have detailed the activity of TAs for a request scenario, but we have a symmetrical scenario for an offer proposition. The list found by Abrose is a list of potential customers interested in the offer given. All the activities between TAs shown, are allowed because the agents are cooperative and because the agents have complementary beliefs about skills of others at a certain time.

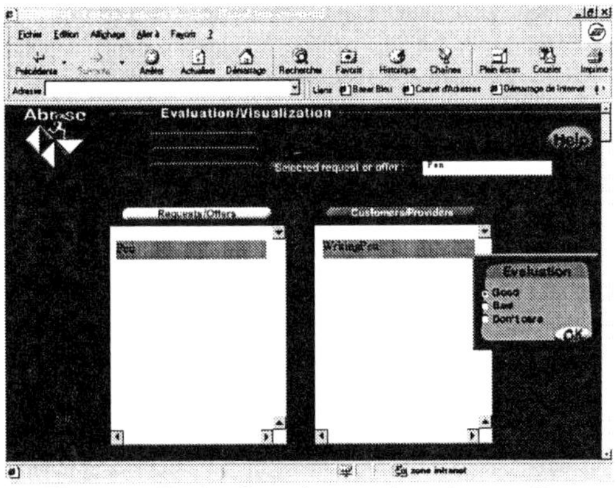

Figure 7. Evaluation of a previous transaction

But in a dynamic domain, a question remains: how have these beliefs been acquired? The beliefs of a TA are stored and managed in a multi-agent system called the belief network. We will focus in the following chapter on this question and will present the architecture and the functioning of a belief network.

3. The adaptation of the TA Beliefs for a dynamic users' profile

3.1. Learning a user profile: a short review

A user profile corresponds to the information about the user and his preferences. It can be constructed explicitly or deduced by the system through the observation of the user's behavior. In order to learn autonomously, the user's agent is "looking over the shoulder" as Maes said [13]. To exemplify the user's profile, we will use the domain of information retrieval in the Internet.

Information filtering describes a variety of processes involving in the delivery of information to people who need it [14]. GroupLens is a system for collaborative filtering of netnews, to help people to find articles they will like in the huge stream of available articles. The rating servers predict scores based on the heuristic that people who agreed in the past will probably agree again. The entire architecture is open : alternative software for news clients and Better Bit Bureaus can be developed independently and can interoperate [15]. MA and TAs in Abrose practice collaborative filtering because they use automatically their own beliefs in order to help others. This behavior is very useful when a new user is logged on, his TA has no initial belief about others, but they increase quickly through the others.

Filtering can reduce the user's information load, provides better coverage of news streams of information, supports ongoing information interests, and provides a mechanism for locating network resources and the people associated to a particular area of interest. Collaborative filters help people to make choices based on the opinions of other people. But mapping the available information corresponding to the users' interests is difficult because of the vocabulary problem. These principles can be applied to electronic commerce.

There are two big problems in using filters concerning the electronic commerce:

1. The large information spaces lead to a great effort involved in creating, maintaining, and evolving filters over time. In order to address this situation, our system manages them automatically without using explicit rule-based agents that recognize a user's usage patterns and make suggestions based on them.
2. The learning starts from zero and it will take quite a long time to train the agent before it becomes useful. Secondly, the agent's competence is necessarily limited to the actions already performed by the user. Collaboration between agents [16] assisting different users can reduce both of these problems [17].

Another electronic commerce system similar to Abrose, Amalthaea, focuses on personalized information filtering and information discovery [7]. It is inspired by an artificial ecosystem of evolving agents that cooperate and compete in a limited resource environment. The Information Filtering agents are responsible for the personalization of the system and for keeping track of (and adapting to) the interests of the user. Information Discovery agents are responsible for information resources handling, adapting to those information sources, finding and fetching the actual information that the user is interested in. The personalization is done in Abrose because each user has its own corpus of beliefs in his TA. In particular, the beliefs about the user's centers of interest are improved after learning during a current transaction as we will show. Through a relevance feedback, a user indicates generally how relevant the documents are in order to improve the filtering process in the future. For example, when an Amalthaea user gives keywords describing a document, the weight of these keywords will be reinforced. The transaction result degree of satisfaction, is provided by feedback. In Abrose, it is obtained when the user manages his list of current transactions: the updating is done when the user indicates if the result is satisfying, uninteresting or does not matter (see figure 7).

Building models of the users' interests is difficult because they all differ with each individual user and are constantly changing. We usually believe that checking keywords patterns is not enough to model the user's interests because semantic and contextual information is required. On the opposite, we think that contextual reasons are too difficult to express and cannot be used in a proper way. This is why we use a theory based on a cooperative self-organization to solve this problem. To do this, only textual description is used.

3.2. The belief network design

The ideal structure of the brokerage domain can be described as a network composed of numerous terms linked the ones to the others and to other elements representing the known customers or content providers. In this ideal view, when a description (a set of terms) is provided, all the relevant users - and only them - are activated. A similar representation is used in the documentation field with the thesaurus approach.

A simplified example of a belief network can be found in the figure 8. If the description of the customer request contains *"Term j"* and *"Term t"* and *"Term k"*, they are activated by the agent frontier. We could suppose that *"Term a"* and *"Term i"* are then activated and in their turn activate the *"User n"* representing a relevant content provider. The lines between all these elements represent the hierarchical organization, expressed with an integer value called the strength. The last parts of the chapter explain this process and analyze the obtained behavior in some examples.

In order to obtain the right behavior in a belief network of a TA, we have defined three types of agents: agent frontier, agent term and agent user.

1. The particular agent called frontier has the role of acting in and perceiving the environment of the system for all the other agents of the society. It activates the corresponding belief agents in order to start the activation of the network. It receives a message from all the activated belief agents representing a user. For convenience, we will present Input and Output Frontier in the figure 8, it is unique in the system.
2. During a previous transaction, the system has spied the content of the request or of the offer, and thus it is able to add a new partial (but probably inexact) representation inside the belief network. All these terms are encapsulated inside the agents term. The belief network is totally empty before the first user interaction.
3. A belief concerns the skill of a particular customer or content provider. Thus, each user has an agent (corresponding to his name) inside the belief network called agent user. Any particular agent term is initially linked with one agent user.

The belief network is used by a TA to find known relevant customers for a given offer or known relevant content provider for a given request. But it is also used to learn new skills of other TAs and skills about itself.

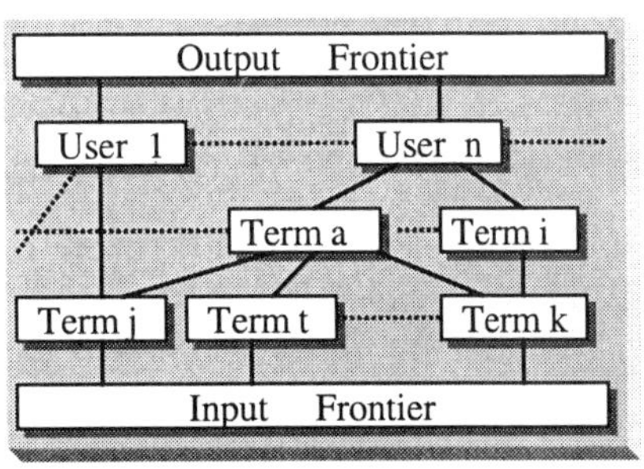

Figure 8. Belief Network organization

3.3. A dynamic Belief Network

A new user does not have enough examples to train his own belief network but he can use the existing ones that have already been evaluated by the other users. This is a main difference with many other approaches like Amalthaea [7]. The code managing the belief network works without any rules about languages (English, French, German, Spanish,...) but is able to obtain a structured representation of a domain from unstructured interactions with the outside. According to the cooperative self-organization theory presented in the part 1.3, this result is reached when all the agents are involved in cooperative interactions with their neighbors. This process is decomposed into three phases:

1. The propagation phase. Any term can be activated directly by the agent frontier when it belongs to the request (or offer) description, or indirectly by other agents which are entries for it.
2. The analysis phase. Now each agent awakened by a request (or an offer) analyses its internal state in order to see if some non cooperative situations occur.
3. The learning phase. After the analysis phase, the concerned agents are informed about the unexpected events occurring to the neighbors. Afterwards, they cooperate in order to solve these undesirable states in modifying the organization i.e. their links with others agents.

To verify the relevance of the learning algorithm, many experiments based on real transactions done by the users in electronic commerce have been realized. The following examples are extracted from used cars domain. We could observe the increasing or decreasing strength of the links between terms and the system converging behavior.

At first the users evaluate some transactions in the used cars domain in order to create the initial links between terms. After, we suppose having interactions only for requests (on this domain and also on other domains very different) to analyze the belief adjustment original process.

3.4. Decreasing links of irrelevant terms

In order to obtain a graph with nodes only composed of a domain significant terms, the self-organization process must lead to the elimination of other irrelevant terms. We observe this phenomenon on the article "a" which is a member of three descriptions acquired by user's feedback in the BN. They have various lengths which imply different initial strengths, expressed on the Y-axis in the figure 9. The X-axis represents the number of requests/offers learnt during this time.

Globally a regular decreasing of the strength is viewed. This occurs because this type of term is frequently used without any particular relevance to the domain of used cars.

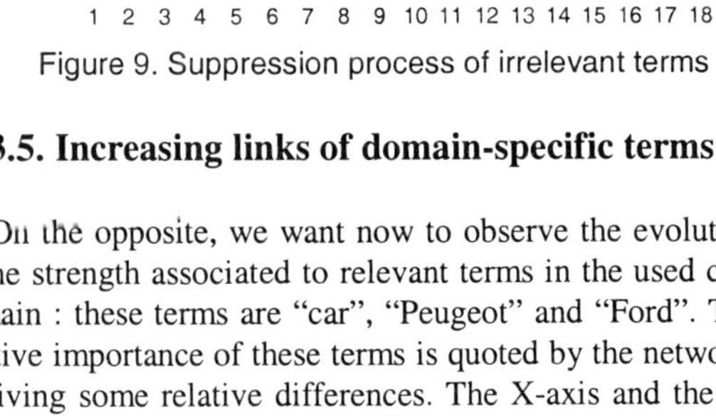

Figure 9. Suppression process of irrelevant terms

3.5. Increasing links of domain-specific terms

On the opposite, we want now to observe the evolution of the strength associated to relevant terms in the used cars domain : these terms are "car", "Peugeot" and "Ford". The relative importance of these terms is quoted by the network, in giving some relative differences. The X-axis and the Y-axis have the same meaning in the figure 10 as in the previous one.

We must have in mind, that all these terms and others such as articles have the same initial strength in a given initial description obtained by feedback. Nevertheless, the system is able to differentiate them, and if "a" disappears (see figure 9), we show here that "Peugeot" and "Ford" are approximately stable and that the very generic term "car" increases a lot.

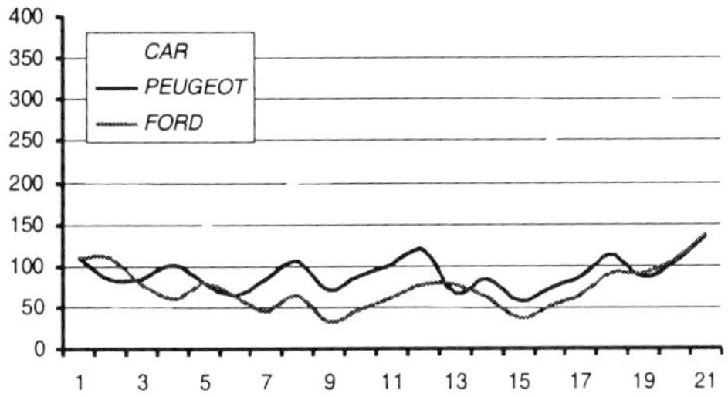

Figure 10. Organization process of relevant terms

3.6 - Analysis

As we have shown in the previous examples, the general behavior of the system leads to the suppression of the useless terms for each domain. The relative increasing strength of significant terms inside domains implies the performance over time because the system diminishes greatly the number of needed reorganizations. This cannot be opposed to the sensitivity of the system, because even after numerous stable interactions it is able to engage a reorganization activity if it detects undesired non cooperative states.

In this approach of a user profile learning, there is only one phase for an explicit user intervention, when he gives his feedback evaluation: this is the way to fill the belief network. Afterwards, the network is able to adapt itself in order to reach an emerging organization between generic and specific terms. It works like a thesaurus. Here, the thesaurus is alive because the new terms added to the network are obtained from the users' habits. The "meaning" of a description is not extracted from a cognitive approach, but emerges from the observation and learning of the users' linguistic habits, which allow to use them whatever the language is, with equally satisfying results.

The belief network which manages all the beliefs of a TA is able to learn all the time without any supervision. It learns new information about the users' preferences in Abrose by taking into account the transactions result. When a TA which controls its own belief network, uses beliefs in order to decide its next behavior, we understand easily why it is more and more accurate over time. The consequence is an improving self-organization process between all TAs in the broker domain. Moreover, the belief network is used by the Navigation Assistant located in the user domain in order to help the customer to formulate his request more accurately.

4. Conclusion and perspectives

The Abrose architecture is based on a multi-agent technology at the TA level and at the belief network level. In this paper, we have described the TA behavior and the learning and adaptation process of a TA to others TA in the system. Each TA represents a user in the system and possesses beliefs about others TA and about itself. The strength of Abrose is to use the set of the beliefs of all the TA and of the MA to improve collectively the brokerage function. This behavior is possible because of the cooperation between the TAs. It works as a large memory enriched by the experience of each user. Each TA stores its beliefs in its belief network which is a multi-agent system. We have shown that this theory based on cooperation allows a good organization between all the agents in the belief network. The results obtained during the questioning of a belief network or during the experiments are very encouraging.

This version of Abrose takes into account only the brokerage function in a highly dynamic environment. Its validation is realized with many scenarios obtained from real brokerage situations. The next stage concerns its concrete integration in the Tradezone application of Onyx with real offers and requests of end-users. TradeZone (https://www.tradezone.onyx.net) provides the secure electronic commerce services to help companies reach a global marketplace via the Internet, increase sales and sales margins, improve customer service and reduce costs. The TradeZone service comprises three main components: a catalogue service, a secure order processing service, and a secure payment processing service.

The associated services like security, billing, payment, delivery and accounting are not currently provided. All these functionalities are already integrated in the existing Tradezone software tool.

Finally, the Abrose experimental service described here has shown that a multi-agent system brings intrinsic innovations for:

- the convergence towards the maximal satisfaction of the users (final customers and service offers) of the mediation service ("win-win" approach),
- the great flexibility to follow the dynamic evolution of the offers-demands context,
- the contextual and personalized help of the customers (e.g. information pushing according to the user profile).

Extensions to others applications are foreseen in the tourism, job research domains and a collective knowledge management system for training [18]. These extensions to new data fields should prove the robustness of the approach. The genericity of the basic functions provided by the multi-agent architecture will be showed, and above all, the added-value of the Abrose multi-agent service to new business domains will be verified.

Acknowledgments

The Abrose project was granted by the European Community. The authors thanks all the partners involved in the development of this software.

5. References

[1] ACM – "Recommender Systems" - Special Issue of Communications of the Association of Computing Machinery – Vol40 N°3 – March 1997

[2] Wiederhold, G., "Mediators in the architecture of future information systems" *IEEE Computer*, Vol25 N.3, 1992

[3] Knoblock C.A., Arens Y. : "An architecture for information retrieval agents", *AAAI Spring Symposium on Software Agents*, Stanford, 1994.

[4]] Chavez A., Maes P., "Kasbah: An Agent Marketplace for Buying and Selling Goods", *The First International Conference on the Practical Application of Intelligent Agents and Muli-Agent Technology*, PAAM'96, London, UK, April 96

[5] Clurman W., Foley T., Guttman R., Kupres K., "Electronic commerce with software Agents, *Electronic Commerce and Marketing on the Internet*, Professors Tom Malone & John Little"

[6] Guttman R.H., Moukas A.G., Maes P.. "Agent-mediated Electronic Commerce: A Survey. ", *Knowledge Engineering Review* June 98.

[7] Moukas A., "Amalthaea : Information Discovery and Filtering using a Multiagent Evolving Ecosystem", *Conference on Practical Applications of Agents and Multiagent Technology*, London, April 1996

[8] Camps V., Glize P., Gleizes M-P., Léger A., Athanassiou E., Lakoumentas N. - A Framework for Agent Based Information Brokerage Services in Electronic Commerce – *EMSEC Conference* – 1998

[9] Gleizes Marie-Pierre, Léger Alain, Athanassiou Eleutherios, Glize Pierre. "Abrose : Self-Organization and learning in Multi-Agent based Brokerage Services" *IS&N 99*

[10] Edmonds B. What is Complexity ? *The philosophy of complexity per se with application to some examples in evolution.* 1995.

[11] Forrest S. Emergent computation : Self-organizing, Collective, and cooperative phenomena in *Natural and Artificial Computing networks* - Special issue of Physica D - MIT Press / North-Holland, 1991.

[12] "FIPA'97 and FIPA'98 : Specification Foundation for Intelligent Physical Agents" – http://www.fipa.org , 1997, 1998.

[13] Maes P. - Agents that Reduce Work and Information Overload. Commun. ACM 37(7, July), 31-40. 1994.

[14] Belkin, N.J; Croft, W.B. (1992): Information Filtering and Information Retrieval: Two Sides of the Same Coin?. *Commun. ACM* 35(12, December), 29-38.

[15] Resnick, P.; Iacovou, N., Suchak, M.; Bergstrom, Peter; Riedl, John - GroupLens: An Open Architecture for Collaborative Filtering of Netnews. In: *CSCW '94*. (Eds: Furuta, Richard; Neuwirth, Christine) ACM Press, New York, 175-186. 1994.

[16] Nwana H.S. – Software agents : an Overview – *Knowledge Engineering Review* Vol 11, N°3 – Cambridge University Press. 1996.

[17] Lashkari, Y.; Metral, M.; Maes, P. - Collaborative Interface Agents. In: Proceedings of *AAAI '94* Conference Seattle, WA July 31-Aug 4, 1994. 1-6. 1994.

[18] Link-Pezet J., Gleizes M-P., Glize P., " FORSIC: A Self-Organizing Training System", *IIIS/SAS* Orlando 22-26 July 2000

DEMOIR: A Hybrid Architecture for Expertise Modeling and Recommender Systems

Dawit Yimam
GMD – German National Research Center for Information Technology
Institute for Applied Information Technology
D-53755 Sankt Augustin, Germany
dawit.yimam@gmd.de

Alfred Kobsa
Department of Information and Computer Science
University of California, Irvine
Irvine, CA 92697-3425
kobsa@uci.edu

Abstract

Although employees' expertise has long been regarded as an important asset in organizations at least on a par with capital, goods and documented information, it is only recently that automated systems to enhance the visibility and traceability of employees with particular expertise started to receive research attention. In this paper, we introduce a systematic classification of alternative architectures for a core functionality of expert finding systems, namely expertise modeling. We also analyze the advantages and disadvantages of each approach and present our hybrid solution. We discuss how this solution addresses the requirements of (1) distributed and heterogeneous organizational and personal expertise data sources and, (2) centralized access to extracted expertise information.

Keywords: expert finders, expert recommenders, expertise modeling, expertise management, knowledge management, knowledge sharing, software architecture

1. Introduction

Expert finders (aka expert/expertise recommenders) are systems that help in tracing people with needed expertise. Such systems are gaining increasing importance as organizations continue to look for better ways to exploit their internal knowledge capital and foster collaboration among their employees for increased productivity. Basically, this trend is predicated on three fundamental premises:

(1) the tacit knowledge held by individuals (like knowledge of organization-specific processes) is at least as important as the information an organization explicitly documents in the course of its day-to-day business;

(2) the attempt to explicate all tacit knowledge held by individuals is not optimal (if it can ever be done); and

(3) making visible (and quickly traceable) the people holding this tacit knowledge in the organization motivates its optimal utilization through sharing and collaboration.

Traditionally, sources like expert databases (sometimes called "knowledge directories"), personal web pages, etc. have been used for this purpose. Recently, more automated systems that primarily work through mining implicit sources of expertise information from electronically available documents are also being developed. These systems can either stand alone or, more effectively, work as parts of, or in integration with, systems like knowledge management systems, information retrieval systems, CSCW systems, collaborative filtering systems, and electronic expertise marketplaces. A number of prototypes have been reported so far, and commercial applications that incorporate expert finding capability as one of their main features have recently come out or are under development (eg., *Knowledge Server*™ from Autonomy, Inc.[1]; *KnowledgeMail* from Tacit Knowledge Systems[2], *Organik*® from Orbital Software[3]; and *Raven* from Lotus Development Corp[4]).

However, there still remain a significant number of challenges that must be addressed to come up with more general solutions for finding experts, as we elaborated in [14]. Although our research is primarily focused on finding efficient techniques for expertise modeling, we have developed an architecture that we named DEMOIR[5]

[1] http://www.autonomy.com/
[2] http://www.tacit.com/
[3] http://www.orbitalsw.com/
[4] http://www.lotus.com/home.nsf/welcome/km
[5] DEMOIR stands for "Dynamic Expertise Modeling from Organizational Information Resources".

to serve as a framework for our solutions and algorithms. The design of this architecture is informed by our in-depth analysis of the expert finding problem and the domain analysis of expert finding systems [14]. In this paper we discuss and compare the various architectural alternatives (centralized and distributed) that we identified. In the next section, we will describe these architectures and point out their advantages and disadvantages. Then we discuss our hybrid architecture in the subsequent sections.

2. Existing alternative architectures

From our extensive review and domain analysis [14], we have learned that expert finding systems generally comprise the following seven features (or "facets"):

(1) *Expertise evidence source recognition* - which can be straightforwardly based on explicit sources (e.g. assertion by experts themselves or their proxies) or involve mechanisms to recognize implicit sources (e.g., document authorship and occurrence of name in documents).
(2) *Expertise indicator extraction* – mechanisms to extract expertise data from implicit sources.
(3) *Expertise models* – representations of extracted and aggregated expertise descriptors.
(4) *Query mechanisms* – explicit or implicit mechanisms to passively acquire or automatically trace information need or "expertise need" of users.
(5) *Matching operations* – mechanisms to match information and/or expertise need with expertise models.
(6) *Output presentation* – modes and contents of expertise information presentation.
(7) *Adaptation and learning operations* – mechanisms to refine expertise models based on user feedback as well as means to tailor expertise information to users' particular requirements.

There are multiple implementation options for each of the above features and a variety of ways of organizing them. In this paper we focus on what is accomplished by the first three features, to which together we refer as *expertise modeling*. The reader is directed to [14] for a complete discussion of the other features (which focus on mechanisms for exploitation of the expertise models). However, we would like to define what we mean by expertise model here. By *expertise model* we refer to representations of an individual's expertise repertoire that are automatically inferred. We distinguish expertise models from *expert models/profiles* by which we refer to the broad representations of an individual's personal details as well as various relations (social, organizational, etc.) that he or she might have with other individuals.

We distinguish four alternative architectural approaches to expertise modeling, which can be systematically placed in a two-dimensional grid (contingency table) as shown in table 1.

Table 1. Expertise modeling time/location contingency table

	Distributed	Centralized
Query-time generated	Dynamic generation by client (at *users'* sites)	Dynamic generation by server
Pre-generated	Personal agents based (at *experts'* sites)	Aggregated expertise model based

The two types of expertise modeling are arrayed along the rows, and the locations where the modeling is done are arrayed along the columns. In the following, we will briefly discuss each of these alternatives individually, pointing out the advantages and disadvantages of each.

2.1 Query-time expertise modeling

In this approach, expertise models are not maintained by the system but are rather dynamically generated at query time. This is done by building the expert finder on top of an information retrieval (IR) engine which would provide access to the organizational sources (databases, Intranets, etc.). The expertise modeling is then done dynamically on the sources returned by the IR engine (e.g. [11]). As shown in the contingency table, one can design the expert modeling to either be co-located with the IR engine on the server or, alternatively, to be done by a client at the user's computer (e.g. as a Java applet). Both options have the following advantages and disadvantages.

Advantages:

- Avoiding the storage and maintenance of large amounts of expertise information that is possibly only infrequently needed.
- Using the most recent information available to locate experts.

Disadvantages:

- High latency in query processing since all the expertise modeling operations are carried out once a user queried the system.
- Limited exploitation of information due to lack of persistent expertise models. This, for example, renders manipulations like the analysis, visualization, browsing and comparison of expertise data computationally expensive, if not impossible.

- Personal sources and non-document sources (e.g. recommendations from people, social relations, etc.) are hard to include.
- Full reliance on the availability of some search engine.

2.2 Distributed personal agents

If we adopt Chandy and Rifkin's [1] dichotomy of distributed systems as being *structured* or *anarchic*, personal agent-based expert finders can be viewed as distributed systems of the latter kind. Here, the whole system is a multi-agent system composed of self-managing, asynchronously operating "personal agents" residing in each expert's computer. These agents, which are endowed with capabilities to find and interact with each other, are the *loci* of all processing and control. Each agent carries out the dual tasks of modeling expertise (from authored documents and other personal sources) as well as assisting its owner in searching other experts. The fact that the principal entities in the expert-finding problem are experts (which themselves can be viewed as distributed knowledge sources) has made the agent-based approach a preferred solution by most works [6][13][10]. This approach has the following advantages and disadvantages.

Advantages:
- Locality and easier preservation of subjective privacy. Everyone's expertise model is locally determined and stored; the overall expertise analysis process is therefore highly decentralized.
- No single point of failure. The low degree of coupling among the agents allows graceful degradation in case of the unavailability of an agent. This decentralization also avoids the need for global system control.
- It allows the exploitation of personal information resources (e.g. emails, work-in-progress, etc.) which would not be made available to a centralized expertise modeling server due to privacy concerns.
- The expert may subjectively have the feeling of being more in control than in the case of the centralized approaches (although any access restrictions that may be imposed on an agent-based model can also be realized for centralized expertise models).

Disadvantages:
- In a strict realization, this approach has the limitation of relying solely on personal information sources of the individual, which excludes other organizational sources.
- The underlying assumption of this approach, namely that expert finders are meant only for supporting networking/sharing among experts, limits the accessibility and usability of the expertise information. Moreover, the fact that the expertise information is distributed results in its sub-optimal exploitation due to the difficulty of working on it in the aggregate. For example, it renders working on expertise data of multiple experts (like in analysis or visualization) inefficient as this would involve pulling expertise models from each agent.
- Coordination overhead may occur. In particular, getting agents to find and interact with one another presents enormous challenges. This situation is aggravated by the fact that agents might appear, disappear, or move at any time.
- In a knowledge-based implementation, this approach requires each agent to maintain its own copy of the central domain model (like in [13]) as well as a matching engine in addition to the expertise models.
- This approach also entails scalability problems as the number of experts grows larger since each query is forwarded to each expert's distributed personal agent – resulting in low query performance. (Foner [3][4] suggests clustering agents to alleviate this problem by limiting each search to a few potential clusters of agents only – an approach that is restrictive and hard to carry out in many cases).

2.3 Aggregated expertise modeling

In this approach, expertise models of individuals are either dynamically aggregated to create a central store of expertise models, or linked to a pre-constructed central expertise model which can be a kind of knowledge structure (ontology), organizational structure, etc. (rudimentary versions of this approach are reported in [9][7]). While this approach fails to provide the locality, easier security, graceful degradation and related advantages of the personal-agent based approach, it however has the following compelling advantages:
- It makes the expertise models widely accessible and easily amenable for efficient multi-purpose exploitation and analysis. For instance, aggregated expertise models make it easy to present each expert as an element within a broad and structured expertise framework which, in turn, can be used for efficient identification and selection of experts through browsing. It also permits interactive refining of queries through browsing, since the expertise models form a closed data set that can be visualized.
- It opens the opportunity to monitor a wide range of expertise data feeds (repositories, databases, Web/Internet resources, etc.)

- It offers better performance due to a single location of information.
- It facilitates using both knowledge-based and statistical expertise modeling. For instance, it allows for the analysis and grouping of experts based on their expertise models, and it facilitates inferences on the basis of relationships among experts and their expertise.

3. Hybrid architecture in DEMOIR

3.1 Requirements

DEMOIR is a framework to develop and test expertise modeling algorithms. Based on the above analysis, we have outlined the following sets of requirements that need to be met by DEMOIR.

1) Distributed monitoring of expertise data sources

We have two broad categories of expertise data sources in organizations: (1) organizational information resources, and (2) experts and their personal resources. Both are essentially *distributed* and *heterogeneous*. Hence, monitoring them requires handling these properties. Here we focus on the distributedness of the sources and we will come back to the heterogeneity aspect later.

So as to be able to exploit both of the above sources, we suggest the use of configurable gatherers for organizational sources while providing expert controllable gatherers (in the form of lightweight agents) for personal sources. Note that the first part of the expertise modeling process is identifying and selecting those sources that can provide expertise evidence from the large mass of sources available. And designing the gatherers in the above fashion decentralizes this particular operation.

The provision of expert controllable gatherers would allow experts to control how their personal sources are mined and let them approve (or specify) what is extracted from their resources. This addresses the privacy issues that arise in monitoring personal resources belonging to experts. Expert finders must find a way to achieve their goal, namely enhancing visibility and collaboration, without compromising the privacy and security of experts' information resources. This is particularly important since many valuable sources of expertise indicators (like emails) are commonly private. As it turns out, privacy and security considerations rank high as factors necessitating a decentralized approach to monitoring private sources, unlike the case of conventional distributed systems where reliability and performance requirements are the prime concerns. In addition to controlling which private sources are used for expertise modeling, experts may also require the expertise data extraction from some of their resources to be done on their own machines. Hence, the architecture should be flexible enough to meet such requirements, too.

2) Centralized expertise information server

This relates to providing a centralized server that aggregates, stores and retrieves the extracted expertise information. In a sense, we can see this as motivated by the need to extend the purpose of expert finders beyond the one advocated in the distributed agents-based approach (i.e. supporting networking among experts) by also incorporating the concept of users (people, organizational functions, etc.). Having the expertise information on a centralized server would make the expertise information readily accessible and useable by these entities. To allow this, the server should provide a generic low-level application programming interface (API). Moreover, this server should provide a "second line of defense" to protect privacy and security of expertise information (i.e. in addition to enabling experts to control how expertise data is extracted from their personal sources) by providing a mechanism to assign access privileges to others. For example, it should allow organizational role-based access control [12].

3) Potentially distributed clients

The approach should delegate application specific exploitation of the expertise information (e.g. searching, browsing, analysis and visualization) to clients. Hence, the system should allow a broad range of possibly distributed clients to interact with the centralized expertise information server. It should also allow integration of expert finding capabilities with other services in the organization (e.g. knowledge management, information retrieval, groupware, recommender systems, collaborative information filtering systems, expertise markets, etc.).

None of the alternative approaches discussed in the previous section can address these three requirements alone. Rather, these requirements suggest a hybrid architecture composed of centralized and decentralized processes. DEMOIR is organized in such a manner to satisfy the above three requirements. Specifically, it is a hybrid of two of the above four alternatives, namely distributed and centralized expertise modeling. It offers a centralized expertise modeling server while also permitting decentralized expertise indicator source gathering, expertise indicator extraction, and distributed clients.

Apart from the above architectural requirements, DEMOIR is also motivated by a fundamental approach to expertise modeling where the heterogeneity of sources is not just a situation to be normalized (homogenized), but rather a source of valuable meta-information that must be exploited. For instance, we want to explicitly capture how the sources relate to experts and where the expertise evidence stems from, and factor this information into the expertise modeling process. For instance, knowing the relation of sources to experts can allow us to weigh the importance of data extracted from each source based on how it relates to the expert. As an example, the occurrence of a phrase in an expert's resume implies a stronger relation to her expertise than its occurrence in one of her articles.

Based on this observation, we can introduce the concept of *source type* to denote the type of relation a given source (e.g. document, database, individual, etc.) has with an expert (or groups of experts). The *format* of a source refers to its syntactic form (e.g. web page, relational database record, etc.). Note that sources of different formats may fall under the same source type and vice versa. Once we identified source types, we can further suggest carrying out differentiated extraction of expertise evidence from each source type. Notice that this approach allows the inclusion of people as distinct source types. This would be valuable in cases that require human input to augment expertise that had been determined by mining documentary sources.

This emphasis on dealing with heterogeneity of expertise indicator sources implies a need to support diverse expertise modeling algorithms. This, in turn, motivates a design goal of developing a flexible modular software architecture. DEMOIR aims to achieve this goal and satisfy the above requirements by partitioning the system into composable modules and defining appropriate interfaces for each module.

3.2 DEMOIR components

We designed the DEMOIR architecture, shown in Figure 1, as a flexible architecture composed of modules for source gathering, expertise modeling and expertise model exploitation. The DEMOIR modules can be implemented separately and readily combined to suit an application environment. These modules, while conceived to meet the aforementioned requirements, also draw from the features we isolated in the domain analysis and listed in section 2. What is more, they are aimed at allowing multiple instantiations of these features and an easy extension of their functionality. Defining appropriate interfaces, these modules can also be distributed across computers if necessary. Below, we briefly describe the components of DEMOIR, grouping them into three general functions.

Expertise indicator source gathering. The gatherers are essentially robots and personal agents which have expertise data source recognition logic built into them. They are envisaged to be independent, adaptable to local needs and constraints of the expertise indicator sources and are not controlled by any central system. At the same time, these agents should have the common goal of acting as "informers" to the centralized server wherein the expertise data is aggregated and made available for easy exploitation and analysis by users and client systems.

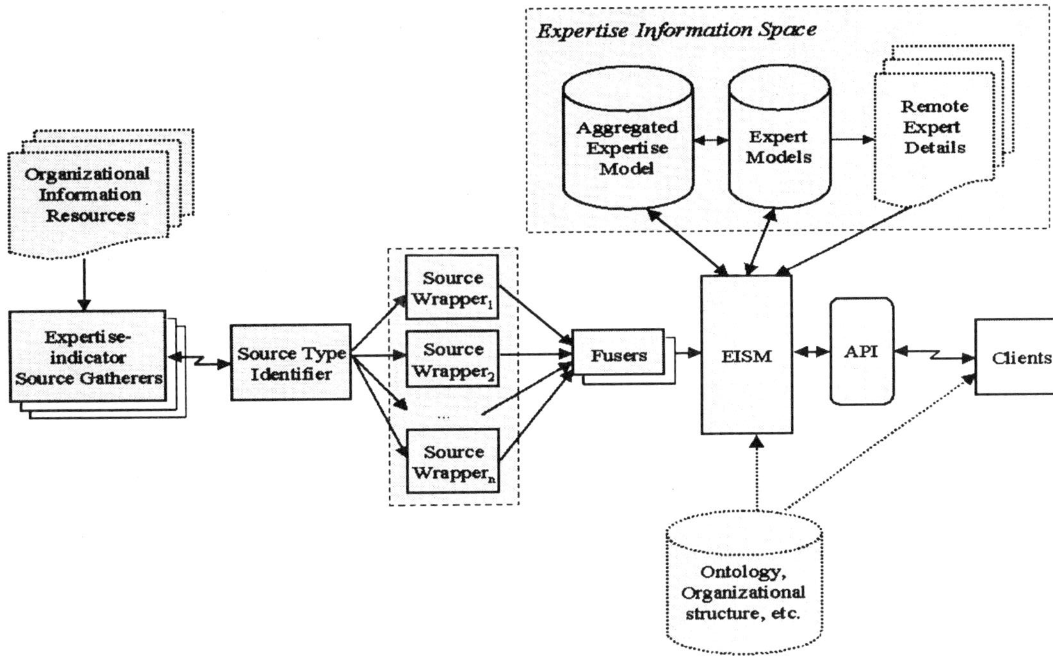

Figure 1. The DEMOIR architecture

Expertise modeling. For this, DEMOIR provides four components that are aimed at meeting our desire to factor provenance, expertise indicator source types, etc. into the expertise modeling. As shown in Figure 1, these components are:

- a *source type identifier* (which determines with which experts each gathered source relates to, and in what way),
- *source wrappers* (source type specific extractors of expertise indicators),
- *fusers* (that aggregate expertise indicators from the wrappers for storage as expertise models),
- and the *expertise information space manager* (EISM) which handles the storage and retrieval of the expertise information.

The source type identifier, wrappers, and fusers are configurable/pluggable and extensible. Hence, one can add new source wrappers and new rules for source type identification or fusing.

Expertise model exploitation. The DEMOIR server is designed as a collaborative system without anticipating particular types of clients. This means that the exploitation manner of expertise information is not limited. This is achieved by *APIs* that can be used to access the expertise information. Any kind of *client* which can be located anywhere in the organization can use the API to provide customized usage of the expertise information. Besides, applications which have appropriate interfaces to interoperate with other applications can make use of the server.

Furthermore, DEMOIR permits flexible partitioning of its modules as server and client operations. Currently we are adopting an approach where the expertise modeling is implemented as a server operation while the expertise indicator source gathering and expertise model exploitation can be distributed. These two client processes differ in their interaction with the server. While the expertise indicator source gatherers need to register with the server, the user clients don't need to do so.

But in cases where privacy issues prohibit the gathered sources from being brought to the expertise modeling server, some portions of the modeling modules (for example wrappers) can also be included in distributed gatherers. Furthermore, one can also envisage a deployment where the document type identifier, wrappers, fusers and the EISM are distributed across computers on a network interacting through a middleware like CORBA's ORB.

4. Current implementation status

As we indicated earlier, our implementation is at the moment mainly focused on the expertise modeling modules of DEMOIR. Specifically, we are implementing and experimenting with source wrappers, fusers and the EISM.

As shown in the DEMOIR architecture, classifying expertise sources based on how they relate to experts permits one to apply tailored extraction of expertise data using the wrappers. But, this is not all there is to it. The goal is to infer the expertise models by combining the inferred relation of experts to sources (i.e. source type) with expertise descriptors contained in, or implied by the sources. One strategy to achieve this goal is to employ matrices as representations of the above relations and develop an algorithm to drive the expertise models through a series of matrix merging. Hence we call this algorithm *matrix fusion*. Crudely put, this algorithm involves the following five steps:

1. Using expertise indicator source gatherers which are presently implemented as web robots, sources (documents) that are deemed to contain expertise data are gathered and a source-to-expert matrix that maps these sources to associated experts is generated. This matrix contains source type codes as its elements (note that a single source may be mapped to multiple experts).
2. For the time being, the gathered documents are then classified into three source types, namely documents produced by experts, document profiling experts and documents mentioning experts (this step is presently done manually).
3. Then, each source is passed to the respective wrapper that employs a set of heuristic algorithms to analyze its content and structure to select/identify key expertise descriptors and note their statistical features. The wrappers output these data as descriptor-to-source matrices.
4. The matrices generated by the wrappers are then fed into a fuser that merges them applying appropriate weighting which takes their source type into account. This is done by parameterizing the term weights by heuristically determined coefficients that quantify the relative importance of the source types.
5. Finally, the descriptor-to-source matrix produced by the fusers is merged with the source-to-expert matrix that was generated by step 1. This merging generates a direct mapping of expertise descriptors to experts. This mapping, which we call the *expertise model*, is also stored as a matrix (a descriptor-to-expert matrix).

How does this algorithm map onto the expertise modeling components of DEMOIR? The source type identifier is implemented to contain an *Expert-to-Source matrix generator* (that presently relies on manually tagged source types) and a *wrapper launcher* that traverses the expert-to-source matrix and passes the source to the respective wrappers. Two types of fusers are used to generate the expertise models from the wrappers' outputs. *A Descriptor-to-Source Matrix Fuser* (DSM Fuser) merges the descriptor-to-source matrices generated by the wrappers, while a *Descriptor-to-Expert Matrix Fuser* (DEM Fuser) performs step 5 of the algorithm described above. Presently, the expertise information space manager (EISM) performs basic matrix storage and access functions, and stores and retrieves the expert models (stored as LDAP directories as discussed below) as well as the archives of sources. The API merely provides access to EISM's functionality. Note that the matrix representation of the expertise model only contains plain terms as descriptors of expertise and hence the conceptual relation among these terms needs to be established later (e.g. by a mapping to an ontology, by a client that does dynamic clustering, etc.)

The implementation also aims to fulfill DEMOIR's goal of flexibility and configurability. To this end, we are currently making use of design patterns [5], specifically factory and prototype patterns, to develop the wrappers as pluggable components that are registered to, and invoked by, a central control. This has enabled us to configure these components to be loaded at runtime. It also has made it possible to control the behavior of wrappers through configurations and to add new wrappers with minimum change needed. The source type identifier components and the fusers, too, are based on configuration files enabling extensibility and reconfiguration (for example, using different parameterization strategies during fusing). In general, our preliminary results in this regard are encouraging.

The *Expert models* that presently contain limited details of individual experts (like name, URL, etc.) are stored as LDAP directories and linked to the expertise model. This approach, in addition to benefiting from the features of LDAP directories, is expected to facilitate the integration of expertise models to directories already available in organizations as well as other related systems like user modeling servers [2]. These directories can also be distributed. The expertise models, too, can be placed on a separate host than the one storing the LDAP directory.

5. Future work

Once we completed our implementation and evaluation of the above components, the next step will be to automate the source type identification part. A candidate approach to performing this is to apply categorization techniques that are based on supervised learning. This will also include the consideration of more fine-grained source type as well as source format classifications that reflect the wide variety of sources commonly encountered in real world organizations (eg. human resource databases which can indicate experts' formal educational backgrounds, professional careers, current job description, etc.; skill databases profiling people's competency areas; employee performance evaluations; e-mails/discussion groups; queries for IR systems/document repositories; expertise recommendation by people; etc.).

Once the expertise models are properly generated, a range of interesting possibilities of exploitation arise. For instance, we plan to develop a client that integrates an ontology definition framework [8] being developed in our research department to dynamically categorize experts. We also plan to investigate the application of clustering techniques to visualize both expert clusters as well as clusters of expertise descriptors. We also intend to incorporate mechanisms to refine the expertise models based on social feedback/ranking.

Extending the current expert models/profiles to incorporate more sophisticated representations of additional attributes of individual experts is also necessary. For example, we should be able to represent attributes like social, organizational, co-authorship, citation, and other relations among experts, which would be valuable augmentations of the expertise models.

6. Summary

In this paper we identified and analyzed four approaches to expertise modeling. With particular reference to three of these alternatives, we have shown that each has its advantages and disadvantages. Consequently, we have proposed an architecture called DEMOIR that tries to combine the advantages of two of the identified alternatives. DEMOIR combines centralized and decentralized processes to create a hybrid approach to expertise modeling. In addition to this architectural requirement, DEMOIR is also motivated by the goal to perform expertise modeling that takes into account the differing importance of various sources as suppliers of expertise evidence.

We also described the approach we adopted to implement DEMOIR using a matrix-based representation of the relations between experts and documents, and the fusion of these matrices to generate the expertise models.

References

[1] K. M. Chandy and A. Rifkin, "Systematic Composition of Distributed Objects: Processes and Sessions", *The Computer Journal*, 40(8), 1997, pp. 465 – 478.

[2] Fink, J., *User Modeling Servers – Requirements, Design, and Implementation,* Ph.D. Thesis, Dept. of Mathematics and Computer Science, University of Essen, Germany, forthcoming.

[3] L. Foner, "A Multi-Agent Referral System for Matchmaking". in *The First International Conference on the Practical Applications of Intelligent Agents and Multi-Agent Technology (PAAM96)*, London, UK, 1996.

[4] L. N. Foner, *Political Artifacts and Personal Privacy: The Yenta Multi-Agent Distributed Matchmaking Systems,* Ph.D. Thesis, Massachusetts Institute of Technology, 1999 (http://foner.www.media.mit.edu/people/foner/PhD-Thesis/Dissertation/)

[5] Gamma, E., R. Helm, R. Johnson and J. Vlissides, *Design Patterns: Elements of Reusable Object-oriented Software*, Addison-Wesley, Reading, MA, 1995.

[6] H. Kautz, B. Selman and A. Milewski, "Agent Amplified Communication", in *The Proceedings of the Thirteenth National Conference on Artificial Intelligence (AAAI-96)*, Portland, OR, 1996.

[7] H. Kautz and B. Selman, "Creating Models of Real-World Communities with ReferralWeb", In *Working Notes of the Workshop on Recommender Systems, held in conjunction with AAAI-98*, Madison, WI, 1998.

[8] R. Klemke and A. Nick. "*brokersLounge: An Ontology – based Knowledge Management Environment*" (in preparation).

[9] B. Krulwich and C. Burkey, "The ContactFinder Agent: Answering Bulletin Board Questions with Referrals". In *Proceedings of the 1996 National Conference on Artificial Intelligence (AAAI-96)*, vol. 1, 1996, pp. 10 – 15.

[10] H. Libermann, A. Vivacqua, "Agents to Assist in Finding Help", *Proceedings of the CHI 2000*, The Hague, The Netherlands.

[11] D. Mattox, M. Maybury and D. Morey, "Enterprise Expert and Knowledge Discovery", In *Proceedings of 8th International Conference on Human-Computer Interaction (HCI International'99)*, 1999, pp. 303-307.

[12] Schreck, J., *Security and Privacy in User Models*, Ph.D. Thesis, Dept. of Mathematics and Computer Science, University of Essen, Germany, forthcoming.

[13] A. S. Vivacqua, "Agents for Expertise Location", in *The Proceedings of the AAAI Spring Symposium on Intelligent Agents in Cyberspace*, Stanford, CA, March 1999.

[14] D. Yimam and A. Kobsa, "Expert Finding Systems for Organizations: Problem and Domain Analysis and the DEMOIR Approach", In M. Ackerman, A. Cohen, V. Pipek and V. Wulf, eds.: Beyond Knowledge Management: Sharing Expertise, forthcoming.

Position Paper on Integrated Broadband Environment for Personalized TV Experience (IBEX)

Yoshihisa Gonno Fumihiko Nishio Tomohiro Tsunoda Yasuaki Yamagishi
Information Broadcasting Laboratories, Inc. Sony Corporation
email: {ygonno, nishio, yasu}@ibl.co.jp, tsunoda@arch.sony.co.jp

1. Introduction

Digital broadcasting systems have been coming into wide use all over the world. Efficient use of bandwidth allows us to transport hundreds of TV programs through a single broadcasting satellite to millions of user terminals simultaneously. On the other hand, millions of multimedia contents, including TV-like streaming live programs, are just going to be distributed over the Web. In order to make the most use of the digital information infrastructure, various forms of information must be well-structured in common ways between TV and the Web environment from every point of view such as authoring, delivery, browsing, searching and retrieval. Well-structured information will make it possible for us to be well navigated in floods of services between TV and the Web seamlessly. In these senses, we have reported basic ideas on a future framework for integration of TV and the Web[1][2][3][4].

As a next step towards the integration of TV and the Web environment, we started a new project on integrated broadband environment for personalized TV experience (IBEX). This is a position paper on IBEX describing an architectural overview of future multimedia environment. The IBEX project also intends to provide a service model for the TV-Anytime[5] framework. The concept of the IBEX features three major viewpoints towards the future TV experience. To release audience from time constraint scheduled by broadcasters is the first target. Then to get seamless and adaptive access between TV and the Web environment from anywhere in the world is also important. In addition, such TV experience is to be securely personalized for individual audience. In order to achieve open framework, these viewpoints must be properly developed in conjunction with well-organized data models and system architecture based on de facto standard technology. The IBEX will provide a prototype system model built on upcoming integrated broadband digital TV infrastructure.

2. General Requirements

In order to provide integrated broadband environment for personalized TV experience among heterogeneous digital infrastructures, such as digital broadcasting networks and the Internet, we raise following general requirements for the system framework.

2.1. Integrated Broadband Network

While growing bandwidth of the Internet rapidly, digital TV infrastructure is still taking advantage to deliver TV-like live programs efficiently because of the optimized transport protocols and codecs. Since both network resources are not inexhaustible, each network resource must be dynamically allocated under the heterogeneous and distributed environment. The seamless and distributed resource management is the most important issue. For efficient delivery of contents and metadata, Web-originated resources and TV-originated resources must be well organized and resource allocation processes must be decentralized. This also means content and metadata should be handled in the same manner between TV and the Web environment.

2.2. Universal Contents Identification

Contents must be uniquely identified, properly located and associated with metadata on the integrated network. The uniform resource locator (URL) scheme with the domain name service (DNS) is widely used on the Web environment and seems to work well so far to identify and locate Web objects. However, it cannot maintain the link consistency against unexpected removal or replacement of objects because the URL scheme itself does not provide global registration mechanism for individual objects. For the proper use of distributed resources over the integrated heterogeneous network, global resource registration and address resolution mechanisms must be installed. This will also provide a proper referencing mechanism to maintain links between names and instances.

2.3. Universal Metadata Description

Metadata must provide structured information not only about contents but also about context how contents are used. The structure of metadata, which is defined by a schema, must be shared between service applications. Well-structured metadata will provide proper APIs to access application specific metadata. This will help search engines and content browsers to find proper contents and to adapt contents to service environment. Each piece of metadata description will be associated with other resources, e.g. multimedia contents, network devices,

0-7695-0798-9/00 $10.00 © 2000 IEEE

individual users, by referencing proper identifiers of the resources. Designing schemas in common way will allow us to develop common APIs for every application and then to reduce the cost of developing new metadata applications.

3. IBEX System Components

From the service-oriented point of view, we raise three general service components for IBEX system in order to simplify and clarify the operation of multimedia delivery services. Each component is connected with each other through the integrated broadband networks as illustrated in Fig.1. Basic functions of each service component are described briefly.

3.1. Contents Provider

Content creation and registration: All contents will be provided by contents providers. Once a piece of contents is created, it must be registered acquiring a contents reference identification (CRID).

Metadata creation and registration: Metadata may be created conformable to certain metadata schemas and registered associating with the CRID of the contents.

Resource reservation: Since a CRID represents only a reference to contents, certain delivery resources, such as broadcasting bandwidth or web archive, must be allocated in order to provide contents instances for the audience through the integrated network.

3.2. Resource Administrator

Content registration: While contents will be registered as a reference that can be identified by a CRID, instantiated contents that can be accessed will be registered as locators with certain media types.

Metadata registration: Metadata with a metadata schema will be registered. While each metadata will be associated with a CRID, each metadata schema will be identified by a namespace URI. All available metadata will be provided for contents providers and content browsers.

Delivery resource management: Comprehensive access interfaces will be provided for heterogeneous resource reservation in order to provide seamless access for distributed contents providers and contents browsers. All resources will be operated based on the reservation.

User profile management: User profiles of subscribers will be registered, and audience ratings and other statistics will be logged for statistical use.

3.3. Contents Browser

Metadata acquisition and content adaptation: Metadata will be replicated from resource administrators. Referring contents metadata to user profiles and resource capabilities, the list of contents will be personalized for each user and adapted for the access environment.

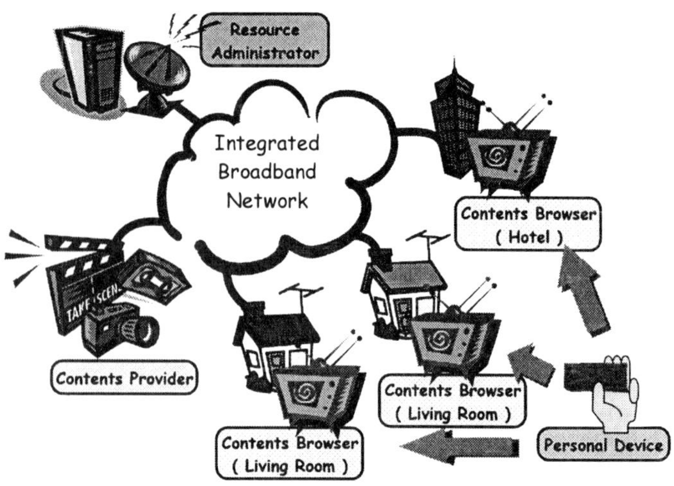

Fig. 1: IBEX System Overview

Content acquisition and local resource management: Local resources such as storage devices will be utilized for contents acquisition along with user profiles.

3.4. Personal Device

User authentication: This is an additional component, which secures user profiles with biometric authentication such as fingerprint identification, and activates customized personal environment on content browsers anywhere. This device will enhance the portability of user profiles.

4. Current Status and Future Plan

The IBEX project has just been started, however, we already made a conceptual demo representing an IBEX service model for the TV-Anytime Forum (TVAF) at NAB2000, April 2000. We will make technical proposals for the TVAF based on the IBEX system architecture, especially focusing on name resolution and metadata replication. Moreover, we will improve the demo system implementing such fundamental mechanisms.

5. References

[1] Y. Gonno, "A View to the Broadcasting and the Internet". W3C Workshop "TV and the Web" Position Paper, June 1998, <http://www.w3.org/Architecture/1998/06/Workshop/paper03/>.
[2] Y. Gonno, et al., "Metadata Structuring of Audiovisual Data Streams on MPEG-2 Systems". Metastructures1998, August 1998.
[3] F. Nishio, et al., "Transporting RDF Metadata Associated with Structured Contents". Metastructures1998, August 1998.
[4] Y. Gonno, et al., "Data Models for Distributed Multimedia Contents Associated with Structured Metadata". ICCC99, September 1999.
[5] TV-Anytime Forum, <http://www.tv-anytime.org/>.

Workshop

Evaluating Collaborative Enterprises

Co-Chairs

Robert Allen, University of Maryland, USA

Michelle Steves, National Institute of Standards and Technology (NIST), USA

Workshop on Evaluating Collaborative Enterprises - Workshop Report

Amy J. Knutilla, Michelle P. Steves and Robert H. Allen
Knutilla Technologies, National Institute of Standards and Technology, and University of Maryland, College Park
{knutilla, msteves, rhallen} @nist.gov

Abstract

The workshop, Evaluating Collaborative Enterprises,[1] explored the issues surrounding the evaluation of collaborative systems including methods and tools for evaluating collaborative software as well as application-specific evaluation experiences. This paper describes the workshop's mission, summarizes the workshop papers and discussions, and concludes with future research needs.

Keywords: CSCW, groupware evaluation, collaborative enterprise evaluation

Acknowledgments

The following people participated in this workshop and contributed to the contents of this report: Janet Allen, Evan Atkinson, Prasun Dewan, Carl Gutwin, David Hallenbeck, Steven MacGregor, Emile Morse, David Pinelle, Catherine Plaisant, Jean Scholtz, monica schraefel, Jonathan Sevy, Eswaran Subrahmanian and Angran Xiao.

In addition to the editors, the following people participated on the program committee. We gratefully acknowledge their time and energies: Jill Drury, The MITRE Corporation; Tom Finholt, University of Michigan; Saul Greenberg, University of Calgary; Carl Gutwin, University of Saskatchewan; Doug Johnson, Hewlett Packard; Srinivas Nidamarthi, Cambridge University; Leysia Palen, University of Colorado; Jennifer Preece, University of Maryland, Baltimore County; Jean Scholtz, U.S. Defense Advanced Research Projects Agency; Eswaran Subrahmanian, Carnegie Mellon University; Marian Williams, University of Massachusetts Lowell.

Introduction

Effective collaboration involves people sharing information. Web technology has enabled basic communication infrastructures needed for collaborative applications to facilitate people working together over the Web. However, using the basic infrastructures has proven much more difficult in enabling effective collaboration within and among enterprises than the hype would suggest. Although higher technological layers are being developed and a general, deeper understanding of collaboration is slowly evolving, progress on efficient and effective Web-based collaboration lags behind these other gains. Researchers need tools to measure the incremental progress towards developing useful collaborative systems, as well as methods to evaluate the impact of specific technologies on the effectiveness of collaboration. We believe effective evaluation and appropriate standardization are mechanisms that will facilitate progress in Web-based[2] collaboration.

This workshop continues themes emanating from previous WETICE workshops held over the last several years. In general, these workshops addressed a number of issues, including:

- How can Web techniques be used to achieve or to improve collaboration within or among organizations?
- Can the Web serve as an infrastructure for both developing and implementing business applications in globally distributed, collaborative business environments?
- Can Web-based software answer the challenges that globally operating companies are facing?

This session continues in the vein set forth in previous workshops and extends it by exploring issues surrounding the evaluation of collaborative systems: When and how do we achieve collaboration successfully? When do we not? Why? With the increasing connectivity of the Internet and the increasingly distributed nature of organizations, groupware[3] is an increasingly attractive method for

1. For the purpose of this workshop, collaborative enterprises are systems of people and software technology involving group work, where more than one person is moving toward a common goal.

2. The term Web-based should not be interpreted as referring only to World Wide Web technology, i.e., technology requiring Web browsers for use. This workshop addressed the evaluation of distributed technologies for collaboration.

collaboration. Effective evaluation of collaborative systems holds one key to improving groupware effectiveness. This workshop explored methods and tools for evaluating collaborative systems as well as application-specific evaluation experiences.

The primary goal of this workshop was to facilitate the progress of distributed collaboration through improved development and use of methods for the evaluation of collaborative enterprises. The workshop also highlighted the value of bringing together people who are addressing the unique and challenging needs of collaborative enterprise evaluation. Plans for further information exchange among researchers, software developers and users of collaborative enterprises to improve the development and use of methods for the evaluation of collaborative enterprises were made.

In this report, we present a summary of the nine papers presented, which fell roughly into two categories: Collaborative System Evaluation Methods and Tools and Application-Specific Evaluation Experiences. These papers discussed evaluation methods and approaches (established and visionary), tools for evaluation (existing and prototype) and research needs. This report summarizes the papers and discussions and concludes with future research needs.

Summary of Papers

This section briefly summarizes the presentations of papers and highlights some of the comments and issues generated by workshop participants as a result of the individual presentations.

Collaboration System Evaluation Methods and Tools

A Review of Groupware Evaluations, by David Pinelle and Carl Gutwin, provides a review of all papers from the Association of Computing Machinery (ACM) Computer-Supported Cooperative Work (CSCW) conferences (1992-1998) that introduced or evaluated a groupware system. The main findings from the review are that almost one-third of the groupware systems were not evaluated in any formal way, that only about one-quarter of the evaluations involved a practical setting and that a wide variety of evaluation techniques are in use. The main conclusions from the review are that more attention must be paid to evaluating groupware systems, and that there is room for additional evaluation techniques that are simple and low in cost. This paper provides a good classification framework for collaborative evaluations that was found useful for further workshop discussions:

- Type of evaluation
- Placement of the evaluation in the software development cycle
- Evaluation techniques
- Focus of evaluation

The Mechanics of Collaboration: Developing Low Cost Usability in Shared Workspaces, by Carl Gutwin and Saul Greenberg, introduces a conceptual framework that addresses the mechanics of collaboration for shared-workspace groupware: the low level actions and interactions that must be carried out to complete a task in a shared manner. These include communication, coordination, planning, monitoring, assistance and protection. The framework also includes three general measures of these mechanics: effectiveness, efficiency and satisfaction. The underlying idea of the framework is that some usability problems in groupware systems are not inherently tied to the social context in which the system is used, but rather are a result of poor support for the basic activities of collaborative work in shared spaces. Gutwin believes that existing, low-cost, evaluation methods–heuristic evaluation, walkthroughs, user observations and questionnaires–can be modified to include this framework in a way that helps a groupware evaluator uncover these usability problems.

During post-presentation discussions for this paper, another group behavior was proposed: people in group situations quickly switch between activities, going back and forth quickly. Several general challenges in groupware evaluation were also discussed. For example, it is difficult to ascertain satisfaction levels for specific behaviors, it is difficult to identify precise measures and it can be difficult differentiating cause and effect. However, it was proposed that if all the correct questions were asked, many deficiencies would be uncovered.

Techniques for Evaluating Collaboration Toolkits, by Prasun Dewan, states that the most reliable approach to evaluating collaboration toolkits is to carry out field studies. This approach has the problem that it requires each toolkit project to create a complete, working system. More importantly, this approach does not allow a project to converge incrementally towards a complete solution. The paper identifies several other techniques for evaluating collaboration toolkits, including inspecting the design to see if requirements have been met, simulating other systems, implementing complete solutions to standard problems and performing self and lab studies. This paper discusses these techniques, points out their pros and cons, identifies the influential projects in which they have been used, and shows how they fit together. The presentation described a list of needs in collaboration toolkit evaluation, including the need to understand the value and cost of different evaluation approaches. It was pointed out that

3. Groupware is defined here as software and technology that enhances collaboration.

there are two aspects to toolkit evaluation: first, how to tell if the toolkit under evaluation can support a certain range of collaborative applications and secondly, how well these applications support collaborative tasks. The paper addressed the first aspect, leaving the second aspect for the workshop. The workshop participants also discussed the need for benchmark scenarios, applications and requirements to help developers and evaluators.

In *CollabLogger: A Tool for Visualizing Groups at Work* by Emile Morse and Micky Steves, a visual tool has been developed to support usability analyses of human-computer interaction of log data from a groupware system. The groupware was instrumented to log users' interactions with the system and each other. The CollabLogger addresses the problem of helping investigators analyze the volumes of log data that groupware tools can generate. Visual tools are powerful when large amounts of diverse data need to be explored.

The workshop participants discussed and concluded that there is real value in determining appropriate sets of events that groupware systems should log so that tools such as the CollabLogger can be employed to help evaluate groupware. Sets of events would be linked to characteristics of the groupware systems so that groupware system developers could easily determine which events to log. Further, a mapping of these events to the mechanics of collaboration identified by Gutwin and Greenberg in the previous paper was determined to be of value.

The paper, *An Evaluation and Comparison of the Industrial and Educational Usage of CSCW Within the Design Process,* by A. I. Thomson, S. P. MacGregor and W.J. Ion, describes the findings of three recently completed research projects conducted at the University of Strathclyde, Scotland. Each of the projects involved the implementation and usage of CSCW technology within the design process. Two of the projects described were education-based while the other was conducted in collaboration with industry and based on live industrial projects. The paper describes the methods adopted to evaluate the impact of the technology together with the findings of each of the projects in the form of implementation guidelines to promote effective and efficient technology adoption. Opportunities for cross-sector lessons were also presented.

In *Towards an Evaluation Methodology for the Development of Research-Oriented Virtual Communities* by Mark Chignell, Janet Ho and m. c. schraefel, a virtual community is defined as a group of people whose shared needs and/or interests are largely communicated within, and mediated by, Web-enabled interactions, e.g., within a website. In order to design effective virtual communities, methods are needed to evaluate the usability and effectiveness of collaborative environments and the degree to which they function as virtual communities (VCs). In this paper the authors explore, through the discussion of a pilot study of a research-purposed VC, how to evaluate a VC infrastructure. Workshop participants posed the question, In what ways can we increase the effectiveness of collaboration system evaluation while reducing the cost?

Application-Specific Evaluation Experiences

The paper, *Deploying and Evaluating Collaborative Studios* by Jonathan Sevy, Vera Zaychik, Thomas T. Hewett and William C. Regli, describes a vision of a collaborative engineering environment, the Collaborative Design Studio. It considers issues and questions relating to the effective design and evaluation of such systems, and describes proposed studies for evaluating and evolving the current environment. While preliminary development of the studio has proceeded using relatively informal input from professional design engineers, it is essential to incorporate direct evaluation by intended users of the system to ensure that it meets their needs accurately and fits into their work environment. Such information will be obtained through surveys and observation of participants as they complete specified tasks. The information will then be analyzed and used to guide further development of the system. Researchers also used archived communication and search (pattern) activity analysis during evaluation for tool development. One important issue raised as a result of this presentation is that long-term use of systems for field studies is very difficult to sell to industry.

In *A Method to Design Process Architecture in the Distributed Product Realization Environment* by Angran Xiao, Janet Allen, David Rosen and Farrokh Mistree, a distributed process structuring method (DPSM) was presented to design the process architectures in a distributed environment. With DPSM, a process is represented as a hierarchy by partitioning the process and reorganizing the activities. Four typical architecture templates are introduced: sequential, parallel, integrated and distributed. The process architectures are constructed by mapping the process representation into the templates. This method is a state-of-the-science method to structure a process in the distributed environment, while ensuring modularity and robustness of the architecture. Finally, an engineering case is investigated with this method and the distributed architecture is implemented using agent technology. The evaluation involved testing the validity of the dependencies within the context of a task and ranking the templates based on effectiveness relative to the context. Workshop participants discussed the issue that it is often difficult to determine what is really happening when things go wrong because of participant group dynamics.

Evaluation Challenges for a Federation of Heterogeneous Information Providers: The Case of NASA's Earth Science Information Partnerships by Catherine Plaisant and Anita Komlodi, presented an experiment to assess the ability of a group of widely heterogeneous, earth-science data or service providers to self organize and provide improved and cheaper access to an expanding, earth-science, user community. As it is organizing itself, the federation is mandated to set in place an evaluation methodology and collect metrics reflecting the health of the Federation and benefits to the public. The authors described the challenges of organizing self-evaluation of such a federated partnership and discussed the issues encountered during the metrics definition and early data collection phases. Some metrics used were changes over time of identified measures, for example: number of delivered data products, number of rendered services, number of Web page hits, number of promotional products, volume of available data and number of available services. One lesson learned was that metrics must be chosen carefully to reflect the goals of the organization, because resources were diverted to enhance the products and services with associated metrics leaving other offerings to languish. Another lesson learned was that while good metrics were difficult to identify, collect and assess, anecdotal information had significant impact in reports. Challenges identified were 1) identifying useful and obtainable metrics, 2) the relative unavailability of baseline data and 3) trying to use metrics gathered from very diverse entities within an enterprise to compare how those entities are performing and collaborating among themselves and with their respective constituencies.

Summary of Discussions

Three main questions were addressed during the discussion portion of the workshop:

- What are the approaches to evaluating collaborative systems?
- What are the current problems with collaboration system evaluation?
- What are future research needs?

The remainder of this report summarizes the discussions and conclusions related to these issues.

What are the approaches to evaluating collaborative systems?

One useful goal for this workshop was to identify the methods and techniques for evaluating collaborative systems and to discuss how those methods are best applied. The participants noted that it will also be important to ascertain when in the development cycle each method is best applied, although it was acknowledged more research needs to be done in this area. In an attempt to frame the scope of the discussion, we first outlined a statement on context for evaluation of collaborative enterprises.

The evaluation of a collaborative enterprise should be set in some context, e.g., a particular application or problem space. Effective evaluations do not take place out of context.[1]

We then turned to what we know of where single-user system and collaborative system evaluation diverge. A major difference between single user system evaluation and collaborative system evaluation is that we are trying to do more than traditional usability testing when evaluating groupware. Testing must also consider the usefulness of the software in addressing the needs of the collaborative enterprise. Sufficient guidelines for understanding how software meets collaborative enterprise *needs* do not exist. (Note, that the workshop participants were being intentionally vague in the use of the term *needs*, it should be defined in future research.)

There are essentially two basic reasons people use groupware: they need to collaborate or they want to improve an existing collaboration. Some form of separation, either geographical or temporal, often drives the incorporation of groupware to facilitate collaboration. Evaluation provides an important method for understanding how to improve the groupware-supported collaborative experience. Given the need to evaluate a collaborative enterprise, there are several approaches that have been used, including exploratory methods, field experiments, laboratory experiments, field and case studies. Building on McGrath's work [4], Pinelle organizes these evaluation types based on the level of manipulation and the setting, see Figure 1. Further research needs to be

Setting \ Manipulation	Rigorous	Minimal/ None
Naturalistic	Field Experiment	Field Study, Case Study
Controlled	Laboratory Experiment	Exploratory

Figure 1: An organization of evaluation types

1. It was also noted that the context needs to be reasonably well understood by the evaluator(s) to identify and examine pertinent variables during analysis.

performed to determine if some approaches are more applicable to the evaluation of collaborative systems than others.

In gathering metrics, evaluators are interested in assessing the effectiveness, efficiency and satisfaction with the product and the process. Gutwin describes these measures in his workshop paper with respect to usability testing,

"Effectiveness considers whether the activity was successfully completed, and the number and severity of errors made during that activity. A usable groupware system will not prevent the mechanics of collaboration from taking place, and will not cause group members to make undue errors in those activities.

Efficiency considers the resources (such as time or effort) required to carry out the activity. A good groupware system will allow the activities of collaboration to proceed with less time and effort than will a system with usability problems. Note that any measures of efficiency must be carefully focused on task activities, since groups often engage in off-task activities that are not detrimental to the overall shared work. Satisfaction considers whether the group members are reasonably happy with the processes and outcomes of each of the activities of collaboration. Satisfaction will sometimes overlap with efficiency and effectiveness (that is, problems in the other areas are likely to reduce satisfaction)."

There are many methods and techniques for evaluation. The workshop participants generated the list below, acknowledging that these methods and techniques are to be used in combination, at different stages of the trial, and have varying levels of effectiveness depending on the situation being evaluated. There is clearly a need for research to understand and to document these (and potentially others) with respect to groupware evaluation:

- Archival analysis
- Informal discussion
- Heuristic evaluation
- Real-time
    - Walkthroughs
    - Participant observations
- User Questionnaires
    - Numerically scaled
    - Free response
- Inspection
- Simulation
- Standard problems (scenarios)
- Automatic data logging/visualization tools
- Think-out-loud studies
- Interaction protocol analysis
- Interviews

Developing useful metrics is key to successful evaluation. Ideally, we would like to be able to match the type of collaboration and the type of tools being evaluated with approaches, methods and tools to generate useful metrics. There is room for considerable research to enable the measurement of product and process efficiency, effectiveness, and satisfaction in a collaborative enterprise. There are issues related to gathering baseline data. This certainly must be done, but often evaluations are done in an environment where metrics have never been identified or gathered. After an attempt to match qualitative and quantitative measures to groupware and collaboration characteristics, the workshop participants decided that this is an area ripe for additional research.

What are the current problems with collaboration system evaluation?

Workshop participants rapidly developed a list of problems and challenges associated with collaborative system evaluation. Then we tried to identify existing and potential solutions for these problems.

Long-term evaluations are difficult and expensive. This problem occurs in collaborative enterprise evaluations where tasks are spread out over many months. The field study evaluation method is particularly prone to this problem. One solution is to incorporate automated data collection with only periodic evaluator involvement during the data gathering phase of the field study.

Evaluating many participants is difficult. As opposed to single-user evaluation, with its documented techniques [5], collaboration system evaluation can involve many participants. It is necessary to develop evaluation techniques that can be performed requiring few or no participants while the software is in early development phases to minimize the number of trials involving lots of people. It was noted that some scaling issues may not always be detectable with only a few participants and that some tests with large numbers of participants will still have a role.

Evaluation costs are high. These costs include researcher costs, access time and participant costs. These costs may be keeping effective evaluations from being completed, resulting in more failures when deploying ineffective collaborative systems. It is important to develop alternative, low-cost methods and tools for evaluation. Furthermore, guidelines for collaborative-software graphical user interfaces (GUIs) like those existing for single-user GUIs, would enable less expensive and evaluation and development of collaborative systems. Along these lines, we also need to develop groupware benchmarks, scenarios and requirements against which to complete future evaluations. There is also a need to develop data-collection tools with data-viewing capabilities to reduce the time required to understand the vast amounts of data gathered. Further, we need to educate users on how their costs can be reduced with implementation of application-appropriate groupware systems. An interesting area for research is in the development of groupware design patterns [1, 2, *et al.*], like those used for single-user software engineering.

Getting participants for field studies is difficult. Field studies of collaborative systems offer the opportunity to truly understand a system's effectiveness, efficiency and satisfaction levels. However, potential participants are wary of inviting evaluators into their shop for fear of productivity losses due to these evaluations. Some useful techniques to minimize this would be automated data collection and embedded, infrequent, random, short, on-line questionnaires. There is also a need to collect success stories in order to "sell" the value of the implementation of a collaborative system as well as the knowledge gained in identifying enterprise processes to potential participants.

Field study evaluation is difficult. While there are many challenges with all types of collaborative system evaluations, field studies are particularly difficult. Obviously, it is necessary to simplify methods for field studies and to develop cheaper field methods. The value in the use of design ethnography [3] was noted. Two potential solutions include: more instrumented beta testing and more robust instrumented feedback.

Cultural and organizational issues affect ability to evaluate cause and effect. When something does not work, is it because of the software or is it due to cultural or organizational effects? Often, studies fail to ascertain the source of success or failure or, worse yet, attribute it incorrectly. We need research to categorize group characteristics and then be able to match appropriate groupware characteristics. We also need to know what to look for so that cultural and organizational issues can be properly attributed during evaluation. Furthermore, evaluations and publication of field studies should include cultural and organizational issues, even if the discussion of such things is merely anecdotal.

Evaluators may have unclear understanding of the technical applications in use in a collaborative system. In other words, those who may be familiar with the groupware being used or with group collaboration evaluation techniques may not understand the end-users' disciplines, resulting in additional evaluation challenges. It would be useful to develop a typology that addresses how categories of log data correlates with specific metrics, e.g., tag log data so that it relates to user activities. This would facilitate intelligent logging of data.

There are insufficient heuristics for collaborative software evaluation. There are no basic groupware design principles, and therefore, there are no basic heuristics that can be used for collaborative software evaluation, as opposed to basic design principles and heuristics for single-user, software systems. There is a need to develop and document heuristics for use in groupware evaluation.

Conclusions and Future Research Needs

Most discussions held during this workshop eventually recognized the need for future research to better understand the complexities and nuances of collaborative enterprise evaluation. A common theme for future work is that there needs to be a better understanding of the characteristics of the collaborative enterprise of interest and then what evaluation approaches, methods and techniques and the associated metrics and tools are most appropriate for use. Additionally, there is an opportunity to exploit some of the work done with single-user systems, for example the design patterns[1] work recently applied to HCI (Human Computer Interaction) was cited.

Ideally, there needs to be some sort of framework or taxonomy that can answer:

- Which evaluation approaches are best for the evaluation of different types of collaborative systems?
- When in the design cycle of collaborative software development are particular approaches most effective?
- What combination of methods and techniques for gathering metrics are most effective for the situation under evaluation?
- Which approaches, methods and techniques address product and process effectiveness, efficiency and satisfaction?
- Which metrics address product and process effectiveness, efficiency and satisfaction of the collaborative enterprise under study?
- What evaluation tools and mechanisms are best for generating specific metrics?
- What categories of log data generated within collaborative software correlate with specific metrics?

Additional notes:

- There is a need to develop collaboration evaluation methods and tools that are low cost and can be done with few or no participants and that use design ethnography.

---

1. http://www.gespro.com/lafrenid/PSA.pdf

- Research is needed in the area of groupware design heuristics.
- As noted earlier, specifications of groupware event sets need to be generated to facilitate automated data collection/logging. Similarly, there is much work to be done in event tagging to enable intelligent data logging and visualizations of logged data.
- Benchmark collaboration scenarios and their associated evaluation measures need to be developed to help developers assess their groupware systems during design and development phases.

An issue in collaborative enterprise evaluation is that it is a multi-disciplinary activity and it is very often difficult to effectively accomplish a thorough evaluation. A significant outcome of this workshop is that NIST will be establishing a forum for information exchange and an on-line repository for useful information about collaborative system evaluation. An email distribution list (eval-ce@nist.gov) will further enable information exchange among interested participants. This workshop formalized initial discussion in an area of great importance to the future success of collaborative enterprises.

References

[1] Erickson, T., Putting It All Together: Pattern Languages for Interaction Design Workshop, Proceedings of the ACM's CHI 97 Conference, Atlanta, GA, 1997.

[2] Foote, B., Harrison, N., et. al., *Pattern Languages of Program Design 4,* Addison Wesley, 1999.

[3] Ford, J. and Wood, L., An Overview of Ethnography and System Design. In *Field Methods Casebook for Software Design,* Wixon, D. and Ramey, J. (eds.), John Wiley & Sons, Inc., New York, 1996, pp. 269-282.

[4] McGrath, J.E., Methodology Matters: Doing Research in the Behavioral and Social Sciences. In *Readings in Human-Computer Interaction: Toward the Year 2000,* 2nd Ed., Baecker, R.M., Grudin, J., Buxton, W.A.S., Greenberg, S. (eds.), Morgan Kaufman Publishers, San Francisco, 1995, pp. 152-169.

[5] Neilsen, J., *Usability Engineering,* Morgan Kaufmann, San Francisco, 1994.

A Review of Groupware Evaluations

David Pinelle and Carl Gutwin
Department of Computer Science, University of Saskatchewan
[dlp849, gutwin]@cs.usask.ca

Abstract

A better understanding of how groupware systems have been evaluated in the past can help to frame the discussion of what methods and techniques should be considered for future evaluations. We reviewed all papers from the ACM CSCW conference (1990-1998) that introduced or evaluated a groupware system. Forty-five papers were included in the review. The main findings are that almost one-third of the groupware systems were not evaluated in any formal way, that only about one-quarter of the articles included evaluations in a real-world setting, and that a wide variety of evaluation techniques are in use. Our main conclusions from the review are that more attention must be paid to evaluating groupware systems and that there is room for additional evaluation techniques that are simple and low in cost.

1. Introduction

As groupware systems become more common, more attention is being paid to the question of how to evaluate multi-user systems. Researchers and developers have employed a range of techniques including scientific, engineering, and social science methodologies, but there is no clear consensus on which methods are appropriate in which circumstances. In addition, groupware is traditionally considered to be difficult to evaluate because of the effects of multiple people and the social and organizational context [14, 39].

In order to gain a better understanding of how different evaluation techniques have been used in the past, and of the strengths and weaknesses of the different methods, we reviewed a sample of CSCW research that discussed groupware systems and evaluations of groupware. This review provides a foundation from which we can consider questions of when and how to evaluate future systems.

This paper presents our review of 45 papers from the ACM CSCW conference 1990 – 1998. Articles were included in this survey if they introduced a new groupware application or contained an evaluation of an existing groupware application. We only considered applications if they were intended to support specific task goals; basic tools such as email systems were not included.

We begin by outlining a set of categories and criteria that we used to analyze the papers, and then detail the results of the review.

2. Classifying groupware evaluations

We analyzed each article in five areas: type of evaluation, characteristics of the evaluation, data collection techniques, placement of the evaluation in the software development cycle, and type of conclusions drawn from the evaluation. Each of these areas is described below.

2.1. Type of evaluation

McGrath's [29] classification scheme for research strategies was used as a starting point for assessing the type of evaluation carried out. The major differentiating characteristics between the strategies are level of experimental manipulation and evaluation setting (Figure 1).

Two additional categories were added to McGrath's scheme. First, most field studies entailed involvement by the authors in the development and implementation of the software. However, a portion of these involved an "after the fact" evaluation in which the authors were not involved in development and implementation but instead evaluated a piece of groupware software that had been implemented in a work setting by others. These were classified as case studies.

Figure 1. Evaluation types

		Manipulation: Rigorous	Manipulation: Minimal / None
Setting	Naturalistic	Field Experiment	Field Study, Case Study
	Controlled	Laboratory Experiment	Exploratory

0-7695-0798-9/00 $10.00 © 2000 IEEE

Second, articles that did not contain formal evaluations were separated into two groups. Articles that drew conclusions based only on the researcher's experience were classified as introspective studies. Articles without formal evaluations that did not draw conclusions about the software were placed in the no evaluation category.

2.2. Characteristics of the evaluation

Evaluations were further classified according to the rigor of the experimental manipulation and the type and rigor of measurements. Twidale, Randall, and Bentley's [49] dimensions for classifying evaluations were combined with McGrath's [29] techniques for experimental manipulation and techniques for measuring experimental results to produce the classification scheme below.

- Formative vs. Summative
- Quantitative vs. Qualitative
- Manipulation:
- Formal / rigorous
- Minimal manipulation
- No manipulation
- Measurement:
- Formal / rigorous
- Informal

2.3. Techniques for data collection

We also assessed each evaluation's data collection techniques. There were seven main techniques:

- User Observation
- Interview
- Discussion
- Questionnaire
- Qualitative work measures
- Quantitative work measures
- Collection of archival material

2.4. Placement of evaluation in software lifecycle

Grudin [14] stresses the importance of evaluation over a period of time following groupware implementation. He also argues that evaluations of partial prototypes in laboratory settings are not able to address complex social and organizational issues. These arguments motivated the collection of data on the placement of the evaluation in the software's lifecycle. We considered six potential placements of the evaluation:

- Periodic evaluations throughout development process
- Continuous evaluation throughout development
- Evaluation of a prototype
- Evaluation of a finished piece of software
- Periodic evaluations after software implementation
- Continuous evaluation after software implementation

2.5. Focus of the evaluation

A set of categories was developed to identify the focus of the evaluation. An initial set of categories was found in the three categories of benefits cited by Baeza-Yates and Pino [2]. These were extended to include concepts from a multi-stage evaluation process discussed by Beuscart-Zephir et al [4]. Types of evaluation focus include:

- Organizational impact / impact on work practices
- End product produced through using the software
- Efficiency of task performance using software
- User satisfaction with the software
- Task support provided by the software
- Specific features of the groupware interface
- Patterns of system use
- User interaction while using the software

3. Results

We include results from our analyses in each of the areas outlined above.

3.1. Characterizing the software

Table 1: Characterizing the software

	#	%	References
Distribution in time			
Synchronous	26	70	[3, 5, 7, 8, 10, 11, 15, 17, 18, 19, 21, 22, 25, 28, 30, 31, 35, 37, 38, 42, 43, 44, 47, 48, 49, 50]
Asynchronous	11	30	[1, 7, 10, 33, 38, 39, 41, 42, 44, 45, 51]

Implementation type			
Academic / Research	19	59	[8, 11, 15, 17, 18, 21, 22, 25, 28, 31, 33, 35, 37, 42, 43, 44, 48, 49, 50]
Real world	13	41	[1, 3, 5, 7, 10, 19, 30, 38, 39, 41, 45, 47, 51].

The majority of the papers introduced synchronous applications. Most of the systems were academic or research implementation, and a smaller number of implementations were installed with in a real world setting. Results are summarized in Table 1[1].

3.2. Evaluation type

The two main types of evaluations seen in the review are laboratory experiments and field studies. However, several other types of evaluation were seen that are related to field methods. When these groups are taken together, the ratio of field to laboratory studies is even (see Table 2).

Almost forty percent of the articles contained no formal evaluation at all. Of these 17 papers, four contained introspective evaluations, and nine did not report on any study. Four more did not include enough information to determine if an evaluation had been carried out.

Table 2: Studies by evaluation type

Evaluation Type	#	%	References
Laboratory Experiment	13	28	[11, 15, 17, 18, 21, 25, 28, 33, 35, 37, 43, 48,49]
Field Study	8	17	[1, 3, 19, 30, 38, 41, 45, 47]
Case Study	4	9	[5, 7, 39, 51]
Exploratory	3	7	[8, 44, 49]
Field Experiment	1	2	[10]
Introspection	4	9	[16, 24, 34, 36]
No Evaluation	9	20	[6, 9, 13, 20, 26, 27, 32, 40, 46]
Not enough information	4	9	[22, 31, 50, 42]

3.3. Characterizing the evaluation

Formative evaluations were more prevalent than summative evaluations (see Table 3). The high number of prototype systems accounts for this in part, as many of the authors were conducting the research to further enlighten system development. In all, 15 evaluations were of prototype systems and 11 were of completed software packages (see table 4). Only a small number of articles contained evaluations that were distributed throughout the software lifecycle.

[1] Tables show the number of studies (#) and percentage of the total (%). Classifications are not necessarily mutually exclusive, and percentages may not always add to 100%.

Table 3: Characterizing the evaluations

Formative vs. Summative			
Formative	18	56	[3, 8, 10, 15, 17, 19, 22, 25, 28, 33, 35, 41, 42, 43, 44, 47, 48, 49]
Summative	12	38	[1, 5, 7, 11, 18, 21, 30, 37, 38, 39, 50, 51]
Both	2	6	[31, 45]

Quantitative vs. Qualitative			
Quantitative	2	6	[18, 21]
Qualitative	23	72	[3, 5, 7, 8, 10, 11, 15, 17, 19, 22, 30, 31, 35, 37, 38, 39, 41, 42, 43, 44, 45, 49, 50]
Both	7	22	[1, 25, 28, 33, 47, 48, 51]

Manipulation			
Formal / Rigorous	14	47	[10, 11, 15, 17, 18, 21, 25, 28, 33, 35, 37, 43, 48, 49]
Minimal	2	7	[1, 44]
None	14	47	[3, 5, 7, 8, 19, 30, 38, 39, 41, 42, 45, 47, 49, 51]

Measures			
Formal / Rigorous	18	60	[1, 7, 10, 11, 15, 17, 18, 19, 21, 25, 28, 33, 35, 37, 41, 47, 48, 51]
Informal	12	40	[3, 5, 8, 30, 31, 38, 39, 42, 43, 44, 45, 49]

Table 4: Placement of evaluation in lifecycle

	#	%	References
Periodic throughout development	3	9	[19, 31, 42]
Continuous throughout development	2	6	[41, 45]
Evaluation of a prototype	15	47	[3, 8, 10, 15, 17, 21, 22, 25, 33, 35, 43, 44, 47, 48, 49]
Evaluation of finished software package	11	34	[1,5,11,18,28,30,31,37,38, 50,51]
Periodic after implementation	0	0	[]
Continuous after implementation	3	9	[7, 39, 45]

3.4. Evaluation Techniques

Observation was by far the most frequently used evaluation technique with 24 studies utilizing this technique, and this was coupled with videotaping of the users in 10 of these cases (see Table 5). Interviews were the next most frequently utilized technique, with 12 occurrences noted. This was followed by questionnaire (9 articles) and quantitative work measures (9).

Table 5: Summary of evaluation techniques

Technique	#	%	References
Observation	24	83	[1, 3, 7, 8, 10, 11, 15, 17, 19, 21, 25, 28, 30, 35, 37, 39, 41, 42, 43, 44, 45, 47, 48, 49]
Observation with Videotape	10	34	[10, 11, 15, 17, 19, 21, 25, 28, 35, 47]
Interview	12	41	[1, 5, 7, 11, 15, 17, 19, 35, 38, 39, 41, 51]
Questionnaire	9	31	[1, 10, 15, 19, 25, 33, 37, 47, 48]
Quantitative work measures	9	31	[1, 18, 21, 25, 28, 33, 37, 48, 51]
Qualitative work measures	5	17	[18, 25, 33, 37, 48]
Collected Archival Materials	4	14	[5, 7, 39, 47]
Discussion	3	10	[8, 30, 45]

3.5. Focus of the evaluation

Only a small number of studies examined the organizational impact or impact on work practices in a user group when a piece of groupware was introduced. This category obviously pertains to "real world" software implementations. However, with a total of 13 articles with real world implementations, only 8 of these evaluated the impact the software had on the user group itself and on its work patterns (see Table 6).

Carrying out an evaluation of this type can be quite time consuming since new work patterns evolve over time. For that reason, the amount of time each researcher was in contact with the user group (regardless of whether this was continuous or intermittent) and gathering this type of evaluation data was recorded. Although 2 of the 8 studies did not specify time [5, 30], the other 6 did, and ranged from 4.5 to 36 months.

Table 6: Focus of the evaluation

Conclusion	#	%	References
Patterns of system use	16	50	[1, 11, 15, 19, 25, 28, 31, 37, 41, 42, 43, 45, 47, 48, 50, 51]
Support for specified task	15	47	[1, 3, 8, 11, 15, 17, 19, 28, 31, 33, 41, 43, 44, 45, 49]
User interaction through the system	14	44	[8, 11, 17, 19, 21, 25, 28, 35, 37, 38, 43, 47, 48, 51]
Specific interface features	12	38	[11, 15, 17, 22, 25, 28, 31, 33, 43, 48, 49, 50]
User Satisfaction	12	38	[1, 5, 7, 8, 10, 15, 19, 22, 35, 37, 45, 47]
Organizational / Work impact	8	25	[5, 7, 30, 38, 39, 41, 45, 47]
End product	5	16	[25, 37, 42, 49, 51]
Efficiency of task performance	4	13	[18, 25, 33, 48]

4. Discussion

Twidale, Randall, and Bentley [49] stress the importance of context in groupware evaluation. However, they point out the usefulness of less authentic evaluation techniques early in development as part of an ongoing formative evaluation. This allows for the elimination of larger, glaring problems early in the development process so that more subtle issues can be dealt with when the software is evaluated with the target user group.

The developer, then, could begin with multiple controlled evaluations to shape the initial prototypes. Many of the problems that would surface early on are obtrusive enough that they would pose difficulties for any user group. As these are overcome, the developer can then move into the naturalistic setting with a piece of software that is refined enough that the target users can begin offering feedback on issues that are unique to them.

From the articles that include enough information to allow classification along these lines, 29 combinations were recorded to allow comparison between placement of evaluation in the software lifecycle and type of evaluation conducted. Of these, 17 were ongoing formative evaluations or evaluations of prototypes [3, 8, 10, 15, 17, 19, 21, 25, 33, 35, 41, 43, 44, 45, 47, 48, 49] and 12 were evaluations of finished products [1, 5, 7, 11, 18, 28, 30, 37, 38, 39, 45, 51]. The formative evaluations were overwhelmingly carried out separately from any kind of work or organizational context. In all, 65% of these were in controlled settings (lab experiment, exploratory) [8, 15, 17, 21, 25, 33, 35, 43, 44, 48, 49], and the remaining 35% were field based (field study, field experiment) [3, 10, 19, 41, 45, 47]. Similarly, evaluations of completed groupware applications were largely carried out in naturalistic settings. In all, 67% of these were carried out using field based evaluations (field study and case study) [1, 5, 7, 30, 38, 39, 45, 51], and the remaining 33% used controlled settings (lab experiments) [11, 18, 28, 37].

These findings are in agreement with Twidale, Randall, and Bentley's hypothesis. This suggests that there may be real value in evaluations conducted out of context early in the development phase. But, as development progresses and the applications become more refined, it becomes increasingly important to move evaluations into the target work setting.

4.1. Evaluation in the work place

Many of the complicating factors associated with groupware implementation stem from the difficulties introduced by context. In particular, it is difficult to predict how the software will fit into the organizational and work practices of a group of end users. Therefore, evaluating the impact of a groupware implementation in these areas should be a priority for developers. However, from the studies included in this survey, 41% of the articles that included evaluations were of actual real world software implementations, but only 25% considered the software's organizational and work impact.

In order to gain an understanding of how these evaluations can be better carried out, further research needs to be done on longitudinal field based evaluation. The focus must shift toward the users and the organization. Grudin [14] has emphasized the difficulty of learning from previous evaluations due to the broad range of organizations and users that must be dealt with. In spite of this, further work should be done on refining data collection methodologies with a focus on conducting these longitudinal studies in a way that is time and cost efficient.

4.2. New techniques for groupware evaluation

An effort should be made to develop new evaluation techniques in order to make evaluation more practical in terms of time and cost. By improving techniques used prior to workplace evaluations, many problems can be eliminated early on, thus improving the efficiency of evaluation as it progresses into the workplace.

One means of developing intermediate level evaluation techniques may be through adapting techniques used to evaluate single user applications. Ereback and Hook [12] attempted this using cognitive walkthrough, but the results were mixed and somewhat inconclusive.

5. Conclusions

This paper explores groupware evaluation trends and techniques by surveying a wide variety of articles from the ACM CSCW conference. We closely analyzed all articles that introduced or evaluated groupware applications. After analyzing forty-five papers, we discovered that almost one-third of the groupware systems were not evaluated in any formal way and that only about one-quarter of the evaluations involve a real-world setting. We suggested future directions for groupware evaluation. In particular, evaluation techniques should be developed to help eliminate problems with the application before it progresses into situated workplace-centered evaluations.

6. References

[1] Ackerman, M.S. Augmenting the Organizational Memory: a Field Study of Answer Garden. *CSCW '94*, 243-252.

[2] Baeza-Yates, R. and Pino, J.A. A First Step to Formally Evaluate Collaborative Work. *SIGGROUP '97*, 56-60.

[3] Bergmann, N.W. and Mudge, J.C. Automated Assistance for the Telemeeting Lifecycle. *CSCW '94*, 373-384.

[4] Beuscart-Zephir, M.C., Molenda, S., Grave, C., Dufresne, E. Usability Assessment of Interactive Multimedia Medical Workstation. *Proc. IEEE Engineering in Medicine and Biology Society*, p. 1358-9, vol.2.

[5] Bikson, T.K. and Eveland, J.D. Groupware Implementation: Reinvention in the Sociotechnical Frame. *CSCW '96*, 428-437.

[6] Boland, R.J., Maheshwari, A.K., Te'eni, D., Schwartz, D.G. and Tenkasi, R.V. Sharing Perspectives in Distributed Decision *Making*. *CSCW '92*, 306-313.

[7] Bowers, J. The Work to Make a Network Work: Studying CSCW in Action. *CSCW '94*, 287-298.

[8] Brave, S., Ishii, H. and Dahley, A. Tangible Interfaces for Remote Collaboration and Communication. *CSCW '98*, 169-178.

[9] Brinck, T. and Gomez, L.M. A Collaborative Medium for the Support of Conversational Props. *CSCW '92*, 171-178.

[10] Brothers, L., Sembugamoorthy, V. and Muller, M. ICICLE: Groupware for Code Inspection. *CSCW '90*, 169-181.

[11] Dourish, P. and Bellotti, V. Awareness and Coordination in Shared Workspaces. *CSCW '92*, 107-114.

[12] Ereback A.-L. and Hook, K. Using Cognitive Walkthrough for Evaluating a CSCW Application. *CHI '94*, 91-92.

[13] Goldberg, Y., Safran, M. and Shapiro, E. Active Mail--A Framework for Implementing Groupware. *CSCW '92*, 75-83.

[14] Grudin, J. Groupware and Social Dynamics: Eight Challenges for Developers. *Commun. ACM* 37, 1, 92-105.

[15] Gutwin, C., Roseman, M. and Greenberg, S. A Usability Study of Awareness Widgets in a Shared Workspace Groupware System. *CSCW '96*, 258-267.

[16] Haake, J.M. and Wilson, B. Supporting Collaborative Writing of Hyperdocuments in SEPIA. *CSCW '92*, 138-146.

[17] Hindmarsh, J., Fraser, M., Heath, C., Benford, S. and Greenhalgh, C. Fragmented Interaction: Establishing mutual orientation in virtual environments. *CSCW '98*, 217-226.

[18] Hymes, C.M. and Olson, G.M. Unblocking Brainstorming Through the Use of a Simple Group Editor. *CSCW '92*, 99-106.

[19] Isaacs, E.A., Morris, T. and Rodriguez, T.K. A Forum for Supporting Interactive Presentations to Distributed Audiences. *CSCW '94*, 405-416.

[20] Isaacs, E.A., Tang, J.C. and Morris, T. Piazza: A Desktop Environment Supporting Impromptu and Planned Interactions. *CSCW '96*, 315-324.

[21] Ishii, H.; Kobayashi, M. and Grudin, J. Integration of Inter-Personal Space and Shared Workspace: ClearBoard Design and Experiments. *CSCW '92*, 33- 42.

[22] Ishii, H. TeamWorkStation: Towards a Seamless Shared Workspace. *CSCW '90*, 13-26.

[23] Johnson-Lenz, P. and Johnson-Lenz, T. Groupware: The Process and Impacts of Design Choices. In *Computer-Mediated Communication Systems: Status and Evaluation*. Kerr, E. and Hiltz, S. (eds.), Academic Press, 1982, 42-55.

[24] Kaplan, S.M., Tolone, W.J., Bogia, D.P. and Bignoli, C. Flexible, Active Support for Collaborative Work with ConversationBuilder. *CSCW '92*, 378-385.

[25] Kraut, R.E., Miller, M.D. and Siegel, J. Collaboration in Performance of Physical Tasks: Effects on Outcomes and Communication. *CSCW '96*, 57-66.

[26] Lee, J. SIBYL: A Tool for Managing Group Decision Rationale. *CSCW '90*, 79-92.

[27] Lee, J.H., Prakash, A., Jaeger, T. and Wu, G. Supporting Multi-User, Multi-Applet Workspaces in CBE. *CSCW '96*, 344-353.

[28] Mark, G., Haake, J.M. and Streitz, N.A. Hypermedia Structures and the Division of Labor in Meeting Room Collaboration. *CSCW '96*, 170-179.

[29] McGrath, J.E. Methodology Matters: Doing Research in the Behavioral and Social Sciences. In *Readings in Human-Computer Interaction: Toward the Year 2000*, 2nd Ed. Baecker, R.M., Grudin, J., Buxton, W.A.S., Greenberg, S. (eds.), Morgan Kaufman Publishers, San Francisco. 1995, 152-169.

[30] Moran, T.P., van Melle, W. and Chiu, P. Tailorable Domain Objects as Meeting Tools for an Electronic Whiteboard. *CSCW '98*, 295-304.

[31] Myers, B.A., Stiel, H. and Gargiulo, R. Collaboration Using Multiple PDAs Connected to a PC. *CSCW '98*, 285-294.

[32] Neuwirth, C.M., Chandhok, R., Kaufer, D.S., Erion, P., Morris, J. and Miller, D. Flexible Diff-ing In A Collaborative Writing System. *CSCW '92*, 147-154.

[33] Neuwirth, C.M., Morris, J.H., Regli, S.H., Chandhok, R. and Wenger, G.C. Envisioning Communication: Task-Tailorable Representations of Communication in Asynchronous Work. *CSCW '98*, 265-274.

[34] Newman-Wolfe, R.E., Webb, M. L. and Montes, M. Implicit Locking in the Ensemble Concurrent Object-Oriented Graphics Editor. *CSCW '92*, 265-272.

[35] Okada, K., Maeda, F., Ichikawaa, Y. and Matsushita, Y. Multiparty Videoconferencing at Virtual Social Distance: MAJIC Design. *CSCW '94*, 385-393.

[36] Olsen, D.R., Hudson, S.E., Phelps, M., Heiner, J. and Verratti, T. Ubiquitous Collaboration via Surface Representations. *CSCW '98*, 129-138.

[37] Olson, J.S., Olson, G.M., Storrøsten, M. and Carter, M. How a Group-Editor Changes the Character of a Design Meeting as well as its Outcome. *CSCW '92*, 91-98.

[38] Olson, J.S. and Teasley, S. Groupware in the Wild: Lessons Learned from a Year of Virtual Collocation. *CSCW '96*, 419-427.

[39] Orlikowski, W.J. Learning From Notes: Organizational Issues in Groupware Implementation. CSCW '92, 362-369.

[40] Pacull, F., Sandoz, A. and Schiper, A. Duplex: A Distributed Collaborative Editing Environment in Large Scale. *CSCW '94*, 165-173.

[41] Prinz, W., Mark, G. and Pankoke-Babatz, U. Designing Groupware for Congruency in Use. CSCW '98, 373-382.

[42] Roseman, M. and Greenberg, S. TeamRooms: Network Places for Collaboration. *CSCW '96*, 325-333.

[43] Shu, L. and Flowers, W. Groupware Experiences in Three-Dimensional Computer-Aided Design. *CSCW '92*, 179-186.

[44] Sohlenkamp, M. and Chwelos, G. Integrating Communication, Cooperation, and Awareness: The DIVA Virtual Office Environment. *CSCW '94*, 331-343.

[45] Star, S.L. and Ruhleder, K. Steps Towards an Ecology of Infrastructure: Complex Problems in Design and Access for Large-Scale Collaborative Systems. *CSCW '94*, 253-264.

[46] Streitz, N.A., Geißler, J., Haake, J.M. and Hol, J. DOLPHIN: Integrated Meeting Support across Local and Remote Desktop Environments and LiveBoards. *CSCW '94*, 345-358.

[47] Tang, J.C., Isaacs, E.A. and Rua, M. Supporting Distributed Groups with a Montage of Lightweight Interactions. *CSCW '94*, 23-34.

[48] Toth, J.A. The Effects of Interactive Graphics and Text on Social Influence in Computer-Mediated Small Groups. *CSCW '94*, 299-310.

[49] Twidale, M., Randall, D., Bentley, R. Situated Evaluation for Cooperative Systems. CSCW '94, 441-452.

[50] Watabe, K., Sakata, S., Maeno, K., Fukuoka, H. and Ohmori, T. Distributed Multiparty Desktop Conferencing System: MERMAID. *CSCW '90*, 27-38.

[51] Whittaker, S. Talking to Strangers: An Evaluation of the Factors Affecting Electronic Collaboration. *CSCW '96*, 409-418.

Techniques for Evaluating Collaboration Toolkits

Prasun Dewan
University of North Carolina, dewan@unc.edu

Abstract

The most reliable approach to evaluating a collaboration toolkit is to carry out field studies. This approach has the problem that it requires each project to be interdisciplinary and create a complete, working system, which seems too costly given the budget for a typical research project and the complexity of a collaboration toolkit; and more important, does not allow a project to converge incrementally towards a complete solution. Based on the lessons learned from our work and that of others on collaboration toolkits, we have identified several lower-cost techniques for evaluating collaboration toolkits including inspecting the design to see if requirements have been met, simulating other systems, implementing complete solutions to standard problems, and performing self and lab studies. This paper discusses these techniques, points out their pros and cons, identifies the influential projects in which they have been used, and shows how they fit together.

1. Introduction

One of the trickiest questions faced by a research project developing a collaboration toolkit is how to evaluate the system. Apparently, the answer is very simple: Carry out studies of the system in use, ideally involving researchers from disciplines other than computer science who are experts in carrying out such studies. This approach seems to be the only one guaranteed to satisfy all researchers in this field, because many of them will not settle for anything else.

There seems to be good reason for holding this view point. As Fred Brooks points out, builders of computer systems are toolsmiths, and the only way to judge how good computer tools are is to involve users in their evaluation [2]. In physical sciences, users do not have to be involved because the goal is to discover nature's laws — evaluation, thus, requires checking whether hypothesized laws are consistent with reality. In computer science, on the other hand, the mission is to create new kinds of worlds solely for the purpose of making life easier for humans — evaluation, thus, seems to imply involving the users to verify that this is indeed the case. It seems to be particularly important to adopt this philosophy to evaluate collaborative systems, since their objective is to fundamentally change the way people do their work.

On the other hand, the vast majority of influential research projects on collaboration toolkits have not used this approach. The main problem with it is that it requires each project to be interdisciplinary and create a complete, working system, which seems too costly given the budget of a typical research project and the complexity of a collaboration toolkit; and more important, does not allow a project to converge incrementally towards a complete solution.

Nonetheless, it is not enough to simply write-up a design and leave the evaluation to its reviewers - it is necessary to do an explicit evaluation of the system.

What other techniques exist for evaluating collaboration toolkits, and how do they relate to each other? This paper addresses this question by identifying the methods that have been used for evaluating collaboration toolkits, pointing out their pros and cons, identifying the projects in which they have been used, and showing how they fit together.

2. General Requirements

It is not possible to evaluate a system without considering its requirements. In general, different systems are designed to meet different requirements. For instance, a shared window system is designed to support synchronous collaboration, while Lotus Notes is designed to support asynchronous collaboration. In order to reason, in a general fashion, about how a system should be evaluated, we must be able to abstract out system-specific requirements into generic requirements.

Three generic requirements followed in the design of collaboration (and other) software systems are the requirements of efficiency, flexibility, and ease-of-specification. The efficiency requirement implies that storage and time costs be kept low. It is the main requirement in the design of computer systems such as compilers and operating system kernels that address implementation of existing, well-accepted designs.

The other two requirements have more abstract semantics. The flexibility requirement implies that users of the system find that it meets their needs. For a collaboration toolkit, it implies that programmers be able use the toolkit to develop the kinds of collaboration functions they are asked to implement such as synchronous or asynchronous coupling.

A flexible system must offer its users primitives to exercise choices. The easc of specification of a system measures the effort required to use these primitives. Thus, in the case of a toolkit, it would measure the effort required to implement applications it is designed to support. A system requiring less specification effort than another is often termed higher-level than the other.

Besides these three requirements, other pragmatic requirements must also be considered. In particular, an important requirement for several collaboration toolkits is reuse of some class of existing single-user applications. In its most extreme form, this requirements implies that the single-user applications be shared by multiple users without any changes to them. Several collaboration toolkits have been designed to support this requirement.

Some of these requirements can conflict with each other. In particular, the ease-of-specification and reuse requirements can conflict with the flexibility requirement. The ease-of-specification requirement is often met by making certain assumptions in the toolkit, which conflicts with the flexibility requirement. Similarly, the extreme case of the reuse requirement implies that existing single-user applications be shared without adding any collaboration-aware code in them, which implies that these applications do not have the flexibility to determine how their collaboration functions are carried out. Therefore, designers of collaboration systems must often tradeoff the flexibility requirement for the ease-of-specification and reuse requirements.

As a result, it is often difficult to prove that a system is "better" than another because the two will typically make different tradeoffs in meeting conflicting requirements. Often the challenge in the design of collaborations systems is finding new, useful ways to make these tradeoffs. For instance, most of the research in collaboration toolkits has involved finding new compromises between the complete automation offered by a shared window system and the complete flexibility offered by a general-purpose distributed programming environment. Such a compromise must be justified by showing that it supports some set of collaboration functions that would require more effort in all other systems that are flexible enough to support it. For instance, only a shared X window system can support WYSIWIS sharing of collaboration-transparent single-user X applications. Similarly, Suite [4] supports a set of coupling policies that would require more effort to specify in all other systems that supported it.

The definitions of ease of specification, reuse, and efficiency requirements are independent of the collaboration function (such as access control, coupling and concurrency control) and do not need further qualification. On the other hand, the meaning of the flexibility requirement depends on the exact function being considered, because it must specify the part of the design space of the function that is to be supported, which is dependent on the function. As a result, the flexibility requirement must be decomposed into simpler function-specific requirements. For instance, in the case of Suite, a coupling-specific requirement is that it should be possible for a user to be coupled differently with different users; and a concurrency-control specific requirement is that variable-grained locking granularity should be supported. Together, all the function-specific requirements of Suite define its top-level flexibility requirement.

If a system is be evaluated, it is important to explicitly identify all of its (function-specific and general) requirements. In fact, in this author's experience, the main difference between a toolkit paper that is accepted for publication and one that is not is whether the paper explicitly shows that the system satisfies a unique set of requirements.

3. Evaluation Techniques

Evaluation of a system determines how well the system meets its requirements, and whether these requirements reflect actual users needs and/or meet well-accepted principles. We might want to know absolute evaluation information such as the exact response times of user commands, or relative information such as whether the response times of a system are better than those of another one implementing the same functions. There are several ways to evaluate a toolkit.

3.1. Inspection

A simple but effective evaluation method is to inspect the toolkit design to determine if a requirement has been met. For instance, it is possible to determine if the requirement of variable-grained locking has been met by simply inspecting the system design.

Most research efforts use this mechanism to some extent. Our work on Suite and Roseman and Greenberg's work on GroupKit [11] uses it as the main evaluation mechanism. Among all the evaluation mechanisms discussed here, inspection has apparently the lowest-cost, since it simply involves checking the design. This is indeed the case if the requirements have been carefully selected up front. In our experience, as this mechanism is used to identify what is unique about a completed design, it is often necessary to refine the original flexibility requirements to make them more specific. For instance, when we started our work on Suite, an open problem was how to support flexible coupling among the views of different users sharing an object. This became the first requirement of Suite. At about the time we met this requirement in Suite, Rendezvous [9] also did so. Therefore, when writing the papers on coupling, we had to refine this requirement into several more specific requirements such as the ability to see different representations of an object and the ability to decide when synchronization of changes to the shared object takes place. Explicitly identifying and motivating these requirements of the Suite coupling model seemed to take almost as much time as its design did! We have found this process equally challenging when evaluating other aspects of Suite such as access control, concurrency control, and merging. Thus, indirectly inspection is a fairly costly evaluation mechanism. On the other hand, it is also perhaps the most fruitful, because it helps explicitly identify the inspected requirements, which then carry forward to other projects. It is probably not fair, therefore, to charge the cost of identifying these requirements to this evaluation scheme.

Inspection of the design can also be used to determine if the requirements themselves are valid by checking if they satisfy well-accepted principles. We used this technique in our access-control work by explicitly showing that many of our access-control requirements could be derived from well-accepted access control principles, such as the need-to-know principle, which says that users should not be able to gain access to information they do not need to perform their task [7].

This approach compares toolkits based on the kinds of applications they support. Thus, it can be used to evaluate some of the specific requirements regarding the flexibility of the system and also for the reuse requirement. However, it cannot be used for the ease of specification and efficiency requirements, which require other evaluation mechanisms.

3.2. Simulations

A technique to evaluate both the flexibility and ease of specification of a toolkit is is to determine if some function of it can simulate the corresponding function of another existing system. This mechanism can be used to determine if the simulating toolkit is at least as flexible as the simulated system with respect to the function. It can be also used to determine how easy to specify the former is compared to the latter, because the size of the simulation gives an indication of the effort required to describe a functionality in the former that is provided directly by the latter. To illustrate, we used the Suite coupling function to simulate, with a few parameter settings, the coupling functions of most collaborative toolkits thereby showing that the former is more flexible than the simulated systems without being unduly low-level. We have similarly simulated existing access-control policies, merge policies, and concurrency control policies. To the best of our knowledge, no one else has adopted this evaluation approach, which we have found highly effective for evaluating a toolkit that is more general than one or more existing toolkits.

3.3. Standard Problems

Another technique to evaluate the ease of specification of computer systems is to create complete solutions to standard problems and let the evaluators of the system judge it based on these solutions. Since it is difficult to agree on the semantics of complex real problems or to understand and evaluate solutions to them, these standard problems tend be simple, toy problems, such as the dining-philosopher problem used to evaluate concurrent programming languages. However, it is an efficient technique for evaluating an system, because it gives the evaluators complete information regarding the solution to the problem without requiring them to use the system. It is particularly useful when a large number of toolkits have to be compared with each other and none of them simulates another.

Malone et al identify several candidates for standard asynchronous collaborative applications such as gIBIS and Coordinator; and describe their experience with implementing these applications using the Oval infrastructure [10]. Roseman and Greenberg have identified an interesting candidate for synchronous collaborative applications - a true "hello world" program that actually greets the "world" rather than a single user [11], and have given the complete code required to implement it using GroupKit. We have identified several other candidates for several synchronous collaborative applications including a simple multiuser talk application, text editor, outline editor, and spreadsheet; and explained how they can be implemented using Suite abstractions [4].

It may not be possible to implement all of the standard applications using a particular infrastructure. For instance, a graphical whiteboard of the kind supported by GroupKit would be a good candidate for a standard application but cannot currently be supported by Suite. The list of standard tasks/applications that can be supported by a system is an evaluation of its flexibility.

None of the evaluation steps described so far involve actual use of the toolkit by programmers. As a result, they can be taken incrementally, as each function is researched. Programmer studies, discussed below, require systems that are complete enough to be usable by programmers to build applications.

3.4. Programmer Studies

The actual experience of the programmers with a collaboration toolkit can determine whether they found the toolkit abstractions to be high-level. These data can be collected by recording the subjective answers of the programmers to questions or observing measurable data such as lines of code or time required to implement applications.

It is possible to gather programming data in several stages, by varying the target programmers and applications. There are three main kinds of programmers to consider:

- *Self*: the developers of the toolkit.
- *Lab programmers*: programmers specially recruited to evaluate the toolkit.
- *Field programmers*: programmers for whom the toolkit is intended.

There are three main applications to consider:

- *Prototypes:* applications designed for purely demonstration purposes.
- *Lab applications:* applications that are evaluated by users in controlled environments.
- *Field applications:* applications meant to be used for solving real tasks.

The reason why it is important to distinguish among these applications is that this area is so new it is not clear that programming data gathered about applications that have not been successfully evaluated in the lab or in the field is as useful as data gathered for those that have.

We have followed some of these steps by doing self implementation of a visitor scheduling application [5], which was developed by the author and used in the field for a short while to gather usage feedback; lab prototyping of the FLECSE collaborative debugger [6]; and lab implementation of the FLECSE software inspector [6], which was evaluated by lab users. Urnes and Nejabi have done lab implementations of prototype applications for several toolkits including Suite [4], GroupKit [11], and Clock [8] to compare the capabilities of these toolkits [12]. Field applications have been created using the GroupKit technology, which is widely used and is now part of a commercial product called TeamWave.

3.5. Performance Data

There are two classic measures of the efficiency of a system, space and time usage. Given the fact that memory is relatively cheap, at least on desktop and laptop computers, space usage has not been an issue in the design of most collaboration toolkits. Perhaps the only exception is our XTV extension to support migration [3], which migrates a server by replaying its log at the new machine. Since sizes of logs of window-level events can become fairly large, special techniques are used in the system to reduce their size. As collaboration toolkits are ported to handheld devices and used to generate logs of user actions (for migration, evaluation and other purposes), the space issue can be expected to become more important in their design.

Several kinds of timing measurements are significant for a collaboration toolkit:

- *local and remote responses time:* the time it takes to give feedback to a user action to the local user initiating the action and other, remote, users, respectively;
- *local and remote jitter*: the difference between the rate at which actions are issued and the rate

at which local and remote responses, respectively, are given to these actions.

- *job completion time:* the time it takes to complete a task.

The job completion time is, of course, related to the two response times but cannot be determined completely from them. The reason is that it is influenced by the dependencies among the actions of users: if a user's action does not influence the actions of other users, then the remote response time of the action does not contribute to the job completion time; otherwise it does. While some systems such as [1, 8] have measured local and remote response times, to the best of our knowledge, none of the papers published so far have reported job completion times.

Local and remote response times are also related to each other in that reducing one can increase the other. Local response time is often reduced by giving local feedback to an action without synchronizing it with the actions of other users. The likelihood of conflict, thus, increases when the actions is played at another site, and resolving it at the other end can substantially increase the remote response time. This argument assumes that the toolkit tries to maintain consistency. Instead of trading remote response time for local response time, it is also possible to trade it for consistency, as mentioned in [1]. Finally, remote jitter is reduced by buffering actions at the remote sites, which however, increases remote response times.

Two main approaches have been used to evaluate the performance of collaboration toolkits. One is to ask users of the system if they find the performance "adequate" and the other is to use benchmarks for evaluating the performance of systems. For instance, we have evaluated the performance of our toolkits by determining whether the response times were adequate in the self and lab studies. Currently, no set of general accepted benchmarks exist for collaboration systems, but once a set of standard scenarios and applications is defined, suitable benchmarks could be identified. So far, limited, simple scenarios have been used to gather performance data such as moving a node in a shared drawing window [8] and typing spaces in a shared text window [3]. At least one project has used synthetic workloads, generated by varying usage and system parameters such as number of users, inter update time and network latency [1].

	Cost	Flex.	Spec.	Effic.	Reuse
Inspection	1	1			1
Simulation	2	2	1		
Stand. Prob.	3	3	5	4	5
Self Stud.	10	6	4	3	4
Lab Stud.	100	5	3	2	3
Field Stud.	1000	4	2	1	2

Table 1: Cost and Benefits of Evaluation Techniques

4. Conclusions and Future Work

While few people today question the importance of collaboration systems, there is considerable debate as to how these systems should be evaluated. In this paper, we have identified the design space of evaluation methods for collaboration toolkits, explaining the role played by each.

Given that a requirement can be evaluated by more than technique, it would be useful to do a cost-benefit analysis of these techniques. Table 1 is a first-cut at such a "meta evaluation" based on this author's experience and intuition: a lower-number implies greater benefit and lower cost. Thus, a technique is superior to another in evaluating a requirement if the cost and benefit of the former are lower than those of the latter.

Field studies are associated with an order of magnitude more cost than lab studies because of the effort required to make the system robust and documented enough to be usable by target programmers. Lab studies are considered to have an order of magnitude more cost that self studies since they involve documenting the system, recruiting subjects, and possibly involving researchers from other disciplines to help perform the studies. Self implementation is considered to take an order of magnitude more effort than implementation of standard problems, because these problems are expected to be toy applications.

Inspection is associated with the lowest cost because the effort to identify the inspected requirements is not charged to it. As mentioned before, this effort is useful for other purposes also - describing the goals of the system and deriving requirements for follow-up projects. In the Suite project, simulating the functionality of other toolkits was more or less trivial-hence the associated cost is less than that of implementing standard toy applications. This may, of course, not be the case in other toolkits.

Inspection is considered the best technique for evaluating the flexibility and reusability of a system because its results are not application-specific. The results from simulating an entire toolkit are more valuable than those from implementing all the standard problems that can be solved by the latter - hence the relative scores for the two evaluation mechanisms. It can be expected that a carefully chosen set of standard problems will better represent a wide range of collaborative applications than those a particular project addresses. Hence a flexibility evaluation based on it is considered to more valuable than those based on the three studies. On the other hand, because the problems are toy, a specification evaluation based on it is considered less valuable than those based on the studies.

The values of the three kinds of studies are not considered to be proportional to their costs. This is because, in this author's experience, few or no surprising results have resulted from going from self to lab and field studies. This is a counter intuitive conclusion, which will hopefully start a debate in the workshop and lead to future work that explores this issue. Further work is also needed to identify other evaluation mechanisms, standard problems, and performance benchmarks; and a well accepted set of specific flexibility requirements.

Acknowledgments

The inclusion in this set of evaluation methods of inspection, standard problems, and simulations was motivated by the work of Rajiv Choudhary, Jon Munson, and Honghai Shen on undo, access control and merging, respectively, and lab implementations/studies was motivated by Vahid Mashayekhi's work on the FLECSE software inspection application. This research was supported in part by National Science Foundation grants IRI-9627619, IIS-9977362, and CDA-9624662; and by DARPA/ONR grant N 66001-96-C-8507.

REFERENCES

[1] Sumeer Bhola, Guruduth Banavar, and Mustaque Ahamad, "Responsiveness and Consistency Trade-offs in Interactive Groupware," *Procedings of ACM Computer Supported Cooperative Work*, 1998, pp. 79-88.

[2] Frederick P. Brooks, "The Computer Scientist As Toolsmith II ," *Communications of the ACM* 39:3 (1996), pp. 61-68 .

[3] Goopeel Chung and Prasun Dewan , "A Mechanism for Supporting Client Migration in a Shared Window System," *Proceedings of the Ninth Conference on User Interface Software and Technology*, October 1996, pp. 11-20.

[4] Prasun Dewan and Rajiv Choudhary, "A High-Level and Flexible Framework for Implementing Multiuser User Interfaces," *ACM Transactions on Information Systems* 10:4 (October 1992), pp. 345-380.

[5] Prasun Dewan, "Designing and Implementing Multi-User Applications: A Case Study," *Software-Practice and Experience* 23:1 (January 1993), pp. 75-94.

[6] Prasun Dewan and John Riedl, "Toward Computer-Supported Concurrent Software Engineering," *IEEE Computer* 26:1 (January 1993), pp. 17-27.

[7] Prasun Dewan and HongHai Shen, "Access Control for Multiuser Interfaces," *ACM Transactions on Computer Human Interaction* 5:1 (March 98), pp. 34-62 .

[8] T.C. Nicholas Graham, Tore Urnes, and Roy Nejabi, "Efficient Distributed Implementation of Semi-Replicated Synchronous Groupware ," *Proceedings of the Ninth Conference on User Interface Software and Technology*, October 1996, pp. 1-10.

[9] Ralph Hill, Tom Brinck, Steven Rohall, John Patterson, and Wayne Wilner, "The Rendezvous Architecture and Language for Constructing Multiuser Applications," *ACM Transactions on Computer Human Interaction* 1:2 (June 1994).

[10] Thomas W. Malone, Christopher Fry, and Kum-Yew Lai, "Experiments with Oval: A Radically Tailorable Tool for Cooperative Work," *Proceedings of CSCW'92* , 1992, pp. 289-297.

[11] Mark Roseman and Saul Greenberg, "Building Real-Time Groupware with GroupKit, A Groupware Toolkit," *ACM Transactions on Computer-Human Interaction* 3:1 (1996).

[12] Tore Urnes and Roy Nejabi, "Tools for Implementing Groupware: Survey and Evaluation," Tech Report CS-94-03, York University, 1994.

The Mechanics of Collaboration: Developing Low Cost Usability Evaluation Methods for Shared Workspaces

Carl Gutwin[1] and Saul Greenberg[2]
[1]*Department of Computer Science, University of Saskatchewan*
[2]*Department of Computer Science, University of Calgary*
gutwin@cs.usask.ca, saul@cpsc.ucalgary.ca

Abstract

We introduce a conceptual framework that articulates the mechanics of collaboration for shared-workspace groupware: the low level actions and interactions that must be carried out to complete a task in a shared manner. These include communication, coordination, planning, monitoring, assistance, and protection. The framework also includes three general measures of these mechanics: effectiveness, efficiency, and satisfaction. The underlying idea of the framework is that some usability problems in groupware systems are not inherently tied to the social context in which the system is used, but rather are a result of poor support for the basic activities of collaborative work in shared spaces. We believe that existing low-cost evaluation methods—heuristic evaluation, walkthroughs, user observations and questionnaires—can be modified to include this framework in a way that helps a groupware evaluator uncover these usability problems.

1. Introduction

With the increasing connectivity of the internet, the increasing power of the world-wide web, and the increasingly distributed nature of organizations, multi-user computer systems (groupware) are becoming increasingly common. Despite this growth, many groupware systems have serious usability problems. At best, working in groupware is awkward and frustrating compared to face-to-face collaboration.

There are many reasons for this poor usability. We have only sketchy knowledge of how people collaborate, and translating what we do know into effective designs is difficult. As well, the effort involved in assessing prototypes and final systems is onerous because there are no simple but effective evaluation techniques for groupware. In this paper, we will concentrate on this evaluation problem. In particular, we will propose a conceptual framework that will help us develop discount usability evaluation techniques that can be readily applied to the iterative development cycle (design, implementation, and evaluation) of groupware.

Traditionally, researchers and developers consider groupware evaluation a difficult problem, especially when compared to the relative ease of evaluating single-user systems. An oft-cited factor is that groupware acceptance is far more likely to be affected by social factors such as organizational culture, differences in personalities, and group dynamics (e.g. [7]). These combine to make the task of understanding group interaction a 'wicked problem' [5]. Consequently, traditional experimental and laboratory methods that remove the software from its context of use may obtain simplistic results that do not generalize well to real-world situations.

As an alternate to the laboratory, many groupware researchers now advocate the use ethnographic and sociologic methods that explicitly consider culture and context (e.g., [10,16]). While these methods have been successfully applied to real situations, they tend to be expensive and somewhat limited. They demand considerable time and evaluator experience. They work best at the beginning of design (to uncover and articulate existing work practices) and at the end (to evaluate how systems already deployed in the work setting are used). Because they are unsuited for rapid prototype evaluation, they are rarely appropriate for iterative design.

We agree that contextual considerations are extremely important. However, we also believe that there is pragmatic value in a complimentary perspective. Specifically, we claim some groupware usability problems are not strongly tied to social or organizational issues, but rather are caused by insufficient or mismatched support for the basic activities of collaboration. These activities, which we call the mechanics of collaboration, are the small-scale actions and interactions that group members must carry out in order to get a shared task done. Examples include communicating information, coordinating manipulations, or monitoring one another.

The activities that form these mechanics of collaboration are particularly important in shared-workspace groupware, where the group task involves objects, artifacts, and tools in a visual workspace. In

0-7695-0798-9/00 $10.00 © 2000 IEEE

systems like this, if a group is unable to communicate effectively and efficiently about the task, or is unable to smoothly and easily coordinate their actions, performance and satisfaction are likely to suffer. The mechanics of collaboration are by and large separate from organizational politics or group dynamics, and usability problems in the mechanics can therefore be discovered and ironed out during iterative design. Although appropriate support for the mechanics of collaboration will not guarantee a system's suitability in the real world, failure to support them will almost certainly guarantee its demise.

In this paper we develop a conceptual framework defining groupware usability for shared-workspaces that is based on the mechanics of collaboration. We describe these mechanics, and propose that various single-user usability testing schemes can be applied to groupware by having them assess support for the mechanics. We believe that evaluating for these mechanics provides a middle ground between the brittleness of controlled experimentation and the expense of field techniques. While not complete on their own, they will provide a useful addition to the practitioner's toolbox.

2. Shared-Workspace Groupware

Groupware allows people to work together across time and distance. An important class of groupware systems is that of applications that support distant collaboration though a shared workspace— a medium sized flat work surface where people collaborate by manipulating visible tools and task artifacts.

Common applications in this class include shared editors, drawing programs, and multi-player games. For example, a shared design application could allow engineers from several different sites to plan, view, and

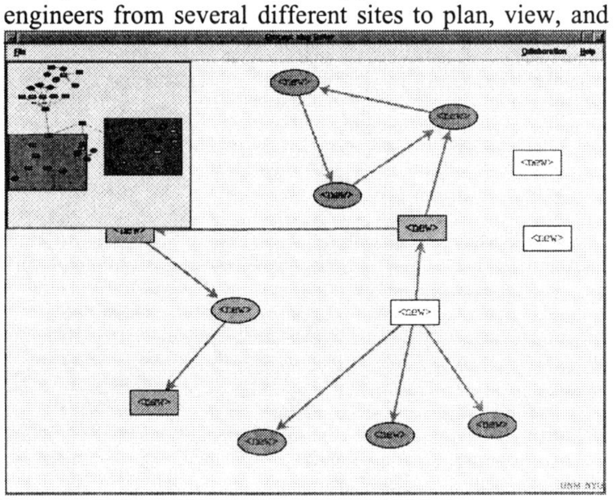

Figure 1. An example shared-workspace groupware system for creating and editing concept maps. A radar overview [8] is visible at top left.

manipulate new parts for a manufacturing process. Similarly, a group troubleshooting system could allow expertise from many locations to be gathered together to investigate a problem and explore possible solutions (e.g. [19]).

The group tasks that happen in these systems tend to be of a few types. Based on McGrath's (1984) task circumplex, tasks in shared workspaces usually involve:

- creation of new artifacts,
- organization of existing artifacts,
- exploration of the space or of a set of artifacts,
- construction of larger objects from component pieces,
- the management of an autonomous system represented in the workspace.

3. The Mechanics of Collaboration

For a collaborative task to be accomplished in a shared workspace, a variety of activities must happen. First, the actual execution of the task must occur— words put on paper, objects placed in order, or parts fixed together to form a whole. This part of the task is no different for a group than it is for an individual, since the same actions still have to happen if the job is to get done. However, most group work involves another set of entirely different activities as well. If we consider task execution to be the *taskwork*, then this other set of activities is the *teamwork*— the work of working together— and a groupware system must support both taskwork and teamwork if it is to be truly usable.

Teamwork can be further divided into two areas: the social and affective elements that make up group dynamics, and the mechanics of collaboration. Although affective elements are important, we will not consider them further here. This leaves us with the mechanics— the things that groups have to do, over and above what an individual has to do, in order to carry out a task.

From our previous research on shared-workspaces (e.g., [9]) and from the literature (e.g., [1,20]), we have identified seven major activities that comprise the mechanics of collaboration.

Explicit communication. Group members intentionally provide each other with information, and verbal and written communication is a cornerstone of collaboration. In a visual workspace, however, the workspace and the artifacts themselves are crucial supports to explicit communication. In particular, people often use deictic references (e.g. "this one") in combination with pointing to an artifact.

Consequential communication. In addition to explicit communication, people also pick up considerable information that is unintentionally "given off" by others as they go about their activities. This is called consequential communication [17] and is also important in smooth group operation. Two main types of consequential communication involve information given off by artifacts as they are manipulated by others (also called feedthrough – [3]), and information given off by the characteristic actions of a person's embodiment in the workspace.

Coordination of action. People organize their actions in a shared workspace so that they do not conflict with others. Shared resources and tools require that turns be taken, and some tasks require that actions happen in particular orders. In addition, people also learn to predict one anothers' actions and use those predictions to make the group more effective or efficient. Symptoms of poor coordination include people bumping into one another, duplicating actions that another person has just completed, or attempting to take shared resources at the same time.

Planning. Some planning activities are too high-level to be considered mechanics of collaboration, but others happen repeatedly inside the shared workspace. For example, people divide and redivide the task as they go along, reserve areas of the workspace for their use, or consider various courses of action by simulating them in the workspace (e.g. indicating a path with a pointer before construction begins).

Monitoring. Many of the other mechanics of collaboration rely on the ability to monitor and gather information about others in the workspace. Much of this information is simply workspace awareness information [9]: who is in the workspace, where they are working, and what they are doing. In addition, there are situations where people monitor one another more explicitly. For example, in an apprenticeship situation, the expert must monitor the activities and whereabouts of the novice even if they are not always working in the same place.

Assistance. Group members provide help to one another when it is needed. Assistance may be opportunistic and informal, where the situation makes it easy for one person to help another, or it may be explicitly requested; either way, appropriate help requires that people understand what others are doing and where they are at in their tasks.

Protection. One danger in group work is that others may inadvertently alter or destroy work that you yourself have carried out. People must therefore keep an eye on their own work, noticing what effects others' actions could have and taking actions to prevent certain activity.

4. The Mechanics & Groupware Usability

The mechanics of collaboration, and the concept of teamwork more generally, allow us to state a definition of groupware usability that goes beyond what is normally included in single-user usability studies. We define groupware usability as:

> ... the degree to which a groupware system supports the mechanics of collaboration for a particular set of users and a particular set of tasks [8].

This definition assumes that a groupware system is already usable from a single-user perspective, and concentrates specifically on usability aspects of group interaction. From this definition, we can now begin to consider ways of evaluating for the mechanics of groupware specifically, and for groupware usability in general. In particular, we believe that we can test for the mechanics of collaboration by examining if a group can perform them effectively, efficiently, and pleasantly (e.g. [14]). Each is described in turn below.

Effectiveness considers whether the activity was successfully completed, and the number and severity of errors made during that activity. A usable groupware system will not prevent the mechanics of collaboration from taking place, and will not cause group members to make undue errors in those activities.

Efficiency considers the resources (such as time or effort) required to carry out the activity. A good groupware system will allow the activities of collaboration to proceed with less time and effort than will a system with usability problems. Note that any measures of efficiency must be carefully focused on task activities, since groups often engage in off-task activities that are not detrimental to the overall shared work.

Satisfaction considers whether the group members are reasonably happy with the processes and outcomes of each of the activities of collaboration. Satisfaction will sometimes overlap with efficiency and effectiveness (that is, problems in the other areas are likely to reduce satisfaction).

Matching the seven mechanics of groupware against these three criteria measures provides a conceptual framework for evaluating groupware (see Table 1).

	Effectiveness	Efficiency	Satisfaction
Explicit communication			
Consequential communication			
Coordination of action			
Planning			
Monitoring			
Assistance			
Protection			

Table 1. The conceptual framework.

Using this framework, we will briefly revisit several discount usability techniques originally developed and successfully applied for evaluating singleware usability. Others are also pursuing the goal of low-cost evaluation techniques for groupware (e.g.[2]), and these efforts are complementary. Our approach can be seen as a bottom-up method that originates from a fixed set of face-to-face collaborative behaviours rather from a top-down analysis of groupware features and characteristics.

With each technique, we will ask if it could be used to test if a group can perform a particular mechanical activity effectively, efficiently, and pleasantly. We caution that this discussion is quite preliminary, and we have not yet evaluated these evaluation methods.

5. Revisiting Discount Evaluation Methods

Because we are interested in techniques that can be done rapidly, we do not consider quantitative measures that require experimental methods or extensive analysis (e.g. performance measures or data-log analysis). Instead, we rely on interface inspection techniques such as heuristic evaluation and task-centered walkthroughs (e.g., [13]), observational methods (e.g., [4]) and subjective assessments by realistic participants (e.g. [15,18]). We describe each below, and assume that an evaluation of these interfaces from a single-user perspective (perhaps done earlier or in parallel) have already uncovered and repaired conventional usability problems.

5.1 Heuristic evaluation

Heuristic evaluation is a widely-accepted discount evaluation method for diagnosing potential usability problems in user interfaces. It defines a particular interface inspection process where several evaluators examine an interface and judge its compliance with recognized usability principles called 'heuristics' [12]. Heuristics draw attention to usability problems often found in single user systems, such as how feedback is provided, how errors are minimized, how help is provided, and so on. Non-compliant aspects of the interface are captured as interface bug reports, where evaluators describe the problem, its severity, and perhaps even suggestions of how to fix it.

We can apply heuristic evaluation techniques to groupware usability by replacing the current set of heuristics by rephrasing those activities that comprise the mechanics of collaboration[1]. For example, groupware heuristics can now be statements such as "Provide the means for explicit communication" and "Allow people to monitor and gather information about others in the workspace". The inspector can then judge the interface by seeing if the means for groups to achieve a particular heuristic is available; if the means are there, the inspector can then ask if the group can use it effectively, efficiently, and with satisfaction.

The high-level nature of these heuristics as well as the small number of them (7) fits with Nielsen's (1994) view of how heuristics should be crafted. As with conventional heuristic evaluation, issues to consider include: how inspectors can be trained to the nuances of these heuristics; whether inspectors can use them effectively to uncover interface problems; how many inspectors are needed to discover the majority of interface problems, and whether these heuristics actually cover a large proportion of the usability problems typically found in groupware.

5.2 Walkthroughs

Another inspection technique is based on the notion of an interface walk-through. While there are many variations of how to perform a walkthrough, in all of them the inspector begins with a realistic and detailed task description, a description of the user, and an interface to evaluate. The inspector then 'walks through' the interface step by step by imagining each action the user would take while performing the task on the particular system. During each step the inspector asks a series of questions. In a task-centered walkthrough [11] the questions include:

1. Can you build a believable story that motivates the user's actions?
2. Can you rely on the user's expected knowledge and training about the system?

If the inspector believes that these questions cannot be answered satisfactorily, then a potential interface problem has been located. The inspector notes it, assumes it has been solved, and goes on to the next step.

Other variations of walkthroughs ask different questions, but almost all are concerned with how single users understand the system and use it to achieve a particular goal. In groupware, it may be possible to perform a walkthrough by articulating tasks that exercise the mechanics of groupware, and by asking questions related to the criteria. For example, a detailed task description would now include activities such as 'Saul and Carl are modifying an architectural floor plan. They examine the current floor plan, and discuss what needs to be changed. Carl makes the living room two meters larger. Saul sees this, and suggests that this would compromise the amount of cupboard space… 'For each step in this process, the inspector would then ask:

1. Can the person/group perform the activity of groupware implied by this step effectively i.e., does the interface supply the means to do it?
2. Can it be performed efficiently i.e., is it believable that the person/group would go through the effort

[1] We have also developed another set of heuristics based on the Locales Framework that could be applied to groupware [6].

required by this interface to perform this step?

3. Can it be performed with satisfaction i.e., is it believable that the person/group would be motivated to do this step, and would they be happy with the outcome?

Of course, there are several issues. First, it is much easier to define a 'typical person' than it is to define a 'typical group'. The richness and variety of group interactions makes them much harder to typify. Second, we don't know if the task descriptions that drive the walkthrough can be expanded sufficiently to include not only taskwork, but to articulate teamwork as well. Finally, we expect that it will be harder for an inspector to answer the three questions above because of the difficulty of predicting particular group interactions.

5.3 Usability testing through observations

Observational user testing is done by observing how people perform particular tasks on a system in a laboratory setting [4]. The evaluator typically tries to observe where people have problems performing a task, and monitors people's talk to see where their conceptual model of the system is at odds with the actual system model. To get people to talk, the evaluator often asks them to 'talk-aloud' i.e., to say what they are doing as they are doing an action. Alternatively, the evaluator would have two people perform a task together, and monitor their speech for insights into what each was thinking.

Groupware evaluation would be similar, with the exception that the evaluators would be trained to observe and analyze the collaboration through a set of criteria based on the conceptual framework presented in Table 1. This could be done either on-the-fly (perhaps noted on a coding sheet), or after the fact (i.e., through video analysis using video annotation software). For example, the criteria for the first row of Table 1 (explicit communication/effectiveness, efficiency, satisfaction) can be partially restated as:

Intelligibility and interpretability of spoken-written-gestural communication:

a) Did the system make it difficult to hear/read what others were saying/writing?
b) Did the system make it difficult to understand what others were saying/writing?
c) Did the system make it difficult to gesture and refer to items in the workspace?
d) Did the system make it difficult to see and understand what others were pointing to?

Of course, there are several issues with this method. First is the difficulty of acquiring suitable people for observations: it is harder to schedule, and harder to predict the expected group interaction. If the software expects a certain level of intimacy between collaborators, then the subject pool may be quite small. Second is the difficulty of interpreting a scene based on these questions. While people may be having problems, groups are remarkably resilient at adapting their interactions to succeed in even awkward collaborative situations.

5.4 User questionnaires

Several researchers advocate evaluation through questionnaires that are filled in by the people using the system (e.g. [15,18]). This could be done after a usability observation (as described above), where the participants would complete the questionnaire. The evaluators could then conduct a group interview to follow up both their observations and the questionnaire answers, perhaps including discussions of possible solutions to the problems.

Similar to our other methods, we would create a groupware questionnaire by organizing it around the seven activities of collaboration. These include questions that consider effectiveness, efficiency, and satisfaction in each area. Since the data is largely subjective, observations or answers should be used as indications that problems may exist in a particular area rather than definitive assessments; agreement between multiple participants or observers, of course, is a stronger indication of a problem.

The questionnaire would be similar to the ones used by evaluators (Section 5.3) but rephrased to be answered from the person's experiences. For example, the criteria for the first row of Table 1 can be partially restated as:

Intelligibility and interpretability of spoken-written-gestural communication

a) It was easy to hear/read what other people were saying/writing
b) It was easy to understand what others were saying/writing
c) It was easy to gesture and refer to items in the workspace
d) It was easy to see and understand what others were pointing to

Issues here are similar to those discussed in Section 5.3. Additional issues are that we have to pay particular attention to the wording of these questions (both to make them understandable and to reduce any implicit bias), and that we cannot afford too many questions as this may make people reluctant to answer them.

6. Conclusions

In this paper, we introduced a conceptual framework for developing discount usability evaluation techniques that can be applied to shared-workspace groupware. The framework is based on support for the mechanics of collaboration: the low level actions and interactions that must be carried out to complete a task in a shared manner. These include communication, coordination, planning, monitoring, assistance, and protection. The framework also includes gross measures of these mechanics: effectiveness, efficiency, and satisfaction. The underlying idea of the framework is that some usability problems in groupware systems are not inherently tied to the social context in which the system is used, but rather are a result of poor support for the basic activities of collaborative work in shared spaces. We believe evaluation schemes based on this framework will occupy a middle ground between brittle experimental techniques and time-consuming field techniques, where they will provide the kind of formative information valuable in an iterative groupware development process.

This is initial work. We have performed only limited testing of how well particular evaluation methods can be adopted to the framework in Table 1. In particular, we have drafted a set of detailed questions to drive user observations and user questionnaires, available from www.cs.usask.ca/projects/hci/. Early indications are that the scheme does provide people with a framework for considering issues that they would have otherwise missed. However, the questionnaires are still being revised, particularly to reduce the number of questions and to improve the clarity of the questions.

As our work matures, we plan to evaluate the various groupware evaluation methods in two ways. First, a particular testing scheme will be applied to a system with known groupware usability problems; afterwards, we will analyze how well evaluators using the scheme could uncover particular problems. In this approach, the testing scheme could also be compared with other evaluation techniques; if a scheme can identify problems that other methods cannot, then the scheme has some value. Second, we will use the various schemes in the context for which it was intended— iterative design of groupware. We will observe its use on a realistic development project, and determine whether the development team finds the scheme to be useful in improving the usability of the final product.

Acknowledgments. We gratefully acknowledge the support of the National Institute of Standards and Technology (NIST), Microsoft Research, and the Natural Sciences and Engineering Research Council (NSERC).

[1] Clark, H. (1996) *Using Language*. Cambridge University Press, Cambridge.

[2] Drury, J., Damianos, L., Fanderclai, T., Kurtz, J., Hirschman, L., and Linton, F. (1999) Methodology for Evaluation of Collaborative Systems. Technical Report (version 4.0), The Evaluation Working Group of the DARPA Intelligent Collaboration and Visualization Program.

[3] Dix, A., Finlay, J., Abowd, G., and Beale, R. (1993) *Human-Computer Interaction*, Prentice Hall.

[4] Dumas, J.S. and Redish, J.C. (1993) *A Practical Guide to Usability Testing*. Ablex, 1993.

[5] Fitzpatrick, G. (1998) *The Locales Framework: Understanding and Designing for Cooperative Work*. PhD Thesis, Department of Computer Science and Electrical Engineering, The University of Queensland

[6] Greenberg, S., Fitzpatrick, G., Gutwin, C. and Kaplan, S. (1999). Adapting the Locales Framework for Heuristic Evaluation of Groupware. *Proceedings of OZCHI'99 Australian Conference on Computer Human Interaction*, Wagga Wagga, NSW Australia, November 28-30.

[7] Grudin, J. (1990) Groupware and cooperative work: Problems and prospects. In *The Art of Human Computer Interface Design*, B. Laurel, Ed. Addison-Wesley, 171-185.

[8] Gutwin, C. and Greenberg, S. (1999). The Effects of Workspace Awareness Support on the Usability of Real-Time Distributed Groupware. *ACM Transactions on Computer-Human Interaction (TOCHI)* 6 (3), 243-281.

[9] Gutwin, C. and Greenberg, S. (1999) A Framework of Awareness for Small Groups in Shared-Workspace Groupware. Research Report 99-2, Computer Science Department, University of Saskatchewan.

[10] Hughes, J., King, V., Rodden, T. and Andersen, H. (1994) Moving out of the control room: Ethnography in system design. In *Proc CSCW'94*, p429439, ACM Press.

[11] Lewis & Reiman (1993) *Task Centered User Interface Design*. From ftp.cs.ucolorado.edu/pub/cs/distribs/clewis/

[12] Nielsen, J. (1994) Heuristic Evaluation. In Nielsen and Mack (1994)

[13] Nielsen, J. and Mack, R. (editors) (1994) *Usability Inspection Methods*. Wiley and Sons.

[14] Olson, J. S., Olson, G. M., Storrosten, M., and Carter, M. (1992). How a group-editor changes the character of a design meeting as well as its outcome, Proc. CSCW'92, Toronto, Ontario, 1992, 91-98.

[15] Ravden, S. and Johnson, G. (1989) Evaluating Usability of Human-Computer Interfaces. John Wiley & Sons.

[16] Rogers, Y. and Bellotti, V. (1997) Grounding blue-sky research: How can ethnography help? *Interactions*, 4(3), 58-63.

[17] Segal, L. (1995) Designing Team Workstations: The Choreography of Teamwork, in *Local Applications of the Ecological Approach to Human-Machine Systems*, P. Hancock, J. Flach, J. Caird and K. Vicente ed., 392-415, Lawrence Erlbaum, Hillsdale, NJ.

[18] Shneiderman, B. (1997) Designing the User Interface. Addison-Wesley, 1997.

[19] Steves, M., and Knutilla, A. (1999) Collaboration Technologies for Global Manufacturing, Proceedings of ASME Symposium on Manufacturing Logistics in a Global Economy, Nashville TN.

[20] Tang, J. (1991) Findings from Observational Studies of Collaborative Work, *International Journal of Man-Machine Studies*, 34(2), 143-160.

CollabLogger: A Tool for Visualizing Groups At Work

Emile Morse & Michelle Potts Steves
National Institute of Standards & Technology
100 Bureau Drive
Gaithersburg, MD 20899
(301) 975-8239
{emile.morse, msteves}@nist.gov

Abstract

The CollabLogger is a visual tool that has been developed to support usability analyses of human-computer interaction in a team environment. The participants in the computer-mediated activity were engaged in a small-scale manufacturing testbed project. Interactions of the group were mediated by Teamwave Workplace[1] and the members performed both synchronous and asynchronous activities depending on their availability, project requirements, and due to chance meetings in the collaborative space. The software was instrumented to log users' interactions with the system and each other. The CollabLogger addresses the problem of helping investigators analyze the volumes of log data that groupware tools can generate. Visual tools are powerful when large amounts of diverse data present themselves. The place-based collaboration environment offered by Teamwave Workplace provided a level of organization that allowed us to create a visual interface with which to perform exploratory sequential data analysis.

Keywords: collaboration environments, software usability, visualization, exploratory sequential data analysis

Introduction

The current state of computing environments has changed remarkably from the days of single-user applications to one in which data, applications and users are distributed and interconnected. Increasingly, organizations are creating virtual teams that may be not only working at different locations but might also work asynchronously. At other times these same users may be collocated, working synchronously either by plan or by accident. Computer-mediated workspaces can be populated with a diverse assortment of objects; the states of all these components are subject to change depending on a myriad of actions by the users and the system. Although groupware systems can be instrumented to capture system and user actions, it is clear that the types of interactions in collaborative systems are more complex than in single-user applications, if only due to the multiple users.

Evaluation of human-computer interaction is the purview of usability professionals. They need arsenals of appropriate tools to perform the functions of determining whether an interface is supporting the goals and objectives of the system. The extra complexity of groupware systems involves detection and processing of not only human-computer interactions but also human-human interactions. A powerful tool for performing complicated data analysis is provided by the use of visualization.

Subsequent sections of this paper describe 1) previous, related work in the areas of exploratory sequential data analysis, data logging granularity issues, time-based visualizations, 2) the scenario which led to our development of the CollabLogger, and 3) the logging tool itself. Finally some conclusions and directions for future work will be discussed

Background and Related Studies

Pertinent literature related to the current topic comes from two main areas:

- What data can be captured vs. what data is useful to capture in time-based situations, and
- Other studies that have applied a visual approach to analyzing time-based data.

[1] Teamwave Workplace [1]is a commercial product identified in this document for the purpose of describing a collaborative software environment. This identification does not imply any recommendation or endorsement by the National Institute of Standards and Technologies.

Data issues

The work of Sanderson & Fisher [2] on exploratory sequential data analysis (ESDA) discusses the range of event types in human-human interaction. These authors note that the granularity of capturable events range from eye movements and gestures which change many times per second, while turn-taking and topic changing occur over intervals ranging from several seconds to about 10 minutes. Meetings last between a minute and several hours, while projects may extend for months or even years. The enormous variability in the granularity and duration of these events from a user-centric perspective lead to a consideration of the parallel set of computer-centric events that are possible to capture.

Indeed, the answer to this question can be found in the work of Hilbert & Redmiles [3]. They have studied how user interface events can be categorized to yield high-level usability data. These authors describe the types of abstractions in user interactions in a hierarchy whose levels are physical events, input device events, user interface (UI) events, abstract interaction events (e.g., providing values in input fields), domain/task related events and goal/problem-related events. Attention to all these levels at one time is as difficult as addressing all the levels of human-human interaction. They suggest that visualization is useful for presenting the results of transformations and other data reduction techniques to leverage the human visual abilities to detect relationships among events.

Regardless of whether a human- or computer-centric yardstick is used to measure the scale of the problem, it is clear that the data set created from interactions of a user with a computer system is likely to be very large. In addition, multi-user, collaboration systems will necessarily experience a combinatorial explosion due to potential and actual interactions between the multiple users. Such data-rich environments are obvious targets for visual solutions [4].

Time-based visualizations

LifeLines was developed by Plaisant, Milash, Rose, Widoff & Shneiderman [5] as a mechanism for displaying personal histories. They describe medical and juvenile justice scenarios implemented with the interface. Overview, zooming, and filtering are all facilitated in the LifeLines display. The data comprises information about single individuals and it is not apparent how the interface could be extended to cope with data from collaborative settings with many individuals.

Morse & Spring [6] presented a set of visualizations that were based on data gathered using the CASCADE (Computer Augmented Support for Collaborative Authoring and Document Editing) system. Although the environment was collaborative in nature, the data in the visualizations that they describe were filtered by user before rendering. This filtering leads to a situation in which relationships among team members can not be detected.

The Multi-Modal Logger was developed at MITRE [7] to record, retrieve, annotate and visualize data from a variety of sources, including audio and video. The visualization tool that is part of the MML toolkit presents the usability engineer with a timeline on the x-axis and a set of objects along the y-axis. Objects may represent users, audio logs, collaborative tool invocations or other significant components of the team environment. Filtering the data to select only the users yields a display that indicates when each user was active (i.e., creating loggable events) but makes it impossible to determine what the users were doing. On the other hand, if the display is not filtered then inferences about users' activities are possible but are made difficult due to the potentially large number of object (i.e., timelines).

Kimber et al [8] have presented a time-based visualization that handles data derived from audio sources. Their system is capable of detecting boundaries between multiple speakers and other sounds. Their graphical display shows the identities of the speakers and attributions for other sounds (e.g., laughter). It also uses a sliding marker to indicate the current position in the playback of the audio; the marker can be dragged to wind the media to a particular area of interest. In addition, the interface has mechanisms for overview and zoom.

The literature related to data classification leads us to believe that it is important to consider that log data for collaborative activities must be gathered at sufficient granularity to support all possible uses that might be made of the data but, more importantly, that mechanisms need to built into the interface to the data to accomplish dynamic filtering of the data. The work on visualizations validates this approach to the treatment of time-based data, while showing that none of the interfaces developed thus far has provided a full answer to the problems of handling multi-user, interaction data.

Manufacturing Collaboratory Scenario

The CollabLogger was developed to support usability analyses of human-computer interactions in a manufacturing research project at NIST involving an automated gas-metal robotic welding testbed. NIST welding researchers are a geographically dispersed team, working to define interface standards between welding work cell components, controllers and power supplies. To achieve this, a functioning welding testbed has been implemented for testing the interfaces between components, equipment and power supplies. Analysis of

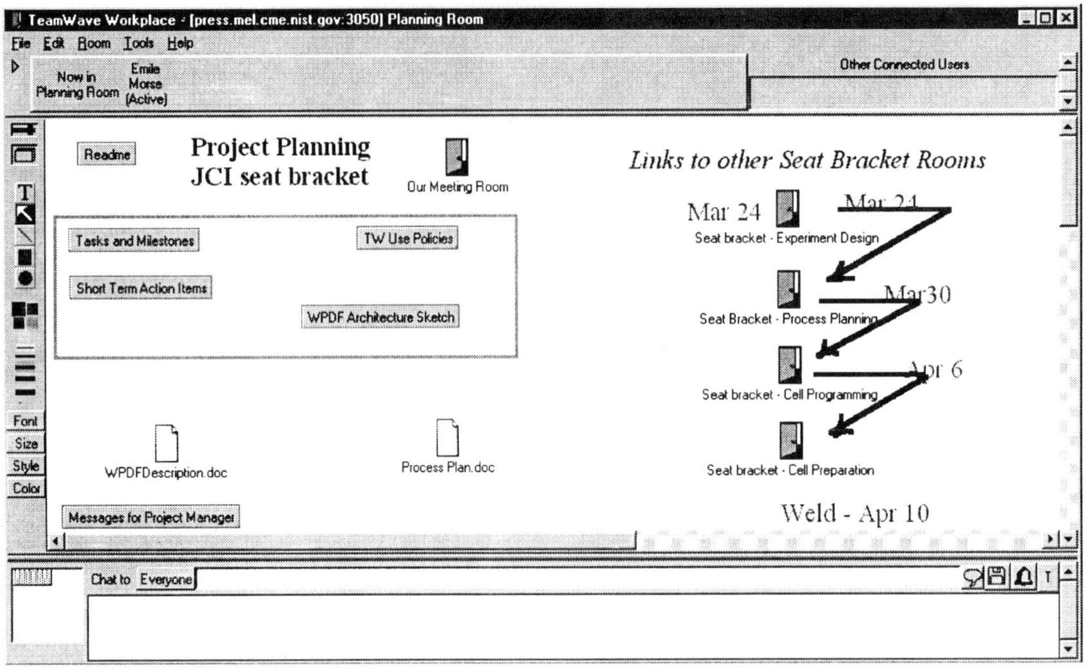

Figure 1: Teamwave Workplace environment for welding project

welds is performed to verify effective operation of interfaces, etc. [9]

The core welding research team is comprised of five people with six roles divided among them and additional guest researchers, who may be distantly located from the physical location of the welding testbed itself. Typically, a welding experiment can be characterized by the following set of tasks:

- Define the experiment (select experimental or developed interface standards and equipment, select the part to be welded -- e.g., automotive bracket, ship plate, select types of welds to be performed, etc.).
- Conduct a synchronous meeting to establish an experiment timeline and deadlines.
- Perform relatively sequential and primarily solitary tasks to set-up the experiment, e.g., procure and prepare the materials, program the robot, test the program using simulation, etc.
- Perform the initial weld(s), with most team members present, some virtually.
- Review the weld data; this is typically performed synchronously by the team if no difficult problem welds are detected. If difficult problem welds occur, typically the welding engineer reviews the weld data asynchronously to analyze the problem and report his finding back to the group.
- Iterate performing welds, varying experiment parameters as defined in the experiment plan until weld results indicate success.

This set of tasks is representative of how many groups work, i.e., in a variety of ways to best achieve their work objective(s). [10]

The CSCW Environment

Each of the participants in the welding collaboratory has access to a Teamwave Workplace[2] client from his desktop computer as well as computers in the welding testbed. Teamwave Workplace (Figure 1) is a shared, room-based collaborative system with a WYSIWIS (what you see is what I see) whiteboard backdrop. Rooms provide boundaries for data groupings and user interactions and a metaphor for easing the transition in groupware [11]. Doorways provide portals to other rooms. Data organization within rooms is configurable by its occupants in how they organize various tools housing their data, such as file viewers, PostIt™ notes, and message boards. FileHolders and ImageHolders are used for linking documents and graphics that may have been created outside of Teamwave Workplace. The system provides for synchronous and asynchronous user interactions, but importantly,

[2] Teamwave Workplace [1] is a commercial product identified in this document for the purpose of describing a collaborative software environment. This identification does not imply any recommendation or endorsement by the National Institute of Standards and Technologies.

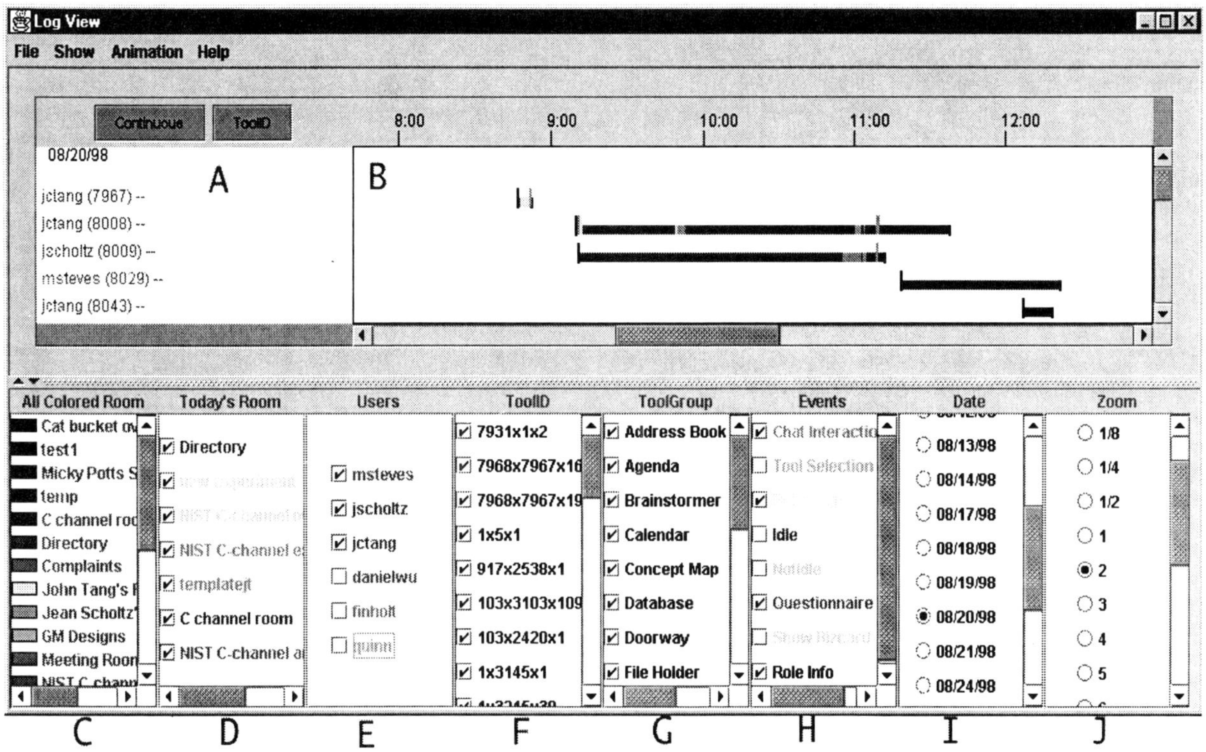

Figure 2: CollabLogger using User ID mode

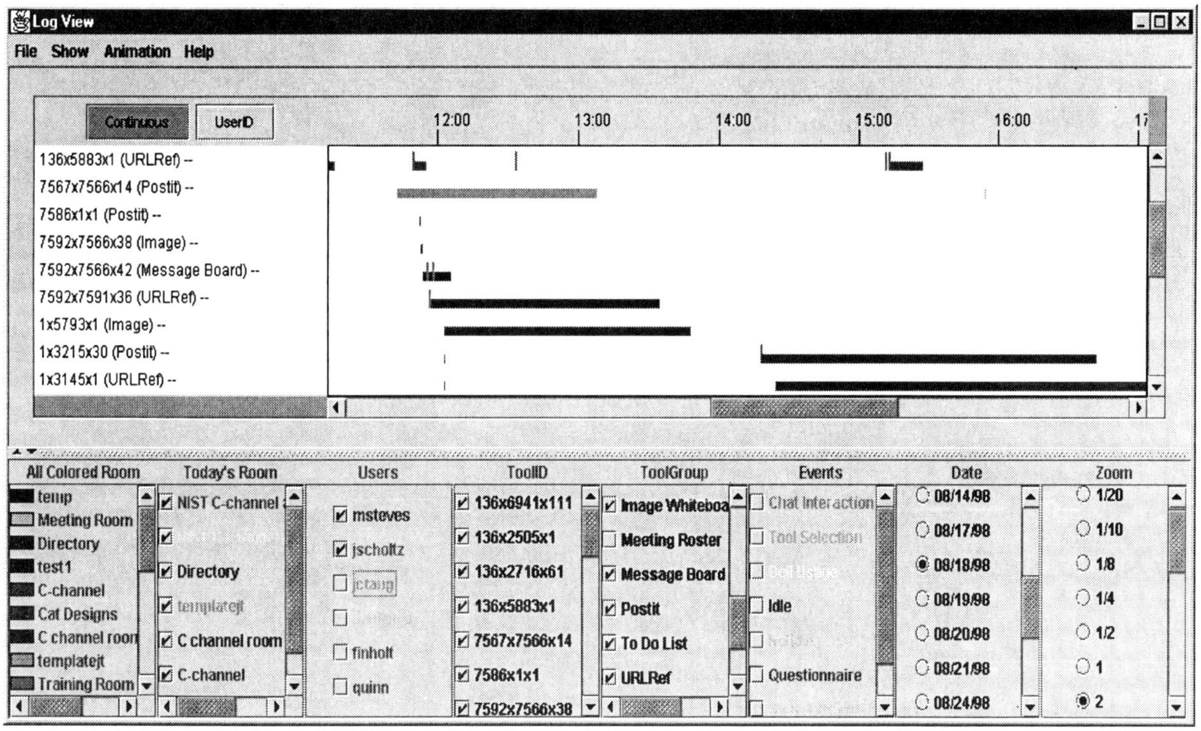

Figure 3: CollabLogger using Tool ID mode

these interactions are in the context of relevant data [12].

The version of TeamWAVE used in this project has been instrumented to capture information about users, TeamWAVE tools, and rooms. Each event is time-stamped by the server and keyed by user.

CollabLogger Description and Functions

The CollabLogger application (Figures 2 and 3) is written in Java 1.2. The menu bar provides access to specialized functions such as replay and symbol overlay. The leftmost panel (A) provides labels for the timelines shown in the main panel of the display. These labels can be toggled between a user-centric view (Figure 2) and a tool-centric one (Figure 3). The figures show log data zoomed in to a 4-hour time slice. The toggle button for user/tool mode is located immediately above the label list. The other button is a toggle that allows an overview of the entire log or a view of a single day.

The lower portion of the Logger window contains the controls by which the analyst interacts with the display. Checkboxes provide a mechanism to show or hide data in a particular view. Each room is color-coded and the panel C displays the mapping for all rooms in the log regardless of whether the current view has information about a particular room. The panel D shows the list of rooms that were occupied during the current day. Panel E allows selection of a subset of users. Information in the panels F and G is related to tool ID. Each instance of a tool is associated with a unique ID and these are displayed in panel F. Panel G allows hiding of tool information at the level of type of tool. For instance, the analyst may want to view all invocations of the 'Address Book' tool only. Events are shown in panel H and the user can delimit the set of markers by checking boxes next to the event type. Panel I allows selection among time segments based on days found in the current master log. Panel J provides a crude zoom tool.

The main display panel (B) of Figure 2 shows that 5 sessions occurred during the time period under investigation. The bars show which room(s) each user occupied during his/her session. Tick marks colored to map to an event type are overlaid on these bars. The particular session shown here reveals that more than one worker was present in the collaborative environment during most of the time. It also shows that these users engaged in multiple chat sessions. By filtering the data with the controls, it is possible to explore the information space. Inferences can be drawn and hypotheses can be formed that might be subjected to statistical treatment. Usability analysts working on collaborative data sets might be interested in answering the following kinds of questions:

- How often do multiple users occupy the space simultaneously?
- Which rooms are the most frequently visited?
- Are there patterns in the paths that users take within a set of rooms?
- Do particular users appear to be leading the activities?

Although the answers to the above questions could certainly be answered definitively using a statistical approach, visualizations allow the formulation of the questions themselves. Detecting patterns, outliers, densities, and gaps are innate abilities of the human visual system.

Figure 3 gives a different perspective of the data; it shows a list of tool invocations relative to time. An analyst using CollabLogger could manipulate the display by filtering and zooming to investigate:

- Are there combinations of tools that are often used in conjunction with one another?
- What tools are used in a room during joint occupancy vs. single occupancy?
- Are doorways an effective navigation tool? (# of hops, etc.)
- Which communication tools are used the most?

Once again the interface serves as a way to rapidly decide how best to formulate relevant hypotheses.

Summary and Future Directions

Usability analyses of collaborative environments are difficult to perform partly due to the potentially complex interactions between the users of the groupware. Users interact not only with each other but also with information objects and tools provided by the environment. The CollabLogger has been useful in allowing usability professionals to detect subtle interactions, which can then be subjected to more quantitative methods of analysis. One example of a use for the CollabLogger is in characterizing asynchronous interactions. That is, how can you tell when people have created something in a room with the intent to communicate to others later on? The onset of a chat or of desktop conferencing is easily flagged as a synchronous episode, but problems arise when trying to make inferences about the contributions of asynchronous activity to the overall workflow. The logging tool supports detection of trails of tool usage that might prove to be sufficient to infer asynchronous communication.

Use of the visual logging tool has raised a few usability issues on its own. Since the log records cover large time spans, there needs to be a more intuitive way to access the parts of the record that correspond to user activity. Other navigational problems are related to 1) the excessive amount of scrolling that is used in the controls and the main display, and 2) the use of a discrete rather than continuous zoom.

The work on CollabLogger has to this point depended on the fact that the TeamWave Workplace version that was used for these studies was instrumented to provide the kinds of information that were deemed to be useful in usability analyses. Future versions of the logger will need to be decoupled from the underlying collaboration environment in order to allow its application across a broader range of applications.

Acknowledgements

Many thanks to Dr. Ruijun Wu for succeeding in mapping the ideas of a large group of investigators into the application now known as CollabLogger.

References

[1] Roseman, M. 2000. http://www.teamwave.com/

[2] Sanderson, P.M. and C. Fisher. 1994. Exploratory Sequential Data Analysis: Foundations Special Issue on Exploratory Sequential Data Analysis. Human-Computer Interaction. 9:251-317

[3] Hilbert, D.M. and D.F. Redmiles. 1999. Extracting Usability Information from User Interface Events. David M. Hilbert and David F. Redmiles. Technical Report UCI-ICS-99-40, Department of Information and Computer Science, University of California, Irvine.

[4] Tufte, E.R. 1990. Envisioning Information. Graphics Press, Cheshire, CT

[5] Plaisant, C., B. Milash, A. Rose, S. Widoff, and B. Shneiderman. 1996. LifeLines: Visualizing Personal Histories. CHI 96, 221-227.

[6] Morse, E.L. and M.B. Spring. 1996. Visualizations that Support Group Work. IEEE Symposium on Visual Languages, Boulder, CO, September 3-6, 1996.

[7] Mitre Multi-Modal Logger. 1997. http://www.mitre.org/technology/logger/

[8] Kimber, D.G., L.D. Wilcox, F.R. Chen and T.P. Moran. 1995. Speaker Segmentation for Browsing Recorded Audio, Proceedings of CHI '95, 212-213.

[9] Rippey, W. and J. Falco. 1997. The NIST Automated Arc Welding Testbed, Proceedings of the Seventh International Conference on Computer Technology in Welding.

[10] Gutwin, C. and S. Greenberg. 1998. Design for Individuals, Design for Groups: Tradeoffs Between Power and Workspace Awareness. CSCW 98, 207-216

[11] Greenberg, S. and M. Roseman. 1998. Using a Room Metaphor to Ease Transitions in Groupware, Research Report 98/611/02, Department of Computer Science, University of Calgary, Calgary, Alberta, Canada.

[12] Steves, M. and A. Knutilla. 1999. Collaboration Technologies for Global Manufacturing, Proceedings of the ASME International Mechanical Engineering Congress and Exposition (IMECE): Symposium on Manufacturing Logistics in a Global Economy.

An Evaluation and Comparison of the Industrial and Educational Usage of CSCW Within the Design Process

A I Thomson, S P MacGregor*, W J Ion
DMEM, University of Strathclyde, Glasgow, Scotland G1 1XJ
avril@cad.strath.ac.uk, {steven.macgregor, w.j.ion} @strath.ac.uk

This short paper presents the findings of three recent research projects carried out at the University of Strathclyde. Two of the projects, ICON & ICON2 investigated the usage of CSCW tools by disparate engineering design students whilst, a Design Council funded research project investigated the introduction and usage of shared workspace technology within the design process of three companies and their supply chain. This is followed by a comparative reflection of the results allowing identification of generic findings together with opportunities for cross-sectoral lessons.

ICON (Institutional Collaboration Over Networks) began in June 1997 with a weeklong collaborative design project involving four pairs of students. The students came from the Product Design Engineering course at Strathclyde University and the same course run jointly at Glasgow School of Art/Glasgow University. The students tackled different design briefs and were asked to provide a solution and present their findings at the end of the week. They were restricted to the use of network technologies such as audio/video conferencing and chat tools and were prohibited to communicate by any other means. Although difficulties were encountered through the week, the project was considered a success in that it proved virtual collaborative design projects were feasible. The difficulties encountered were also examined and resultant changes made to the system for the second project, ICON2, which ran for eight days in September 1998. This iterative process resulted in modifications being made to the system in terms of the methodological approach and project organisation, in the pursuit of ensuring future success.

The underlying philosophy to the ICON projects involved improving the accessibility of CSCW tools in order that policy makers in academia could implement similar projects easily, efficiently, and with as little as possible start up.

The industrial involvement came through the *Integration of Design Specialists Through Shared Workspaces* projects.

*Corresponding author

This recently completed research, funded by the UK Design Council, investigated the introduction and usage of shared workspace technology within the design process of a number of small and medium sized enterprises (SME's). Within this context shared workspaces included video and data conferencing, real-time application sharing, shared whiteboards and file transfer.

Development and use of such technology to date has been dominated by large multinational companies. Ford, for example, have used the latest collaborative technologies to allow their seven design centres, each of which specialises in different aspects of design, to communicate effectively across great distances and different time zones.

The research approach adopted is best described as a series of industrial case studies involving a number of companies from a range of industries, specifically Product Design, Construction and Electronics Manufacture.

The general methodology adopted within each of the companies was to run successive case studies each building upon and testing the findings of the previous. Therefore, each case study followed a different methodology focusing on slightly different aspects. The first company case study commenced in May 1997 with a series of trials being carried out in Hulley & Kirkwood, a mechanical and electrical building services consultancy. This was followed by a product design company, Devpro starting in December 1997. Finally, the Keltek electronics case study began in June 1998.

Recording methods used in both projects for post-evaluation included pre and post questionnaires, support-staff logs, on-line diaries, and interviews.

The main findings of the educational research can be classified in the following areas:

- System and tool usage
- Benefits
- Barriers

It is crucial that the process of evaluation is correct in these projects, otherwise barriers and benefits will be inaccurate. Furthermore, it is important that we pinpoint 'what' to evaluate. In this research, communication,

0-7695-0798-9/00 $10.00

relationships and learning – particularly central in an academic sense, were examined and mapped to results.

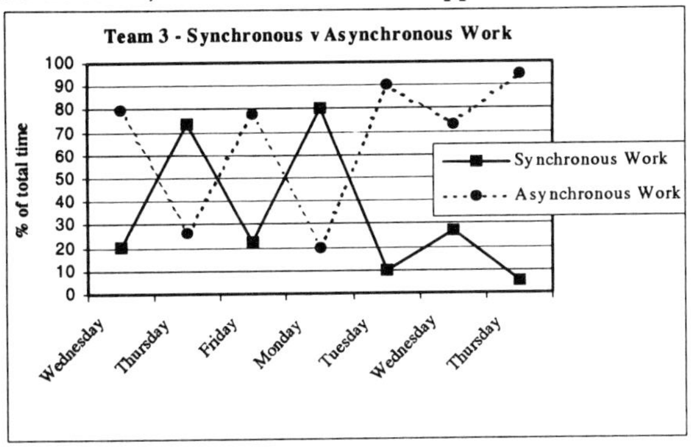

Figure 1 Team 3 Communication Cycle

The above chart evaluates communication through the daily synchronous/asynchronous split for one team in ICON2. Important questions include what is the ideal split and what patterns are required for different tasks.

Furthermore, from examination of the personal log and on-line diaries in ICON2 it became apparent that the participants, generally, displayed the same work mode at each of the various stages. By examining this it may be possible to maximise benefits and ease teething trouble in future projects. To this end, figure 2 is proposed.

Stage	Induction	Familiarisation	Expert
Attitude	Keen	Content	Frustrated/ Stressed
Tools Usage	Using a wide variety	Narrowing usage	Whatever appropriate to deliverables
Attitude to tools	*"open to anything"*	*"open to what works"*	*"nothing works"*
Level of back-up	Tools instruction needed	Software support only	Moderate software support

Figure 2 Work-modes and Attitudes

Barriers identified during the introduction and use of the shared workspaces in the educational *and* industrial settings can be classified under *management*, *psychological*, *technology* and *training*. In both cases the technology was used to *augment* rather than replace current activities. Implementation guidelines produced followed similar paths including the gamut of activities from identification through installation to monitoring. The majority of findings from both projects are common. However, both projects provide scope for lessons to be transferred from industry to education and vice versa.

Industry to Education:

- More barriers were identified in the industrial based projects, due to the artificial "sheltered" nature of the ICON projects. These additional barriers have been developed in to guidelines which could prove useful in future educational projects;
- Industrial case studies can be used as material within educational environments in order to provide students with a realistic overview of "the real world";

Education to Industry:

- Both ICON projects were well managed and prepared for well in advance of commencing. As a result, system usage was smoother than within the companies. Industrial case studies show that companies are keen to commence usage in order to achieve the perceived benefits and tend to gloss over the preparation and management stage, often to the detriment of successful technology implementation;
- The ICON projects showed that students adopted high levels of synchronous work to cope with short project deadlines. Results from industry showed users tended to "back off" employing technology when tight deadlines were looming often resorting to conventional asynchronous modes which are more time consuming.
- In ICON particular attention was paid to the learning process that the students went through. As CSCW technologies are new to most people in education and industry, the latter can learn from the former in methods that maximise quick and efficient uptake of the new systems - all engage in the learning process.

The role of evaluation was crucial to the iterative development of the research and formed the crucial phase prior to the creation of guidelines, barriers and benefits of the technology. However, evaluation still needs to be faster, more reflexive - able to cope with the different demands and pressures that the design process will create through the life cycle - and cheaper.

Finally, the research has shown that two main elements of evaluation are the 'what's' – specific elements of work that we are evaluating such as communication and learning, and the 'how's' – the methods by which we can achieve that evaluation. Some preliminary key features of future approaches have been identified as transparency, flexibility and interoperability.

Acknowledgements

The corresponding author would like to acknowledge the generous support of the Royal Academy of Engineering (RAE) and the Institution of Mechanical Engineers (IMechE) in sponsoring the author's attendance and participation at WET-ICE 2000.

Towards an Evaluation Methodology for the Development of Research-Oriented Virtual Communities

Janet Ho, m.c. schraefel, and Mark Chignell
Knowledge Media Design Institute, University of Toronto
10 King's College Road, SF4306
Toronto, Canada. M5S 3G4

Abstract

This paper is part a case study of collaborative environment use and part a proposition for a methodological approach for evaluating virtual environments based on the findings from that case study. We review the literature on evaluating collaborative environments and we also report on a usability study carried out on a research oriented virtual community. The report includes a cluster analysis of the questionnaire results and the use of those results in profiling user attitudes. We propose that this type of differential cluster analysis should be used in the future to identify people who are generally better able to make discriminating judgments, and also to identify people who are able to analyse the usability of different components of an environment rather than just the overall environment.

1. Overview

As part of a recent project with Bell University Labs, our research group inherited a collaborative environment that had been previously built in an attempt to facilitate Research/Industry collaboration. The environment supported several groupware features such as the ability to define a work space (lab) within the environment; add members to this space; control visibility of the created Lab to non-members. The environment also maintained a discussion space (similar to newsgroup postings), and some document management. The environment had not been evaluated for usability for wider use prior to this project.

To begin to understand *how* to evaluate this collaborative environment, we took two main approaches which we present here: reviewed the literature in virtual communities for evaluative approaches, and ran an evaluation of the environment itself. We promoted use of the environment by establishing it as the designated workspace for a graduate project course in Mechanical and Industrial Engineering at the University of Toronto. There were 22 participants in the course. We used both the system use logs from that group as well as questionnaires and interviews with that group to understand the strengths and weaknesses of the environment. The environment was also used by other researchers, and by a small number of people from industry.

In both the review of previous work, as well as in our own evaluation, we found stickiness to be a significant problem: people may engage such an environment initially, but their use tapers off. If the environment were useful in supporting work, why would use taper off?

One of the significant findings of our work is that, while we began the studies of the environment focused on discovering the strengths and weaknesses of that environment, our findings lead us to consider the problem in terms of user profiles rather than simply usability. We describe these findings below.

In the following sections, we present: previous work in this space; some working definitions of virtual communities based on that work; previously discovered usability problems. We provide an overview of our approach to evaluating our collaborative environment in that context, an analysis of that evaluation, and a proposal stemming from that work for a methodology of evaluation, focused on user profiling.

2. Previous work

In recent years there has been an accelerating trend towards research partnerships between universities and industry as the advantages of applied research and technology transfer become ever more apparent [14]. Infrastructure is required to support these collaborative endeavours. In some cases, industrial research parks (e.g., in Oxford, England) have been created to facilitate interaction. However, the facilitation of research collaboration between university and industry continues to be a challenge, particularly in cases where it may be too expensive or otherwise impractical (e.g., due to geographic dispersal) to collocate researchers in shared office and meeting space. This has led to a number of initiatives for creating online communities that can provide some of the sense of the community that is normally gained by working together in the same location. A variety of relevant technologies are described in Baecker [1] and elsewhere (e.g., in the ACM conference on Computer Supported Collaborative

Work, CSCW). In this paper we focus on the development of online collaborative spaces as an important component in building a virtual community for research collaborators. Alternately referred to as virtual, online, or networked communities, the creation and use of digital spaces for research practices have been investigated along several paths:

- what constitutes the sense of "community" in these virtual spaces [11][8]
- how virtual research spaces are distinct from non-research virtual spaces [8][14] [6]
- what the attributes of an entity are that can be considered a virtual "community" [8][11][9]

The above questions address various components and properties of virtual spaces, but not the relationships between those properties and actual use. We need to know what it is about virtual spaces that make them more or less likely to "work" by being sufficiently engaging or useful to encourage active usage over a period of time. Thus we are particularly interested in the question: how well have these constructed spaces been used, in terms of exploitation of available services and "stickiness"? By stickiness, we mean, the amount of activity (both in terms of duration and transactions) that a person carries out in such a community over time. A recent survey of online communities such as the Palace and Agora, for instance, shows that maximal use of such spaces is approximately two weeks [7]. This small time frame begs the question: if you build it, they may come, *but will they stay?* And if they won't, what's the value of the service? The design challenges raised by this question need to be addresses as a matter of urgency in light of increasing trends towards the world of work "becoming virtual" [6].

2.1 Attributes of vrtual communities?

The research literature on Virtual Communities (VCs) considers many types of VCs: those used primarily as places for social exchange; those used in education contexts and those used primarily for work or research. This paper focuses on the latter mission. Within this research, definitions of the attributes for VCs differ according to one key element: whether or not synchronous communication is needed.

Much VC research centers around highly constructed text-based virtual environments like Multi User Domains (MUDs). Consequently, VCs are often constructed to utilize not only regular net tools like email, ftp and web for posting and reading of communications, but also some type of real time communication environment.

In this work, a VC is defined as *a technologically mediated, persistent, environment which supports: multiple interaction styles, capability for realtime interaction, and multi-user engagement* [8]. These last two points are seen as critical, since they distinguish this type of VC from strictly "point to point" communication. A MUD, for instance, facilitates persistence of environment for interactions by presenting a persistent meeting room. The MUD also allows for synchronous one to one, one to many, or many to many communications. When this environment was tested in a classroom environment however, its "multiple interaction styles" were not seen as multiple enough [8]. The technical communication students using the MOO criticized it as time-consuming and exhaustive when typing in text. They also had difficulties following overlapping and multiple conversations presented in a single text window. Moreover, the tool did not support WYSISYG manipulation of text, since MOO works only with ASCII text. This was seen as reducing the value of tool use [8]. So while the MUD/MOO environment supports multiple types of synchronous communication, it uses a single limited text tool for doing so. This limitation restricts the environments viable support of "multiple interaction styles", and hence compromises its utility.

Teresa Roberts's work questions the synchronous requirement for VCs. Her work on newsgroups suggests that the user's sense of community may not depend on real time interaction, but on the richness of asynchronous participation opportunities. These are measured in the following dimensions, rated by Newsgroup participants across a variety of groups: cohesion, effectiveness, help, relationships, language and self-regulation [11]. Cohesion considered the stability of the Newsgroup: long time members to new users. Interestingly, gender played a role in the prediction of cohesion. For women, frequency and thoroughness of reading group posting were significant predictors. For men, the predictors were presence of women in the group, and the respondents' frequency of reading the group [11].

Effectiveness refers to how well a group is perceived by its users to meet its own stated purpose. Help indicates how helpful the group is at providing types of information or support within the topic area. Relationships investigates ways in which group postings lead to one on one type communication. Language refers to the specific identifying jargon associated with a group, and whether this was an attractor or detractor for participation. Self-regulation refers to how well the group handles inappropriate behaviour [11]. In each case above, Roberts suggests that frequency and thoroughness of use of a group are what lead to a group user describing that group as a community [11]. We may extrapolate Roberts' finding to suggest that, for a virtual environment to be perceived as a virtual community, it needs to facilitate frequent and broad use of its resources.

Related to the above position, our group's recent work [13] proposes a heterogeneous approach to VC construction/experience. Based on individual and group need within the VC, work group or research communities may need to interact in a variety of ways among different levels of the virtual work space, leading to a variety of tool requirements. As the lab grows to include new members from more locations, it may be necessary to add Chat-style services. Thus, the availability or otherwise of asynchronous communication cannot be a defining trait of virtual communities. Rather, a sense of community is promoted through appropriate tools for extending the styles of interaction relevant for that community.

3. Study environment

Once we have a working definition of the attributes of a VC we can come back to our earlier question. "If we build our ideal mix of tools and flexible infrastructure, and users come to use it once, will users keep using it?" The Evaluation component of the paper below shows how we have begun to address this question.

3.1 Overview of environment for study

The VC that we examined brings together an industrial partner with various research institutions to collaborate in the performance of research that is of both academic and industrial interest. The front end of the environment is a website. This virtual campus creates an institutional environment where participants can interact with each other in the site's conference and research centers. The participants can post documents, appointments, deliverables, etc. on the website. The works posted on the site are under the explicit control of the originator in order to protect and properly recognize the contribution of each participant.

The VC has five general areas: Labs, Pubs, Commons, Conference Center, and Library. The 'Labs' is a secure area where participants can discuss work in progress in private groups, allowing collaboration and technology transfer between the commercial and academic settings in focused teams. The content is secure until the work is published in the 'Library' or elsewhere by the author(s). The 'conference centre' is the area where a broader audience or the general public can participate in the work discussions. The 'Pub' is a free form-discussion area of the site. This area is completely open to new topics and many forms of discussions. The 'Commons' is a public event announcement area.

One of the features of the site is that it is designed to manage intellectual property so that different researchers and groups can post information to different labs, and different projects within the labs, in privacy, with the researchers determining who can see what information. The following section reports on initial evaluation of the site's first few months of operation.

4. Evaluation

During a period of approximately five months, seven labs were set up on the site, each containing one or more projects. Lab 1 was a collection of four research projects on a common theme that was carried out by teams of professors and research students, with some input from the industrial personnel. Lab 7 was set up towards the end of the evaluation period as a tool to support projects within a graduate class on mobile computing (participation in the lab was encouraged, but optional for the students). Of the eight project groups in that class, three groups chose to use the website during the evaluation period. Part of their course work was to consider and respond to a usability questionnaire as they interacted (or not) with the site. A number of evaluation methods were used, including analysis of server logs, and usability questionnaires, which will be the focus for this paper. Server logs were collected over a period of five months. Discarding all login duration which are less than 5 minutes, during the 5-month period, there was a total of 161 logins. The average login time for the users in the period was 17.6 minutes, where the longest login time was 79.68 minutes. Fifteen of the users of the collaborative environment filled out usability questionnaires.

Web site development is not solely the development of a single 'page'; it is the close interaction of the content, navigation, and appearance of the website, so that separate evaluation of any part of the web site alone is not enough [12]. Consequently, the questionnaire used to evaluate the VC was based on Nielsen's ten heuristic for the web [10], Garzotto and Matera's SUE methodology [4], and the modified cognitive workload analysis [5].

The questionnaire was divided into the following six categories (a copy of the questionnaire is available from the authors upon request):

- structure of the content's organization
- navigation of links used to explore the website's structure
- behaviour of functions and links of the website
- user control of available interaction components
- presentation of features shown to users, e.g. layout and visual appeal, and
- functionality of the component and amount of effort required

Each of the items in these categories consisted of a statement with an associated rating scale for responses (a Likert type scale was used with five categories: strongly disagree, disagree, neutral, agree, strongly agree).

The sample size for the data reported below (approximately 160 log-ins and 15 usability questionnaire respondents) reflects the relatively low utilization of this version of the collaborative environment. The analysis focused on the following questions:

- Which functions were used most frequently?
- Were users consistent in how they answered the questionnaire?
- Were there identifiable groups of users that could be differentiated based on their patterns of response (this question was addressed using cluster analysis)?

Cluster analysis was carried out using K-means (an iterative partitioning approach) and Ward's Method (a hierarchical agglomeration technique). All the analyses reported in this paper were carried out using SPSS for Windows, version 10.

The activity measurement of the virtual campus tabulated the number of postings in the various projects in the 'Labs' section. Postings include the number of word documents, discussion items, deliverable records, calendar events, and notes placed on the virtual campus. Inside the 'Labs' webspace, each project group has its own notice boards, deliverables, and workspace sections. The workspace section is further separated into discussion, document publishing, and calendar sub-sections. The number of postings in each section is recorded and is shown in the following results section.

4.1 Results

The number of sub-groups (projects) varies between the seven labs, which are relabeled alphabetically, e.g. Project 1A for the first project in lab 1. The profile of activity for each of the projects across the tools/functions in the workspace is shown in Table 1, below.

Lab	Project		Workspace			
		Deliver-ables	Discuss-ion	Document Publish-ing	Calendar	Notice-board
1	A	2	0	7	0	0
1	B	0	0	2	0	0
1	C	0	0	0	0	0
1	D	0	0	2	0	0
2	A	7	0	0	0	0
3	A	0	0	1	0	0
4	A	0	0	5	0	0
4	B	0	0	24	0	0
5	A	2	7	1	7	0
6	A	0	0	2	0	0
7	A	0	1	2	0	2
7	B	0	0	6	0	0
7	C	0	0	3	1	0

Table 1. Web site overall postings

It can be seen in Table 1 that only one group used the notice board, and that the profile of tools used by each project varied considerably. Table 1 shows that document publishing was the most frequently used tool, with relatively low usage of the other tools. There was considerable variation in overall usage of the site and its tools between the different labs. Lab 4 was the largest user of the lab, using the document publishing feature exclusively.

Figure 1 shows how much time users spent on each of the twelve listed features. In addition to document management category, users also spent a relatively large amount of time reading the information available on the webpage ("about").

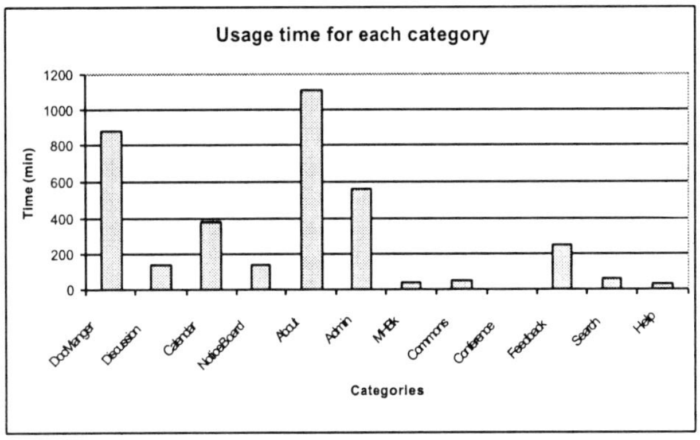

Figure 1. Cumulative Usage Times

The third most accessed was the 'Administration' category. This reflected the relatively large amount of administration that was required to create labs, project groups, and to set up member access rights.

The first cluster analysis used all the questions in the questionnaire. Using Ward's method, subjects were grouped into three main clusters (Table 2). The numbers corresponded to the subject ID numbers and used in this case to signify cluster membership.

Cluster 1:	Cluster 2:	Cluster 3:
1, 5	2, 4, 6, 8, 11, 12	3, 7, 9, 10, 13, 14, 15

Table 2. Cluster membership for subjects using Ward's method

A similar grouping was obtained using k-means cluster analysis with k=3 (Table 3). There were only three differences in the groupings obtained using the two methods, subject 3 was grouped with the first cluster (in k-means, but not Ward's clustering) and subjects 12 and 15 were swapped between two clusters for the two methods. The overall similarity between the two clustering methods increased confidence in the groupings obtained.

For interpretational purposes, the k-means clustering solution was chosen for further analysis. ANOVA was used to identify which of the questionnaire items contributed to the questionnaire effect (with cluster membership being used as a pseudo-factor). Question 2, 3, and 4 of the presentation section, questions 2-6 of structure section and question 3 of the navigation section all were significant questionnaire items (in terms of cluster membership).

The people in cluster one had 3-5 years of both Internet and collaboration software experience, used Internet more than once a day and used Internet collaboration software at least once a day. This group of users liked the screen layout (agreed to the statement for question 4 of presentation section: "The screen layout of the website is appealing"), but otherwise found the site difficult to use and poorly organized.

The second cluster contained people with more than 5 years of Internet experience and with 3-5 years collaboration software experience (using collaborative tools such as chat at least once a day). These users did not like the screen layout but were otherwise mostly positive about the site (they tended to agree with statements such as: "it is easy for me to find desired items on the website" and "the organization of materials on the website is easy to understand").

The people in cluster 3 tended to have less experience (3-5 years of Internet experience but only 1-3 years of collaboration experience) and were generally neutral in their ratings of the site.

Separate cluster analyses were also carried out for different sections of the questionnaire (one for structure+navigation, S/N, the other for presentation+functionality, P/F). Table 3 summarizes the clustering results that were obtained. Subjects 1, 3, and 5 were consistently unfavourable (cluster 1), Subjects 11 and 15 were consistently neutral (cluster 3), and subjects 2, 4, 7, 8, 9, 10, and 12 were consistently positive (cluster 2). Subjects 6, 13 and 14 represented a potentially interesting group of people who differed in their level of approval between different components of the environment (as assessed using the questionnaire).

	Cluster 1:	Cluster 2:	Cluster 3:
S/N	1,3,5,13	2,4,6,7,8,9,10,12	11,14,15
P/F	1, 3, 5	2,4,7,8,9,10,12, 13,14	6,11,15

Table 3 Clustering for different portions of the questionnaire (K-means method).

5. Stickiness and personalization

Increasingly, we expect computer systems to do more for us as the technology advances. We want systems that we can control more easily and that meets our needs rather than vice versa. It will be almost impossible, from an economic point of view, for developers to handcraft a slightly different version for each individual. Personalization, however, is possible with the development of interfaces and environments where users can create their preferred "version" without having major programming skills.

Personalization may also be implemented through adaptation. For an environment to adapt to a user, the system needs to adapt to the differences between individual users across: characteristics, abilities, interests, behaviour, needs and preferences [3]. Specific factors that might be relevant to use of a VC might include the user's level of spatial ability, their preferred learning style or field dependency; and personal 'profile' characteristics such as previous experience, age, gender or job requirement [2].

The value of a VC can be expected to increase as people participate and contribute to the shared information base. In the case of the website that we evaluated, it appeared that there were problems both with usability and with motivation to use the site. As a result, the labs failed to reach a critical threshold where the communicational and information value of content on the site overcame the psychological and practical "barriers to entry". The lack of stickiness for the VC that we observed may have been partly due to usability problems and to the way in which participants were motivated (or not) to use the site. However, our early findings suggest that lack of personalization may also have played a role. The site tended to be used in different ways by different labs, and perhaps stickiness would increase if lab leaders were able to personalize each lab according to the needs and interests of the lab members and the joint tasks they perform. A personalized site would then assist in motivating and training group members, as there would be a consistent conceptual model of group activities reflected in the structure and functionality of their personalized view of the site.

6. Conclusions

The methodological outcome seems to be a proposal that has several components: one is a way to help determine, in the high cost operation of usability testing, who is likely to produce the most useful feedback for a given set of attributes. Profiling based on clustering, as illustrated in this paper, can be used to differentiate between subjects that have a more uniform attitude (e.g., favourable) to the environment being tested, and those that show more discrimination between the different sections of a usability questionnaire. The cluster analysis identified different groups of users with respect to attitudes towards site usability. We identified three groups of users, one with generally positive attitude, another containing people with generally negative views, and a third group of less experienced users with more neutral attitudes. In addition, we identified a number of individuals who were able to discriminate between different constructs (e.g., structure and navigation, versus presentation and functionality) when making their usability judgments.

We can characterize these subjects as "holistic" vs. "analytic" (discriminating) in nature. Based on understanding how people rate usability, and their requirements or expectations for different components of usability, it may be possible to build the *kinds* of customization needed for the groups into the environment, with some insights on how to make these tools accessible to those populations.

The relatively low usage in this preliminary study may be due to the prototype nature of the website and also to the fact that researchers were unfamiliar with the site. Researchers often chose alternative means of communication (for most of the researchers it was possible to communicate reasonably easy through other means, including face to face meetings) instead of using the site. This was partly because the information from labs for which a VC participant was not a member were invisible, which generally added to the impression that the site was fairly empty. This problem is somewhat like the catch 22 a restaurant faces when its empty because it has no customers and prospective customers lose interest because it is empty.

However, even with the limited amount of usage we observed it seems that usage varies across labs both in terms of overall activity and in terms of the specific functions or tools that are used.

Overall, the most popular activity was document publishing. This is the space where virtual campus members upload their work in progress to exchange with other members of the same project group. This activity was perceived to have high value because it meant that a single posting could "deliver" the document to anyone who participated in the project, and that group members always knew where to find the latest version of a document. This value was enhanced by the fact that most participants were unwilling or unable to post documents on a Website themselves using HTML or PDF authoring, FTP, etc.

The VC that we studied had a powerful set of tools, but was relatively little used during the observation period. In discussions with some of the site users (or intended users) we identified the following issues:

- Users were reluctant to move from or supplement the tools that they currently used to support their collaboration (file transfers, email, phone, face to face meetings, etc.
- The initial appearance of the Website turned people off because it appeared to be empty of content.

7. References

1. Baecker, R.M. (1993), Readings in Groupware and Computer Supported Cooperative Work: Software to Facilitate Human-Human Collaboration. Morgan Kaufmann Publishers, Los Altos, California.
2. Benyon, D. R. (1993) 'Adaptive Systems: a solution to usability problems'. User Modelling and User Adapted Interaction, v. 3, n1, pp.65-87.
3. Dieterich, H., U.Malinowski, T. Kuhme, and M. Schneider-Hufschmidt (1993) 'State of the Art in Adaptive User Interfaces'. In: M. Scheider-Hufschmidt, T. Kuhme, U.Malinowski (eds.): Adaptive user interfaces: Principles and practice. Amsterdam: North-Holland, pp.13-48
4. Garzotto, F., and Matera, M. (1997) 'A systematic method for hypermedia usability inspection' The New Review of Hypermedia and Multimedia, p.39-65.
5. Hart, S. & Staveland, L (1988) 'Development of NASA-TLX (Task Load Index): Results of Empirical and Theoretical Research', in P.A. Hancock & N. Neshkati (ed's), Human Mental Workload. Elsevier, pp. 139-183
6. Igbaria, M., Shayo, C., Olfman, L., Beniger, J. 'On Becoming Virtual: The Driving Forces and Arrangements' SIGCPR '99, New Orleans LA USA.
7. Long, Barry. (1999) 'Shaping Social Space from Information Space.' Masters Thesis. Dept. of Computer Science, University of Toronto.
8. Mehlenbacher, B., Hardin, B., Barrett, C., and Clagett, J. (1994) 'Multi-users domains and virtual campuses: Implications for computer-mediated collaboration and technical communication' DOC 94, Banff, Alberta, Canada. pp. 213-219
9. Mynatt, E.D., Adler, A., Ito, M., O'Day, V.L. (1997) 'Design For Network Communities' Proc. ACM CHI'97. Atlanta, GA, March, pp. 210-217.
10. Nielsen. J., and Molich, R. (1990) 'Heuristic evaluation of user interfaces'. Proc. ACM CHI'90. Seattle, WA, April, pp. 249-256.
11. Roberts, T.L. (1998) 'Are Newsgroups Virtual Communities?' ACM CHI 98 APRIL, pp. 360-367
12. Scholtz, J., & Downey, L 'Methods for Identifying Usability Problems with Web Sites' September 30, 1998 <http://www.itl.nist.gov/iaui/vvrg/jpaper/final.html> (December 2, 1999).
13. schraefel, m.c., Ho, J., Chignell, M., Milton, M., (2000) 'Building Virtual Communities for Research Collaboration' AIWoRC'00 An International Working Conference and Industrial Expo on new advances and emerging trends in Next Generation Enterprises, Buffalo, NY, April.
14. Steed, A.& Tromp, J., (1998) 'Experiences with the Evaluation of CVE Applications', Proceedings of Collaborative Virtual Environments, 17-19th June 1998, Manchester, UK.

Developing and Evaluating Collaborative Engineering Studios

Jonathan Sevy Vera Zaychik Thomas T. Hewett William C. Regli
Geometric and Intelligent Computing Laboratory
Department of Mathematics and Computer Science
Drexel University
3141 Chestnut Street
Philadelphia, PA 19104
http://gicl.mcs.drexel.edu

Abstract

We discuss a vision of and work in progress on a collaborative engineering environment, the Collaborative Design Studio, being developed at the Geometric and Intelligent Computing Laboratory at Drexel University. This works seeks to integrate Computer-Aided Design (CAD) and communication tools through automatic extraction and embedding of design context into communications, as well as provide archiving and retrieval of informal communications. While preliminary development of the studio has proceeded using relatively informal input from professional design engineers, direct evaluation by intended users of the system will be sought to guide further development of the system to ensure that it accurately meets their needs and fits into their work environment. Such formative user input will be obtained through surveys and observation of subjects as they complete specified tasks. Future summative evaluation will attempt to measure changes in user productivity and efficiency. Discussion focuses on issues and questions relating to the effective design and evaluation of such systems, and describe proposed studies for evolving the current environment.

1. Introduction

We describe our vision of a collaborative engineering environment, the **Collaborative Design Studio**, consider issues and questions relating to the effective design and evaluation of such systems, and describe proposed studies for evaluating and evolving the current environment. This work is being undertaken at the Geometric and Intelligent Computing Laboratory at Drexel University While preliminary development of the studio has proceeded using relatively informal input from professional design engineers, we feel it is essential to incorporate direct evaluation by intended users of the system to ensure that it accurately meets their needs and fits into their work environment. Such information will be obtained through surveys and observation of subjects as they complete specified tasks, analyzed, and used to guide further development of the system.

2. Current Vision of a Collaborative Design Studio

The fundamental goal of the Collaborative Design Studio project is to enhance the design engineering process through the integration of computer-aided design and engineering tools, communication tools, and archiving functions. Design context is automatically extracted from CAD tools for inclusion in communications, and all design-related communications are automatically archived in a searchable database. We are attempting to achieve this while incorporating commercial off-the-shelf (COTS) tools, with underlying integration functions being transparent to users.

The proposed environment should provide a number of enhancements to the design engineering process. A central advantage will be the enabling of efficient and effective distributed design efforts, with geographically separated engineers able to work together effectively. The capabilities of the studio are being specifically targeted to this increasingly important work mode; however, they should prove advantageous in traditional settings as well. A significant benefit should be a reduction in design development time, facilitated by the automatic inclusion of design context into communications. Even frequent and informal forms of communication (such as e-mail) will include precise and unambiguous reference to parts and features in the current de-

0-7695-0798-9/00 $10.00

sign, making it easier for engineers to have detailed discussions without requiring face-to-face meetings. The integration of communication tools and design tools allow these contextual references to initiate the automatic display of the relevant design model or diagram, freeing the receiver of a communication from the task of locating and loading the appropriate file. In addition, the automatic inclusion of specific, unambiguous design references should reduce the number of errors or misunderstandings generated by misinterpretation of designer-produced verbal descriptions of the design feature and context to which the communication applies. Finally, the automatic archiving of all communications, together with embedded design context information, should greatly aid many design activities. Design reuse and adaptation will be facilitated by designers' having access to all communications related to previous design efforts, which can provide valuable insight into tradeoffs and compromises made which might not be reflected in formal documentation. During protracted design efforts, such an archive may provide the only access to rationales used by engineers who have retired or left the project. Manufacturing and maintenance activities should similarly benefit from being able to identify hidden considerations relating to specific part functions.

A side benefit is the opportunity that such a transparent integrated environment presents to researchers wishing to study workgroup interactions. The automatic and transparent archiving of communications provides access to all but the most informal verbal communications exchanged during the design process, in a completely non-intrusive fashion, permitting a researcher to study interactions without perturbing the participants' normal work environment.

3. Studio Architecture

The user-accessible components of the Collaborative Design Studio consists of three groups of tools: **CAD/CAE tools**, **collaborative work tools**, and **archiving tools**. These are integrated through a number of software modules. The design of the environment has been guided by two requirements: standard commercial tools should be incorporated whenever possible, so as to avoid expecting designers to use proprietary software in place of effective and familiar alternatives; and the integration of tools should be as nearly transparent as possible, placing few additional burdens on users. The current prototype utilizes the Structural Dynamics Research Corporation I-DEAS suite as its CAD/CAE package, Netscape Communicator as the email client, Collaborative Virtual Workspace[1] (CVW, developed by the Mitre Corporation) as a video-conferencing tool, and Oracle as the database archive (the search interface to this archive being web-based, allowing the use of any web browser). However, the integrating modules have been designed with an emphasis on "package independence," to allow substitution of alternate packages with relatively minor effort (as long as the substitutes provide a sufficiently rich feature set — for example, CAD/CAE software with an application programming interface permitting the extraction of design information).

Design context is extracted from the current design for embedding into a communication by the client communication module. This module communicates with the CAD/CAE software (using the Open I-DEAS API in the case of SDRC I-DEAS) and creates an XML document incorporating the extracted design data organized according to a design-communication specific *message model*. This message model is central to the integration of the components in the studio: all design and communication context is captured in these messages, which provide the fundamental level of organization of information. A designer initiates a communication through a script which first calls the client module to extract the design context and create the XML document and then starts the appropriate communication tool, with options that associate the generated XML document (as an attachment in the case of email) and automatically include the archiving server as a participant (or recipient) in the communication. The user will observe little of this background processing, being presented with the selected communication tool as in the normal (unintegrated) setting. The client communication module also functions on the receiver side, using the attached XML design context document to display the appropriate design part in the CAD package.

The archiving server extracts design context from the XML document associated with a received communication and uses it to drive storage of the communication in the archive. The server also permits web-based search access to archived communications, returning retrieved information in the form of XML documents which are used by the communication module to display the associated design files.

While we feel the Collaborative Design Studio will provide many obvious benefits for designers, there are still a number of questions to be addressed. One particular issue is the amount and level of design context information to include into the XML documents. The message model has been designed to be extensible, permitting varying types of context to be included; however, this leaves open the question of exactly which information to include, which cannot be adequately answered without some form of input from the intended users of the system. In addition, it will be important to understand the role of the various tools used by designers when they employ the integrated suite in the Collaborative Design Studio. Some questions to be addressed

[1] `http://cvw.mitre.org`

are: to what extent does integration enhance the design process, and how can this be measured; how is the pattern of use of the tools changed when integration is incorporated; and how does access to archived communications influence design efforts. The issue of how we hope to obtain this information is addressed below.

4. Formulating Evaluation Questions and Procedures

There are two levels of criteria that are important in thinking about ways to facilitate use of an engineering design environment. One is the interface or **tactical level**; the second is the interaction or **strategic** level. Interface level criteria address issues such as how interface components and widgets should be built or "shaped" – for example, aircraft cockpit instruments need to show certain necessary information clearly. In contrast, interaction level criteria address the goals of the user and focus on the way the user thinks about the task. Certainly, a concern with interface features is important; however, optimizing these features without attending closely to the overall flow of interaction can lead to unworkable or unusable systems.

Adopting the goal of understanding the designers' tasks and how they proceed in solving their problems immediately commits one to developing explicit answers to several questions. Exactly who are the target users? What knowledge are they assumed to have, and what are their skills? What specific tasks will such users want to complete and are there generic types of tasks or task characteristics? How will successful user performance be measured or assessed? As a number of sources on Task Analysis [10, 14] have pointed out, the user's task can have a significant impact on how tools are used or not used. Consider the use of CAD systems in architecture. It is possible to divide architectural design into two broad categories of activity. One type of activity is associated with preparation of a model or design representation to illustrate the design to a customer. Another type of activity is associated with sketching out and developing a novel design concept. Even casual observation of usage patterns of architectural CAD systems reveals task differences. While it is not unusual to find someone trained in the use of an architectural CAD system putting it to use in polishing and preparing drawings for presentation, it is quite a challenge to find an architect using such a CAD system while creating an original design concept.

4.1 A taxonomy of design activities

As pointed out by Brown and Chandrasekaran [2] and Dym [5], there are three identifiable types of engineering design activity: **routine**, **variant**, and **creative**. **Routine** design involves taking an existing design and making minor tweaks in the artifact being designed to develop an improved artifact. **Variant** design involves using existing components or subassemblies to create a new version of an existing artifact. **Creative** design involves coming up with a new design concept (though existing components or subassemblies may become components of the new artifact).

It is expected that the tasks and activities of designers will vary depending on the type of design being performed. It will thus be necessary to account for this when studying the designers' activities and evaluating a collaborative system.

4.2 A role of analogical thinking in design

One place to begin identifying task-critical functionalities for a human centered engineering design environment is with a realistic understanding of current procedures, practices and activities that the environment is meant to augment or replace, as discussed in Hewett and DePaul [7]. For example, there are a variety of reasons for believing analogical thinking is a key process involved in creative advances in science and engineering [9]. Of particular relevance to thinking about the creation of design environments is work on the use of analogy, both in individual problem solving [3] and in generating new insights during the social process of science and engineering [4].

Clement [3] found that the steps used by scientists in developing a problem solution are not necessarily derivational or formal, but often proceed by analogy. He gave a mechanics problem to 10 participants sophisticated in physics but with no extensive experience solving problems from the class, and asked participants to "think aloud" while solving the problem. Examination of videotapes from these sessions revealed that the typical solution procedure involved memory search for an analogous situation with similar characteristics, conducted through association or by examining dimensions of similarity. The problem solver then developed a possible solution on an analog which had been judged to be appropriate; once the solution had been worked out for the analog, the individual then proceeded to test the solution on the original problem.

Dunbar [4] reported on a year-long study conducted in four molecular biology laboratories, where he followed several projects. The processes studied included "planning the research, executing the experiments, evaluating the experimental results, attending laboratory staff meetings and public talks, planning further experiments, and writing journal articles (p. 365)." As Dunbar reports, "analogies were an important source of knowledge and conceptual change (p. 381)."

The researchers Dunbar studied used three different classes of analogy. **Local analogies** were those within the same domain as the research being conducted and were drawn from a previous experiment to the current one. This type of analogical reasoning typically occurred when a scientist would attempt to map a currently unsuccessful experiment onto a similar experiment that had been successful. Local analogies seemed to be one of the main mechanisms for driving the research program forward. **Regional analogies** involved mapping a system of relationships from a similar domain onto the problem domain being studied. This type of analogical reasoning was typically "employed when the scientists were working on elaborating their theory and planning a new set of experiments (p. 383)." These regional analogies seemed to be one of the main mechanisms for allowing the scientists to fill in gaps in their own knowledge and to suggest new questions to ask about the entities being studied. **Long-distance analogies** involved mapping a concept from a very different domain onto the problem domain being studied. Typically, "long-distance analogies were used to highlight features of the research that were salient," and were used to, "bring home a point or to educate new staff members of a laboratory (p. 383)."

This suggests investigating the role of analogical thinking in both individual and collaborative engineering design, exploring the apparent parallel which exists between Dym's categorization of engineering design activities (routine, variant, and creative) and Dunbar's comments about the types of analogy that were used in the research laboratories which he studied — i.e., are routine, variant and creative design characterized or driven by the use of local, regional, and distant analogies, respectively. Our preliminary hypothesis is that the role of analogy in collaborative engineering design is analogous to its role in scientific research. At an individual level it is a way to generate alternatives and solve the problem of selection of alternatives. At a social level it is a way to extend knowledge, to ask new questions about a design, and to communicate with design team members in working out novel solutions to design problems. Consequently, one issue in developing measures and metrics will be finding ways of assessing when and to what degree analogical thinking takes place.

In the event that data support the hypotheses that analogical thinking plays a critical role in design and that different types of design problems (routine, variant, and creative) involve different types of analogies (local, regional, and long-distance), it would be valuable to determine how analogical thinking can be supported in a collaborative design studio. One approach would be to provide a library giving access to local and regional design analogs (somewhat along the lines of the design repository described by Regli, [13]). Such design examples could be stored as modifiable templates, adaptable for use in solving analogous design problems. The design repository should contain examples drawn from more than one related design problem domain, to support and facilitate regional and long-distance analogical thinking. In addition, these inquiries into characteristics of the engineering design process will guide the development of the message model used to archive design decisions and provide design context during communication. It is expected that the type of design context information most useful to designers will vary somewhat depending on whether design is routine, variant or creative.

It is apparent that a collaborative engineering design environment presents a wide array of questions to be addressed. There are questions concerned with interface level details, i.e., are the tools usable and useful given their intended purpose, as well as those about facilitating interaction, both a single designer's interaction with the tool set and the social interaction among members of a team. In addition, a collaborative studio simultaneously creates an environment in which questions about the nature of design and collaborative design can be formulated and answered. Answers to these questions, such as the role of analogical thinking in design and its relation to the basic types of design, can in turn be used to evolve the studio to better support design functions.

5. Proposed Approaches to Evaluation of the Collaborative Design Studio

5.1 Survey of working engineering designers

In order to develop baseline data about how design engineers currently think they collaborate, we have under development a survey which we propose to circulate to working engineering designers. In this survey we explore both the types of knowledge which engineering designers feel they use and the nature of how they store, retrieve, and/or exchange that information to other designers (e.g., use of analogical thinking). This survey is being structured based upon both our own experience and some of the work of others (e.g., [11, 12, 15]). Once the survey document has been pilot tested to improve its wording, etc., we intend to disseminate the questionnaire to a large number of design engineers in New Jersey, Pennsylvania, Delaware and Maryland in conjunction with our collaborators with the Delaware Valley Industrial Resource Center (DVIRC)[2]. Not only will this survey provide us with normative data about what designers currently think about what they do, it will also be used to seek volunteers to participate in further studies in which experienced engineers are the most appropriate participants. In short, the survey provides us with a "map of the terrain," an indication of tasks that need to be studied and questions to be answered.

[2]dvirc.org

5.2 Thinking out loud studies

In order to capture snapshots of the actual working and collaborative practices of engineers, we currently anticipate the need for one or more studies in which engineers and/or student engineers participate, working on real or simulated design problems. Again, these studies will allow us to establish a baseline for existing collaborative procedures and then to learn more about the weaknesses of the tools and environment at the interface level when infelicities or outright errors are identified for us by people engaged in a design task — e.g., is there an unusable tool or feature? In addition, we anticipate the need for one or more studies focusing on the interaction level of analysis so that we can improve the cognitive engineering of the environment and tools — e.g., have we structured the environment in such a way that the designer is forced to hold more information in memory than a human being can maintain in an active state?

Protocol analysis, or thinking out loud, is a technique to obtain subjects' verbal reports about a task being performed concurrent with the process of completing that task. It has been shown that this technique can produce valuable data while not altering subjects' mental processes [6]. Subjects are instructed to verbalize their thoughts while performing the task being studied — i.e., to think out loud. It should be noted that this is somewhat different from having participants explain their actions while they are engaged in the task; in particular, it is relatively unobtrusive to the problem-solving process (except in certain exceptional cases, such as time-critical activities). The technique gives insight into subjects' mental processes, course of thought and problem-solving approach in addressing the specified task. This real-time verbal report will also be supplemented with retrospective reports and interviews of the type reported by Hewett and Scott [8]. The retrospective reports provide an indication of what participants "think they were doing" during the activity; the former gives evidence of what they "actually were doing."

It is generally desirable that subjects employed in such a study have prior familiarity with the process being studied to gain any reliable insight into that process. Thus if the process of designing a mechanical artifact is being studied, the participants of the study should be people familiar with mechanical design, perhaps industrial designers or design engineers. If in addition what is being evaluated is not the CAD software itself, but the integration of that software into an environment including other applications, then the participants should be familiar with the use of a CAD package (though not necessarily the specific package used in the study, since most CAD applications are similar in behavior, at least in those components likely to be relevant for the study). Considering that each test group should consist of at least 10 teams of subjects to guarantee an acceptable level of confidence in the results, it becomes clear why such studies are seldom done: it is very hard to get appropriate subjects.

For our particular problem, the main task assigned to users would be to solve a design problem as a group, collaboratively, while being spatially separated. The chosen problem needs to be relatively simple, able to be solved in a matter of hours, while still requiring active collaboration of members of the design team. The activity to be observed is how CSCW tools are used in the process of design, and how their integration with design authoring tools influences the activity — in particular, is such integration beneficial, and what kinds of information about the design should be incorporated into communications. A control group of designers will work on a design problem under "normal" conditions, in which design authoring and CSCW tools are both present but not bound together in any way; another group will be given access to the Collaborative Studio, with communication tools integrated with CAD software. Experimenters will observe subjects, recording what kind of information is being exchanged, how, in which cases, and for what purposes participants use the communication tools at their disposal, and other pertinent data. The observers will record in addition how long it takes to complete the task, the frequency and amount of information exchanged, and the classification of that information. The types of measures and metrics which are relevant here include such things as quality of the design and suitability of the design, as assessed by judges who are unaware of which type of groups did the design. Also relevant will be measures of participant satisfaction with the end result and the work progress.

For our particular problem, the main task assigned to users would be to solve a design problem as a group, collaboratively, while being spatially separated. The chosen problem needs to be relatively simple, able to be solved in a matter of hours, while still requiring active collaboration of members of the design team. The activity to be observed is how CSCW tools are used in the process of design, and how their integration with design authoring tools influences the activity — in particular, is such integration beneficial, and what kinds of information about the design should be incorporated into communications. A control group of designers will work on a design problem under "normal" conditions, in which design authoring and CSCW tools are both present but not bound together in any way; another group will be given access to the Collaborative Studio, with communication tools integrated with CAD software. Experimenters will observe subjects, recording what kind of information is being exchanged, how, in which cases, and for what purposes participants use the communication tools at their disposal, and other pertinent data. The observers will record in addition how long it takes to complete the task, the frequency and amount of information exchanged, and the classification of that information.

5.3 Interaction Process Analysis

Another aspect of the Collaborative Studio design that we intend to study is the categorization of exchanged communications. We have developed a preliminary set of categories for the types of design communication that could be exchanged: request for change, change notification, information request, information reply, etc. However, the study will help to improve and augment the classification. The communication tools require the user to select the type of communication being sent, with the ability to supply a user-defined type if none of the options are appropriate. However, there is often a difference between what a subject says he or she is doing, and what is actually being done. Thus protocol analysis will be used to try to determine the intention which lies behind the sending of each communication, which should help identify possible classification schemas. Linguistic analysis will also be performed on the subjects' verbal reports to determine patterns, significant and preferred words (such as action verbs [1]), and the like.

6. Conclusion

The Collaborative Design Studio is being designed to provide features and functions likely to prove valuable in any engineering environment, whether traditional or distributed. However, until user studies are undertaken, the value of the system as a whole and the relevance of specific features remain unproven. To guide further development, we have proposed several evaluation strategies, which will serve as a primary source of information for the evolution of the design environment.

Acknowledgements. This work was supported in part by National Science Foundation (NSF), Knowledge and Distributed Intelligence in the Information Age (KDI) Initiative Grant CISE/IIS-9873005 and Grants ENG/DMI-9713718 and CISE/CDA-9729827.

Any opinions, findings, and conclusions or recommendations expressed in this material are those of the author(s) and do not necessarily reflect the views of the National Science Foundation or the other supporting government and corporate organizations.

References

[1] J. L. Austin. *How To Do Things With Words*. Harvard University Press, Cambridge, Massachusetts, 1962.

[2] D. C. Brown and B. Chandrasekaran. *Design Problem Solving : Knowledge Structures and Control Strategies*. M. Kaufmann Publishers, Loas Altos, CA, 1989.

[3] J. Clement. Observed methods for generating analogies in scientific problem solving. *Cognitive Science*, 12:563–586, 1988.

[4] K. Dunbar. How scientists really reason: Scientific reasoning in real-world laboratories. In R. J. Sternberg and J. E. Davidson, editors, *The Nature of Insight*, pages 365–395. The MIT Press, Cambridge, MA, 1995.

[5] C. L. Dym. *Engineering Design: A Synthesis of Views*. Cambridge University Press, New York, NY, 1994.

[6] K. A. Ericsson and H. A. Simon. *Protocol Analysis: Verbal Reports as Data*. The MIT Press, Cambridge, Massachusetts, revised, third printing edition, 1999.

[7] T. T. Hewett and J. L. DePaul. Towards a human-centered scientific problem solving environment. In E. Houstis, S. Gallipolous, J. R. Rice, and R. Bramley, editors, *Enabling Technologies for Computational Science*. Kluwer Scientific Publishers, Boston, MA, 2000.

[8] T. T. Hewett and S. Scott. The use of thinking-out-loud and protocol analysis in development of a process model of interactive database searching. In H.-J. Bullinger and B. Shackel, editors, *Human Computer Interaction–INTERACT '87*, pages 51–56. Amsterdam: North-Holland, September 1987.

[9] K. J. Holyoak and P. Thagard. *Mental Leaps: Analogy in Creative Thought*. The MIT Press, Cambridge, MA, 1995.

[10] B. Kirwan and L.-K. Ainsworth, editors. *A Guide to Task Analysis*. Taylor and Francis, London, England UK, 1992.

[11] M. L. Maher, S. J. Simoff, and A. Cicognani. *Understanding Virtual Design Studios*. Springer Verlag, 2000.

[12] S. E. Poltrock and G. Engelbeck. Requirements for a virtual collocation environment. *Information and Software Technology*, 41(6):331–340, April 1999.

[13] W. C. Regli and V. Cicirello. Managing digital libraries for computer-aided design. *International Journal of Computer Aided Design*, 32(2):119–132, Februrary 2000. Special Issue on *CAD After 2000*. Mohsen Rezayat, Guest Editor.

[14] T. L. Seamster, R. E. Redding, J. R. Cannon, and J. M. Ryder. Cognitive task analysis of expertise in air traffic control. *International Journal of Aviation Psychology*, 3(4):257–283, 1993.

[15] J. C. Tang and L. J. Leifer. A framework for understanding the workspace activity of design teams. In *Proceedings of the Conference of Computer-Supported Cooperative Work*, 1988.

A Method to Design Process Architecture in a Distributed Product Realization Environment

Angran Xiao, Janet K. Allen, David Rosen and Farrokh Mistree
Systems Realization Laboratory, The George W. Woodruff School of Mechanical Engineering
Georgia Institute of Technology, Atlanta, GA 30332-0405
gte790f@prism.gatech.edu,janet.allen@me.gatech.edu,david.rosen@me.gatech.edu
farrokh.mistree@me.gatech.edu

Abstract

Globalization, collaboration and competition are forcing product realization processes to become faster and more distributed. The requirements for higher efficiency, lower cost, and better product quality lead to challenges in the design of a product realization process in which concurrency and distribution are important. A distributed process structuring method (DPSM) is presented to help engineers design process architectures, based on characteristics of the distributed environment. DPSM also provides a framework for managing collaboration. With DPSM, a process is represented hierarchically by partitioning the process and reorganizing the activities. Four typical architecture templates, sequential, parallel, integrated and distributed architectures are presented. Process architectures are constructed by mapping the process representation into the templates. DPSM is a state-of-the-science method for structuring the distributed product realization process, while ensuring its modularity and robustness. An engineering case is investigated, and the distributed architecture is implemented using agent technology.

1. Designing Product Realization Processes

The modern marketplace has forced industries to compete not only by improving product design methods, but also new strategies. By considering characteristics of distributed product realization in design of these processes, a flexible, robust and efficient process architecture can be designed to support collaborative product development.

1.1 The Product Realization Process and the Process Architecture

A product realization process is a group of product development activities that occur from conceptual design through manufacturing. The product realization is becoming a complex, collaborative process. In design, engineers collaborate in order to accomplish a concurrent product realization process. To accomplish this, information is shared, and resources must be managed systematically, etc. Therefore, designing the collaborative process is actually designing a computer-supported framework to help engineers in product development.

A product realization process can be decomposed hierarchically into phases, events and tasks. *Phases* are the distinct stages of a product's development. [1]. An *event* is a group of product development activities that must occur so that the solution of a problem or sub-problem can be achieved [2]. A *task* is an activity in the event in which a specific problem is solved or a decision made. After representing the process, the next step is to structure the process architecture, that is, create a graphical representation of the product realization process, including all activities and their relationships, information and material flows, and the engineer and tool manipulations.

Constructing process architecture constitutes designing the product development process [1, 3]. This involves partitioning the system for function, partitioning the design process into a set of decisions and planning the sequence in which these decisions will be made [1]. Distribution causes additional difficulties, hence traditional process design methods are not effective. In this paper, a process structuring method, the Distributed Process Structuring Method (DPSM) is introduced to design collaborative process architectures.

1.2 Distributed Product Realization

Since the early 1990's, product realization process has changed dramatically. Globalization, cooperation and competition is forcing the process to become faster and more distributed [4], Figure 1. The requirements for higher efficiency, lower cost, and better product quality lead to challenges in the design of product realization process in which concurrency and distribution are important [5-6]. Five important characteristics of distributed product realization are:

1. Engineers are geographically distributed;
2. Product development activities are accomplished concurrently;
3. Heterogeneous software tools and platforms are integrated;
4. Information and data are distributed and knowledge is shared at request ;
5. The control of the product realization activities is distributed [4].

0-7695-0798-9/00 $10.00 © 2000 IEEE

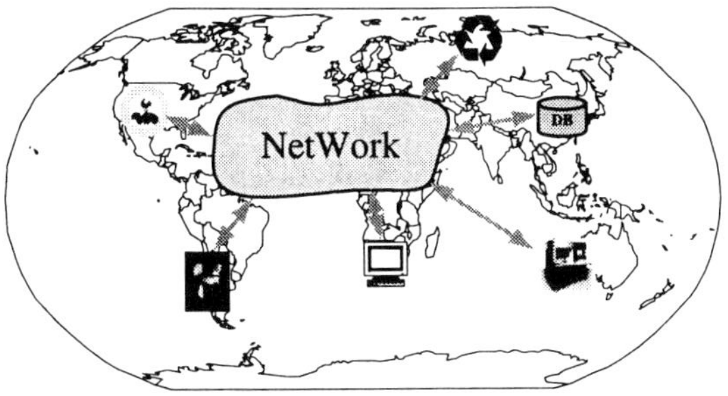

Figure 1. Distributed product realization

Physically, a distributed process is composed of computers, machines, software, etc., at different locations and connected by network in which information and control are shared.

1.3 Challenges in Process Structuring

Distribution can greatly improve the flexibility, robustness, and efficiency of the product realization process. However, engineers working in a distributed environment may only consider their own objectives while making decisions. Therefore, a coordination mechanism must be designed into the distributed process architecture to implement collaboration.

Coordination between engineers is supported by specific communication tools or methods. There are a variety of approaches in the literature for supporting such coordination, e.g., developing new communicating tools [6-7] and new languages to express activities [8], and constructing knowledge sharing approaches [9]. However, collaboration can also be structured by rigorously designing the collaboration process by specifically identifying and supporting appropriate patterns for communication while limiting or restricting collaboration where it does not contribute to the overall goal of product development. That is, by properly assigning tasks, planning activities, and constructing the process framework carefully, a collaboration coordination mechanism is "designed into" the process framework to ensure greater efficiency, lower cost and higher product quality.

Traditional process analysis methods are based on experience. Another challenge is the topological structure of the distributed process architecture. Standard architectures, e.g., a sequential architecture, highly reduce the process flexibility, robustness and efficiency. Therefore, we present a new topological model of the distributed product realization process. This new model is flexible, modular, robust, and easily implemented.

2. FRAME OF REFERENCE

System partitioning is one of the most important methods to analyze and solve engineering problems, thus the original problem is broken in to sufficiently simple modules that finding solutions is a manageable process. At the same time, the problem and its model must be a close-enough approximation of the real world that satisficing solutions yields useful results" [3].

In mechanical engineering, system partitioning methods are categorized into product and process partitioning methods. Products are partitioned based on geometric shape, functions, or assembly constraints, etc. Pahl and Beitz propose a hierarchical function architecture to represent the elements of a product, the relationships between them are tracked by the transformation of matter, energy and information [10]. Ulrich defines product architectures by mapping functional elements onto physical components and relating them to the performance of the firm [11]. Rosen investigates the use of discrete mathematics to design modular product architecture, a subset-superset is proposed to identify all possible fragments of product architecture which can serve as building blocks for an overall product architecture [12].

Process partitioning methods are used to distinguish activities and their relationships in product development. Fujita and Ishii improved the hierarchical architecture for this purpose and their method improves system integration and scalability [5]. The Decision Support Problem Technique (DSP Technique) is presented by Bras and Mistree to design the design process based on "the needs of Concurrent Engineering", within which the design process is partitioned hierarchically into system, phases, events, tasks, and decisions [13]. Kusiak and Wang developed a system decomposition approach to decide tasks and parameters in the detail design process of a product [14]. The process partitioning method presented here is based on the need for collaboration in a distributed environment.

3. CASE STUDY: THE RAPID TOOLING TESTBED

Rapid prototyping and injection modeling are product fabrication technologies which can be used to build products with almost any geometric shape. Rosen and colleagues are developing the Rapid Tooling TestBed (RTTB) as an experimental system to investigate methods for product design and realization [4].

As shown in Figure 2, the RTTB is divided into three phases: design, design for manufacture (DFM), and manufacture. During the design phase, requirements including part representation and specifications are entered. In the DFM stage, suitable part and mold materials, rapid prototype technologies, and injection molding technologies, are selected. In addition, injection molding tooling is designed and the part is tailored to facilitate the manufacture of both the mold and part. The final stage involves the actual manufacture of the tooling and part.

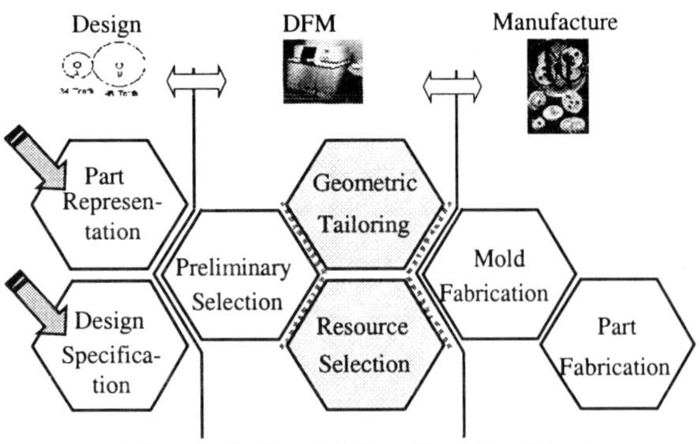

Figure 2. Rapid Tooling TestBed

4. DISTRIBUTED PROCESS STRUCTURING METHOD

In this paper, the three steps of DPSM are presented to design the product realization process architecture. These steps are:

1. Analyzing and partitioning the product realization process;
2. Presenting typical templates for process architectures;
3. Mapping activities into the process architecture.

4.1 Analyzing a Product Realization Process

In the RTTB, we are developing a philosophy of implementing collaboration by managing the couplings between the activities. This coupling is due to dependence between these two activities so that they must be accomplished simultaneously. Local collaboration is different from that in the distributed environment, in which independence and concurrency are dominant characteristics. Dependence relationships across phases are a principal reason for iteration and errors in product development. Compared to dependence within a phase, dependence across phases usually causes greater cost, longer product development time and worse product quality. Therefore, the objective of the first phase is, *partitioning and organizing the product realization process into an uncoupled hierarchy architecture in which the activities can be accomplished independently and concurrently.* Process partitioning consists of three steps:

Step1: Partitioning the product realization process hierarchically into phases, events, and tasks.

Decomposing the activities into phases, events and tasks is a recursive analysis process, it is fairly straightforward to represent a process hierarchically. A process should be partitioned hierarchically into a level such that each activity at the leaf nodes of the process representation can be accomplished independently, using a single resource in the product realization environment, with input only at the beginning of the activity. The challenge here is to determine how finely the elements should be decomposed, while retaining independence.

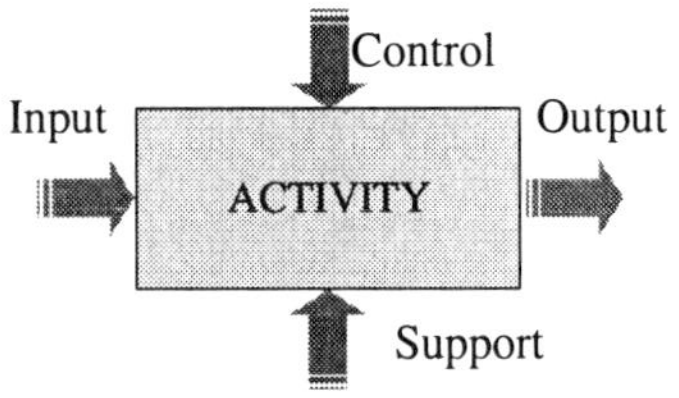

Figure 3. Basic model of activity

In Figure 3, an activity is shown, if the activity can be accomplished without interfering with other activities it is independent and therefore can be carried out concurrently with other activities. Using this model, a hierarchical process representation is obtained by partitioning the processes, deciding the inputs, outputs, controls and support required for the activities. We propose two rules for partitioning activities:

Rule 1: Further partitioning the activity if the tools supporting it consist of multiple resources, e.g, computing tools, software packages, equipment, etc.;
Rule 2: Further partition the activity if information has to be input in the middle of it.

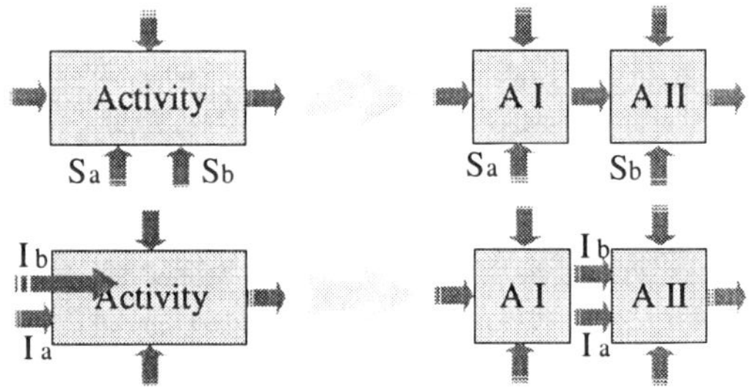

Figure 4. Partitioning activity for distribution

Rule 1 is proposed to eliminate coupling due to resource use. When two software packages are required for an activity and they are distributed, information must be exchanged between these packages frequently, and coupling occurs between the computers running packages. However if this activity is decomposed into two sub-activities, both are independent. Rule 2 is introduced for a similar reason. In Figure 4, although sub-activity II still depends on information I_b, sub-activity I does not.

Step2: Tracking dependence relationships between activities.

In order to design the distributed process architecture, dependence relationships between activities should be eliminated. Information and matter flows are usually used to track them. Two tentative rules are proposed:

Rule 3: Only dependence relationships between end node activities are counted.
Rule 4: Only dependence relationships across phases are counted.

Rule 3 is presented because activities at a higher level must be further decomposed, it is unnecessary to track their relationships. Rule 4 is presented because only the dependence across phases needs to be investigated, it is the most significant and causes iteration and errors.

Step3: Reorganizing the activities into uncoupled hierarchy architecture.

The purpose of reorganization is to construct a process architecture in which most of the significant dependence relationships are eliminated [15]. Presently, this work is done based on three tentative rules.

Rule 5: If an activity is independent from others, it should be moved to the first phase;
Rule 6: If the coupling between two activities is unavoidable, cluster the activities into one phase such that the iterations happened within the phase;
Rule 7: If an activity is dependent on other activities in the downstream phases, moves this activity backward behind the other activities. That is, if A depends on B and C, move A behind B and C.

Rule 5 is introduced because independent activities should be accomplished as early as possible, so that other dependent activities can be accomplished earlier. Rule 6 is introduced to make the coordination of the architecture as simple as possible. Finally, Rule 7 is applied to reduce information and matter flows from the downstream phases forward in order to reduce iteration.

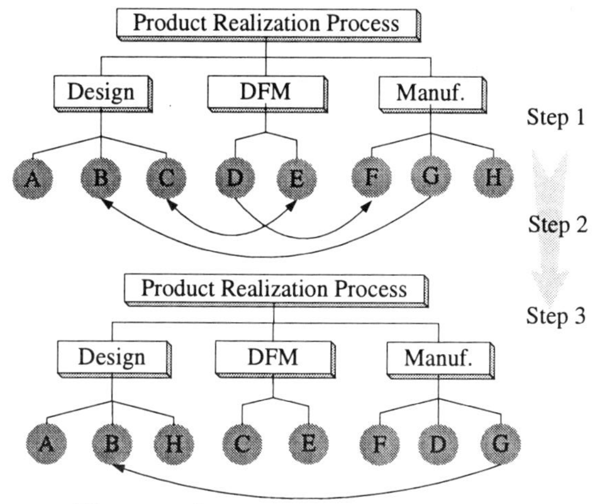

Figure 5. Steps in process partitioning

An example is shown in Figure 5 in which dependence relationships are indicated by arrows. Activity H is moved to the design phase based on Rule 5. C and E are coupled and therefore clustered based on Rule 6. From Rule 7, D is moved to the manufacturing phase, thus eliminating most of the coupling relationships. Next typical templates for organizing the process architectures are introduced.

4.2 Presenting Typical Templates of the Process Architecture

Process architecture is the framework representing the logical relationships, management structure, and the information and material flows within the process. Different process architectures can be constructed based on different design philosophies.

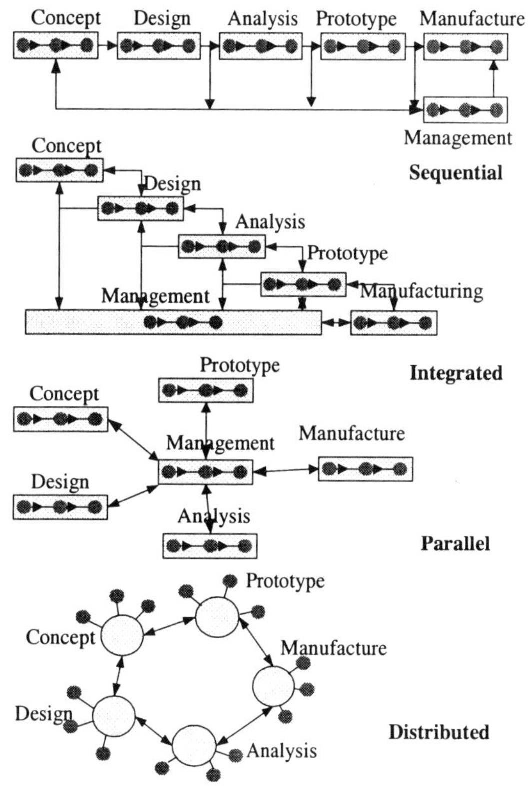

Figure 6. Typical process templates

Four templates, sequential, parallel, integrated and distributed process architectures, are presented. Given a process consisting of concept design, design, analysis, prototyping, manufacturing and management, the four typical process architectures are illustrated in Figure 6. In the figure, a box represents a phase and a circle represents an event. The arrows represent information and matter flows. Process architecture can be easily developed into a product realization framework, in which the circles represent agents or activities, and the arrows represent communication channels and material flow among the agents.

Figure 6(a) is a sequential architecture in which activities are organized linearly. The parallel architecture (b) improves the concurrency of the product development by overlapping activities. But it is still essentially a linear architecture and one single manager or management team controls all other activities. This integrated architecture increases product development efficiency because activities are carried out concurrently under the supervision of manager. On the other hand, it does have some shortcomings. (1) If the manager is not on-line, all activities must pause. (2) A centralized manager forms a bottleneck of information flow in the whole process. (3) All coordination tasks are integrated within the management node, this greatly reduces the process modularity. Thus any change or mistake made by the central node will cause changes in other activities and vice versa.

The distributed process architecture is presented as the next-generation process architecture for product realization in the worldwide environment. It consists of two levels of nodes, the larger ones representing phases and the smaller nodes are events. A coordinator, an automated independent information-handling agent, is within each phase node. Engineers are working within the event nodes. Event nodes within a phase communicate directly with each other, and transfer information and matter through phase agents to event nodes in other phases. Phase agents can talk directly without passing other nodes. As an example, first, engineers receive requirements from higher nodes. After working independently using their own tools, they share knowledge with other engineers in the same phase directly. If an engineer needs to communicate with another in different phase, the request is sent to its phase agent. With the help of the phase agent, the engineer receives information, without worrying about the details.

The distributed architecture is not only a flexible model of process architecture, it is also a model of information communication, activity planning, and resource management, etc.

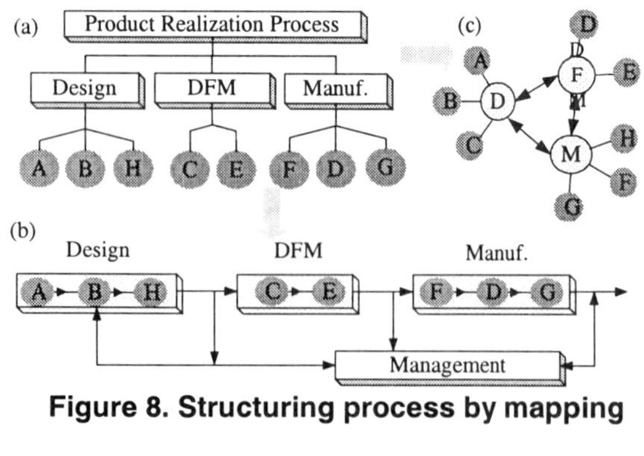

Figure 8. Structuring process by mapping

4.3 Mapping the Hierarchical Representation into the Process Architecture

With the process representation and templates, it is easy to map the activities into process architectures. In Figure 8, (b) represents a sequential process architecture and (c) a distributed process architecture. The coordinators are represented with large circles. These coordinators:

- provide information-communicating supports. Information can be shared or broadcast to all other nodes.
- track the information flow and the versions of product development.
- support task selection. An agent (controlled by engineers) can select the most suitable activity as its task.

With graphical representation of the process architecture, it is easy to develop a distributed product realization process using agent technology.

5. CASE STUDY

In the case study, the design of a gear in the RTTB, the available resources are common CAD software, rapid prototyping tools and equipment in a distributed product realization environment. Using the Distributed Process Structuring Method, the first phase is to analyze the gear development process. The detailed process representation is illustrated in Figure 9.

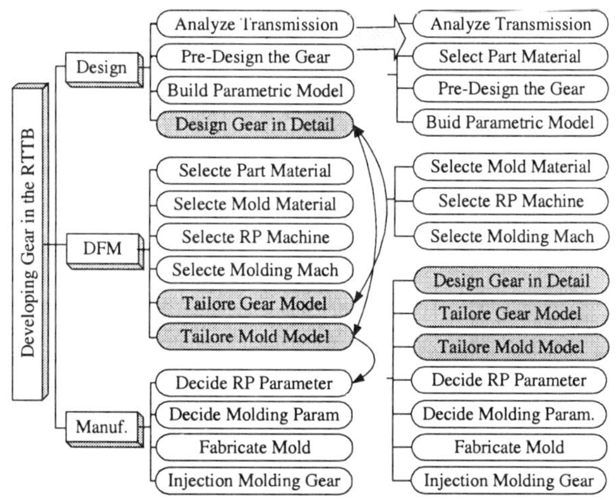

Figure 9. Process representation of case study

First, the gear developing process is partitioned into independent activities. For example, the gear design phase is partitioned into four events, analyzing transmission ratio, preliminary design, building a parametric model, and designing the gear. The analysis of the transmission ratio is accomplished with the package DESIDES (developed by SRL). Building a parametric model is accomplished using a CAD software package, such as Pro/E,

CATIA, etc. These software packages are and distributed within different computers. The dependence relationships between events is shown in the figure. *Design Gear in Detail* is highly coupled with *Gear and Mold Tailoring*, represented with double arrows. Therefore this event is shifted into the same phase as the *Gear Tailoring* and *Mold Tailoring* events, the manufacturing phase. They are not moved into the DFM phase because the *Mold Tailoring* depends on *Decide RP Parameters*. Finally, *Select Part Material* is moved to the design phase because it is independent of the other activities. The process is thus re-organized into a de-coupled hierarchical structure.

Given the templates of the process architectures, the activities in the hierarchical representation of the process can be mapped into different process architectures. In the distributed environment, the process architecture can be implemented using agent technology. The process architecture of this example is illustrated in Figure 10.

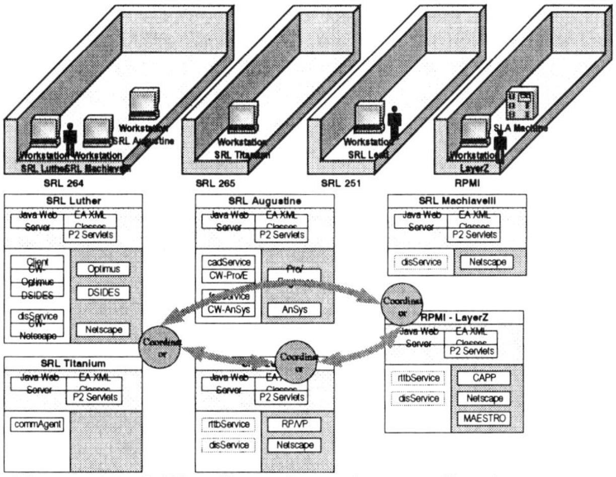

Figure 10. A Distributed product realization process in the RTTB

6. CLOSURE

In this paper we introduce a new process design method, Distributed Process Structuring Method. DPSM is a state-of-the-science method used to design the process architecture in the distributed product realization environment. Designing distributed process architecture is a complex research question, in this paper, we only present part of our on-going research. In the future, more experiments will be designed to validate this method. Also, the rules should be validated mathematically.

ACKNOWLEDGMENTS

We gratefully acknowledge NSF grant 96-12365 and funding from NIST 70NANBOH0024. The cost of computer time is underwritten by the Systems Realization Laboratory at Georgia Tech.

REFERENCES

[1] F. Mistree, W.F. Smith, B.A. Bras, J.K. Allen, D. Muster, D., "Decision Based Design: A Contemporary Paradigm for Ship Design", *Transactions of the Society of Naval Architects and Marine Engineers*, 1990, pp. 565-587.

[2] M. Hale, *An Open Computing Infrastructure that Facilitates Integrated Product and Process Development from a Decision-Based Perspective*, Ph.D. Dissertation, Aerospace Engineering, Gerogia Institute of Technology, Atlanta, GA, 1996.

[3] F. Mistree, D. Muster, J.A. Shupe, J.K. Allen, "A Decision-Based Perspective for the Design of Methods for System Design", *Recent Experiences in Multidisciplinary Analysis and Optimization*, Hampton, VA, 1989.

[4] J.K. Allen and D.W. Rosen, "Design Methodology Issues in a Distributed Studio for Rapid Tooling and Molded Parts," *CIRP Proceedings: Multimedia Technologies for Collaborative Design and Manufacturing,* Los Angeles, CA 1997, pp. 21-28.

[5] K. Fujita, S. Akagi, "Agent-Based Distributed Design System Architecture for Basic Ship Design," *Proceedings of 5th ISPE International Conference on Concurrent Engineering (CE98),* July, 1998, Tokyo, Japan.

[6] H. Park, M.R. Cutkosky, A.B. Conru, S. Lee, "An Agent-Based Approach to Concurrent Cable Harness Design", *AIEDAM* Vol. 8, No.1, March 1994, pp. 45-61.

[7] M.R. Cutkosky, R.S. Engelmore, R.E. Fikes, M.R. Genesereth, T.R., Gruber, S. William, J.M. Tenenbaum, and J.C. Weber, "PACT: An Experiment in Integrating Concurrent Engineering Systems", *IEEE Computer*, Vol. 26 No. 1, 1993, pp. 28-37

[8] C. Schlenoff, A. Knutilla, S. Ray, "Unified Process Specification Language: Requirements for Modeling Process", NISTIR 5910, September 1996.

[9] G. Toye, M.R. Cutkosky, L.J. Leifer, J.M. Tenenbaum, J. Clicksman, "Share: A Methodology and Environment for Collaborative Product Development", Infrastructure for Collaborative Enterprise *(CDR-TR #19930507)*, IEEE Press, 1993.

[10] G. Pahl and W. Beitz, 1996, *Engineering Design: A Systematic Approach*, 2nd Edition, Springer-Verlag, NY.

[11] K.T. Ulrich and S.D. Eppinger, *Product Design and Development*, McGraw-Hill Inc., NY, 1995.

[12] D.W. Rosen, "Design of Modular Product Architectures in Discrete Design Spaces Subject to Life Cycle Issues," *Adv. In Design Automation*, Irvine, CA, ASME, Paper No. 96-DETC/DAC-1485, 1996.

[13] F. Mistree, B.A. Bras, W.F. Smith, and J.K. Allen, "Modeling Design Processes: A Conceptual, Decision-Based Approach," *International Journal of Engineering Design and Automation,* Vol. 1, No. 4, 1996, pp. 209-221.

[14] A. Kusiak, J. Wang, D.W. He, "Negotiation in Constraint-Based Design", *Journal of Mechanical Design*, Vol. 118, No. 4, 1996, pp. 470-477.

[15] T.U. Pimmier, S.D. Eppinger, S. D., "Integration Analysis of Product Decompositions", *DE-Vol.68, Design Theory and Methodology,* DTM'94, ASME 1995, Page 343 - 351.

Evaluation challenges for a federation of heterogeneous information providers: The case of NASA's Earth Science Information Partnerships

Catherine Plaisant[%], Anita Komlodi[#%], Francis Lindsay
University of Maryland
Institute for Advanced Computer Studies
[%]Human-Computer Information Laboratory
[#]College of Information Studies

plaisant@cs.umd.edu, komlodi@glue.umd.edu, flindsay@geog.umd.edu

Abstract

NASA's Earth Science Information Partnership Federation is an experiment funded to assess the ability of a group of widely heterogeneous earth science data or service providers to self organize and provide improved and affordable access to an expanding earth science user community. As it is self-organizing, the Federation is mandated to set in place an evaluation methodology and collect metrics reflecting the outcomes and benefits of the Federation. This paper describes the challenges of organizing such a federated partnership self-evaluation and discusses the issues encountered during the metrics definition phase of the early data collection. Our experience indicates that a large number of metrics will be needed to fully represent the activities and strengths of all partners, but because of the heterogeneity of the ESIPs the qualitative data (comments accompanying the metric data and success stories) becomes the most useful information. Other lessons learned include the absolute need for online browsing tools to accompany data collection tools. Finally, our experience confirms the effect of evaluation as an agent of change, the best example being the high level of collaboration among the ESIPs which can be in part attributed to the initial identification of collaboration as one of the important evaluation factors of the Federation.

1. Introduction

Beside the obvious need to evaluate any experiment to measure its positive and negative impact the U.S. Government Performance and Results Act (GPRA) [1] is slowly changing the way federal projects are being conducted. Quantitative and qualitative metrics are being defined by projects but large and heterogeneous programs and experiments present a serious evaluation challenge.

The U. S. Government Performance and Results Act was created in response to complaints and findings of waste and inefficiency in federal programs stemming from 'insufficient articulation of program goals and inadequate information on program performance'. Among the goals of the GPRA is promoting a new focus on results, service quality, and customer satisfaction. It mandates the creation of strategic plans, including provisions for program evaluation. Annual performance plans and reports are another area covered by the Act. Each agency is required to create annual performance plans for each program. Goals need to be expressed in objective, quantifiable and measurable form.

GPRA calls for the establishment of 'performance indicators to be used in measuring or assessing the relevant outputs, service levels, and outcomes of each program activity'[1], and for the provision of a basis for actual program results with the established performance goals. It also requires a description of the means to be used in verifying and validating measured values. In cases where performance cannot be measured by objective and quantifiable terms, special arrangements can be made for alternative performance evaluation methods, such as descriptive statements of minimally effective and successful programs. The GPRA gives general definitions of output and outcome measures, performance goals and indicators.

In this paper we focus on one of NASA's Earth Science Enterprise experiments. The goal of NASA's Earth Science Enterprise (ESE) is to further develop our understanding of the total Earth System, including the effects of natural or human-induced changes to the global environment. The program draws upon the full range of NASA's technical and scientific capabilities to achieve this goal. The ESE distributes this information to both the public and the private sectors in order to promote productive use of the gathered data.

The Earth Science Information Partners Federation (or ESIP Federation) is an experiment – or working prototype – funded to assess if such a Federation could be the viable enterprise model to facilitate the public availability of Earth science data from geographically dispersed providers, and to foster the development of new services to the user community. The Federation itself is charged with collaboratively developing this new enterprise model. It is charged to define a governance structure that encourages cooperation as well as create a community of ESIPs that are dedicated to the continued success of the Federation.

The most striking characteristic of the Federation is the diversity of its partners:

- 10 "Veteran" Distributed Active Archive Centers (DAACs) who have been operational for years and deal with the archiving and distribution of Earth science data (called ESIP Type 1s).
- 12 new data-enhancing ESIPs, generally run by Earth scientists themselves at Universities. They create new products and services for the research community (called ESIP Type 2s). Examples of ESIP2s include the University of Maryland ESIP specializing in new data products and services for land cover studies, and the DODS ESIPs offering data interoperability software components.
- 12 commercial entities, from startup companies to established educational entities like museums, provide practical applications of Earth science data for a broader community (called ESIP Type 3s – they are only partially funded by NASA, and meant to become rapidly self sustaining). Examples of ESIP Type 3s goals vary from developing educational materials to developing new services for commercial shipping and fisheries.

This paper describes the challenges facing the ESIP Federation in organizing its own evaluation, and discusses the issues encountered during the metrics definition phase of the early data collection.

2. The Role of Evaluation

Marchionini [2] differentiates evaluation as a research process from product or system testing. Evaluation research examines the interaction of complex phenomena using qualitative and quantitative methods, studying the object of the evaluation from many different angles. The current evaluation aims at similar methods, as the application area and the organizational experiment are both new and complex phenomena.

The object of the current evaluation is a web-based information system. Methods of evaluation suggested for more traditional information systems can be applied, although the technology is different and this should be taken into account. In both cases, information is the commodity that is collected and processed and provided to users. The overall goal and mission is the same for both, thus evaluation methods will have to be similar Lancaster [3] suggests defining inputs, outputs, and outcomes in information system evaluation. The long-term objective of any such system is to achieve certain outcomes in the community it serves. Inputs are processed in order to generate outputs, in the case of information systems the goal is to turn financial input into information services output.

Griffiths and King [4] emphasize the importance of measuring not only performance, but also user satisfaction, purpose of use, consequences of use, etc. They suggest four kinds of measures: input costs, outputs, effectiveness, and domain. They define information system functions as user-related, operational and support functions. The four measures are collected in all these functional areas. In these terms, the evaluation reported here focuses on output, outcome and impact measures in user-centered functions.

Marchionini [5] provides one of the best examples of long term digital library evaluation. An evaluation of the Perseus Project, an evolving digital library of resources for the study of the ancient world was carried out. The evaluation was extensive and covered several distributed sites with different practices but they were all using the same multimedia system and the data could be collected fairly homogeneously. The author describes methodology, results and implications.

In the domain of geographical information systems Hill [6] reports on the evaluation of a single site and how it improved usability and user satisfaction. Other digital library evaluation discussions can be found in the D-Lib Magazine article of July/August 1998 [7] , and in Bishop et al. [8].

3. The Earth Science Information Partnership Federation

One challenge for the ESIP Federation is the prototyping of alternative ways of developing, producing, and distributing Earth science data. The Internet, the World Wide Web, and other rapidly developing technologies enable the public to access vast quantities of information. Developing practical applications of advanced information technologies such as these is vital to the discipline of Earth System Science. Current research in the Earth sciences has the potential to yield a variety of new scientific insights and practical benefits - from monitoring deforestation or understanding global environmental changes, to providing customized reports to farmers or fishermen, or offering services to local government and land owners. The ESIP Federation provides the means to facilitate data access, exchange, and enhancement.

The Federation was launched in 1998 with the competitive selection of the initial 24 ESIP Type 2s among candidates from the academic, government and private sectors.

ESIPs have different levels of funding and cost sharing, they are at different stages of developments – from the well established ESIP Type 1s, to others who are not to date fully operational. Some offer data only, other services but no data, and some both. Some ESIPs have a handful of employees, other several dozens. Some ESIPs easily reach thousands of users via a popular website (e.g. the NBC4 weather page) while others cater to a smaller number of high-end scientists who may use their service extensively. Finally another peculiarity of the Federation is that it will be evaluated by the level of cooperation among ESIPs. Individual ESIPs were selected following a competitive process and will have to recompete to receive continuing support. Because of its self-organizing principle, the Federation receives limited guidance from NASA, which leaves room for experimentation but can also lead to confusion in the early stages of organization.

In simple terms the goal of the Federation can be described as the provision of improved and affordable access to Earth science data, and the development of new user communities attracted by new types of data and services.

4. Challenges of Evaluation

4.1 Leadership and Coordination in Evaluating Distributed Systems

The development of an evaluation plan, and its execution can be originated on different levels of a heterogeneous, distributed systems. It is important to clearly define responsibilities and coordinate actions among the different evaluation activities in order to minimize effort. An individual project can be collecting evaluation information for their own use, or collect data for reporting and management.

The development of evaluation metrics across all ESIPs will inevitably involve representation from these ESIPs. This is necessary to insure the inclusion of all the different types of activities and accomplishments of the different units. The management of this process was setup by NASA management decision and voluntary selection. The team at the University of Maryland took responsibility for defining and developing metrics, and devising ways to collect them. In the development of the metrics, we built on several different evaluation efforts in the ESIP projects, and collected several existing sets of metrics. We defined a new set based on these and on our evaluation experience with our own ESIP, the Global Land Cover Facility (http://glcf.umiacs.umd.edu). Another ESIP volunteered to use their existing web tools to develop prototypes of online data collection and viewing tools.

4.2 Including all aspects of what the partners do

The 34 ESIPs grouped under the aegis of the Federation differ considerably in their profiles. They vary in size, infrastructure, mission, and services. The heterogeneity makes it difficult to find a balance between (1) limiting the number of metrics, and (2) identifying metrics that truly represent the activities and strengths of all ESIPs.

Our strategy evolved over time. The first approach involved defining a small, common set of mandatory metrics that all projects would provide, later we added the notion of a larger group of optional metrics. We also considered including yet another level of metrics: custom metrics defined and collected by the individual ESIP in order to monitor and improve their own activities (e.g. what part of the website or dataset is most used? is the help system being used?).

This multilevel approach was rejected mainly due to the lack of agreement on a small set of common "mandatory" metrics. Instead, a single larger set of common metrics was developed, acknowledging that not all ESIPs will be able to collect all metrics and would just mark them as Non Applicable.

Examples: The initial list of metrics included measuring the amount of data delivered, the volume of data etc. because this was a traditional way of measuring ESIP Type 1s (DAACs) activities. Some of the ESIPs do not have any data per se, and instead provide valuable services (i.e. processing data provided by users, or providing interoperability capabilities and software components). In response we had to also measure the number and type of services.

One of the initial metrics was the total number of users, but in our first attempt to collect metrics data we realized that we were adding up science users downloading data, kids using education materials, and the general public reading web pages. It became clear that a better classification was needed to reflect the diversity and richness of the activities so we separated consumers (e.g. museum patrons, web page readers) from data and service users (who download or order data).

Qualitative data. In order to accommodate the variety of the ESIPs, we collected both quantitative data (metrics) and qualitative data referred to as nuggets. Nuggets are short descriptions reporting on the special activities and accomplishments of the ESIPs. There are currently twenty categories of nuggets defined, based on discussions with the different projects.

Even after adding many metrics to our list of metrics there was still a strong feeling of not being able to completely capture the richness of activities and the nuggets have become the most important reporting method. For example one of the ESIPs did not have much data, very few users but generated results that could be better evaluated by the number of lives they saved! Clearly not a metric applicable to many ESIPs but could be reported via a nugget.

Examples of nugget types

- New science:
  - New type of data use
  - Data quality achievement
- Federation activities
  - Notable results from working group
  - Example of federation collaboration
  - Collaboration with other institutions
- Federation reactiveness
  - Rapid response to adverse event
  - Rapid dissemination of data or service
- Dissemination:
  - Publications written by ESIP users
  - Mention of ESIP in press
- Education
  - New K-12 education activities
  - New higher education activities
  - Student graduated
- Miscellaneous
  - Steps toward sustainability
  - Impact on citizens, business
  - Quotes

Examples of metrics:

Number of data and service users
Number of information consumers
Note: Consumers are all users who come to find information or learn from ESIP information but do not necessarily download data or use services
Number of repeat users
Data volume
Total data volume in archives, including data not available to users
Number of Datasets
Number of Data Products delivered
Volume of products delivered
New datasets not available before the federation
Number of services available to users
Number of services that were not available before the federation
Number of services rendered
Delivery time of data or service

4.3 Dealing with parallel collection efforts

Because of heterogeneity of the ESIPs subsets of ESIPs are also part of additional metrics collection efforts. For examples the DAACs (ESIP Type1s) have been in existence for years and many metrics are already being collected. The more "commercial" ESIPs are part of a larger group of projects required to submit special metrics related to their economic impact or financial well-being. Those concurrent metrics collection efforts use different collection mechanisms (e.g. interview, web form), have different time periods (e.g. monthly, yearly) and different due dates. Some metrics are compatible and can be re-used while others are not. When possible we try to reuse the data, format it to our metrics schema and then ask for feedback and corrections from the responsible ESIPs. The impact of this coordination was that the total number of metrics increased. For example the DAACs had always been reporting on the volume of data delivered so we also included that metrics to allow longitudinal comparisons even though we already had a similar (and preferable) metric for the number of products delivered.

Without coordinated metrics collection, the data metrics data providers become rapidly annoyed by the multiple requests for data. Coordination is rarely achieved because it is difficult, and because it does not benefit the decision-makers who are sponsoring the data collection.

4.4 Baseline Definition

The definition of the baseline presented difficulties as our evaluation efforts began after the start of the Federation. Data related to the baseline measure before the inception of the federation is sparse and mainly anecdotal - the exception being the DAACs which existed before the start of the other ESIPs. Their performance data could be used as a basis for comparison, however, the mere number of projects grew and thus performance is expected to multiply, this comparison would not be adequate.

Many baseline items consisted of vague complaints (such as "it took too long to get data", or "too long to make new data available"). Even though no good baseline numbers are available (e.g. number of days or months), it was useful to review this information and choose metrics or nugget categories that would help back up our claim that we were doing "better than before". As an example, the delivery time became a required metrics (average delivery time for different types of media). For the 'time to dissemination' comparing average times would be useless, we thought of counting the number of complaints - but formal complaints are rare, so instead we added a category of nuggets "Examples of rapid dissemination of new data" in which ESIPs are encouraged to report success in this direction.

In summary, even though the baseline is hard to define and not quantitative, attempting to describe it is very useful in formalizing goals and selecting metrics.

4.5 Coercing Participation in the Data Collection

The GPRA makes evaluation and metrics collection mandatory but how much effort is to be dedicated to it will remain a matter of interpretation. Some ESIPs have more resources than others and will be more likely to have staff and resources for generating good metrics data. ESIPs with poor results may not report, which might muddy the metrics summary, but those ESIPs will suffer the consequences later on when renewal time comes, so in the long term this problem should recede.

We found that merely asking the ESIPs to submit data would not be successful without providing a way for the ESIPs to also view their own data and the data of other ESIPs. Therefore we are working on password-protected data viewers that let federation participants review the collected data.

On the other hand, it was suggested that the qualitative data, such as nuggets, would be better reported globally, i.e. at the federation level, to avoid the bias favoring large ESIPs who would have more resources and could assign more staff time to enter nuggets.

4.6 Internal vs. External Evaluation

The current metrics were developed and defined with the evaluands, the organization being evaluated. These metrics are reported to the management of the project, which presents a contradiction of interests. The projects are not likely to suggest metrics that will present a negative image of their performance, as this would be against their best interests. An external evaluation body ('judge') would need to be appointed in order to insure impartiality.

4.7 Evaluation as an agent of change - You become what you measure!

Metrics collection can effect the phenomena itself. For example asking for the volume of data delivered encourages ESIPs to create large chunks of inseparable data to boost this metrics. But having files too large to download was a complaint identified in the baseline, so instead it seemed important to measure the number of items delivered, which would encourage smaller chunks so that users can download only what they need. It seemed important to favor metrics that "if abused", would have a positive overall effect on Federation activities. (note that we ended up using both metrics to remain compatible with another collection effort -see 4.3).

The best example of evaluation as an agent of change might be the high level of collaboration among the ESIPs. This can be in part attributed to the initial identification of collaboration as one of the important factors in the evaluation of the Federation by NASA.

5. Conclusion

We have described some of the challenges facing the ESIP Federation in organizing its own evaluation, and discussed the issues encountered during the metrics definition phase of the early data collection. This is just the beginning. We are currently collecting the first round of data and feedback on the appropriateness of the proposed metrics via personal telephone interviews. Tools are being implemented to allow online data collection and review. We know that this early evaluation will only provide a crude overview of the early activity of the Federation but will also provide a crucial tool to its vitality.

Our experience indicates that a large number of metrics will be needed to fully represent the activities and strengths of all partners, but because of the heterogeneity of the ESIPs the qualitative data (comments accompanying the metric data and success stories) becomes the most useful data. Other lessons learned include the need for evaluation data viewing tools to accompany collection tools. Finally, our experience confirms the effect of evaluation as an agent of change.

6. Acknowledgements

This work is supported in part by NASA (NCC5300). We want to thank all the Federation members that helped define the evaluation challenges presented here, Joseph Ja'Ja' and John Townshend, principal investigators of the Maryland ESIP, Ben Shneiderman and Gary Marchionini for their helpful feedback.

7. References

[1] GPRA 93: Government Performance Results Act of 1993 http://www.whitehouse.gov/OMB/mgmt-gpra/gplaw2m.html

[2] Marchionini, G. Evaluating Digital Libraries: A Longitudinal and Multifaceted View. Technical Report, June 2000. http://ils.unc.edu/~march/perseus/lib-trends-findraft.pdf

[3] Lancaster, F. W., If you want to evaluate your library. Imprint, Champaign, IL : *University of Illinois, Graduate School of Library and Information Science*, 1988.

[4] Griffiths, J.-M. A manual on the evaluation of information centers and services by Jose-Marie Griffiths and Donald W. King. New York : AIAA, 1991.

[5] Marchionini, G., Crane, H., Evaluating hypermedia and learning: Methods and results from the Perseus project. *ACM Transactions on Information Systems,* vol. 12, 1 (Jan. 1994) 5-34. also: Evaluation of the Perseus Hypermedia Corpus. http://www.perseus.tufts.edu/FIPSE/report-final.html

[6] Hill, L. et al. (1997) User Evaluation: Summary of the Methodologies and Results for the Alexandria Digital Library, University of California, Santa Barbara. In: *ASIS '97. The Annual Meeting of the American Association for Information Science.* http://www.asis.org/annual-97/alexia.htm)

[7] National Research Council. Computer Science and Telecommunications Board. Design and Evaluation: A Review of the State of the Art. *D-Lib Magazine*. July/August 1998. http://www.dlib.org/dlib/july98/nrc/07nrc.html

[8] A. Bishop, B. Buttenfield, & N. VanHouse (Eds.) *Digital library use: Social practice in design and evaluation*. MIT Press, Cambridge, MA (2000)

8. Related Sites

Federation website: http://www.esipfed.org/

Federation evaluation resources and metrics documents website: http://esip.umiacs.umd.edu/documents/eval/

Workshop

Enterprise Security

Chair

Yahya Al-Salqan, Sun Microsystems, USA

Co-Chairs

Wu Wen, Science University of Tokyo, Japan

Mourad Debbabi, Laval University, Canada

Summary Report on Enterprise Security Workshop

Wu Wen
Science University of Tokyo

Yahya Al-Salqan
Sun Microsystems

1. Introduction

This report summarizes the presentations of the 5th IEEE Enterprise Security Workshop. As the title indicates, in the enterprise security workshop, the emphasis is on applications of security technology in areas related to virtual and real enterprises, E-commerce and Internet. The following topics are the focus of this workshop:

- Secure computing;
- Intrusion detection;
- Internet Protocols;
- Malicious code;
- Access control;
- Workflow security.

Although the participants come from a varied background and institutions, including NASA, NIST, Entrust, NRL, Sun and various universities, many returning participants were present. It is also noteworthy that Entrust and RSA used this workshop to announce their new product. The workshop, as its predecessors, went on in discussion mode through out. In this report, we intend to highlight interesting and provocative topics that generated the most discussions in each session. We hope it serves as thought provoking questions that are seeking answers from the readers. In addition, we hope this summary report can be used to privide some additional information for the readers when reading the technical papers.

2 Secure Computing

Two of the presentations were concerned with providing a security framework for enterprise wide applications. One approach is to use risk assesment related methodology and tools to reduce specific security risks when integrating various security technology with enterprise wide applications. The other approach emphasises on taking advantages of available security solutions and integrate them into enterprise wide applications. The audience seem to appreciate the necessity of the tasks. Most of the discussions and comments were related to the scalability of such approach. The applications as well as the security technology varies greatly and there seem to be no effective way to deal with them in a unified manner. The other presentation describes a Web-based inter-operability testing system for IPSec. One of the concerns was how to make sure that the testbed itself satisfies the specifications. The presenter has acknowledged that due to mistakes in the testbed, implementors have changed their implementation to meet with the testbed specifications "wrongly". However, it is agreed that it is better to flush out such mistakes in both specifications as well as implementations using an open testbed than leaving the specifications vague.

3 Intrusion Detection

Two papers were presented in this session. One concerns with alerting users when tapping activities were present in both local and remote networks. The authors seem to have presented an effective approach toward discovering a type of tapping which involves actively changing the host software on which such tapping is conducted. However, its effectively against physical tapping, which are easier to do on LAN, is questionable. When questioned whether there are similar work done in discovering such tapping, the author was unable to give any significant reference. The other presentation on intrusion detection concerns with the use of graphical interface and machine learning to present and analyze Unix log information for the purpose of detecting abnormal activities on Unix hosts. Although still in early stages, the graphical presentation of log file seems to have generated most interests from the audience. The ability for users to see and to interact with specific activities recorded in the log

0-7695-0798-9/00 $10.00 © 2000 IEEE

file provides an unique approach not available in other intrusion detection systems.

4 Internet Protocols

This session is concerned with new protocols and attacks on existing protocols used on the Internet. The initialization vector attack on IPSec protocol seem to be quite serious and have been reported in other similar protocols. Most of the questions were directed at whether the new version of IPSec will incorporate known and well publicized methods to prevent such attack. The second presentation on "server-assisted generation of a strong secret from a password" was voted the best paper of this workshop. It aims at solving a very practical problem: how to make human centered password more secure. The approach presented in this talk combines multiple servers with simple user-friend password to generate a strong secret to be used for a particular secure session. This protocol has been implemented as a product by Verisign and RSA. There are many recent work in providing strong encryption yet allowing users to use the human-friendly password. It appears that a standard protocol, simillar to SSL for certificate based authentication, is needed for simple password-based protocol. The third presentation concerns with a fix of SSL/TLS handshake protocol which prevent a certain type of attack that uses a compromised server certificate.

5 Malicious Code

The first presentation on "Secure Self-certified COTS" generated most discussion and controversy. One controversy is related to the use of "self-certified" phrase. It appears to many audience that certification must be done independently. Self-certification implies that Microsoft is certifying that Windows98 is working properly and will not steal secret from your machine. It appears that the approach advocated by the authors is to provide a platform for the developer as well as the end-user, so that by agreement and cooperation, it is possible to provide certain certification without active involvement of the third party. The author further stated that this technology has been mostly used to help eradicating bad programming practices at the developer side for the sake of the end user, such as the government. Other questions were regarding what is the meaning of unsafe, malicious and bad programming in a unsafe language such as C. It appears to be very difficult if not impossible to enforce the type of security checking such as those available to typed language such as Java. The second presentation concerns with a stand alone Java Bytecode Verifier. The motivation for this work is to allow the end users to customize the type of things that needed to be checked, but were not provided by the standard JVM.

6 Access Control

Access control has always been a very interesting topic but difficult to handle in practice. The first presentation describes work in the familiar track: UML modeling of RBAC. It is an attractive topic, but very hard to venture deeper than the simple RBAC model. Unlike other UML models which are used to directly generate code, the RBAC model seem to be quite separated from the underlying application to be of any use in generating code directly from the UML model. The author has claimed in future work to provide specific case studies such as medical systems with detailed UML model, but until them, how effective UML is to RBAC remains to be seen. The second presentation describe an unique spin on access control. It aims at protecting privacy when performing access control policies. As the presentation progresses, it appears that the type of access control described in their work really resembles a ticket for obtaining some service. In many access control applications, it is required for the service provider to audit the user information. In such applications, privacy will not and can not be protected. In the ticket based service access scenario, digital cash is another similar approach, in which the user can remain anonymous when access certain services. The final presentation is concerned with secure software delivery using multi-cast. One shortcoming that was pointed out was that, although the software were delivered using multicast, the initial key distribution etc was performed peer to peer, which can be very time-consuming.

7 Workflow Security

Workflow security is perhaps one of the most appropriate area for enterprise security. Unfortunately, not much research has been conducted in this area. This is an area, similar to access control in large organizations, appears to be very interesting but hard to tackle. The first presentation describe an approach which uses standard software engineering methodology to describe the security requirements of a specific workflow system. The second presentation describe an abstract way of calculation trust relationship in distributed organizations. The third presentation describe a futuristic infrastructure for providing various e-services to users at home.

Reducing Software Security Risk Through an Integrated Approach

David P. Gilliam
Caltech, Jet Propulsion Laboratory
david.p.Gilliam@jpl.nasa.gov

John C. Kelly
Caltech, Jet Propulsion Laboratory
john.c.kellyw@jpl.nasa.gov

Matt Bishop
University of California at Davis
bishop@cs.ucdavis.edu

Abstract

This paper discusses new joint work by the California Institute of Technology's Jet Propulsion Laboratory and the University of California at Davis sponsored by the National Aeronautics and Space Administration to develop a security assessment instrument for the software development and maintenance life cycle. The assessment instrument is a collection of tools and procedures to support development of secure software.

The toolset initially will have a Vulnerability Matrix (VMatrix) with severity, frequency, platform/ application, and signature fields in a database keyed on the Computer Vulnerability Enumeration (CVE) number. The toolset also will include a property-based testing tool to slice software code looking for specific vulnerabilities using signatures from the VMatrix. A third component of the research underlying this toolset will be an investigation into the verification of software designs for compliance to security properties. This is based on model checking approaches initially researched together with analytical verification of formal specification.

Keywords

Security Toolset, Vulnerability Matrix, Property-Based Testing, Model Specification Checking, Security Verification

1. Introduction

Security vulnerabilities in software on networked systems provide attackers an avenue to penetrate those systems. The source of these security weaknesses are usually traced to poor software development practices, non-secure links between computing systems and applications, and mis-configurations. An otherwise secure system can be compromised easily if a system or application software on it, or on a linked system, has vulnerabilities.

Currently, there is a lack of security assessment tools for use in the software development and maintenance life cycle to mitigate these vulnerabilities. The National Aeronautics and Space Administration (NASA) has funded the Jet Propulsion Lab in conjunction with the University of California at Davis (UC Davis) to begin work on developing a software security assessment instrument for use in the software development and maintenance life cycle.

The goal of this work is to use a formal analytical approach to integrate security into existing and emerging techniques for developing high quality software and computer systems. The approach will be multifaceted, with activities and prototype tools in the following sub-domains:

– Assessment instrument for reducing risk during development, configuration, and installation of secure systems

0-7695-0798-9/00 $10.00 © 2000 IEEE

- Models based development and verification for secure software architectures
- Security testing, and verification and validation (V&V) techniques

Assessments of high profile NASA systems believed to be vulnerable to attack will provide a metric to determine the effectiveness of these activities and prototypes.

2. Securing the Computing Environment

The computing environment upon which this work is based consists of multiple computer systems connected by a network and running or supporting network-aware applications. A vulnerability on any one of the systems puts all the systems sharing the computing environment at risk (due to the notion of the weakest link, or, more formally, the principle of least common mechanism [A]). It is imperative to secure the computing environment to ensure NASA's computers, and hence missions and research, function as expected. One key element of securing the environment is knowledge of the systems, the software running on them and their potential vulnerabilities. Unfortunately, new exploits are being discovered daily. Consequently, maintaining the security of a computing environment is a constantly moving target that consumes institutional resources.

Developers and maintainers of software need an integrated approach to prevent security vulnerabilities from being introduced during the software development and maintenance life cycles. Much like preventing application fault errors, preventing conditions that allow the code to be exploited through race conditions, buffer overflows and the like, requires an extendable and modifiable toolset to assist developers to write code not containing these problems.

As stated in the National Institute of Standards Technology (NIST) handbook on computer security, "Security, like other aspects of a computer system, is best managed if planned throughout the computer system life cycle." ([2], p. 74) This life cycle includes planning and implementing software security. It is much less costly to plan and implement software security from the beginning of the development effort than to implement and add it later. It also ensures that security is included in the ongoing software life cycle development, including maintenance, system upgrades and the design of new modules. Life cycle management also helps document security-relevant decisions, in addition to assuring management that security is fully considered in all phases. Security management should begin early in the software life cycle and continue throughout, including during the maintenance and upgrade phases.

Our approach is to develop and implement a software security assessment instrument that can be used in the software development and maintenance life cycle to reduce risk through an integrated approach.

The assessment instrument under current development includes a Vulnerability Matrix (VMatrix), a property-based testing tool, and model-based security specification and verification mechanisms.

3. Vulnerability Matrix

The VMatrix is a dataset ranking severity of vulnerabilities against frequency of occurrence by platform. The matrix suggests where to best expend effort in minimizing security risks in the computing environment.

Its purpose is twofold: 1) to provide system administrators metrics that show where best to expend their efforts in protecting their computing environments; and 2) to provide vulnerability specifications for the property-based testing tool, enabling developers to test for vulnerabilities in code during the software development and maintenance life cycle.

The VMatrix will be stored in a SQL searchable database so its users can search for particular vulnerabilities and obtain different views of the data. The database can also be searched by platform, application, or vulnerability, so users can examine existing tools and systems as they develop new ones, or bring on line entities described in the database.

An effort to provide a unique identifier to each vulnerability is currently underway, headed by MITRE and the SANS Institute. Numbered vulnerabilities are stored in a Common Vulnerabilities and Exposures (CVE) list. A number of companies selling security products use the CVE numbers to identify vulnerabilities.

The VMatrix will use the CVE assigned identifiers as the primary key in the database. The fields will include the CVE identifier, vulnerability name, type, platform(s), application, severity, frequency, and vulnerability signatures, as well as preconditions for the vulnerability to arise. The vulnerability signatures will have multiple subfields to break up the signature into specific components. This allows the database to contain fine-grained details of the attacks to exploit the vulnerability.

The signature fields will provide developers the ability to import the signature(s) into intrusion detection tools. From those signatures, developers can derive low-level specifications to give to the property-based testing tool. This tool will use those specifications to test software for specific vulnerabilities.

4. Property-Based Testing

The role of property-based testing is to bridge the gap between formal verification and *ad hoc* verification. This provides a basis for analyzing software without sacrificing usefulness for rigor, yet capturing the essential ideas of formal verification. It also allows a security model to guide the testing for security problems.

Property-based testing [4] is a technique for testing that programs meet given specifications. The tester gives the specifications in a language that ties the specification to particular segments of code. The specification has *assertions*, which indicate changes in the security state of the program, and *properties*, which describe a specific security state (that, in this context, is considered secure). The idea is to ensure that the properties always hold.

To simplify the testing procedure, the program is *sliced* to delete those parts of the program unrelated to the properties being tested. The result of the slicing is a compilable program that satisfies the properties if, and only if, the unsliced program satisfies the properties.

The sliced program is then modified to function as a simple state machine by inserting code to emit information about assertions and the need to check properties. A monitor collects this information and updates the state of the program. When a property statement is reached, the monitor determines if the property holds. If not, the monitor reports that the program failed to meet its specification, and the tester can take appropriate action.

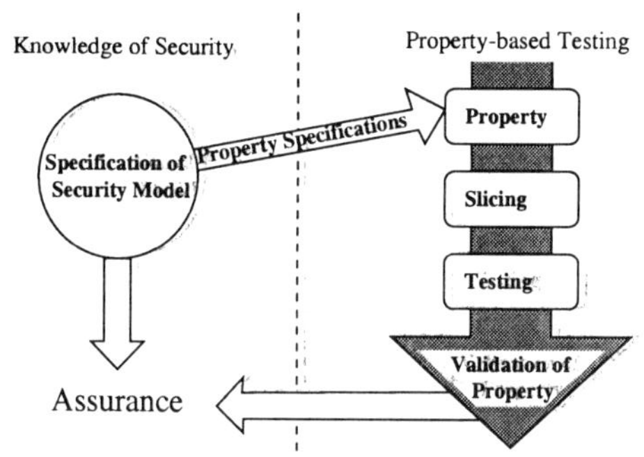

Figure 1

Figure 1 above graphically portrays how the procedure works. The circle on the left represents an accurate specification of the security model (which says what you are, and are not, allowed to do). The goal is to analyze the software to determine the level of assurance, or belief that the program does what it is supposed to do. The arrow going from the left to the right shows that the security property specifications, written in a low-level specification language called TASPEC, represent the requirements of the security model. The arrow goes to the property box on the right to emphasize that the properties we test for are taken directly from the security properties of the model. It is expected, and must be tested, that the code will honor these properties.

Next, the program is sliced, or the smallest program equivalent to the original with respect to the stated properties is derived. Then the program is instrumented and tested, as described earlier. The testing either validates the properties or shows they do not hold. This helps determine the level of assurance of the program, as captured by the arrow going from the right to the left.

As an example, consider Fink's implementation of property-based testing. He defined a language called TASPEC that expressed specifications in terms of C code (which was the environment in which his tool was to be used). This differs from more familiar specification languages such as Z [B], which work at a more abstract level. For example, consider the high-level requirement (stated in English) that "a user must authenticate himself or herself before acquiring privileges." The low-level specification (again in English) for a UNIX program written in C would be:

```
Is password corrrect? {
        Compare user's password hash to hash stored
                for that user name
        If match, set UID to user's uid
        If no match, set UID to ERROR
}
if privileges granted {
        compare UID to the uid for which privileges
                are granted
        if match, all is well
        if no match, specification violated
}
```

Translating this into TASPEC gives [3]:

```
location func setuid(uid) result 1
        { assert privileges_acquired(uid); }
location func crypt(password, salt) result encryptpwd
        { assert password_entered(encryptpwd); }
location func getpwnam(name) result pwent
        { assert user_password(name,
                pwent->pw_passwd, pwent->pw_uid); }
location func strcmp(s1, s2) result 0
        { assert equals(s1, s2); }
password_entered(pwd1) and
        user_password(name, pwd2, uid) and
                equal(pwd1, pwd2)
        { assert authenticated(uid) ; }
authenticated(uid) before privileges_acquired(uid)
```

The set of statements with **assert** in their associated blocks are the set of TASPEC statements that indicate changes of state. From the top, they say that when the program makes a *setuid* system call with an argument of *uid*, the process acquires the privileges of that *uid*; when the process calls the UNIX function *crypt*, the result is a hashed password; when the process calls the *getpwnam* function, it gets back information about the user, her (hashed) password, and UID; and the UNIX function *strcmp*, when called, compares two strings and returns 0 if they are equal. Code is added to the named functions so that, for example, when *setuid* is called, the assertion *privileges_acquired(uid)* is added to the current security state. When all of *password_entered(pwd1)*, *user_password(name, pwd2, uid)*, and *equal(pwd1, pwd2)* are in the state, the monitor will add *authenticated(uid)* to the state.

The last line says that when the assertion *setuid(uid)* is added to the state, the property that *authenticated(uid)* is already in the state, for the same *uid*, must hold; in other words, if *authenticated(uid)* is not in the current security state, the monitor will raise a warning that a property has not been satisfied.

This example shows how property-based testing can take advantage of the specifications of vulnerabilities in VMatrix to detect problems. The key is to represent the vulnerability in the low-level specification language. That explains the subfields in the matrix; they must capture the essence of the problem. As a side benefit, this work feeds directly into the Davis model for vulnerabilities [C], because the assertions are the preconditions of that model.

A second advantage of the properties being stored in VMatrix is that they form the core of a library that can be used for testing the security of programs other than those in the NASA suite. In essence, we extend the notion of software reuse to properties and assertions [D].

We will apply the property-based testing tool to the NASA environment. Hence, the prototype property-based testing tool will be written for C++ and the UNIX environment. Success will be determined by performing static analysis of several programs of interest. Flaws not known to those performing the testing will be injected into the program to provide a baseline of measurement. Once this is completed, we will develop and prototype an engine to perform testing on programs in a production type environment.

At this point we will examine the use of a run-time testing tool similar to the static property-based testing tool (the difference being the omission of slicing).We will determine how much its use degrades performance, and how much extra overhead the testing adds to the system in general. We will also perform "friendly" penetration attacks on the relevant software, and determine if the run-time testing environment detects these attacks .

The property-based software tool, Tester's Assistant–Next Generation (TANG), will benefit users by giving them increased confidence in the programs' correctness with respect to the stated (security) specifications. If non-security properties (such as safety) are of interest, the testers will have access to TANG to perform similar testing for their own set of properties. But the focus of this study is on security-related properties.

5. Model-Based Security Specification and Verification

Analyses based on models can be used to verify and check compliance to desired security properties. Many security properties cannot be verified by test activity alone, however verification through analyses and modeling at the design stage can increase the confidence that the specification provides a sound base for developing a secure program or communication protocol. The analysis and modeling process can begin early in the software development life cycle and provides a machine-readable model, which can be probed through various tools. Analyses and models should be updated periodically, as requirements and designs become more mature. Analyses and models can contribute to the verification by testing programming code through consistent collaboration of test logs.

Software model checkers automatically explore all paths from a start state in a computational tree. The computational tree will contain repeated copies of subtrees. The objective is to verify models over as many scenarios as feasible. Since the models are selective representation of functional capabilities under analysis, the number of feasible scenarios are much larger than the set that can be checked during testing. Model Checker differ from traditional formal techniques by the following characteristics:

- Model checkers are operational as opposed to deductive
- Model checkers provide error traces
- Their goal is oriented toward find errors as opposed to proving correctness (since complete state space exploration is usually infeasible)

<u>Model based security specification and verification</u>:
Model checking addresses issues in security protocols by examining a large number of ways to circumvent the security mechanism. In contrast to purely analytic methods, model checking is capable of examining the larger venue by validation of the over-all-security system

in local, regional, or global environments. These methods have more leverage since they model real world scenarios, and they embrace more than just the mathematics of the protocol. For example, the Needham-Schroder protocol (1978) was proven secure using the BAN logic for protocol specification. However, Lowe (1998) and Wu (1998) using the model checking system SPIN, have discovered successful attacks abrogating the effectiveness and usefulness of this protocol. We propose to extend this approach to protocol validation by (1) proposing models of security protocol systems, and (2) validating those configurations. These modeling techniques have developed around a multi-agent programming paradigm that has emerged as a convenient framework around which internet applications can be successfully validated Mitzoguchi(1998).

Consider two concurrent processes P1 and P2 depicted by the following state machine diagrams (example adapted from Callahan*)

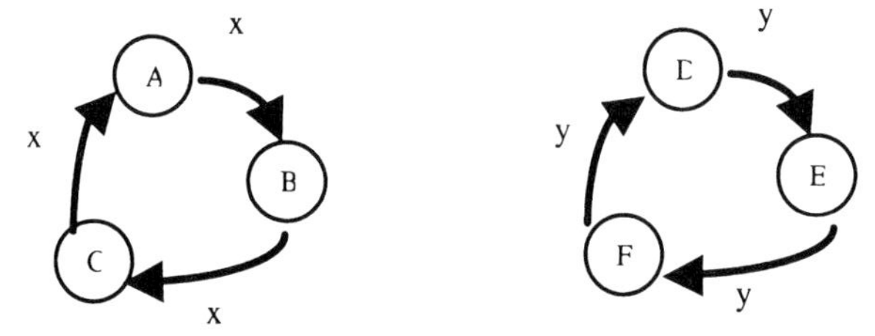

Process P1 Process P2

Figure 2

A partial state transition diagram for the joint process machine would be:

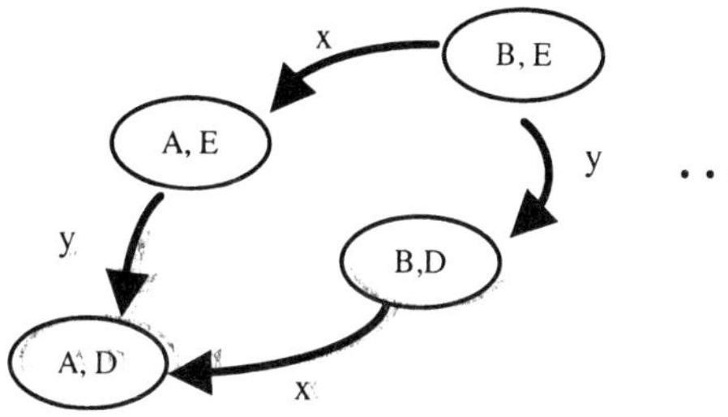

Processors P1, P2

Figure 3

Model checkers effectively and automatically explore a large number of paths from a start state in a computational tree. In Figure 4 below we have diagramed the paths of the model checking. Note we have not listed in the tree any state that was reached in a prior level. The computational tree will contain repeated (perhaps infinitely many times) copies of subtrees. We've arbitrarily chosen state (A,D) as the start state for this computational tree.

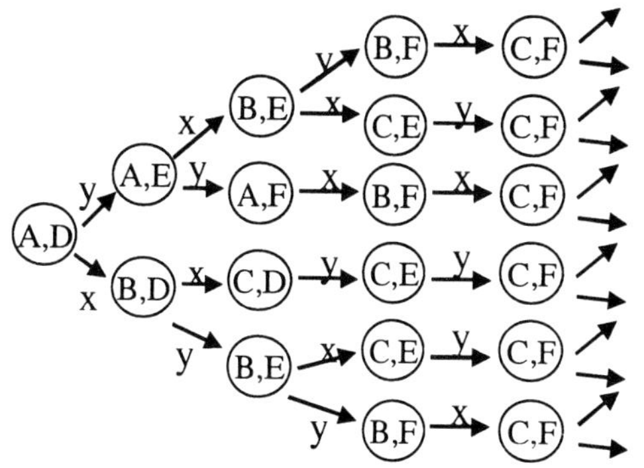

Figure 4

Considered together, the joint process machine has nine states (the Cartesian product of the state space for P1 with the state space for P2):

(A,D)	(B,D)	(C,D)
(A,E)	(B,E)	(C,E)
(A,F)	(B,F)	(C,F)

State Space for Joint Process Machine*

(* Examples is from a presentation by J. Callahan entitled *Automated Testing via Model Checking*, West Virginia University, 1997)

Figure 5

Three common properties to check for are:

Invariant – always p

- p is a property the model must always have

Safety – not ever q

- q is a property the model must never have

Liveness – r implies s will be "true" now or in the future

- always the case that if property r holds at the current state, then property s will hold at some state now or in the future
- used to guarantee that significant sequences take place

Security verification of new architectures:

Architectures that support change and facilitate maintenance are essential to secure systems. However, these architectures are inadequately tested by traditional verification techniques. Model Checking offers ways to begin modeling and investigating the behavior of the planned system, and to validate that key properties hold invariantly in the system as modeled. This technique will be explored in collaboration with security vulnerabilities and property based testing as part of this study.

6. Conclusion

The three parts of this work form a coherent technique to examine new and existing systems for security flaws. The vulnerability matrix drives the selection of security properties that the Tester's Assistant – Next Generation will look for. The matrix contains the problems of greatest concern to NASA at the moment. Model checking will refine the selection of properties by moving their selection from an ad hoc technique to an analytic technique based upon the needs of the systems. So, the Vulnerability Matrix and model-pased checking provide the properties that the software must meet; the property-based tester checks that the programs do indeed meet these properties.

This project suggests several other area in which fruitful research may be conducted.

* The model-checking methodology requires a secure model to check against. Developing such models is an open research issue.
* Property-based testing requires properties expressed in TASPEC to test against. The vulnerability matrix forms the beginning of a library of TASPEC properties. How to develop other properties worth adding to a library of properties is another open research issue.
* Training in the writing of more secure programs flows directly from the library of security properties and the system-specific models. Placing these in the context of a particular language and environment is an important part of improving the quality of software and systems.

Porting the toolset to alternate environments (such as Windows 2000) and languages (such as scripting languages and Java) requires revisiting the models used to develop the tools as well as the models of systems.

7. Acknowledgements

The research described in this paper is being carried out by the Jet Propulsion Laboratory, California Institute of Technology, under a contract with the National Aeronautics and Space Administration.

The research described in this paper is also being carried out by the University of California at Davis under a subcontract with the Jet Propulsion Laboratory, California Institute of Technology.

8. References

[1] M. Burrows, M. Adbadi, and R. Needham. A Logic of Authentication. Technical Report 39, DEC Systems Research Center, February 1989.

[2] "An Introduction to Computer Security: The NIST Handbook," National Institute of Standards and Technology Administration, U.S. Department of Commerce, 1995.

[3] G. Fink, M. Bishop, "Property Based Testing: A New Approach to Testing for Assurance," *ACM SIGSOFT Software Engineering Notes* **22**(4) (July 1997).

[4] G. Lowe. Breaking and Fixing the Needham-Schroeder Public Key Protocol Using CSP and FDR. In TACAS96, 1996.

[5] F. Mizoguchi, H. Ohwada, H. Nishiyana, and H. Hirasishi. An Integrated Agent Architecture for Smart Office Robot Collaboration. Technical report, Information Media Center, Science University of Tokyo, 1998

[6] "Panel I: Issues in Requirements Definition for Survivable Systems," Chair: R. C. Linger, Proceedings of the 3rd International Conference on Requirements Engineering (ICRE '98), Apr, 1998, Colorado Springs, CO, pp. 198-199.

[7] A.B. Smith, C.D. Jones, and E.F. Roberts, "Article Title", *Journal*, Publisher, Location, Date, pp. 1-10.

[8] W. Wen and F Mizoguchi. Model checking Security Protocols: A Case Study Using SPIN, IMC Technical Report, November, 1998.

[A] J. Saltzer and M. Schroeder, "The Protection of Information in Computer Systems," *Proceedings of the IEEE* **63**(9) (1975) pp. 1278-1308.

[B] A. Diller, *Z: An Introduction to Formal Methods*, John Wiley and Sons, New York, NY (1990).

[C] M. Bishop, "Vulnerabilities Analysis," *Proceedings of the Recent Advances in Intrusion Detection* (Sep. 1999).

[D] J. Dodson, "Specification and Classification of Generic Security Flaws for the Tester's Assistant Library," M.S. Thesis, Department of Computer Science, University of California at Davis, Davis CA (June 1996).

IPsec-WIT: The NIST IPsec Web-based Interoperability Test System

Rob Glenn, Sheila Frankel, and Doug Montgomery
Information Technology Laboratory
National Institute of Standards and Technology
{robert.glenn, sheila.frankel, dougm}@nist.gov

Abstract

NIST is an active participant in the Internet Engineering Task Force (IETF) efforts to develop Internet Protocol Security (IPsec) technology. Our ultimate goal is to expedite the rapid commercialization and ubiquitous deployment of IPsec protocols. As initial IETF IPsec specifications began to emerge, it became apparent that the availability of interoperability testing would be the critical barrier to the rapid evolution of early prototypes into commercial products. In this paper we describe the design and development of the NIST IPsec Web-based Interoperability Tester (IPsec-WIT). IPsec-WIT is an experimental test system aimed at exploiting WWW technology to provide remote interoperability testing services anytime and anywhere without requiring any distribution of test system software, or relocation of the systems under test. We conclude with a discussion of the potential future evolution of the system based on observations gained through putting our experimental system on-line and providing IPsec and Internet Key Exchange (IKE) testing services to the IETF research and development community for several months.

Keywords: interoperability testing; protocol testing; IPsec; IKE.

1 Introduction

While it might be prudent to provide a brief history of the development of the Internet Engineering Task Force (IETF) Internet Protocol Security (IPsec) and Internet Key Exchange (IKE) standardization effort, for the sake of brevity and scope, the history of this project begins at the first IPsec interoperability workshop sponsored by RSA Security Inc. In a tower of a Dallas hotel, overlooking the historical Dealey Plaza, a dozen vendors and researchers cobbled together a network of computers with IPsec prototypes based on early IETF draft specifications. After an entire day of configuration, debugging, and testing, a few prototypes successfully interoperated. This initial "bakeoff" was followed by numerous ad-hoc, one-on-one interoperability trials. These trials typically involved calling a testing partner, poking holes through corporate firewalls, and exchanging testing parameters over the telephone. Testing would then consist of a series of quick tests, followed by long debugging sessions that required the parties to negotiate a future time to resume testing. Over time, the increasing demand for Internet security products and the growing number of new vendors has resulted in the organization of more large interoperability workshops where dozens of vendors and organizations send large engineering teams to test their emerging IPsec products. Today, these workshops involve building complex networks, establishing formal testing procedures, and testing both hardware and software products, while watching packet exchanges through sophisticated protocol analyzers. Even at these large workshops, many test sessions still consist of a few quick tests followed by long code debugging sessions. Many times the debugging sessions occur back in hotel rooms and go on late through the night. Unfortunately in these situations, retesting code changes cannot occur until the next morning when the workshop resumes.

Based on our observations made during these testing trials and workshops, and a general call for better IPsec testing tools from the IETF community, NIST designed and developed an IPsec Web-based Interoperability Tester (IPsec-WIT). Our primary goal was to develop and interactive, web-based test system that would allow implementers to test their products between organized bakeoffs. We wanted to design a system that would support the kind of testing that implementers need early in the product development cycle. As such, we wanted a system that would provide ubiquitous remote access and support asynchronous testing where the time and order of tests are controlled by the user and do not require coordination with those operating the test system.

The remainder of this paper provides a technical overview of the design and implementation of the IPsec-WIT system. This is followed by a brief discussion of the potential future evolution of the system and our conclusions and observations about its use to date.

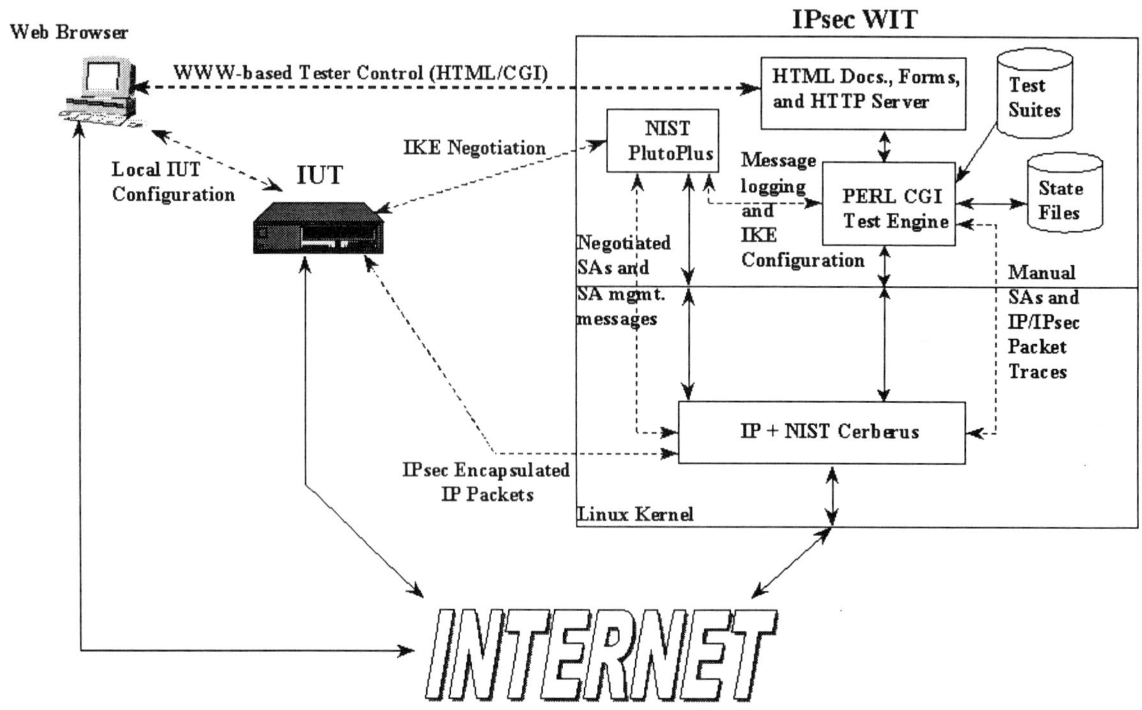

Figure 1 IPsec-WIT System Architecture

2 Design and Implementation

IPsec-WIT is a web-based IPsec and IKE interoperability test tool designed to solve some of the inherent problems with more traditional forms of interoperability testing. Our design objectives were to provide IPsec interoperability testing "anytime and anywhere", without requiring distribution of tester software, physical relocation of the implementation under test (IUT), modification of the IUT, or human coordination among those participating in the tests. Our targeted audience consists of security researchers, product implementers and highly technical users such as network engineers and administrators. This user community is primarily interested in highly available, lightweight and flexible test systems that provide detailed technical diagnostics, more so than fully automated certification systems typically used in protocol conformance testing. Figure 1 depicts the resulting IPsec-WIT architecture. The remainder of this section discusses the design decisions and components embodied in this architecture.

In order to achieve interoperability testing anytime and anywhere, IPsec-WIT was designed to be deployed as a standing service on the public Internet. Such remote interoperability testing is possible because IPsec and IKE are peer-to-peer protocols that are tunneled and/or encapsulated in normal IP packets.

Given that IPsec-WIT and IUT may be on opposite sides of the global Internet, one must decide how individual users can interact with and control the test system and how the IUT can be controlled for testing. Here our guiding philosophy was to minimize the testing specific requirements on, and assumptions about, the IUTs. As a result it was decided not to automate the test system's control of the IUT (e.g., the use of architectures with upper testers and test management protocols as is typical for conformance test systems [1], or require the use of standardized test harnesses and APIs). Instead, we opted to leverage the ubiquitous nature of world wide web (WWW) technology to provide the user's control and diagnostic interface for the test system and to simply convey any test specific IUT configuration requirements through the browser interface.

IPsec-WIT is a novel use of WWW technology for the purposes of protocol interoperability testing. While the WWW has been used as a testing tool to test other WWW related technology [2], and as a simple configuration and control interface for remote protocol implementations [3], we are unaware of other distributed protocol interoperability test systems that are completely web based. Using a common web browser, an IPsec-WIT user can easily navigate through directories of pre-defined test cases, configure the test system, execute tests, and view detailed test results.

2.1 Embedded Reference Implementations

A critical factor in the practical utility and community acceptance of IPsec-WIT is that the test system is based upon NIST developed, publicly available reference implementations of IPsec (*Cerberus*) and IKE (*PlutoPlus*). Cerberus [4] is a Linux kernel reference implementation of the IPsec [5] protocol, including both the Encapsulating Security Payload (ESP) [6] and Authentication Header (AH) [7]. ESP and AH are encapsulation protocols that provide cryptographic confidentiality (ESP), and authentication (AH), to individual IP packets. PlutoPlus [8] is a Linux reference implementation of IKE [9], a dynamic key management protocol used to negotiate security associations (SAs) and keying material between two systems. Fundamentally, the IPsec-WIT system is a wrapper and front end that drives the Cerberus and PlutoPlus reference implementations and analyzes their output.

Cerberus and PlutoPlus reference implementations were designed to be completely operational stand-alone prototypes. Before they could be used in IPsec-WIT they had to be extended with additional control and diagnostic capabilities specifically for protocol testing. Cerberus is a stateless IPsec protocol engine that resides in the Linux kernel. While it was easy to determine where in the code to place testing diagnostic statements and control hooks, it was more difficult design how to convey and correlate this information between the kernel and the testing processes in user space. In the end this was accomplished by using the existing Linux *klogd* utility extended with special tags to allow the test system process to correlate packet traces with test sessions among multiple simultaneous users.

PlutoPlus is a complex, stateful key management daemon. This complexity allows for interoperability problems to occur at many different places in the protocol. Testing diagnostic statements were added extensively to the PlutoPlus implementation. To allow the test system to be used simultaneously by multiple users, PlutoPlus had to be modified to operate in a single negotiation mode in addition to its normal daemon mode. In single negotiation mode, the PlutoPlus process exits after each IKE negotiation (i.e., a single test). This new mode allows the IPsec-WIT test system to independently control IKE behavior and correlate outputs for each user of the system. Having multiple IKE processes complicates the interactions between IKE and IPsec. Because PlutoPlus binds itself to a socket to communicate to the Linux IPsec kernel, it is possible for one PlutoPlus test execution to block another. Fortunately the negotiations conclude quickly and the chance that one execution would start before another finished is very slim.

2.2 Core Test System Implementation

The main engine of the IPsec-WIT system is a Perl cgi-bin script that ties the user interface HTML forms, directories of test cases, and prototype reference implementations into a working interoperability test system. Interoperability testing scenarios usually involve an iterative series of quick tests and long debugging periods. One interesting design decision was how to allow users to retain state regarding test configurations and progression through test directories between debugging sessions. In some cases, users may go off line for days then want to resume the test session they had in progress. In the end, after considering the use of cookies, and other client side approaches we opted for maintaining simple state files that contain control parameters (e.g. tester configuration variables, IUT addresses, current test case, etc.) and are indexed by a user provided unique user-id / password. These state files allow users to resume testing after a debugging session, from any browser location, by simply typing in their unique user-id.

Perl's ability to easily parse and manipulate strings was particularly useful in customizing test cases with the user specific control information in the state files. This allowed for the development of a generic set of test cases that could be dynamically instantiated for each specific user. These parsing features were also useful in processing the results of the Cerberus and PlutoPlus diagnostic statements. The IPsec-WIT engine can take these results, determine which test session they belong to, augment the results with HTML formatting and deliver the results back to the user's browser. Finally, Perl's ability to execute system commands, combined with its parsing features, allowed us to develop a generic testing language that could be converted into system commands. This allowed the test cases to be self-documenting as well as executable.

2.3 Test Description Language

The test description language is made up of simple test system directives and Unix system commands. The language is implemented as extensions to HTML. The IPsec-WIT engine pre-processes the extension tags to perform variable substitutions and invoke Unix commands. A given test case typically consists of a sequential set of commands that define and explain the test, document the IUT configuration requirements, configures the security state and policies for the embedded IPsec and IKE implementations, executes a series of simple connectivity tests (e.g., ping), and displays the output from the reference implementations back to the user.

To make the results of the test more intuitive to the user, the test directive ***Expect*** was defined. ***Expect*** simply describes the expected output of the command that follows it. The results of executing a test command are compared against the prior expect directive. Upon a successful execution of a test command the statement ***Expected Results Occurred*** is displayed with the test results. A failure results in the statement ***Expected Results Did Not Occur***. In addition, color was used to emphasize the results, green for a success and red for a failure. **Figure 2** depicts and example test case using the expect directive.

Once a test case has executed the output from executing each command and the output from the instrumented reference implementations is displayed back to the user on a single results page. In addition, the results page also includes a packet dump of the ping packets, before and after IPsec processing, between the two systems. For implementers, this detailed packet dump is the most valued form of diagnostic information.

The simplicity of the test language makes it convenient in documenting tests. Unfortunately, it also restricts the type of testing IPsec-WIT can perform. A more capable testing language would allow for more sophisticated tests. For example, a looping construct would allow IPsec-WIT to perform multiple tests within a single test case. Defining a more extensive test description language was left as a future activity.

```
test name: km.init.ah.md5-trans

test summary

Initiate AH:HMAC_MD5_96 SA with replay check in transport mode.

test case description

Test km.init.ah.md5-trans negotiates inbound and outbound IPsec Security Associations
(SAs) for the Host to Ping (DEST) with this system (TESTER) as the Initiator and the Host
to Ping (DEST) as the Responder. The resulting SA is a transport-mode SA with replay
check. The peers authenticate each other through a pre-shared secret key.

The test first deletes any existing SAs with DEST and saves the pre-shared secret key.
After PlutoPlus completes negotiations with DEST, the test displays the parameters of the
negotiated SAs, pings DEST, and awaits the response. If the PlutoPlus negotiation was
successful, and both systems' security policies and SADB entries are configured
correctly, and if DEST is reachable, ping should return a positive response. The test
then deletes the negotiated SAs and the pre-shared secret key.

test script

expect {nothing}
sadb delete d dest all

save pre-shared secret key for dest (value = presharedsecret)

expect SUCCESSFUL NEGOTIATION
plutoplus  -i -a 2   2>&1

expect {something}
sadb get d dest all

expect pingcount packets transmitted, [^0] packets received
ping dest

expect {nothing}
sadb delete d dest all

remove pre-shared secret key for dest (value = resharedsecret)
```

Figure 2 Example Test Case

2.4 Test Cases

The test cases are perhaps the most significant contribution of our work. They are the primary component that sets this system apart from those WWW systems that act as remote configuration user interfaces. When dealing with protocols with many optional features, it is necessary to organize the test cases into context relevant categories. For IPsec, the majority of interoperability problems are the result of non-interoperable or incorrect application of the cryptographic algorithms. Because of this, the IPsec test cases were organized into test directories based upon cryptographic algorithm (e.g. DES, 3DES, etc.). Organized in this way, users can easily test variations of a particular algorithm before moving on to the next algorithm.

For IKE, it was difficult to identify any particular feature that causes the majority of interoperability problems. In any IKE negotiation there are several message exchanges involving multiple cryptographic algorithms. A failure at any point in the exchange will cause interoperability problems. For the sake of expediency, the question of how to better organize test directories for IKE was left as a future activity. IKE test directories are also organized based on the different cryptographic algorithms. However, because of the complexity of IKE, the ability to make additional configuration changes to a given test was provided. This allows the users the flexibility to test for a given negotiated algorithm and then make subtle changes to the test configuration to test for more IKE specific problems.

As mentioned above, the test cases serve as both documentation and executable. The test cases were written in HTML to easily convey to the user the test purpose, how to configure the IUT for the test, and exactly how the test will be executed. The test cases are enriched with special tagged variables that the Perl script replaces with user specific control information, creating a test case tailored for a particular user.

3 Future Directions

Over the past few years the test system has evolved from an IPsec test system with a handful of test cases to a robust test system that includes hundreds of IPsec and IKE test cases. This evolution resulted from the continued support and development of the NIST prototype implementations, feedback from IPsec-WIT users, changes and clarifications in the IPsec and IKE specifications, observing how IPsec-WIT was being used, and new ideas from the developers of the test system. Additional ideas have been discussed that, in some cases, would involve a complete re-design and development of a new test engine. The following is a brief discussion of some of the potential future directions.

One of the limiting factors of the test system is its simple language. A ***looping*** directive would allow users to test multiple, consecutive executions. A ***timer*** would allow users to test complex issues like key re-negotiation, and IKE timeouts between messages. Through the use of a ***not*** directive, IPsec-WIT could be used to verify that implementations responded properly to error conditions. To implement these complex directives, significant changes may be required to the underlying reference implementations.

IPsec-WIT currently contains test cases reflecting the implemented features of the reference implementations. IKE is a very complex key negotiation protocol with many optional features. PlutoPlus implements the core components of IKE as well as some of the optional features. As PlutoPlus is expanded, new test cases and configuration options are added. One of the planned near-term future additions is incorporating public key certificates to provide authentication for PlutoPlus. To allow users to test their implementations using this mode of authentication, IPsec-WIT will have to be integrated with a certificate server in new test cases and configuration options will need to be added. As new features are added, careful thought must be given on how to incorporate the changes. It is often difficult to determine which changes should be implemented as new test cases as opposed to configuration options. Observations and user feedback are used heavily in making these decisions.

The design of IPsec-WIT forces users to test a complete execution of a protocol. To assist users in finding problems more quickly, the test system could be modified to execute a specific portion of a protocol. For example, if after having problems in testing an IKE implementation, a user could test a single phase or even a single message exchange to identify the location of the problem. This would require a significant change in both the test system and the reference implementations.

Most of the changes discussed so far are focussed on assisting implementers in debugging their software. A significant change focussed on expanding the scope of our interoperability testing would be to design an interface that would allow the test system to be incorporated with other IPsec and IKE implementations. Users could then test against an array of implementations increasing their confidence in the products they are implementing or deploying. To accomplish this, an interface would have to be specified and standardized. IPsec-WIT would have to be re-designed to operate through this interface, which would be less tightly coupled to the implementations since they will typically be operating on separate platforms. And finally implementers would have to be encouraged to include this interface in their code.

4 Conclusions

Multi-vendor interoperability has been the corner stone for the explosive growth of the Internet. The increasing complexity of new protocols, such as that found in Internet security protocols, makes developing interoperable products very difficult. Implementers and standards organizations require tools to better facilitate the development of interoperable products. IPsec-WIT is an example of one such tool, used to assist in the development of IPsec and IKE products.

The IPsec-WIT architecture is comprised of several components welded together through the use of Perl and HTML. By themselves, the components are not revolutionary in the context of testing technology. Integrated, as defined by the IPsec-WIT architecture, they become an innovative approach toward meeting our basic design goals as well as meeting our primary objectives of making IPsec and IKE interoperability testing easier, more effective, and less expensive. Our design trade offs in the capabilities of the tool versus the complexity of its use seem to have hit a sweet spot with the research and development community.

To date, over 350 implementers and users attempting to deploy IPsec and IKE product have used IPsec-WIT. Through its use, IPsec-WIT has helped improve the quality of emerging implementations and identify ambiguities in the IETF specifications. IPsec-WIT has made formal testing sessions more productive. Implementers use IPsec-WIT to test their code prior to attending these sessions. While attending the sessions, implementers use IPsec-WIT as a stable reference point to verify that code changes have not introduced new interoperability problems.

While IPsec-WIT was specifically designed to facilitate the development of interoperable IPsec and IKE implementations, the observations and insights found in this paper could easily be applied to developing testing tools for other protocols. We are currently exploring ways to expand and evolve the test system.

IPsec-WIT is on line and available for IPsec and IKE interoperability testing at:

http://ipsec-wit.antd.nist.gov/

Acknowledgements

Many thanks go to Stephen Nightengale who provided the core design and implementation of the test system. Thanks to Hsin Fang who worked with Stephen in developing many of the initial test cases. The authors would also like to thank the users of IPsec-WIT who provided feedback that helped with the evolution of the test system.

References

[1] Linn, R.J., "Conformance Testing for OSI Protocols", Computer Networks and ISDN Systems, Vol 18, 1990.

[2] L. Rosenthal, M. Skall, M. Brady, M. Kass, and C. Montanez-Rivera, "Web-Based Conformance Testing For VRML", StandardView, Vol. 5, No. 3, September 1997.

[3] http://isakmp-test.ssh.fi The SSH Communications Security IPsec and IKE test page.

[4] NIST Cerberus, An IPsec Reference Implementation for Linux, http://www.antd.nist.gov/ipsec/

[5] Kent, S., and R. Atkinson, "Security Architecture for the Internet Protocol", RFC 2401, ISOC, November 1998.

[6] Kent, S., and R. Atkinson, "IP Encapsulating Security Payload", RFC 2406, ISOC, November 1998.

[7] Kent, S., and R. Atkinson, "IP Authentication Header", RFC 2402, ISOC, November 1998.

[8] NIST PlutoPlus: An IKE Reference Implementation for Linux, http://is2.antd.nist.gov/plutoplus/

[9] Harkins, D., and D. Carrel, "The Internet Key Exchange (IKE)", RFC 2409, November 1998.

Walking the Web of Trust

Germano Caronni

Sun Microsystems Laboratories, Palo Alto
Email: <gec@acm.org>

Abstract

Most currently deployed Public Key Infrastructures (PKIs) are hierarchically oriented and rely on a centralized design. Hierarchical PKIs may be appropriate solutions for many usage-scenarios, but there exists the viable alternative of the 'Web of Trust'. In a web of trust, each user of the system can choose for himself whom he elects to trust, and whom not.

After contrasting the properties of web-of-trust based PKIs to those of hierarchical PKIs, an introduction to webs of trust and to quantitative trust calculations is given. The paper concludes with the presentation of an efficient, sub-exponential algorithm that allows heuristic computations of trust paths in a web of trust.

Keywords: Web of Trust, PKI, Heuristic Trust Calculation.

1 Introduction

The current boom in e-commerce relies to a certain extent on our ability to communicate securely. The slow but steady progress of IPSEC, the ongoing deployment of VPN firewall technologies and the ever-widening use of SSL for secure transactions over the world-wide web are just a few examples for this. But as the communication infrastructure offers more and more security-related functions, the limitations of the overlaying key management frameworks become more and more visible.

The ultimate purpose of key management is to assure its users that they are securely communicating with whom they want to communicate, and nobody else. A user of the framework must be able to get satisfying answers to the following questions:

- Is the person or service I am talking to really the one she claims to be?
- Is there somebody in the middle, relaying everything?
- How sure can I be about this?

Those and more questions translate into the realm of key management and trust calculations. In contrast to this, traffic authentication (message authentication codes and asymmetric signatures), covers only the most basic necessities on the communication side, and secure systems offer required properties on the systems side. These two aspects will not be further discussed in this paper.

The most fundamental aspect of trust that is involved covers the participants (i.e. the peer authentication). All other trust relations, mechanisms and system components are created to support this fundamental one. In particular, Public Key Infrastructures (PKIs) are supposed to provide a satisfactory answer to above three questions.

Most currently deployed PKIs (with the notable exception of PGP, see section 3) use centralized and hierarchical models for their trust computations, accepting certain drawbacks coming with them. An interesting and viable alternate solution is, for some applications, the web of trust. This well-known model can be used to allow users to derive trust parameters without involving certification authorities (CAs) or the like.

The remainder of this paper discusses some issues with current PKI solutions, gives an overview over existing work, and then introduces the web of trust as an alternate solution to the peer authentication problem. The use of quantitative trust calculations is illustrated, and a viable heuristics to do fast calculations in a web of trust is given.

2 Hierarchical PKI vs. Web of Trust

Depending on the environment of the targeted user community, different needs exist, which lead to different schemes for key management.

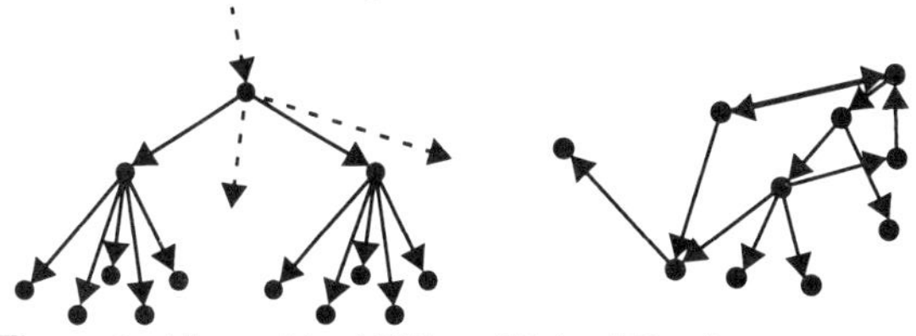

Figure 1: Hierarchical PKI vs. Web of Trust

Figure 1 illustrates the principal difference of two solutions, namely the rigid structure of the traditional hierarchically organized PKI, in contrast to the flexible, distributed nature of the web of trust, which makes it at the same time a more generic solution, and potentially more difficult to manage.

In the following subsections, three usage scenarios will be explored, leading to different requirements for a PKI.

2.1 The Hierarchical Organization

Assume that the infrastructure of a large bank or industry is to be made secure. All participants have the need to authenticate their communication partner, and to transfer data privately over a public infrastructure. At the same time, they are embedded in an environment where rules of trust and dependencies are well specified. Thus, a central certification authority (CA) or a small hierarchy of those can be employed to provide certificates to all communicating peers. The peers can easily verify their authenticity and thus communicate securely.

Naturally the situation becomes more difficult when several usually competing entities, each owning its own certification hierarchy, want to enter a limited collaboration, and use each others certificates to secure communications.

2.2 The Divided Community

This is an actual and interesting scenario. Everybody who has established a link to a Web server using 'secure' http has experienced it. Customers of an on-line service usually want to be sure that they are talking to the real service provider, and not an impostor. On the other hand, the service provider does not have an immediate need for the authentication of the customers. They authenticate themselves e.g. by giving appropriate payment information. As a result, this scenario can be modeled as representing two distinct sets of entities. The first set provides services, and owns well known identities, the second set uses the available services, and wants to authenticate the service provider.

There currently exists a set of commercial certification authorities, whose public keys have been made widely available, and where service providers can buy certificates (e.g. for their web servers). Potential customers can retrieve such certificates containing public keys from the service providers and verify the correctness using the public key of a commercial CA which they have received by out-of-band methods.

In this scenario, several issues can be observed. Firstly, service providers tend to become dependent on the CA services, having to buy new certificates regularly. Secondly, users need to get root certificates through a trusted channel — for now this is simply the distributed software (i.e. netscape) itself. Tampering with the software, malevolent configuration, or malevolent proxies can easily lead the user to believe things that are not what they seem to be. Additionally, it is quite hard for the average user to verify the correct configuration of his browser.

One may also be concerned about the strong segregation into service providers and service users that has evolved in recent years. It is hard for a user to gradually become a trusted and authenticated service provider, instead he has to invest substantial effort and/or money to make the switch from one class to the other.

2.3 The Unstructured User Community

Last, but not least, individuals that to not pertain to one organization, and are not embedded in a certification hierarchy may still want to encrypt and authenticate their communications. They can achieve this by using traditional key agreement methods such as Diffie-Hellman, or use a public key infrastructure that represents a web of trust (e.g. PGP). This gives the communicating peers privacy, and authenticity, if the correctness of the employed public keys is verified out-of-band.

Again, to do this correctly can be hard for the average user, and it is a problem to create globally valid models to establish the same amount of trust into differently verified public keys. Additionally, each user needs to hold more data than in the hierarchical PKI scenarios.

2.4 Summary

Key management schemes that want to reach maximum deployment may have to provide mechanisms that suit all three of those scenarios and the policies associated with them. Public keys, as managed by a public key infrastructure (PKI), are bound to identities by CA's (which may in themselves be normal users of the system), must be easily retrievable, replaceable and revocable. Only this is the function of a PKI; whether it be hierarchically organized or based on a web-of-trust architecture.

The advantages of a web-of-trust based PKI are the possible (but not mandatory) genericity of trust relations, the ability to fit whatever organizational structure is present, and to easily evolve into other layouts when the users needs change. In the special case of webs of trust that map to hierarchical systems, trust calculations become easy, and the system shows the same properties as purely hierarchical PKIs, with more flexibility as a bonus.

3 Related Work

The primary issue of existing PKI solutions is to establish trust in the identity of the communication peers. Current trust relationships either work in a hierarchical manner ([X.509] for example), with one or more certification roots from which all participants derive their respective trust, or by using the model of web of trust, as it was introduced, for example, by PGP [PGP95], or, sometimes, using a mixture of the rigid hierarchies and freely interconnecting certifications. A formal definition of trust relationship networks and the quantification of trust can be found in [Maurer96a]. Although the approach given there is the most comprehensive formal and understandable solution to date to the expression of trust, the calculation of trust values is very expensive ($O(n^2)$). Additionally, a means of binding trust values to real-world authentication processes (such as passport verification) is not yet agreed upon.

The expression of trust into prospective peers is but the first step in establishing a secure connection to this peer. As a next step, the peer needs to be authenticated, using one of many possible protocols that achieve this, see also [Caronni96]. For an overview of authentication in distributed systems, see [Liebl93]. For an in-depth discussion of other issues related to flexible and secure communication frameworks see [Caronni99], and for group communication key management issues, see [Waldvogel99]. [Maurer96b] gives an extended formal definition on the theory of authentication, and [Maurer94] introduces a intuitive and comprehensible method to formally express the state of associations. A selection of architectures that deal with the issue of peer authentication will now be explored.

3.1 PEM, PGP and Verisign

Privacy Enhanced Mail (PEM) [RFC1421] and Pretty Good Privacy (PGP) [PGP95] are two packages that provide mail security. Verisign provides certificates to WWW servers and clients. They all use asymmetric cryptography (RSA or Diffie-Hellman based) to provide peer authentication. Although electronic mail and web access seem unrelated, participants use the same mechanism (signed certificates) to insure peers of their respective identities. PEM and Verisign choose to limit themselves to the use of traditional certification hierarchies, PGP allows the establishment of a web of trust and unlimited cross certification.

3.2 Secure DNS

The Domain Name System (DNS) [RFC1033], [Albitz92] is a critical component of the Internet. It is implemented as a distributed database on a global scale, provides the translation of domain names to Internet addresses and also performs diverse other functions, *e.g.* the mapping of mail addresses to mail handling agents. Recently, an extension to the DNS that allows for data authentication through digital signatures and key distribution has been proposed [RFC2065]. The proposal expects that in most cases a single private key (the "zone key") will generate all the signature records for a given zone. The zone would act as its own CA, its authority coming from its super-zone. The keys additionally stored in the DNS are accompanied by information such as for what to use the key, and a signature of the certifying authority. The secure DNS allows cross-certification between zones, eliminating the need for a root key. Such cross-certification is impractical on a large scale, but it does allow for an organization with several domains to set up a secure DNS in the absence of keys for the higher-level domains.The secure DNS extensions are new and time will tell whether they succeed in providing a general public key infrastructure that does more than add security to the DNS database.

3.3 Kerberos

Kerberos [RFC1510], [Neuman94] is a system of trusted entities, offering authentication to single users on unsecured workstations. The system relies on initial authentication, where the trusted entity provides user's workstations with a credential ticket. This ticket may be used to request services from servers. Linking together different Kerberos-realms is possible by cross certification. Open problems are the limits imposed on the infrastructure (either a trusted computing base is employed, or only one user may be allowed to have access to a workstation at a time) and the delegation of rights. The usability of the system is somewhat reduced because all remotely operating applications must be made Kerberos–aware; this drawback is taken into account in favor of a more secure environment.

3.4 X.500

Within the OSI infrastructure, the directory service X.500 [X.500] is an important element. A general authentication framework for this service is specified in X.509 [X.509], together with a certifying hierarchy. Authorization issues are also considered by the X.500 recommendations, principally in X.501, Annex F [X.501]. Most components are only roughly sketched out, and details for implementation purposes of many mechanisms are at the care of the implementors. The certificate data format that has been defined by X.509 is coming into widespread use as a vessel to create interchangeable certificates.

3.5 Authentication and Trust

As illustrated by above subsections (and several more solutions exist), authentication and trust frameworks abound, and no basically new aspects are to be added to the field of knowledge in this area. In contrast to the basic aspects, practical Web of Trust computation offers space for improvement. One area of innovation specifically lies in the method how trust into a peer is calculated, and this is the focus of the coming sections.

4 The Web of Trust

Concepts and ideas presented here are, in much more complete form, elaborated in [Maurer96a]. The goal of the presentation in this subsection is to shortly familiarize the reader with the necessary concepts for web of trust calculations, and to introduce some trivial simplifications to Maurer's model, as later implemented by the heuristic approach in section 5.

Assume the existence of a public key infrastructure, where a global database holds public keys of participants, together with claimed identities and signatures thereon, performed by other participants. This very well matches the current state of the PGP public key server infrastructure. The result is a web of trust where key holder can make publicly known whose keys they trust to be authentic. As a member of this infrastructure, one can decide whom to trust as an introducer of new keys, to a lesser or stronger degree. If the resulting web of keys and trust relationships allows one to establish a link between oneself and the target identity, then communication can take place. The general concept of a web of trust can be made to fit any certification hierarchy model, or it can be used without additional constraints, leading to a grass-roots approach.

The next logical step is to assign to each link in the web of trust a probability indicating its correctness. Thus finding the total trust from a starting point towards a desired key becomes a series of random experiments, and, at least in the model, is governed by probabilistic laws.

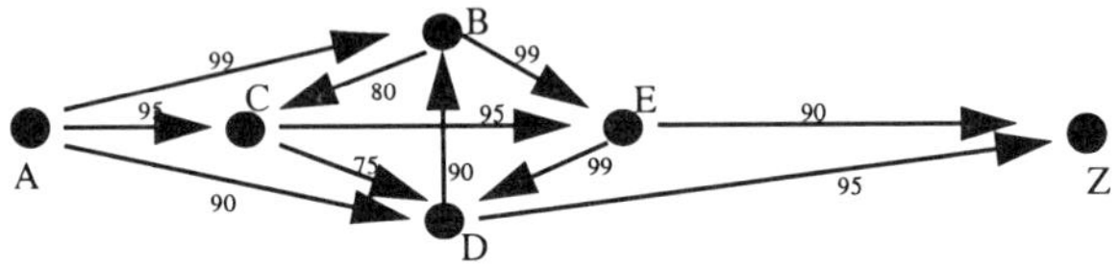

Figure 2: Sample Web of Trust

Figure 2 gives an illustration of such a web of trust. Point A is represents the user Adam as starting point, and Z (or Zacharias, if you want a name) is the target point. This translates as user A holding the keys of B, C, D, E, and Z, having signed keys B, C, and D himself, and wanting to communicate with Z. The values in the figure represent trust invested in links, represented as percentile values, or in other words, a value bound to a signature, assigned by the signer, and indicating how high an probability he assigns to the signee really being whom he claims to be.

This promptly gives raise to some concerns. For example, for such a model to be valid, the way trust is determined must be standardized, as to make clear what a probability value actually means. Probability values could be assigned to a close acquaintance being whom she claims to be, or to a stranger whose passport and drivers license have been inspected being whom he claims to be. Methods to derive such values must be globally known, and, if there are different ones, conversion functions have to be assigned.

Additionally, one must not only examine the value of trust bound to individual links, but also the trust one must invest in intermediate nodes to introduce third ones. While this aspect is not further covered here, it is very important to make a valid model, please see Maurer's paper for a complete treatment. This aspect has been neglected here as it does not significantly add to the complexity of the technical problems that are to be solved.

In the next section both the theoretically correct (but expensive) method, and a cheaper heuristic method of calculation on the simplified model will be introduced.

5 Heuristics for Trust Calculations

To further illustrate the behavior of trust in remote peers, some simple scenarios will be visited first:

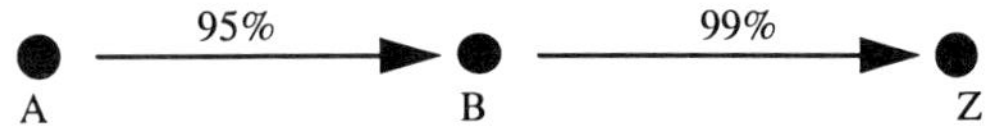

Figure 3: Serial Trust Path

Figure 3 shows a very reduced web, containing only one path with one intermediate entity. Trust in the final destination decreases when more entities lie between the start and the target node. In terms of probabilities, the resulting trust (about 94%) is the result of the product of the separate trusts. In contrast to serial trust, a scenario

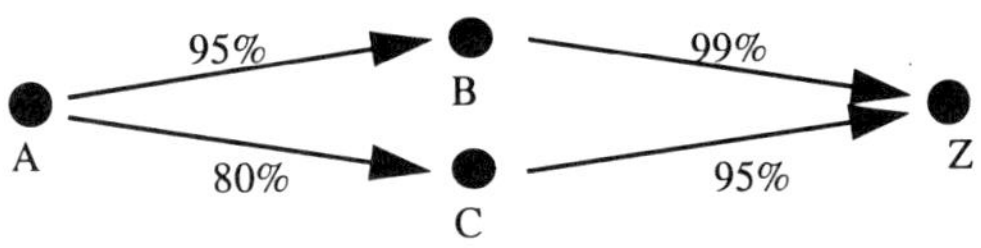

Figure 4: Parallel Trust Paths

with parallel paths, such as the one in Figure 4, is supposed to lead to increased trust in the destinations authenticity. Again, this translates nicely to probabilities, since the destinations key can be used if at least one of the paths leading to it is correct. If there are more, it is for the better. This reinforcement may be treated like independent probabilities in statistics. Thus A is sure about the identity of Z with $T_{AZ} = 1-(1-0.99 \cdot 0.95)(1-0.80 \cdot 0.95)$, that is about 98.6%. Up to now, the examples would allow for the iterative calculation of trust (this is what the heuristic approach tries to achieve, see below), but some more peculiarities have to be accounted for first.

In the real world, a web of trust will contain loops and interdependent paths, as illustrated in Figure 5 and Figure 6. In fact, the example with interconnected paths is

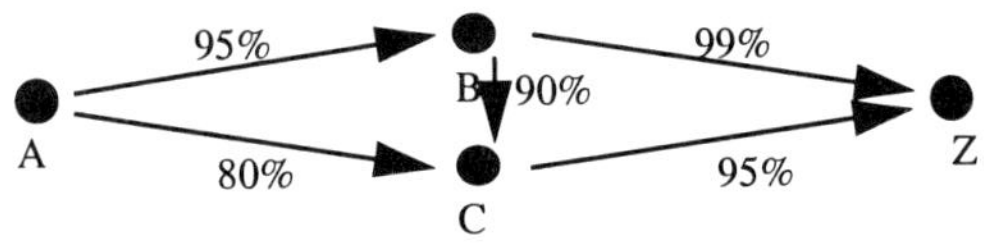

Figure 5: Interconnected Paths

the most simple scenario where all heuristic approaches fail to correctly model the theoretically correct approach. If one refrains from using a purely probabilistic model, different ways of reasoning would be possible: The optimistic approach would be to assume that B reinforces A's trust in C (like 'Parallel Trust Paths' above). The pessimist could argue that B could use C (without its knowledge) to reinforce As trust in Z. But that is okay, as C believes in Z independently of B (but then again, what if they do cooperate?).

There are different ways to look at this scenario: B reinforces A's belief in C and/or C reinforces B's belief in Z. Some links in the path are used more than once, dooming iterative processing.

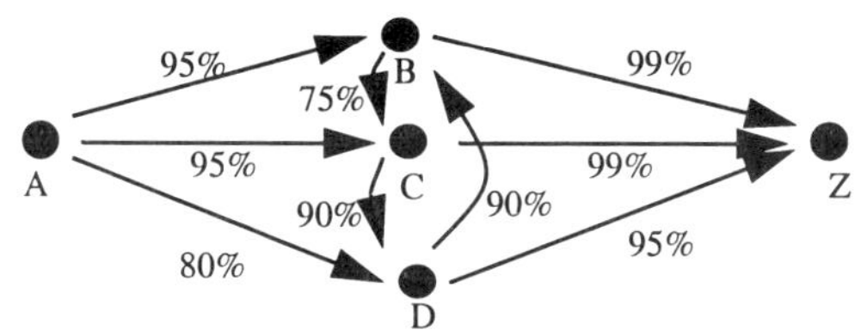

Figure 6: Looping Path with Intermediate

Figure 6 represents an even more general case of trust webs, where arbitrary complex loops are bound to occur.

Now, how is such a web of trust evaluated using only probabilistic laws? In fact quite easily. One must consider each event (of a link either being there, or being absent, with the given probability), and the sum of random experiments where all those events are combined obviously has the probability of 1. From this universe, all experiments where at least one path from the start to the target remains intact are noted, and their probability is added. The resulting value indicates the trust that the starting point can invest in the target really being whom he is supposed to be. In pseudo-code the algorithm looks like this:

```
Input: Web w, Node start, Node target
Set result to 0.0
Treat links in the web as states in a binary vector
Set the vector to 'all 1', meaning all links are up
While the vector is not all zeros do
      If a path from start to target can be found
            Calculate product of all 'up' and 'down'
            probabilities
            Add product to result.
      Decrement vector by one, thereby enumerating
      all possible states
Return result
```

As can easily be seen, the algorithm is of exponential complexity. Evaluation time explodes with the size of the web, and a well connected web with more than a few hundred participants certainly evades computability in the foreseeable future. To increase efficiency, one may collate all purely sequential elements in a first pass, and all purely parallel elements in a second pass, until neither of the passes can achieve a simplification, see also the heuristic approach below.

As an alternative, different (some non-probabilistic) interpretations of the web of trust have been sought:

- The worst path: Only consider the worst available path leading from start to target. Nonsensical, since much crucial information is discarded. This certainly is the pessimistic approach.
- The best path: Even when only the trust over the best available path is computed, discarding parallel paths leads to significant distortion of the result. Even optimists would suffer.
- Find all independent paths and calculate their mean value: This keeps some of the information provided by the web of trust, and simplifies it sufficiently to make the computational solution easily feasible. It is not clear how taking a mean of different paths would relate to reality.
- Hull: Select the best path from start to target, calculate and remove it. Repeat until no more paths can be found. This gives you all possible independent paths, which are then combined via their distrust. Hull makes sense if someone wants to get an result which does neither favour nor punish cooperation of intermediate links. Efficient calculation is given.
- All: Calculate the probability of all possible paths. Combine them via distrust. Not very useful, as the same link may be used for different evaluations. The resulting values that are combined via distrust are not independent, which is bad. You break fundamental rules of probability calculus by doing this.
- Cooperative ('Coop'): This is like 'Int' below, with one addition. Starting from the neighbours of A you record the nodes passed on the paths. If two paths come together later on, and if they share earlier nodes you average them instead of using the reciprocal value. This actually weakens paths were the partners trust each other.
- Interleaving ('Int'): Use iterative processing, first finding the trust to direct neighbours from the start node, and the build on these results to finally reach the target node. As long as the web of trust suffices certain laws of non-interdependence, the result is equal to the theoretically correct one – thus making it an acceptable heuristic. The approach is fast and has been found to be of practical use. Its pseudo-code description follows:

```
For all direct neighbours to target node Z do
      If direct neighbour X is a start node
            Multiply trust into X with the trust into
            the link from X to Z
            Calculate new trust into Z as:
            Z := 1-(1-X*link)(1-Z)
      Else
            Create a copy of the web
            Drop target node Z in the copy
            Designate node X as new node Z in the copy
            Recurse in the copy
            Add returned value to trust into Z as:
            Z := 1-(1-return)(1-Z)
      Endif
Endfor
Return resulting trust in Z
```

It is important to note that the initial trust in the target node is initialized as 0 and the trust in the start node is set to 1. Creating a copy of the web that is used for the recursion assures that the computational results to derive the trust in one neighbor do not influence the trust in any other neighbor of Z. Even though the algorithm starts close to Z, it will first compute the trust in direct neighbors of the start node, due to the recursion, and from there move on to derive the trust into their neighbors, and so on until the target node is reached.

The examples given above, and additionally Figure 7 computed with both approaches yield the following trust values:

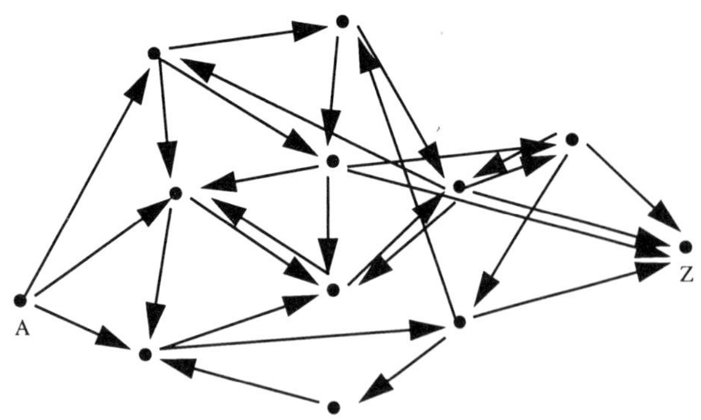

Figure 7: Complex Scenario (all links set to 90%)

Table 1: Web of Trust Computation Results

Scenario	Complete	Heuristics
Figure 2, example scenario	0.99486	0.99494
Figure 3, serial paths	0.94050	0.94050
Figure 4, parallel	0.98572	0.98572
Figure 5, interconnected	0.98734	0.99538
Figure 6, loop	0.99944	0.99997
Figure 7, complex scenario, uniform probability, 90%	.0.99721	0.99985

As is well visible, results differ in some scenarios. The lower the absolute link probabilities are, and the more 'interconnected' paths exist, the stronger the deviations are, the heuristic approach usually being more optimistic than actually granted. It is possible to detect in advance when the heuristic approach leads to wrong results (every time when the direct neighbors of the starting node can not be computed without re-assigning them target node status), and it is also possible to mix both calculation methods to minimize errors. Ideally, the problem would be simplified by using the heuristic approach, and then be segmented such that the resulting segments can be computed with the correct algorithm.

6 Summary

A variety of issues connected to trust and authenticity has been examined. The focus was placed on fast of web of trust computations.

For web of trust computation, a heuristic has been presented that allows computation in subexponential time (depending from the makeup of the web of trust, this can be linear cost), in contrast to preexisting algorithms with exponential cost. As a severe drawback, the found solution is not exact in all cases, but tends to be overly optimistic when trust paths contain looping structures or are otherwise interconnected. Both algorithms were implemented, and tested on small web of trust configurations.

Availability

Source code for trust computations (both Maurer-style and heuristic) is available, just send email to <gec@acm.org> with a subject of 'web of trust source'.

Acknowledgments

Many thanks go to Dr. Daniel Bauer (now at IBM), Prof. T. Plagemann and the UNIK in Oslo, Prof. B. Plattner, and Prof. U. Maurer, both at the ETH Zurich, for interesting discussions during the evolution of this work.

I am also very thankful for the critical review that Dr. Susan Landau gave this paper.

References

PGP95: P. R. Zimmermann: The Official PGP Users Guide; MIT Press, Boston, Massachusetts, U.S.A., 1995.

Maurer96a: U. Maurer, "Modelling a Public-Key Infrastructure", ESORICS'96, 1996.

Maurer94: U. M. Maurer, P. E. Schmid, "A Calculus for Secure Channel Establishment in Open Networks", ESORICS '94, Nov. 1994.

Maurer96b: U. Maurer, "A Unified and Generalized Treatment of Authentication Theory", LNCS 1046, pp. 387-398, STACS 96, Springer Verlag, 1996.

Liebl93: A. Liebl, "Authentication in Distributed Systems: A Bibliogrphy", Operating Systems Review 1993.

RFC1421: IETF, "Privacy Enhancements for Internet Electronic Mail (Part 1)", Internet Engineering Taskforce RFC 1421, 1993.

RFC1033: IETF, "Domain Administrators Operations Guide", Internet Engineering Taskforce RFC 1033, 1987.

Albitz92: P. Albitz, C. Liu, "DNS and BIND", O'Reilly & Associates, 1992.

RFC2065: IETF, "Domain Name System Security Extensions", Internet Engineering Taskforce RFC 2065, 1997.

RFC1510: IETF, "The Kerberos Network Authentication Service (V5)", Internet Engineering Taskforce RFC 1510, 1993.

Neuman94: B. C. Neuman, T. Ts'o "Kerberos: An Authentication Service for Computer Networks", IEEE Communications Magazine, v. 32, n. 9, pp. 33-38, Sept. 1994.

Caronni96: G, Caronni, H. Lubich, A. Aziz, T. Markson, R. Skrenta, "SKIP – Securing the Internet", Fifth Workshop on Enabling Technologies (WET ICE '96), 1996.

Caronni99: G. Caronni, "Dynamic Security in Communication Systems", doctoral thesis no. 13156, ETH Zurich, 1999.

Waldvogel99: M. Waldvogel, G. Caronni, D. Sun, N. Weiler, B. Plattner: "The VersaKey Framework: Versatile Group Key Management", IEEE Journal on Selected Areas in Communications, vol 17 no. 9, Septemeber 1999.

X.500: CCITT, "X.500 Directory Services", Blue Book, VIII.8, Geneva, 1988.

X.501: CCITT, "X.501 Authorisation", Blue Book, VIII.8, Annex F, Geneva, 1988.

X.509: CCITT, "X.509 The Directory – Authentication Framework, Blue Book, VIII.8, Geneva, 1988.

Tapping Alert Protocol

Gookwhan Ahn, Kwangjo Kim, and Hee Yong Youn
Information and Communications University
Taejon, Korea
{tachyon, kkj, youn}@icu.ac.kr

Abstract

This paper proposes a new protocol called tapping alert protocol (TAP), *which detects if any computer is eavesdropping on the network. When tapping is detected, it alerts the network users on the danger of tapping. In designing the protocol, a model for an attacker is developed who sniffs the network and breaks down the proposed protocol, and the requirements on the protocol in terms of efficiency and security are defined. We also describe how to detect if a network interface card on a remote computer is in the sniffing mode. The proposed protocol employs cryptographic schemes to guarantee authentication of the code monitoring tapping operation and integrity of the data being sent. Finally, the proposed protocol can protect authorized users from illegal eavesdropping on the network.*

Keywords: cryptography, network security, promiscuous mode, sniffing, tapping alert protocol.

1. Introduction

Numerous techniques have been devised that allow attackers to break into the network, and then steal, forge, and destroy data in the target computer system. Tapping is one of the most popular network attacking methods appeared since early 1980s. In this paper we propose a new protocol, which protects the system from tapping. It provides a local area network with a mechanism by which it can detect if any computer is eavesdropping on the network. Upon detection, it alerts the network users on the danger of tapping that can leak the information of the users.

Tapping has been called by several different terminologies - snooping, sniffing, eavesdropping, etc. Tapping in a local area network is relatively easy since Ethernet is a shared network and all the packets on the network are broadcast. When someone eavesdrops on a session of a connection while data are transferred between the computers, the person can easily extract the data. In addition, if the user-ids and the corresponding passwords are extracted through tapping, the person eavesdropping can even break into the computer system. Due to this, tapping has been one of the most popular and easiest ways to penetrate a computer system. A number of sniffing programs on the Internet have been developed, and many attackers have used them for breaking into computer systems and networks.

Tapping is possible by taking advantage of the *promiscuous mode* of network interface. Promiscuous mode is a condition when the network interface controller (NIC) of a computer system passes all frames up to the higher network layers regardless of the destination address. Normally, a network controller passes up only the frames having the destination address to that device. However, when it is in promiscuous mode, the destination address is not checked. In other words, if an NIC is set to the promiscuous mode, it means that the computer is running the sniffing or tapping program [1]. Of course, when a network administrator needs to analyze the network performance, the promiscuous mode is also used. However, it can still collect the host and user authentication information in addition to the data on network operation, which can be used for tapping.

There are some countermeasures developed to avoid tapping as follows [1].

- Do not use the NICs that support promiscuous mode.
- Use one-time password for connection.
- Encrypt a user's connection by using SSH (secure shell) program, *etc.*
- Use a switching hub so that an attacker cannot tap the network easily.
- Use tools such as "cpm" to detect the promiscuous mode of NIC on a local computer [9,10].

Previously, to the best of our knowledge, it has been possible to detect the promiscuous mode of only the computers on LAN with the countermeasures above. If someone is running a sniffing program on a remote computer system, nobody could detect it. For this reason, we propose a new method for detecting the promiscuous mode even on remote computers. The new method, called TAP (Tapping Alert Protocol), uses cryptographic schemes [2,3] in order to provide authentication of module checking and integrity of data.

The rest of the paper is organized as follows. Section 2 discusses the background issues related to tapping. In Section 3, the proposed protocol is presented which prevents the local area network from being tapped by any attacker. We analyze the protocol in Section 4. Finally, conclusions are given in Section 5.

2. Background

In this section, we first present the requirements on the protocol detecting promiscuous mode. Next, we describe how to check if an NIC is in sniffing mode. We also examine the types of attackers breaking into the network with some sniffing tools and build assumptions by which the attackers break down the proposed protocol.

2.1. Requirements on the Protocol

Here we do not consider how to prevent the root permission from being compromised. There are many techniques protecting a computer from the attack on the root permission through Internet. Under this assumption, we consider the requirements on the protocol in terms of security and efficiency.

Security requirements

- *Authentication*: If legitimate routines are needed to run normally and they are not to be forged, authentication is necessary.
- *Integrity*: If the data transferred through the network are not to be forged, integrity is also necessary.

The main objective of public-key encryption is to provide privacy or confidentiality. However, public-key encryption alone does not provide either data authentication or data integrity. Therefore, in building a scheme handling tapping, some additional mechanisms need to be employed in addition to public-key encryption scheme in order to provide authentication and integrity. They are message authentication code (keyed hash function) and signature function [2,7].

We also need to employ the three-pass variation of the basic Diffie-Hellman protocol to provide a shared secret key between two entities involved when a message authentication code is used [13].

Efficiency requirements

- *Low congestion*: If any computer runs a tapping program, this information needs to be broadcast so that other computers in the network can be aware of the fact. In the case that there exist many computers in the network, this may cause the network congested. In order to avoid this problem, the scheme developed for handling tapping needs to use UDP or IP address for broadcast in the network [4-6].

2.2. Detecting the Promiscuous Mode

Here we present how to detect if an NIC operating under Unix is in promiscuous mode. The following C code describes the routine for NIC running in SunOS 4.x [9]. If the value of the underlined *if*-statement is true, then the NIC is in promiscuous mode.

```
int fd, itf;
struct ifreq buf[MAXINTERFACES];
.
.
.
if (!(ioctl(fd, SIOCGIFFLAGS, (char *) &buf[itf])))
{
   if (buf[itf].ifr_flags & IFF_PROMISC) {

  /* This network interface is in promiscuous mode */

   }
}
```

2.3. Possible Attacks

When a protocol handling tapping is installed on a network, an attacker may tackle that in the following ways:

- The attacker obtains the root privilege in order to eavesdrop the network or stop the protocol. If an attacker has no root permission on the computers, it cannot tap the network.

- The attacker forges the routine checking the network interface. If an attacker wants to deceive the network users and computer system, it replaces the original checking routine with a forged one. The forged one conducts as the original routine does, and the network users and computers will misjudge that it is a legitimate one.

- The attacker forges the data sent to other computers. Here if an attacker wants to provide the network with the routine checking the network interface and wants it to run normally but still wants to deceive the network users and computers, it forges the data sent.

We next present the proposed protocol.

3. The Proposed Protocol

In this section we present a new protocol preventing a network from tapping. We describe the notations, message formats, and message flow supported by the proposed tapping alert protocol (TAP).

The TAP is designed to alert other computers to the danger of sniffing in the local area network if any computer runs a sniffing program in the environment of a shared network. Until now, there has been no method checking if a computer in a remote network is running a sniffing program. With the proposed TAP, the promiscuous NICs running sniffing program remotely can be detected.

3.1 Notations

We employ the following notations to represent the messages used in the proposed protocol.

- $\|$ — Concatenation of messages.
- ***I*** — Initiator, who sends a message.
- ***R*** — Responder, who responds to a message.
- $A \rightarrow B : M$ — Entity A sends a message M to entity B.
- $DEC_X()$ — Decrypt data with the private key of entity X.
- $ENC_X()$ — Encrypt data with the public key of entity X.
- $K = g^{xy}$ — Session key by Diffie-Hellman Key agreement.
- $h_K(\,)$ — Keyed hash function.
- $IPaddr_X$ — IP address of entity X.
- $MachineTypes_X$ — A kind of OS and CPU (Linux, Solaris, AIX, etc.) of X.
- PK_X — Public key of entity X.
- SK_X — Secret key of entity X.
- $Sign_X()$ — Signature data with the private key of X.
- ***Routine()*** — The program checking the promiscuous mode of an NIC on the main memory.
- $TimeStamp_X$ — Timestamp of entity X.
- ***'Y' or 'N'*** — 'Y' means that the computer is in sniffing mode. 'N' means it is not.

3.2. Message Formats

We design a set of message formats as follows:

- msg_n : messages transmitted among the entities

$msg_1=(h_K(Routine()) \| \text{'Y' or 'N'} \| IPaddr_R \| TimeStamp_I \| TimeStamp_R \| MachineTypes_R)$

$msg_2= \text{'Y' or 'N'} \| IPaddr_R \| TimeStamp_R \| MachineTypes_I$

- **TAPinit**: This message is first sent to ***R*** to build a session key using the Diffie-Hellman key exchange setting between two entities, ***I*** and ***R***.

  $(\text{'TAPinit'} \| g^x)$

- **TAPack**: This is used for precluding man-in-the-middle attack against building the session key as a shared key.

  $(\text{'TAPack'} \| g^y \| g^x \| h_k(g^y \| g^x))$

- **TAPagree**: This is used as the final step to setup a session key. As this message is sent to ***R*** which is one of the two entities on the key agreement protocol, it is said that the two entities share a session key without any attack.

  $(\text{'TAPagree'} \| h_k(g^x \| g^y))$

- **TAPreq**: Query message for requesting a check of a computer, which may be running a sniffing program.

  $(\text{'TAPreq'} \| TimeStamp_I)$

- **TAPreply**: Reply message to the checking routine above.

  $(\text{'TAPreply'} \| ENC_K(msg_1))$

- **TAPalert**: Advertisement message for alerting the hosts on the danger of sniffing. This message is advertised by using the broadcast IP address on the local area network.

  $(\text{'TAPalert'} \| Sign_I(msg_2) \| msg_2)$

- **TAPreqpk**: To verify '**TAPalert**', other computers on the network request the public key of entity ***I*** that has broadcast '**TAPalert**'

  $(\text{'TAPreqpk'} \| TimeStamp_O)$

- **TAPackpk**: This is sent to the computer that has requested '**TAPreqpk**'.

  $(\text{'TAPackpk'} \| PK_I \| TimeStamp_O \| TimeStamp_I)$

3.3. Message Flow

3.3.1 Overview

Figure 1 shows that the TAP runs on the computers on a local area network to detect whether any computer is in sniffing mode. It is assumed that the TAP has been installed on all the computers on the network. If a computer does not support the TAP and thus it cannot reply to the TAP messages when other computers requests it, it is recognized as a one being compromised.

In the figure, assume that the computer marked as `TAP1' wants to know whether any computer from TAP2 to TAPn is in sniffing mode. We assume also that a sniffing program is running in TAPi, which is depicted by a bomb symbol. Here TAP1 sends a request message to all other computers one by one in order to detect the sniffing computer as the solid line arrows indicate. All other computers do the same operation as TAP1. Here the check operation by TAPn, for example, is shown by the dotted line arrows. The requested computers should send the reply message to the initiator of the TAP.

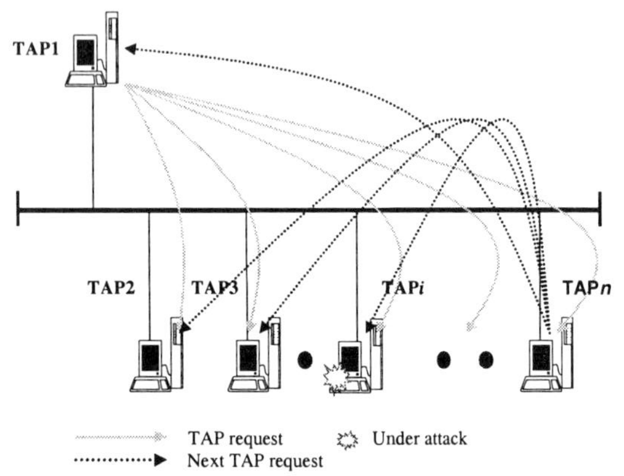

Figure 1. The TAP operation among computers.

3.3.2 Procedure

We here present the procedure employed for the TAP. Figure 2 illustrates the flow of the messages with the TAP.

STEP 1: Initialization

$I \rightarrow R$: **TAPinit** (1)
$R \rightarrow I$: **TAPack** (2)
$I \rightarrow R$: **TAPagree** (3)

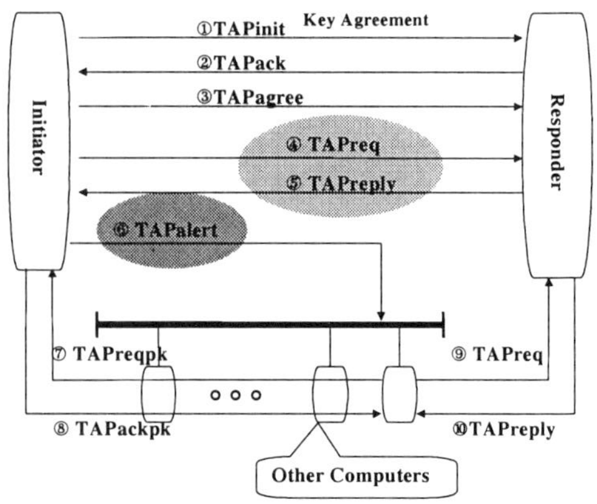

Figure 2. The flow of TAP messages.

This step is for establishing a session key between two entities, ***I*** and ***R***, as a three-pass variation of the basic Diffie-Hellman protocol. When a computer boots up, it is initiated for just once. The detailed actions are as follows:

(1) ***I*** generates a secret random number x and sends ***R*** '**TAPinit**'.

(2) ***R*** generates a secret random number y and computes the shared key $K = g^{xy}$. ***R*** hashes the concatenated exponents ordered as in '**TAPack**', and sends '**TAPack**' to ***I***.

(3) ***I*** computes the shared key $K = g^{xy}$, and uses ***K*** to verify the received value as the hash value on the cleartext exponent received and the exponent sent in '**TAPinit**' message. Upon successful verification, ***I*** accepts that ***K*** is actually shared with ***R***, and sends '**TAPagree**' to ***R***. Finally, ***R*** verifies ***I***'s hash value. If successful, ***R*** accepts that ***K*** is actually shared with ***I***.

This step allows the establishment of a shared secret key between two entities with mutual authentication and explicit key authentication. Due to this, the communication of the two entities is protected from eavesdropping.

Finally, it is assumed that the shared key is put in a private area of the entity such as smart card.

STEP 2: Request and reply

$I \rightarrow R$: **TAPreq** (4)
$R \rightarrow I$: **TAPreply** (5)

(4) If ***I*** wants to check the promiscuous NIC of ***R***, ***I*** sends '**TAPreq**' to ***R***. The '**TAPreq**' message is sent to each other one by one periodically. ***R*** should reply with '**TAPreply**'.

(5) If ***R*** receives '**TAPreq**' message, ***R*** should reply to the initiator with '**TAPreply**'. Since the checking routine has a shared secret key with ***I***, the routine can encrypt the checked result with the shared secret key after the routine hashes itself. Next, the routine sends '**TAPreply**' to ***R***. If ***R*** does not send '**TAPreply**' to ***I*** within a predetermined time limit or ***R*** sends an invalid '**TAPreply**' to ***I***, then ***I*** recognizes that ***R*** is running a sniffing program.

In case that ***R*** does not reply with '**TAPreply**', we should consider the following two cases:

- One is the case that the computer does not reply since it is dead.
- The other case is that the computer is compromised.

To distinguish the two cases above, 'Ping' command is used. To be sure, we assume that the TAP is implemented in the OS kernel such as TCP/IP stack.

STEP 3: Alert

$I \rightarrow$ Local Network **: TAPalert** (6)

(6) If any message format is invalid or any computer identifies a promiscuous NIC, the computer advertises the '**TAPalert**' message on the local area network by using the broadcast IP address.

In this step, a signature function is used for precluding data-forgery attack. If all the formats are valid and all the computers identify no promiscuous NIC, no '**TAPalert**' message is broadcast on the network. Suppose that a computer has already received '**TAPreply**' with '**Y**', which means that a sniffing program is running. If the computer also receives '**TAPreply**' message with '**N**' which means that a sniffing program is not running, the computer advertises the '**TAPalert**' message including 'N' on the network.

STEP 4: Verification

$O \rightarrow I$: **TAPreqpk** (7)
$I \rightarrow O$: **TAPackpk** (8)
$O \rightarrow R$: **TAPreq** (9)
$R \rightarrow O$: **TAPreply** (10)

(7) ***O*** means that other computers received '**TAPalert**', and ***O*** requests ***I***'s public key to verify '**TAPalert**' including the signature value.
(8) ***I*** sends its public key to ***O***.
(9) ***O*** also sends ***R*** 'TAPreq' to verify that the '**TAPalert**' value is 'Y'.
(10) ***R*** replies to ***I*** with '**TAPreqply**', but do not advertise the '**TAPalert**' message.

This is the step for verifying that '**TAPalert**' is not forged. If '**TAPalert**' has been forged, this step will detect it and alert the users on the compromised ***I***.

In addition, the TAP possesses the following properties:

- If a computer wants to check the promiscuous NIC on the remote network, the TAP can be processed by the same procedure.
- In case that a user does not want to receive tapping alert message, it can turn off the TAP by using the program supporting the TAP. However, the computer must still be capable of transmitting '**TAPreply**'.
- The initiation time of each computer can be changed manually or automatically in order not to congest the network with the TAP packets.

4. Analysis of TAP

In this section, we first analyze the performance of the proposed TAP in terms of security. The merits and demerits of the TAP are then discussed. The implementation issue is also discussed.

4.1 Security Analysis

After TAP is initiated, suppose that an attacker wants to stop the routine. In this case a computer will send '**TAPalert**' out on the network. Other computers in the network will then recognize that the computer is malicious and thus alert the users.

An attacker may want to forge the routine so that the forged routine can conduct as the original one. Note, however, that even though the attacker may be aware of the hash value of ***R***, the attacker cannot generate the signature value if it does not know the shared secret key of ***I*** and ***R***. Due to this, any attacker cannot forge the routine.

If any attacker wants to forge the data from the checking routine, the attacker should get the shared secret key of ***I*** and ***R*** because the data is encrypted with a shared secret key. Since the shared secret key of ***I*** and ***R*** is put in a private area, however, it is very difficult for the attacker to get the key. Therefore, the attacker can hardly forge the data being sent.

4.2. Merits and Demerits

The proposed TAP allows a system to check if a sniffing program is run on a remote computer. It was previously impossible to check if a sniffing program is run in a remote computer.

IDS (Intrusion Detection System) [11,12] is a famous system which detects any intrusion on the network. In comparison with the TAP, IDS does not check the network interface on the remote computer but analyzes the packets on the network. Therefore, IDS cannot check the promiscuous mode of the network interface on a remote computer.

Since additional packets are generated periodically for supporting the TAP, this may slightly degrade the network performance if the network bandwidth has already been fully utilized for regular traffic. This is the only overhead incurred in the implementation of the TAP.

4.3. Implementation Issues

Figure 3 shows a structure where the TAP is assumed to be implemented under Linux platform. Here a routine in the Linux kernel need to keep in close contact with the routines of other computers for authentication and integrity using public-key encryption and keyed hash function. When the TAP identifies tapping, it broadcasts an alert message to the network by using broadcast IP address.

To insert the TAP into the kernel and check promiscuous mode, we update the *dev_set_promiscuity*() function of linux kernel. Since the TAP is implemented in the kernel like TCP/IP stack, there is no way to kill the TAP without killing the kernel.

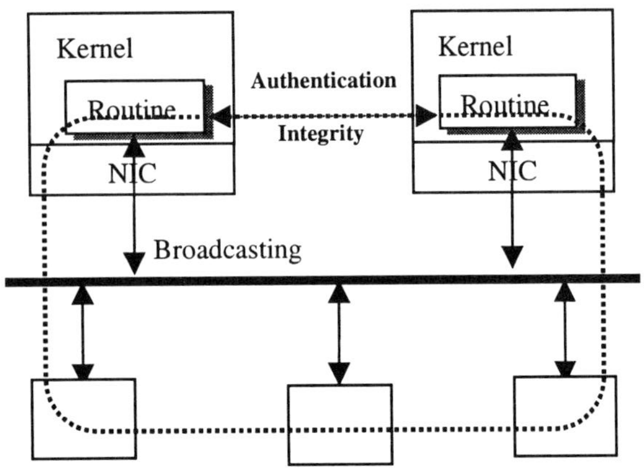

Figure 3. Implementation with Linux kernel.

5. Conclusion

In this paper we have presented a new protocol that provides the network with the capability of checking if the network interface in a local or remote computer is tapping. The protocol works based on a hash function and a public key scheme with the properties of authentication and integrity. Due to this, it is very difficult for an attacker to forge the checking routine and the data being sent.

We will implement the TAP in Linux as a future research.

Acknowledgements

The authors would like to thank Prof. Ben Lee at ICU for his proofreading of this paper.

References

[1] http://www.cert.org/ftp/cert_advisories/CA-94:01.network.monitoring.attacks, Feb. 1994.

[2] W. Diffie, M. Hellman, "New Directions in Cryptography," IEEE Transactions on Information Theory, 22, pp. 44-654, 1976.

[3] FIPS 180-1, Secure Hash Standard, NIST, US Department of Commerce, Washington D.C., April 1995

[4] Postel, J.,"Internet Protocol," RFC 760, USC/Information Sciences Institute, Jan. 1980.

[5] Postel, J., "Transmission Control Protocol," RFC 761, USC/Information Sciences Institute, Jan. 1980.

[6] Postel, J., "User Datagram Protocol," RFC 768, USC/Information Sciences Institute, Aug. 1980.

[7] Alfred, J. M., Paul, C. O., Scott, A. V, "Handbook of Applied Cryptography," CRC press, pp.25-28, 1997.

[8] Douglas, R. S., "Cryptography Theory and Practice," CRC Press, pp. 232-236, 1995.

[9] http://www.certcc.or.kr/tools/network/cpm/cpm.1.2.tar.gz

[10] ftp://coast.cs.purdue.edu/pub/unix/tools/ifstatus/ifstatus.tar.gz

[11] Mukherjee, B., Heberlein, L. T., Levitt, K. N. "Network Intrusion Detection," IEEE Network Volume: 83, pp. 6–41, May-June 1994.

[12] Helmer, G.G., Wong, J.S.K., Honavar, V., Miller, L. "Intelligent Agents for Intrusion Detection," IEEE Information Technology Conference, pp.121-124, 1998.

[13] W. Diffie, P. van Oorschot and M. Wiener, "Authentication and Authenticated Key Exchange," Designs, Codes and Cryptography, 2, pp.107-125, 1992.

Anomaly Detection using Visualization and Machine Learning

Fumio Mizoguchi
Information Media Center, Science University of Tokyo
Noda, Chiba, 278-8510, Japan
mizo@imc.sut.ac.jp

Abstract

Unauthorized access from inside or outside an organization has become a social problem in the last few years, making a system that can detect such accesses desirable. We therefore monitor normal activities using inductive logic programming (ILP) which is one of machine learning and detect anomalies. To ensure effective monitoring, we think the following two points must be considered. One point is automation of detection by ILP system, which is a rule generation engine, that always induces and updates effective rules. The other point is providing a visualization tool that reflects induced rules to the detection system. This tool enables an administrator to understand detection situations. For automated detection, we provide the ILP system with an automatic parameter adjustment function. For the visualization tool, we apply the visualization technology of a hyperbolic tree.

1 Introduction

Unauthorized accesses to computers or networks are increasing every year. In addition, according to an investigation of CSI-FBI in 1999 [1], many organizations have been greatly damaged by internal and external crime. For this reason, there is increasing interest in intrusion detection. One type of intrusion detection is anomaly detection that determines the normal use state using statistic or machine learning and detects exceptions. This includes research that rule-izes usual telephone-call records by machine learning and monitors such records to detect telephone fraud [2], and that analyzes the sequence of the command logs by using machine learning [3].

However, the existing anomaly detection systems are in the examination stage for automatic generation of an optimum rule and automatic renewal, as well as its application method. We have resolved this problem by using an inductive logic programming (ILP) system with a function to automatically adjust parameter as the rule generation engine [4]. This paper also examines anomaly detection using the system.

It is difficult for an administrator to comprehend the voluminous audit data when trying to detect anomalies. Therefore, we propose a visual browser in order to support an administrator browsing analyzed results or raw data. Furthermore, we seek to detect anomalies visually through interaction of the browser and a visual tool, and to bring out the structure of audit data. As the visual tool, we use WebMap [5], which is a visual tool added the concept of the height to a hyperbolic tree. This paper presents research relevant to the Cuckoo Egg Project [6], which seeks to detect intrusion by machine learning and visualization techniques.

This paper is organized as follows: Section 2 describes the architecture of our intrusion detection system, Section 3 explains the Visual browser that plays the most important role in our system. Section 4 describes the method of generating user profiles by using ILP, Section 5 provides the experimental results and final section contains our conclusions.

2 Intrusion Detection System with Visual browser

We designed Intrusion Detection System with Visual browser (IDS-V). The figure 1 shows the system architecture of IDS-V that consists of Log database, Profiling engine, Log checker and Visual browser.

Log checker monitors user events which are collected in the Log database as audit log. The Log database is the center of IDS-V. The log data is referred by Profile engine and Log browser.

The Profile engine generates profiles of each users. We adopt Inductive Logic Programming (ILP) to induce a rule from audit data. The generated profiles is sent to the Log checker and Visual browser. Log checker filters the user events using the profiles and we can edit the profile using Visual browser. The Log checker detects anomaly event based on the profiles and notify the fact that anomaly event happens to Visual

0-7695-0798-9/00 $10.00 © 2000 IEEE

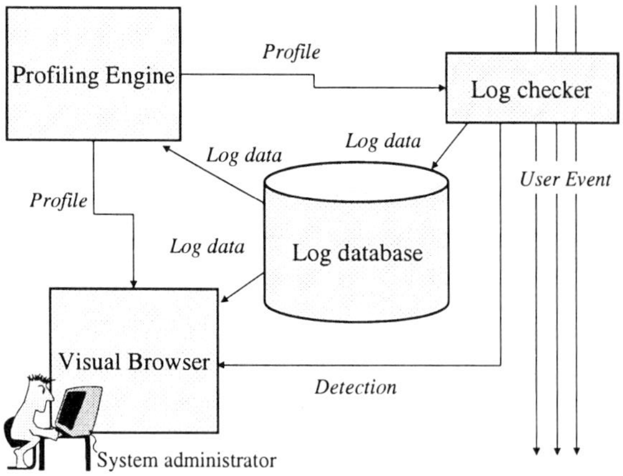

Figure 1: System architecture of IDS-V

browser. Visual browser also get the log data from the Log database and it shows us the log structure and classification based on the profiles from the Profiling Engine.

The Log checker is able to reduce the log data, however, it is hard to generate perfect profiles to detect anomaly event using the machine learning. So, we should use rough rules rather than strict rules not to lose anomaly event. Therefore, there are some cases that the Log checker reacts on normal log as anomaly event. In these case, an administrator must judge whether the detected log is real anomaly or not. The Visual browser helps an administrator to check the log leaking from the Log checker.

Our IDS-V deal with command logs as user events and collects the following data set:

- User name (who)
- Host name (where)
- Executed command name (what)
- Parameter of the executed command (how)
- data and time (when)

Thus, IDS-V can monitor user behaviors in the network. The data set is stored in the Log database.

3 Visual browser

Visual browser help an administrator for log browsing, and clarify the structure of audit data visually by using a hyperbolic tree as the visualization to perform effective browsing and help the troublesome task to find the track of an intruder.

The figure 2 shows our Visual browser[1]. The text field is to input the query to get log data from Log database and it has three browsing buttons: "Get" is to get the log data corresponding to the query, "Clear" is to clear the text field and "Back" is to show the previous log data.

There are four tabbed panels on this system: Log browser, Visualize, Profile, and Property. The Property panel is not shown in figure 2, it is to set some properties such as hostname of each servers (Log database, Log checker and Profile engine) and timing getting log data such as getting logs before 60 seconds from current time. Other panels are explained in the following sections.

3.1 Log browser

Log browser is to browse logs that are listed on the spread sheet in the order of new log. The showing log is user command: the first column is the user name, the second one is the host name where the user execute the command, third one is the executed command and the last column is the time when the user execute the command.

Notified anomaly event from the Log checker, the cuckoo icon start moving and let us know the detection by the cawing of a cuckoo. The log associated to the anomaly event is listed in red.

The logs corresponding to the query in the text field are returned by Log database. For example, if we can get the log related to the user "hiraishi" "AND" machine "imct451", we just set the following query:

```
usr(hiraishi) & hst(imct451)
```

And we can also set " | " for the "OR" operation. If we set empty as the query, the database returns all logs contained the time range setting in the Profile.

When we click on the text on the spread sheet, The item is also appended to the query and down load logs from the database automatically. So, we can browse and go close up to the intended logs.

3.2 Visualize

The most important role of visualization is to enable us to easily understand the use status of devices and networks. Therefore, it is important to design a browser for visualizing audit data. "Audit work bench [?]" developed at the University of California is one such attempt. Although the objective of this paper is

[1]It is implemented by Java Language jkd1.2.2.

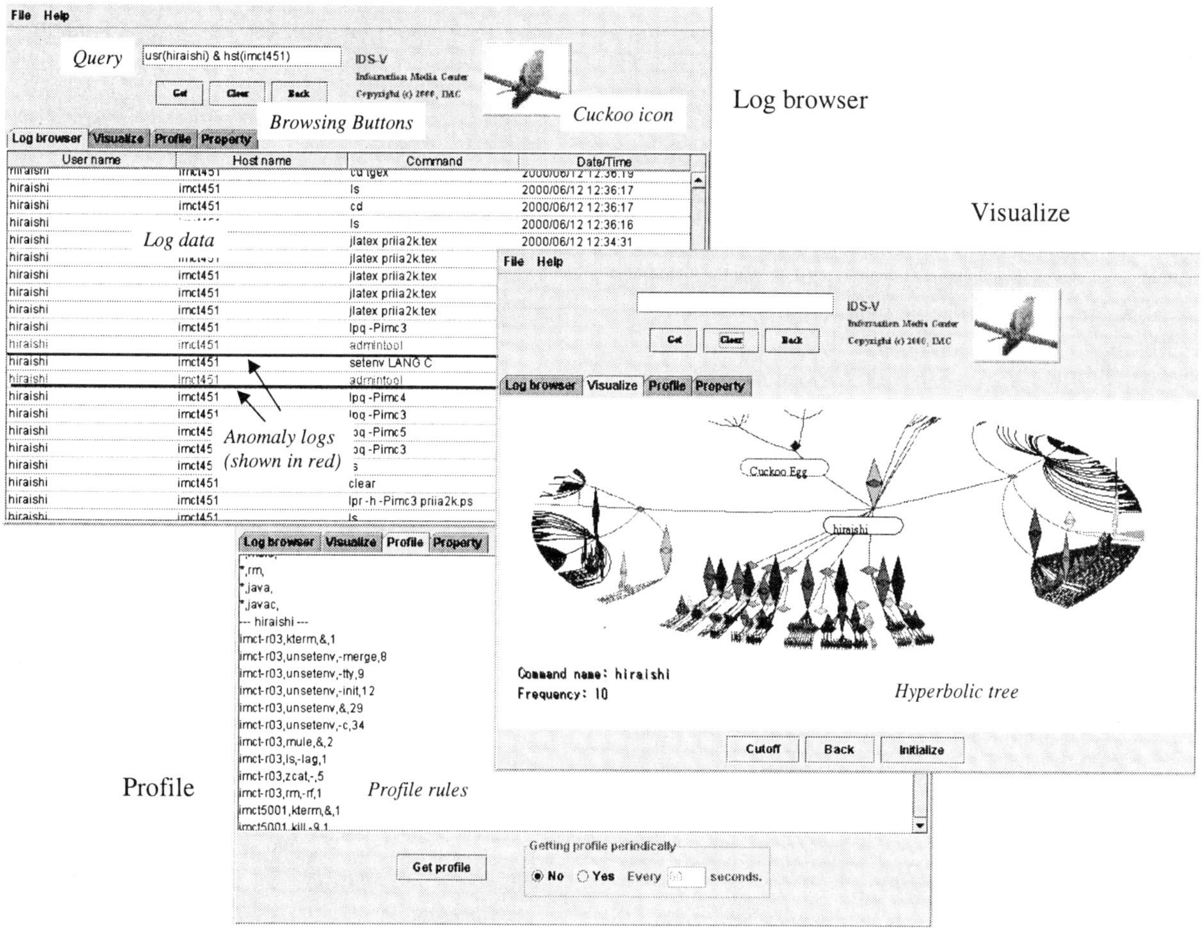

Figure 2: Visual browser

close to that of using their visual browser to audit data, we focus on extracting and visualizing the information from data in data mining.

In order to visualize audit logs, we adopted the WebMap visualization technique [5], which maps Web URLs onto a hyperbolic plane. Our visualization makes hierarchy basically in the following order: "User name", "Host name", "Command name" and "Parameters". However, in the "Command name" level, we divided into four categories as the characteristics of command:

- Un-ruled command

  This category is the most dangerous. The commands does not conform to the profile is classified into this category. So, they may be commands an intruder executes.

- Danger command

  Commands that imply the use of the network and commands that system administrators frequently use (su, finger, ftp, telnet, rlogin, alias, configure, nmap, etc.) tend to be used to intrude into the network and stole password data. We make this category in order to become aware of the executing such commands.

- Safety command

  This category includes the commands corresponding to the profile and plain safety commands like ls, cd, jlatex, java, etc.

- Unknown command

  Commands except for any of the above belong to this category. This includes many cases of typing mistakes and also includes the original command of users.

We should first checks the un-ruled command, If many branches have grown from the node of un-ruled commands, We should regard the user as an intruder. Then if the danger command has many branches and the user is not an administrator, it indicates that the user might do illegal use and there is a possibility that the intruder pretends to be the user. Even if there are many branches in safety command, it is not necessary to care about it. It is quite normal phenomenon. Instead, a few commands mean anomaly. When many commands are in the unknown command, the administrator should check whether the command is mistyping or not.

A hyperbolic tree can be changed arbitrarily by mouse operations. Focus is changed by clicking the mouse on a node. Mouse dragging can be accepted at any position, making it easy for users to change the viewpoint of the tree. We can also cutoff branches above the clicked node by using "Cutoff" button. The new hyperbolic tree consisting of only branches under the clicked node is reconstructed. This allows us to make the tree focusing on the special purpose like the command category as mentioned above. In this way, the administrator can browse and understand huge logs visually.

3.3 Profiling

The profiles generated by Profiling engine is also shown in the text area of our visual browser. The profiles are listed every users in the following form:

```
--- hiraishi ---

imct-r03,kterm,&,1

*,java,
```

The first line indicates the user name and the following lines contains the profiles of the user. The second line means that the user "hiraishi" uses the command "kterm" at the machine "imct-r03" and he sets the parameter " & " at the first argment. The " * " is the wildcard, the third line indicates he uses "java" command at any machines.

Since the profiles generated by Profiling engine is not complete for anomaly detection. We can edit and create the profiles in the text area of our browser.

4 Generating Profiles

In order to induce the rules, we apply an inductive logic programming (ILP) system, and use it as the rule generation engine, in other words, the profiling generation engine. The ILP system learns from an example, enables relational learning, and produces a result for incremental learning. The framework of ILP is represented as following:

$$B \wedge H \models E^+$$

$$B \wedge H \wedge E^- \not\models \phi$$

where, E^+ is the positive examples, E^- is the negative examples and B is the background knowledge. Thus, the purpose of ILP induces the hypothesis H.

In the method like decision tree general used in data mining, we must combine target tables to generate the relational rules. However, ILP can generate rules from the distributed tables. It is natural that the logs is distributed such as the computer is distributed in the network. So, the ILP is more suitable for the log data analysis.

This learning system is implemented in Java language, and references both Muggleton's Inverse Entailment [7] and the GKS algorithm [8]. This system uses the objective function by including positive examples and the hypothetical length, and gives the rate of negative examples (Error rate), which the user establishes, as the constraint, and determines the best hypothesis (rules) from the most special case.

However, existing ILP systems, including this system, must set up a search parameter. Therefore, when the users induce the rules from data by ILP system, they must adjust the parameters, considering the performance of rules. This becomes an obstacle, when we incorporate a learning system into the detection system and automate it. We therefore define a function by which the system automatically adjusts search parameter by observing the value of a performance measure (parameter). We call this function 'parameter tuning'. When we implement this function, we use the result of Cross-validation and Bootstrap method [9] of re-sampling method. Our system then adjusts the parameter by learning them. Thus, we seek to perform effective rule generation for large scale audit data by harvesting the re-sampling technique. Furthermore, we use the induced rules as profiling.

4.1 Automatic parameter adjustment method

The ILP system that we apply must set up an orror rate that implies how the hypothesis can include negative examples. The performance (Table 1) of a rule is influenced by the setup, so we automatically adjust the error rate so that it may maximize the performance measurement specified by a user.

Table 1: Performance measurement

	A hypothesis regards as a positive example	A hypothesis regards as a negative example
E^+	True Positive	False Negative
E^-	False Positive	True Negative

$$\text{Sensitivity} = \text{True Positive (TP)} \;/\; E^+$$

$$\text{Specificity} = \text{True Negative (TN)} \;/\; E^-$$

$$\text{Accuracy} = (\text{TP} + \text{TN}) \;/\; (E^+ + E^-)$$

At this time, it can provide the remaining parameters that are not specified as constraint conditions. The parameters that it can maximize are accuracy, sensitivity, and specificity. These parameters are obtained from the re-sampling technique. The parameters are such that the error rate tends to increase when sensitivity increases and decrease when specificity increases. The error rate that yields the best parameter values is obtained by binary search considering the relation of the error rate and the parameter.

A practical processing procedure is as follows. First, a user selects a parameter (Table 1) to maximize and sets the remaining parameter as constraint conditions. The system then generates a training set and a test set by a re-sampling process like Cross-validation or bootstrap. Next, it learns the training set, tests the test set, asks for the performance evaluation shown in Table 1, and checks whether the ILP system satisfies the constraint. If the constraint is satisfied, the system updates the error rate so that the target parameters may be maximized (maximization process). If the constraint is not satisfied, the system updates the error rate so that the constraints are satisfied (adjustment process). The system then updates the error rate repeatedly until the parameters becomes constant.

5 Experimental results

In order to clarify the effectivity of our visualization and profiling, we simulated the situation that an intruder pretends to be a user. Using logs of two users A and B, we added logs of the user A to logs of the user B little by little.

The user A and B use about 900 commands in one month. The main work of the user A is editing the text and Java programming. In contrast, the user B is the administrator in our network. He often uses the command for system administration and writes program by using C language. So, the user A tends to behave such as an intruder.

We derived profiles with ILP in the three methods:

1. logs of the target user is set as the positive example, in contrast, logs of other users is set as the negative example and we gave the use way of commands and login status as the background knowledge In this case, the rules emphasizing how the target user use commands are derived. For example,

   ```
   user_A(X) :- login(X, ''imctX'', Y),
           type(Y, ''mule,&,1'').
   ```

   In the machine "imctX", the user A use the command "mule" with the parameter " & " at the first argument.

2. Inducing rules from only logs of the target user. we gave the use way of commands as the background knowledge. In this case, the rules the target user frequently uses are derived. For example,

   ```
   user_A(X) :- type(X, ''ls,-al,1'').
   ```

   This means user A uses the command "ls" with the parameter "-al" at the first argument.

When a rule that incorporates the login status is generated, we can learn that a user logs in from a specific host to another certain host with a decided format such as telnet login. I When we analyzed command logs, we found that the order of the arguments and how to use command are unique.

The figure 3 shows the changing of tree structure. First we generated profiles of the user A using 1000 commands. The tree structure of the fist step is the (A) in the figure 3. The (B) is the structure after adding 20 commands. At this time, we can find the change of tree structure easily, the number of branch at the un-ruled command is increased. Since the user B is not a system administrator, there is no such a command in his profiles and the command "su" is categorized in the un-ruled command.

The (C) is the result after adding 100 commands of the user A. The "su" command is in the danger command. This means the profile that the user B use "su" command is generated by ILP. If an administrator can not notice the intrusion and the ILP induces from logs contains anomaly events, the ILP may generate the rules infected with the anomaly logs. As a result, the profiles can not work effectively any longer. In our experiment, the 100 logs correspond to the logs collected for 3 days. The administrator should check logs once 3 days at least.

However, since we set the four command categories, even if the rules infected with the anomaly logs are generated, the commands associated such rules is classified into danger command or unknown command. We can find the trace of intrusion by checking their branches.

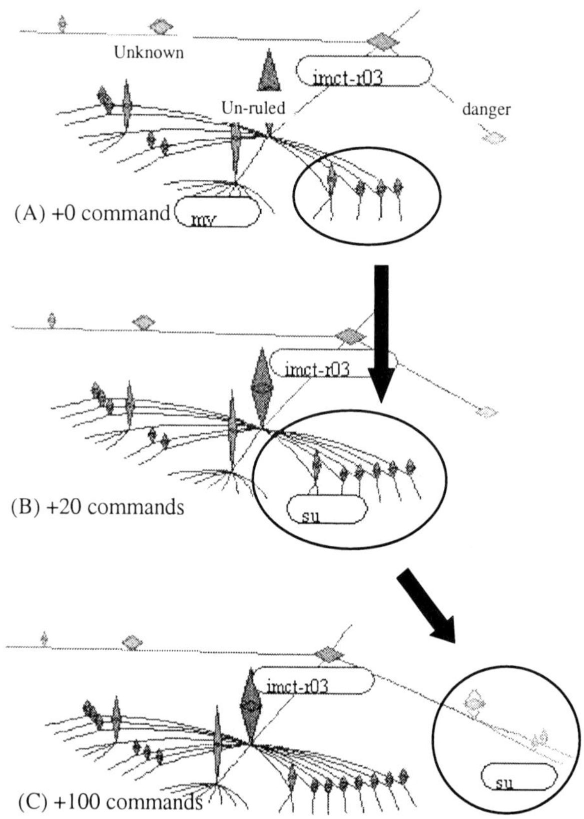

Figure 3: Changing of tree structure

6 Conclusion

We design the intrusion detection system with the visual browser that helps an administrator for log browsing, and clarify the structure of audit data visually by using a hyperbolic tree as the visualization to perform effective browsing and help the troublesome task to find the track of an intruder. We implemented the following two functions

- Visualization function that reflects rules induced by ILP system
- Automatic parameter adjustment for search on ILP system

By implementing these two functions, we attempted to automate a system and facilitate visual perusal of a situation. In short, we proposed a framework of anomaly detection using such technologies.

References

[1] CSI-FBI, 1999 CSI-FBI Survey Results, http://www.gocsi.com/summary.htm, 1999.

[2] T.Fawcett and F.Provest, Adaptive fraud detection, Data Mining and Knowledge Discovery1, 291-316, 1997.

[3] B.D.Davison and H.Hirsh, Predicting sequences of user action, In Predicting the Future: AI Approaches to Time Series Problems, AAAI Press, pp.5-12. WS-98-02, 1998.

[4] F.Mizoguchi, H.Ohwada, J.Tuchiya, Development of agent type datamining system, Information-Technology Promotion Agency, Japan, 1999.

[5] H.Sawai, H.Ohwada, F.Mizoguchi, Incorporating a navigation tool into a browser for mining WWW information, The First International Conference on Discovery Science, 1998.

[6] F.Mizoguchi, Visual browser for intrusion detection - Cuckoo egg project, CSS'99, 1999.

[7] S.Muggleton, Inverse Entailment and Progol, New Generation Computing, 13:245-286, 1995.

[8] F.Mizoguchi and H.Ohwada, Using Inductive Logic Programming for Constraint Acquisition in Constraint-based Problem Solving, Proc. Of the 5th International Workshop on ILP, 297-322, 1995

[9] M.Weiss and A.Kulikowski, Computer Systems That Learn, Morgan Kaufmann Publishers, 1991

Initialization Vector Attacks on the IPsec Protocol Suite*

Christopher B. McCubbin   Ali Aydın Selçuk   Deepinder Sidhu
Maryland Center For Telecommunications Research
Department of Computer Science and Electrical Engineering
University of Maryland Baltimore County
Baltimore, MD 21250, USA
E-mail: {cmccub1,aselcu1,sidhu}@umbc.edu

Abstract

In this paper, we analyze the security of IPsec against a class of attacks known as the IV attacks, which are based on modifying the initialization vector (IV) of a CBC-encrypted packet during transmission. We show that IV attacks can be a serious threat for IPsec if IPsec is not used carefully. We also discuss the defense methods against these attacks.
Keywords. *Internet security, IPsec, IV attacks, cryptanalysis.*

1. Introduction

IPsec is a security protocol suite that provides encryption and authentication services for IP messages at the network layer of the Internet [6, 4, 5]. Two major protocols of IPsec are the Authentication Header (AH) [4], which provides authentication and integrity protection, and the Encapsulating Security Payload (ESP) [5], which provides encryption as well as (optional) authentication and integrity protection of IP payloads.

IPsec offers a number of advantages over other protocols being used or proposed for Internet security. Since it operates at the network layer, IPsec can be used to secure any protocol that can be encapsulated in IP, without any additional requirements. Moreover, IPsec can also be used to secure non-IP networks, such as Frame Relay, since operation of many parts of IPsec (e.g., ESP) do not necessarily require encapsulation in IP.

IV attacks are a security risk of the CBC encryption mode of block ciphers [8] which can be applied to IPsec [1]. This class of attacks makes use of an unauthenticated IV in CBC encryption, so that the attacker can do controllable changes on the first block of the decrypted plaintext by modifying the IV. We discuss IV attacks in more detail in Section 2.

When encryption is done at an intermediate layer of the protocol stack (e.g. IPsec is at the network layer) the first block modified by an IV attack includes parts of the upper-layer protocol header. In those cases, an attacker can do extraordinary things (like obtaining the whole decrypted message, as we show in Section 3) by just modifying the IV. The specifics of the results that can be obtained by such attacks depend on the upper-layer protocol in use.

In this paper, we analyze the security risks posed by IV attacks on IPsec with several possible upper-layer protocols, including TCP, UDP, (tunneled) IPv4 and v6, and L2TP. In our analysis, we consider two common block sizes: 64-bit block size, which is the block size of many popular encryption algorithms, including DES, IDEA, and Blowfish; and 128-bit block size, which will be the block size of the Advanced Encryption Standard (AES) [7]. Analysis results show that IPsec encryption can be very vulnerable to IV attacks if used carelessly. We also discuss the defense methods to protect IPsec encryption against IV attacks.

The rest of this paper is organized as follows: We describe the IV attacks and CBC encryption in Section 2. In Section 3, we analyze the impact of IV attacks on a number of protocols that are typically encapsulated in IP. In Section 4, we discuss possible defenses against the IV attacks.

2. IV Attacks against CBC encryption

In the *Cipher Block Chaining* (CBC) encryption mode of block ciphers, the data stream to be encrypted is divided

*This research was supported in part by the Department of Defense at the Maryland Center for Telecommunications Research, University of Maryland Baltimore County. The views and conclusions contained in this document are those of the authors and should not be interpreted as representing the official policies, either expressed or implied, of the Department of Defense or the U.S. Government

into plaintext blocks $P_1, P_2, \ldots$, and each plaintext block is encrypted as

$$C_i = f_K(P_i \oplus C_{i-1}),$$

and decrypted as

$$P_i = f_K^{-1}(C_i) \oplus C_{i-1},$$

where f_K and f_K^{-1} denote the block cipher encryption and decryption, and "$\oplus$" denotes the bit-wise exclusive-or. For the special case of the first block, where there is no ciphertext C_0 to xor, an *initialization vector* (IV) is used instead:

$$\begin{aligned} C_1 &= f_K(P_1 \oplus IV) \\ P_1 &= f_K^{-1}(C_1) \oplus IV \end{aligned} \qquad (1)$$

IVs are usually chosen randomly by the sender, and sent to the receiver along with (or before) the encrypted message. If an IV is sent in clear and is not protected by an authentication mechanism, an attacker can modify the IV, and therefore, can modify the first block of the decrypted plaintext according to Equation (1). We refer to such attacks, which are based on modifying the value of the IV, as the *IV attacks*. If encryption is done at an intermediate layer of the protocol stack, then the first plaintext block includes parts of the the upper-layer protocol header, and the results of an IV attack can be much more serious than just modifying a single block of plaintext. In certain cases, the attacker can obtain the whole decrypted text, as in the examples we give on IPsec in Section 3.

IV attacks can be a serious problem for IPsec encryption. IPsec has many possible configurations that enable IV attacks. First, all the IPsec encryption algorithms proposed so far use a block cipher in CBC mode. Moreover, almost all of these algorithms allow the use of cleartext unauthenticated IVs. Also in the ESP RFC [5], it is mentioned that the IV "may be carried explicitly in the Payload field" and "usually is not encrypted per se". Although [5] recommends always using authentication whenever encryption is used, which would prevent the IV attacks, authentication with ESP encryption is neither mandatory nor is it the default mode. Therefore, in practice, IPsec encryption can be very vulnerable to IV attacks. The exact results an attacker can obtain will be dependent on the protocol encapsulated in IPsec.

3. IV Attacks against IPsec

In this section we examine how IV attacks can be used against protocols encapsulated by IPsec. The protocols we examine are TCP, UDP, IPv4, IPv6, and L2TP. For the encryption block size, we consider two common sizes: 64-bit block size, which is the block size of many popular encryption algorithms, including DES, IDEA, and Blowfish; and 128-bit block size, which will be the block size of the AES [7]. Throughout the discussion, we assume that the attacker is capable of intercepting and modifying packets during transmission over the network.

The attacks in this section show that the impact of IV attacks on IPsec can be extremely serious. Our attacks include several examples where the attacker can obtain the whole decrypted message, totally defeating the encryption.

A possible complication for IV attacks comes from the upper layer protocol (e.g., TCP, UDP) checksums, which detect changes made to those protocol headers. However, these checksums are computed as a 16-bit one's complement sum, which is not one-way and can be fixed quite easily. What is needed to fix the checksum is a 16-bit scratch field that can be modified without affecting the reception of the packet, which will be used to compensate for the changes made to the fields under attack. The difference that is "added" to the checksum by the changes on the attacked fields can be "subtracted" by changing the scratch field accordingly. The method is relatively straightforward and we leave out the details.

Another complication for the IV attacks is that, in order to be able to change a header field in a desired way, first of all the original value of the field should be predictable. The fields we consider for an attack, as shown in [2], are indeed mostly predictable.

3.1. TCP

If the packet encapsulated in IPsec is a TCP packet, and a 64-bit block cipher is used to encrypt it, the fields of the TCP header that fall into the first encryption block are the Source Port, Destination Port, and Sequence Number fields. If a 128-bit block cipher is used, the fields in the first block also include the ACK Number, Data Offset, and Window Size fields, and the TCP flags.

The most significant IV attack on these fields is an attack on the Destination Port. If the attacker has a login on the same machine as the legitimate receiver, by changing the destination port number of a TCP packet, the attacker can have the packet delivered to a port of his own after the IPsec decryption. In this way, the attacker obtains the decrypted message, totally defeating the IPsec encryption. In this attack, the changes made to the TCP header do not affect the correct decryption of the packet. The decryption key is identified by the fields in the ESP header and does not depend on the fields in the inner TCP header.

Other useful attacks on TCP can be obtained by modifying the Sequence Number and the Window Size fields. By modifying the Sequence Number field, the attacker can change the ordering of the packets, which may have significant implications depending on the content of the packets. By modifying the Window Size field, the attacker can change the perceived buffer size of the connection, which may lead to the flooding or stalling of the connection.

Another possibility for an attack is to modify the Data Offset field. The Data Offset field in TCP indicates how long the TCP header length is. Modifying this field will give the attacker the ability to make part of the payload of the packet appear as a TCP option. Although not very likely, obtaining meaningful results by this kind of attack may be possible, depending on the contents of the TCP header and the payload.

The other fields in the TCP header are not likely to be useful for an attack. They can be better used to fix the checksum to compensate for the changes made to the more useful fields.

3.2. UDP

With a 64-bit block cipher, the first block of an encrypted UDP packet will consist of the whole UDP header, including the Source Port, Destination Port, Length and Checksum fields. If a 128-bit block cipher is used, the first block will additionally include the first 64 bits of the data payload. An important advantage the attacker has with UDP, as compared to TCP, is that the Checksum field is in the direct control of the attacker.

Among the fields in the first block, an attack on the Destination Port has the most significant effects. If the attacker has a login to the victim's machine, he can obtain the decrypted message by modifying the Destination Port field, similar to the attack on TCP.

Another field which can be attacked with significant impacts is the Length field, which indicates the length of the UDP packet. By decreasing the Length value, the meaning of the packet can be changed significantly; for example, "Pay Alice $10,000" may become "Pay Alice $1".

With a 128-bit block cipher, the first 64 bits of the payload is also included in the first block. So, the attacker can modify the first 64 bits of data by an IV attack. Clearly this is a very troubling prospect. The meaning of a message can be significantly altered by changing the first 64 bits. Also, the attacker conceivably has control over the *Maximum Transmit Unit* (MTU) negotiation at the lower levels of the network. If the attacker sets the MTU so that the packets will have no more than 64 bits of data, then he will have the ability to control all the data over the lifetime of the connection.

3.3. IPv4

Besides securing higher-layer protocols such as TCP and UDP, IPsec can also be used to tunnel IP packets. In case of tunneled IPv4, the fields that would be included in the first block with a 64-bit cipher are the Version, Header Length, Type of Service, Total Length, Identification, Flags, and Fragment Offset. With a 128-bit cipher, the Time to Live (TTL), Protocol, Checksum, and Source Address fields are also accessible to the attacker.

An attack on the Total Length field of IPv4 is analogous to the attack on the UDP Length field; i.e., an attacker can truncate a packet and change its meaning by changing this field.

A novel attack on IPv4 is possible by modifying the Protocol field. If the attacker has a login to the same machine as the legitimate receiver, and gets the same port number for a protocol, say UDP, as the receiver's port number for another protocol, say TCP; then by changing the Protocol field from TCP to UDP, the attacker will get the decrypted packets delivered to his UDP port, and the IPsec encryption will be totally defeated.

Another possibility for an attack is to modify the Identification and Fragment Offset fields. These fields are used to identify the location of the parts in a fragmented packet. An attack on the Fragment Offset field can change the ordering of the parts in a reassambled packet. An attack on the Identification field can swap parts between packets. Results of such attacks can be significant depending on the content of the packets.

The Flag bits can also be used to attack fragmented IP packets. If the flags are changed from a fragment setting to a whole packet setting, the receiver will accept the modified packet not as a fragment, but as an entire packet. Use of this packet for an attack will be dependent on the data contained in the packet. An attacker may also set the Last Fragment flag indicating that the fragment in question is the last fragment. This will have the effect of shortening the reassembled packet. However, in the case of transport layer being TCP or UDP, these attacks are not very useful since TCP and UDP have upper layer Length and Checksum fields.

Attacks on other fields of the IPv4 header are possible, but they are not likely to produce useful results for the attacker. These fields can be better used for checksum fixing.

3.4. IPv6

In case of tunneled IPv6, the fields accessible to the attacker with a 64-bit cipher include Version, Priority, Flow Label, Payload Length, Next Header, and Hop Limit. With a 128-bit cipher, the first 64 bits of the Source Address are also accessible.

The Next Header field replaces the Protocol field of IPv4; and an attack on this field can yield the decrypted message to the attacker, similar to the attack on the Protocol field of IPv4. Attacks on other fields are not likely to produce much useful results.

Note that IPv6 has no checksum and, therefore, modifications to the IPv6 header can be done at will.

3.5. L2TP

The Layer Two Tunneling Protocol (L2TP) is a protocol to tunnel PPP connections over wide-area networks and is used with IPsec to establish *virtual private networks* over the Internet. L2TP data packets are typically encapsulated in UDP. As we have seen from the section on UDP, a 128-bit block size will make IV attacks possible on the first 64 bits of the UDP payload, which in this case will include the Length, Tunnel ID, and Call ID fields of the L2TP header.

The most significant attack on these fields is obtained by modifying the Call ID field. In L2TP, many calls (users) can be connected to a location through the same tunnel, where each call is identified by the Call ID number. If the attacker has access to the same tunnel as the victim, he can get the decrypted packets routed to his connection at the endpoint of the tunnel by modifying the Call ID field, in a spirit similar to the attack on TCP port numbers. This attack is likely to be effective in practice since all traffic in a tunnel usually uses the same IPsec Security Association and the same key.

Another possibility for an attack is to modify the Length field. The Length field in L2TP indicates the length of the L2TP header. An attack on this field will result in a change in the perceived length of the L2TP header. Although not very likely, obtaining meaningful results by this attack may be possible, depending on the contents of the L2TP header and the payload.

An attack on the Tunnel ID field is not likely to produce any useful results, since each tunnel typically has a different encryption key. Therefore, changing the Tunnel ID will probably cause the packet to be decrypted as garbage.

4. Prevention of IV attacks

Modification of the IV in a controllable way is central to all attacks outlined in this paper. The attacker can undetectably modify the IV because the IV is sent in the clear and is not protected by cryptographic authentication.

Controllable modification of the IV can be prevented by sending the IV encrypted in the ECB mode or by sending a value that is hashed via a one-way hash function into the actual IV. Or, alternatively, modification of the IV can be totally prevented by using a constant agreed-upon IV, such as 0. Then the first block will receive only ECB protection but this is better than having the first block be modifiable.

Although there are many ways to prevent an IV attack, probably the best protection method is to always use authentication whenever encryption is used. Many reasons for authenticating secret data are present in the literature for reasons besides IV attack prevention. For example, in the case of IPsec, several attacks are known which are due to use of unauthenticated encryption [1]. Typically authentication is computationally less expensive than encryption, which also makes this solution practical. Therefore, our recommendation is to never use encryption without authentication in IPsec.

5. Conclusions

We showed that IV attacks can be a serious threat for IPsec, if IPsec is not used carefully. In the absence of authentication, an attacker may be able to totally defeat the IPsec encryption by the techniques we described in Section 3. Although there are many ways to prevent these attacks, we recommend always using authentication whenever encryption is used. Our conclusion is also supported by other attacks on IPsec, most importantly those discovered by Bellovin [1], which also make use of the fact that IPsec permits encryption to be used without authentication.

An ordinary IPsec user will not be aware of the attacks we described in this paper or the attacks Bellovin described in [1]; nor will he be aware of the recommendations in the IPsec RFCs [6, 5] to always use authentication whenever encryption is used. So, in practice, IPsec in its current form can be very vulnerable to these attacks. To prevent such failures, we recommend making authentication a mandatory feature of an IPsec operation.

Acknowledgments

We would like to thank Gargi Banerjee, Andrea Colegrove and Kim Morgenstern for many helpful discussions and suggestions.

References

[1] S. Bellovin. Problem areas for the IP security protocols. In *Sixth Usenix Unix Security Symposium*, pages 1–16, 1996.

[2] S. Bellovin. Probable plaintext cryptanalysis of the IP security protocols. In *Symposium on Network and Distributed System Security*, pages 155–160, 1997.

[3] D. Comer. *Internetworking With TCP/IP, Volume I: Principles, Protocols, and Architecture*. Prentice Hall, 1995.

[4] S. Kent and R. Atkinson. IP Authentication Header, November 1998. Internet RFC 2402.

[5] S. Kent and R. Atkinson. IP Encapsulating Security Payload (ESP), November 1998. Internet RFC 2406.

[6] S. Kent and R. Atkinson. Security Architecture for the Internet Protocol, November 1998. Internet RFC 2401.

[7] National Institute of Standards and Technology. *AES: A Crypto Algorithm for the Twenty-first Century...* http://www.nist.gov/aes.

[8] V. Voydock and S. Kent. Security mechanisms in high-level network protocols. *ACM Computing Surveys*, 15(2), June 1983.

Server-Assisted Generation of a Strong Secret from a Password

Warwick Ford
VeriSign, Inc.
wford@verisign.com

Burton S. Kaliski Jr.
RSA Laboratories
bkaliski@rsasecurity.com

Abstract

A roaming user, who accesses a network from different client terminals, can be supported by a credentials server that authenticates the user by password then assists in launching a secure environment for the user. However, traditional credentials server designs are vulnerable to exhaustive password guessing attack at the server. We describe a new credentials server model and supporting protocol that overcomes that deficiency. The protocol provides for securely generating a strong secret from a weak secret (password), based on communications exchanges with two or more independent servers. The result can be leveraged in various ways, for example, the strong secret can be used to decrypt an encrypted private key or it can be used in strongly authenticating to an application server. The protocol has the properties that a would-be attacker cannot feasibly compute the strong secret and has only a limited opportunity to guess the password, even if he or she has access to all messages and has control over some, but not all, of the servers.

1. Introduction

Network users potentially need to access sensitive private data, digitally sign transactions, and strongly authenticate to application servers. To support these requirements, client systems typically store the user's private key(s), secrets shared with servers, and/or other private user data on the client system hard drive, encrypted under a password-derived symmetric key. However, this model does not provide for the roaming user, that is, a user who accesses the network from different client terminals. For such a user, the terminal holds no initial user-specific state information. The roaming user is a common phenomenon in many workplace environments and some consumer environments, such as consumer kiosks.

There are two basic alternatives for launching a secure environment for a roaming user – smartcards (or other types of hardware token) and password-only mechanisms. While the smartcard approach is very sound from the security perspective, it is not currently practical in many real-world environments because of cost and convenience factors. This paper focuses on the password-only approach, which does not require special client hardware hence does not suffer from the cost inhibitors of smartcards.

Password-only methods leverage assistance from a *credentials server* in launching a secure environment. Typically, the user first authenticates to the server, which consequently enables strong security in a wider context. Examples of credentials server designs are the family of roaming system protocols described by Perlman and Kaufman [PK99], in which the server securely delivers private data (such as a private key) to the client, or Kerberos [KN93], where the server issues a ticket that can be used in strongly authenticating to other servers.

The fundamental problem with passwords is that a password needs to be easily memorable (otherwise there is a strong tendency to write it down) which often also means that it may be easily guessed by an attacker. Good credentials server designs can do a great deal towards combating password guessing attacks — the protocols can be designed such that no information about the password is revealed to an eavesdropper, and the server can limit the number of tries an attacker can make by throttling or locking out an account in the face of repeated unsuccessful authentication attempts.

However, all known credentials server designs to date suffer from one significant shortcoming: *the server represents a major vulnerability*. The server operator, or someone who compromises the server, can always mount an exhaustive attack on a user's password, in either of two ways. First, if the attacker gains access to the server's database, stored values can be attacked directly. For example, if the server stores a key or verifier derived from a user's password, the attacker can exhaustively guess passwords, apply the derivation function, and compare the results with the stored value. Second, if the attacker can disable the throttling or lockout mechanism, that attacker can make unlimited tries at penetrating an account without having direct access to the database. Since the existence of the credentials server may have created the expectation that reasonably user-friendly passwords are secure, one can anticipate that attacks of these types might often be successful. Furthermore, since one credentials server will typically support a significant population of users, an attack on a credentials server may

0-7695-0798-9/00 $10.00

result in penetration of a large proportion of a user community.

We present a solution to this problem, based essentially on the idea that multiple servers, potentially in different locations and operated by different personnel or even different organizations, need to be compromised, or their operators all need to collude, in order to successfully mount a password-guessing attack.

In addressing this issue, we focus on solving the problem of generating a strong secret (that is, one that cannot feasibly be guessed) from a weak secret (typically a password), in a way that does not expose the weak secret to an exhaustive guessing attack. The solution to that problem can then be leveraged in various ways. For example, the strong secret can be used as a symmetric encryption key to recover encrypted private data stored in a widely accessible directory. Alternatively, the strong secret might be used in securely authenticating to an application server.

2. Server vulnerabilities in existing protocols

For the purposes of this paper, we can assume the state of the art in credentials server designs to be the family of protocols described by Perlman and Kaufman [PK99]. The protocols described in that work are primarily variants or derivatives of Bellovin and Merritt's EKE protocol [BM92, BM94] and Jablon's SPEKE protocol [Jab96, Jab97]. Other credentials server protocols have been proposed by Gong et al. [GLNS93, Gon95], Wu [Wu98], Halevi and Krawcyzk [HK98], and MacKenzie and Swaminathan [MS99].

All these protocols are designed so that the protocol exchange hides information about the password, preventing off-line attacks. To determine whether a password guess is correct, an outside attacker must engage in repeated, on-line exchanges with the server. The server can likewise determine whether a password guess is correct, and can thus throttle or lock out further exchanges after some number of failures.

The server's ability to test passwords is a double-edged sword. While an outside attacker is effectively defeated, an *inside* attacker who compromises the server can directly test a list of passwords. This is true even if the server does not store the password directly, but rather a one-way function of it (as is the case in the most of the protocols mentioned). This vulnerability is a particular concern from the perspective of non-repudiation.

It appears that a single server alone does not provide the assurances we want. Yet if multiple servers are employed in the protocols above, each providing a share of the strong secret, the vulnerability remains, because the user will have to provide something derived from the password to each server, which will thus be able to test whether the password is correct. Related to this, Gong [Gon93] has described an approach to increasing security of credentials servers by having multiple servers, but each server still holds a key for each user which, in a password-only scenario, needs to be derived from the password.

3. A new paradigm

To address the above concerns, we now describe a new paradigm by which a user can obtain one or more strong secrets from a password – the protocol involves multiple servers but no server alone can determine whether a password guess is correct. The paradigm is based on a new *password-hardening protocol,* described further below, by which a server interacts with the user to *harden* the user's password into a strong secret, without learning either the user's password or the hardened result. The hardened passwords can then be combined to obtain additional strong secrets, which none of the servers can determine alone.

The basic protocol is as follows:

1. For each of one or more servers $S_1, \ldots, S_n$, the user engages in a password-hardening protocol with server S_i to obtain a hardened password R_i from the password P. None of the servers learns the password and none of the servers learns the hardened passwords. Note that the hardened password R_i will be the same each time the user runs the protocol with a given password P.
2. The user derives strong secrets $K_1, \ldots, K_m$ where $m \geq n$ from the hardened passwords $R_1, \ldots, R_n$, for instance with a key derivation function KDF:
$$K_i = \mathrm{KDF}\,(R_1, \ldots, R_n, i)\ .$$
3. For each server $S_1, \ldots, S_n$, the user authenticates to the server S_i with K_i.

To protect against on-line attacks, each server keeps track of the number of password hardenings in step 1 and the number of successful authentications in step 3. If there are significantly more password hardenings than successful authentications, the server can throttle or lock out further requests.

We now argue that the protocol meets our design objectives:

- $K_1, \ldots, K_m$ are strong secrets, because they depend on the hardened passwords. Since each one will be the same each time the user runs the protocol, and can be established with the servers when the user first registers. The additional secrets $K_{n+1}, \ldots, K_m$ can be used for other purposes, for instance to authenticate to other servers, to decrypt credentials, and so on.
- The servers collectively can determine whether a user knows the password, and hence can lock out attackers who are attempting to guess the password.

- No combination of n-1 or fewer servers can determine alone whether a password guess is correct, and hence no such combination can determine the secrets $K_{n+1}, \ldots, K_m$. This is because there will be at least one hardened password that the servers cannot determine without interacting with another server, and each strong secrets depends on *all* the hardened passwords.

The interaction in step 1 remains to be defined; we address this point next.

4. Password-hardening protocol

We now suggest a method for hardening a password by interacting with a server. Our goals are as follows: the user should obtain a value R from a password P, it should not be possible for an outside attacker to determine R by exhaustive search, the server should not learn R or P, and the same value R should be obtained each time the user runs the protocol with a given password.

We accomplish these goals as follows. The server selects a prime p such that $p = 2q+1$ where q is a prime, and for each user U selects a secret exponent d_U between 1 and q-1. The server also publishes a function f that maps passwords to elements of multiplicative order q in $\mathbf{Z}_p^*$. For instance, $f(P)$ might be defined as $\text{MGF}(P)^2 \bmod p$ where MGF is a mask-generation function.[1]

Each time the user wants to harden the password, the user engages in the following interactions with the server:

1. The user computes $r = f(P)^k \bmod p$, where k is a random exponent, $1 \leq k \leq q-1$, and sends U and r to the server.
2. The server computes $s = r^{d_U} \bmod p$ and returns s to the user.[2]
3. The user computes $R = s^{1/k} \bmod p$, where $1/k$ is the inverse of $k \bmod q$.

As a result of this protocol, the user obtains $R = f(P)^{d_U} \bmod p$. The exponent k in step 1 serves as a blinding factor: all values of r are equally likely, so the server does not learn any information about the user's password from r, and consequently does not learn the hardened password R. The value R is a strong secret since it depends on the secret exponent d_U.

This protocol should preferably be implemented in such a way that the integrity of the exchange is protected; that is, so that the user is assured that the value of s obtained was computed correctly from r. For instance, the user might protect the exchange with SSL/TLS [FKK96][DA99] and trust the server to perform the computation correctly. Alternatively, the user might require the server to give a proof of knowledge that s was computed from r with the correct exponent. The motivation for this is that otherwise an attacker could cause the user to compute $R = f(P)^{d^*}$ for some different d^* selected and known to the attacker, by replacing s with r^{d^*}. This removes the password-hardening server's influence from the secret and can result in the secrets $K_1, \ldots, K_m$ being directly derivable by the attacker from the password. If any of the secrets is employed in a way that enables the attacker to verify its value (e.g., by authenticating to a server), the attacker will also be able to verify the password.

If the protocol is implemented without integrity protection on the exchange, then the user needs some way to check that at least one of the secrets is correct without enabling the attacker to verify its value. For example, if a secret K_i is used to decrypt credentials and the credentials have sufficient redundancy, the user can check that the secret K_i is correct by decrypting the credentials. The user should do this prior to employing the other secrets.

The parameters p and q and the function f can be built into client software as they are common to many users. If they are not built in, the client should ensure that they are valid (i.e., that p and q are prime and $p = 2q+1$) before using them to prevent a compromised server from providing p and q values for which the blinding property in step 1 does not hold. This assurance of validity may also be provided by a third party, for instance if the primes are provided in a certificate.

The secret exponents for different users should be unrelated. For convenience of implementation, the server may derive the secret exponent for different users from a common secret value, rather than storing a separate value for each user. Alternatively, the secret exponent might be provided by the user during a registration operation.

The protocol described here is based on discrete-logarithm cryptography and can be easily extended to elliptic curve cryptography. It is also possible to construct a protocol based on the RSA algorithm where the blinding operation has the form $r = f(P)\ k^e \bmod n$ for a random k (see [Cha83]). In this case, the client can

---

[1] From a security perspective, it is important that the mapping be independent of the other cryptographic operations involved, and should map to the sufficiently large values mod p. Jablon [Jab97] has observed weaknesses if $f(P)$ is defined as $g^P \bmod p$ for some base g; attacks such as [CNS99] may apply if $f(P)$ is too small. A "random" mask generation function addresses these concerns.

[2] It is possible that an attacker can obtain the least significant bit of d_U by supplying an r value that does not have multiplicative order q and observing whether the resulting s value has order q. Other than this, no information about d_U is obtained by this exchange. (See [Zuc99] for related discussion.)

check directly that the blinding operation has been performed correctly, but must also ensure that the RSA modulus and exponent are valid before using them.

5. A special case

The discussion so far has assumed that two or more password-hardening servers are involved. We observe that it is also possible for the user to obtain a strong secret with only one password-hardening server, with the assistance of a credentials server. In this special case, the user obtains strong secrets T_1 and T_2 from a hardened password R_1. The first strong secret is used to authenticate to the credentials server, and the second is used to encrypt one or more strong secrets $K_1, \ldots, K_m$, with appropriate redundancy, where the encrypted secrets are stored on the credentials server. The protocol is as follows:

1. The user interacts with one password-hardening server S_1 to obtain a hardened password R_1 from a password P.
2. The user derives strong secrets T_1 and T_2 from the hardened password R_1:
$$T_i = \text{KDF}(R_1, i)$$
3. The user authenticates to a credentials server with T_1, then downloads the encrypted secrets $E_{T_2}(K_1, \ldots, K_m)$. This must be done in such a way that it is not possible for an attacker to determine whether T_1 is correct by observing protocol exchanges or to observe the encrypted secrets. For instance, the authentication and download could be done within an SSL session.
4. The user decrypts the encrypted secrets with T_2 to recover $K_1, \ldots, K_m$.
5. The user authenticates to the password-hardening server S_1 with K_1. (This key might, in fact, be the user's private key; the server would hold the corresponding public key.)

The additional secrets $K_2, \ldots, K_m$ can be used for other purposes, for instance to authenticate to other servers, to encrypt other credentials, and so on.

As in the previous protocol, the password-hardening server keeps track of the number of password hardenings in step 1 and the number of successful authentications in step 5. The credentials server also keeps track of the number of unsuccessful authentications in step 3. If the secret T_1 is provided directly to the credentials server in step 3 (e.g., within the SSL session), then for the reasons noted in Section 4 the exchange in step 1 needs to be integrity-protected. The redundancy in the encrypted secrets enables the user to check that the secrets are correct before employing them.

It is easy to see that the design goals are met in this special case as well:

- $K_1, \ldots, K_m$ are strong secrets.
- The servers can lock out attackers who are attempting to guess the password.
- Neither server can determine alone whether a password guess is correct, and hence neither can determine the secrets $K_2, \ldots, K_m$. If K_1 is a private key and the password-hardening server only holds the public key, then neither server can determine K_1 either.

This special case is particularly attractive because the credentials server could be an ordinary directory server. By adding a single password-hardening server to a system that already has a directory, the user can obtain significantly better security, without any other protocol changes.

6. Conclusion

This paper has described a new class of protocol for obtaining a strong secret from a weak secret such as a password. It is particularly suitable for supporting roaming users who need to execute secure transactions but do so from stateless, shared client terminals. The protocol leverages multiple independent servers that hold user-specific secret data components and that monitor their environments for likely attacks on specific accounts. The protocols have the property that a would-be attacker cannot feasibly learn either the weak secret or strong secret for a user by monitoring communications and/or by compromising servers, unless all servers are compromised. This includes resisting password-guessing attacks as a consequence of server compromise. Variants of the protocol based on both the discrete logarithm problem and RSA problem exist. The protocols can be used as the basis of launching various security contexts, including recovering sensitive private data and/or strongly authenticating to application servers.

References

[BM92] S. Bellovin and M. Merritt, "Encrypted Key Exchange: Password-based Protocols Secure against Dictionary Attacks", *Proc. IEEE Symposium on Research in Security and Privacy*, May 1992.

[BM94] S. Bellovin and M. Merritt, *Augmented Encrypted Key Exchange: A Password-Based Protocol Secure against Dictionary Attacks and Password File Compromise*, AT&T Labs Technical Report, 1994.

[Cha83] D. Chaum, "Security without Identification: Transaction Systems to Make Big Brother Obsolete", *Communications of the ACM*, 28 (1985), 1030–1044.

[DA99] T. Dierks and C. Allen, *The TLS Protocol Version 1.0*, IETF RFC 2246, http://www.ietf.org/rfc/rfc2246.txt, Internet Activities Board, January 1999.

[FKK96] A. Frier, P. Karlton, and P. Kocher, *The SSL 3.0 Protocol*, Netscape Communications Corp., Nov 18, 1996.

[GLNS93] L. Gong, T.M.A. Lomas, R.M. Needham, and J.H. Saltzer, "Protecting Poorly Chosen Secrets from Guessing

Attacks", *IEEE Journal on Selected Areas in Communications*, vol.11, no.5, June 1993, pp. 648-656.

[Gon93] L. Gong, "Increasing Availability and Security of an Authentication Service", *IEEE Journal on Selected Areas in Communications*, vol. 11, no. 5, June 1993, pp. 657-662.

[Gon95] L. Gong, "Optimal Authentication Protocols Resistant to Password Guessing Attacks", *Proc. 8th IEEE Computer Security Foundations Workshop*, Ireland, June 13, 1995, pp. 24-29.

[HK98] S. Halevi and H. Krawczyk, "Public-Key Cryptography and Password Protocols", *Proceedings of the Fifth ACM Conference on Computer and Communications Security*, 1998.

[Jab96] D. Jablon, "Strong Password-Only Authenticated Key Exchange", *ACM Computer Communications Review*, October 1996.

[Jab97] D. Jablon, "Extended Password Protocols Immune to Dictionary Attack", *Proc. of the WETICE '97 Enterprise Security Workshop*, June 1997.

[KN93] J.T. Kohl and B.C. Neuman, *The Kerberos Network Authentication Service*, RFC 1510, http://www.ietf.org/rfc/rfc1510.txt, Internet Activities Board, September 1993.

[MS99] P. MacKenzie and R. Swaminathan, *Secure Network Authentication with Password Identification,* submission to IEEE P1363 working group, http://grouper.ieee.org/groups/1363/, July 30, 1999.

[PK99] R. Perlman and C. Kaufman, "Secure Password-Based Protocol for Downloading a Private Key", *Proc. 1999 Network and Distributed System Security Symposium*, Internet Society, January 1999.

[Wu98] T. Wu, "The Secure Remote Password Protocol", *Proc. 1998 Network and Distributed System Security Symposium*, Internet Society, January 1998, pp. 97-111.

[Zuc99] R. Zuccherato, *Methods for Avoiding the "Small-Subgroup" Attacks on the Diffie-Hellman Key Agreement for S/MIME,* IETF RFC 2785, http://www.ietf.org/rfc/rfc2785.txt, Internet Activities Board, March 2000.

A Delayed Commitment Scheme to Enhance Public Key Certificate Based Protocols

Wu Wen
Science University of Tokyo
2641 Yamazaki, Noda
Chiba, Japan 278-8510
wen@imc.sut.ac.jp

Abstract

Public key certificate based protocols depend on the freshness of the certificates for their security. It has been pointed out by various authors that current Public Key Infrastructure (PKI) does not provide effective freshness proof for certificates. An "ex-employee" who has access to the private key of a compromised server certificate can mount an attack on the SSL/TLS handshake protocol and eavesdrop the subsequent secret communication even if the server uses a fresh certificate[2]. In this paper we propose an improved handshake protocol which requires minimum change to the current SSL/TLS handshake protocol, yet practically prevent the above "ex-employee" attack.

1. Introduction

Public key certificate based protocols depends on the validity and freshness of the certificates for their security. Validity of a certificate is concerned with whether a particular certificate is issued by a trusted CA or not, and can be checked with the CA's verification key. It is a static property and SSL/TLS supports and enforces the check. On the other hand, freshness of a certificate is concerned with it status of revocation. It is a dynamic property and need to be checked in real time just before a certificate is used. In [1] it was stated that:

> It is the responsibility of any party that trusts another's certificate to check with the certificate authority to make sure the certificate has not been revoked. This function is not the responsibility of the SSL protocol, ... It is noteworthy to consider, though, that the current Web commerce infrastructure does not have an effective (and widely supported) means for systems to check a certificate against a Certificate Revocation List (CRL). For that reason, there is no practical way to revoke a traditional Web commerce certificate.

2. SSL/TLS Handshake Protocol

In the following, we give a brief description of the SSL/TLS handshake protocol by listing the messages communicated between the client and the server[1]. The basic mode of the SSL/TLS protocol is the "named-server, anonymous-client" version of the protocol, in which only the server, such as an Internet shopping mall, is authenticated. This protocol generates a master secret between an anonymous client and a named server. We use well known notations[2] for the messages:

$$C \to S: \quad (N_C, T_C) \qquad (M_1)$$
$$S \to C: \quad (N_S, T_S) \qquad (M_2)$$
$$S \to C: \quad \{S, K_S^+\}_{K_{CA}^-} \qquad (M_3)$$
$$C \to S: \quad \{N'_C\}_{K_S^+} \qquad (M_4)$$
$$S \to C: \quad \{H(K_{CS}, CS_5, (M_1, M_2, M_3, M_4))\}_{K_{CS}} \qquad (M_5)$$
$$C \to S: \quad \{H(K_{CS}, CS_6, (M_1, M_2, M_3, M_4))\}_{K_{CS}} \qquad (M_6)$$

The messages can be summarized as follows:

- M_1: C sends a timestamp and a nonce to S;
- M_2: S sends another timestamp and nonce to C;
- M_3: S sends its certificate to C;
- M_4: C returns the " pre-master secret" N'_C encrypted under K_S^+;

0-7695-0798-9/00 $10.00 © 2000 IEEE

- M_5: S sends the hash of the session key, a tag CS_5 indicating the protocol stage , and all preceding messages sent by S to C;
- M_6: C sends the hash of the session key, a tag CS_6 indicating the protocol stage, and all preceding messages sent by C to S.

3. "Ex-employee" Attack

In the following, we describe the steps showing how an intruder with a compromised certificate can learn the master secret even if the server has updated its certificate. Message in the form of "... $\rightarrow (X)I$" indicates that a message intended for X is intercepted by I. Message in the form of "$(X)I \rightarrow$ ..." indicates a message faked by I as from X. Note that $\{S, K_S'^{+}\}_{K_{CA}^-}$ is the compromised certificate of S while $\{S, K_S^+\}_{K_{CA}^-}$ is the fresh and valid certificate of S.

$$
\begin{array}{lll}
C \rightarrow S: & (N_C, T_C) & (M_1) \\
S \rightarrow C: & (N_S, T_S) & (M_2) \\
S \rightarrow (C)I: & \{S, K_S^+\}_{K_{CA}^-} & (M_3') \\
I(S) \rightarrow C: & \{S, K_S'^{+}\}_{K_{CA}^-} & (M_3'') \\
C \rightarrow (S)I: & \{N_C'\}_{K_S'^{+}} & (M_4') \\
(C)I \rightarrow S: & \{N_C'\}_{K_S^+} & (M_4'') \\
S \rightarrow (C)I: & \{H(..., (M_1, M_2, M_3', M_4''))\}_{K_{AB}} & (M_5') \\
(S)I \rightarrow C: & \{H(..., (M_1, M_2, M_3'', M_4'))\}_{K_{AB}} & (M_5'') \\
C \rightarrow (S)I: & \{H(..., (M_1, M_2, M_3'', M_4'))\}_{K_{AB}} & (M_6') \\
(C)I \rightarrow S: & \{H(..., (M_1, M_2, M_3', M_4''))\}_{K_{AB}} & (M_6'')
\end{array}
$$

Note that the purpose for M_5 and M_6 in the original SSL/TLS handshake protocol was designed to prevent attacks that are based on interception and faking of messages. For example, if M_5' is allowed to reach C, C will find out that the hash of all messages doesn't match because C expects (M_1, M_2, M_3'', M_4') but instead receiving (M_1, M_2, M_3', M_4''). We can see from above that it is ineffective in preventing the interception and faking described above because the master secret K_{CS} is known to the intruder. After the verification steps, an SSL/TLS session is regarded securely established between C and S. Unfortunately the master secret is now known by the intruder I. The consequence of this attack is severe. The secrecy and integrity of the protocol is totally destroyed.

4. Delayed Commitment Scheme

One way to stop this attack is to provide certain unique identity for the "anonymous" client. A public key pair is generated by the client for each session. The handshake protocol now look as follows:

$$
\begin{array}{lll}
C \rightarrow S: & (N_C, T_C, K_C^+) & (M_1) \\
S \rightarrow C: & (H(\{N_S\}_{K_C^+}), T_S) & (M_2) \\
S \rightarrow C: & \{S, K_S^+\}_{K_{CA}^-} & (M_3) \\
C \rightarrow S: & \{N_C'\}_{K_S^+} & (M_4) \\
S \rightarrow C: & \{N_S\}_{K_C^+} & (M_{4.1}) \\
S \rightarrow C: & \{H(..., (M_1, M_2, M_3, M_4))\}_{K_{AB}} & (M_5) \\
C \rightarrow S: & \{H(..., (M_1, M_2, M_3, M_4))\}_{K_{AB}} & (M_6)
\end{array}
$$

It is beyond this short paper to show why it is secure against the "ex-employee" attack, which we hope to present in another paper. The original SSL/TLS handshake protocol has gone through intense scrutiny since it is published. However, most analysis assumes that the validity and freshness of the certificate can be guaranteed. We have basically improved the "named-server, anonymous-client" mode of the protocol so it is as strong as the "named-server, named-client" mode with respect to the "ex-employee" attack.

5. Conclusion

In this paper, we have proposed a "delayed commitment scheme" to prevent the "ex-employee" attack on the "named-server anonymous-client" mode of SSL/TLS handshake protocol. Due to the fact that most of the SSL/TLS implementation are using the "named-server, anonymous-client" mode, the proposed approach effectively enhance the protocol against the serious "ex-employee" attack without requiring the upgrading of SSL/TLS to the more costly "named-server, named-client" mode. This has practical implications for small and mobile devices which may be constrained from implementing such mode even if they are available. In addition, the proposed improved protocols can be made compatible with the original protocol. This means that the improved version can be made to co-exist with the current version of SSL/TLS. For example, an option can be added to the "negotiated cipher" specification of the current SSL/TLS protocol. So the improved version of the handshake protocol will be used after both client and server agrees.

References

[1] S. Thomas. *SSL and TLS Essentials*, chapter Basic Cryptography, pages pp 34–35. Wiley Computing Publishing, 2000.

[2] W. Wen, T. Saito, and F. Mizoguchi. Security of public-key based authentication protocol. *LNCS, Springer Verlag*, 1751:196–209, January 2000.

Secure Self-Certified COTS*

M. Debbabi & E. Giasson & B. Ktari & F. Michaud & N. Tawbi
LSFM Research Group,
Computer Science Department,
Science and Engineering Faculty,
Laval University,
Quebec, Canada
{debabi,giassone,ktari,michaudf,tawbi}@ift.ulaval.ca

Abstract

With the advent and the rising popularity of networks, Internet, intranets and distributed systems, security is becoming one of the major concerns in IT research. An increasing number of approaches have been proposed to ensure the safety and security of programs. Among those approaches, certified code seems to be the most promising. Unfortunately, as of today, most of the research on certified code have focused on simple type safety and memory safety, rather than security issues. We therefore propose to extend this approach to the security aspects of a program. Our intention is to use such an approach as an efficient and realistic solution to the problem of malicious code detection in COTS. In this paper, we present our progress in defining and implementing a certifying compiler that produces a secure self-certified code that can be used to ensure both safety and security of the code.

1. Motivation and Background

Nowadays, there are many information infrastructures based on the so-called Commercial Off-The-Shelf (COTS) components. Actually, many organizations are undergoing a remarkable move from legacy systems towards COTS-based systems. The main motivation underlying such a migration is to take advantage of cutting-edge technologies and also to lower the program life-cycle costs of computer systems. Nevertheless, this migration phenomenon poses major and yet very interesting challenges to the currently established computer system technologies in terms of security, reliability, integration, interoperability, maintenance, planning, etc.

In our current research, we are concerned with malicious code that could exist in COTS software products. In a preliminary study of the domain [2], we considered different approaches suitable to address this problem. Among those approaches, certified code seems to be the most promising. Given a certified program provided by an untrusted source, a host can determine with certainty that this program may be safely executed. Unfortunately, as of today, most of the research on certified code have focused on simple type safety and memory safety, rather than security issues. We therefore propose to extend this approach to the security aspects of a program.

In this paper, we present our progress in defining and implementing a certifying compiler that produces a secure self-certified code that can be used to ensure both the safety and security of the code. We used LCC [3], a C compiler, as the starting point for our certifying compiler to which we added a type system based on TALx86 [5].

The rest of the paper is organized as follows. Section 2 presents the certified code approach, which guarantees that COTS components may be safely executed. Section 3 focuses on the code generation process that produces annotated assembly code. Section 4 follows with the verification process, which aims at formally certifying that the generated annotated code satisfies well defined safety properties. Section 5 proposes an extension to both the generation and verification processes to include security properties. Section 6 presents related work. Finally, a few concluding remarks and a discussion of future research are ultimately sketched as a conclusion in Section 7.

2. Certified Code

Certified code is a general framework that aims at guaranteeing COTS components compliance with the functionality and security requirements. It allows a host, which is re-

*This research is funded by a research contract from the Defense Research Establishment, Valcartier, DREV, Quebec, Canada.

0-7695-0798-9/00 $10.00 © 2000 IEEE

ferred to as the *code consumer*, to determine with certainty that a program supplied by an untrusted source, which is referred to as the *code producer*, can be safely executed. The code producer must attach a collection of annotations (the *certificate*) to the code it produces. The certificate can be made of proofs, types, or any other kind of formal or informal information about program dynamic behaviors properties. Once the code consumer holds both the code and the certificate, it checks the certificate to ensure that it is safe to execute the associated code.

To its full extent, the certified code approach brings several key characteristics that draw a clear advantage over more traditional approaches for malicious code detection:

- First, the overall certification process is shared between the producer and the consumer code. Thus, as the code verification is much easier than the code and certificate generation, this could be beneficial for the consumer compared to other approaches, such as a full blown, lengthy static binary code analysis.
- Second, approaches using cryptography and authentication, in order to ensure that the code has been produced by a trusted source and has not been altered during the transmission, are not required. If either the code or the certificate is altered, the verification process will fail. Moreover, if both are altered in such a manner that the verification still succeeds, then the code remains safe, provided that the certificate still satisfies safety and security properties.
- Third, since a certificate is attached to the low-level code and the former contains additional information regarding the code (proofs, types, etc.), the verification process could take advantage of this additional information, as opposed to a raw binary code verification.
- Lastly, the verification process is performed off-line and only once, no matter how many times the code is executed. Thus, there are no run-time penalties, which makes this approach more efficient than others.

The certified code approach first appeared in the JAVA programming language. The JAVA compiler produces statically typed Java Virtual Machine Language (JVML) code, which includes typing annotations that a verifier can use to ensure the type safety of the code. More recently, three interesting and more general approaches have been proposed:

- Proof-Carrying Code (PCC) [7]: The certificate represents a proof. The producer supplies along with the code a proof attesting that the code satisfies a formally defined security policy publicized by the consumer. The consumer then gets the code and its proof, and validates the proof in order to execute the code safely.
- Typed Assembly Language (TAL) [6]: The certificate is made of typing annotations. Along with the assembly code, the compiler produces typing annotations that can be used to ensure the safety of the assembly code. Thus, the verification process consists of type-checking the annotated assembly code.
- Efficient Code Certification (ECC) [4]: The certificate corresponds to structured annotations that merely direct the verification process. Annotations are limited to a fixed and relatively basic level of security (control flow, memory and stack safety) since the motivation of the author was to propose a simple and efficient system that would be relatively simple to incorporate into existing compilers.

3. Code Generation

To implement our certifying compiler, we modified an existing compiler instead of building a new one from scratch. We chose LCC since its source code (about 15 000 lines) is available for free and the book [3] covers it nicely.

LCC is a retargetable compiler for ANSI C that generates code for the following processors: ALPHA, SPARC, MIPS R3000 and Intel x86. To allow compilation for different processors, LCC is designed in two parts: a general front end and a processor-dependent back end. The front end does the C language analysis and produces an intermediate representation of directed acyclic graphs. Afterwards, the back end uses this intermediate representation to generate the assembly code.

Taking back the idea of a typed assembly language, which is the TAL project (throughout this paper, the TAL acronym refers to this particular project, instead of "typed assembly language", its actual meaning), the first step in our certified compilation process is to generate a typed assembly output from an ANSI C source file. Basically, typed assembly is an annotated assembly code. Annotations, created and inserted automatically by a compiler, describe the types of each data and piece of code in a given source file as well as types of variables and functions imported from other files or libraries. Types are built from a type algebra that allows a low-level description of both low-level concepts such as integers and hardware registers, and higher level concepts such as structures and functions. Such a type system must be closely related to both the source language (here ANSI C) and the destination platform hardware (32-bits code on an Intel x86). Indeed, types serve as the missing link between structured and functional source code and machine dependent assembly language.

Our type algebra was largely inspired by TAL type system, at least textually, though semantics were widely redefined and tailored to our needs. While TAL types were based on the Popcorn language (a sort of a C subset and ML hybrid language), ours were meant to fully describe ANSI C elements, such as pointers, integers of different sizes, floating-point numbers, etc.

Both data and code labels need to be annotated, as well as instructions that branch to code labels, namely calls and jumps. On the data side, there exists an almost one to one relation between ANSI C data types and low-level types. Furthermore, the type algebra allows different kinds of basic types composition and grouping to build complex types representation such as structures, unions, or types like "pointer to an array of 25 integer pointers" for example. Therefore, the implementation in the compiler is a rather straightforward translation.

On the code labels side, type generation is not that obvious. As code is meant to be executed in a dynamic context, label annotations need to describe a state, a context that must hold, i.e. be true, when execution reaches that point. To its largest extent, a context would hold the state of "everything" accessible by a running process, like processor registers, every byte of stack and heap memory, and all other possible resources. Obviously, describing "everything" is far out the compiler reach and doesn't make much sense in practice. So as the TAL approach suggests, we focus only on registers and stack state, which nevertheless hold all local variables in a C function and all values to be manipulated within functions. Heap usage tracking is part of our future research work.

Before annotating labels, code must be split into basic blocks. A basic block begins with a label, followed by zero or more assembly instructions, up to the next label or jump (conditional or not) whichever comes first. A jump to the following label is implied at the end of any block that doesn't explicitly end with a jump. The entire source code thus appears as a bunch of labelled blocks of code and the function concept becomes meaningless at this point. Also, code generated by LCC is not globally optimized and the x86 back end stores intermediate results and common subexpressions into temporary variables on the stack rather than registers. It can then be assumed that values are not carried across basic blocs boundaries by registers. The only exception is the EAX register that is often use to hold the return value of a function. Consequently, other registers are never considered as initialized at the execution point following any label (except for ESP and EBP which point to the stack). The registers annotation has thus been left out in code label annotations.

Typing the stack state requires a good knowledge of x86 back end stack management and a complete control flow analysis of the code. Stack management is similar to common commercial compilers. Control flow analysis computes the semantic content of this stack frame at the beginning of every basic bloc, i.e. at every label. A deeper analysis provides information about uninitialized, initialized or read-only variables, which is added to the semantic information to build the stack state type. In the case where multiple paths in the control flow graph lead to the same block and carry different information about variables state, we use a worst case approach. For example, a variable may or may not be initialized in different paths, therefore it is considered uninitialized where the paths meet in the control flow graph.

```
int function( parameters ) {
    variables declarations (A)
    complex code (uses temporaries)
    if ( condition )
    {
         variables declarations (B)
         simple code (no temporaries)
    }
    return value
}
```

Figure 1. Simple C code example.

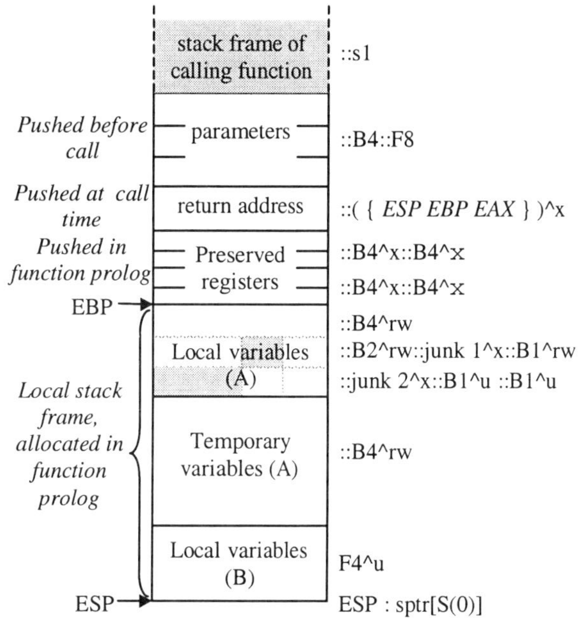

Figure 2. Stack configuration.

Figure 1 shows a simple C code example. Some variables are declared at the function level while some other are declared in an inner compound-statement. Also, some temporary variables are generated by the compiler to hold temporary results in the "complex code" part. Such variables are semantically equivalent to local variables. In this example, both EBP and ESP registers point to the stack frame and therefore, are typed in label annotations. ESP always points at the end of the function stack frame or further if arguments are pushed onto the stack before a call, but EBP always points at the beginning of the stack frame, as shown in Figure 2.

This figure shows a hypothetical stack content when execution reaches the "simple code" point. The actual label annotation for this block of code describes among other things the type of the ESP register, which is shown on the right side of the figure, written from bottom to top. Roughly speaking, this type means that ESP points to the stack, where there is several variables of different types and access. Among them, the return address is expressed as the type of several registers that must hold on function return. Their actual type was removed from the figure given their complexity. It is worth noting however that ESP is also typed in this part of ESP type. A typed relation can then be expressed between the actual stack type and the caller stack type. The complete stack state of a running process is somehow the sum of local stack frames of all called and not yet completed functions since the process was started. As functions in the actually compiled source file may be called in an order that is well often not known statically, and since they might also be called from functions in other source files compiled separately, the complete stack state cannot be computed during compilation.

However, type variables are used in annotations as placeholders for yet unknown types. In the stack figure, the "s1" type variable holds for the stack content before the actual function was called, which can't be computed at this point. Actually, unknown types include the stack type before the actual function was called and an arguments list for functions such as `printf` which take a variable number of arguments. Other information from the calling function required to type both ESP and EBP registers is also represented by type variables. Namely, this other information is needed to type EBP and ESP as they should be at the beginning and the end of the function that is, before the local stack frame is allocated, and right after a return instruction is executed. Such information is only known within blocks that call the actual block, and is probably quite different from one block to the other if those blocks formerly belonged to different functions. Also, different labels may require a different kind of type variables. Each call or jump must therefore provide the appropriate information to complete the destination label type in a macro with parameters fashion. The verification process will take care of variables substitution.

4. Code Verification

Ultimately, the verification process will match a certificate against its corresponding binary executable to detect any malicious alterations to either one, and will then match this certificate against a local security policy to prevent unwanted behaviors from the executable. Any security policy includes de facto low-level security (safety) properties that deal mainly with memory and stack safety.

The actual implementation of both the compiler and the verifier only address the safety issue, as covering security properties is currently an ongoing work on both the compiler and the verifier. Furthermore, certified binary executable are not yet generated and we are still working on the assembly language output code along with its type file generated by the compiler. But since there is almost a direct relation between the assembly code and binary code, as well as between a type file and a certificate, our actual verifier does pretty much the same job as the targeted final verifier, although its implementation is quite simpler. Actually, safety properties covered by generated annotations and their verification are proper use of stack and CPU registers.

The verification process is split into three main steps: files parsing, type consistency check and instructions verification. Parsing was done using a Flex and Bison++ generated lexer and parser. Type consistency does some basic check about types in annotation that we assume to be of any given kind. For example, user-defined C types such as structures are stored in the type file as a "kind" and a "type". In that case, the kind specifies that the associated type is a "piece of memory of n bytes". The type consistency step computes the size of the structure in memory and matches it against the kind. This step prevents some malicious alterations in the type information and ensures that the compiler and the verifier are both correct or both wrong. Given the relative complexity of both process, it is unlikely that they are both wrong "in the same way". All parsed types must be consistent to continue with the next step.

The last step is the core of the verification process. Blocks of code are verified one by one, independently. Each block of code is a basic block, made of a label followed by zero or more assembly instructions. A label annotation describes a context under which all instructions are to be executed. Starting from this context, instructions are verified one by one, in order. A transition rule is associated to every assembly language mnemonic (instructions) known by the verifier. Some mnemonic might have different meanings depending on the type of their operand and are thus associated with more than one rule.

A transition rule states pre and post-conditions that must hold when executing the corresponding instruction. The preconditions describe what could be considered as valid operands, if any, and a context state that must be valid before executing the instruction. Post-conditions tell how the context is to be modified after executing the instruction.

Each instruction is verified by applying the corresponding transition rule down to the last instruction of the block, which is always a jump, either explicit (a jump instruction) or implicit (in the case a jump to the following block of code is implied when the last instruction is not a jump). Transition rules for calls and jumps are slightly more complex than others since they must also substitute type variables in the destination label annotation and make sure that this new context (the modified version of the label annotation) can exist under the current context.

Any unverified condition automatically aborts verification with an error. No recovery scheme is actually implemented. Such an error may occur if there was malicious modifications of the assembly code and/or annotations, or if the code generated by the compiler is wrong. In fact, annotation are generated before the generated code, still in a structured form, is translated into assembly language by the back end. We could then detect some errors in the back end if there were any. But fortunately, the version of LCC we use seems so far to be error free.

5. Secure Self-Certified Code

As explained before, actual certifying compilers have focused on simple type safety properties. However, the security issue is of paramount importance. The consumer code accepting an untrusted code must check that the latter will not affect the secrecy (by leaking sensitive information), integrity (by corrupting information), authentication (by impersonating authorized principals), availability (by denying service to legal users), etc. Consequently, we need to extend our certifying compiler in order to consider the security aspects of a program.

As mentioned in [6, p. 530], the ideal system would contain both the compiler support and compact annotations of TAL, and the flexibility of PCC. On one hand, PCC uses a general-purpose logic, and can encode more expressive security properties. On the other hand, TAL provides compiler writers with a higher-level set of abstractions than PCC.

Our intended approach take advantages over both approaches (TAL and PCC).

First, on the code producer side, we use type annotations provided by TAL to generate a secure self-certified code. However, in order to consider security aspects of the code, we plan to extend the type system with effect discipline [9]. This extension consists of an inference type-system that propagates the security effects that result from accessing private resources, sending sensitive information over the network, etc. The idea is to consider security effects as part of the static evaluation of the code. The resulting annotations constitute valuable information for static analysis purposes, especially for verification, and correspond to the certificate that is delivered with the generated code.

Second, on the code consumer side, two verification process steps are needed. The first step corresponds obviously to the validation of the certificate. The purpose of this validation is to check, with certainty, that the certificate corresponds to the associated code. It is done by type-checking the code under the certificate constraints. The second step involves a model-checking verification technique. It consists of the extraction of a model from the information contained in the certificate. This model provides an abstraction of security aspects of the program. Afterwards, this model is matched against a logical specification of security policies. We plan to use a modal μ-calculus based logic to specify security policies.

Figure 3 shows the typical process of generating and verifying secure self-certified code.

6. Related Work

Recently, a surge of interest has been devoted to the security aspect of programming languages, especially through the compilation process. Moreover, we report two different research projects that are based respectively on TAL and PCC approaches.

In [10], the authors present an extension to the TAL approach that allows the generation of certified code for expressive security policies. In their proposed approach, security policies are specified using security automata [8]. One of the particularities of security automata is that its specifications can always be enforced by inserting run-time checks. Thus, during compilation, they dictate when to insert run-time checks. Especially, the compiler places run-time checks around every call to sensitive operations to ensure that the program uses these operations according to the specified security policies. The program is then optimized, removing run-time checks wherever it is possible to do so. The resulting code is then verified (type-checked) for its safety before being linked with a secure annotated interface of the system.

This approach seems to be very promising and useful. However, it is not clear how efficient the optimizer is in removing the dynamic checks. Furthermore, while security automata seem to be adequate to specify any *safety property* [8], it remains that they fail to capture some interesting security policies like information flow.

In [1], the authors propose an extension of the PCC approach to support high-level security policies. Among others, the main novelty in this research is the security policy component. They intend to bring together ideas from proof-carrying code with ideas from authentication logics. By doing so, they intend to build a system that is practical and handles sophisticated high-level security policies.

This approach has a number of advantages over other ones [1]. However, while the use of logics to specify se-

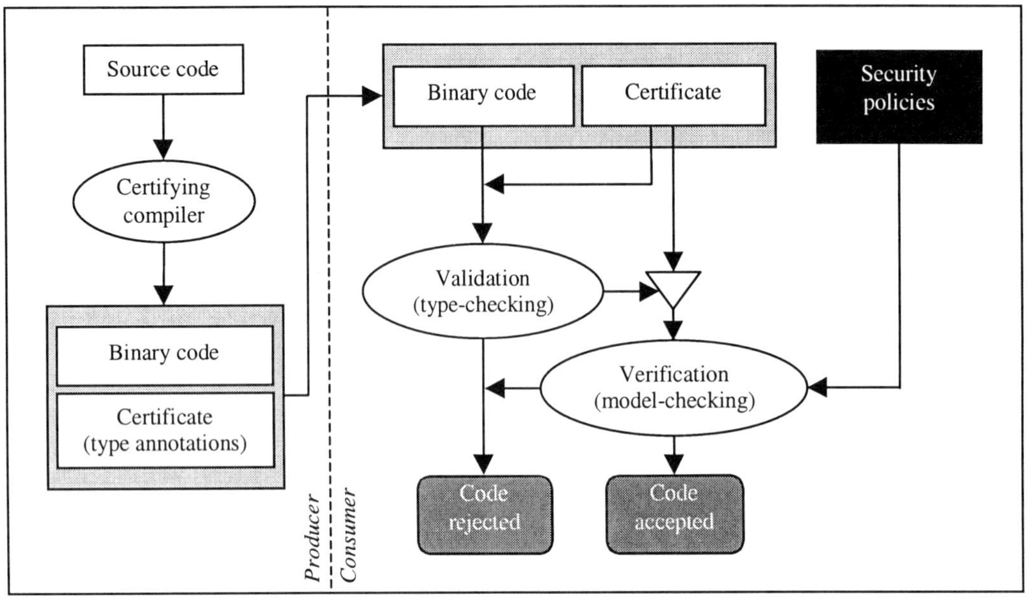

Figure 3. Secure self-certified Code.

curity policies seems to be more expressive than security automata, it is not clear how efficient authentication logics are to express security policies related to malicious code.

7. Conclusion

In this paper, we have reported our progress in defining and implementing a certifying compiler that produces a secure self-certified code that might be used to ensure both safety and security of the code. The current implementation of both the compiler and the verifier only addresses the safety issue, as covering security properties is currently an ongoing work. We intend to use a modal μ-calculus based logic to specify security policies and to address the verification problem through model-checking. The main idea is to match the model, extracted from the program through effect annotations, against a security policy specification.

As future research work, we plan to emphasize on the elaboration of the formal definition of the logic. Also, we aim at achieving efficient and practical program checking of potentially malicious code against security properties specifications. Finally, we hope to come up with practical tools and technologies that address the automatic detection of malicious code in COTS.

References

[1] A. W. Appel, E. W. Felten, and Z. Shao. Scaling proof-carrying code to production compilers and security policies. `http://www.cs.princeton.edu/sip/projects/pcc/whitepaper/`, Jan. 1999.

[2] J. Bergeron, M. Debbabi, J. Desharnais, B. Ktari, M. Salois, and N. Tawbi. Detection of malicious code in COTS software: A short survey. In *First International Software Assurance Certification Conference (ISACC'99)*, Washington D.C, Mar. 1999.

[3] C. Fraser and D. Hanson. *A retargetable C Compiler: design and implementation*. Adison-Wesley, 1995.

[4] D. Kozen. Efficient code certification. Technical Report TR98-1661, Cornell University, Jan. 1998.

[5] G. Morrisett, K. Crary, N. Glew, D. Grossman, R. Samuels, F. Smith, D. Walker, S. Weirich, and S. Zdancewic. TALx86: A realistic typed assembly language. In *1999 ACM SIGPLAN Workshop on Compiler Support for System Software*, Atlanta, GA, USA, May 1999.

[6] G. Morrisett, D. Walker, K. Crary, and N. Glew. From system F to typed assembly language. *ACM Transactions on Programming Languages and Systems*, 21(3):528–569, May 1999.

[7] G. C. Necula. Proof-carrying code. In *Proceedings of the 24th ACM Symposium on Principles of Programming Languages*, Paris, France, Jan. 1997.

[8] F. B. Schneider. Enforceable security policies. Technical Report TR98-1664, Cornell University, Jan. 1995.

[9] J. Talpin and P. Jouvelot. The type and effect discipline. *Information and Computation*, 111(2):245–296, June 1994.

[10] D. Walker. A type system for expressive security policies. Technical Report TR99-1740, Cornell University, Apr. 1999.

On the Implementation of a Stand-Alone Java™ Bytecode Verifier*

Frédéric Painchaud
LSFM Research Group
Laval University
painchaf@ift.ulaval.ca

Mourad Debbabi
LSFM Research Group
Laval University
debbabi@ift.ulaval.ca

Abstract

A member of our research team has already produced a well-organized, clear, technical and complete specification of the Java Bytecode Verifier. We are now using this specification to implement a stand-alone version of the Verifier that totally complies with Sun's specification. We are also integrating static checks that are currently absent from their implementation. In this paper, we share our experience on that development work. As an introduction, we depict the main goals of the Verifier, followed by an overview of its verification process. We then present the major steps that we followed to develop our Verifier, in order to explain the problems that we have encountered and to summarize their solutions. Finally, we show a screenshot of our Verifier's interface and enlighten its most interesting features.

1. Introduction

Java compilers perform extensive compile-time checking on the source code they compile. Among other verifications, they enforce type safety, impose a strict adherence to the Java language rules, ensuring that no classes try to access other classes' private members for example, and carry out class interdependency analysis.

However, the Java Virtual Machine cannot rely on compile-time checking because it has no way of determining whether the class files it interprets were produced by a trustworthy Java compiler or by a malicious user.

Therefore, the JVM needs to verify loaded class files to ensure that they do not compromise the security of the system by either

- disrespecting the Java language rules or
- corrupting its integrity.

This task is actually fulfilled by the Bytecode Verifier. In other words, the Verifier serves to make sure that classes loaded into the JVM respect certain security-related properties or constraints, which bear on:

- the class' syntax
- the behavior of its code and
- the potential interdependencies that it has with other classes.

The particulars of the verification process will provide more details about these properties and constraints.

2. Overview of the verification process

When a class file is submitted to verification, not only that file but also all the class files it references, like its superclass and implemented interfaces, are verified. This verification process, incompletely defined in [6] but presented thoroughly by Stéphane Doyon in [3], is actually quite recursive. For example, before verifying a given class file, all its ancestors must be recursively verified. This is also true for their implemented interfaces and all the superinterfaces of these interfaces.

The suggested steps of the verification of each class file are as follows. For the sake of brevity, we assume that the reader already knows the basics of the Java language, detailed in [2], and the class file format, defined in [6].

1. Class file syntax

1.1. Class file format: The first step of the verification process involves checking that the loaded file is really a class file, and not simply a renamed file with a *.class* extension, and that it basically respects the class file format. The Verifier checks that the class has the expected name, that all entries in the constant pool are valid and that the length and number of recognized attributes are appropriate. Tests related to the superclass and implemented interfaces are also performed so that their definition can also be loaded.

1.2. Class file consistency: This step encompasses all remaining checks except those dealing with the bytecode instructions composing method bodies. It

* Supported by the *Defence Research Establishment Valcartier* (DREV), National Defence, Canada.

0-7695-0798-9/00 $10.00 © 2000 IEEE

involves checking the consistency of the constant pool, validating the access flags of the class and of each field and method, as well as verifying their name and signature. This step also performs tests related to the class' method table: it checks that the class declares or inherits the necessary methods to fully implement each interface it claims to implement, that it does not declare to be a subclass of a "final" class and that it does not override any "final" methods. Once a class has successfully passed this step, the information about its declared fields and methods can be used safely.

2. Bytecode verification

2.1. Code layout: The layout of the code in method bodies is now checked: basically, the Verifier parses the code, ensuring that all opcodes are valid and that it does not contain garbage. This step is also responsible for checking the methods' exception table.

2.2. Operands: Checks are performed on the operands of each instruction. At this point, the targets of branch instructions can be verified (control flow safety). For every operand that is a reference to the constant pool, the verifier ensures that the pointed entry is of the appropriate type for the current instruction. The number of the target register of "load" and "store" instructions is also checked to be within the range of the method's declared number of used registers (register safety).

2.3. Dataflow analysis: A dataflow analysis is then performed on the code. For more information about dataflow analysis in general, see [1]. For in depth explications of the dataflow analysis performed by the Bytecode Verifier, see [3], [4], [5] and [7]. This is the most complex yet most significant part of the verification process. The dataflow analysis serves to determine, at each instruction, what types of values are present in each stack location and in each register. This information makes it possible to check that no value is taken from an uninitialized register (register safety), that there are no stack overflows (stack safety) and that the arguments of all instructions are of the right type (type safety). It is also verified that the values passed as arguments when invoking methods and the values put into fields are of appropriate types (type safety), that no newly allocated object is used before it is initialized (object safety) and that subroutines do not disrupt control flow safety.

3. Resolution: This final step deals with checks that must be performed when resolving a reference to another class, field or method. Among others, existence and accessibility of the target should be verified. These tests are usually performed lazily, at run-time, in a JVM that integrates a Verifier. Since our Verifier is stand-alone, we perform them during the dataflow analysis, in step 2.3.

Now that you have a better idea of what the verification process involves, we present our Bytecode Verifier implementation work.

3. Major steps of our development work

Since the Java Bytecode Verifier is already a rather complex piece of software, we tried to keep our design and implementation straightforward. We wanted the design to be simple and easily extensible. Furthermore, the source code should not sacrifice clarity for efficiency. Our Verifier is implemented in Java.

3.1. Class file disassembly

We began our development work by figuring out how to disassemble a class file. This task did not cause many problems since the class file format is very well documented in [6] and it has been designed with verification in mind. Therefore, class file disassembly is simply a matter of defining proper data structures and filling them with the right information taken from that class file. This is probably why there are so many class file disassemblers and assemblers freely available on the Internet.

Although, in the context of the production of a Verifier, the only thing to be careful about at this stage is to make sure that you do appropriate checks before trying to load any given information from a class file because you cannot assume that it is not corrupted. These tests correspond to the step 1.1 of the verification process and constitute a class file syntactic analysis. For example, before attempting to load the information contained in a constant pool entry, you must verify that this entry's tag is valid, i.e. that its value is either 1, 3, 4, 5, 6, 7, 8, 9, 10, 11 or 12. By specification, it cannot be 2.

3.2. Verifier's engine

When you study the Java Virtual Machine and its Bytecode Verifier in details, you realize that they are complementary. Indeed, the JVM loads class files as it needs them and passes them to the Verifier in order to ensure that they are safe for interpretation. Consequently, when you develop a stand-alone implementation of the Verifier, you need to design an engine that simulates the JVM class file dynamic loading behavior.

This engine is not so difficult to devise but it has to be well designed because it constitutes the core of the Verifier. It initiates and controls the verification of every class file.

We give a summarized UML representation of our class, named *Verifier*, that plays the engine role in our implementation:

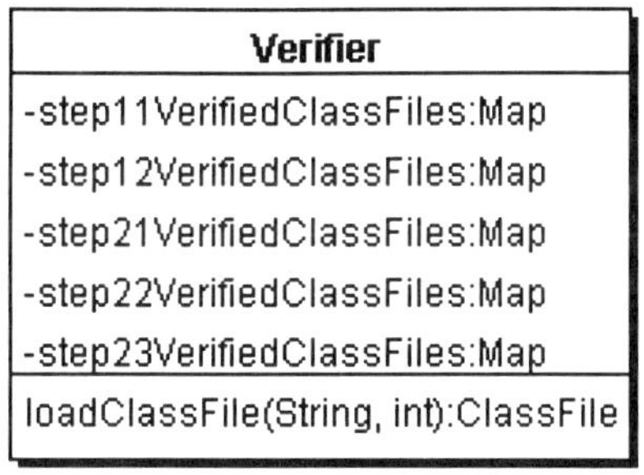

The most important thing to explain about this class is that it has five maps, named *stepXYVerifiedClassFiles*, corresponding to the five substeps of the verification process, in order to remember which class files have successfully passed which verification step. Each of these maps associates strings to representations of class files in memory. The strings are class file names like "java.lang.Object", for example. Hence, these maps tell us which class files have successfully passed a given step of the verification process and also prevent us from verifying a certain class file twice. This is of paramount significance considering how the verification process operates. Indeed, since we need to examine all the ancestors of a class file to certify it, without appropriate tests, we could repeatedly verify the same class file over and over again.

We also want to draw your attention to the method, named *ClassFile loadClassFile(String, int)*, that this class possesses. It has generated the major problems that we have encountered in this part of our development work. This method searches for specified class files on the user's file system, loads them into memory and directs their verification up to the given step. Using the maps presented above, it determines if the specified class file has already successfully passed the given verification step. If so, it simply returns the associated object, interrogating the proper map. If not, it initiates the proper examinations on the class file.

It is consequently the core of the Verifier's engine. The major problem is that it has to be implemented extremely carefully because it is called recursively throughout the whole verification process. Indeed, you must take very good care about where you call that method in this aforesaid process because you can easily cause infinite recursion. For example, suppose that verification step 2.3 is being performed on a class file. Assume also that this step provokes the verification of the same class file because the latter makes a reference to itself. If this is not controlled, we could have infinite recursion.

A simple solution to this problem is to memorize, by some mean, the class files that you are currently verifying. Using this strategy, you can detect a reentrant control flow and avoid it.

3.3. Verification step 1.2

We performed checks involved in step 1.1 while disassembling class files. It is now time to implement tests comprised in step 1.2. They basically constitute a class file semantic analysis. Since they are fully described in [3] and [6], they were not problematic.

3.4. Dataflow analysis-related classes

To sum up, we were then able to disassemble class files and parse them syntactically and semantically, performing verification steps 1.1 and 1.2. The next thing on our list was to define the classes related to the dataflow analysis.

Without giving all the details, which are out of this paper's scope, the dataflow analysis needs to know, for each instruction in every method of every class, the type of each operand stack location and register of a method. We definitely needed a rather complex data structure to hold those types. We have named that class *StateInfo*. Moreover, there are some restrictions on these operand stack and registers that were required to be modeled. Thus, we had to define a customized stack, named *DataflowStack*, and a vector, called *DataflowVector*, to represent operand stacks and registers.

We now present summarized UML representations of these classes:

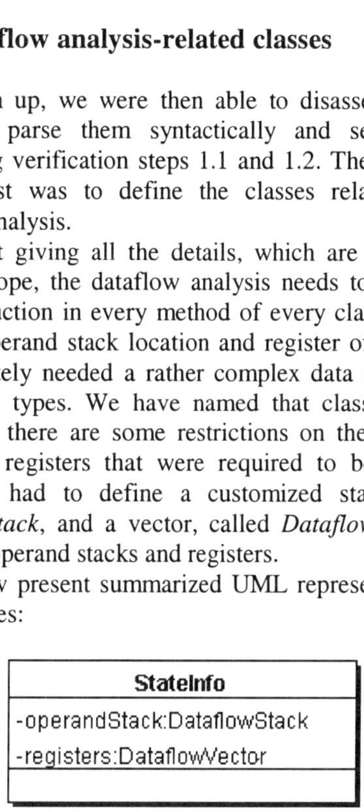

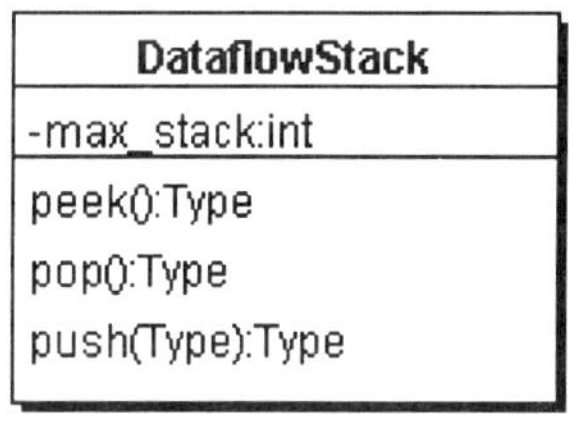

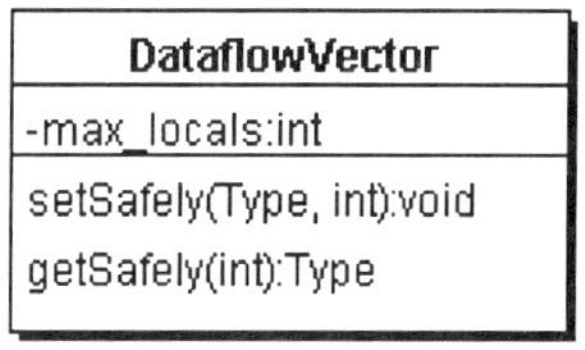

We see that *StateInfo* basically contains a *DataflowStack* and a *DataflowVector*. They are both used to store representations of the types that the dataflow analysis needs.

In order to guaranty stack safety, the dataflow analysis needs to know the maximum depth of any operand stack. This information is present in class files, computed by the Java compiler. *DataflowStack* takes this maximum depth into account by testing whether the stack is full before pushing an element on its top. If the stack is already full, an exception is raised and verification stops, because we have detected a stack overflow in the current method.

DataflowStack also deals with stack underflows by verifying if the stack is empty before popping or peeking an element. If so, another exception is raised and verification halts. This is all very straightforward.

Although, we must be careful about 64 bits primitive types: *long* and *double*. Indeed, since the operand stack and registers in the JVM are 32 bits wide, those types take up two consecutive 32 words in them. So when we push a type representing a *long* or a *double* into *DataflowStack*, we must ensure that it logically takes two stack spaces, one for the high order bits and the other one for the low order bits.

The restrictions placed on *DataflowVector* are conceptually similar. There is a maximum number of registers for each method, specified in class files, that we must enforce in *DataflowVector*. When storing 64 bits primitive types, we make sure that we use two consecutive vector locations and ensure that it is impossible to read only the high order or low order bits.

Once the design and implementation of these fundamental classes were finished, we had to concentrate on the dataflow analysis itself. Indeed, it necessitates a lot of work, especially at the implementation stage. The dataflow analysis algorithm is not so tricky to understand but you have to devise many classes to make it work in practice. For example, we needed to group the 201 bytecode instructions into families in order to create a generic class for each family and implement a transfer function in each of these classes. See [1] for an explanation of transfer functions.

Tests implied in verification steps 2.1 and 2.2 were also implemented at this stage of our development process.

3.5. Dataflow analysis implementation

Everything was in place to begin the implementation of the dataflow analysis. After a couple of days working on some corrections of our dataflow analysis algorithm, we have implemented it. At this point, our Verifier was able to disassemble class files, perform syntactic and semantic analysis and guaranty stack safety, certain aspects of type safety and a portion of control flow safety. Control flow safety was partially managed by the fact that the dataflow analysis verifies that no instructions make the execution go outside of the method's body. We will see in section 3.7 that we must also manage subroutines to totally guaranty control flow safety. Type safety was partly assured by the numerous transfer functions shattered around the classes generically representing all the 201 bytecode instructions.

We say that type safety was *partly* assured because an important characteristic of the JVM and the Bytecode Verifier must be well understood to produce a stand-alone implementation of the Verifier that really certifies bytecode: in Sun's Verifier implementation, interface types are handled dynamically, not statically. This means that, during the dataflow analysis, their Verifier allows any interface or class type to be assigned to an interface type. Their JVM then performs a run-time check that occurs when an interface method is invoked. Before searching the target class' method table, the JVM verifies that the target class implements the interface from which the method is taken.

This is certainly an efficient solution in the situation of a JVM that integrates a Bytecode Verifier. Although, if you are planning to develop a stand-alone Verifier, your dataflow analysis must handle interface types statically to proclaim that it rigorously guarantees type safety.

We have used a solution explained in [3] to handle interface types statically in our dataflow analysis. The detailed presentation of this solution being rather lengthy to explain, we only mention that it consists essentially in:

- using sets of interfaces as a new type and that
- merging two sets of interfaces types produces a set of interfaces containing the interfaces that the superinterface trees of the interfaces from both sets have in common and
- merging a class type and a set of interfaces type produces a set of interfaces containing the interfaces implemented by the class or its superclasses and interfaces whose subinterfaces are implemented by the class or its superclasses.

A significant portion of verifications implied in step 2.3 was then implemented. In particular, we have had implemented tests comprised in step 3, which we had to include in step 2.3.

Stack safety, type safety and a portion of control flow safety were managed. We had to move on object safety and to finish control flow safety.

3.6. Object safety

In the Java language, object allocation and initialization is done in a way similar to this:

```
Object obj = new Object();                    (1)
```

Note that both the allocation and the initialization are done in one atomic operation, at least for the programmer's eyes. Indeed, you cannot code something like this in Java:

```
Object obj = new Object;
obj.myConstructor();
```

i.e., you cannot separate object allocation from object initialization.

At the bytecode level though, they are always divided into two distinct phases. For example, the line of Java source code labeled (1) is typically compiled into bytecode similar to this:

```
new <Object>
dup
<potentially, push the constructor's arguments>
invokespecial Object.<init>()
```

We realize that there is a period of time, between *new* and *invokespecial*, when a reference points to an uninitialized object in memory. So it is technically possible to use this object, by invoking one of its methods for example, before it gets initialized by one of its constructors. If this happens, the bytecode would break the object-oriented principle that says that any object begins its life cycle in a state defined by one of its constructors.

Hence, the Verifier has to check that no objects are used before getting initialized. The best moment to accomplish this task is probably during the dataflow analysis.

We present a summary of our solution using the aforementioned simple bytecode example:

	Bytecode instruction	Operand stack
...	...	...
7	new <Object>	..., uninit(7,Object)
8	dup	..., uninit(7,Object), uninit(7,Object)
9	invokespecial Object.<init>()	..., Object

We see that our dataflow analysis considers that the *new* instruction generates a reference of the type *uninit(o,Class type)*, where *o* is the offset of the *new* instruction in the method's body and *Class type* is the freshly allocated object's class name. We need to record the instruction offset to distinguish two different references pointing to the same object type.

However, this is not sufficient in the presence of subroutines. See [3] for more details about this problem and a complete explanation of the solution.

We also need the *Class type* to change the *uninit()* reference types back to normal initialized reference types, after the invocation of an appropriate constructor.

This *uninit()* reference type can be manipulated by the instructions *aload*, *astore*, *swap* and the variants of *pop* and *dup*. This is due to the fact that the bytecode needs to be able to copy and move those references around in the operand stack and the registers. Though, all the other instructions that manipulate references, like the ones that invoke methods, cannot use this special uninitialized reference type. This is guaranteed by their transfer function.

The dataflow analysis finally detects the invocation of an appropriate constructor and searches the operand stack and registers to change any *uninit(7,Object)* type to *Object*. The initialized reference can then be used normally.

We want to put the emphasis on the fact that there are many more problems that we do not discuss in this paper. Type aliasing, interactions with exception handlers and with subroutines are all very delicate subjects. Once again, please refer to [3] to get all the details.

3.7. Subroutines

The Java language includes a feature called *finally*. Here is an example of its usage:

```
try
{
   preheatOven();
   bakeTripleChocolateCake();
}
finally
{
   turnOffOven();
}
```

The Java language guarantees that the oven is turned off, even if an exception occurs or if the protected code does a "return" while preheating the oven or baking the delicious triple chocolate cake.

The source code included in the *finally* block is compiled as a subroutine in the corresponding bytecode. A subroutine is simply a piece of bytecode that can be called from any places in the enclosing method. Currently, it is used only to compile the *finally* feature. However, it could be exploited in the future to optimize bytecode by factorizing it into subroutines.

As we already mentioned, subroutines are problematic to control flow safety. Indeed, they are really a new control flow entity that we need to manage in the Verifier. Once it is called using a *jsr* instruction, the subroutine will have to return, sooner or later, with a *ret* instruction, to the instruction following the calling *jsr*. This return from a subroutine is precisely what we have to control via the dataflow analysis. The *ret* instruction takes a register number as an argument in which it should find the return address. The latter is simply the offset of the instruction following the calling *jsr*. Since many return addresses can be simultaneously present in different registers, the dataflow analysis must verify that subroutines return to valid addresses. In particular, it must ensure that any subroutine returns to a subroutine that is in its call chain or to its enclosing method.

Essentially, the dataflow analysis must know, for any subroutine *s*, to which subroutines this subroutine *s* can return. To summarize a possible solution, let us mention that you can associate a set named *returnable* to every instruction that is part of a subroutine in the dataflow analysis state information. By propagating and augmenting this set from one subroutine call to another, you can make it store all the return addresses of subroutines that are part of the current subroutine's call chain. The valid return addresses for that current subroutine would then be the ones listed in the *returnable* set of its *ret* instruction.

More problems and solutions concerning subroutines are elucidated in [3].

4. Screenshot and interesting features

We begin this section by presenting a screenshot of our Bytecode Verifier's interface:

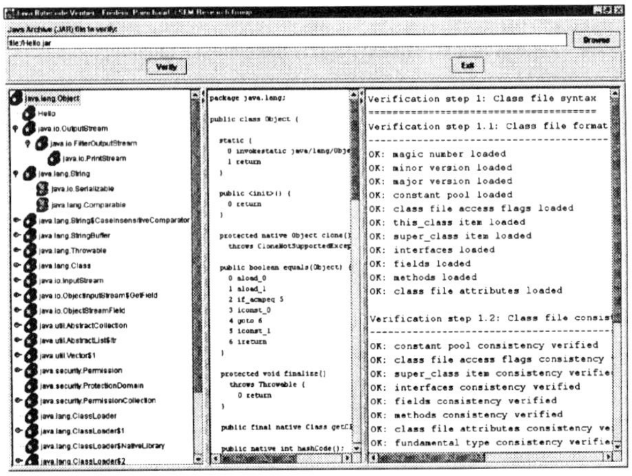

We can see that the user is invited to enter the name of the JAR file containing the class files that s/he wants to verify. This is done via a URL so the JAR file can be anywhere on the Internet.

In the left window, a hierarchy of the verified class files is presented to the user. A blue 'C' represents classes and a green 'I', interfaces. Subclasses are placed right below their superclass; interfaces below the classes that implement them. An offending class or interface would have a red "no sign" over its representing letter.

By selecting one of these classes or interfaces, the user can see, in the middle window, the corresponding class file disassembly, expressed in a language that is similar to Java, except for the bytecode that is not reverse engineered. In the right window, s/he is able to read the verification report generated for this class file. If the latter has failed the examination, a detailed error explanation is given.

At the time of writing this paper, our stand-alone implementation of the Bytecode Verifier is not yet totally completed. This is why we cannot publish benchmarks.

5. Conclusion

We have successfully used our well-organized, clear, technical and complete specification of the Java Bytecode Verifier to develop our own 100% Sun's specification compliant, stand-alone, documented and complete version. Our Verifier performs extensive syntactic and semantic analysis on class files and guarantees stack and register safety, type safety, object safety and control flow safety by statically managing interface types, which is not done statically in Sun's implementation, ensuring proper object initialization and fully supporting subroutines.

6. References

[1] Aho, A. V., R. Sethi, and J. D. Ullman, *Compilers: Principles, techniques, and tools*, Addison Wesley, Massachusetts, 1986.

[2] Campione, M. and K. Walrath, *The Java Tutorial Second Edition: Object-Oriented Programming for the Internet*, The Java Series, Addison Wesley, Massachusetts, 1998. Available from http://web2.java.sun.com/docs/books/tutorial/.

[3] Doyon, S., *On the Security of Java: the Java Bytecode Verifier*, Master Thesis, Laval University, April 1999.

[4] Freund, S. N. and J. C. Mitchell, "A Type System for Object Initialization In The Java Bytecode Language", In *Proceedings of the 1998 ACM SIGPLAN Conference on Object-Oriented Programming Systems, Languages and Applications*, October 1998. Available from http://www.informatik.uni-trier.de/ley/db/conf/oopsla/oopsla98.html.

[5] Goldberg, A., "A Specification of Java Loading and Bytecode Verification", In *Proceedings of the 5th ACM Conference on Computer and Communications Security*, November 1998. Available from http://www.kestrel.edu/HTML/people/goldberg/.

[6] Lindholm, T. and F. Yellin, *The Java Virtual Machine Specification Second Edition*, The Java Series, Addison Wesley, Massachusetts, 1999. Available from http://java.sun.com/docs/books/vmspec/index.html.

[7] Stata, R. and M. Abadi, "A Type System for Java Bytecode Subroutines", In *Proceedings of the 25th ACM SIGPLAN-SIGACT Symposium on Principles of Programming Languages*, January 1998. Available from http://www.luca.demon.co.uk/POPL98/Program.html.

[8] Yellin, F., "Low Level Security in Java", In *Proceedings of the Fourth International World Wide Web Conference*, December 1995. Available from http://www.javasoft.com/sfaq/verifier.html.

UML-Based Representation of Role-Based Access Control [†]

Michael E. Shin and Gail-Joon Ahn
ISE Department
George Mason University
4400 University Dr.
Fairfax, VA 22030, U.S.A.
{eshin,gahn}@isse.gmu.edu

Abstract

In role-based access control (RBAC) permissions are associated with roles, and users are made members of appropriate roles thereby acquiring the roles' permissions. The principal motivation behind RBAC is to simplify administration. Several frameworks for the development of role-based systems have been introduced. However, there are a few works specifying RBAC in a way which system developers or software engineers can easily understand and refer to develop role-based systems. The Unified Modeling Language (UML) is a general-purpose visual modeling language in which we can specify, visualize, and document the components of a software system. In this paper we represent the RBAC model with this well-known modeling language to reduce a gap between security models and system developments. We specify the RBAC model with three views: static view, functional view, and dynamic view. In addition, we briefly discuss about the future directions.

1. Introduction

In RBAC permissions are associated with roles, and users are made members of appropriate roles thereby acquiring the roles' permissions. This greatly simplifies management of permissions. Roles are created for the various job functions in an organization and users are assigned to roles based on their responsibilities and qualifications. Users can be easily reassigned from one role to another. And the access of users to the information is regulated on the basis of the roles which are assigned to the users.

Since RBAC has become widely accepted as the proven technology, many security researchers and secure system developers have spent their time to develop role-based systems. Several frameworks for the development of role-based systems have been introduced [2, 11, 12]. These prior works were sometimes hard for system developers to understand because some are too abstract and formal, and others are ad-hoc solutions which are focused on application-oriented or domain-specific frameworks. These frameworks are not good enough to give a sound blueprint to system developers.

Our main objective here is to reduce such a gap between security models and system developments. In this paper we represent RBAC with a general-purpose visual modeling language UML. We choose the UML because it has been a standard language in the modeling community. Our representation includes static, functional, and dynamic views of RBAC model to achieve our objective.

This paper is organized as follows. In section 2 we describe a well-known model for role-based access control, commonly known as RBAC96. Section 3 briefly overviews UML. In section 4 we represent RBAC96 model with UML. Section 5 concludes this paper.

2. RBAC Model

RBAC has recently received considerable attention as a promising alternative to traditional discretionary and mandatory access controls (see, for example, [3, 4, 6, 9]). As MAC is used in the classical defense arena, the policy of access is based on the classification of objects such as top-secret level. The main idea of

[†]All correspondence should be addressed to: Dr. Gail-Joon Ahn, Information and Software Engineering Department, Mail Stop 4A4, George Mason University, Fairfax, VA 22030; email:gahn@isse.gmu.edu; phone:+1-703-993-1668; fax:+1-703-993-1638.

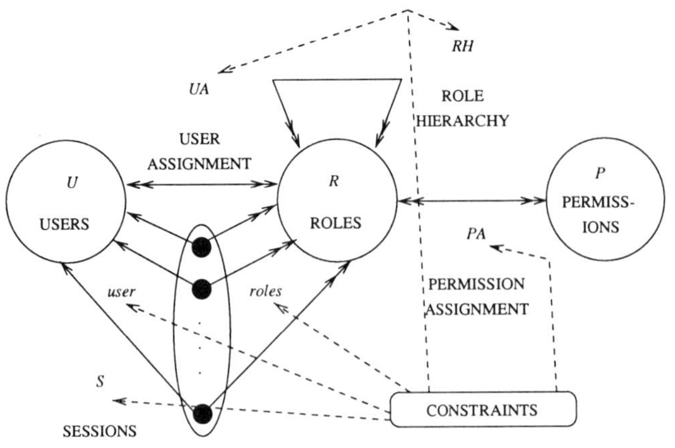

Figure 1: RBAC Model

DAC is that the owner of an object has discretionary authority over who else can access that object. But RBAC policy is based on the roles of the subjects and can specify security policy in a way that maps to an organization's structure.

A general family of RBAC models called RBAC96 was defined by Sandhu et al [9]. Figure 1 illustrates the most general model in this family. Motivation and discussion about various design decisions made in developing this family of models is given in [9].

Figure 1 shows (regular) roles and permissions that regulate access to data and resources. Intuitively, a user is a human being or an autonomous agent, a role is a job function or a job title within the organization with some associated semantics regarding the authority and responsibility conferred on a member of the role, and a permission is an approval of a particular mode of access to one or more objects in the system or some privilege to carry out specified actions. Roles are organized in a partial order $\geq$, so that if $x \geq y$ then role x inherits the permissions of role y. Members of x are also implicitly members of y. In such cases, we say x is senior to y. Each session relates one user to possibly many roles. The idea is that a user establishes a session and activates some subset of roles that he or she is a member of (directly or indirectly by means of the role hierarchy). The RBAC model has the following components and these components are formalized from the above discussions.

- U is a set of users,
- R is disjoint sets of roles and administrative roles respectively,
- P is disjoint sets of permissions and administrative permissions,
- $UA \subseteq U \times R$, is a many-to-many user to role assignment relation,
- $PA \subseteq P \times R$ is a many-to-many permission to role assignment relation,
- $RH \subseteq R \times R$ is partially ordered role hierarchies (written as $\geq$ in infix notation),
- S is a set of sessions,
- $user : S \rightarrow U$, is a function mapping each session s_i to the single user $user(s_i)$ and is constant for the session's lifetime,
- $roles : S \rightarrow 2^R$ is a function mapping each session s_i to a set of roles $roles(s_i) \subseteq \{r \mid (\exists r' \geq r)[(user(s_i), r') \in UA]\}$ (which can change with time) so that session s_i has the permissions $\cup_{r \in roles(s_i)} \{p \mid (\exists r'' \leq r)[(p, r'') \in PA]\}$, and
- there is a collection of constraints stipulating which values of various components of the RBAC model are allowed or forbidden.

A user can be a member of many roles and a role can have many users. Similarly, a role can have many permissions and the same permissions can be assigned to many roles. Each session relates one user to possibly many roles. Intuitively, a user establishes a session during which the user activates some subset of roles that he or she is a member of. The permissions available to the users are the union of permissions from all roles activates in that session. Each session is associated with a single user. This association remains constant for the life of a session. A user may have multiple sessions open at the same time, each in a different window on the workstation screen for instance. Each session may have a different combination of active roles. The concept of a session equates to the traditional notation of a subject in access control. A subject is a unit of access control, and a user may have multiple subjects (or sessions) with different permissions active at the same time.

3. Overview of UML

The Unified Modeling Language (UML) is a general-purpose visual modeling language in which we can specify, visualize, and document the components

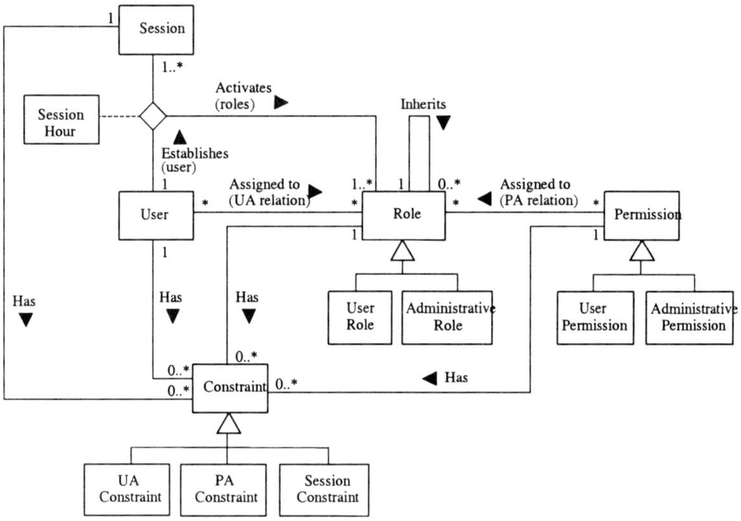

Figure 2: Class Diagram: Conceptual Static Model

of a software system. It captures decisions and understanding about systems that must be constructed [7]. It has been a standard language in the field of software engineering.

The UML consists of *use case modeling*, *static modeling*, and *dynamic modeling*. In *use case modeling*, the functional requirements of systems are specified with use cases and actors. A use case is initiated by actors and it defines interactions between the actors and the systems. *Static modeling* provides a structural view of information in the systems. In such a view, classes are defined in terms of attributes, as well as relationships with other classes. The relationships include association, generalization/specialization, and aggregation of classes. *Dynamic modeling* shows a behavioral view of the systems. It can be described with object collaboration diagrams, sequence diagrams, or statecharts. Object collaboration diagrams and sequence diagrams are developed to show how objects collaborate with each other to execute the use cases. State dependent views of objects are defined in statecharts [5].

In this paper, we take class diagrams, use case diagrams, and object collaboration diagrams for a static view, a functional view, and a dynamic view of the RBAC model, respectively. In the rest of this paper, we use UML notations which were introduced in [1, 7, 10].

4. UML-Based RBAC Presentation

Major components in RBAC are users, roles, permissions, sessions, and constraints. In order to represent RBAC model using UML, we analyze each component with a notion of object class. In the subsequent sections, our analysis is specified by three different views such as a static view, a functional view, and a dynamic view.

4.1. Static View

The conceptual static model for RBAC is depicted in Figure 2. It contains classes, relationships between classes, and cardinalities in relationships. The basic entities are user, role, permission, constraint, and session classes. The role and permission classes, respectively, may be specialized to two categories: user and administrative. This specialization depends on the level of users' qualification. The constraints in the RBAC model can have various forms, which are dependent on application systems. In order to simplify

«entity» User	«entity» Role	«entity» Permission	«entity» Session	«entity» SessionHour
user : String roleList: List	role : String subrole: String	permission : String roleList: List	sessionName String roleList: List	sessionName String startTime: List

Figure 3: Attributes of Entity Classes

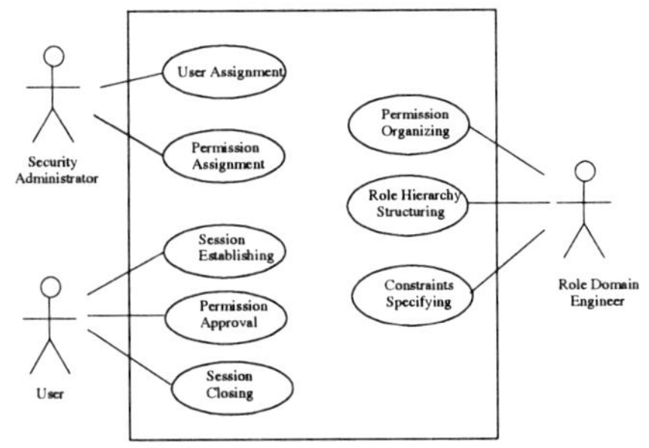

Figure 4: Use Case Model

the analysis model, the constraint in our static model has only three constraints such as user constraint, permission constraint, and session constraint. Also, the static model has a special class called session hour. This class is used when a user establishes a session to activate her/his roles. This notion is useful to express session-based constraint. For example, an organization may require that a user can establish her/his session only during the certain amount of time. In order to enforce this kind of constraints, we need to keep track of session hours for each session. Attributes of entity classes are defined in Figure 3.

In the static model, UA relation and PA relation are represented as "Assinged to" relation with a many-to-many cardinality. User-session relation is viewed as a user can establish one or more sessions to activate at least one or more roles per each session with the constant session lifetime. The role inheritance relation is shown as a role inherits the other roles.

4.2. Functional View

In this paper, we also make more concrete functional requirements to represent the functions that RBAC systems should provide are not clearly defined in section 2. The functional view is depicted in Figure 4 using the use case model that has three actors such as a security administrator, a user, and a role domain engineer. The role domain engineer who extracts the foundational knowledge from application systems may organize a set of permissions, construct role hierarchies, and specify constraints. The security administrator who administrates a role-based system may assign users to roles and assign permissions to roles. The user who would be real persons or external systems may establish sessions, request permission approval, and close sessions.

The following shows the brief specification of the session establishing use case:

> **Use case**: Session Establishing use case
> **Actors**: User
> **Precondition**: System idle
> **Description**: A user presents an information for establishing a session. System displays the roles that a user can activate. A user selects roles to activate. System activates a session with the roles that a user selected.

After a user establishes her/his session with selected roles, a user may need to access the system resources requiring authorization procedures that should be based on her/his role information. In other words, the permissions that are associated with her/his roles should be approved by the system. The following shows the brief specification of such a use case, called permission approval use case:

> **Use case**: Permission Approval use case
> **Actors**: User
> **Precondition**: A session was previously activated for a user.
> **Description**: A user presents an information for permission approval. System notifies a user whether or not the permission is approved.

In this paper, the limited functions are inferred from the RBAC model. We may also consider other situations because the functions in the RBAC system can be articulated. For example, we may require additional functions for monitoring sessions initiated by a security administrator or inquiring a user's status initiated by a user.

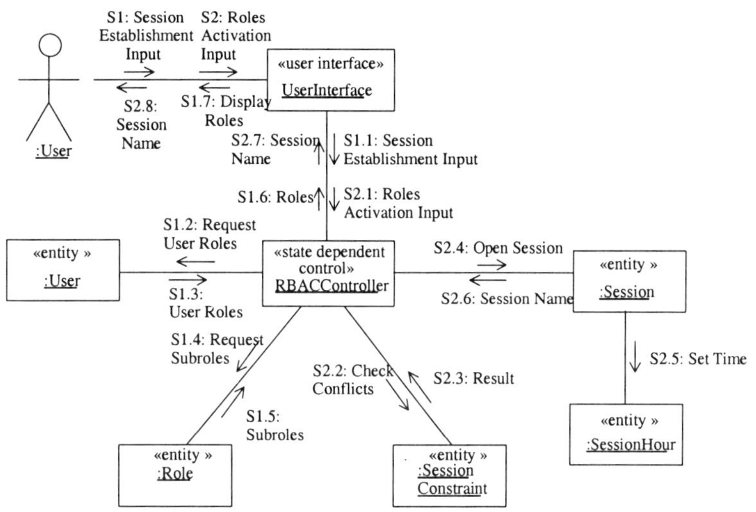

Figure 5: Collaboration Diagram: Session Establishment

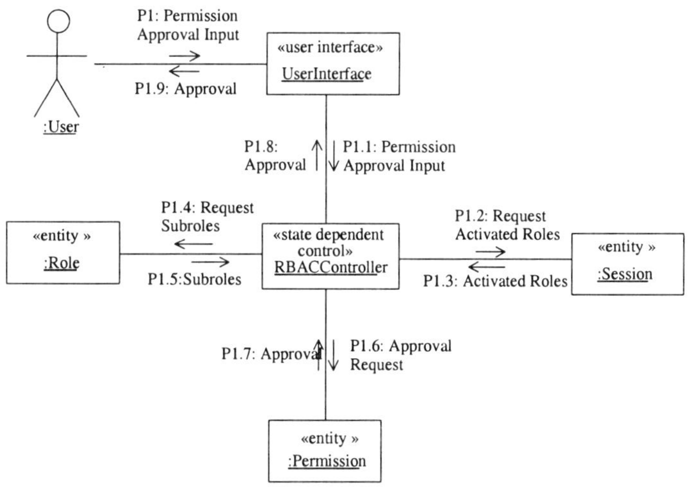

Figure 6: Collaboration Diagram: Permission Approval

4.3. Dynamic View

In the dynamic view, the use cases are refined to show the interactions among the objects that participate in each use case. The collaboration diagram for the session establishment is depicted in Figure 5 where a user initiates the use case through a user interface and RBACController coordinates interactions between the objects in the use case. The collaboration diagram for permission approval is illustrated in Figure 6 where it requires a precondition that a session has been activated before the execution of permission approval use case. The complete descriptions of each diagram are omitted for the simplicity.

5. Conclusion

In this paper, we briefly described a well-known model for role-based access control. We specified this model using the visual modeling language UML. Rather than simply enumerating each component in RBAC model, we showed UML-based analysis model using class diagrams, use case diagrams, and object collaboration diagrams. This is the first attempt for specializing RBAC model using a modeling language. We believe that our work can help system developers to understand RBAC model more easily and to build role-based systems. Also we could identify useful functions and constraints which were ruled out at the beginning of the security model.

Based on this work, we would investigate how the UML-based model can be accommodated to specify each component in RBAC model. It may include how to represent role hierarchies and constraints with some possible extensions of the UML. Because models help us understand the system by simplifying some of the details, this direction will be of practical interests.

Acknowledgements

The authors would like to thank Mr. Jaehong Park for his assistance on reviewing this paper.

References

[1] G. Booch, J. Rumbaugh, and I. Jacobson. The Unified Modeling Language User Guide. Addison Wesley, 1999.

[2] Pete Epstein and Ravi Sandhu. Towards A UML Based Approach to Role Engineering. In *Proceedings of the 4th ACM Workshop on Role-Based Access Control*, pages 135–142, Fairfax, VA, October 28-29 1999.

[3] David Ferraiolo and Richard Kuhn. Role-based access controls. In *Proceedings of 15th NIST-NCSC National Computer Security Conference*, pages 554–563, Baltimore, MD, October 13-16 1992.

[4] M.-Y. Hu, S.A. Demurjian, and T.C. Ting. User-role based security in the ADAM object-oriented design and analyses environment. In J. Biskup, M. Morgernstern, and C. Landwehr, editors, *Database Security VIII: Status and Prospects*. North-Holland, 1995.

[5] Hossan Gomaa. Object Oriented Analysis and Modeling for Family of systems with the UML. Technical Report, ISE Dept. George Mason University, 1999.

[6] Imtiaz Mohammed and David M. Dilts. Design for dynamic user-role-based security. *Computers & Security*, 13(8):661–671, 1994.

[7] J. Rumbaugh, G. Booch, and I. Jacobson. The Unified Modeling Language Reference Manual. Addison Wesley, Reading MA, 1999.

[8] Ravi S. Sandhu. Lattice-based access control models. *IEEE Computer*, 26(11):9–19, November 1993.

[9] Ravi S. Sandhu, Edward J. Coyne, Hal L. Feinstein, and Charles E. Youman. Role-based access control models. *IEEE Computer*, 29(2):38–47, February 1996.

[10] National Software et al. Unified Modeling Language Notation Guide, Version 1.1. September 1, 1997.

[11] Charles Youman, Ed Coyne, and Ravi Sandhu, editors. *Proceedings of the 2nd ACM Workshop on Role-Based Access Control*, Nov. 6-7. ACM, 1997.

[12] Charles Youman, Ed Coyne, and Ravi Sandhu, editors. *Proceedings of the 3rd ACM Workshop on Role-Based Access Control*, Oct. 22-23. ACM, 1998.

Privacy-Enhanced Access Control by SPKI and Its Application to Web Server

Takamichi SAITO   Kentaro UMESAWA   Hiroshi G. OKUNO
Department of Information Sciences, Science University of Tokyo
Yamazaki 2641, Noda, Chiba 278-8501, JAPAN
{saito,okuno}@is.noda.sut.ac.jp, kentaro@cs.is.noda.sut.ac.jp

Abstract— **For providing a privacy-enhanced access only for an appropriate user, anonymous access such as anonymous FTP is too weak because a service provider cannot know about a client, while authentication-based access control such as PKIX (Public Key Infrastructure with X.509) is too strong because ID information on a client is exposed to a service-provider. Instead, we present a new access control scheme by using SPKI (Simple Public Key Infrastructure), since an authorization certificate based on SPKI does not carry any ID information. This scheme needs additional mechanism for the server and clients such as issuing, delegating, validating, and revoking certificates. A web-based privacy-enhanced access control is designed on the basis of the proposed scheme and implemented by Java. The resulting system shows that the proposed scheme works well with a small amount of overheads being introduced into a normal web server.**

I. Introduction

Recently there are strong demands for privacy in using Internet aplications. A client usually does not want to expose his/her individual information such as ID information, age, blood, family, affiliation and so on. Once a client accesses service with presenting his/her individual information, he/she must be anxious about leakage of his/her information to a third party, malicious or not. If one can access services without individual information, one need not worry about such leakage and associated troubles. Consequently, we focus on enhancing privacy in access control protocol without ID information. However, when an unrestricted access to the server is permitted, the resource of the server is dangerously bleached. Therefore, we want to be securing necessary information for the emergency. However, because which service the client enjoyed comes to light, it is undesirable that the server has the information.

In this paper, we provide the design and implementation of the privacy-enhanced system which provides appropriate service only to the eligible client, in the distributed client-server model on the network. This system meets secure in our sense. As one of the methods for valuing privacy and limitting the appropriate access, the client with an appropriate authority should be able to exercise authority without submitting ID information to the server. In a word, it is necessary to offer the service related with the authority only to the user who has appropriate authority, unlike an anonymous FTP which unrestrictedly permits the access to the server. Since SPKI is PKI (Public Key Infrastructure) which uses the certificate without ID information, it is effective to the privacy valuing system.

In SPKI theory, the problem of the authentication remains, for obtaining the system which can do a proper access control, appropriate mechanism should be introduced. The *Issuing Agent* being separated by transferring an appropriate authority, we provide the privacy-enhanced scheme (technique) by the Issuing Agent, which selects a user and offers proper service only to the user has an appropriate authority.

Moreover, to verify the effectiveness of the frame of the privacy valuing system which proposed, the Web-based application system was implemented by Java. The server was constructed by using Servlet on Apache. We use the Java(JDK1.2) and the library of IAIK-JCE(IAIK Java Cryptography Extension) for the implementation of a certificate with an electronic signature and the cryption/decription program. The client moreover is accessing the server by using a Web browser because of the handiness of use, and uses the verification and decryption tool implemented by Java.

From our implementation and the use experience of this application system, if the proposed frame is used, it has been understood easily to be able to achieve, and to be able to use the access mechanism of the privacy valuing for an existing system.

The rest of the paper is organized as follows: Section 2 gives the definition of security and necessary information on the SPKI-based access control proposed in this paper. Section 3 presents our requirements and design of SPKI-based access control. Section 4 presents a privacy-enhanced web server. Section 5 discusses the evaluation of our implementation and Section 6 concludes the paper.

II. Background

A. Network Model

The network model we assume consists of four kinds of subjects, *Authority Server*, *Issuing Agent*, *Client*, and *Intruder* (Fig. 1).

- **Server:** a subject that provides the service or delegates the authority.
- **Issuing Agent:** a subject that issues a certificate to a client, after authentication. This subject has authority or permission to issue a certificate. This autority expressed by a certificate is given by the Server.
- **Client:** a subject that requests the service by submitting a certificate to the server specified by the certificate. The certificate may be issued to the client by

0-7695-0798-9/00 $10.00

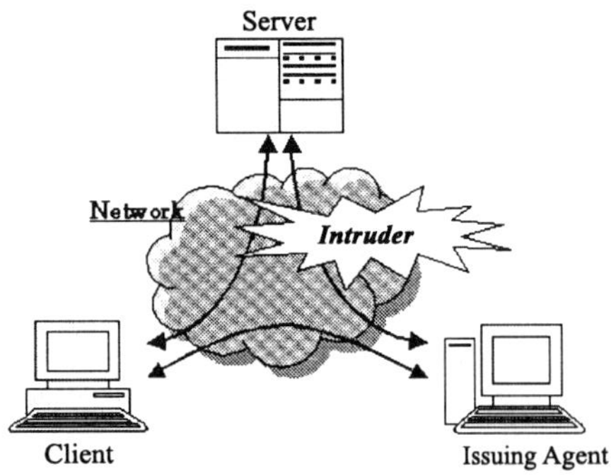

Fig. 1. Network Model assumed in this paper

the Issuing Agent.

- **Intruder:** a subject that may intercept messages from some subject, modify them, and/or transmit messages by masquerading other subject.

Possible menaces caused by intruders are summarized as follows (these are based on [3]):

- **Interruption:** Some system resources are destroyed or become unavailable or unusable.
- **Interception:** An unauthorized party gains access to some system resources.
- **Modification:** An unauthorized party not only gains access to but also tamper with some system resources.
- **Fabrication:** An unauthorized party inserts counterfeit objects such as messages into the system.
- **Masquerade:** One subject pretends to be a different subject.
- **Replay:** An unauthorized party captures a message and its subsequent retransmission to produce an unauthorized effect.
- **Denial of Service (DOS):** An unauthorized party prevents a normal user from using system resources, in particular, communications.

For secure communication in this model, the exchanging messages should be defended from these menaces using by cryptogram, digital signature and so on.

In this paper, when these menaces except interruption and DOS is eliminated, we call *the communication is secure*. It is easy to detect interruption and DOS, but much difficult to prevent them. So we omit them from our argument.

B. SPKI Certificate

The SPKI, which was triggered by Ellison's paper [6], proposes to realize a concise scheme for access control with a public key. The proposal of SPKI focuses mainly on naming of identity [5]. However, we emphasize that the importance of the SPKI resides in the separation of authentication and authorization. *The privacy enhanced access control can be achieved, because SPKI certificate doesn't contain an identity of client.*

The useful properties of the SPKI for our purpose, privacy-enhanced access control and so on, are summarized below:

(1) **Based on Authorization Certificate:** Since an SPKI uses an authorization certificate which is no ID information, ID information cannot be inferred from the certificate. Therefore, it provides good privacy. And also, the life span of certificate depends on that of authority. There is no need to maintain a kind of infrastructure like PKIX.

(2) **Light & Efficiency:** Since public key is not mapped to ID in an SPKI certificate, public key can be generated for a service or a set of services and discarded after its usage or lifetime. This disposable key scheme alleviates the management of public keys.

(3) **Delegatability:** Like currency, it can be delegated more easily. Shortly, without modification of server's database, a certificate can be delegated from a client to a client. However, there is the concept of ownership in this certificate. Then, unlike currency, only proper client can use his certificate.s

(4) **Independence from Specific Services:** Unlike the SET (Secure Electronic Transactions) [10], which is a payment system by credit card on the Internet, the SPKI scheme is not dependent on specific services.

(5) **Self-Verifiable Certificate:** In the SPKI scheme, there is a chain of verification: without a server's or a third party's help, a client can verify a certificate using by themselves (see (4) in III-B).

(6) **Closed Delegation:** The authorization certificate finally returns to the authority server. Then authority server can revoke the authority without a certificate revocation system. And also, unlike PKIX based system, the infrastructure like PKIX's CA is not needed.

(7) **Secure:** In addition to the above conditions, this scheme is secure exchanges in communication in our sense.

B.1 SPKI Certificate Format

SPKI certificate is defined in [5]. It consists of the following 5-tuple.

$$\langle I, S, D, A, V \rangle$$

Each field is defined as follows:

- **Issuer** I**:** This field specifies the *issuer* of the certificate who has created and signed it. The issuer is represented as a public key or hash of a public key.
- **Subject** S**:** This field defines the *subject* of the certificate, to whom the certificate has been issued, or to whom the certificate has been delegated. It is represented by a public key or a hash of a public key.
- **Delegation** D**:** This field specifies whether the authority specified in the certificate is delegatable or not. It is represented by a Boolean value, $TRUE$, or $FALSE$.
- **Authorization** A**:** This field specified the *authority* of the certificate, which defines the access right, represented by S-expression, to the server.
- **Validity** V**:** This field defines how the certificate is valid. For example, a period of time.

For example, the following 5-tuple

$$\langle P(I), P(S), TRUE, (file_1, file_2), (7/Jan/2000)\rangle$$

indicates that the subject I has issued this certificate to the subject S. As mentioned earlier, the subject is represented by its public key, say $P(I)$ for I. The Delegation Flag, $TRUE$, indicates that the subject S can delegate it to a third party. The Authentication of this certificate specifies that the subject S can access $file_1$ and/or $file_2$, and that this access permission will be expired on Jan. 7, 2000.

When SPKI certificate is issued, 5-tuple is signed by the secret (private) key of the issuer. The secrete key of I is represented by $S(I)$, then SPKI certificate is represented as follows:

$$\langle P(I), P(S), TRUE, (file_1, file_2), (7/Jan/2000)\rangle_{S(I)}$$

In this paper, an authorization certificate is represented by an SPKI certificate. Hereafter, we use an SPKI certificate as an authorization certificate.

B.2 Reduction Rule

All or some parts of the authority specified in an SPKI certificate can be delegated by a subject to other subject. This may cause a deluge of certificates. Therefore, the reduction rule is used to make a concise certificate [5].

Given two certificates:

$$\langle I_1, S_1, D_1, A_1, V_1\rangle, \quad and$$
$$\langle I_2, S_2, D_2, A_2, V_2\rangle.$$

If $S_1 = I_2$ and $D_1 = TRUE$, the following authorization certificate is acquired:

$$\langle I_1, S_2, D_2, AIntersect(A_1, A_2), VIntersect(V_1, V_2)\rangle$$

Here, $AInersect(A_1, A_2)$ indicates the intersection of two authorities A_1 and A_2, and $VInersect(A_1, A_2)$ indicates the intersection of two validities V_1 and V_2. Note that a server is the only subject that can reduce certificates, because rules for computing intersection $AInersect$ depend on the applications. We will show some examples later.

III. Requirements and Design of Our SPKI-based Privacy-Enhanced System

In this section, we describe the requirements of our SPKI-based system, and also define its design for the requirements.

A. *Requirements of Our SPKI-based Privacy-Enhanced System*

(1) The client with an appropriate authority exercises its authority to the Authority Server without offering ID information.
(2) When the authority is exercised, the authentication is not needed in the Server.
(3) The authority should be able to be transferred without third party's help.

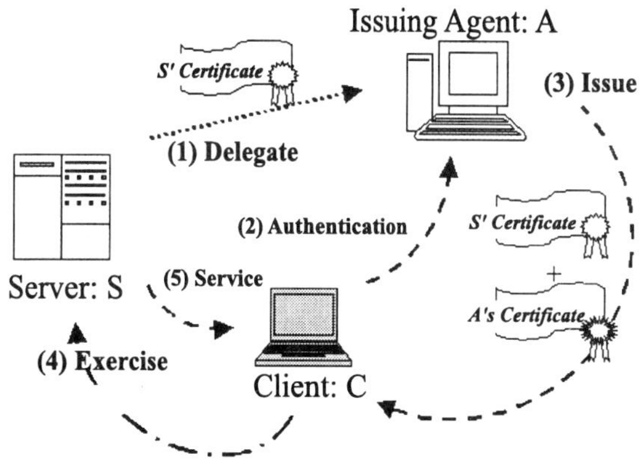

Fig. 2. Whole Image of Our SPKI-based Privacy-Enhanced System

(4) The validity of the authorization certificate should be able to be proven only by themself.
(5) The authority can be revoked easily.
(6) The result of the exercised authority makes sense only for an appropriate client.
(7) Continuous management of a certificate is not demanded.
(8) All of the above-mentioned are securely done.

Since the system which uses an ID certificate with an ACL in the server can get to know who enjoys the service, we do not adopt this scheme. A client only has to show to have the appropriate authority when the authority is exercised. Then, in exercising an authority, there is no need authentication.

Since the life cycle of the authority ends at the exercise, continuous management of the system is not needed. So, we don't prepare magnificent infrastructure, like PKIX (PKI with X.509).

Our system is made to be filled the demand above based on our definition of the above-mentioned security.

B. *Design of Our SPKI-based Privacy-Enhanced System*

From the viewpoint of privacy, our objective is the role of issue should be separated from the service-provinding server. By this dividing, a client's ID can be protected from the server. We provide Issuing Agent for this purpose. And also, for administering the transaction, the Issuing Agent should store the correspondence of ID information and authority. The most important point of our system is the existence of Issuing Agent. Owing to Issuing Agent, the administrator of the system can specify who enjoyed service, according to the information provided by the Issuing Server and the Authority Server when something trouble happen.

In this subsection, we describe the design of our SPKI-based system. Actually, this sytem consists of the following three subjects: Authority Server, Issuing Agent, Client(see Fig. 2).

B.1 Authority Server

An authorization certificate can be issued by the Server S (Fig.2.(1)). This S' certificate shows the permission that the Issuing Agent A can issue the certificate for authority not exceeding the original authority.

The Server S obtains the Issuing Agent's public key $P(A)$. Where we assume the Issuing Agent is trustable for S. Secondly, it decides the authority, e.g. $(file_1, file_2)$, which means this certificate can access $file_1$ and/or $file_2$. And also, it decides the term of validity, e.g. $(7/Jan/2000)$, and a Boolean which settle its permit of delegation. This field is $TRUE$ because this certificate can be delegated.

Then, S adds its own public key $P(S)$ in this certificate. Finally, it creates 5-tuple composed of them and signed 5-tuple by its own secret key $S(S)$ for the certificate $Cert_1$:

$$Cert_1 = \langle P(S), P(A), TRUE, (file_1, file_2), (7/Jan/2000)\rangle_{S(S)}$$

B.2 Issuing Agent

After authentication (Fig.2.(2)) in the Issuing Agent A, the agent authorized by the certificate $Cert_1$ creates an another certificate $Cert_2$ and issues the certificate $Cert_1$ and $Cert_2$ (Fig.2.(3)).

As a more important role, the agent A decides the authority not exceeding the original authority.

After verifying the $Cert_1$, the Issuing Agent A specifies the client C. Using by authentication, A can detect C and obtain a public key $P(C)$ for C. Then it decides the delegating authority $(file_2)$, the term of validity $(5/Dec/1999)$, and an Boolean $FALSE$. Next, A obtains its own public key $P(A)$. Finally, it creates another 5-tuple composed of them and signs 5-tuple by its own secret key $S(A)$ for the certificate $Cert_2$:

$$Cert_1 = \langle P(S), P(A), TRUE, (file_1, file_2), (7/Jan/2000)\rangle_{S(S)}$$

$$Cert_2 = \langle P(A), P(C), FALSE, (file_2), (5/Dec/1999)\rangle_{S(A)}$$

The Issuing Agent must hold the mapping of the client's ID to its public key, i.e. holding the knowledge $P(C)$ is a public key for C in this case.

B.3 Client

The Client C submits the certificates $Cert_1, Cert_2$ for enjoying its service (Fig.2.(4,5)). The Server S verifies them. If the certificates are proper, S interprets the authority and provides the service (Fig.1.(5)).

Now, we presume the server is received the following $Cert_1, Cert_2$. Note that $P(A)$ in $Cert_1$ and $P(A)'$ in $Cert_2$ are different:

$$Cert_1 = \langle P(S), P(A), TRUE, (file_1, file_2), (7/Jan/2000)\rangle_{S(S)}$$

$$Cert_2 = \langle P(A)', P(C), FALSE, (file_2), (5/Dec/1999)\rangle_{S(A)}$$

At first, the server S verifies the properness of certificates by the following process:

(1) Assuming that the server's public key is $P(S)'$, it compares its own public key $P(S)'$ and $P(S)$ in $Cert_1$.
(2) If the keys are the same, it verifies if the signature $S(S)$ is not altered or modified, using by $P(S)$.
(3) If it is proper, the server verify $Cert_2$. It compares the public key $P(A)$ in $Cert_1$ and $P(A)'$ in $Cert_2$.
(4) If same, it verify $S(A)$ in $Cert_2$ not to be altered, by $P(A)$.

Note that the certificates are verified by themselves except using the server's key $P(S)$. After above verification, the following reduced certificate can be obtained:

$$\langle P(S), P(C), FALSE, (file_2), (5/Dec/1999)\rangle$$

Finally, by interpreting the authority that shows the $file_2$ can be downloading, the Server S provides it to the client C. Since it can utilize the public key to transmit messages $(file_2)_{P(C)}$, which means $file_2$ is encrypted by $P(C)$, it can do secure downloading.

IV. Implementation

In this section, we explain about our implementaion. It consists of the Java classes related with the followings: an authorization certificate, Authority Server, Client, and Issuing Agent.

The Authority Server holds text files for serving to the qualified client. After selecting a service, the Issuing Server issues a pair of certificates. When excersing certificates in the Authority Server, the Client submits them by HTTP communication, achived by Servlet's uploading. Then, the Authority Server provides a file to the Client if the certificate is valid. Downloading text files are encrypted by the Client public key.

A. *Authorization Certificate*

The Java class that treats the authorization certificate is prepared, and also the methods for doing the operation are implemented in it. In this class, the data structure for an authorization certificate is defined. Moreover, the methods are prepared with the following constructor:

(1) The constructor of generating authorization certificate: a secret key for signature and its 5-tupple's items are given, and then a signed certificate is generated.
(2) The method of encoding Base64: this method encode a certificate to Base64, because of all transaction being by HTTP communication.
(3) The method of decoding Base64: the Base64-encoded certificate is decoded by this method.

In our system, we generate the RSA 512 bytes public key pair using by IAIK-JCE's liberary.

Concrete treatment of the authority becomes as follows: since the server provide text files as service, the file name, represented like `file-1`, is put in the item of the authority. More concretely, we prepare four text files: `file-1`, `file-2`, `file-4`, and `file-4`. For instance, when generating a certificate in server, a file name is put in the item of the authority in the authorization certificate.

B. Issuing Agent

This server is implemented using by Apache, Apache-Jserv, JSDK2.0, IAIK-JCE, and JDK1.2. Concretely, the Issuing Agent is constructed on the Apache server by using Servlet. Receiving HTTP's GET request from a client, this server returns the input form for selecting a file. Receiving HTTP's POST request, which contains the client's selection of service, this server returns certificates made by Java classes. This server, Issuing Agent, is composed of the following Java classes:

(1) The Java class that deals with the access from the client: this class consists of the following methods:

(1-1) The method of returning response for GET request in HTTP communication: it generates HTML form for selecting a file, and return it to Client's Web browser.

(1-2) The method of returning response for POST request in HTTP communication: after receiving the client's request of service, it creates a certificate using by the following class.

(2) The Java class that issues an authorization certificate: this class is extention of the thread class. The authorization certificate corresponding to the request is issued using by this class. And then, it creates the 5-tuple corresponding to the service, and the 5-tuple is signed with the Issuing Agent's secret key. Moreover, it stores the correspondence of the client's ID information and the public key. Finally, the authorization certificates are converted into Base64 code.

In our implementation, the public key pair are generated on the server side at this time. As one of other ways, Client generates the public key pair, and passes it to the Issuing Agent.

And also, we assume the communication between the Client and the Issuing Agent is secure, for example, using by SSL. Then we omit an implementation of authentication at this time.

C. Authority Server

This server is also implemented by using Apache, Apache-Jserv, JSDK2.0, IAIK-JCE, and JDK1.2.

After receiving HTTP's GET request from a client, this server returns the input form. Receiving POST request, which contains the client's submitting certificates, this server returns proper service, encrypted by the client's public key. Where certificates are verified, and service are decided by the certificates. The system consists of the following three Java classes:

(1) The Java class which controls answer of access from the client: this returns service corresponding to the authority by using the classes: a verification and an authority decision class. This class consists of the following methods:

(1-1) The method of returning response to GET request in HTTP communication: it generates HTML form for selecting a file, and return it to a client.

(1-2) The method which returns response when receiving POST request: this verifies the authorization certificate submitted from the client by using the verification class. Then, proper authority is decided by the authority decision class. It returns the file encrypted by DES algorithm by using the encrypting class. This file is downloading to the clients's Web browser.

(2) The verification class: this class verifies the validity of the authorization certificate. This class is composed of the following methods.

(2-1) The method which verified the each item of the authorization certificate: it verifies the validity term of the authority, order from which the certificate is issued, and the value of Delegation's item. Moreover, the validity of the public key is checked.

(2-2) The method of verifying digital signature of authorization certificate: it verifies a signature of the authorization certificate by public keys contained in each certificate. Since the public keys are encoded by Base64, it decode them at first.

(3) The authority decision class: this decides the proper authority from the authority of two authorization certificates, and offers appropriate service. This class consists of the following methods:

(3-1) The method of deciding authority: when the authority is decided, this decides the text file's name by referring to the file in the authorization server.

(3-2) The method of encrypting data: after the text file is decided by (3-1), the file is encrypted by using DES. Then it encrypts its DES's key by the client's public key. This encryption is done using by class of IAIK-JCE. Finally, they are encoded by Base64 to the character string data.

D. Client

The user as Client accesses the Issuing Sever or the Authority Server using by the Web browser as an interface. Moreover, he/she, at hand, utilizes Java application *Decrypter* to decrypt the data, and Java application *Verifier* to verify the certificates.

(1) Verifier: Java application program by which authorization certificate is verified.

(2) Decrypter: Java application program which decode the encrypted data served from the Authority Server. Since serving data is encrypted by Client's public key, the text data can be decrypted using by the client's own secret key.

V. Evauation

In this section, we evaluate our implementation.

From the aspect of server-client model, our system is divided into two phase: issuing the authority, and excercising authority. In this paper's implementation, the authorization certificate from the Authority Server to the Issuing Agent will be handed over by off-line.

In these two phases, we evaluate our implementation. The execution environment is as follows: our sysmtem consists of three entity in the above-mentioned network model. Moreover, the Client is assumed to have Decrypter and Verifier. And also, basically, the Issuing Agent is assumed

TABLE I

COMPUTATION TIME

Operation	Issuing a certificate	Verifying a certificate
CPU time	9.66 sec	0.62 sec

to keep the correspondence of the authority and ID information secretly.

A. *Authority Issue Phase*

Although the mechanism of the authentication was not introduced in our implementation at this time, the following two are thought as examples of implementations:

(1) It is assumed that the Issuing Server be ISP (Internet Service Provider), and it authenticate the client. Then, ISP can properly select a suitable authority depending on each client, and issue the authorization certificate. Thinking communication on the telephone line, the server can sacurely issue the authorization certificate to the client.

(2) The authorization certificate is issued by communication on SSL (Secure Socket Layer) between the client and the server.

Since the correspondence of the ID information and the authority is preserved in Issuing Agent, the Client which the authority exercised can be specified. However, the information should be secret in usual.

And also, the Client can evade the trouble of using certificates in the exercise because it can verify the authorization certificate with a tool at hand. Since they exist for protecting the Client's interests, they can't provide anythig for cheating, even if they are modified with malice.

B. *Authority Exercise Phase*

It is clear that our requirements are satisfied because of the theory of SPKI and our implementation such as the Issuing Agent.

Actually, when the authority is exercised, in which raw data is trasmitted by using HTTP communication, the modification or fabrication can be detected by an electronic signature. Since the returning data is encrypted with the Client's own public key, even if it can be tapped by the third party, only the proper Client can enjoy service. On the other, the Authority Server can prevent the fabrication or modification only by verifying the validity of the authorization certificate itself even if it is data transmitted by HTTP communication.

C. *Overheads*

The overheads introduced by our SPKI-based privacy-enhanced system can be divided into two categories: communication and computation. Extra communication is needed only for Issuing Agents, but this overhead is difficult to measure because it depends on the network topology.

Extra computation is needed in issuing a certificate by the Issuing Agent and in verifying a certificate by the Authority Server. The average computational time in our implementation is summarized in Table I. The current system is running on SUN Microsystems Ultra 10 (UltraSPARC I-Ii 333MHz, 128Mbyte) under Solaris 2.6 operating system. These overheads may be smaller than PKIX, but we need to reduce computational overheads.

VI. Conclusion and Future Works

In this paper, we provide the design, implementation and evaluation of the privacy-enhanced system which provides appropriate service only to the eligible client. For privacy of a client and steady management of system in a secure way, we used the SPKI theory and introduced the Issing Agent. As a result of the implementaion of the system, according to the design, we were good at implementaion of a target system.

There is a lot of things to do and some of them are listed below:

1. Implementation of authentication on Issuing Agent.
2. Implementation of issuing from Issuing Agent to Client in secure way by SSL.
3. Mechanism of revoking a certificate in any time.
4. Delegation or transfer certificates between Clients.

Acknowledgments

The authors would like to acknowledge Prof. Wu Wen of Media Center, Science University of Tokyo, for his discussion.

References

[1] S. Farrell, R. Housley, An Internet Attribute Certificate Profile for Authorization, IETF Internet Draft, Oct. 1999. `draft-ietf-pkix-ac509prof-01.txt`

[2] M. Kaeo, *Designing Network Security*, Cisco Press, 1999.

[3] W. Stallings, *Cryptgraphy and Network Security -Principls and Practice- (2nd ed.)*, Prentoce Hall, 1999.

[4] C. Ellison, SPKI Requirements, RFC2962, 1999.

[5] C. Ellison, *et al.* SPKI Certificate Theory, RFC2963, 1999.

[6] C. Ellison, Establishing Identity Without Certification Authorities, *USENIX Security Symposium*, July 1996.

[7] H. Kikuchi, and Y. Kawakura, Student discount problem in electonic tickets and SPKI/SDSI framework for authorization, C-SEC, May 1999.

[8] B. Schneier, *Applied Cryptgraphy (2nd ed.)*, John Wiley & Sons, Inc.

[9] T. Saito, K. Umesawa, W. Wen, and H.G. Okuno, Access Control by SPKI Certificate, *Proc. of The Joint Workshop on Information Security and Cryptology 2000*, Okinawa, Japan, Jan. 2000.

[10] *SET Secure Electronic Transaction Specification, Book 1: Business Description*, `http://www.setco.org/`, May 1997.

[11] I. Lehti, P. Nikander, Certifying Trust, *Proc. of First International Workshop on Practice and Theory in Public Key Cryptography, PKC'98*, 83–98, Feb,1998.

Secure Multicast Software Delivery[1]

Lin Han Nahid Shahmehri
Laboratory for Intelligent Information Systems
Department of Computer and Information Science
Linköping University, Sweden
Email: {linha, nahsh}@ida.liu.se

Abstract

Nowadays, purchased software is delivered via sending CD-ROMs or downloading from the Internet. These solutions are either time-consuming or not scalable when the number of end-users becomes large.

In this paper, we explore the use of multicast technology as an option for software delivery. We present a global structure for multicast software delivery and look into security issues, mainly focusing on access control in establishing a secure multicast recipient group. A communication schema between each entity in a multicast software delivery system is described in detail. We also describe briefly the implementation of our current prototype for a multicast software delivery system.

Such electronic software delivery is the first phase of our ongoing project towards unattended software installation, configuration and upgrade.

1. Introduction

Due to the increasing availability of computers and novel technologies for accessing the Internet, electronic services (e-services) have attracted a great deal of attention. Using electronic means, services can be provided conveniently and economically without geographical limitations.

In order to enable e-services, service providers sometimes need certain software to be available and functional on the end-user side. Thus, efficient software delivery is imperative for e-services where a large number of end-users involved.

Generally, purchased software is delivered via sending CD-ROMs or downloading from the Internet. The former is time-consuming and counted in days. The latter is using "pull" technology - software is published at a web site, and can be pulled (downloaded) on the end-users' initiative. This usually can be done within minutes and is more efficient than sending CD-ROMs. However, when downloading software over the Internet, the number of simultaneous users is limited by server capacity and network bandwidth. Especially, when there are a huge number of users downloading software from the same web site at the same time, the resources in both network and the software provider's web site are consumed heavily. This might result in a slowdown in service, or even denial of service.

Alternatively, "push" technology can also be used, which means software providers actively push (send) software to end-users. With this approach, server capacity can be saved by using one instance of server response to serve multiple awaiting end-users. This method is suitable for serving a large number of end-users who need to receive certain software at a particular time.

Facing the huge number of end-users and given network bandwidth, pushing software still needs to employ an efficient transfer protocol. Compared to unicast, IP multicast provides a more efficient technology to support one-to-many group communication [1][2][3]. Applying multicast technology to electronically pushing software is quite promising.

Security is sensitively viewed as a major issue in content delivery [4], e.g., electronic software delivery. However, in recent years, much effort was put on developing a variety of multicast transfer protocols and not much work has been done to add security management into these protocols. The fact that security is lacking for existing multicast applications [5] makes this technology not very useful for electronic software delivery.

In this paper, we explore the use of multicast technology as an option for software delivery and focus

1 This work has been supported by ECSEL (Excellence Center in Computer Science and Systems Engineering in Linköping) and NUTEK (Swedish National Board for Industrial and Technical Development).

0-7695-0798-9/00 $10.00 © 2000 IEEE

on security issues involved. We develop the group management system [6][7] and present a global structure for multicast software delivery. The communication schema for a multicast software delivery session is described in detail. The work reported here is part of a large project aiming at unattended software installation, configuration and upgrade.

The rest of the paper is organized as follows. Basic process in multicast software delivery is introduced in section two. In section three we present the architecture of a multicast software delivery system. Section four details the communication schema for a software delivery session. It is followed by a description of our current implementation. Section six reviews some related work. Finally, we summarize the paper and give pointers to our future work.

2. Basic process in multicast software delivery

During a session of multicast software delivery, there is usually only one sender (software provider), but multiple recipients (subscribed end-users). For example, in the case of software upgrade, the company that owns the software takes the responsibility to send the upgraded software. The recipients are the subscribers who want to upgrade their software.

A multicast software delivery session can be divided into two phases. One is the recipient group establishment phase, and the other is the data delivery phase. In the first phase, the sender announces a delivery session, and subscribers register for the session. The recipient group should be composed of the subscribers who are interested in this software delivery session. The recipient group establishment is the basis for securely distributing software.

According to common practice, we make the following assumptions:

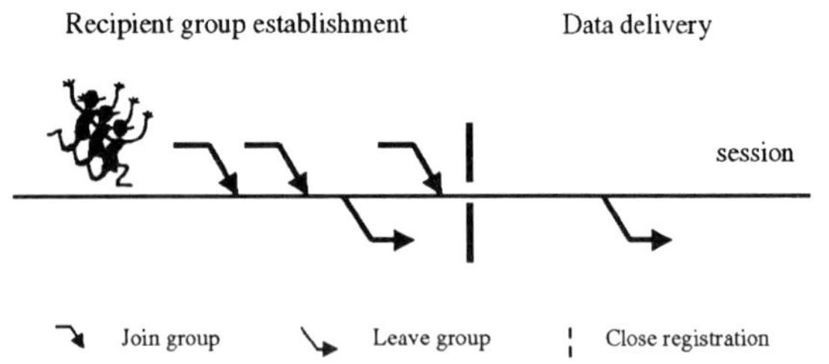

Figure 1. Membership changes in a software delivery session

- Subscribers join the recipient group during the recipient group establishment phase (see figure 1). Once this phase is over, no registration is allowed.
- All the members in the recipient group can be trusted. They will not disclose their keys to any outsiders even if they might leave the recipient group during a session.

3. Architecture of a multicast software delivery system

As shown in Figure 2, a multicast software delivery system consists of two parts, a sender manager and multiple recipient managers. The former is on behalf of the sender and composed of a controller, a delivery agent and a sender security agent. Each of the recipient managers represents a recipient and consists of a controller, a receiving agent and a recipient security agent.

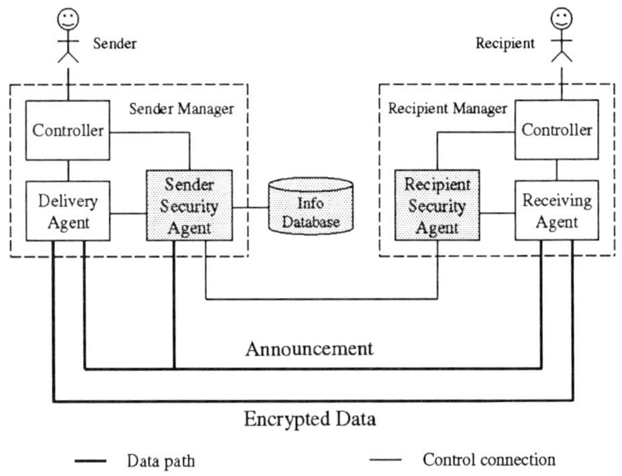

Figure 2. Architecture of a multicast software delivery system

The proposed group management system is responsible for security management during a software delivery session [6][7]. It consists of the sender security agent, recipient security agents and a database which is connected to the sender security agent and stores information about all authorized recipients.

Control connections are completely separated from the data paths used for software delivery. These control connections exist throughout the whole procedure of a software delivery session.

The main functionality of each entity in a multicast software delivery system is shown in Table 1 and Table 2.

Table 1. Functionality of each entity in the sender manager

Entity	Functionality
Delivery Agent	• build subscriber list • announce a software delivery session • encrypt and send the software • re-send the missing or corrupted packets
Sender Security Agent	• collect subscriber information • authenticate subscribers • issue a session key • forward response messages
Controller	• manage the two agents • provide an interface to the sender

Table 2. Functionality of each entity in a recipient manager

Entity	Functionality
Receiving Agent	• listen for the announcement • prepare the end-user's environment, e.g., detecting disk space, RAM, and network error • receive the delivered software
Recipient Security Agent	• assist the sender security agent when the subscriber is authenticated • decrypt the delivered software • report the recipient status
Controller	• manage the two agents • provide an interface to a recipient

4. Communication Schema

As mentioned above, a multicast software delivery system mainly has four components: the delivery agent, the sender security agent, recipient security agents and receiving agents. Figure 3 shows an example with a single recipient. The numbers in the figure represent the steps for a multicast software delivery session.

Among these steps, steps 1 through 5 constitute the recipient group establishment phase while steps 6 and 7 constitute the data delivery phase.

Detailed communication and some time sequence diagrams in the two phases are described in section 4.1 and 4.2, respectively.

4.1 Recipient group establishment phase

The delivery agent initiates a session of multicast software delivery by issuing an announcement to a public multicast group address where all potential receiving agents and the sender security agent are listening. This address can be obtained when end-users make their subscriptions.

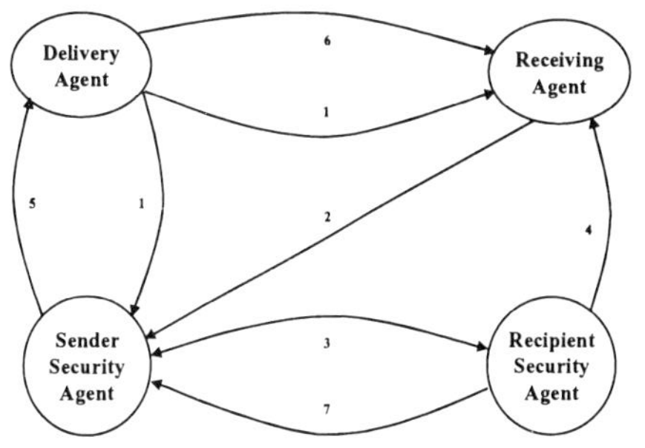

Figure 3. System components and their communications

Step 1:

In an announcement, the delivery agent provides information about the delivered software and specifies a response address where all registration messages will be sent. This response address can be different from the delivery agent's address. In our proposal, the address of the sender security agent is set to be the response address.

Step 2:

According to the environment configuration, such as disk space and RAM, all receiving agents should send a response message to inform whether they will join the recipient group. If a receiving agent does not send any response during the recipient group establishment phase, it is considered as rejecting to receive the software in this session.

Meanwhile, the sender security agent collects the subscribers' information and stores it in the database.

Step 3:

When the sender security agent receives a response message, it initiates a process of authentication and authorization. Recipient security agents are required to connect to the sender security agent and show their subscriptions. The sender security agent checks whether the subscriptions are valid. If a subscriber is successfully authenticated, the sender security agent sends to the corresponding recipient security agent a session key which is used to decrypt the delivered software. Otherwise, the recipient security agent is informed that the subscriber is not allowed to join this software delivery session.

Step 4:

After receiving the response from the sender security agent, a recipient security agent instructs its receiving agent to continue or stop the application. For example, if the subscriber does not pass authentication, the recipient security agent should stop the receiving agent.

Step 5:

The sender security agent forwards to the delivery agent the aggregated response messages coming from qualified subscribers. The delivery agent sends out a confirmation, directing corresponding qualified subscribers to join the multicast recipient group, and informing the sender security agent to update the current status of each subscriber.

After all expected subscribers have sent their responses or the announcement duration is over, the recipient group establishment phase finishes. No registration is allowed any more.

Figure 4 shows the time sequence diagram for successful recipient group establishment. The delivery agent, sender security agent, recipient security agent and receiving agent are application level users.

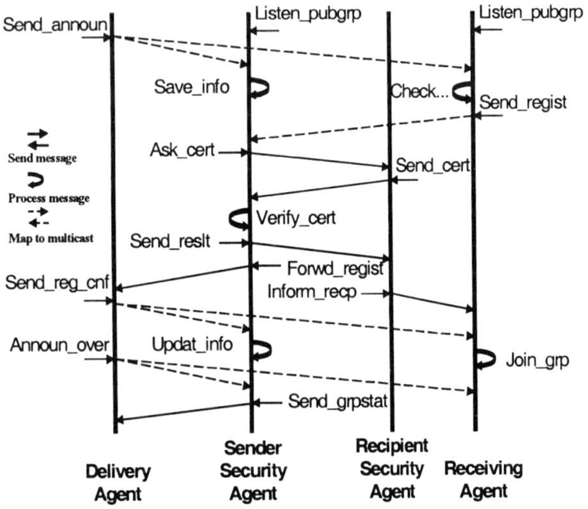

Figure 4. Time sequence diagram for successful group establishment

When establishing a recipient group, some establishment policies can also be involved. The sender security agent may check whether these policies are achieved. For example, if no more than a pre-defined number of subscribers can join the group, the sender security agent sends a message to the delivery agent, requesting to close this session. No software is transferred in this situation.

The procedure for group dismissal is shown in Figure 5.

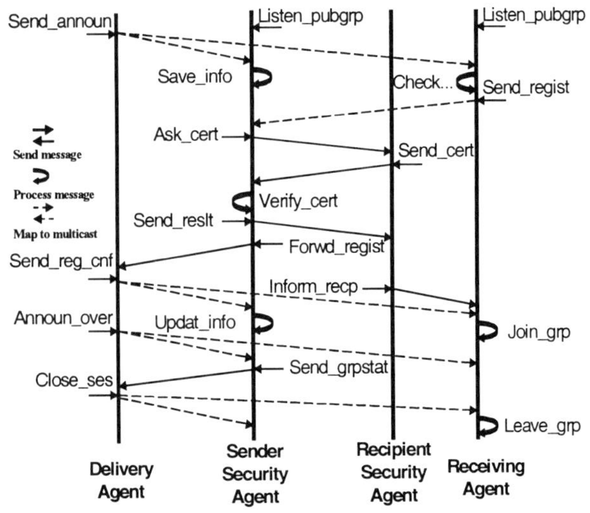

Figure 5. Time sequence diagram for non-successful group establishment

4.2 Data delivery phase

After the recipient group establishment phase is over, the data delivery phase starts. This phase is the main part of a software delivery session. As mentioned before, we employ a reliable multicast transfer protocol to meet the efficiency requirement.

Step 6:

To keep the transmitted data confidential, the delivery agent encrypts the delivered software using the session key (we assume that the delivery agent and the sender security agent share the session key before a software delivery session begins), and sends the encrypted data to the multicast recipient group address.

If some packets are missing or corrupted, the delivery agent re-sends those packets. This is realized by the employed reliable multicast transfer protocol.

Step 7:

Since the recipient security agent holds the session key if a subscriber has been successfully authenticated, it is in charge of decrypting the delivered software.

The final status of each recipient is reported by the recipient security agent to the sender security agent. The sender security agent then updates the subscriber information.

Figure 6 shows the communication in the data delivery phase.

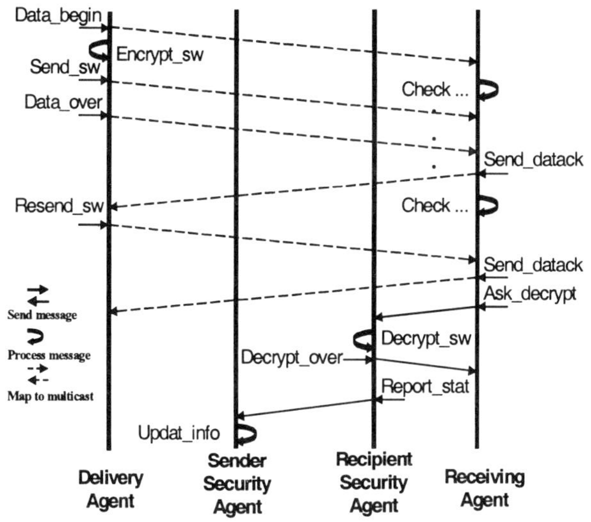

Figure 6. Time sequence diagram in the data delivery phase

5. Implementation

We have implemented a prototype for a multicast software delivery system in order to verify the practical feasibility of our proposed approach. In our implementation, the delivery agent and the receiving agent are coded using StarBurst Software's AutoCast API, which is built on top of a reliable multicast transfer protocol. The group management system is implemented using the openssl 0.9.2b library. Authentication is achieved by the use of extended X.509 certificates with attributes encoded inside. Communication between the sender security agent and a recipient security agent is secured by SSL (Secure Socket Layer).

The prototype confirms our intuitive expectation that multicast delivery can greatly reduce response time when the number of recipients becomes big. In the testing environment which is composed of two LANs, the prototype's response time in the data delivery phase is nearly N times less than the corresponding response time used in unicast (N is the number of recipients). The details about the testing results can be found in [8].

6. Related work

Many multicast applications have been presented in the literature [9][10][11]. However, little is mentioned on authentication and authorization.

de Rezende and Mauthe suggest in [12] a method for supporting group communication which is called M-Connection Service. They emphasize on QoS (Quality of Service) negotiation and group communication policies. Unfortunately, little security management issues are mentioned in their work.

Group key management has been the main issue for establishing a secure multicast group. Some frameworks are proposed [13][14]. These approaches fit well the dynamic multicast group where members join and leave the group dynamically during the whole session. However, multicast software delivery has different requirements for multicast group establishment (see section 2). In this multicast application, there is no need to prevent past members from understanding current and future communication. Thus, rekeying after group members' leaving is unnecessary.

7. Summary and future work

In our proposal, we introduce a group management system into the recipient group establishment and apply multicast technology to the data delivery. The introduced group management system emphasizes on authentication and access control so as to establish a secure group which demands that only subscribers should join the transmission group. This system is independent of the multicast transfer protocol we employ.

We have implemented and tested a prototype of a multicast software delivery system. The testing results show that our prototype is feasible in the testing environment.

Our next step is to implement the sender manager and the recipient manager using agent technology, test and evaluate the system in a large-scale environment.

In the future, we intend to develop a method for unattended software installation, configuration and upgrade.

Acknowledgement

We are deeply grateful to StarBurst Software for providing AutoCast API. We would also like to thank Claudiu Duma for his help in implementing our prototype.

References

[1] S. Deering, "Host Extensions for IP Multicasting", *RFC 1112*, August 1989.

[2] S. Deering, "Host Extensions for IP Multicasting", *RFC 988*, July 1986.

[3] S. Deering, "Host Extensions for IP Multicasting", *RFC 1054*, May 1988.

[4] M. Butler, and D. Leach, "IBM in the e-Business Market", June 1999.

[5] C. K. Miller, *Multicast Networking and Applications*, Addison Wesley Longman, Inc., 1998.

[6] L. Han, and N. Shahmehri, "Establishing a Secure Multicast Group for Remote Software Delivery", *Proceedings of the*

Eighth IEEE International Workshops on Enabling Technologies: Infrastructure for Collaborative Enterprises, IEEE, Palo Alto, CA, USA, June 1999, pp. 194-195.

[7] L. Han, and N. Shahmehri, "Towards Remote Software Delivery Using Secure Multicast Group Establishment", *Proceedings of the Second Conference on Computer Science and Systems Engineering in Linköping*, Norrköping, Sweden, October 1999, pp. 85-91.

[8] L. Han, C. Duma, and N. Shahmehri, "Electronic Software Delivery Service", in submission.

[9] E. Hinsch, A. Jaegemann, I. C. Roper, and L. Wang, "The Secure Conferencing User Agent – A Tool to Provide Secure Conferencing with MBONE Multimedia Conferencing Application", *Proceedings of Interactive Distributed Multimedia Systems and Services.* Springer Verlag, Berlin, Germany, March 1996, pp. 1-14.

[10] K. Bahr, E. Hinsch, and G. Schulze, "Incorporating Security Functions in Multimedia Conferencing Applications in the context of the MICE Project", *Proceedings of Multimedia: Advanced Teleservices and High-Speed Communication Architectures.* Springer Verlag, Heidelberg, Germany, September 1994, pp. 1-7.

[11] W. Geyer and R. Weis, "A Secure Accountable, and Collaborative Whiteboard", *Proceedings of Interactive Distributed Multimedia Systems and Telecommunication Services.* Springer Verlag, Oslo, Norway, September 1998, pp. 3-14.

[12] J. F. de Rezende, A. Mauthe, D. Hutchison, and S. Fdida, "M-Connection Service: A Multicast Service for Distributed Multimedia Applications", *Proceedings of Teleservices and Multimedia Communications.* Springer Verlag, Copenhagen, Denmark, November 1995, pp. 1-18.

[13] G. Caronni, M. Waldvoget, D. Sun, and B. Plattner, "Efficient Security for Large and Dynamic Multicast Group", *Proceedings of the Seventh IEEE International Workshops on Enabling Technologies: Infrastructure for Collaborative Enterprises,* IEEE, Palo Alto, CA, USA, June 1998, pp. 376-383.

[14] T. Hardjono, B. Cain, and N. Doraswamy, "A Framework for Group Key Management for Multicast Security", *Internet Draft*, Internet Engineering Task Force, February 1999. Work in progress. Available at: ftp://www.ietf.org/internet-drafts/draft-ietf-ipsec-gkmframework-01.txt.

EWS – a Case Study on Access Control in Workflow Systems

Åsa Hagström
Viiveke Fåk

Information Theory Group
Department of Electrical Engineering
Linköping University
581 83 Linköping – SWEDEN
asa@isy.liu.se

Mark Vandenwauver

Tivoli Secure Business Unit
9020 Capital of Texas Highway North
Building 1, Suite 270
Austin, Tx 78759 – USA
mark.vandenwauver@tivoli.com

Abstract

EWS is a workflow engine under development with specific requirements for the access control. We study a subset of these requirements, concerning work assignment, lockups and delegation issues. Three other systems – Changengine, FloWare and the Two-Schema Architecture – have been studied with respect to these problems, and we use the insights gained from these studies to give our own solutions to the problems. Changes that are made in the design of the system include new access modes, a structure for which access modes to use for which objects, a process document folder, and a delegation relation.

1. Introduction

The background of this study is a master thesis [1] carried out at the University of Linköping in 1999. A company called Ida Systems [2] planned to create a workflow engine with specific requirements for access control, designed to fit into their platform PAX Enterprise. Therefore, a number of different workflow engines were examined in order to find solutions to use, as well as pitfalls to avoid.

This paper is organized as follows: This section introduces the company Ida Systems and gives a brief explanation of the concepts of workflow and access control. In section 2, the system modules handling user and access permissions in the platform are presented. Section 3 specifies some of the requirements that were stated for the access control of Ida Systems' new workflow engine EWS – requirements concerning work assignment, lockups and delegation. EWS itself is presented in section 4. In section 5, we refer to some other workflow systems and their solutions for access control, examining how those solutions could enhance EWS. Section 6 constitutes the main part of the paper. Here, we give our proposed solutions to the discussed problems. We conclude with a summary.

1.1. Ida Systems

Ida Systems is a company that specializes in document management systems as well as systems for collecting, processing and distributing information. The former systems constitute the company's traditional product type, and are based on the platform PAX Enterprise, a framework for information and document processing with workflow support. The new workflow engine, EWS, should be a part of the PAX Enterprise system and function together with other platform modules. The company's clients are mainly government agencies and public institutions.

1.2. Workflow

The Workflow Management Coalition [3] defines *workflow* as "the computerized facilitation of a business process, in whole or in part, during which documents, information or tasks are passed from one participant to another for action, according to a set of procedural rules" [4]. This computerized facilitation is handled by a *workflow management system*, which "completely defines, manages and executes 'workflows' through the execution of software whose order of execution is driven by a computer representation of the workflow logic" [4].

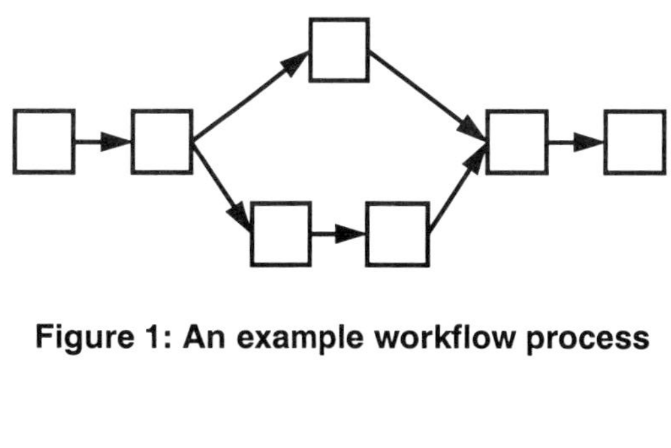

Figure 1: An example workflow process

0-7695-0798-9/00 $10.00 © 2000 IEEE

In other words, a workflow management system handles business processes by shipping them through workflow maps (see Figure 1). A workflow map consists of a set of activities, individual pieces of work, which may be handled manually or automatically.

There are different ways to manage workflow-related data. Often, documents are a vital part of the business cases processed in a workflow system, and the protection of these is just as important as the protection of workflow activities. Ideally, the workflow engine interacts with the document management system to make sure that the protection of documents and the protection of workflow objects (processes, activities,...) agree.

1.3. Access control

As hinted above, a workflow typically involves a number of different users with different responsibilities. Therefore, access control is needed in order to define the permissions of each actor involved in a workflow system.

Access control is about controlling and enforcing who in a system may access which of the system's resources, and how. The reason for requiring access control is to protect information integrity (the quality of data), as well as to ensure the confidentiality of it.

A number of different access control paradigms have been used throughout the history of multi-user computer systems. The one that is studied here is a variant of RBAC (Role-Based Access Control) [5], due to the fact that Ida Systems' platform uses this kind of access control. The key feature of RBAC is that permissions are granted to roles, rather than to users directly – users can take on different roles, and get the permissions corresponding to the roles they currently function as. In this scenario, however, permissions can be granted both to individuals and to roles.

2. The platform

PAX Enterprise is a large and complex system, and we will only give a brief overview of the modules that handle user information and access permissions: GRU and AC.

GRU is the group-role-user service, handling information about relationships between actors in the system. The basic entity is the user, i.e. a single person or process. Users can be assembled in groups; a user can be part of many groups, and groups can be part of other groups. Roles are instantiated as group-roles, which are coupled to a group and zero or more users. A user can take on several different roles, but does not need a role to be member of a group.

For each subject in GRU, an *access object set* can be derived. This is the set of all subjects that the subject is related to, following all relations recursively.

AC is the access control service, handling permissions for objects within the PAX Enterprise system. The entries in the AC database simply consist of subject-object-permission triples. It is possible to specify access permissions for any combination of subject, constituted by an entry in GRU, and object, constituted by a system resource.

The access permissions for a subject S is the set of all access permissions held by subjects in S's access object set. Since this model is additive, only permissions that are specific and personal to S need to be stored directly with S. The other permissions are inherited through the access object set.

When S wants access of type T to an object O, the system module handling O asks AC if access should be allowed. AC asks GRU for S's access object set, checks whether any member of the set has the T access permission for the object O, and returns the answer.

The scope of our work has been limited because of the restrictions placed by the nature of the problem – first and foremost, our model had to fit the existing platform. That goal motivates many of the choices made in our design.

3. Requirements for a workflow system

Originally, the requirements for the access control of EWS were stated in a list of 52 items, many of them specifying different access modes for the different entities in the EWS data model. In this paper, we concentrate on the issues of *work assignment, lockups* and *delegation*. First, we introduce some important concepts relating to these problems.

3.1. Concepts

A process has a set of *responsible handlers* and a set of *capable handlers*. The responsible handlers are those users that primarily should be chosen by the system to handle activities. If there are no responsible handlers available to assign an activity to, a handler should be chosen among the set of capable handlers. The purpose of responsible and capable handlers is to have default groups of users to compare with the settings for specific instances. These sets are a way for the workflow security administrator to make sure that no unwanted access permissions are issued, even though they have no direct control over each instance.

A process can also have a set of *supervisors*. These users do not handle activities, but merely monitor the workflow.

We define a *lockup* as the situation where there is no workflow participant that can handle a process. There are two types of lockup: *assignment lockups,* which occur when there are no workflow participants allowed to handle an activity at all, and *read lockups*, which occur when the possible workflow participants do not have the appropriate permissions to access workflow related data (such as documents).

3.2. Requirements

The work assignment requirements specify properties relating to the assignment of responsibilities for activities. There should be responsible as well as capable handlers defined for each process type, and it should also be possible to designate a set of supervisors. The handlers and supervisors should only get the needed permissions when they are actually assigned an activity.

The lockup problems resulted in requirements for verification. On process creation and modification, it should be possible to verify that no read or assignment lockups will occur. If, nevertheless, a lockup should occur, the system should be able to realize that so has happened.

There was a need for delegation functionality in the workflow engine. A user should be able to delegate all of their responsibilities, a subset of them, or single activities, to another workflow participant (such functionality is needed for example during vacations or sick leave).

3.3. Comments

The possible solutions to the problems given in Section 3.2 differ in many aspects. As for the work assignment requirements, they could be achieved either through the use of access modes, giving those an interpretation of responsibility and capability, or through some dedicated construct such as responsibility rules.

The requirements regarding lockups impose a control structure on what modifications of the granted access permissions that should be allowed in order for the system to function as intended. Some kind of rules and control mechanisms are needed to solve the problem.

There is no obvious way to tackle the problems involved in delegation. Somehow, the delegate should inherit the needed permissions from the delegator, but only for the amount of time that the delegation is valid.

4. The embedded workflow services

The embedded workflow services (EWS) is the workflow engine under development at Ida Systems. It is intended to be a general-purpose workflow engine, but needs to fit into the rest of the PAX Enterprise platform.

The data model used to represent workflows in EWS is shown in Figure 2. The entities are drawn with boxes, their relations are represented by diamonds, and for each relation, the minimum and maximum number of entities involved are shown in parentheses. Some entities are drawn with a dashed line to indicate that they exist only for a short time and for a specific business case.

A process definition includes a number of activity definitions. These are linked to each other by transitions. When a process is instantiated, the start activity is instantiated. By following the transitions, EWS finds the next activity (or activities) in the flow and instantiates it (or them) when necessary.

The process definition and process type entities differ. The process definition describes the graphical representation of a process, whereas the process type is used as a template for process instances.

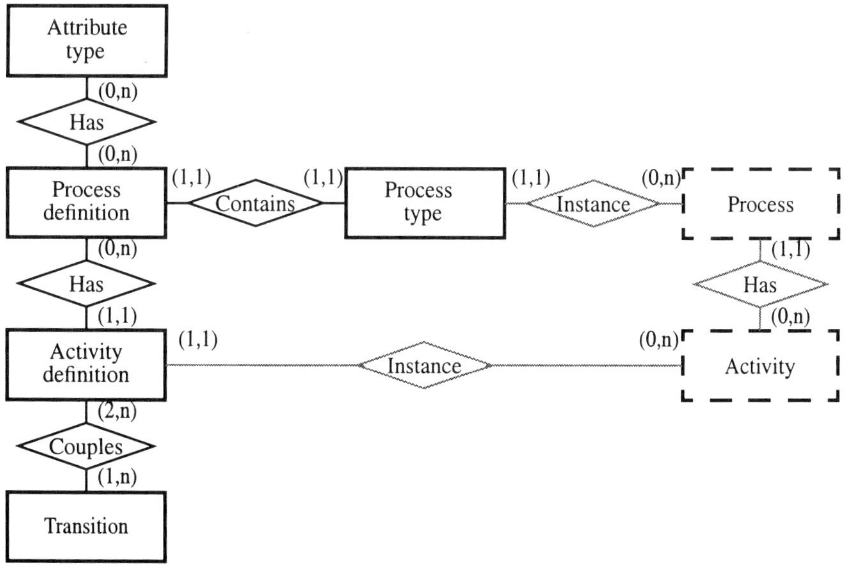

Figure 2: The EWS data model

5. Solutions in existing systems

Three existing workflow engines were analyzed with respect to access control in order to see if our requirements on work assignment, lockups and delegation were met in these systems, and how the problems had been solved. The studied systems were FloWare from Banctec [6], Changengine from Hewlett-Packard [7], and the Two-Schema Architecture, described in a doctoral thesis [8].

5.1. Work assignment

In Changengine and the Two-Schema Architecture, permissions for specific process instances cannot be set – the permissions for a process type are used for all instances of that type. Therefore, responsible and capable handlers are not needed in these systems, since the administrator has direct control over which users are allowed access. The users with access to a process or activity as specified in the process definition will always get access to each instance. There is no difference in priority between different users with access permissions to an activity or process.

In FloWare, it is possible to set permissions for specific instances, including or ruling out the default handlers for a process. Default permissions are set on the process definition level, but each process instance has a so-called *courier* that follows the instance through the workflow activities. The courier holds a list of users to include or exclude from the default permissions. It is possible to implement the functionality of responsible and capable handlers in FloWare, using groups (e.g. called 'responsible' and 'capable'). The handler for an activity is found by taking the intersection of the courier access list and the group of responsible handlers (primarily) and capable handlers (secondarily).

5.2. Lockups

Lockups constitute a problem that is either circumvented or ignored in the examined systems.

In Changengine and the Two-Schema Architecture, permissions cannot be changed for specific instances of processes or activities. Any anomalies in the granted permissions will therefore be discovered shortly after process design, and the permissions can then be adjusted accordingly. This applies for both types of lockups.

In FloWare, permissions can be set for specific process instances, and the lockup problem is thereby more immediate. Through the use of courier access lists, the default permissions can be overridden in a way that is impossible to analyze beforehand, and assignment lockups can easily occur.

It is noteworthy that none of the analyzed systems handle the protection of workflow-related data in a satisfactory manner.

5.3. Delegation

Changengine is designed in a very flexible manner, using databases and allowing the users to design the schemata for these. Since the system imposes no specific structure on the stored information, it is possible to express such constructs as delegation by introducing new relations and their interfaces in the system.

The other systems do not implement delegation, but Bichler proposes the use of relationships between objects to solve part of the problem.

Delegation does not seem to be an important issue for most workflow system designers. The examined systems lack consistent structures for such functionality, and much remains to be done in this area of workflow research.

6. Our solution

After reviewing these models, we used the gained insights to improve EWS's access control. Different solutions were used for the three studied problems.

6.1. Work assignment

The work assignment requirements could have been solved either with access modes or assignment rules. We chose to use access modes in conjunction with a set of rules specifying how the permissions should be inherited in the object model. The access modes used for each entity are shown in Figure 3.

The access modes are interrelated as follows. For process types, responsible handlers are given 'execute' permission, capable handlers are given 'back up' permission and supervisors are given 'read' permission. These permissions are inherited by the instances of this process type (but may possibly be changed during runtime), and the 'read' permission is inherited by the activity instances as well. Those handlers that should handle individual activities get 'instantiate' permission for the corresponding activity definitions. To find a handler for an activity, the intersection of users with 'instantiate' permission for the activity definition and users with 'execute' or 'back up' permission for the process is calculated. This solution gives the same sets of handlers for each process instance; there are no dynamic changes that can influence this model. However, for each process instance there should be a two-dimensional list (one list for each activity in the process) with the users wanted as handlers for that specific process instance. These users can only be chosen among the responsible and capable handlers with instan-

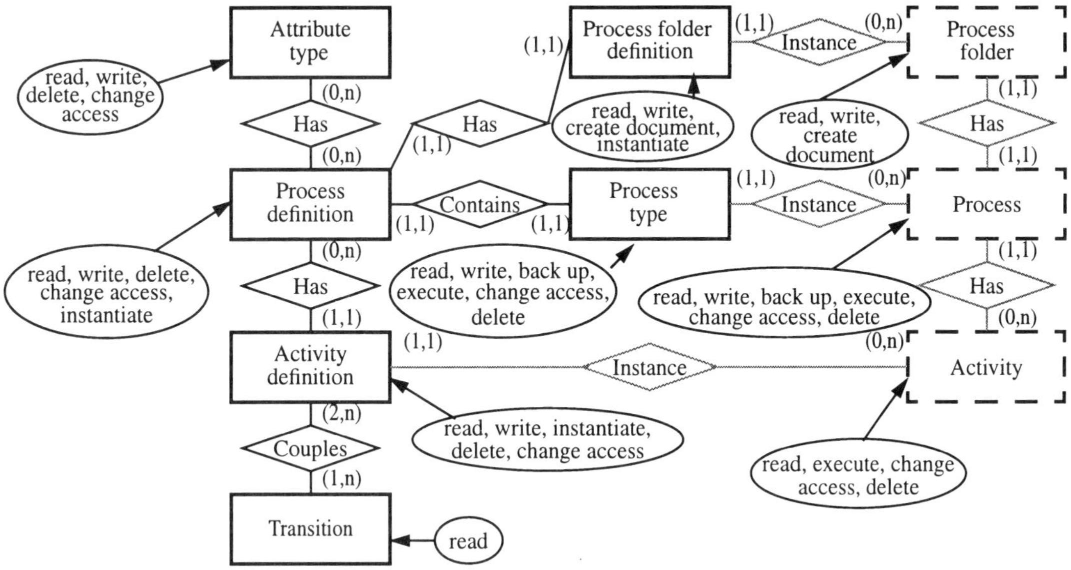

Figure 3: Access modes in EWS

tiate permission for the activity, and when there is such a list, those users are primarily chosen as handlers.

There are a number of rules specified to clarify the relationships between the different access modes [1].

6.2. Lockups

There is a need for linking documents to workflows. This concerns documents that are created during a process and probably only used by process handlers, as well as general documents that may be accessed by several processes and even by users outside of EWS. In order to organize the documents used by a process, a process folder is added to the data model (see Figure 3, top right corner). The folder holds references to the documents needed in the process (see Figure 4). This folder needs access protection; the 'read', 'write' and 'create document' access modes are applicable for the folder entity. Responsible and capable handlers are allowed all access to the process folder, while supervisors get 'read' permission.

Documents that are created during a workflow don't have a UID at process definition time, and must therefore be dereferenced when the process is running. As illustrated in Figure 4, the process folder keeps references to a table of document UIDs, which in turn can be used to find the corresponding AC entries. When a certain document is created, the process folder entry is dereferenced and linked to the document UID list.

This structure makes it possible to avoid read lockups. In each activity definition, a list of the needed documents is kept together with information on the access permissions required by a handler for that activity. Now, a lockup analysis can be performed. For each activity, the possible handlers are calculated and their permissions are compared to the permissions required for the documents in that activity. If there are no handlers that can access the documents as

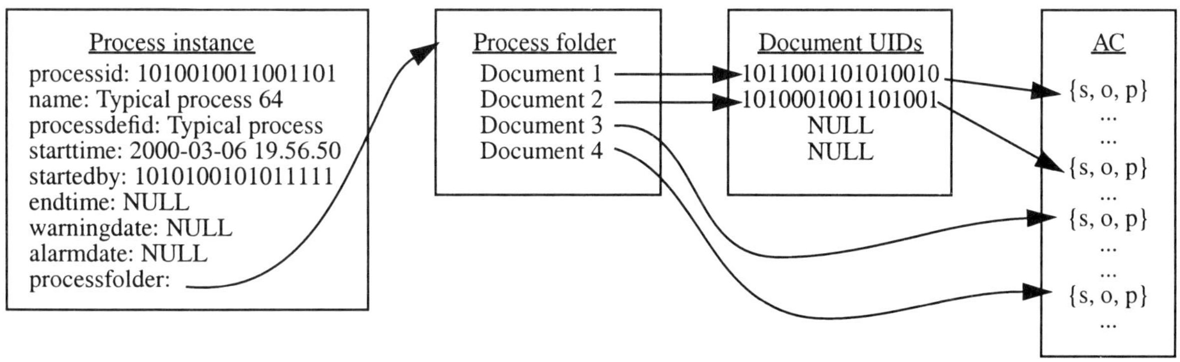

Figure 4: The processfolder attribute and dereferencing of document UIDs

required, a lockup has been found. This analysis can be performed at process definition time, and at any time the settings are changed.

With the given set of access modes for the system, it is possible to analyze a process in order to find assignment lockups. The sets of responsible and capable handlers must be compared to the set of users with 'instantiate' permission for each activity definition. This should be done at process definition time, but an analysis should also be performed:

- when the sets of responsible or capable handlers for a process are modified
- when the set of users with 'instantiate' permission for an activity definition is modified

When a process includes subprocesses, the analysis is more involved, but the principle remains the same.

6.3. Delegation

It is possible to add delegation to the platform's user model by using a dedicated delegation relationship in the GRU database where user information is stored. Every user can delegate his or her responsibilities and the accompanying access permissions to another user. A given user can be the delegate of many other users, but only one delegate can be chosen for each delegator. When a user delegates responsibility to someone else, the state of the delegator is set to 'delegated'. The delegate can be found through the relation in the database, and if that user is chosen to handle an activity on behalf of the delegator, the access object set of the delegator is added to that of the delegate.

Although this model would be easy to implement, it does have obstacles. Problems that arise with this model include:

- Delegation loops – if two or more users delegate their tasks to each other, there is no one to handle the tasks.
- Blind delegation – if a user delegates their tasks to a user who in turn delegates their tasks to somebody else, it may be unclear to the first delegator who will handle these tasks.
- Delegation chains – if delegation occurs in many steps, it may get undesired consequences. If a user high in the hierarchy delegates to someone on a lower level, and this is repeated several times, the first user's tasks may end up at a user who is unqualified for the tasks, or – worse – should not be allowed access to the data involved.

The problem of delegation loops can be avoided by making it impossible to delegate to users who are already delegating their tasks (this would also solve the problem of blind delegation in a simple way). Another way is to analyze each delegation, looking for loops, before allowing them. Blind delegation can also be avoided by making it open-eyed: the delegation information for each user could be readable by all, or to users with a specific permission.

The problem of delegation chains is more subtle. Either, the system can be based on trust, so that the delegator relies in the delegate not to pass down their tasks to untrusted parties, or there could be some form of control of the delegation chains (e.g. length).

No matter how these problems are addressed, it is unavoidable that the concept of delegation involves and is closely related to that of trust. A user must trust the person to whom they delegate their tasks; otherwise there could be no delegation.

7. Conclusions

The problems of work assignment, lockups and delegation were not solved in a satisfactory way in the studied systems – FloWare, Changengine and the Two-Schema Architecture. However, by adjusting the architecture of EWS and adding the needed structures, we were able to find solutions to the three problems. For the work assignment issues, we specified access modes and rules for inheritance of these. To solve the problems with lockups, we added a process document folder and perform lockup analysis. The delegation problem was addressed by adding a delegation relationship to the GRU database. However, a number of problems involving delegation in several steps arise, and cannot be completely eliminated.

References

[1] Å.Hagström. *Access Control Models for Workflow Systems*, Linköping University, November 1999. Available from http://www.it.isy.liu.se/~asa/.

[2] The Ida Systems web site: http://www.idasys.se/.

[3] The WFMC web site: http://www.aiim.org/wfmc/.

[4] The WFMC/D. Hollingsworth. *The Workflow Reference Model*, 1995. Available from http://www.aiim.org/wfmc/.

[5] R. Sandhu et al. *Role-Based Access Control Models*. IEEE Computer, Volume 29, Number 2, February 1996. Available from http://www.list.gmu.edu/journal.htm.

[6] The FloWare web site: http://www.plx.com/html/floware_scaleable_workflow.html.

[7] The Changengine web site: http://www.ice.hp.com/cyc/af/00/index.html.

[8] P. Bichler: *Conceptual Design of Secure Workflow Systems – An Object-Oriented Approach to the Uniform Modeling of Workflows, Organizations, and Security*. Johannes Kepler University of Linz, Austria. Available at http://www.ifs.uni-linz.ac.at/ifs/research/publications/phdtheses/finished.html.

A Framework for Secure Enterprise Computing

Myong H. Kang and Judith N. Froscher
Information Technology Division
Naval Research Laboratory
Washington, DC 20375

{mkang, froscher}@itd.nrl.navy.mil

Abstract

Distributed computing that supports cooperation among enterprises tends to be large and complex. Hence, it is not a trivial task to make enterprise computing secure and flexible. We have developed a prototype that supports flexible, secure, and recoverable enterprise computing. In this paper, we briefly describe the prototype secure enterprise application-building tool.

Keywords: Enterprise computing, security

1. Strategy for Enterprise Computing

Enterprise applications tend to be large and complex. Usually a team of programmers has to work on different parts of a program, which have to be assembled to provide the IT support for the enterprise cooperation. Hence, it is not a trivial task to make enterprise computing secure and flexible. Once the application is completed, it has to be installed and executed across enterprise boundaries. Monitoring the status of such large-scale application provide another challenging opportunity for system builders.

We have developed a prototype enterprise application-building tool that supports flexible, secure, and recoverable enterprise computing. The philosophy behind our system is as follows:

- Make use/reuse of existing components and services as much as possible.
- Separate mission (meta) logic from component/service logic. A designer can program mission logic and specify interactions with underlying components.
- Support abstraction. Since enterprise computing tends to be large scale, different designers and users tend to think about the problem at different levels of abstraction.
- Maximum use of Commercial-off-the-shelf (COTS) security solutions. There are many existing COTS security solutions for distributed computing, such as CORBA Security, Secure Socket Layer (SSL), Role-Based Access Control (RBAC), etc. We make use of them as much as possible. Only when existing solution cannot provide the fine-grained control that is needed do we extend them [2, 3].

2. System Organization

There are three major building blocks in the prototype of the secure enterprise application-building tool (see figure 1).

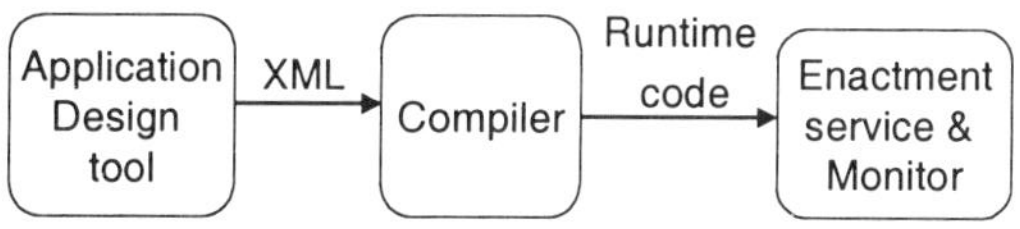

Figure 1: Internal structure of secure enterprise application building tool

The GUI-based enterprise application design tool allows application designers to specify mission/application logic. In other words, the designer can specify each task[1] (e.g., inputs, outputs, invocation method for the underlying component/service), and control logic and data flow among tasks. This tool also allows application designers to hide complexity by providing a way to group related tasks into a higher-level task (i.e., supporting abstraction). The design tool saves the specification in XML (eXtensible Markup Language) [1]. When the application design is completed, the compiler reads the XML representation of the design, and performs the necessary design analysis and

[1] In this context, the task is a unit of work that interacts to an underlying component/service and other tasks.

0-7695-0798-9/00 $10.00

validation. Finally it generates runtime code for enactment services.

3. Security Services

As we mentioned in section 1, our philosophy is to use COTS security solutions whenever they are suitable. We use SSL for HTTP connections (HTTPS), CORBA security for IIOP connections, and RBAC for user authorization. However, we have found that existing security solutions have many limitations because they are designed independent of applications. In other words, application specific, fine-grained access control cannot be achieved by the naïve use of existing security solutions. Consider the following application (see figure 2). In this example, there are six tasks that are executed in three enterprises that participate in the cooperation.

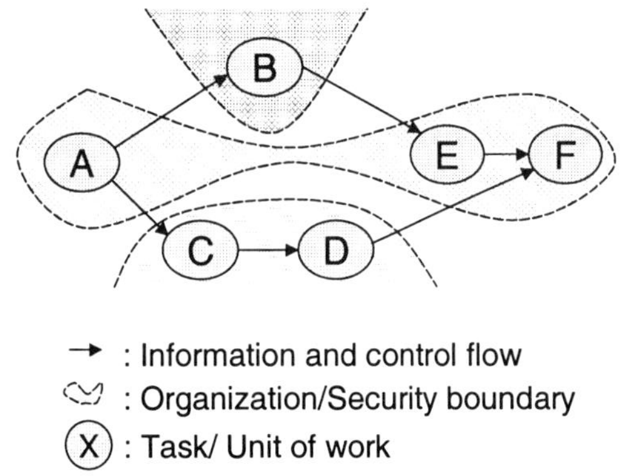

Figure 2: An enterprise-computing example

Naïve use of existing security solutions may not satisfy the following security requirements.

1. Tools need to provide different views of the application based on users' needs to know. For example, users in enterprise 3 may not need to know the existence of other tasks such as task A, B, E, or F that are under the control of other enterprises. Also a user may not need to know the existence of other tasks even if they are under the control of the same enterprise.
2. Fine-grained access control that can control what task can access which data and which portions of data can be read and modified by each task.
3. Need to enforce 2-mem rule such as the person who performed the task C cannot perform task D even if they have the required role.

The above requirements are application specific security requirements that can be easily enforced by the application [4]. However, implementing application specific security mechanisms and supporting infrastructure in each application may not be a cost-effective way of building and maintaining applications. Hence, embedding those application specific security mechanism so that any application that was built using the tool also supports those fine grain security mechanisms is a cost-effective way of building and maintaining applications.

4. Conclusion

In this paper, we have presented a way to construct a secure application that spans enterprises. Security mechanisms that were constructed independent of applications are limited in satisfying application specific security requirements. Adding security mechanisms to each application is not a cost-effective method. We propose a secure application-building tool that reduces the burden of enterprise application design and supports fine-grained security mechanisms.

References

1. "Extensible Markup Language (XML) 1.0," World-wide-Web Consortium, http://www.w3.org/TR/1998/REC-xml-19980210.html

2. M. H. Kang, J. N. Froscher, B. J. Eppinger, and I. S. Moskowitz, "A Strategy for an MLS Workflow Management System" Proceedings of 13th IFIP Conference on Database Security, Seattle, WA, 1999.

3. M. H. Kang, B. J. Eppinger, and J. N. Froscher, "Tools to Support Secure Enterprise Computing," Proceedings of the 15th Annual Computer Security Applications Conference, (1999).

4. M. H. Kang, J. S. Park, and J. N. Froscher, "A Strategy of Security Services for Enterprise Applications," Submitted for publication, (2000).

Towards Secure e-Services

Claudiu Duma   Almut Herzog   Nahid Shahmehri
Laboratory for Intelligent Information Systems
Linköping University, Sweden
Email: {cladu, almhe, nahsh}@ida.liu.se

Abstract

The networked home with refrigerators and washing machines connected to the Internet and reachable through Web browsers will be reality soon. Following this development, the market for electronically deliverable services will evolve. Companies that want to provide electronic services cannot be expected to deal with cable, network and routing problems – they need to rely and build on a common, secure hard- and software infrastructure that allows services to reach the customers' homes. We call such an infrastructure an e-services system (e-SS).

In this paper we present the infrastructure of an example e-SS, highlight a number of specific security issues and show how they can be addressed in the early stages of the design of an e-SS.

1. Introduction

Virtually any area of life can be subject to electronic services. Application areas for e-services are vast and can comprise e.g. entertainment, remote (Internet) control of home devices, meter reading, home care and other fields of home automation. e-services need a common platform to run on. We call such a platform an e-services system (e-SS).

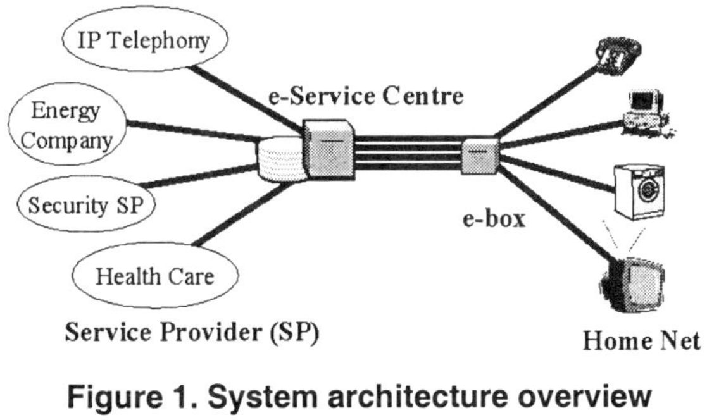

Figure 1. System architecture overview

Our reference of an e-SS that we will use throughout the paper is Ericsson's e-box system [1] in which we have identified four main components: (1) *Service Providers (SPs)* develop, maintain and bear responsibility for electronic services. Services can either be off-the-shelf products (house lights controllable over the Internet, games etc.) or services that require data transmissions between the end user and the SP (meter reading, medical data transmission, etc.). (2) An *e-Service Centre (e-SC)* is an access gateway between SPs and e-Boxes. It maintains a list of available e-services, can run services and manages e-Boxes. (3) An *e-Box*, installed in the end user home, is an access gateway between an e-SC and home devices. (4) *Home devices* in this context means devices that can be accessed through a network (e.g. Ethernet, but also power line) [2].

To summarise, the architecture in figure 1 makes home devices reachable from the Internet through e-Box gateways. e-Boxes are administrated by a third party, namely the e-SC, and not by the end user who need not necessarily be capable to operate a computer.

We will now present a model of our reference e-SS developed in UML and continue with an investigation of important security issues that are integrated by our model. The paper concludes with an outlook on our future work.

2. Model

We aim at an intuitive but formalised representation of an e-SS by developing a model of our e-SS using the Uniform Modelling Language (UML) [3]. The model is intended to lead to an implementation of a prototype.

While the architecture in figure 1 describes the main system components, the UML model identifies, in addition, properties of the system. New entities are introduced and relations between parties are established. Rules, expressed as associations and constraints, define the policy of the system.

Figure 2 is the conceptual view of our e-SS. It describes parties and their relations as a UML class diagram. The main parties are *SP*, *ESC*, *EBox*, *User* and *Device* which are all brought together by their mutual use or management of *Services* that consist of *Applications*.

0-7695-0798-9/00 $10.00 © 2000 IEEE

3. Security issues in the e-SS model

According to Gollmann [4] the definition of security covers the aspects of *confidentiality*, *integrity* and *availability*. The aspect of availability is of highest priority in an e-SS: If a service is not available, no revenue is generated for its providers, and also users simply might not use services which suffer from repeated periods of unavailability.

Availability can be threatened by e.g. denial of service attacks, bandwidth or network problems but also power failures. There must be rules about how shared resources such as bandwidth and other network parameters are to be handled to ensure that all applications can run the way they were designed for.

Our model addresses this by stating that each service depends on a number of resources that must be available for the service to function as intended (association *depend* between *Service* and *Resource* in fig. 2). Resource availability could be controlled by a manager service that can check, allocate, distribute and limit system resources.

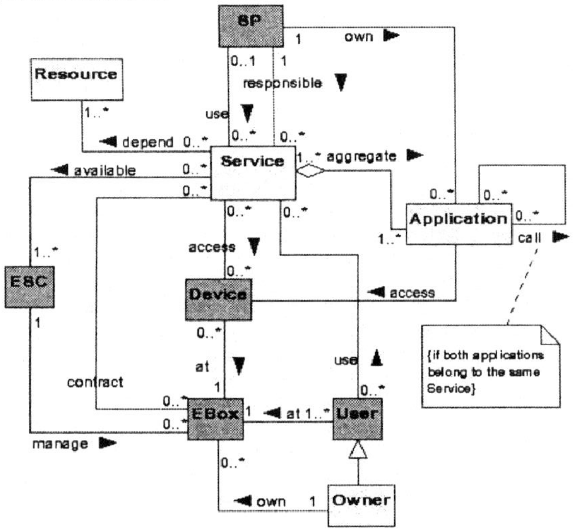

Figure 2. e-SS Model View with Example Constraint

An available system will still not be used widely if its users cannot rely on the *confidential* treatment of their data.

If medical data is transmitted in an e-service concerning home care, this data must only be accessible to authorised people [5], i.e. the user and the trusted SP. In the model, the rule is to let only SPs and end users run services (and, implicitly, have access to data generated by a service), as shown (in fig. 2) by the association *use* between *User*, *e-box* and *Service* and association *use* between *SP* and *Service*). e-SCs are allowed to manage services (association *manage* between *ESC* and *EBox* in fig. 2) but they are not automatically enabled to run them. Access control [6] measures make sure that these rules are obeyed.

Access control must also be used on the application level to ensure that applications only communicate with trusted applications. It is a horror scenario to imagine that an alarm system is fed with replayed input data covering burglars in the house. Applications must only send and receive data from authorised and clearly identified applications belonging to the same service. This is shown (in fig. 2) as a constraint to the association *call* that connects two *Applications*.

Data should not only be guaranteed to be treated confidentially but also correctly while going through the e-SS. That is, data must not be modified accidentally or maliciously – its *integrity* must be preserved. Our rule for communication between applications ensures integrity at a high level of design. Cryptography and error detection are measures on lower levels to guard integrity.

Integrity is a very basic security requirement. But it cannot be the aim of an e-SS to guarantee data integrity from the source (being e.g. a device bought by the end user). If a device generates incorrect data or has been tampered with, this can not be detected by the e-SS.

4. Conclusion and future work

We described a system architecture overview of an e-SS, presented a conceptual UML model for our e-SS and showed security issues in our model concerning the issues of availability, confidentiality and integrity.

UML has been employed in modelling and design of a variety of systems, but little work has been done for specifying security in UML. Epstein and Sandhu [7] present a UML approach to Role Engineering of an RBAC model. With our work we will also investigate the versatility of OO methodology, and especially the UML, as support for security requirements and specification.

[1] http://www.ericsson.com/wireless/products/ebox/pubrel/brochure.shtml, 23-Mar-2000

[2] A. Dutta-Roy, "Networks for Homes", IEEE Spectrum, 1999, pp. 26-33

[3] G. Booch, J. Rumbaugh, I. Jacobson, *The Unified Modeling Language User Guide*, Addison Wesley Longman, Massachusetts, 1999

[4] D. Gollmann, *Computer Security*, John Wiley and Sons, Chichester, 1999, pp. 4-10.

[5] R. J. Anderson, "Patient Confidentiality – At Risk from NHS Wide Networking", *Proceedings of Health Care 96*, March 96

[6] R. Sandhu, P. Samarati, "Access Control: Principles and Practice", *IEEE Communications Magazine* Volume: 32 9, 1994

[7] P. Epstein, R. Sandhu, "Towards a UML based approach to role engineering", *Proceedings of the fourth ACM workshop on Role-based access control* October 28-29, 1999, Fairfax, VA USA, pp. 135-143

Workshop

Web-Based Infrastructures and Coordination Architectures for Collaborative Enterprises

Organizers

Kirstie L. Bellman, Aerospace Integration Science Ctr., USA
Gabriele Kostis, University of Vienna, Austria
Christopher Landauer, Aerospace Integration Science Ctr., USA
Gustaf Neumann, University of Essen, Germany
Robert Tolksdorf, Technische Universität Berlin, Germany
Franco Zambonelli, Università di Modena e Reggio Emilia, Italy

Report On Major Themes And Issues Arising From The Workshop

Kirstie L. Bellman, Chris Landauer
The Aerospace Corp.
{bellman,cal}@aero.org

Robert Tolksdorf
Technical Univ. Berlin
tolk@cs.tu-berlin.de

Alois Ferscha
Univ. Vienna
ferscha@ani.univie.ac.at

Abstract

The WETICE Workshop on Web-based Infrastructures and Coordination Architectures for Collaborative Enterprises continued two threads of workshops in the WETICE series that were held over the last four years. These workshops addressed the question of how Web techniques can be used to achieve or to improve collaboration within or between organizations, and which coordination mechanisms could be used in such an architecture.

The papers presented at the workshop and included in the proceedings contributed to all areas mentioned. They triggered several discussions on the addressed topics. This report present the views expressed and conclusions drawn.

The Workshop Chairs voted Alois Ferscha's paper "Workspace Awareness in Mobile Virtual Teams" as the best paper in the workshop.

1 Introduction

The problem area raises several questions of both technical and organizational nature. How can a system enable the participants to support flexible and effective collaboration? Should we concentrate on developing an infrastructure for sharing artifacts (e.g., documents, files, data)? Should we develop a shared language (e.g., XML, RDF) to exchange business information which represents an external representation of the private artifacts? Or will we need a richer communication infrastructure supporting shared virtual spaces (e.g., tuple spaces, MUDs and related Virtual Worlds), where people are "in the system", rather than purely using or sharing the artifacts of a system? Is it important to make the infrastructure seamless, ubiquitous, and unobtrusive, or should it allow user-level access to internal processes, for fine-tuning, efficient access, and instrumentation?

Higher-level mechanisms and procedures have to be considered as well. A collaborative application can reflect the real-world organizations that overlay the system or even become part of the organization itself. The system must therefore both enforce specific organizational rules (e.g., workflow rules) and facilitate knowledge management and exchange. Thus, the workshop looked not only at collaborative systems, but also at the models and infrastructures needed for enabling human organizations, or hybrid organizations made up of both human and software agents / processes, to effectively interact and cooperate.

The papers presented at the workshop and included in the proceedings contributed to all areas mentioned. They triggered several discussions on the addressed topics. This report present the views expressed and conclusions drawn.

The Workshop Chairs voted Alois Ferscha's paper "Workspace Awareness in Mobile Virtual Teams" as the best paper in the workshop.

2 Workshop

2.1 Basic Agreements

Providing user-oriented collaborative systems and infrastructure includes both technology and social issues. As an example, privacy issues within environments include both social issues (what to make private and how to manage the amount of privacy / distribution), and technical ones (how to implement a system with this granularity and level of control).

We need to make this technology useful to humans; it should not just be a set of tools looking for a problem. We therefore need to represent the problems that people have and their goals for collaborative technology. We also need to develop methods to co-evolve and support the correct "concepts of operations", that is, styles of use of the collaborative systems.

Frameworks, methods, and tools are needed that enable the use of each other's collaborative work and results. So far, there is little transfer of tools or results from one project to another.

An infrastructure for collaboration needs to retain different entry levels and modes, so users coming from very different interaction means can still collaborate (e.g., text-based, web, 2D and 3D, mobile, etc.)

We need to define one or more development paths from single user systems to multi-user tools and environments.

0-7695-0798-9/00 $10.00 © 2000 IEEE

Otherwise, collaboration tools will be much more difficult to make popular.

We need to balance standards and standard technology with necessary heterogeneity and methods for allowing specializations.

2.2 Quick Poll

We asked our Workshop participants why they want collaborative technologies (21 respondents).

- 8 To support meetings
  - 6 Especially small, personal ones, communities of interest, and spontaneously composed ones
  - 2 Community-oriented, widely distributed services, such as infrastructure for "the good of the community"
- 7 To conduct distributed projects, such as virtual enterprises - Especially knowledge management, identifying resources for and experts for some project, and eventually coordinate with external environment
- 4 To support collaborative manufacturing Sharing both data and process products
- 4 To share data for collaborative authoring
- 2 To share non-verbal skills (e.g., training, telemedicine)

2.3 Cooperative Work Dimensions

Figure 1 shows the Cooperative Work Dimensions which represent different kinds of cooperation, and some of the technologies relevant to them. The original of this slide was borrowed from [1].

3 Technical and Philosophical Issues for Infrastructure

3.1 Purpose

The purpose of the infrastructures that were discussed in this Workshop is to support multi-user interactions at a number of different levels of intimacy. They should allow individuals to control their own time and tools in planning, organisation and execution of their work, business, and private activities, freed from unnecessary time, geographical, media, and device barriers.

We need to characterize, define, and support them, and explain the differences between coordination, collaboration, cooperation, and related concepts. These distinctions lead to different specifications and uses of the resulting models. There are many different descriptions of the differences, but none has taken a dominating position.

3.2 Examples

Games are currently one of the most successful and popular forms of collaborative computing environments, for several reasons.

- Players know their roles and can choose an appropriate level of difficulty.
- There are generally well-defined outcomes (when you're dead, you're dead).
- There is a level of functionality that matches the game story.

The critical mass that is needed for any collaborative system to be effective is relatively easy to get with games. However, the reliability and robustness of these games is adequate for games but not for real life situations, especially for safety-critical systems. Also, creating Collaboration Worlds is harder than "playing" in existing worlds, so most players simply use other people's game worlds. For us, this means that developing appropriate collaboration environments is (and will remain) much harder than just using them.

Business and Economic applications and models offer a rich history of methods and theory, which certainly make a good start for e-commerce and other distributed business applications, since they provide criteria and hence metrics of success. They are not necessarily appropriate for other applications, such as education, medicine, games, etc.. For each application, these models need to be examined to determine whether they are adequate or not; this applicability does not transfer well.

Security (of information, access, and processes) is a dominating issue and inherently contradicts many of the flexibilities we want to have in collaboration systems. They must handle heterogeneity, flexible starting points for different actors, and recognize and exploit opportunities as they arise. Each of these is a potential security problem, and will need to be addressed as such. The semantics of "just business" is challenging enough for now.

XML is certainly a useful approach, and it is clear that it will happen. It has been pretty useful in examples, because as simple as it is, at least it gets to a first level of agreement. The potential problems are the same as in other languages and arise from misunderstanding of the use for XML for more than syntax. It will not by any means automatically solve semantic integration issues. Different user groups will still have to set up their own conventions for semantic

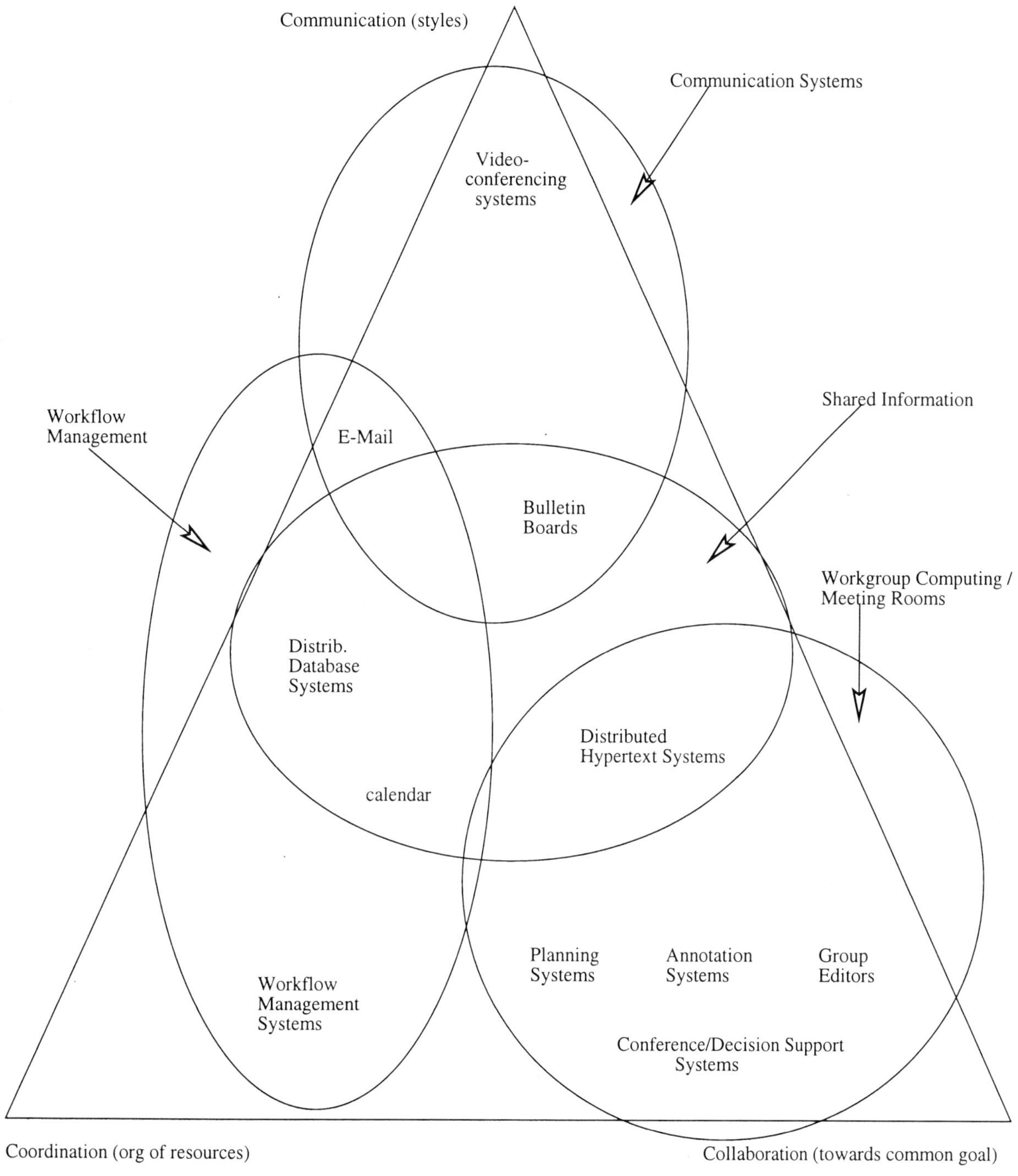

Figure 1: Cooperative Work Dimensions

integration, via an agreed upon mapping of XML-defined syntax into conventional semantic units that are common in the application domain. Many groups are doing this now, and we predict a great deal of difficulty in integration across these domains.

3.3 Future Directions

The workshop compiled the following list of issues that lead to research questions in the field of collaboration:

What services and capabilities should be distributed and what should be centralized? What metrics should be developed so we can eventually decide which to do in a given architecture for a given purpose? The user and developer viewpoints of distribution need to be separated, and the corresponding issues for client and server architectures need to be identified. The distribution question interacts with the choice of spatial metaphor that is used, and the emphasis within different implementations of "location" in these architectures.

What is the role of collaboration beyond the box, that is, collaboration infrastructure for mobile, ubiquitous, or wearable computing, and the digital assistants that will provide it? We want an infrastructure for all of our devices and file systems, no matter where or what they are, so that we do not have to manage them all separately and keep them consistent ourselves. We want something like a "Universal Remote Control", that would query the devices within its range, and present a device-specific menu of functions, so that the user need not learn the device details. This level of integration will be hard, especially among different cultures: consider the current difficulties among different standards for just sharing text among different languages.

The individual utility of wireless appliances and other infrastructure services will be greatly increased when they are

- personalized, i.e., user-centered and dynamically adapted to user preferences;
- location-aware, i.e., multimodal and multifunctional according to the environment; and
- time-dependent, i.e., dynamically variable and with timely responses.

We should consider a "pervasive" web infrastructure that links together people in different "modes" (at work, in private, etc.) with devices of different shape / form factor / functionality, at different places (fixed, remote, roaming).

3.4 Properties

Observability in several senses is a big issue. Here the group was split on how crucial they considered "mutual observability" to be as a property of collaborative environments. Not everyone observes the system in the same way at the same time, and these multiple viewpoints are key feature of agents. Even if mutual observability is not emphasized, there are crucial issues of instrumentation of a system, so its developers and users can observe its behavior, for modification and understandability.

Time management issues are crucial to coordination and collaboration - and hard! Time management is needed to organize both causality and observability. It shows up here in e-commerce, manufacturing, telemedicine, games, and meetings. The problem is to find methods to let a distributed system evolve over time in a consistent manner, since such concepts will impact our "user models" that are so necessary in collaboration. Many methods exist for time management in some applications (e.g., for distributed simulation, etc.), but in these collaborative systems, we are combining both virtual and real clock times, and that is much harder than managing either one separately.

One of the difficulties in analyzing collaborative systems is our difficulty in representing what we want to DO collaboratively in a computer mediated environment, and how it fits into our organization or other work environments. We need methods that are flexible, expressive (enough), and analyzable. The Workshop heard some promising formal work on collaborative protocols.

It is clear that whether as protocols, places, or special agents, part of collaboration requires representing social rules and conventions, since we are generally expecting the collaborating entities to be humans. We need to distinguish among the different kinds of constraints (social conventions, coordination constraints, etc.), and among the different degrees of enforcement and style of enforcement of those constraints (e.g., chosen by players, the "physics" of a place, etc.).

Finally, we get to standards, where we have a direct conflict between the variability of human behaviors and the rigidity of computing behaviors. We need to determine what the correct role is for standards, and especially what the correct level of control is. We need to decide when they should be used in this community, how soon we can leverage off the advantages of standard languages, and when we should leave the coordination to the participants. We need to decide what kind of standards are appropriate for what part of the infrastructure: open standards seem much more desirable than proprietary ones. We started in the Workshop a wish list on the characteristics of the kinds of languages we want.

4 State of the Art?

We need more roadmaps and better overall visions for collaborative environments and frameworks. They will lead to planning and investment strategies. We need help in mapping problems and uses of collaboration to current and future capabilities, since there is no plan for transitioning to more use of current and future collaborative tools.

We need modeling and studies of the impact of these technologies on workplaces. For example, there are few studies of how technologies impact work styles. We need much more experimentation on how humans use these tools. We need more information models, process models, and much more data.

We need to scale up the size of applications We are past toy problems, but we are not past small or simple problems. Large collaboration services are being provided in versioning systems, mailing lists, email, chat groups, MUDs, and the web, but all of them address a relatively homogeneous problem, using either post and access style, or explicit distribution to a known list. Neither of these support small groups in personal, specialized, or sophisticated fashion. It is also not yet possible to analyze them.

We need to collaborate ourselves, because of the rising number of devices in use per person. We are building up a body of knowledge by using some common approaches and some somewhat composable approaches. We need to compare these and understand where each provides an essential capability.

The continuing virtualisation of organisational structures in "virtual communities" and "virtual enterprises" is a direct consequence of the availability of new networking technologies and the advanced mobility of people, devices and services. Facing today's maturing of these and other networking technologies, particularly the wireless Internet, as the fastest growing economic and industrial fields of information technology, it is important to develop new views on how organisational structures, human relationships, responsibility and trust, work and lifestyle can be redefined and manifested, as time, geographic, media and mobility boundaries become less and less important.

We need to develop the understanding to support these views, the methods to understand and model them, and the infrastructure to implement them.

References

[1] S. Teufel, C. Sauter, T. Mühlherr, K. Bauknecht, *Computerunterstützung für die Gruppenarbeit*, Addison-Wesley, Bonn 1995 (in German)

A Coordination Infrastructure for Agent-based Internet Applications

Enrico Denti Andrea Omicini

LIA - Laboratorio di Informatica Avanzata
DEIS - Università di Bologna
Viale Risorgimento, 2 40136 – Bologna, Italy
{edenti,aomicini}@deis.unibo.it

Abstract

Internet applications are often structured as collections of interactive, heterogeneous agents, which have to coordinate to pursue the application goals. These applications require design methodologies that are far from being well established, and new standard technologies, models, languages, technologies and tools specifically tailored to the agent metaphor and to agent-based systems. This article presents LuCe*, a coordination infrastructure for the design and the development of agent-based distributed applications on the Internet, which integrates Java, logic-based languages, and tuple-based coordination models. We discuss the impact of this approach on the design both of the single agents and of Internet applications, then suggest how it could be exploited in the design/development/test cycle.*

1 Agents and the Internet

The Internet is definitely becoming *the* vehicle to innovative services and applications. Whether they are the result of previously-existing systems being brought to the Internet, or new systems built from scratch, their construction often implies several heterogeneous information sources and consumers to inter-operate and cooperate.

Due to the intrinsic decentralisation and unpredictability of the Internet, *autonomy* is a fundamental feature required to all the system components (processes, objects, agents): each component should be an independent *locus* of control, encapsulating its own control flow. However, designing a distributed multi-component system in a control-driven fashion is unnatural, and can easily become impractical when the system size scales up, because of the difficulty in mastering all components' activities. By leaving control issues apart, the *information-driven* approach, where the design is based on the available knowledge and on the information flows, seems to be more adequate to complex interactive systems.

Autonomy is one of the typical properties of *agents*, active computational entities featuring enough control autonomy to be charged of specific, clearly-identified *task(s)*, which they try to pursue *pro-actively* [15]. Autonomy, task-awareness and interactivity (the ability of reacting to the environment) are the key features distinguishing an agent from an operating-system process, and make agents quite a natural metaphor to design distributed, decentralised systems.

Agents within an application are typically heterogeneous from several viewpoints: their essence (human agents, offices, software agents), technology (from the newest to the oldest legacy system), abilities (mere executive agents vs. intelligent agents), role (coordinators, executors, transformers, etc.), communication abilities (communication language, protocol), mobility (static agents vs. mobile agents), etc. Dealing with heterogeneity is a desirable property of any multi-agent system, but becomes a must in Internet applications, where the nature of remote systems is often unpredictable. So, communication and interoperability middleware standards and infrastructures are necessary, and have clearly emerged in the last years (TCP/IP, HTTP, SSL on the one side, and CORBA [5], DCOM, Jini [1] on the other side, to cite only some of the most known ones).

However, these alone are not enough, since a society (of human beings, of agents) is more than just a sum of individuals carrying out their *individual tasks*: it also features a *collective behaviour*, aimed to pursue some *social tasks*, while guaranteeing that the proper *social rules* are respected. While agents' communication and interoperability is a matter of standards to *enable* communication, and are covered by the current development methodologies via middleware services, mastering interaction and embodying the collective behaviour so as to enforce the social rules is much a less established area. Yet, its role is fundamental in modern systems, and proper guidelines are needed so as to avoid that "spaghetti interaction" becomes the modern version of the well-known "spaghetti programming" issue of the Sixties. In short, we need a way to actually *rule* communication, which is what *coordination* is meant for.

0-7695-0798-9/00 $10.00 © 2000 IEEE

2 Coordination

The coordination dimension is conceptually orthogonal to computation: as computation languages allow the inner working algorithm of an agent to be expressed, coordination languages focus on the agent's observable behaviour. In the same way agent languages and architectures provide for abstractions and tools to design and build single agents, *coordination models, languages and architectures* provide for abstractions and tools to manage and rule interaction.

A *coordination model* is a conceptual framework to model the space of component (object, agent) interaction. So, it is the natural source of abstractions and tools to manage the *interaction dimension*. Defining a coordination model amounts to defining three major entities: *(i)* the *coordinables* - that is, the entities it is supposed to coordinate, *(ii)* the *coordination media* - that is, the media used to support inter-agent communication, and *(iii)* the *coordination rules* - that is, the laws that govern agent interaction.

For instance, in Linda [9], probably the most widely known coordination model, the coordinables are any entity able to adhere to its coordination language, made of the three basic primitives *in*, *rd*, *out*. The coordination medium is the *tuple space*, and the coordination rules follow from the intended effects of the above primitives, along with the pattern-matching mechanism for tuple selection: *out(t)* adds tuple *t* to the tuple space, while *rd(tpl)* and *in(tpl)* try to select from the tuple space a tuple *t* matching tuple template *tpl* (removing it from the tuple space in the latter case).

The choice of the coordination model has a strong impact on the application design (Section 3): in particular, *tuple-based* models seem well suited to the design of open, distributed applications because they inherently promote an information-driven design approach [3].

However, no coordination model or abstraction can actually help in the development of interactive [14] applications, like the Internet ones, unless supported by a suitable and reliable *coordination technology*, supplying the typical distributed programming technologies (monitoring, debugging, multiple views, etc.) but tailoring them to the interaction framework of the selected coordination model.

What is needed is a *coordination infrastructure* that defines a coordination architecture and provides design, deployment, maintenance and incremental development tools that be *tailored* to the model's metaphors, so that developers can choose at any time the system abstraction level that is the most suited to a specific development phase.

3 Design issues

An effective design approach for agent-based system is to start from the tasks to be achieved, delegating each task to the responsibility of an agent [4]. This view naturally decouples agents from each other, shifting focus onto agents' observable behaviour: agents' inner structure is left aside, letting designers free to adopt for each agent the most proper structure and implementation language.

The next step is to make agents interact so as to build an ensemble. In many contexts, interaction traditionally rhymes communication, and interaction histories are just the result of the random (and chaotic) interleaving of the observable agents' behaviour. No surprise, then, that interaction is perceived as a source of complexity in many programmers' experience. Actually, this is just the the superficial effect of focusing only on the tasks and the related agents, neglecting the true role of the interaction dimension: governing the social tasks & rules.

Instead, social rules can be a potential source of further intelligence (*the global intelligence*) which goes beyond the single agents', and represents the natural place where to embody the global system properties. Engineering the social aspects becomes then *at least as relevant* as engineering the single agents: interaction is no longer something to be "added on" an already-designed system, but a crucial design issue to be accounted for since the earliest design phases.

Social tasks are often implemented as a special agent, charged of managing the tasks that do not actually belong to any agent: however, this seems more to suggest a lack of abstractions, than a convincing design choice. Instead, focusing on the social aspects of interaction naturally suggests that the coordination medium might be a separate, stand-alone component, holding the global coordination rules.

Embedding explicitly-represented coordination rules in a coordination component leads to automatically achieve another fundamental property: the incremental refinement / specialisation of the social behaviour of agent societies. In fact, storing social tasks in their natural store where they conceptually belong, instead of spreading and embedding them among several agents, means that the social rules may be changed - in principle - without touching the single agents at all, by just updating the coordination laws, in the same way as any change to an individual task naturally leads to modifying only the delegated agent.

This is where infrastructures play a fundamental role: social infrastructures, meant to encapsulate global rules and policies, can be naturally implemented upon coordination infrastructures, providing multi-agent systems with the abstractions to embed the coordination rules.

4 LuCe Model and Architecture

In LuCe (Logic Tuple Centres), agents interact by exchanging *tuples* (in particular: logic tuples) through a multiplicity of communication abstractions, called *tuple centres*. These are basically Linda-like [9] tuple spaces, enhanced with the notion of *behaviour specification*.

A tuple space is a shared memory abstraction containing tuples (ordered collections of information chunks) which can be accessed by means of three basic operations: *out*, *in*, and *rd*. These operations respectively add, remove, and read a tuple to/from a tuple space. In particular, LuCe adopts a communication language based on first-order logic: so, a tuple is a Prolog ground fact, any unitary Prolog clause is an admissible tuple template, and unification is the tuple matching mechanism. Moreover, each tuple centre is identified by a unique name, which is a ground Prolog term.

In LuCe, agents need not care about tuple centre existence / creation (*coordination transparency*): a tuple centre is automatically created when first used. So, it can be thought as an ever-existing entity, with no need for primitives (like York Linda's `tsc`) for explicit creation.

From the agent's viewpoint, a tuple centre looks like a tuple space, since it is accessed through the same interface (`out`, `in`, `rd`, `inp`, `rdp`): the difference lays in the notion of *behaviour specification*, which defines how a tuple centre *reacts* to an incoming/outgoing communication event. Unlike a tuple space, the tuple centre's behaviour in response to communication events is not fixed once and for all, but can be defined according to the application needs.

The language adopted to express behaviour specifications is independent of the tuple centre notion; in LuCe, tuple centre behaviour is defined in terms of *reactions*, specified as first-order logic tuples called *specification tuples*. The resulting specification language, ReSpecT (Reaction Specification Tuples), is briefly recalled in the sidebar.

The chance to define tuple centre behaviour makes it possible to keep the agent's perception of the interaction space distinguished from the actual state of the coordination media, and to relate them according to the required coordination laws. For instance, the reaction

```
reaction( out(p(X)), (
  in_r(p(X)), rd_r(toggle), out_r(q(X)) )).
```

alters the standard semantics of the `out(p(a))` operation, which would just add `p(a)` to the tuple centre, redefining it so that, if the `toggle` tuple is present, `p(a)` is replaced by `q(a)` before `p(a)` can ever be perceived. In other words, according to the agents' perception, `p(a)` never appears in the tuple centre at all – `q(a)` does, instead.

Since they can change the expected effects of a communication operation to the agents' eyes, reactions can alter the standard cause/effect relationships of Linda primitives: for instance, if `toggle` is present, the above `out(p(a))` can no longer wake up a suspended `in(p(a))` operation. In the same way, an `in(p(X))` may be suspended even in presence of a potentially-matching tuple, if a reaction removes such a tuple before the agent can perceive it. As a further example, suppose that some agents are based on the assumption that a numbered token can be taken by reading a tuple such as `number(N)`. To ensure that the same number is never read twice, such a tuple may not actually exist: it may be synthesised by the tuple centre dynamically, as a response to the agent's `in(number(n))` operation:

```
reaction( in(number(N)), ( pre,
  rd_r(counter(N)), out_r(number(N)),
  Next is N+1, out_r(counter(Next)) )).
```

ReSpecT's Turing-equivalence ensures that any computable coordination law can be encapsulated into the coordination medium. Since agents interacting through the same tuple centre are subject to the same coordination laws, coordination laws are implemented *locally* to a tuple centre, but spread their effect *globally* throughout the system.

The Architectural Model. The LuCe architecture is based on the notion of *cell*. This is a collection of *interacting entities* hosted by a physical node of the distributed system, and defines a *local interaction space*. Each node of a LuCe sys-

---

ReSpecT: Language and Model

ReSpecT is the language adopted in LuCe to define tuple centre behaviour via specification tuples of the form `reaction(`*Op*`,`*R*`)`, which associate a communication event generated by operation *Op* to the *reaction R*.

Communication events. A communication event is anything that crosses the tuple centre's boundary. Since `out` is a one-way operation, just adding a tuple, it endorses one communication event only. Instead, `in`, `rd`, `inp`, and `rdp`, which are two-way operations, first providing a tuple template (*query phase*), then awaiting a matching tuple (*answer phase*), endorse two distinct communication events. By *pre phase* we refer to both the single event of `out` and the query phase of the above primitives, while *post phase* denotes the answer phase of the the above primitives only.

Reaction structure and semantics. Each reaction behaves as a transaction: so, it either succeeds, performing all its intended effects, or fails, yielding no effect at all. Structurally, a reaction is a sequence of *reaction goals*, which may access properties of the occurred event, perform simple term tests, and operate on tuples in the tuple centre (see [7]). In particular, `out_r`, `in_r`, `rd_r`, `no_r` operations work on the tuple space similarly to communication operations (`no_r` tests the absence of a given tuple), and can trigger further reactions in a chain.

Execution model. Reaction goals are executed sequentially, each with a transactional semantics: the reaction succeeds only if all its reaction goals succeed. For agents to perceive *only the final result* of the execution of the communication event *and* the set of all the triggered reactions, all the reactions triggered by a communication event are executed *before* serving any other communication event. This allows a new observable behaviour to be embodied in a tuple centre, transparently to agents.

tem hosts at least one cell, but multiple cells can be hosted by the same node. An interacting entity can be either an agent or a tuple centre.

A LuCe *space* consists of a collection of cells, possibly spread over the Internet, and is denoted by a globally unique identifier (by default, `LuCe Space` – see Figure 1). Within a given LuCe space, interaction takes place in a fully transparent way: that is, agents can access tuple centres *by name*, with no need to know anything of their actual location and existence. The information needed to handle transparency, such as the name and location of each cell, the name and location of each interacting entity, etc. constitutes the *environment* of the LuCe space, and is stored in an homonymous system tuple centre, which is handled by an ad-hoc system process, the *environment process*. Since the existence of an environment process characterises the existence of a LuCe space, the first cell willing to join a previously-unnamed LuCe space also causes the corresponding environment process to be created: such a first cell is called the *main cell* of that space. Further cells willing to join an already-existing LuCe space have to specify the host name and port number of the corresponding environment process when the new cell is started up. This is how LuCe conjugates network transparency at the coordination level with *network awareness* at the architectural level, which is often required for network control purposes.

5 The LuCe Technology

In LuCe, the Java technology is used for the system development, for the Web interface, and to face the heterogeneity of Web nodes. Prolog, instead, is used as the communication language, exploiting first-order logic to mediate among heterogeneous Web agents. In addition, a Java-based Prolog engine is used to build the LuCe top-level, and makes it possible to exploit the inferential capabilities of Prolog for the construction of intelligent agents.

A new LuCe space is created by starting a main cell, thus creating the respective environment, too. The environment host name/port, which are the global ID of the new space, are set according to the user input (Figure 1, top left). After the cell joins a LuCe space, its *console* appears (Figure 1, bottom left), providing a command line interface.

5.1 The LuCe support tools

The LuCe coordination infrastructure defines a set of support tools specifically tailored to the LuCe metaphors. Since a tuple centre is characterised at any time by the set T of its tuples, the set W of its pending queries, and the set S of its reaction specifications, LuCe *Inspectors* make it possible to view, edit and control tuple centres from the data, the pending query and the specification viewpoints.

The T Inspector. The T Inspector is the tuple tracer/editor (Figure 1, bottom right): a `tinspect(`*`Insp`*`,`*`TC`*`)` command at the cell console activates inspector *`Insp`* on tuple centre *`TC`*. As a tracer, it can capture all the state transitions of a tuple centre, and show the current state of the space T of tuples. As an editor, it allows the user to add, read or remove tuples by means of the standard LuCe communication primitives, showing the operation result, if any.

In order to make user operations indistinguishable from agent-triggered operations, users cannot add or delete tuples directly: they can only operate via the classical tuple space operation (*in*, *out*, *rd*, etc). This choice ensures that the associated reactions, if any, are properly triggered, as needed to make tracing useful. So, the tuple centre behaviour can be tested separately from agents.

The other controls are used to configure according to the desired user views. So, the `Freq` field allows the user to define how often (in terms of observable tuple centre transitions) the view should be updated. Moreover, since a too fine-grained trace may result confusing, due to the plethora of tracing messages, the `Pattern` field allows the user to specify a filter template: then, only unifying tuples are shown. Of course, the user is free to force an update of the tracing view at any time, by means of the *`Update`* button.

The W Inspector. The W Inspector (not shown) is the pending query tracer, and works like the T Inspector. By showing the pending query queue (the W set), it provides users with the communication viewpoint in a *control-oriented* fashion, unlike the *data-oriented* fashion of the T Inspector.

The S Inspector. The S Inspector is the specification editor. Unlike the T and W Inspectors, it has no *`Out`*, *`Rd`*, *`Rdp`*, *`In`*, *`Inp`* buttons, since its purpose is to let users write programs (reactions) in a file, edit them, and reload the new specifications when done. So, its buttons enable to *`Consult`*, *`Edit`*, *`Update`* and *`Save`* a specification (Figure 1).

5.2 LuCe Agents

Prolog Agents. Due to the built-in Prolog engine, writing Prolog agents in LuCe is straightforward: any standard Prolog program can perform tuple centre operations (`out, in, rd, inp, rdp`) according to a syntax like `TC ? out(`*`Tuple`*`)`, where `TC` is the tuple centre name.

Java Agents. Any LuCe/Java agent class is a subclass of the `LuCeAgent` class, written according to a very simple (applet-like) design pattern, based on the definition of two methods: `Init` and `mainLoop`. `Init` is where initialisations can be performed, while `mainLoop` expresses the agent body. This method is repeatedly executed until either it returns `false`, or the `Stop()` method is called.

A Java agent may be launched from the operating system shell, or invoked from the LuCe console via an

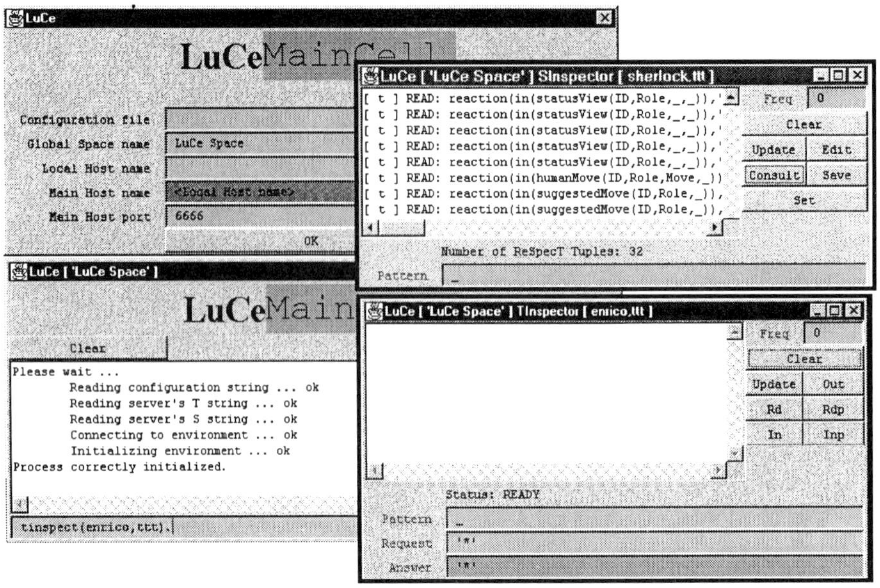

Figure 1. Starting (top) and using (bottom) a LuCe Main Cell, and some LuCe tools (right)

`agent(Name,Cmd)` statement. *Cmd* is a Prolog term whose functor is the Java name of the agent class: it may be either just the class name, or a structure such as `AgentClass(ArgList)`, in which case the `Parm(int n)` can be used to retrieve the *n*-th argument in `ArgList`. Communication operations are methods like

```
public void Out(mpStruct tuple, mpStruct tc);
```

the `Inp` and `Rdp` methods return a `boolean`. All methods use `mpStruct` objects to manipulate the Prolog structures in Java. The unified tuple can be retrieved by calling the public method `Tuple`, which returns an `mpStruct`.

The very simple agent below just performs an `out(p(0))` operation on tuple centre `tt`:

```
import Luce.Agent.*;
import microProlog.Term.*;
public class MyAgent extends LuceAgent {
  private mpStruct tc, tuple;
  public void Init() {
   tc = new mpStruct("tt");
   tuple = new mpStruct("p", new mpInt(0)); }
  public boolean mainLoop() {
   try { Out(tuple,tc); }
   catch(Exception e){ System.err.println(e); }
   return false; }
}
```

This agent is invoked as

```
agent(Name, 'Examples.LuCe.MyAgent').
```

Optionally, the agent might take the tuple centre name or the tuple from console arguments:

```
agent(Name, 'Examples.LuCe.MyAgent'(TC,Tuple)).
```

6 Development in LuCe

The LuCe infrastructure has a strong impact on the design of an agent-based application, since it enables *(i)* agent interaction to be designed in an information-driven fashion, *(ii)* agents to be designed independently from each other and agent interaction protocols to be designed separately from the agents, and *(iii)* charging tuple centres of "bridging the gap" between the different agent perceptions of the information space and the different interaction protocols.

So, once agents are assigned a task (see *(i)*), their interaction protocols can be defined according to simple information-oriented criteria – which information is available / needed and when, etc. Designing agent protocols means then to define how agents exchange tuples with tuple centres, in function of their current state: the agent fundamental activity is therefore to *get the information it needs* and behave accordingly: an imperative approach, based on issuing commands, would contradict the information-oriented methodology, and would make the agent and the protocol design less natural and unnecessarily complex.

To glue things together (*(iii)*), specification tuples must provide each agent with its own perception of the information space, and with the interaction protocol it expects: as a basic design principle, each specification should handle one single case, and should be simple enough to easily understand which interaction condition it is meant to capture.

The application development process sketched above shows that each agent can be designed independently of the other agents, and regardless of the specific information representation adopted in the tuple centre. This is the key feature of tuple centre coordination, as it supports incremental application development and testing: in fact, the designer can start implementing one single agent category, and use the LuCe inspectors to simulate the missing ones by operating on the tuple centres as the missing agents would.

This approach actually separates the agent implementation (a computation issue) from the design and test of the interaction protocols (a coordination issue). So, the check of the interaction protocols can be performed *a-priori*, before implementing agents at all.

7 Related Works and Conclusions

Coordination technology on the Web is a currently hot research topic [3], as shown by the recent work by Sun Microsystems and IBM, with the JavaSpaces [8] and the T Spaces [16] projects. In particular, Javaspaces clearly show how a coordination service can be embodied into a general-purpose network infrastructure, namely Jini [1]: however, no development tools specifically tailored to the coordination abstraction are provided. This is why we are currently involved in an affiliated project aimed at porting the LuCe technology on the Javaspaces/Jini platform.

Integrating logic-based and object-oriented technology for Web-based coordination is the starting point of LogiMOO [13], Linda Interactor [12], and Jinni [11], too. In particular, the Jinni model exploits a logic-based scripting language to glue Java objects and knowledge processing components together in networked applications, as well as a shared blackboard with Linda-style primitives as the communication and coordination support.

With respect to all the above approaches, LuCe provides a technology to effectively support the application development phase, by means of specialised tools based on the coordination model's metaphors. This feature is crucial for application maintenance and incremental development, which may be as critical as the design of the application itself.

The MARS project [2], developed independently of LuCe by a different research group in the context of mobile agent systems, also adopts reactive tuple spaces for mobile agent coordination, though the reaction specification language, which is Java-based, and the reaction model are different. Our research groups are currently joining the efforts to address some of the major open problems, such as the support for mobility, security, and network topology. The TuCSoN coordination model [10], joint-developed, is meant to supply a coherent conceptual framework and a single infrastructure where coordination is taken as the unifying paradigm accounting for authentication, authorisation, and support for intelligent agent exploration [6].

References

[1] K. Arnold, B. O'Sullivan, R. W. Scheifler, J. Waldo, and A. Wollrath. *The Jini Specification*. The Jini Technology Series. Addison-Wesley, 1999.

[2] G. Cabri, L. Leonardi, and F. Zambonelli. Reactive tuple spaces for mobile agent coordination. In *Proceedings of the 2nd Workshop on Mobile Agents*, volume 1477 of *LNCS*, pages 237–248. Springer-Verlag, September 1998.

[3] P. Ciancarini, A. Omicini, and F. Zambonelli. Coordination technologies for Internet agents. *Nordic Journal of Computing*, 6(3):215–240, Fall 1999.

[4] P. Ciancarini, A. Omicini, and F. Zambonelli. Multiagent system engineering: the coordination viewpoint. In N. R. Jennings and Y. Lespérance, editors, *Intelligent Agents VI — Agent Theories, Architectures, and Languages*, volume 1767 of *LNAI*, pages 250–259. Springer-Verlag, February 2000.

[5] CORBA home site. `http://www.omg.com/corba/` .

[6] M. Cremonini, A. Omicini, and F. Zambonelli. Multi-agent systems on the Internet: Extending the scope of coordination towards security and topology. In F. J. Garijo and M. Boman, editors, *Multi-Agent Systems Engineering – Proc. of the 9th European Workshop on Modelling Autonoumous Agents in a Multi-Agent World; (MAMAAW'99)*, volume 1647 of *LNAI*, pages 77–88. Springer-Verlag, June 30 - July 2 1999.

[7] E. Denti, A. Natali, and A. Omicini. On the expressive power of a language for programming coordination media. In *Proc. of the 1998 ACM Symposium on Applied Computing (SAC'98)*, pages 169–177. ACM, 1998. Track on Coordination Models, Languages and Applications.

[8] E. Freeman, S. Hupfer, and K. Arnold. *JavaSpaces: Principles, Patterns, and Practice*. The Jini Technology Series. Addison-Wesley, 1999.

[9] D. Gelernter. Generative communication in Linda. *ACM Transactions on Programming Languages and Systems*, 7(1):80–112, January 1985.

[10] A. Omicini and F. Zambonelli. Coordination for Internet application development. *Journal of Autonomous Agents and Multi-Agent Systems*, 2(3):251–269, September 1999. Special Issue: Coordination Mechanisms for Web Agents.

[11] P. Tarau. Jinni: a lightweight Java-based logic engine for Internet programming. In *Proc. of Post-JICSLP'98 Workshop and 1998 Compulog Net Area Meeting on Parallelism and Implementation Technology for (Constraint) Logic Programming Languages*. June, 15–19 1998. Invited talk.

[12] P. Tarau, V. Dahl, and K. De Bosschere. A Logic Programming infrastructure for remote execution, mobile code and agents. In *Proc. of the 6th IEEE Workshops on Enabling Technologies: Infrastructure for Collaborative Enterprises*, pages 106–112. IEEE Computer Society, June 1997.

[13] P. Tarau and K. De Bosschere. Virtual world brokerage with BinProlog and Netscape. In *Proocedings of the 1st Workshop on Logic Programming Tools for Internet Applications, JICSLP'96, Bonn (D)*, September 1996.

[14] P. Wegner. Why interaction is more powerful than computing. *Communications of the ACM*, 40(5):80–91, May 1997.

[15] M. J. Wooldridge and N. R. Jennings. Intelligent agents: Theory and practice. *The Knowledge Engineering Review*, 10(2):115–152, 1995.

[16] P. Wyckoff, S. W. McLaughry, T. J. Lehman, and D. A. Ford. T Spaces. *IBM Journal of Research and Development*, 37(3 - Java Techonology):454–474, 1998.

On the Design of a Mobile Agent Web for Supporting Virtual Enterprises

Ad Aerts, Nick Szirbik, Dieter Hammer, Jan Goossenaerts, Hans Wortmann
Eindhoven University of Technology, Postbus 513, 5600 MB Eindhoven, The Netherlands
{a.t.m.aerts ; d.k.hammer}@tue.nl, {n.b.szirbik ; j.c.wortmann ; j.b.m.goossenaerts}@tm.tue.nl

Abstract

In this paper we discuss the design of a mobile agent based infrastructure for monitoring and controlling activities in a Virtual Enterprise (VE). We define the concepts of the Virtual Enterprise and the Mobile Agent Web (MA-web).

1. Introduction

New organizational concepts pose new challenges to the ICT systems supporting them. In a Virtual Enterprise (see section 2) one of the challenges is to provide flexible support for the co-ordination and integration of the ICT systems of each of the participant enterprises without imposing excessive demands on the systems of these participants. In section 3, we discuss a design for the integration of the ICT support systems for a Virtual Enterprise (VE). The design is based on the mobile software agent paradigm [8] and is one of the results of an interdisciplinary research project, named ROVE (**R**easoning about **O**perations in **V**irtual **E**nterprises) at the Eindhoven University of Technology. We have started to develop a Concordia [1] platform-based prototype named PROVE (Prototype for ROVE [10]). The role of the prototype is to identify the problems, which appear in the Virtual Enterprising process, and to find the best architectural patterns for the flexible integration of ICT support systems for VE's. We do not discuss alternatives for the mobile software agent paradigm in this paper (see [8]). Section 4 concludes the paper with some open issues.

2. The Virtual Enterprise

The concept of the Virtual Enterprise is rather novel and there exist different views about it. We will first present two examples of Virtual Enterprising and then discuss the VE and the requirements it poses on its ICT support. The formation of the VE is not a topic of this paper. We assume it to be in place. In particular, we assume that the participants are willing to cooperate and share data.

2.1 Two examples of Virtual Enterprising

Consider the case of a commercial jet that needs replacement of a high-value part like an undercarriage, because the old one was damaged in a rough landing. International regulations prohibit the airline to repair this part of the plane by replacing only the severely damaged components and tinker with the slightly damaged ones. They ask for a full replacement of the landing gear. Because the airline companies usually do not keep spare undercarriages in stock, the airline has to order a new undercarriage in this situation. The problem is that 80% of the global commercial fleet consists of aircraft, which are no longer in production. Worse still, many of the companies who built the planes are not on the market any more.

However, the market of high-value replacement parts is very active. The manufacturing of such parts requires the collaboration of a number of companies, which join forces for this particular purpose. For an undercarriage, about a dozen companies are involved, which are typically located on different continents. Note that this case is characterised by a one-of-a-kind assemble-to-order style.

Consider now the case of a group of specialized enterprises that sells office furniture, such as desks, filing cabinets, computers, and other accessories, and has started a collaboration to offer complete office solutions via the Internet. Through a Web-portal, complete workplaces for one or several office workers are offered, with a choice of popular colours and styles. Customers, who want to expand an existing branch office or open a new one, can order any number of workplaces at a time. The order is split at the Web portal into sub-orders for the participant companies, depending on such factors as product and availability of resources. The products are assembled and sent to a distribution centre near to the customer, where the order is collected for delivery. This case is batch oriented.

0-7695-0798-9/00 $10.00 © 2000 IEEE

2.2. A definition of the Virtual Enterprise

From the examples above we see that a VE caters to markets that the individual participants by themselves cannot access: they need to collaborate. Moreover, the VE is not their main business, but just a collateral activity that helps them to fill the gaps in the usage of their resources, to participate actively in new, global markets, and to virtually extend their resource types. This is due to the fact that opportunities leading to Virtual Enterprising are hard to forecast. For example, it is impossible to forecast when a landing gear will break and need replacement. The participants thus will commit only a small fraction of their resources to the VE. Virtual Enterprising requires a lot of flexibility and therefore is based on a global agreement, not on detailed contracts. To increase the flexibility of the VE and to avoid orders from being rejected, because the required resources aren't available at the right time, some redundancy of resources should exist and more than one company with a given production capability should participate in the VE.

Our definition of a Virtual Enterprise is related to the concept of *virtual capability* [9]:

"A group of enterprises, which has the ***capability*** *of realising in a collaborative manner, items or services from a limited portfolio of products, is a Virtual Enterprise."*

The composition of the group is dynamic. Enterprises may join or leave the group. The definition above does not capture the state of a given VE at a certain moment in time. We introduce a new concept for that:

"A group of enterprises, members of a bigger Virtual Enterprise, which is currently involved in the execution of an order for a customer, is a Cluster."

Many Clusters can be simultaneously active in a Virtual Enterprise. The selection of the members of a Cluster depends on how their resources can be used, in terms of available time-slots, stocks, past performance, prices, and possibly customer preference.

For the ICT support of collaborative processes, we need a structured approach to identify the requirements, the architecture, and the problems of Virtual Enterprising.

2.3 Requirements for ICT support for a VE

The business process in a VE starts with an order by a customer for a composite product, be it a landing gear or the complete furnishing of an office. The order has to be decomposed into suborders, which are dispatched to the participants in the VE, which may be regarded as subcontractors for a specific component. The decomposition will follow the BOM (Bill of Material) of the product ordered by the customer, until a component is reached that can be produced by a single enterprise. In a VE, one wants to monitor the process of the decomposition of the order of a particular customer and the production of the product ordered [10]. In addition, one wants to provide *decision support* for the management of problems, originating for example from the fact that one enterprise cannot meet its delivery date, and has to be replaced by another one in the VE. The resolution of such problems requires co-operation among the participants, e.g., to reach an agreement about who will pay for possible additional costs incurred by a tardy delivery [11, 12].

In this project, we have chosen to use the mobile agent paradigm to implement the support for the monitoring and control of the activities of the enterprises. Mobile agents can migrate from one computer to another and execute their code on different locations, by their own "will". Because this implies a high degree of portability, mobile agents are usually coded in Java [5]. To allow the mobile agents to run on a computer, we need specialised software, which in literature is called "mobile agent server", "mobile agent dock" or "mobile agent platform". There are now many mobile agent development systems, which provide the functionality of the dock and a basic structure for the agent, such as IBM's Aglets [3] and the Mitsubishi Concordia Mobile Agent Framework [1], which we use in this project. The development and deployment of agent-based VE integration includes the installation of *docks at all enterprises involved*. The integration task then amounts to making the agents able to identify and *invoke* local functionality. The Mitsubishi Concordia Mobile Agent Framework has specialized skeleton modules (Service Bridges) to help making the interfaces between the agents and the local software. The installation of such a service bridge is fairly simple and also the coupling to, e.g. a database, is based on a broadly accepted standard such as JDBC.

In our project, we have assumed that the members of the VE are all linked to the Internet, and have mobile agent docks installed on their computers. We call such a group of enterprises an *MA-web* (Mobile Agent Web).

2.4 Design outline

Figure 1 shows an object diagram, depicting the information needed to support the deployment of agents to provide monitoring and control at a global level (i.e. the level above the enterprises). In a mobile agent system, agents need a Trader to tell them which resources (machines, stock, or operators) can be found in the system and their availability. Resources may be

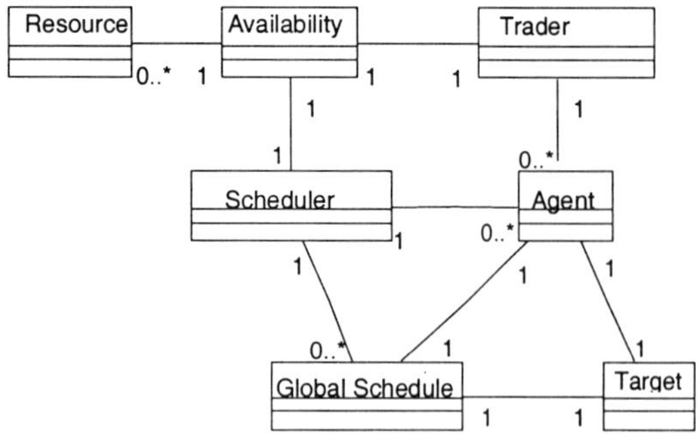

Figure 1. Co-ordination in the VE.

free for specific periods of time (see Figure 2). When an agent wants to use a resource, it is reserved for that agent and becomes unavailable for other agents. When the enterprise in control of the resource agrees to participate in the execution of an order, the resource becomes committed and is no longer available.

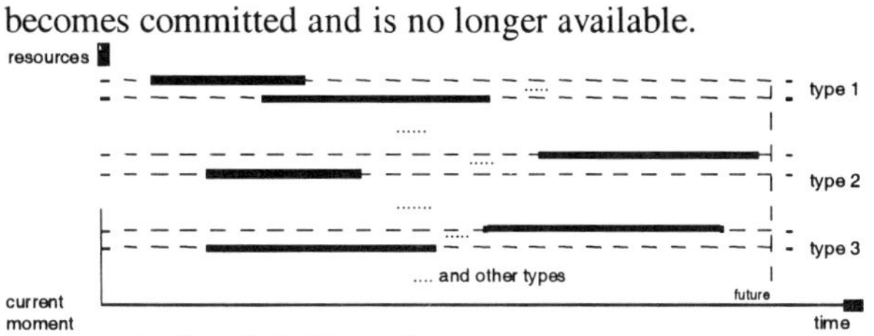

Figure 2. Availability of resources.

In addition to a Trader, a Scheduler is needed at a global level to support the realisation of the Target. The Target object contains the information about the product that has been ordered: its composition (BOM) and the routing needed to manufacture it. An agent is put in charge of the target and submits the routing data to the Scheduler, which combines it with the availability data to produce a (modification to the) Global Schedule. The global schedule is returned to the agent in charge of the target. This agent decomposes the order into components to be manufactured, creates an agent to monitor the production of each component, and uses the schedule to send these agents to the enterprises in control of the resources reserved to manufacture the particular component. It co-ordinates the activities of these agents, communicating with them to resolve any problem that may arise, until the agents return with their component and the final product is assembled. This process repeats itself until a sub-component is produced as a whole by a single enterprise (see also [10]).

3. Design Decisions

We can define two levels of decisions: business and architecture related decisions, respectively. The business decisions concern the structure the VE business process. The VE needs take commonly agreed decisions about how co-operation and overall performance (especially in terms of customer satisfaction) can be improved. The architectural decisions are related to the ICT support development for a VE. They are, however, strongly based on the business decisions that determine the design variables of a software system. The architecture decisions are taken by the software and system architects in co-operation with the stakeholders.

3.1 Business decisions

Decision B1: Adopt a *mixed initiative interaction* system based on human and software agents. This decision is the basic idea in ROVE. It entails the following consequences:

- Software agents are empowered to take supply chain control decisions.
- The human-to-human interaction, which underlies current supply-chain control systems, is replaced by an agent-mediated scheme in which some of the decisions are initiated by humans and some by the software agents.

The first consequence implies that humans will trust the decisions taken by the agents. To ensure this, it is absolutely necessary that the human users understand how the agents work. This puts requirements on the subsequent architectural decisions (see, e.g., A10).

In our opinion, the main challenge of the ROVE project is to see how agents can develop more initiative and take some of the routine decision making burden in the VE control system from the human actors.

Decision B2: For agent-oriented IT support, the parties in a VE rely on a *common software provider*. This SW provider plays a role similar to that of an Internet provider or a provider of complex software who provide a reliable and trustworthy product. In this case, the agents (dedicated to perform uniform tasks over a large area) are developed by a single provider, which we call the SACP (software agent common provider). Such a specialized firm can be provider for more than one VE. The SACP could be an independent party, which enjoys a high level of trust and should have the following responsibilities:

- Develop the required agents and necessary support services and keep record of the parties who are using them (the VE).
- Help the parties to install the software and teach users how to use it.
- Maintain and upgrade the system.

- Help the users with expertise to enact the service bridges, in order to make local data available to the agents.

Decision B3: The security of the agent system is entrusted to a *(trusted) third party* that provides monitoring and detection of hostile activities. Because of the dynamic composition of the VE and its distributed nature, it is best to contract secure communication channels as a service, e.g. in the form of a Virtual Private Network, from a trusted, specialized provider. This approach is also used for Extranets.

Decision B4: *Centralization* of common services. In the ROVE framework, a central site has, amongst other things, the following functions:

- Maintain a central repository of data about the available resources in the VE, updated as often as possible.
- Calculate Global Schedules for orders.

The rationale behind this decision is that one consistent body of global information makes it simpler to generate optimal global schedules, and to avoid the resource conflicts, inconsistencies and inefficiencies implied by distributed alternatives. It furthermore relieves the participant enterprises from the hard task of developing and maintaining a distributed version of these services themselves, and lowers the threshold for participation in the VE.

Decision B5: Enact a Web portal for the VE for the interaction with the customers. This portal exposes the portfolio of the VE and permits customers to issue orders. The roles of SACP, of trusted third party, and of maintaining a central site and a Web portal may be attributed to a single company.

Central solutions always have the risks of congestion (because the central services create bottlenecks) and of central system breakdown. We envisage about hundreds to thousands of agents to be active at any time. Since the agents invoke the central services only in certain, rare situations, we regard the probability to reach a state of real congestion as rather low. Also, the system is not subject to real-time constraints. Since the agents rely on an asynchronous interaction mechanism, and can wait a while for the Trader to respond, a small degree of congestion can be tolerated.

The asynchronous nature of the system also helps to avoid problems if the central site needs to recover in case of hardware or software failures.

3.2 Architecture related decisions

Decision A1: *Central* Repository for Resource Availability Data. This decision can be viewed as a natural consequence of Business Decision B4. The rationale is that the overall functionality of the system is simplified. It offers the possibility to have *global knowledge* about the status of the "controlled" system. A central repository allows agents to access necessary data (via the Trader) immediately. In addition, Global Scheduling can take place using local data, without the need to collect every time the necessary information. Also, when the Web portal has access to the global data, it can provide quick order confirmation including information about, e.g., delivery dates. If the resources in the VE are almost fully committed, it is very easy to refuse orders without keeping the customer waiting.

Because it always takes a finite amount of time to reflect changes of the local resource availability in the repository, the latter may not always reflect the latest state of the VE (the update mechanism is discussed in the context of decision A4). This is not a real issue, because resources must be *committed* locally before usage. When an agent finds the information kept in the central repository to be outdated or inconsistent with the local reality, (because the local scheduler has assigned the resource to a local production process) an exception is raised. The agent can invoke the Trader to find a new available resource of similar type and time-slot, or it can ask for a calculation of a new Global Schedule.

The alternative to centralization is to keep the availability data local (i.e. in the enterprises). In this case, the scenario of using the agents is quite different. Each time a customer issues an order, the portal deploys agents to all sites, where they search and select the best offers. It is still possible to make a global schedule, but only after the agents have collected the data. In architectures without a central repository, the main activity of the agent will be *searching*. For instance, when an agent needs a new resource it has to send agents throughout the entire VE to find one. Also in case of *delay management*, in order to obtain the value of the penalty to be paid to the customer, a Global Schedule has to be calculated, which implies collecting all data again. Also the optimization of the Global Schedules for different products is very difficult, because this requires the entire Availability Gantt chart to be constructed. Another consequence is that the agents need more functionality (for searching, navigating, co-ordination, etc) in order to compensate the lack of a central Trader.

Since the Central Repository is only a (redundant) copy of the local data, this data can easily be reconstructed after a failure.

Decision A2: *Centralized* Global Scheduling. One of the reasons why Virtual Enterprising exists is better customer satisfaction, especially in terms of fast order execution, which is supported by a central scheduler that uses global knowledge about the available resources to produce optimal schedules with, e.g., minimal lead-times.

The way the schedules are constructed depends on architecture decision A1. Without a central repository, the schedules will have to be calculated by the agents after they have collected all necessary information about resource availability. Schedules may now be produced concurrently at different sites for different orders, based on the same availability data. Independent construction of schedules can lead to the allocation of the same resources to different targets. It is quite difficult to see how these conflicts can be avoided or how conflict resolution can be done.

A Central Repository for Availability data, Global Scheduling capabilities and a Trader represent the minimal centralized infrastructure, leaving unaltered the inherently distributed nature of the system.

Decision A3: *Serial* calculation of schedules. Global Schedules can be calculated at the central site in parallel or serially. The choice depends on the scheduling load. The simplest variant is to calculate the schedules serially. Since the number of sites, of tasks per product and of available resources is expected to be low, it should be possible to produce the schedules within a sufficiently short time. To support parallel scheduling, a concurrency control mechanism must be implemented. Also this should not present any problems, because the schedule generation is taking place at a single site based on a single set of data.

Decision A4: Use *Polling* for data collection. There are two basic approaches for collecting the data for the central repository: polling and publisher/subscriber. In a polling approach, the central site has a list of all sites, and it asks them, via messages or by sending agents, whether any changes in the availability of the local resources have occurred within the production horizon of the VE. This approach has the disadvantage of complicating the functionality of the central site. It also increases the communication volume between the local sites and the central one, and thus the possibility of congestion. A new updating service is needed.

In a publisher/subscriber approach, the local sites have to send the information about relevant changes to the central site. This approach complicates the functionality of the local service bridges. These service bridges are pieces of software, which have to be developed by local programmers and it is better to keep them as simple as possible. The service bridges are basically only an interface between docked agents and local data repositories or humans. Furthermore, if all sites send the information at the same time, also in this case congestion can occur. In view of the maintainability of the system, and the ease of installation and use we have chosen the polling approach.

Decision A5: Use *Roaming Agents* implementation of the polling approach. We have chosen for the option to let the central site send agents to gather the information. It is possible to use only one agent for this task, when the number of sites is not very high. If changes have occurred, the agent can send a message to the central site, or it can reduce the communication load by storing the data in his own data repository and uploading the information when it visits the central site. If the number of sites is high, the VE can be partitioned in areas, each one with its own roaming agent. In the event that a site is down, an agent who can wait, until the communication channel is operational again, is preferable. Roaming agents have been proven an efficient mechanism for collecting data in the context of the World Wide Web [4], where they are known as spiders or crawlers.

Decision A6: *Message* Based Communication between agents. In the Nucleus model [5], the agents have been able to communicate only through the dock. When two agents want to communicate, they have to move to the same dock. In most systems, including Concordia, Grasshopper, Odyssey, Voyager and BOND [3], agents have a unique identity and can communicate via messages between themselves. Because Concordia is our target implementation tool, and the architecture must be general enough for other implementations, direct messaging between agents is used.

Also, it is logical to use message-based communication for co-ordination tasks. The agents, who participate, are docked at various sites, tracking the production of the parts they are responsible for. There is no need for them to move to another location just to communicate with another agent.

Decision A7: Use a pull model for the **migration** of the agents. There are three possible models [6] for mobile agent migration in a distributed environment:

Pull: the agents are sent from buyers (assemblers) to suppliers to look for opportunities.

Push: the agents are sent from suppliers to buyers with offers.

Broker: both buyers and suppliers are sending agents to a virtual marketplace, where agents can participate in auctions and exchange information in various ways.

According to [6] the broker model is best suited for e-commerce applications and not for VE support. Since a VE is a customer (buyer) driven environment, the best model seems to be the pull model. Also the monitoring task of the agents implies a pull model.

Decision A8: Limit the *interaction* between agents to pair wise interaction. The rationale behind this decision is simplicity. An alternative is teamwork interaction, but this is extremely difficult to model. Auction based schemes are using broadcast interaction, but there is, at present, no need for this in PROVE.

Decision A9: Use *BDI* as Agent Behavioral Model. The BDI (Beliefs - knowledge, Desires - goals, Intentions - agenda) model is the most popular model in the agent researcher community. In our context, it has the advantage that the results of the ROVE project can be compared with other similar approaches.

The agent internal structure has to be developed keeping in mind the process they have to support [7]. In our case, timely delivery of the product is a business goal. This is reflected in the agent by designing it around the delay management process [12].

Decision A10: *Rule-Based Systems* for the implementation of Agent Behavior. This design decision de-couples the agent behavior from its implementation. When the behavior is coded directly in a procedural way (as methods), any modification to the behavior of the agents implies code re-writing. Using a rule interpreter [2], we have the possibility to specify the behavior at a level that is understandable by the human VE controllers. These users then are more likely to trust the agents to take (low level) decisions. The main advantage of rules is that they are much easier to read than code and have clear semantics even for non-programmers. Furthermore, we only have to modify the rule base of the agents to change the application we want to support. The disadvantage of this approach is that is quite difficult to see if a specific rule base is correct or not. In a later stage of the project a proof mechanism will be developed for this purpose.

4. Conclusions and future work

In this paper we have presented an approach to the design of ITC support systems for VE's, which have as principal requirement a minimal impact on the local systems in terms of additional work load and software development effort. We have argued that architectures based on mobile agents are well suited for this task. The agents provide support for the dispatching, monitoring, tracking and negotiation processes. We have given strong arguments that some centralisation of data and services for the agents will simplify and improve the processes and the system structure. We have identified several of these: a software agent common provider, a trusted third party to provide security, and a central site to provide support for trading and scheduling.

Our future work has two horizons. The short-term work will comprise mixed initiative experiments with one-of-a-kind ordering style. In these experiments the number of simultaneous targets will be kept low. After that, we will have to deal with batch ordering and conflicting resource allocation for multiple targets.

5. References

[1] Mitsubishi Concordia Mobile Agent Framework, http://www.concordia.mea.com/concordia/

[2] "The Java Expert System Shell", http://herzberg.ca.sandia.gov/jess/

[3] "Agent Construction Tools", http://agentbuilder.com/AgentTools

[4] Bowman, C. M. et al. *The Harvest Information Discovery and Access System.* Second International World-Wide Web Conference, Chicago, 1994.

[5] Dalmeijer M., Rietjens E., Soede M., Hammer D.K., Aerts A.T.M., (1998*), MAF: A Java-Based Implementation of a Mobile Agent Architecture* 1st IEEE International Symposium on Object-oriented Real-time distributed Computing (ISORC), April 1998, Kyoto, Japan.

[6] Dasgupta, P., Narasimhan, N., Moser, L.E., Melliar-Smith, P.M., (1999), "Mobile Agents for Networked Electronic Trading", in *IEEE Transactions on Knowledge and Data Engineering*, vol. 11, no. 4, pp.509-525.

[7] Goossenaerts, J.B.M., Aerts, A.T.M., Hammer, D.K., (1998), "Merging a Knowledge Systematisation Framework with a Mobile Agent Architecture", in *Information Infrastructures for Manufacturing II*, (Mills & Kimura, eds.), Kluwer, The Netherlands.

[8] Hammer D.K., Aerts A.T.M., Dalmeijer M., (1998), *Mobile Agents Architectures: What are the design Issues?* International Conference on Engineering of Computer Based Systems (ECBS), Jerusalem, Israel, March 1998.

[9] Kornelius, L., (1999), "Inter-Organisational Infrastructures for Competitive Advantage: Strategic Alignement in Virtual Corporations", *PhD Thesis, Faculteit Technologie Management*, Eindhoven University of Technology, The Netherlands.

[10] Szirbik, N.B., Hammer, D.K., Goossenaerts, J.B.M., Aerts, A.T.M., (1999), "Mobile Agent Support for Tracking Products in Virtual Enterprises", in *The working papers of the Workshop on Agent-Based Decision-Support for Managing the Internet Enabled Supply-Chain*, pp.93-100, AGENTS'99 Conference, Seattle.

[11] Szirbik, N., Wortmann, H., Hegge, H., Goossenaerts, J., (1999), "Improving manufacturing cooperation in a virtual enterprise by tracker mobile agents", in *Proceedings of EFTA'99*, pp.1451-8, Barcelona, IEEE Press.

[12] Szirbik, N.B., Wortmann, J.C., Hammer, D.K., Goossenaerts, J.B.M., Aerts, A.T.M., "Mediating Negotiations in a Virtual Enterprise via Mobile Agents", AIWoRC'2000: Mobile Technologies and Virtual Enterprises", Buffalo, April 2000.

Applications of XML and Customizable Components in Building Virtual Places on the Web

Lukasz Beca
Syracuse University
111 College Place
Syracuse, New York 13244
beca@npac.syr.edu

Abstract

The demand for the systems that facilitate human interactions over the World Wide Web is growing. Shared Place is a technology for building collaboration environments tightly integrated with the Web and customized for specific user needs. XML-based Shared Place Definition Language, designed to describe collaboration functionality of the configurable components, can be merged with ordinary Web page content to create specifications of virtual places. This paper discusses basic concepts of the Shared Place technology, the model developed to describe functionality of virtual places, Shared Place documents and the architecture of the system. The discussion is illustrated with the examples of the applications.

Keywords

Collaboration, XML, virtual places, software components

1. Introduction

In recent years, the demand for Web-based collaboration environments is growing. Currently, on-line presentations, distance learning, and customer support are beginning to offer *interactive* applications on the Web. However, many aspects of personal interactions in this environment are awkward and primitive - the most often used collaboration tool is still a chat and sets of static HTML pages. In spite of the enormous potential for building media rich, interactive experiences on the Web, the frameworks that would enable such solution are not widely used. One of the reasons is that HTML was not designed and is not well suited for describing collaboration functionality. It is sufficient for description of the appearance of a Web page but does not address such issues as, for instance, synchronization policy of collaborative applications.

Fortunately, the progress in Web technologies may change this in near future. Important standards such as XML [16] emerged, which enable creating collaboration-oriented languages. Also, of great importance are advances in browser technology. Browser products - Internet Explorer 5.0 and Mozilla currently support XML, Document Object Model (DOM) [15], and other features such as dynamic changes in the structure of the Web page content. Development of component architectures for major programming languages: ActiveX [4] for C++ and Java Beans [13] for Java is another factor. Those advances together create platform for new developments in area of collaboration on the Web.

To explore those opportunities, we launched new research program called Shared Place on the Web. The main assumption we make is that collaboration functionality should be treated as any other Web page content. In this way the Web content can be combined with the collaboration components in order to create new functionality. We believe this approach will enable implementation of efficient Web-based *shippable places* described in [11] as the next generation of the Web content - the places that can be shipped over the Internet. In our work on Shared Place we build on the experience gained during development of the TANGO Interactive framework [1] and component-based solutions employed in this system for creating collaborative applications [2]. Currently, TANGO Interactive Virtual Classroom [14] is actively used by Syracuse University to deliver online courses.

2. Shared Place overview

A *place* consists of two important components: a shared space and a social context. Multiple aspects of place metaphor application in development of collaboration systems are described in [12]. We are convinced that both social and spatial aspects are important for successful collaboration and our solution tries to support both factors equally. Shared Place does not offer collaboration functionality *per se,* rather it supports construction of virtual places on the Web where people can interact and work together. Users of such virtual places can use content and tools that are present at the place for collaborative work. They can bring their own content and share it with others. They can possibly create new content and take it with them to another virtual place or store it in a personal repository for off-line

0-7695-0798-9/00 $10.00 © 2000 IEEE

work. From the user's point of view, the Shared Place application is an ordinary Web page with added collaboration functionality. Let's imagine a place for stock traders. Such place would contain relevant information in HTML or XML form: stock prices, news updates, and latest data about financial state of various companies. It would also contain collaboration tools such as audio conferencing tools for communication, shared spreadsheets for financial calculations, shared whiteboards for analyzing economic trends, and voting tools for making buy/sell decisions. Such a place could be an efficient work environment and could be created by merging HTML content with collaboration components. Countless other places can be imagined, such as the place for discussing results of experiments for scientists or a place for distance learning.

Shared Place offers significant advantages to software developers and Web site builders. It provides mechanisms that allow separation of software components development from process of building virtual places. Software developers can concentrate on creating various types of collaboration tools using Shared Place API. Whereas content developers can use available collaboration components, Web resources, and Shared Place Definition Language (SPDL) to develop virtual places on the Web. Content developers do not have to deal with complexities of the collaboration component implementation. Hence, people without programming background can create interactive virtual places according to their needs.

3. Model

Collaborative applications must usually satisfy a large set of requirements. It would be convenient to have a model that allows specification of those requirements in abstract terms relevant to the collaboration functionality. Our model is a tool for making the transition from the domain of high-level software requirements to more structured specification of the virtual place. The model is designed in such a way that the description of the application in terms of model entities can be easily transformed to an SPDL document, which in turn is used by the Shared Place framework to create a virtual place with desired functionality. The model is a result of analysis of needs of various collaboration applications (such as distance learning and virtual meeting tools) and is influenced by especially successful MUD and MOO approaches [6].

3.1. Model entities

Shared Place model distinguishes several basic entities:

A **Place** corresponds to a physical place in the real world. It provides boundaries where the intended interactions occur. Places can contain Artifacts, Visitors, Agents, Tools, and Gates. Visitors present at the Place can interact directly with Agents, Tools, and Gates gathered here. Visitors interact indirectly (by using Tools) with Artifacts and other Visitors. Places are persistent; its content is preserved when all Visitors leave. They can also provide Gates to other Places. In this way the groups of interconnected Places can be defined. Figure 1 illustrates the Place with Place Artifacts, Visitors, a Gate, and a Tool used by Visitors to work on the Artifact.

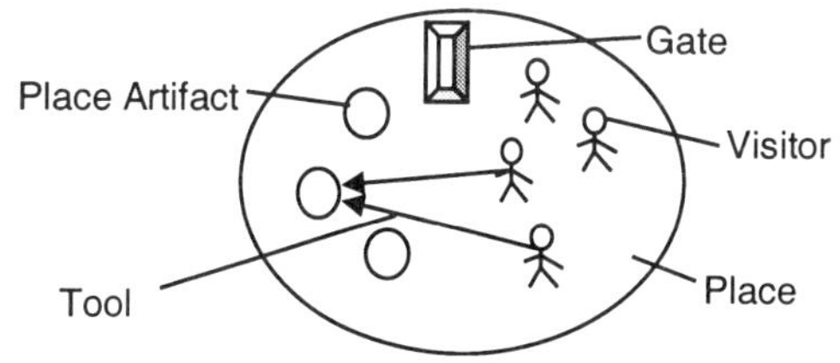

Figure 1. Model entities

A Place possesses a number of customizable properties. First, it is possible to specify Visitors that are allowed to enter the Place and assign them to Visitor groups. The Place also contains description of the place *policy* specified as a set of behavior rules. Policies impose various restrictions on the model entities depending on the desired functionality (see [8] for detailed discussion of policies in collaborative applications). For example, a description of the Place can include allowed and disallowed types of Artifacts and Tools. A description of a Tool can specify the level of control that a Visitor can exercise over the Tool, the level of synchronization that the specific Tool provides, mechanism used for initial state distribution, user interface presented to Visitors, and type of floor control transfer. Rules for Artifacts can describe Visitor's rights to create, store, copy, or delete Artifacts.

A **Visitor** represents the user in a Place and is similar in some aspects to the concept of an avatar in Multi-User Virtual Environments (MUVE) [9]. All actions that a user executes on the content of the Place are performed by the Visitor. Visitors can enter and leave the Place using Gates. The Visitor can interact with Place Artifacts using Tools and carry their own Personal Artifacts. Visitors can interact with Agents and communicate with each other using Tools. One user can have possibly several Visitors present in different Places at the same time. Usually, each Visitor has some role assigned in the Place. A role is used to determine how other Shared Place entities react to the Visitor actions. The Visitor cannot assume several roles in the same Place.

A **Tool** provides means of interaction between Artifacts and Visitors, as well as between Visitors. Whenever the Visitor wants to change state of the Artifact, the Visitor must use a Tool. Tools can be used to perform various tasks such as: providing awareness information, artifact management, communication, collaborative work, or modification of artifacts. Some Places need Tools that implement all these tasks, others will manage to provide required functionality with a subset. Tools may behave in different way depending on the type and mode of the Artifact they operate on, and the role of the Visitor that uses them. Tools can present different interfaces to the Visitors with different roles. Their behavior is defined by the place policy rules. They can be associated with a given Place or brought to a Place by a Visitor.

An **Artifact** represents content of an arbitrary type that can be created and accessed by a Visitor using Tools. It is essentially a data container such as a Web page, a document, an image, a stream of data, an entry point to information stored in database, or a set of links to other Artifacts. Artifacts can be moved from one Place to another by Visitors. However, some Places may put limitations on types of imported and exported Artifacts.

An Artifact can exist in one of two basic modes - as a Personal or a Place Artifact. A Personal Artifact belongs to a Visitor. A Visitor can possess arbitrary number of Personal Artifacts. Personal Artifacts are Place independent and can be carried from one Place to another. Place Artifacts are part of the Place content. They can be visible to the Visitors present at the Place if appropriate Tool for managing Artifacts is provided. The Visitors can change the mode of an Artifact by moving it from the Personal pool to the Place space or from the Place space to the Personal pool if appropriate Tools are present.

Artifacts have a number of properties such as type, expiration date, author information, date of modification, and pointer to a Tool that can be used to access the content. The Tool indicated by the information associated with an Artifact is activated when the Place does not have a specific Tool assigned to this type of the Artifact.

An **Agent** may perform actions on Place Artifacts on behalf of the Visitor while he or she is not present in the Place. Those might be administration tasks - removal of the expired Artifacts, or update of the time-sensitive content of the Artifact. Agents can also act without any authorization of a specific Visitor. Moreover, Agents may have social tasks to perform such as greeting Visitors, or offering instructions about use of certain Tools.

A **Gate** is an entity that enables Visitors to move from one Place to another. It is similar to HTML hypertext link but a Gate can also perform more complicated tasks such as authentication or providing information about the Place that the Visitor is about to enter.

3.2. User's view of the Place

A user perceives a place through a *view*. The view can be very different, depending on the purpose and the functionality of the place. The same entities of the model can be presented to the user in different manner in different places. Another factor that influences the view of the place is the role assigned to the user in the place. A user having the role of an administrator has access to more functionality than a user accessing the place as an ordinary customer. The view may also depend on the used device. For example, a view presented on a palmtop should be simpler than the view presented on a desktop machine.

A view is composed of Tools, Gates, Agents and HTML content. Information about Artifacts and other Visitors present at the place is not shown directly in the place view but it can be displayed by dedicated Tools. For example, a Tool can display a list of Personal or Place Artifacts or show Visitors as icons. The user may see all or certain subset of the place entities. If the designer of the place decides that it should be used only for synchronous communication, Artifacts and Agents may not be necessary.

3.3. Example of place description

In this section we describe a fairly complex collaboration system, a customer support place, using concepts introduced by the Shared Place model. We begin with a view seen by a support person. Such a person enters the place as a Visitor with 'Support' role assigned. Necessary Tools for communication with customers include a chat Tool or an audio Tool and a demonstration area. The chat or the audio Tool (whichever is available in the place) has the ability to create logs of conversations in the form of Place text or audio Artifacts. The demonstration area has the ability to retrieve Place Artifacts with the examples of the offered products and provides whiteboard functionality.

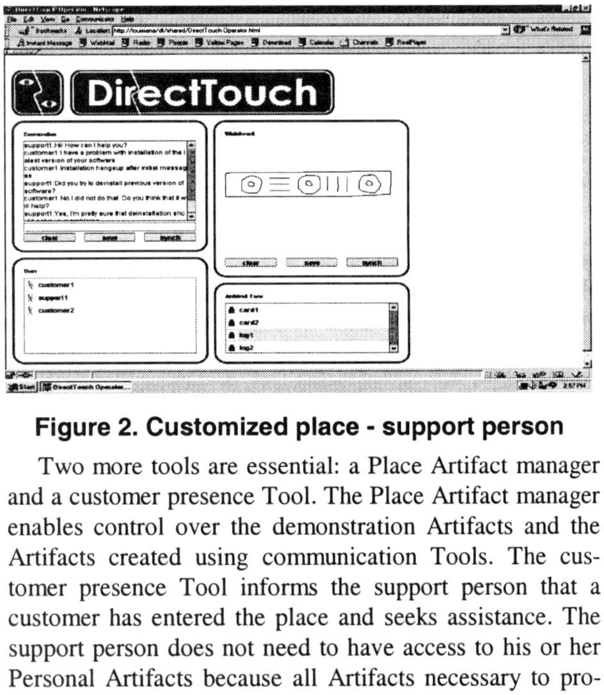

Figure 2. Customized place - support person

Two more tools are essential: a Place Artifact manager and a customer presence Tool. The Place Artifact manager enables control over the demonstration Artifacts and the Artifacts created using communication Tools. The customer presence Tool informs the support person that a customer has entered the place and seeks assistance. The support person does not need to have access to his or her Personal Artifacts because all Artifacts necessary to provide the service are available as the Place Artifacts. No Agents or Gates are necessary for the support person.

A customer enters the place as a Visitor with 'Customer' role assigned. The customer has access to the same communication tools as the support person; they are necessary for asking questions and receiving responses, but their functionality is slightly different. They enable archiving of interaction results in the form of Personal Artifacts that the customer will be able to store and consult later. The demonstration area should offer similar functionality. As a result, a Personal Artifact manager is needed to control created Artifacts. The customer support place can also have a Gate to another place where customers can gather and exchange experiences with other customers who bought the same product. An Agent may greet entering customers and offer some forms of assistance. Finally, the place view is complemented with the context content: HTML with company specific widgets or ads of the latest products.

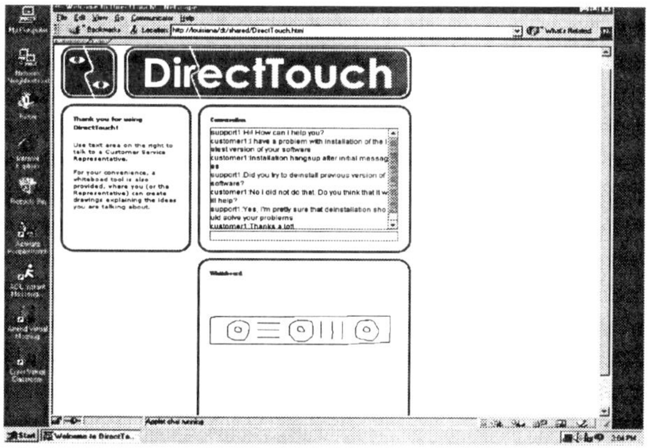

Figure 3. Customized place - customer

Figures 2 and 3 demonstrate the view of the customer support place as seen by the support person and the customer respectively. The screenshots show the prototype implementation of DirectTouch - the customer support system developed by WebWisdom.com using the Shared Place framework. The functionality of the customer's interface presented in Figure 3 is not as rich as described in the example above but it is sufficient for basic communication. It is important to notice that the support person has access to more place resources than the customer does. More Tools are available; apart from a chat and a whiteboard, a list of Place Artifacts and a list of present Visitors are provided. Moreover, the chat and the whiteboard Tools operated by the support person have additional controls that allow saving chat and whiteboard content in form of Place Artifacts. Other controls are used for erasing and synchronizing Tool content. In this prototype, integration of the HTML content with collaboration components allowed to create customized appearance of the place.

4. Shared Place documents

Shared Place documents have crucial role for the Shared Place concept. Most of the content of the documents is specified in Shared Place Definition Language (SPDL) - the XML-based language providing syntax for describing the collaboration functionality of the virtual place. The Shared Place framework recognizes several types of documents. The most important is the document that describes the place itself. It is composed of two parts. The SPDL part defines collaboration functionality of the place. It has ability to define multiple properties such as users allowed to enter the place, roles assigned to specific users, behavior of collaboration tools, or policies regarding persistence of objects created during collaborative work. It contains entries that describe properties of model entities: the place itself, the users, user groups and their roles, artifacts, tools, visitors, agents, and gates to other places. The place policy is specified in SPDL as a set of behavior rules, which are associated with user roles, tools, artifacts and agents to create complete definition of the place policy.

```
<role name="Support">
  <user>John</user>
</role>
<role name="Customer">
  <user>guest</user>
</role>
<behavior_def name="restricted">
  <synchronization>instant</synchronization>
  <control>no_buttons</control>
  <initial_state>none</initial_state>
  <archiving space="none">none</archiving>
  <floor_control>none</floor_control>
</behavior_def>
<behavior_def name="full_access">
  <synchronization>instant</synchronization>
  <control>full</control>
  <initial_state>none</initial_state>
  <archiving space="public">read_write</archiving>
  <floor_control>none</floor_control>
</behavior_def>
<tool_def name="chat">
  <description>Tool for text based communication
  </description>
  <policy role="Customer" behavior="restricted"/>
  <policy role="Support" behavior="full_access"/>
  <implementation>
  http://www.npac.syr.edu/shared/sptool/chat.spdl
  </implementation>
</tool_def>
```

Figure 4. Fragment of place description in SPDL

Figure 4 presents the fragment of the SPDL part of the place description. It declares two roles - the 'Support' role is assigned to the person that enters the place as John, the 'Customer' role is assigned to any other user that enters the place through gate without authentication. Two behavior rules are declared, later associated with user roles to determine behavior of a chat tool. Information about tool contains URL of the tool description document that contains declaration of collaboration properties supported by the chat and a pointer to the actual implementation of the tool.

The HTML part of the place definition document describes the appearance of the virtual place, and can be different for each user role. In this part a developer can utilize all the resources used in building regular Web page. Entities described using SPDL are embedded in the HTML part of the document by using special tags. HTML is not the only choice here. Other applications of XML such as XHTML can be used.

Shared Place also relies on other documents, specified entirely in SPDL. They describe properties that tools, artifacts, agents, and gates expose for customization. This information is used to check validity of the place definition document. The last type of document used by Shared Place provides identity information about a user. It corresponds to a business card presented whenever user accesses specific place. It contains such data as user name, e-mail address, home Web page or place, and a public key used for data encryption.

5. Architecture

Shared Place merges several technologies such as Web infrastructure, Web browser platforms, and component technologies (see Figure 5). Shared Place documents are stored on Web servers and can be downloaded as any other Web resources. The places are accessed using the components implementing gate functionality. Such a component can be embedded in a regular Web page or it can be a part of a virtual place. When activated by the user, it has the ability to fetch a Shared Place document, translate it into a document with embedded collaboration and Shared Place framework components understandable by a standard Web browser, and display the result as a virtual place in a browser window. The collaboration components are visible to the user, whereas the framework components, which implement the collaboration services and expose them to the collaboration components of virtual place, remain hidden. The collaboration services include user authentication, establishing channels of communication, synchronization, access to place properties, access to policy settings, notifications about changes in the state of the place, and management of persistent artifacts. The services implemented by Shared Places framework are available through the set of Application Programming Interfaces (API). The framework components communicate with the Shared Place server that implements most of the services.

The collaboration components (tools, gates, and agents) are customizable pieces of software developed using available component technologies (for example Java Beans or ActiveX) and Shared Place API. They are stored on a Web server together with the SPDL documents that describe their configurable properties. When embedded in a place, they follow rules described in a place definition document and communicate with the Shared Place framework (through exposed API) to access available collaboration services. As a result, it is possible to create multiple places that look and behave in different manner by changing SPDL specifications or place layout while using the same set of the collaboration components.

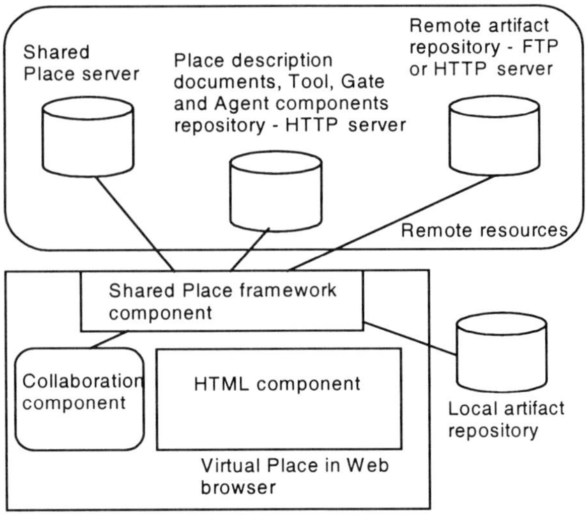

Figure 5. Shared Place architecture

The HTTP or FTP servers are used as the artifact repositories. The servers must be set up in a way that makes updates of artifacts possible. An artifact may also provide an interface to more complex form of storage such as database repository, media streams or access to scientific instrument input and output. In addition, personal artifacts may be stored on a local machine to allow off-line access.

6. Related work

Significant research was conducted in the area of separating the computation and coordination mechanisms in collaborative applications. For example, Describing Collaborative Work Programming Language (DCWPL) [5] allows developers to specify multiple coordination rules for the same application. The execution of applications is controlled by external entity - Control Engine, which can interpret DCWPL programs and impose chosen collaboration policy. Shared Place framework is not so restrictive in controlling behavior of collaboration components. Collaboration components access policy settings during initialization procedure and act accordingly.

Artefact [7] is Web-based framework for building collaborative applications that supports a room metaphor. The rooms are built from set of HTML frames that contain information about applications, objects and users. The applications are launched as separate windows with exception of a chat tool, which is permanently built in the one of the room frames. Artefact provides Artefact Definition Language (ADL) that allows building simple collaboration tools by composing HTML and Tcl constructs. It also offers APIs in several programming languages. Our solution differs in several aspects. Virtual environments built using Shared Place are not restricted to one type of layout, HTML documents with arbitrary structure can be used to define appearance of the place. Moreover, Shared Place allows arbitrary collaboration components to be embedded in the document as interactive content (this approach is preferred over launching tools in separate windows). In addition to collaboration tools, other specialized components can be used such as gates and agents. Finally, SPDL can define the behavior of the individual component as well as the behavior of the whole place.

There are many other environments and systems that employ place metaphor such as Multi User Dungeons (MUD and MOO) [6], Collaborative Virtual Workspace [10] or TeamRooms [12] but they are not integrated with Web environment and usually they do not allow for component customization.

7. Implementation status

The early results of the work on Shared Place were presented at XML Developers' Conference in August'99 [3]. The prototype versions of the Shared Place server and the framework components are already implemented and were used to develop virtual places for customer support service. The first version of the SPDL was created but the work on the improved version of the language and development of the SPDL processor is still under way.

8. Conclusions

Shared Place technology provides place functionality by merging customizable collaboration components and support for persistent artifacts with the Web content. The Shared Place Definition Language (SPDL), based on XML, allows description of collaboration functionality using conventional markup language. The conformance to the Web standards means that SPDL documents can be processed by widely available XML tools and can be integrated with other Web resources.

The level of customizability offered by Shared Place allows developers to create various environments, from social interaction to work and service oriented places. The process of building places is separated from the development of the collaboration tools. One of the advantages of this approach is the possibility of dynamic creation of the virtual places from the libraries of the components. The dynamic construction of the virtual place can be accomplished by generating Shared Place documents according to user preferences, tasks to be executed or available resources. Whenever necessary, the places can be interconnected to build complex Web communities.

Further work is still needed to include support for dynamic changes of users' roles and directory services for finding users distributed among different places. Other important issues that must be addressed include security and privacy of the users accessing virtual places.

9. Acknowledgements

Many thanks to Marek Podgorny and Geoffrey C. Fox for support of my work on Shared Place, to Remek Trzaska for his help in creating the prototype of the customer support service system, and to Kim Mills for his helpful comments on the drafts of this paper.

10. References

[1] Beca, L., Cheng, G., Fox, G. C., Jurga, T., Olszewski, K., Podgorny, M., Sokolowski, P., and Walczak, K., Java enabling collaborative education, health care, and computing, *Concurrency: Practice and Experience*, Vol. 9(6), June 1997, pp. 521-533.

[2] Beca, L., Fox, G. C., Podgorny, M., Component Architecture for Building Web-Based Synchronous Collaboration Systems, *Proceedings of WETICE'99*, June 1999, pp.108-113.

[3] Beca, L., Fox, G. C., Podgorny, M., Shared Places on the Web: XML for Web-based collaboration and Distance Education, Graphic Communications Association, XML Developers' Conference, August 1999, http://www.npac.syr.edu/users/gcf/montrealxmlaug99/.

[4] Chappell D., *Understanding ActiveX and OLE: A Guide for Developers & Managers,* Microsoft Press, 1996.

[5] Cortés, M., Mishra, P., DCWPL: a programming language for describing collaborative work, *Proceedings of CSCW'96,* November 1996, pp. 21-29.

[6] Curtis, P., Nichols, D.A., MUDs grow up: Social Virtual Reality in the Real World, *Proceedings of the 1994 IEEE Computer Conference*, 1994.

[7] Dobridge, T., Lin, J., Rajan, D., Roscoe, T., Brandenburg, J., Byerly, B., Artefact: A Framework for Low-Overhead Web-Based Collaborative Systems, *Proceedings of CSCW'98*, November 1998, Page 189 - 196.

[8] Edwards, W. K., Policies and Roles in Collaborative Applications, *Proceedings of CSCW' 96*, November 1996, pp.11 - 20.

[9] Kauppinen, K., Kivimäki, A., Era, T., Robinson, M., Producing identity in collaborative virtual environments, *Proceedings of the ACM Symposium on Virtual reality software and technology*, November 1998, pp. 35 - 42.

[10] Mosier, J. N., Deus, L. M., Carlson, J. A., Spellman, P. J., Collaborative Virtual Workspace; *Proceedings of the International ACM SIGGROUP Conference on Supporting Group Work*, November1997, pp. 197 - 203.

[11] Orfali, R., Harkey, D., Edwards, J., *The Essential Client/Server Survival Guide,* Second Edition, John Wiley and Sons, 1996.

[12] Roseman, M., Greenberg, S., TeamRooms: Network Places for Collaboration, *Proceedings of CSCW'96*, November 1996, pp. 325 - 333.

[13] Sun Microsystems, *The JavaBeans 1.01 Specification*, http://java.sun.com/beans.

[14] WebWisdom.com, *TANGO Interactive Virtual Classroom*, http://www.webwisdom.com/.

[15] World Wide Web Consortium, *Document Object Model (DOM) Level1 Specification: Version 1.0*, W3C Recommendation, http://www.w3.org/TR/REC-DOM-Level-1, October 98.

[16] World Wide Web Consortium, *Extensible Markup Language(XML) 1.0*, W3C Recommendation, http://www.w3.org/TR/REC-xml, February 98.

Coordinating Work on the Web with Workspaces

Robert Tolksdorf

Technische Universität Berlin, Fachbereich Informatik,FLP/KIT,
Sekr. FR 6–10, Franklinstr. 28/29, D-10587 Berlin, Germany,
mailto:tolk@cs.tu-berlin.de, http://www.cs.tu-berlin.de/~tolk

Abstract

Workflow management systems focus on coordinating work that is situated in the real world. A strong trend towards combining workflow and Internet technologies has recently evolved. Workspaces *combines coordination technology and standard Internet technology to exhibit various benefits of explicit procedure representation, distributed and uncoupled architecture and ease of access. Its architecture is based on workflows as coordinated transformations of documents. Basic steps transform XML documents under the control of an XSL engine. Coordination operations affect the order of execution in the workflow. Finally, a meta step compiles a workflow graph represented in the XML-based Workspaces Coordination Language into a set of XSL rules for single transformation steps. Workspaces uses a Linda-like data space for coordination via XML documents.*

1 Workflow and the World Wide Web

The necessity of integrating workflow and Internet technologies has been discussed in depth by the industry consortium of the major workflow management system vendors, the Workflow Management Coalition WfMC [6]. Workflow systems and the Internet are recognized as complementary technologies whose combination could lead to tremendous changes in the workplace.

Following the paper, the Internet brings to workflow technology zero application deployment costs, ubiquity, integration tools, distribution and virtual enterprise, and electronic data interchange. On the other hand, workflow is expected to enhance the Internet with functions like procedure representation and interpretation, dispatching work to the right participant at the right time, integration of existing applications, assistance with activity execution, monitoring and alerting, and statistics. The WfMC expects the following benefits of the Internet from workflow technologies: increased security, enhanced reactivity, clear progress reports, productivity, and quality and cost control.

In this paper we show how coordination technology in the Linda style [2] can be efficiently combined with recent Internet standards by the World Wide Web Consortium (W3C) – namely XML [7] and XSL [10, 9] – to implement a workflow management system providing the expected benefits of Internet based workflow systems. While it seems clear that both Web technologies do not provide benefits per se, their standardization and their widespread deployment is enabling for a Web based architecture.

2 Coordination by Transforming Documents

Workflow management systems are interesting from a coordination viewpoint, as they represent very general coordination systems. The agents coordinated are a mix of humans and system components. The coordination options are slightly more general as those in a pure computing system because of human involvement and sub-formal work specifications. We want to use coordination technology as described in [2] in the application context of workflow systems to show its usefulness.

Workspaces is based on the *step* as the basic kind of activity. As shown in fig. 1(a), each step is the transformation of one or more documents by an activity into a number of other documents. The emerging documents in turn can

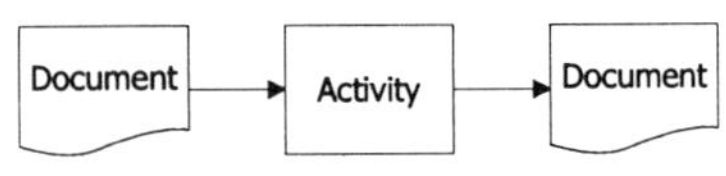

(a) A step in Workspaces

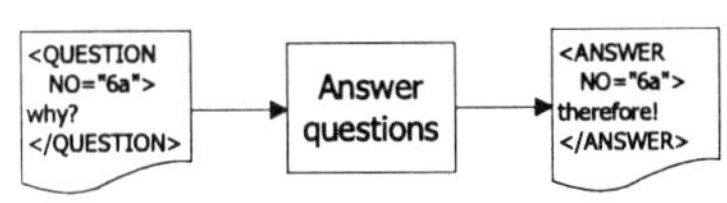

(b) An external step

Figure 1. Transformed documents

0-7695-0798-9/00 $10.00 © 2000 IEEE

cause further activities to start. There are several *kinds* of steps that we distinguish:

- *Automatic steps* are pure document transformations and require only activity of some transformation component within the system. An example is a text formatter that transforms a document from some markup language into a formatted and printable representation.
- *External steps* involve applications that take a document as input, let the user perform some activity on it, and finally generate an output document. An example is an editor used on some text.
- *User steps* are performed by a user without any support by a computing system. An example is the activity to read a book, or to develop an idea. The user has to report the completion of such a step at a GUI.
- *Coordination steps* coordinate the flow of work only. In the process model by the WfMC [5] we find examples of coordination steps with the ROUTE, LOOP and SUBFLOW activities. We consider these as steps and not as topologic attributes of the workflow graph. These explicit coordination steps together are the coordination language of the workflow, as opposed to the set of automatic, external, and user steps that represent the actual work performed.
- *Meta steps* change or generate the structure of the workflow. An example is to introduce a repetition of activities by adding steps.

In the following, we will refer to automatic, external and user steps as *basic steps*.

An *engine* is responsible for the execution of the respective activity upon the presence of an input document and the generation of output. In the Workspaces implementation, it might consist of several processes that can be distributed.

The most dominating format for marking up documents on the Internet will be the *Extensible Markup Language* XML [7], which is a language to describe the grammar of application specific markup languages. For Workspaces, all documents on which work is performed are XML documents that follow application specific grammars.

For the example domain of a university course, we can envision a special markup language for homework assignments. Questions shall me marked up with <QUESTION> and answers shall be marked as <ANSWER>. Fig. 1(b) shows the step of actually doing the homework. It is an external step, because some editor is used to type the answer.

We listed five kinds of steps and introduced the engine responsible to perform a step. However, we want a *generic* engine, not one for calling an editor and another one for asking the user to read a book. *Activity descriptions* define the specific kind of step and are interpreted by the engine. An activity description itself is a document (fig. 2(a)).

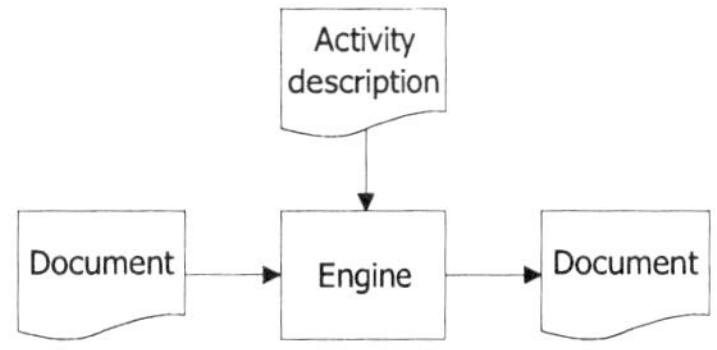

(a) Processing an activity description

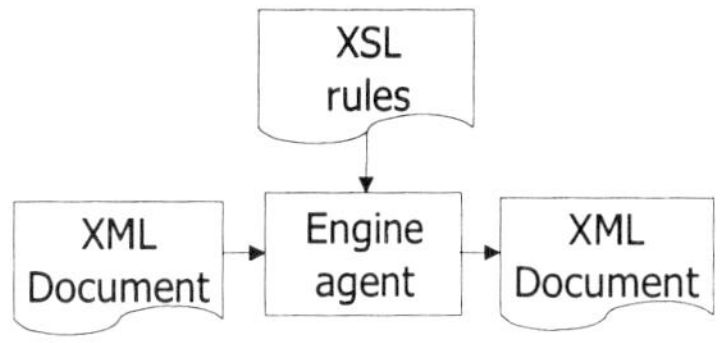

(b) A step as an XSL transformation

Figure 2. Steps with descriptions

The task of transforming an XML document into another one is the very subject of the *Extensible Stylesheet Language* XSL technology currently developed by the W3C [10]. An XSL processor takes an XSL rule set which contains patterns and transformations. It tries to match patterns in the input document and to apply transformations on the match that generate fragments in the output document. In Workspaces, activity descriptions are represented as an XSL rule set and the engine is implemented with an XSL processor, as depicted in fig. 2(b).

3 The Steps and Their Implementation

3.1 Basic Steps

With activity descriptions as XSL rules, the basic steps mentioned above are implemented by an XSL engine:

- *Automatic steps* are the very normal XSL processing that takes a document and outputs another one.
- *External steps* lead to the invocation of an external application by the XSL engine as depicted in fig. 3(a). There are several options for implementing this behavior, such as to use a standardized scripting language within XSL, or a processing instruction built into our XSL engine to perform the invocation.
- *User steps* result in an invocation of a GUI as depicted in fig. 3(b). This can be implemented as either a function built into our XSL engine, by a scripting function,

or unified with external steps by invocation of an external program that only display a small GUI.

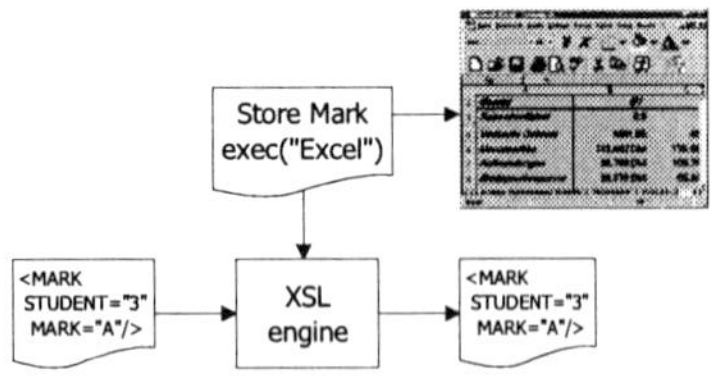

(a) An external step using a spreadsheet

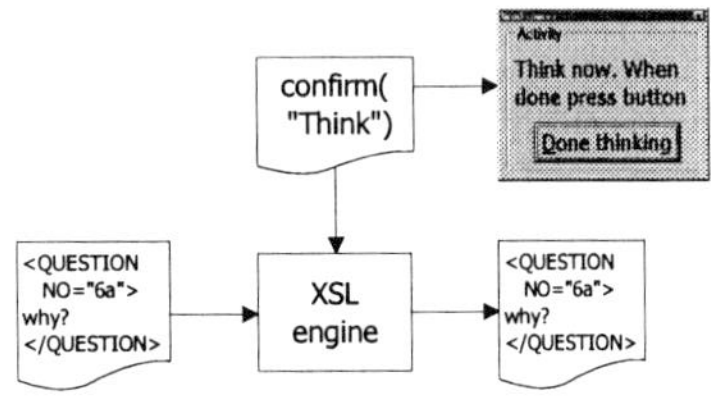

(b) A user step

Figure 3. Steps with external effects

3.2 Coordination Steps

The kind of steps that affect the order of execution in the workflow are called *coordination steps*. Workflow procedures describe temporal and causal dependencies amongst activities represented as steps. Managing these dependencies is the central issue for any workflow system. Following [3], we call this management activity *coordination*.

A simple management of a dependency amongst two activities is their sequential execution which is represented in a workflow graph by one activity being the direct or indirect successor of the activity on which it depends, as in fig. 4.

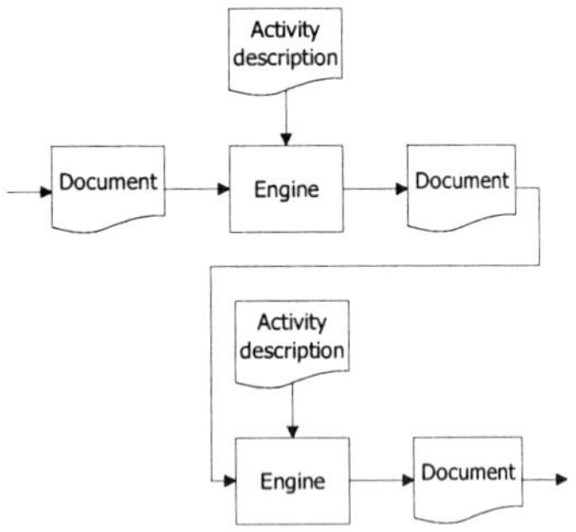

Figure 4. Two steps in sequence

More complex coordination operations are ones that change the direction of threads of work such as XOR-JOIN, start multiple such threads (SPLIT), or synchronize them with a single successor activity (JOIN).

In Workspaces, special XSL rules implement these steps. As all activities are started by the presence of some document, a SPLIT simply generates a number of identical documents that start a set of threads as in fig. 5(a). JOIN is a step that consumes several documents, processes them and outputs a single document as in fig. 5(b).

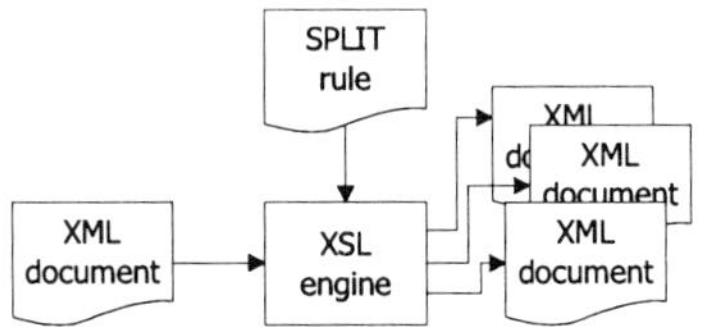

(a) SPLIT

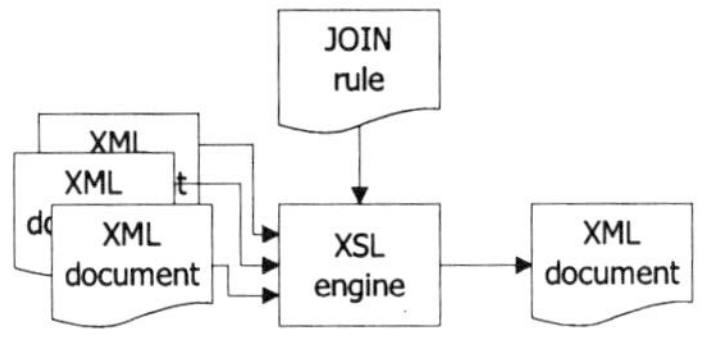

(b) JOIN

Figure 5. Coordination steps in Workspaces

3.3 Meta Steps

Basic steps together with coordination steps can lead to complete workflow graphs. Fig. 6 shows such a graph where some question set is distributed as homework, answered, and finally collected and merged.

In Workspaces, this graph will be represented as an XML document. It will follow a specific grammar, namely the Workspaces Coordination Language (WSCL) that builds heavily on the WPDL proposed by the WfMC. An editor with a graphical interface to model such workflows and to automatically generate the respective WSCL representation is currently being implemented.

The execution of a workflow is the execution of individual steps by the respective XSL engines. This resembles the notion of an "instruction" in microprocessors. The workflow graph can be considered the "program" written in a high level language. The remaining step of "compiling" is performed by *meta steps* in Workspaces. The workflow graph is represented as an XML document following the WSCL-grammar. XSL rule sets are by definition also represented as XML documents following a syntax defined in the

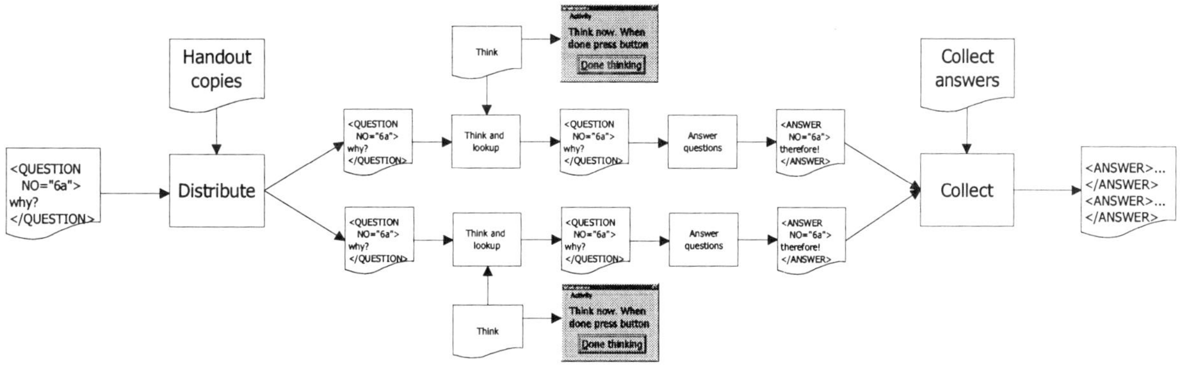

Figure 6. A complete workflow graph

XSL standard. Thus, the compilation of the graph into steps is the transformation of one XML document into a set of XML documents, each containing an XSL rule for one step, as depicted in fig. 7. Each step, then takes an application specific XML-document and performs a step on it, resulting in another application specific document. Workflow-modeler and users will not be confronted with XSL-scripts.

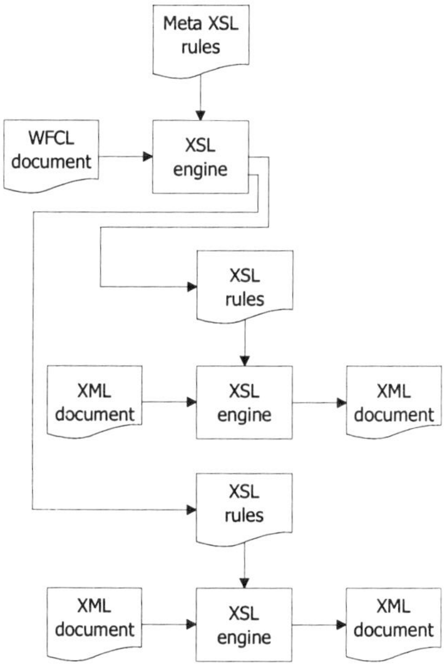

Figure 7. Compiling a workflow graph

As the transformation of XML documents is performed by an XSL engine, the compilation can be described by a set of *meta rules*. The "compiler" is implemented as a complex set of XSL rules that take the graph document and generate a set of step documents.

4 An Architecture for Workspaces

4.1 The Workspaces Coordination Language

A workflow in Workspaces is described as a graph of activities and represented as an XML document following the DTD of the *Workspaces Coordination Language*, WSCL.

In its first version, WSCL is based directly on the Workflow Process Description Language as defined by the WfMC. Changes to the WPDL concern the alignment of the syntax to the rules of XML and the appropriate definitions of tags and their attributes and the usage of references in the workflow definition. As we aim at the Web context, any reference is a global URI resolvable by network access.

Fig. 8 shows an example workflow being marked up with WSCL. The workflow is an excerpt from peer reviewing of conference papers. It involves reviewing forms and the papers as data manipulated. We model two activities, reading the paper and sending the review form to some program committee chair. Reading is marked up as being not supported by a tool and will be implemented as a user step in Workspaces. Sending the form is an external step that uses a browser application to fill out and send it. The only dependency marked up by a transition amongst activities is that the paper has to be read before the form is sent. For brevity, we omit the step of writing down the review.

4.2 The Coordination Medium XMLSpace

The coordination language Linda [2] introduced the notion of a tuplespace that contains data driving coordination and that of a *coordination language* as a set of primitive operations manipulating that space. The tuplespace uncouples

```
<WORKFLOW ID="review">
 <DESCRIPTION>This describes the workflow
  of a reviewer.</DESCRIPTION>
 <DATA ID="form" TYPE="Reviewform"/>
 <DATA ID="paper" TYPE="Paper"/>
 <ACTIVITY ID="read">
  <DESCRIPTION>Read paper, check contents
   and get an opinion</DESCRIPTION>
  <NOIMPLEMENTATION PERFORMER="pcmember"/>
  </ACTIVITY>
  <ACTIVITY ID="sendreview">
   <APPLICATIONS><TOOL NAME="browser"/>
   </APPLICATIONS>
 </ACTIVITY>
 <TRANSITION ID="paperread"
  FROM="read" TO="sendreview"/>
</WORKFLOW>
```

Figure 8. An example workflow in WSCL

the coordinated entities in time and space as they communicate indirectly, anonymous, undirected and asynchronous by one process placing some data into the space (using the `out` primitive) and another retrieving it from there using the `in` primitive with a template describing the desired data. `in` blocks until a matching tuple is present.

Our Workspaces model is very close to that abstraction: One activity generates a document that is taken by another step for further transformation. That other step has to wait for the presence of a matching document. For processes that do not actually involve document as outputs of activities, dummy-documents allow it stay within our framework

Thus, the central coordination medium for documents and steps in our architecture is a Linda-like coordination kernel, *XMLSpace*. While tuples were the elements contained in the coordination medium for Linda, they are XML documents for XMLSpace. XMLSpace is currently under implementation on top of TSpaces [12].

It introduces the usage of multi matching relations to retrieve XML documents in quite different ways. There is a choice of retrieving a document by specifying its DTD in a template, by defining a template that incorporates tag-contexts or values of specific tag attributes etc. For a Workspaces workflow, we use an associative matching by retrieving any document that confirms to the DTD used for describing individual steps. A specific document involved in a specific instance of a workflow will carry a unique identifier in an attribute of the enclosing XML element and thus will be retrieved by a simpler matching routine that checks for equality of specific attributes.

While currently complete documents are the granularity of items in the shared space, upcoming standards like XML-Fragments and XInclude ([8, 11]) will allow finer-grained matching-relations and operations.

Several other Linda-adaptions use XML instead of tuples, eg. [13, 4, 1, 12]. With respect to those, XMLSpaces is unique in its openness for multiple matching routines.

The Workspaces engine is implemented by a number of identical engines located on various machines. As depicted in fig. 9, each of them retrieves some step to coordinate from the XMLSpace. Based on that, it waits for the necessary document by issuing an `in` operation to the XMLSpace. Upon receipt of a matching document, it performs the XSL-based transformation and finally outputs the result with `out`. The engine then can terminate or retrieve another step description.

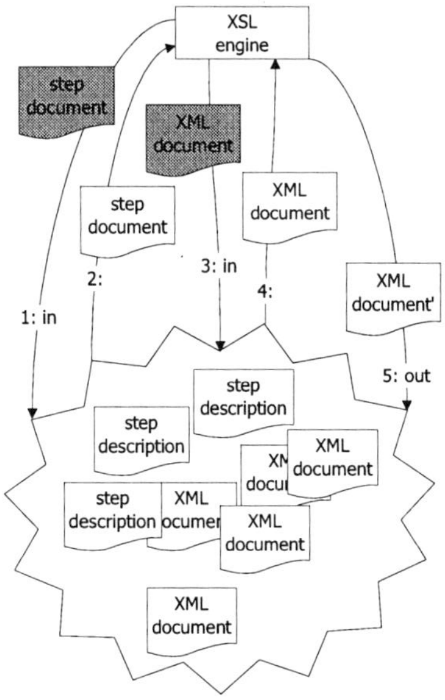

Figure 9. An XMLSpace

Thereby the individual engines are completely uncoupled and can be distributed and mobile. Their number does not have to fixed. The engine that will process future steps does not necessarily have to run when the workflow starts being run. These attractive advantages of our architecture are due to the use of coordination technology.

4.3 Distributed Workspaces

Workspaces are completely modularized in two aspects. First, the decomposition of the workflow graph into atomic steps makes each step a very light and uniform entity. It can be packaged with an engine and moved, replicated etc. Second, the components of the architecture are intended as objects that each encapsulate a specific functionality and can be independently placed at any Internet location. There are several options to optimize the distribution policies, for example by replication of documents, by partitioning the set of XML documents kept, or by clustering documents following the same DTD. A Workspaces client consists of a Workspaces specific communication component, a GUI component and platform specific applications.

5 Conclusion and Outlook

The composition of coordination and Internet technology in Workspaces results in an architecture with various attractive benefits caused by the following characteristics.

All workflows in Workspaces are explicitly notated with a standard syntax, namely XML. This makes them *communicable* just as normal Web pages. Thereby, several useful scenarios are enabled, such as publishing "standard procedures" as a workflow (eg. a IEEE-standardized reviewing process), or as delegating a task by passing it by e-mail.

All of these are implied by the specific representation of workflows, as anticipated in the WfMC white paper mentioned in the beginning. Moreover, we use a standard, machine readable and machine processable representation by using XML and introduce meta steps in which the procedure representation is taken as data.

The Workspaces architecture tries to *decompose* the workflow in its atomic parts – the steps. Thereby the execution of the steps becomes more independent of the execution of others. The condition for a step to be executed is a local one: There has to be a document to be transformed. There is no global control over the complete workflow.

This decomposition is enabling for the distributed execution of steps. It enables mobility of the actors in workflows: As there is no central control, no connection to some server has to be kept established. The decomposition allows for the delegation of steps. The decomposition leads to a higher autonomy of the people that execute parts of the workflow.

The *decoupled* coordination style, indirected by a coordination medium that masks any issues of distribution and synchronization, gives the technical freedom for a distributed and open implementation. With explicit activity descriptions and the extensible meta step, the system is open to accommodate new kinds of steps.

The Workspaces architecture incorporates standard components and *standard technologies* only. We build on XSL, XML and the Java platform – each of which is available without license costs and each of which will be standard components of near future Web systems. Thus, Workspaces does in fact provide zero application deployment costs and ubiquity, as required in the WfMC white paper.

XSL is currently being deployed in its first version and therefore seems the right choice to work on XML documents. Currently, however, it is not finally clear, how SPLIT and JOIN steps can be implemented without relying on additional processing. While XSL mentions the generation of multiple documents, there is no current standard of how to merge multiple documents in one XSL processing step.

While the initial implementation of the Workspaces concepts presented here is currently underway, several further issues are not yet dealt with in a sufficient manner. As most important we mention dealing with exceptions in the workflow and the consistency of the workflow description and data involved in the case of exceptions and adaptation of the workflow. Conditions for the dynamic adaption and potential coordination patterns usable as higher coordination steps are on the mid-term agenda for Workspaces.

Information about Workspaces is available at *www.cs.tu-berlin.de/˜tolk/workspaces*. Acknowledgments go to the TU-Berlin students Marc Stauch, Amarilis Macedo-Aranya, and Dirk Glaubitz who developed initial implementations of the XSL-applications, a graphical editor and the XMLSpace as part of their respective diploma-thesis.

References

[1] G. Cabri, L. Leonardi, and F. Zambonelli. XML Dataspaces for Mobile Agent Coordination. In *Proc. of the 2000 ACM Symposium on Applied Computing*, pages 181–188, 2000.

[2] D. Gelernter and N. Carriero. Coordination Languages and their Significance. *Commun. ACM*, 35(2):97–107, 1992.

[3] T. Malone and K. Crowston. The Interdisciplinary Study of Coordination. *ACM Comput. Surv.*, 26(1):87–119, 1994.

[4] D. Moffat. XML-Tuples and XML-Spaces, V0.7, 1999. http://uncled.oit.unc.edu/XML/XMLSpaces.html.

[5] Workflow Management Coalition. Interface 1: Process Definition Interchange Process Model, 1998. http://www.wfmc.org.

[6] Workflow Management Coalition. Workflow and Internet: Catalysts for Radical Change. WfMC White Paper, 1998. http://www.wfmc.org.

[7] World Wide Web Consortium. Extensible Markup Language (XML) 1.0. W3C Recommendation, 1998. http://www.w3.org/TR/REC-xml.

[8] World Wide Web Consortium. XML Fragment Interchange. W3C Working Draft, 1999. http://www.w3.org/TR/WD-xml-fragment.

[9] World Wide Web Consortium. XSL Transformations (XSLT). W3C Recommendation, 1999. http://www.w3.org/TR/xslt.

[10] World Wide Web Consortium. Extensible Stylesheet Language (XSL) Specification. W3C Working Draft, 2000. http://www.w3.org/TR/xsl.

[11] World Wide Web Consortium. XML Inclusions (XInclude). W3C Working Draft, 2000. http://www.w3.org/TR/xinclude.

[12] P. Wyckoff, S. McLaughry, T. Lehman, and D. Ford. T Spaces. *IBM Systems Journal*, 37(3):454–474, 1998.

[13] B. Y. Zhao and A. Joseph. XSet: A Lightweight Database for Internet Applications. http://www.cs.berkeley.edu/˜ravenben/publications/saint.ps.gz, 2000.

Integrating XML and Object-based Programming for Distributed Collaboration

Vassil Roussev, Prasun Dewan, Naveen Koorakula, Sriram Sellappa
University of North Carolina
{roussev, dewan, naveen, sriram}@cs.unc.edu

Abstract

In this paper, we explore some of the new opportunities for distributed collaborative applications that emerge from the use of XML as a data specification language. We present two different approaches: the first one transparently adds asynchronous collaboration to applications whose persistent state is in XML format, while the second one helps build synchronous collaborative applications starting with an XML schema specification.

Although the two approaches start with different assumptions, they both lead to the same problem—the need for a generic one-to-one conversion between objects and XML constructs. Using object properties, we define two variants of a conversion scheme for the two approaches.

Introduction

Experience shows that writing distributed multi-user applications is a non-trivial task and involves a number of issues not raised by single-user applications. The added complexity stems primarily from the need to coordinate the actions of a group of users working on a common task. Furthermore, the coordination mechanisms must be flexible enough to allow the collaborators to effectively cooperate in a number of different situations where computer aid is desirable.

To illustrate the needs of distributed collaboration, let us consider a simple example of collaborative editing. Users *A* and *B* are planning to write a paper together but would like to do it over the Internet as they live far apart. They could cooperate by sending each other emails with their respective versions of the document. However, this implies that they would have to rely entirely on social protocol to ensure the consistency of the document, and would have to manually reconcile different (and potentially conflicting) versions of it. Instead, they would like to have a collaborative environment where they could work on the paper simultaneously and have an automated mechanism that can ensure consistency and help resolve conflicts.

The development of collaborative applications from the ground up is a costly and error-prone process. Therefore, we need software infrastructures to support this process, as well as simple and intuitive abstractions that can be presented to the user. Ideally, the infrastructures should also be compatible with existing standards.

Traditionally, many distributed collaborative systems have been built around the notion of *sharing*. The basic idea behind sharing is to give each user a copy of the shared entity and to guarantee a certain level of consistency among these copies. In general, users are most familiar with two types of entities on their computers–data files and applications. Therefore, it is intuitive to present shared versions of these abstractions to the user.

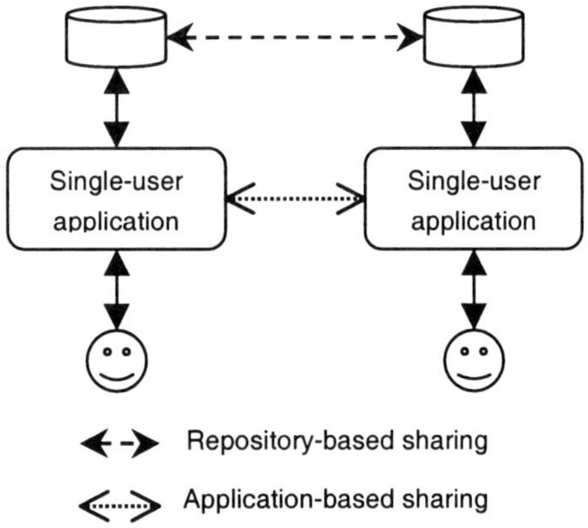

Figure 1 Collaborative sharing

Thus, there are two ways to achieve the abstraction of sharing. One is to create a shared file and allow collaborators to edit it independently. The other is to create a shared application, which allows the collaborators to see the effects of each other's action on the document in real-time. We refer to these models as *repository-based* and *application-based* sharing, respectively.

Our work explores new ways of implementing these two forms of sharing mechanisms based on XML document representation and its integration with object-oriented technologies. The rest of this paper is organized as follows. First, we discuss the use of XML in developing a fine-grained repository-based sharing mechanism. Next, we apply a similar idea to an application-based sharing scheme, and describe an experimental implementation of it. Finally, we summarize our results and future extensions of this work.

Repository-based sharing

The OS has traditionally assumed the responsibility of maintaining the persistent storage of all data. This opens up the opportunity to synchronize the state of applications using the file I/O channel. Indeed, users of distributed file systems have used repository-based sharing for many years. Distributed file systems (DFS), such as *Coda*, allow multiple users to cooperate by repeatedly loading, modifying, and saving the same file. Moreover, *Coda* supports merging of data of disconnected and weakly-connected clients and its recent extension [1] handles user-level operations in an attempt to improve performance.

However, the impressive list of features in traditional DFS comes with a relatively high cost of deployment and maintenance. This makes them inherently unsuitable for spontaneous collaboration over a wide-area network. Currently, a number of freely-available products allow the creation of an application-transparent 'Internet drive'. The importance of these systems with respect to collaboration is that they make wide-area sharing affordable to practically all Internet users.

We see two major advantages in the use of DFS for collaborative sharing:

Transparency. None of the applications has to be aware of the sharing–all of the distribution functions are handled automatically at a lower level.

Interoperability. The sharing mechanism is independent of the application as all applications use the same I/O functions and abstractions provided by the system.

One the other hand, there are some collaboration-specific issues that DFS are not designed to deal with:

Fine-grained sharing. The unit of sharing is a whole file, which often is inadequate if two or more users want to work on it at the same time. Consider our editing example: the authors would like to simultaneously work on different sections of the document. Furthermore, they might want to ensure that the document is consistent by either preventing conflicting updates, or by merging non-overlapping changes.

In the physical world, our users could, for example, work on separate sheets of paper and then simply combine them to get the whole paper. Surprisingly enough, current distributed technologies do not offer such a generic solution to the above scenario in the virtual world. The problem has been that there was no agreed upon standard, such as XML, for representing arbitrary structured data, which made it infeasible to derive the data structure in a generic way and to provide finer-grain services.

Incremental response. In general, file systems do not provide incremental synchronization, access control, concurrency control, and fault-tolerance. The large overhead of file operations effectively prohibits the access to these services incrementally.

Thus, the lack of incremental response is an inherent problem to repository-based sharing. However, the lack of fine-grained sharing can be overcome by breaking away with the canonical treatment of files as opaque entities and assuming that at least some the applications will store their data in XML format. As we discuss in the next section, this allows us to give better sharing services to those applications.

XML-based repository sharing

To illustrate this approach, consider the following XML document:

```
<document title="XML 1.0">
  <section title="1 Introduction">
      <p>Extensible Markup Language …</p>
      <section title="1.1 Origin and goals">
        <p>XML was developed … </p>
      </section>
      <section title="1.2 Terminology">
        <p>The terminology used … </p>
      </section>
  </section>
</document>
```

It presents a definite hierarchical structure that allows us to deduce that the main document consists of smaller units (called "section") that in turn can have even smaller subdivisions ("section" and "p"). (This information can also be derived from the corresponding DTD schema, if present.)

Note that, while we still don't understand the semantics of the data, the standard syntax permits its incremental breakdown into smaller and smaller units. Eventually, we reach the indivisible (leaf) units, which we must treat as atomic entities (in this example the "p" elements). Having derived the structure, we are now capable of providing sharing at a much finer granularity (in fact, at variable granularity).

Looking back at our original scenario, we are now ready to help our collaborators edit their document in a consistent manner by providing generic collaboration services, such as coupling, concurrency control, and fault-tolerance, that follow the document structure.

XML serialization

The previous section showed how XML could be used to implement fine-grained collaboration services in an application-neutral way. However, we expect that applications would rarely operate directly on the textual representation of XML data. More likely, they would convert it into language-specific objects, process it, and then export it back in XML format. Hence, a marshalling/unmarshalling utility that can automate this process would be very useful.

One way to handle these conversions is to use standard representations, such as the DOM, that provide a one-to-one mapping between objects (in different languages) and XML. DOM objects are modeled after XML and any application that uses it must deal with XML-specific objects (document, schema, elements, attributes, etc.). This raises at least two problems:

- The DOM naming does not reflect object semantics in the application context and, therefore, its universal usage would distort programming style. For example, coding a text editor with `element` and `attribute` objects is not as intuitive as doing it with `title`, `section`, and `paragraph` objects.
- Existing applications need to be rewritten to comply with the DOM in order to get the benefits of automation.

Both problems indicate that this is not an approach that can be expected to gain widespread acceptance. In general, we believe that any object-to-XML conversion scheme should fulfil several requirements in order to be successful.

Generality. The conversion scheme must handle generic objects–not just the ones from a particular inheritance tree.

Automation. The conversion should be done automatically with minimal need for program modifications.

Reversibility. It must be possible to execute the reverse XML-to-object conversion. In other words, enough information must be retained to reconstruct the original object in a different address space, and enough information must be stored to resolve any potential ambiguities in the reverse mapping.

No new language support. The solution must work with any implementation of the underlying language. In particular, it should not depend on specialized translators, such as (pre-) compilers or interpreters.

To devise a solution that satisfies the above requirements, especially the last one, we have chosen *Java* as our implementation language.

A *Java* solution

In an ideal solution, developers' effort would be reduced to a single method invocation of the form:

```
XMLSerializer.saveAsXML(rootObject,fileName)
```

with the expectation that the `XMLSerializer` would take the `rootObject`, save it in the file with the specified name (in XML), and then find all other objects to which `rootObject` has a reference and would apply recursively the same procedure. The recursion terminates whenever it reaches a node in the document hierarchy that does not refer to any objects that have not been saved already.

The idea of serializing objects to a persistent store has been explored extensively. In *Java* however, the idea has been brought a step further by embedding it into the language in the form of a standard API.

At a high level, *Java*'s serialization mechanism works as follows. Given an object tagged as `Serializable`, *Java* allows the programmer to store it to a file, or send it over a network connection with a single method call. Moreover, it finds all other objects to which the original object has references and applies the same procedure recursively until the whole graph of related objects is stored/transmitted.

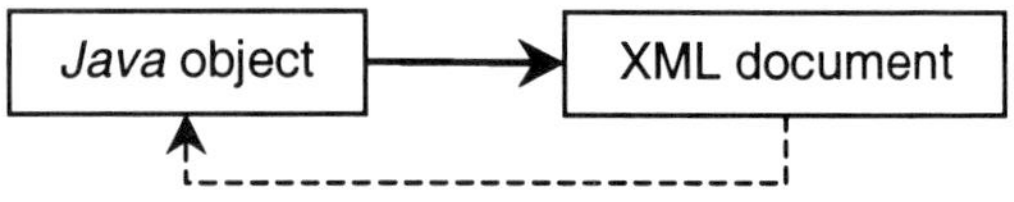

Figure 2 Starting with Java object

This is very similar to what we want to achieve with the exception that objects are not stored in XML format. To be fair, we must say that *Java* provides a mechanism that allows objects to take responsibility of their own serialization. During the serialization process, if an object tagged as `Externalizable` is encountered, *Java* will invoke its `writeExternal` method to export its state. Conversely, when the object is deserialized, its `readExternal` method will be invoked to restore its state. Thus, by implementing the `Externalizable` interface, we can achieve conversion to/from XML and solve our problem.

Unfortunately, this solution does not satisfy our requirement for low programming cost as it necessitates the modification of each and every class whose instances must be serialized. Thus, we are a looking for a solution similar to the standard serialization mechanism but one that can be implemented outside the *Java* virtual machine.

Therefore, we must be able to derive the structure of the object from its external appearance. In general, this is an unsolvable problem so we restrict ourselves to a set of objects called (*Java*) *beans* [2].

A *bean* is a collection of *properties* with well-defined semantics. A *property* is a distinct, named attribute of an object. It can be accessed and/or modified through a set of dedicated methods and its value may be of any type.

Bean objects adhere to a set of programming patterns (naming conventions) that permit the automated discovery of their properties. Furthermore, they may expose standard interfaces through which other objects can receive notifications about specific changes in their state.

The standard bean conventions recognize two types of properties: *simple* and *indexed*. A simple property is characterized by a pair of 'get' and 'set' methods whose purpose is to read and write the property. An indexed property is a simple property of an array type (e.g., an array of strings). In addition to the standard get/set methods, which deal with the whole array, it may have and additional pair of methods for manipulating individual elements by their index.

A property-based solution

Let us now use the property-based view of the application objects to support our automated object-to-XML conversion. We assume that only the values of the publicly accessible properties represent the serializable state of the object. At first glance, this may seem like a severe restriction, but a closer look at good programming practices reveals that it is a valid approach.

First, we believe that the majority of current applications are being developed using the document/view paradigm in which the abstract data structure is separated from its UI representation. For example, Microsoft's development environments advocate this approach and generate skeleton class files to facilitate the process. Thus, it is not overly restrictive to consider the existence of 'data' objects whose main purpose is to store the application's state. Therefore, other application objects must be given access to this information. If we follow the data-encapsulation principle, access must be provided through dedicated methods, and not by exposing the internal structure of the objects. Hence, we should be able to retrieve the state of these objects using only public methods.

Second, the use of method naming conventions (which form the basis for property discovery) is highly desirable from a software-engineering point of view–it greatly simplifies the understanding, maintenance, and further development of the application.

Finally, the serialization of public properties solves the 'fragile serialization' problem. That is, it allows two different versions of the same object to use the same serialized state. We believe that this is not possible to achieve with the standard *Java* serialization process, as the compiled classes do not contain enough data for the system to make an informed decision.

Having adopted properties as our way of describing the object state, we are now ready to define a generic mapping between the object and its XML representation. We map each object to an entity with a name derived from its class name. Next, we map all properties of the object to nested elements. To preserve the semantics of object-to-object relationships, we need to distinguish between literal and reference property values. The former include numbers and strings, whereas the latter include all object references. Literal values can be converted directly to XML's PCDATA, but doing so for references may not preserve the intended application semantics. To illustrate this, consider two `paragraph` objects, each of which has a *style* property, which is a reference to the same `style` object. If we treat objects as literal values, we would end up with two `paragraph` elements, each with a `style` nested element. If we now do the reverse conversion, we would have little choice but to create two equivalent but separate objects for the `style` elements. Therefore, if the application changes one of them, the other one would remain intact, which is probably not the intended semantics. Hence, we need to encode references differently so that object relationships can be properly reconstructed. We encode references, using XML's ID/IDREF attributes, which essentially provide the reference semantic (an IDREF attribute refers to an element with the given ID attribute), and we can expect a standard XML parser to handle these automatically.

Given this background, we can now follow a depth-first-search-based algorithm, similar to the one implemented by the standard serialization process, to serialize the graph of related objects. The only difference here is that we only consider property values when looking for referenced objects.

The reverse conversion from XML is straightforward given the one-to-one mapping defined above and is omitted for the sake of brevity. The only subtlety we will point out is that, in order to faithfully recreate the object, we need to have the binding schema, which maps object classes to XML elements. This information can be stored either as part of the XML file, or as a separate entity. We advocate the second approach as it allows the generated XML data to be interpreted independently of the source object. Furthermore, this leaves the option of binding the serialized state with another (version of the) object.

Let us now focus on a couple of implicit restrictions that result from the fact that we only use the public properties of the object and not its internal state.

First, there is no explicit ordering among the properties of an object. This does not present a problem in the conversion to XML but is a potential setback in recreating the object. A problem may occur if a given property is dependent on another property in the same object and setting the value of the first property before the second would cause an error, or an inconsistency. This is an inherent problem with using object properties and cannot be solved without specific, per-class information. For that reason, we assume that object properties are autonomous and can be assigned independently of each other.

Second, the unmarshalling of the object must start with creating an instance of it. The question is: which constructor should be used, and what argument(s) must be supplied? Again, class-specific information could be used to resolve the issue but we want to avoid the costly effort. Therefore, we always use the constructor with no arguments. To justify this we make two points here:

- Constructors with arguments are a matter of convenience and not of necessity–all classes could be written so that they always have a constructor with no arguments.
- Wherever such constructors are missing, a trivial (empty) implementation can be added automatically either at the source-code level, or at class-load time by using object instrumentation [3].

An example

To illustrate the use of XML-based serialization in distributed collaboration, consider the potential use of the *XMLDiff and Merge Tool* [4] for enhancing repository-based collaboration. The essential diff/merge functions can, for example, be embedded as part of a client/server system:

Whenever the server receives a put request for a particular XML file, the new version is automatically compared with the existing copy and any non-conflicting changes are merged. Similarly, the client must now take into consideration that its copy may not be not be up-to-date, and after saving its copy must immediately request the document back and merge with its own version.

To outline the benefits of using fine-grained XML services over generic file-based solutions, we compare the above approach with the UNIX *diff3* tool. *diff3* takes as input an original text file and two versions of it. It then produces a script that, when applied to one of the versions, reconciles it with the other.

Consider the integration of *diff3* at the server as a means of achieving consistency between, say, two XML documents. It can lead to two types of problems:

• Discovery of irrelevant formatting differences. The simplest example is differences in the spacing of XML constructs. In general, those are ignored with the exception of some data blocks.

• Discarding of non-overlapping changes. For example, very often multiple attributes of an element are defined on the same line. Thus, if one user changes one of them, while the other changes another, *diff3* will detect a conflict and will choose one version of the line over the other. However, a fine-grained diff/merge tool will discover that the updates are independent and will proceed to automatically reconcile them without discarding user updates.

Application-based sharing

Recall that repository-based sharing is inherently unsuitable for synchronous collaboration. Therefore, support must be included in the application at development time. As it turns out, XML can play an important role in this case, too.

The idea is that the data schema of the application is not given in terms of *Java* classes. Instead, it is defined by an XML schema, for which the *Java* classes are derived automatically.

The use of XML for data specification has several advantages over other options:

Intuitive. XML is simple enough so that even non-programmers can produce XML specifications.

Formal. Using a formal language significantly reduces the possibility for ambiguities and misinterpretations. This is an important advantage over using, for example, a description written in plain English.

The described data-centric approach leads us to explore the generation of (parts of) the collaborative application from an XML specification. That is, we start with a DTD schema and we generate a class representation of it. From there on, we are free to follow the standard object-based development process.

Note that this is a different problem than the problem of recreating objects from their XML-serialized state (Figure 2). The differences stem from the fact that now the schema is fixed and object representation can vary. Therefore, we must decide on a suitable class representation of the DTD schema, specifically its elements and attributes. Given our property-based approach, we have little choice but to map them both to corresponding properties. Thus, it is no longer possible to distinguish nested elements and attributes in this class representation. In our view, this does not pose a problem, unless we impose the additional requirement that object instances of the generated classes be convertible into XML structures conforming to their initial schema.

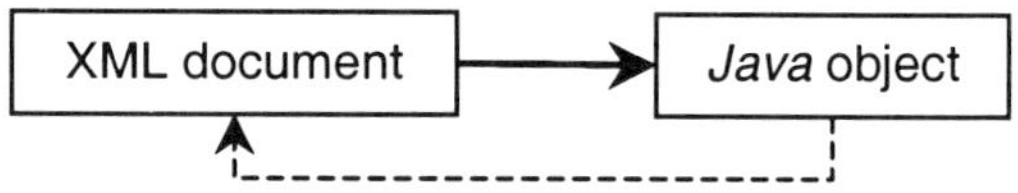

Figure 3 Starting with XML specification

This optional requirement allows us to get two additional benefits from using XML for data specification:

Interoperability. The data output of the application can easily be shared with other XML-enabled applications.

Standard rendering. The XML data can be displayed using a standard viewing utility, such as a web browser.

Given these advantages, we must address the ambiguity mentioned above. To resolve the issue, we use the initial DTD specification by reading the object properties in the given order, and then mapping them to elements, or attributes, according to the schema. As in the previous mapping, we need to store the binding between the DTD and the resulting object(s) to enable the correct XML serialization of the object.

Our XML-to-Java binding schema has a different goal and takes a different approach than most other implementations. While other schemes are concerned with fixing a standard *Java* representations of XML documents, we are more interested in providing a generic two-way conversion between XML and *Java* objects that preserves the natural style of programming. Another difference is that we are not using XML as a means of declarative programming as it is the case with *BML* [5]. To the best of our knowledge, there are no other schemes that provide a model for XML serialization of generic objects.

XML-based application sharing

In this section, we outline the major steps involved generating a collaborative application from an XML data specification. We also use a simple collaborative text editor that we have built to demonstrate a concrete implementation.

• We start by building an appropriate DTD schema for the application. In our case, the basic data structure is the document so we use a simple hierarchical description of nested sections, and paragraphs.

• Next, we generate 'data' object classes that will contain the actual run-time data on which the application will operate. We emphasize the use of naming conventions that closely match the names in the original DTD to facilitate any subsequent modifications to the code.

In the example, we generate a `Document` class, which has a simple *title* property, as well as a list of authors and a list of sections (both indexed properties). Similarly, the `Section` class is generated with a *section* and *paragraph* indexed properties. Finally, the `Paragraph` class has (for the sake of simplicity) a single *text* property containing the actual text of the paragraph.

• Next, using generic window components, we generate a UI that allows the user to create, edit, and store/load the data objects (in XML).

• Finally, we combine the generated objects with generic implementations of collaboration-specific services, such as coupling, access/concurrency control, merging, and fault-tolerance, to achieve the desired collaborative behavior.

In our implementation, we have provided coupling and fault-tolerance as example collaboration functions. We should note that the discussed application was developed manually. We are currently working on an infrastructure that will permit the automation of collaboration services.

Related Work

Let us outline some of the main differences between our approach and other solutions. *CORBA* [6] provides a framework for inter-operating objects that are implemented in different languages. However, its mechanism is relatively heavyweight and requires the individual description of every shared object.

On the other hand, platforms, such as *XML-RPC* [7] and *SOAP*, simply extend the original idea of RPC by using open standards (XML/HTTP) for their implementations.

KOML [8] is most closely related to our work, however, its approach is tied to the specifics of the *Java* serialization format.

Summary and future work

In this work we showed two different ways to utilize XML for the purposes of distributed collaborative applications. The first one enhances existing asynchronous, repository-based sharing by adding fine-grained collaboration services. The second one enables the generation of synchronous collaborative applications from a generic XML schema. We argued that using XML for data specification provides users with an intuitive, yet formal way of starting application development. Furthermore it can help in inter-operating different applications and displaying application data with a generic viewer.

We showed that the successful implementation of both of these schemes hinges on the solution of a more general problem—the generic mapping between XML data constructs and objects. We gave two such mappings, both based on the bean property model. We motivated the differences between the two approaches by showing the different requirements they must satisfy.

In this paper, the presented implementation work is limited to the generation of class files based from a DTD schema. We would like to extend this and build an implementation that allows instances of these classes to be serialized in XML. We would also like to build a prototype implementation of the presented XML-based repository sharing mechanism.

Another direction for our ongoing research is concerned with overcoming the limitations imposed by the bean property model. Space limitations do not permit us to discuss them here in detail but we should not that, currently, many objects cannot be adequately described with simple and indexed properties. For example, the standard `Vector` and `Hashtable` classes have *no* identifiable properties.

Therefore, we are working on extending the bean model to incorporate other types of properties. Our extension is based on the idea of flexible specification and recognition of properties using programming patterns.

Acknowledgements

The reviewers gave several helpful suggestions for improving the quality of this presentation. This research was sponsored in part by National Science Foundation grants IRI-9627619, IIS-9977362, and CDA-9624662.

References

1. Lee, Y., Leung, K., Satyanarayanan, M. *Operation-based Update Propagation in a Mobile File System.* in *USENIX.* 1999. Monterey, CA, USA.
2. Hamilton, G., *JavaBeans Specification.* 1997, Sun Microsystems.
3. Cohen, G., Chase, J. *Automatic Program Transformation with JIOE.* in *USENIX Annual Technical Symposium.* 1998.
4. Birsan, D., Sluiman, H., Fernz, S., *XML Diff and Merge Tool (http://www.alphaWorks.ibm.com).* 1999.
5. Weerawarana, S., Duftler, M., *BML (http://www.alphaworks.ibm.com/tech/bml).* 1999.
6. *http://www.corba.org.*
7. *http://www.xmlrpc.com.*
8. *http://www-sop.inria.fr/koala/koml/.*

Distributed Collaborative Design and Manufacturability Assessment for Extended Enterprise in XML-based Agent System

Joe Y Shiau, Svetan M Ratchev, George Valtchanov
School of Mechanical, Material, Manufacturing Engineering and Management
University of Nottingham, Nottingham NG7 2RD, United Kingdom
epxys@unix.ccc.nottingham.ac.uk

Abstract

The paper reports on a pilot application of a decision-making environment for part manufacturability assessment in extended enterprises using collaborative design and manufacturing agents. The system is implemented as an XML/CORBA based environment for conveying design and manufacture messages across traditional technology boundaries. The approach is based on exchange of manufacturability requests and product information between different agents using a new Manufacturability Mark-up Language (MML). The paper provides an overview of key domain models and their integration within the decision-making environment. The reported research aims to provide the designers with a rapid manufacturability assessment tool to be used at early design stage in extended manufacturing enterprises.

1.Introduction

In order to dramatically reduce the cost at the early stages of product development, the planners need methodologies and tools that would allow them to judge upon the implications of the product design specification on the required manufacturing processes and facilities for its production. As a result, process and facility prototyping is increasingly becoming an essential part of the new product design process. A distinctive feature of the early manufacturability assessment in extended manufacturing facilities is that it depends on successful process knowledge management between closely interrelated domains of products, manufacturing processes and geographically distributed manufacturing resources.

A multi-agent framework facilitating concurrent product design and planning is proposed by Tan et al [1]. The framework draws on design-team behaviour in different domains with the goal of providing the infrastructure to enable designers, planners, and managers from different functional areas to collaborate in improving the initial product design. The methodology is based on integrated blackboard architecture with an intelligent agent network using conflict resolution techniques for design refinement and process plan generation. A concurrent engineering framework based on multi-agent planning environment is also reported by Balasubramanian et al [2]. The approach targets a heterogeneous multi-agent system for concurrent design, manufacturability analysis, process planning, routing and scheduling. The above idea is further developed by Gu et al [3] by integrating design, process planning, and scheduling using a bidding-based approach and STEP based product representation. The proposed methodology assumes an agile manufacturing environment based on intelligent machines capable of making autonomous planning decisions.

In recent years, the principles of concurrent engineering have been widely applied to overcome the lack of communication between product development tasks that often causes consistency problems in the manufacturing enterprise [4][5]. Concurrent Engineering refers to the practice of coordinating various life-cycle product elements at early design stages. Coordination is the key to maintain the consistency of concurrent decision-making and the integrity of information in the product development lifecycle [6]. The coordination of collaborative design activities is time consuming and requires sufficient knowledge support at different decision making levels. One way of supporting collaborative engineering activities is by deploying intelligent agents to assist designers in coordinating the decision making process, manage interactions and provide immediate feedback from others manufacturers. Such approach will contribute to reduction in design lead time and will facilitate designers to focus on the essential problems of design [7]. In agent-supported collaborative design, the designer can coordinate and communicate with manufacturing planners and other stake holders through computer software agents that are applied in a human centred fashion. In this context the human user is also seen as an agent who can interact with other human/software agents via a user interface [8]. An agent

0-7695-0798-9/00 $10.00 © 2000 IEEE

collaboration and communication system, therefore, involves interacting agents that collectively possess the necessary knowledge about manufacturability and enterprise resources for collaborative product design and evaluation [9].

The ARPA Knowledge Sharing Effort has defined the principal components of an Agent Communication Language (ACL), that satisfies these needs. Three components of an ACL have been defined: (1) Knowledge Query and Manipulation Language (KQML), (2) Knowledge Interchange Format (KIF); and (3) Ontology, which function as open-ended dictionaries to define the vocabulary used [10]. Message communication sent using this ACL are KQML queries on KIF expressions using concepts defined in ontology. However, in many cases XML (eXtensible Markup Language) could be used to substitute to KIF as a more broadly understood - albeit less expressive - form of representation [11][12].

The advent of the World Wide Web (WWW) has opened new horizons for collaborative decision-making using agent based technology. The introduction of XML (eXtensible Markup Language) has defined an universal standard for electronic data exchange on the Web [13]. Traditionally the Web pages are constructed using Hypertext Markup Language (HTML) which does not allow structured exchange of information. XML allows the information to be encoded using a meaningful structure and semantics can easily exchanged and understood by software agents. XML is equipped with several powerful hyper-reference functions and it permits semantic tagging and interoperation [14].

Despite the recent developments in the area of concurrent design and manufacture, there is a need of generic methods to support the interactions between different stake holders at the early design stages and provide a basis for mapping design requirements to processing capabilities of the manufacturing systems participating in the extended production environment. An important step in this process is the identification, structuring and formalisation of the product and process knowledge that can allow different levels of knowledge abstraction and exchange.

The paper reports on a XML-based agent communication and knowledge exchange framework applied as a CORBA distributed environment. The reported approach defines product design, process and facility knowledge domains, each supported by an object-relational data model. XML meta-tags linked to domain database tables are used to store structured design and manufacture data. A new markup language MML (Manufacturability Markup Language) is proposed with a specific semantics that support design manufacturability assessment activities. MML provides a format for exchanging ontology definition and communication among different agents in a distributed design environment.

2. Manufacturability Models in the Extended Enterprise

The manufacturability assessment is based on selection of manufacturing processes and resources with processing capabilities that match the product design requirement. The decision making process is supported by manufacturing knowledge models and performance measuring tools for design evaluation. Generic enterprise capability patterns are used to uniquely describe the specific core resources and the unique and shared manufacturing capabilities of the companies collaborating in the extended enterprise.

2.1 Product data model

The input request for design evaluation is based on component data model representing the target components constituting the new product. Components are described using form features and their relationships. Form features are considered as geometric objects that represent geometric patterns and have some significance in the context of component design and manufacturing [15]. Examples of such features are hole, step, pocket, etc., each of which is uniquely classified and described within the component model. Component form features are organised into a hierarchical structure for their definition and classification. The relationships between the component features are described by component connectivity graph representing external access directions for relating individual features to the key component directions. Also at component level, the technological relationships (e.g. geometrical and positional tolerances) between different features are recorded.

2.2 Capability model of an extended manufacturing facility

The approach adopted in this work is to relate process capability to three fundamental levels. The first is a "form generating schema" to be used for describing process knowledge at a level that is independent of the machine tool and machining facility used for process execution. Form generating schema (FGS) is defined as a technologically meaningful combination of tool and relative motion, FGS are machine independent but can be used to provide a generalised description of machine tool capabilities.

The second level of abstraction is the "facility" level that is used to describe the distribution of manufacturing capabilities in each facility belonging to the extended enterprise. The overall capabilities of a manufacturing facility are described by a set of resource elements (RE) [16]. Each RE represents a collection of form generating schemas which uniquely define the exclusive machine tool capability boundary and the shared boundaries between machine tools.

At extended facility level, the distributed of manufacturing capabilities between different geographically distributed facilities is described by technological elements. Technological elements (TE) are collections of from generating schemes which uniquely define the exclusive and shared machining capability boundaries between different business entities/facilities [16]. The TE's are extended facility specific and capture information relating to the distribution of FGSs among the machining shops included in the extended enterprise. Although a TE may be attached to several resources, a form generating schema can belong to only one TE. A machining shop is capable of carrying out all the form generating schemas of the TEs associated with it.

2.3 Product and facility prototyping methodology

The decision-making system for product and facility prototyping in extended manufacturing facility is outlined in Figure 1. The main objective is to provide an early design assessment tool to support design and planning.

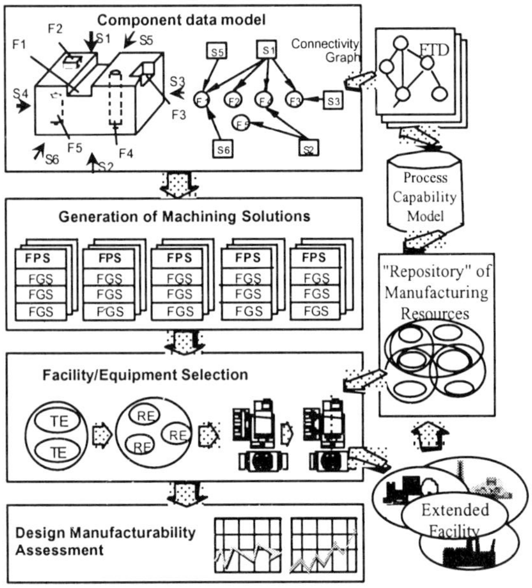

Figure 1. Decision making methodology – an overview

The methodology is based on iterative matching of the product design requirement to the machining capabilities available for selection in the extended enterprise environment. The decision making process is supported by a process capability and manufacturing resource models and performance measuring tools for design and facility evaluation activities in a distributed manufacturing environment.

In an extended manufacturing environment the decision making is based on collaboration between different geographically distributed facilities with a high level of autonomy in the extended enterprise organisation. Such autonomy can be effectively described by using a multi-agent representation of the main decision making modules within the distributed design environment. In the context of the reported research an agent is considered to be autonomous collection of object oriented decision making algorithms, software tools, and data structures to support human-centred decision making process in a well defined domain and provide communication to other agents.

3. CORBA-based Distributed Agent Communication Framework

Communication between agents in distributed systems with different platforms, programming languages and network protocols enables true enterprise product development collaboration. The manufacturability assessment system is developed as a CORBA-based distributed multi-agent environment in Figure 2.

The decision-making agents are implemented using CORBA objects with IDL (Interface Definition Language) interfaces allowing application independent specification of available member functions to a client. To call member functions a client needs to know only the object's IDL definition without any details such as programming language used, object location, or operating system. Each agent is based on communication layer (ORB), parser using KQML/XML message representation and a Java applet user interface.

A client, usually a browser, requests a Java applet. Then the browser initiate a separate TCP/IP session to fetch the applet. The browser loads the applet into the client's main memory, and then executes it. The Java applet will include IDL-generated client stubs, which use the CORBA DII (Dynamic Invocation Interface) to generate server request, e.g. *dynamic agent location*, *knowledge retrieval format for database*, *message repository operation*, *parsed knowledge in XML format*, *KQML message format for agent communication* and *receiving message format for human answer*. The applet also provides functionality that allows the user to browse the product database, view CAD and VRML file, manipulate the reply message in message repository, view sending and receiving message, and put the request in KQML message columns. The ORB is responsible for finding a CORBA object's implementation, preparing it to receive requests, communicate requests to it and carry the reply answer to the client user. In the server side, the XML and component data generator, generate the domain knowledge from the database according to the domain DTD, and the message repository stores the communication messages (Figure 6).

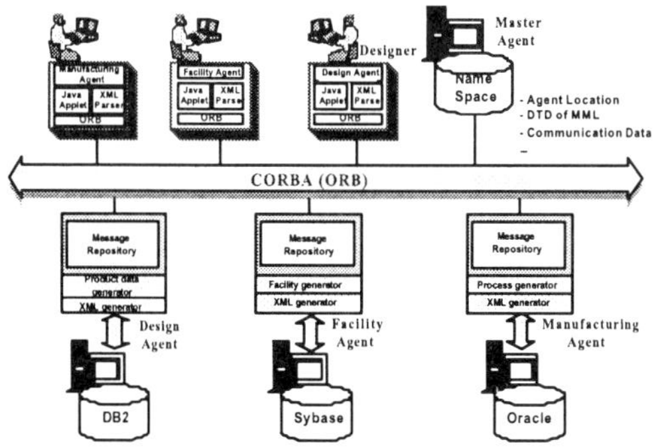

Figure 2. A CORBA-based distributed multi-agent environment

When a design agent needs to send a message to another agent, the main application module first generates a string structured as a KQML message that includes XML content. This message is then parsed by the KQML-XML parser/generator which invokes the required method from the CORBA IDL according to the performative request [17]. The invoked method is then transferred to the ORB, which determines the object to which the invocation will be passed. The call is then sent via master agent server to the target agent. The master agent server stores information about the agents location, data type definitions (DTD) and other communication data. Thus, each client can query the server at runtime to obtain definitions about different available interfaces and then call the member functions of the relevant agent.

The receiving agent parses the message and generates KQML instructions according to the invoked method and its XML content. The generated string is then passed to the main application of the agent which performs the required operations according to the content of the message.

4. The Manufacturability Markup Language (MML)

Since people construct agents, the effect is that the agent's creator must use a specific ontology to represent the agent's knowledge. An ontology is more than a taxonomy of classes, and should describe their relationships. All agents that share the same ontology for knowledge representation have an understanding of the words in the agent communication language.

MML (Manufacturability Markup Language) is a language for exchange of ontology in manufacturability assessment among agents communication. The purpose of MML is intended to be used for transferring ontologies among different databases that exist in extended enterprises, and constitutes a form of knowledge for agent communication.

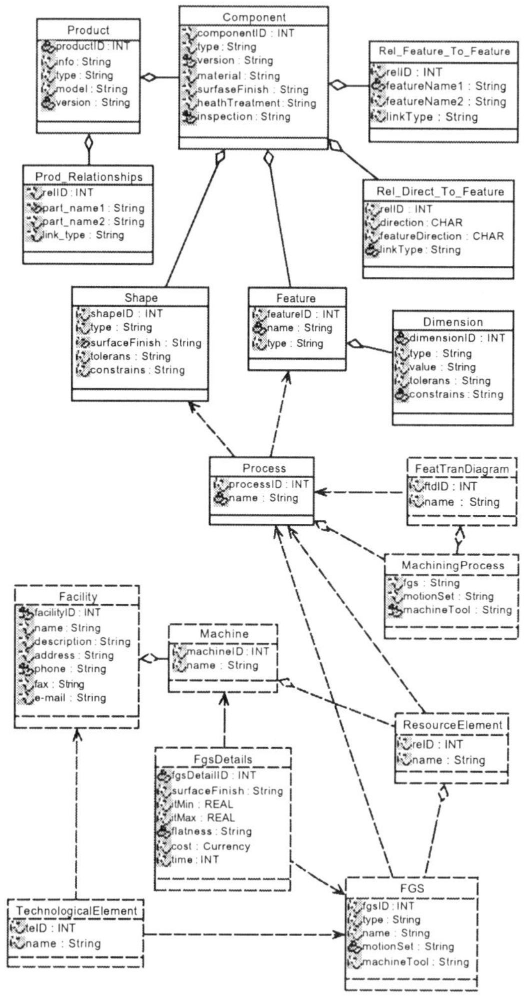

Figure 3. Data model representing the domain knowledge classes for manufacturability assessment support

Figure 3 illustrates the classes of elements and attributes of the product data model, process data model, extended facility data model and the remote link between each model. As represented in Figure 3, the base class of the product data model is classified into three further base classes: *Product*, *Component* and *Feature*. *Prod_Relationship* is one-to-many association relationship for product and sub-assembly. *Rel_Feature_to_Feature* and *Rel_Direct_To_Feature* are associated relationship and define the connection with other components in assembly processes. *Dimension* is a subclass of the class *Feature*.

In the process data model, the *Process* class is dependent link on the *Feature* class, and it could indicate the machining solutions of each feature from the *FeatTranDiagram* class and *MachingProcess* class.

ResourceElement class and *FGS* class, which provide an important link between the facility data model and the process data model, and performs the facility selection from machine tool capability and shares boundaries between machine tools among the association relationship classes.

```
<?xml encoding="US-ASCII"?>

<!-- Revision: 60 1.2 facilities.dtd, docs, xml4j2,
xml4j2_0_15 -->

<!ELEMENT facilities (facility)+>
<!ELEMENT facility (description*,address*,phone*,fax*,e-
mail*,machines)>
<!ATTLIST facility f_name ID #REQUIRED>
<!ELEMENT description (#PCDATA)>
<!ELEMENT address (#PCDATA)>
<!ELEMENT phone (#PCDATA)>
<!ELEMENT fax (#PCDATA)>
<!ELEMENT e-mail (#PCDATA)>
<!ELEMENT machines (machine)+>
<!ELEMENT machine (resource_element)>
<!ATTLIST machine m_name ID #REQUIRED>
<!ELEMENT resource_element (fgs)+>
<!ATTLIST  resource_element re_name ID #REQUIRED>
<!ELEMENT fgs
(tech_elem,motion_set,machine_tool,surface_finish,it_min,it_ma
x,cost,time)>
<!ATTLIST  fgs fgs_name ID #REQUIRED>
<!ELEMENT tech_elem (#PCDATA)>
<!ELEMENT motion_set (#PCDATA)>
<!ELEMENT machine_tool (#PCDATA)>
<!ELEMENT surface_finish (#PCDATA)>
<!ELEMENT it_min (#PCDATA)>
<!ELEMENT it_max (#PCDATA)>
<!ELEMENT cost (#PCDATA)>
<!ELEMENT time (#PCDATA)>
```

Figure 4. An DTD example for facility data model

MML uses XML syntax to represent different object classes of the manufacturability domain models. The models store structured data in XML meta tags linked to database tables. Each tag is defined by DTD (Document Data Definition), and carries semantics that can be used for knowledge retrieval. The DTD create classes of elements and attributes, and defines the type of elements that can be used in relationships among those elements. A example of the basic DTD classes and relationships among the classes in the facility data model is shown in Figure 4. The illustrated DTD declares the content model of XML elements representing facility ontology concept. Sub-elements represent attributes of concepts, e.g. *address* and *machines* are attributes of *facility*. If the attribute represents a relation to another concept, the attribute element has the content of the respective concept element, otherwise its content type is simple PCDATA. Figure 5 is an example for defining one of the resource elements in Bridgeport milling centre with MML.

```
<?xml version="1.0"?>
<!DOCTYPE facilities SYSTEM "facilities.dtd">
<!-- Revision: 61 1.3 facilities.dtd, docs, xml4j2, xml4j2_0_15 >
<facilities>
<facility f_name="Facility_1">
  <machines>
    <machine m_name="Bridgeport_milling_centre">
      <resource_element re_name="RE-1">
        <fgs fgs_name="end_milling_1_rough">
          <tech_elem>"TE#1"</tech_elem>
          <motion_set>"Rk_Ti_tk"</motion_set>
          <machine_tool>" end_mill"</machine_tool>
          <surface_finish>"60"</surface_finish>
          <it_min>"0.01"</it_min>
          <it_max>"0.03"</it_max>
          <cost>"50/hour"</cost>
          <time>"30min"</time>
        </fgs>
      </resource_element>
    </machine>
  </machines>
</facility>
</facilities>
```

Figure 5. An example of resource element in MML

The MML language is designed to provide a mechanism for encoding manufacturability ontologies within a flat file. MML proves not only to be adequate for knowledge representation, but also provides an intermediate language for agent communication in a distributed environment.

5. Illustrative Example

An illustrative example of the decision making interactions between the design, processing and facility agents for manufacturability assessment is shown through the user interface of the Design Agent (see Figure 6).

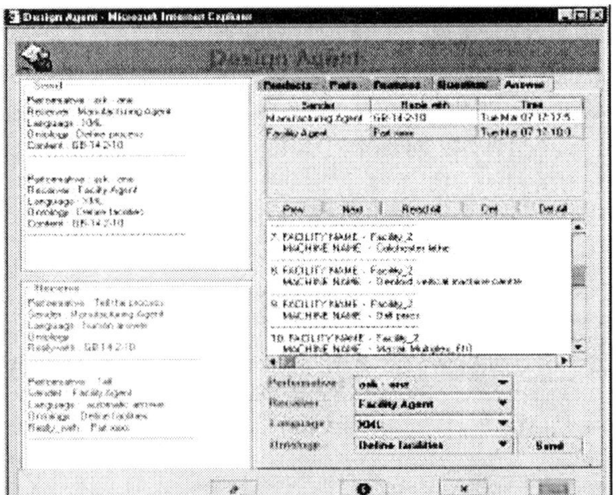

Figure 6. Design Agent - user interface

The example starts with a generation of request for manufacturability assessment by the designer which is transmitted throughout the Design Agent. The message is sent to the manufacturing agent which facilitates the selection of processing alternatives by consulting the issuing the request to the manufacturing planner and proving support for search of the process capability warehouse. As a result a number of possible solutions are generated that are communicated to the facility agent.

The facility agent attaches technological elements to each processing alternatives and provides support for optimisation of the overall set of technological elements and final machining equipment selection. Each proposed processing and equipment solution is evaluated by the project moderator agent (not shown) and performance measure values attached. The preferred solution is then sent to the design agent and issued to the designer who initiated the request (refer to Figure 6).

6. Conclusions

The reported research aims to provide designers and manufacturing planners with a rapid manufacturing feasibility assessment tool to be used at different design and planning stages in extended manufacturing enterprises. It is based on matching the design requirements to the facility capabilities in an extended enterprise environment using generic models for representation of the processes and resource capabilities in an extended virtual manufacturing environment.

The proposed distributed agent-based approach supports simultaneous and collaborative decision making by providing the scope for development of an efficient XML/CORBA based environment for conveying design and manufacture messages across traditional technology boundaries. The reported Manufacturability Markup Language supports the transfer of messages across different data models by providing a meaningful semantic framework for communication between stake holders and software agents in the distributed design process.

The reported methodology is a step towards the development of a generic prototype tool for collaborative design evaluation and rapid assessment of the manufacturing feasibility and resource availability at different stages of the product development process.

References

[1] Tan, G. W., Hayes C. C., Shaw M., 1996, An Intelligent agent framework for concurrent product design and planning, IEEE Transactions on Engineering Management, 43, 297-306.

[2] Balasubramanian, S., Maturana F. P., Norrie D. H., 1996, Multi-agent planning and coordination for distributed concurrent engineering, International Journal of Cooperative Information Systems, 5, 153-179.

[3] Gu, P. Balasubramanian S. Norrie D. H. Bidding-based process planning and scheduling in a multi-agent system. Computers and Industrial Engineering. 1997; 32(1):477-496.

[4] Maturana, F. P. and Norrie D. H. Multi-agent Mediator architecture for distributed manufacturing. Journal of Intelligent Manufacturing. 1996; 7:257-270.

[5] Lee, B. H. and Ishii K. Product-Agents and the Embedded Web: Architectures and Tools for Lifecycle Design. Workshop 8: AGENTS AND WEB-BASED DESIGN ENVIRONMENTS; Stanford University, CA-USA. 1996.

[6] Lottaz, C. and Smith I. Collaborative design using constraint solving. Lausanne, Switzerland: Swiss Federal Institute of Technology (EPFL); 1997.

[7] Murthy, S. Akkiraiu R. Rachin J. and Wu F. Agent-based cooperative scheduling. Yorktown Heights, NY USA: IBM T.J. Wrson Research Center; 1998.

[8] Jim, Y. Lu Stephen C. Y. An Agent-Supported Approach to Collaborative Design. Annals of CIRP. 1998; 47(1):107-110.

[9] Ratchev, S. Shiau, J. Valtchanov, G. Distributed Product and Facility Prototyping in Extended Manufacturing Enterprises. The 15th International Conference on Production Research, ICPR'99, University of Limerick, Ireland; Aug 9-12 1999.

[10] Genesereth, M. R. Ketchpel S. P. Software agents. Communications of the ACM. 1994 Jul; 37(7):49-53.

[11] Lassila, O. RDF Metadata and Agent Architectures. Workshop on Compositional Software Architectures; Monterey, California. Jan 6-8 1998.

[12] Karp, P. Pangea Systems Inc. XOL: An XML-Based Ontology Language for Bioinformatics. Objects in Bioinformatics'99; Silicon Valley, San Jose, Aug 19-21 1999.

[13] W3C, The World Wide Web Consortium. Extensible Markup Language (XML) Available at: http://www.w3.org/XML/, Feb. 1998.

[14] Erdmann, M. Studer R. Ontologies as Conceptual Models for XML Documents, Twelfth Workshop on Knowledge Acquisition, Modeling and Management, KAW'99 Voyager Inn, Banff, Alberta, Canada; Oct 16 1999.

[15] Gindy, N. N. Z. Ratchev, S. M., Component grouping for Cellular Decomposition of Manufacturing Facilities using Resource Elements, Integrated Manufacturing Systems, 8, 215 –222, 1997.

[16] Ratchev, S. M., Resource Capability Modelling for Responsive Process Planning in Extended Manufacturing Facilities, in *Globalisation of Manufacturing in the Digital Communications Era of the 21st Century*, Kluwer Academic Publishers, 1998, pp. 389 – 400.

[17] Mayfield, J., Labrou Y., Finin T., Evaluation of KQML as an Agent Communication Language. Proceedings of the 1995 Workshop on Agent Theories, Architectures, and Language Vol. II - Intelligent Agents, 1995.

A Web Infrastructure for People and Agent Interaction and Collaboration

Giacomo Cabri, Letizia Leonardi, Franco Zambonelli
Dipartimento di Scienze dell'Ingegneria – Università di Modena e Reggio Emilia
Via Campi 213/b – 41100 Modena – ITALY
E-mail: {giacomo.cabri, letizia.leonardi, franco.zambonelli}@unimo.it

Abstract

Internet pervasive services call for flexible supports to enable a wide degree of collaboration. On the one hand, many people are connected to the Internet and surf the Web not only to retrieve information, but also to carry out several kinds of different tasks via the on-line services. On the other hand, the Internet is likely to be soon populated by software agents that will act in behalf of users, "intelligent" enough to achieve the better result without boring their users. In this paper we present a Web-based modular architecture that permits interaction and collaboration among people and agents, leading to a more fruitful exploitation of the capabilities offered by the Internet. A negotiation application based on auctions is used to show the advantages of the proposed architecture.

1 Introduction

A lot of applications is being developed to exploit the positive features that characterize the Internet [3]. Due to the characteristics of openness, heterogeneity and unreliability of the Internet, these kinds of applications call not only for tools and methodologies, but also for appropriate models and supports to make the design of the applications easier and to permit a fast spread of these technologies.

In this context, developers must take into account that the Internet world will be populated by heterogeneous kinds of entities, in particular *people* and *agents*. Many people discover how the use of the Web permits to save time even in performing simple tasks. Moreover, the Web gives a world-scale spectrum of possibilities among which to choose the preferred one, letting people compare and make the best decision. Agents are proposing as other entities that will populate the Internet. They are software entities characterized by the following main features: *autonomy, proactiveness, reactivity* and *sociality* [13]. While the first three features are related to the development of each single agent application (or of classes of applications), the fourth one has a deep impact in the development of Internet services. Moreover, we think that a further important feature for the agents is *mobility*, i.e., the capability of actively changing the hosting execution environment in a network-aware fashion [14].

Even if both people and agents exploit the same Internet services and resources, the ways they do it can be very different, because of the differences between the adopted interfaces, the speeds of elaboration, the intelligence degrees, and so on. This calls for an adequate support to permit heterogeneous interactions and collaborations on the Web [4, 10]. In a previous work, we identified the requirements of a flexible architecture that could support collaborative work on the Web, and we developed PROOF [6], a modular framework that meets such requirements. We now point out that such architecture is adequate for a people-populated Web, but has several limitations when it has to be exploited also in an agent-populated environment. In this paper we propose a more general architecture, designed starting from the previous one, which has been extended to support the hosting of (possible mobile) agents and to be enriched by high-level coordination capabilities. The resulting architecture, called PROOF v2, is very flexible and can be exploited by several kinds of Internet applications. In particular, in this paper we show the concrete use of such architecture in an auction-based Internet application, considered as a case study.

2 The basic PROOF Architecture

The main aim of *PROOF* [6] is to provide a mean to enrich the Web with computational capabilities for CSCW (Computer Supported Cooperative Work) without requiring significant modifications to current servers and clients. In fact, PROOF relies on the concept of *proxy server*, which stands in the middle between servers and clients. While traditional proxy servers are mainly used to provide cache functions, PROOF is much more flexible and can embody several different functionalities. Thus, a

0-7695-0798-9/00 $10.00

such kind of proxy server intrinsically becomes a workplace open to the Internet, where the cooperation between clients can occur without forcing clients to exit the workplace when accessing generic Web servers. Within our PROOF proxy server, any kind of computation can be enclosed, such as caching and dynamic production of result HTML pages, as in the server-side approach. Synchronous interactions between the clients and the proxy server can be enabled by letting PROOF insert specific applets into the pages that it provides to clients (browsers), thus enabling communication among people in the workgroup via the proxy server.

PROOF is based on a modular architecture, composed by a *framework* and several application *modules* (see Figure 1). The framework provides the basic proxy functionalities, such as the connections with the client browsers and with the Web servers, the user identification and authentication; moreover it permits the embodying of different application modules. Each module implements the behavior of one specific application. The framework can load one module a time.

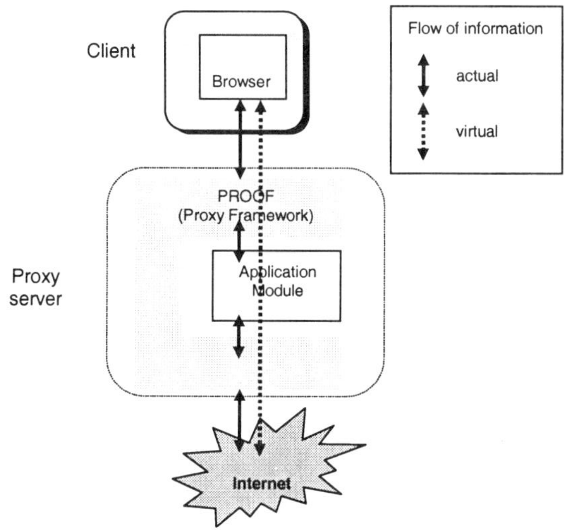

Figure 1. The application-dependent module defines the proxy server behavior

PROOF is written in Java, to achieve portability. It exploits the mechanisms of *interfaces* and *reflection* to achieve modularity and an easy and dynamic installation of application modules into the framework.

The PROOF architecture is very general and it is not tightly bound to any specific application because it is based on the implementation of a framework that offers general-purpose application-independent functionalities. Different application modules can be implemented with a limited coding effort and easily installed within the proxy-framework.

3 Extending the basic PROOF Architecture – PROOF v2

The previously described implementation of the PROOF architecture is satisfactory for the use in a Web inhabited by people. But it could be more useful if it were exploitable also by software agents. In this direction, we present the extensions made to the PROOF architecture in order to be more open and better integrated in the Internet environment. Such extensions have been implemented in the second version of PROOF, *PROOF v2*. In particular, the two most significant extensions are related to *(i)* the capability of hosting mobile agents and *(ii)* the integration of an advanced coordination model to enable high-level interactions and synchronization.

3.1 Adding Mobile-Agent Capabilities

The first important extension to the old PROOF architecture is the addition of the capability of hosting mobile agents. They can significantly improve the design and the development of Internet applications thanks to their characteristics. The *agency* feature [13] permits them to exhibit a high degree of autonomy with regard to the users. The *mobility* feature [14] takes several advantages in a wide and unreliable environment such as the Internet. First, mobile agents can significantly save bandwidth, by moving locally to the resources they need and by carrying the code to manage them. Moreover, mobile agents can deal with non-continuous network connection and, as a consequence, they intrinsically suit mobile computing systems.

Therefore, mobile agents, on behalf of users, can install specific modules to give the proxy server an application-dependent behavior. Since agents are autonomous, the user can give them a possibly high-level task to carry out, and they can proactively search for the needed module(s), perhaps by mean of negotiation with module providers; once they have found the module(s), they can search for the most appropriate – also in terms of costs – proxy server where to install the module(s). The user is then notified of the proxy server (s)he have to use in order to exploit the needed functionalities. As a further advantage, this extension permits to give other entities – besides people – the access to collaborative Web applications. Users can think of not participating directly to an interactive application that requires repetitive actions; instead, they can rely on one or more software agents that act in behalf of them. For example, if a user is interested in buying a good, (s)he can delegate to a software agent the tasks of comparing the different offers, and of negotiating the final price. In this context, the exploitation of mobile agents can make the PROOF v2 architecture very open and flexible. The presence of different kinds of involved entities, introduces several interaction and synchronization issues, and calls for the presence of appropriate coordination models, detailed in the next Subsection.

3.2 Adding Advanced Coordination

Apart from hosting (possible mobile) agents, the PROOF v2 architecture also needs a sophisticated coordination model to permit interactions, collaborations, negotiations and also competitions at a high level. Since programmable tuple spaces are recognized to be a powerful coordination mean that well suits Internet applications, in particular those where mobile agents are involved [11], we have decided to extend PROOF with programmable tuple spaces.

The integration of coordination model based on programmable tuple spaces can be exploited also to store information about the proxy and the installed modules. This has a number of advantages. First, the tuple space is used as a shared repository where different entities can store, retrieve and exchange information in a simple and standard way. Second, the exploitation of programmable reactivity increases flexibility and permits to add whatever computation in the coordination media. For example, a reaction can be in charge of notifying a proxy module about a change in the tuple space; the proxy module, in its turn, can dynamically update the Web pages on the users' browsers accordingly to the new information in the tuple space (see Figure 2).

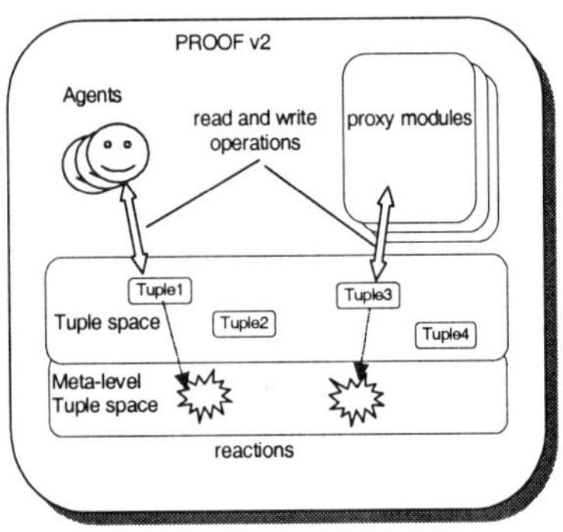

Figure 2. The MARS Architecture integrated in PROOF v2

The concrete coordination system that we choose to be integrated in PROOF v2 is MARS (Mobile Agent Reactive Space) [5], a coordination architecture based on an enhanced Linda-like model [2]. MARS defines tuple spaces as shared repositories of information, used to store and associatively retrieve messages in the form of tuples (see Figure 2) [12]. MARS was originally conceived for mobile agent applications, but it can be fruitfully exploited also by non mobile agents. The MARS architecture supposes that one tuple space is associated to each node.

MARS is JavaSpaces compliant and is written in pure Java. MARS tuples are Java objects that represent ordered sets of typed fields. Tuple classes must implement a specific interface required for tuple management and named Entry in JavaSpaces, or, in a simpler way, can sub-class from the so called AbstractEntry class, which provides for a basic implementation of the Entry interface. A specific tuple field is defined as an instance variable of a tuple class. Each field of the tuple refers to an object that can also represent primitive data. The MARS interface defines five Linda-like operations to access the tuple space:

- **write**, to put a tuple, supplied as parameter, in the space;
- **read**, to retrieve a tuple from the space, on the basis of a request tuple supplied as a parameter and to be used as a pattern for the matching mechanism;
- **take**, which works as the read operation but extracts the matching tuple from the space;
- **readAll**, to retrieve all matching tuples from the space;
- **takeAll**, to extract all matching tuples from the space.

MARS overcomes the limits of the static data-oriented Linda model, by adding programmable reactivity, which means that specific actions can be programmed in response to the accesses performed by agents on the tuple space [7]. In fact, MARS implements a programmable reactive tuple space model in which the effects of the operations on the tuple spaces can be dynamically modified. Agents always access the tuple spaces with the same basic set of Linda-like operations. A meta-level tuple space is introduced in each node to associatively manage reactions. A meta-level tuple in the form (Reaction_object, T, O, I) associates the reaction implemented by Reaction_object with the event of the operation O performed on the tuple T by the agent with identity I. Writing a meta-level tuple in the meta-level tuple space means installing the corresponding reaction, while taking a meta-level tuple means uninstalling the corresponding reaction. Readings on the meta-level tuple space are performed by the system to search for a matching reaction when an operation occurs on the base-level tuple space. Since T can be a template, a single meta-level tuple can be used to associate a reaction with the events related to all the tuples matching with T.

MARS can be exploited to implement agent-based applications in different areas. For instance, information retrieval, distributed management and mobile computing are the context where the MARS features can be exploited in a more effective way [9].

3.3 Implementation Issues

The two above-described extensions do not present hard implementation problems, since PROOF was originally designed taking into consideration modularity and flexibility. Moreover, the MARS coordination architecture has been designed to be very portable and uncoupled from Java-based hosting environments (usually, the agent systems): this makes easier to embody MARS in PROOF. However, some light modifications to the proxy framework are needed in order to achieve the highest usability and to exploit all features. In particular, the most significant one is that PROOF v2 must keep a reference to the local MARS tuple space, and must provide it to the installed modules; other more significant modifications to PROOF are needed in order to accept mobile agent modules; the main ones – detailed in the following of this section – are related to: multi-module capability, and security.

The first significant modification concerns the number of modules that can be loaded concurrently. While the first version of PROOF allowed only one module at a time, the new *multi-module capability* permits one single proxy to be exploited by several clients (browsers or agents) for different applications. Obviously, this capability introduces more complexity in the handling of the incoming requests and the related responses. To deal with more than one module in the framework, an additional software level is needed. Such level is in charge of *demultiplexing* the incoming request to the appropriate application module, so that each connected browser has the correct responses. Moreover, we must take into account the possible coordination among different modules installed in the same proxy framework. While the framework provides a simple mean of communication in the form of a global environment, the use of the MARS tuple space is encouraged to exploit all the advantages of its uncoupled and programmable coordination open also to external mobile agents.

The second aspect requiring modifications is related to *security*. In fact, if agents are allowed to install their own modules, security mechanisms and policies must be provided to control such installations, to avoid agents installing malicious modules, which can compromise the whole system by issuing, for example, a *denial of service* attack. The basic security mechanisms must be provided by the mobile agent system, in terms of identification and authentication of the incoming agents. The information about an agent permit to know whether it comes from a trusted user/site and to decide whether to allow the installation of an application module or not. Anyway, we choose to limit the visibility of the proxy internal state/functions from the agents. Moreover, the access to the internal environment by the application modules must be ruled with care, to avoid that a module has full power on the proxy state that relates also to other modules. So the access to the internal state of the proxy can occur only via a well-defined set of methods, which limits the possibilities of manipulate internal variables and information structures.

4 Application Example

An example of application that can fruitfully exploit the PROOF v2 architecture is an auction manager. *Auctions* are interesting negotiation means [1] where there are entities that make resources available and entities that are interested in using such resources. The former ones are usually called *sellers*, while the latter ones are called *bidders*. Normally, there is an intermediate entity, called *auctioneer*, which actually performs the negotiation. The price of the resources sold by sellers via an auction is not fixed, but it is dynamically determined by the interest of the bidders. The seller can set a *reserve price*, i.e., a price under which it does not want to sell the resource. Intelligent agents can spend time to negotiate the desired resources by using the auction mechanisms, which seem to well fit dynamic and heterogeneous environments. In fact, an auction has a high degree of adaptability, has not any *a priori* fixed price and allows dynamic attending by participants. There are several different forms of auction, depending on the number of participants, on the criteria with which the resources are assigned, and so on. We focus on the auctions with one seller and multiple bidders at a time, ruled by several mechanisms: for example, English, Dutch, first-price and Vickery [1].

Currently, there are several implementations of auctions described in the literature. With regard to human people, auction-based markets are rapidly spreading over the Internet, exploiting the Web infrastructure to permit interested people to interact [17]. With regard to the agent-based applications, auctions can be used both to sell goods and to deal with Web resources [16]. In the following of this section we show how the PROOF v2 architecture can be exploited to build an auction-based application, which permits both people and agents to interact in an Internet environment.

4.1 Implementing Auctions with PROOF

First of all, an appropriate *auction proxy module* has to be implemented and installed in PROOF v2 to deal with the auctions. Appropriate *MARS reactions* are in charge of exchanging information between the auction proxy module and the tuple space, realizing the interactions between agents and people. On the one hand, people can participate by using their usual browsers, which are set to use PROOF v2 as the proxy server. On the other hand, agents can attend the auctions exploiting the tuple space integrated within PROOF v2, where they can find needed information about the goods/resources on sale, such as the price, the current highest bid, the timeout, and so on. Therefore, in this context, the features of the MARS model integrated within the proxy server can be useful exploited in the implementation of the auction mechanisms:

- the Linda-like data-oriented approach permits to access the selling/buying services in a simple and uniform way;
- the programmability property allows to uncouple auction mechanisms, implemented via reactions, from auction policies decided by people or embodied in the agents.

These aspects make possible to rule the agent's behavior depending on the specific auction laws. This achieves the same purposes of the socially adopted conventions of the traditional auctions [15].

The actual implementation of Internet auctions by using PROOF v2 works as follows. Let us suppose the following case for explanation purpose: the seller is represented by a mobile agent, while the bidders are represented by both human people and mobile agents. The bidder people participate by means of standard browsers configured to use PROOF v2 as proxy server. At connection time, they choose the auction module installed in PROOF.

At the negotiation site, the seller agent writes a tuple that contains information about the good/resource it is going to sell (step *a* in Figure 3). This writing triggers a specific pre-installed reaction that acts as the auctioneer, i.e. it is in charge of managing the auction (step *a'* in Figure 3). Such reaction is also in charge of notifying the auction proxy module that an auction has started (step *a''* in Figure 3).

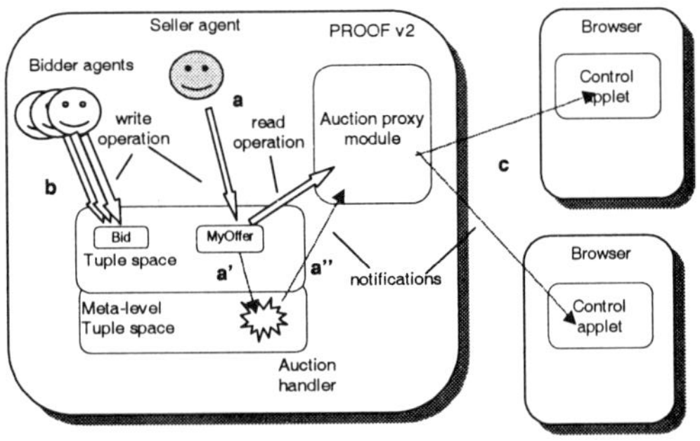

Figure 3. A seller agent puts a good on sale (a), the bidder agents put their bids (b), the auction proxy module updates the users' browsers via the control applets (c)

Once the proxy module and the bidder agents have read the tuple representing the good/resource on sale, people and agents can bid a price to buy the good/resource on sale, respectively by using the applet displayed in the users' browsers or by inserting tuples (step *b* in Figure 3).

In the people case, the control applet communicates the new bid to the proxy module, which is in charge of updating the information in the proxy server environment by writing a tuple in the tuple space.

In the any case, the auctioneer reaction monitors the bids from both agents and people, and notifies the interested agents and the auction proxy module that a change has occurred in the auction. The module is then in charge of updating the information in the user browsers by reading the value of the new bid from the tuple space and communicating it to the control applets inserted in the auction Web page (step *c* in Figure 3).

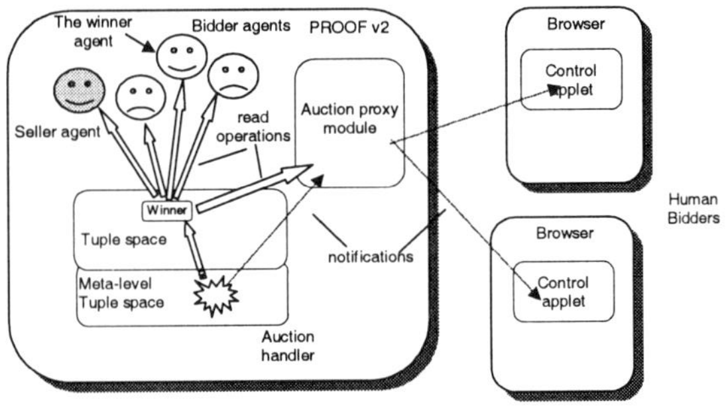

Figure 4. The Auctioneer reaction decides the winner and communicates it via a tuple

When the auction is over, the auctioneer reaction decides the winner and creates a tuple to inform all the participants about it: people are notified via the proxy module, while agents can directly read the tuple (see Figure 4). A detailed description of the implementation of auctions via reactions can be found in [8]. Obviously, the auction implementation must make use of security capabilities provided by the system to authorize only correct readings, takings and writings of tuples.

PROOF v2 permits to handle auctions in which both people and agents are involved, in a very flexible way. In fact, thanks to the modularity of the architecture and the capability of programming the behavior of the tuple space, several kinds of different mechanisms can be implemented by changing (also at run time) the reactions installed in the system. For example, if a good is on sale by English auction rather than Dutch auction, the appropriate reaction can be installed to rule the interactions among participants.

5 Conclusions

In this paper we have presented the PROOF v2 architecture. Our aim is to realize a general-purpose architecture that supports the dynamicity, the heterogeneity and the openness of the applications in the Internet scenario. PROOF v2 is a modular architecture that well fits the Web environment, thanks to its "standing in the middle" between browsers and servers that permit to use existing Web components. The capability of dealing with mobile agents and the integration of an advanced coordination model permit to better exploit all the Internet features. On the one hand, the architecture becomes more open by letting also agents exploit its functionalities in terms of installing/uninstalling modules and interacting with the installed modules. On the other hand, the advanced coordination model based on programmable tuple spaces makes easier the design and the development of Internet applications, where collaboration, synchronization and competition have to be properly expressed and managed.

From the architecture point of view, PROOF v2 can be seen as a sophisticated interface to shared information. In fact, the information represented by tuples stored in the tuple space can be accessed by means of Internet browsers, which rely on an *ad hoc* proxy module. In this way, the module permits users to access and modify the content of the tuple space in an application-dependent way. Different modules can present a different vision of the information, depending on the specific application policies. As a final note, we point out that the presented new PROOF v2 architecture permit also to create a federation of proxy servers, which can be exploited in different ways. For example, the presence of several proxies with the same functionalities permits to perform load balancing by distributing the users towards the less loaded servers.

Acknowledgment

This work was supported by the Italian National Research Council (CNR) in the framework of the project "Global Applications in the Internet Area: models and programming environments".

References

[1] Agorics, Inc., "Going, going, gone! A survey of auction types", http://www.agorics.com, 1996

[2] S. Ahuja, N. Carriero, D. Gelernter, "Linda and Friends", IEEE Computer, Vol. 19, No. 8, pp. 26-34, August 1986.

[3] G. Almasi, A. Suvaiala, I. Muslea, C. Cascaval, T. Davis, V. Jagannathan, "Web*: A Technology to Make Information Available on the Web", Proceedings of the 4th IEEE Workshop on Enabling Technology: Infrastructure for Collaborative Enterprises, pp. 147-153, Berkley Springs (WV), IEEE Computer Society Press, 1995.

[4] R. Bentley, T. Horstmann, J. Trevor, "The World Wide Web as enabling technology for CSCW: The case of BSCW", in Computer-Supported Cooperative Work: Special issue on CSCW and the Web, Vol. 6, Kluwer Academic Press, 1997.

[5] G. Cabri, L. Leonardi, F. Zambonelli, "Reactive Tuple Spaces for Mobile Agent Coordination", Proceedings of the 2nd International Workshop on Mobile Agents, Lecture Notes in Computer Science, No. 1477, Springer-Verlag (D), September 1998.

[6] G. Cabri, L. Leonardi, F. Zambonelli, "A Proxy-based Framework to Support Synchronous Cooperation on the Web", Software, Practice and Experience, Vol. 29, No. 14, pp. 1241-1263, 1999.

[7] G. Cabri, L. Leonardi, F. Zambonelli, "Mobile-Agent Coordination Models for Internet Applications", IEEE Computer Magazine, Vol. 33, No. 2, pp. 82-89, February 2000.

[8] G. Cabri, L. Leonardi, F. Zambonelli, "Auction-based Agent Negotiation via Programmable Tuple Spaces", 4th International Workshop on Cooperative Information Agents, LNCS, Boston (USA), July 2000, to appear.

[9] G. Cabri, L. Leonardi, F. Zambonelli, "Mobile Agent Coordination for Distributed Network Management", Journal of Network and Systems Management, to appear.

[10] P. Ciancarini, R. Tolksdorf, F. Vitali, D. Rossi, A. Knoche, "Coordinating Multi-Agents Applications on the WWW: a Reference Architecture", IEEE Transactions on Software Engineering, Vol. 24, No. 8, May 1998.

[11] E. Denti, A. Natali, A. Omicini, "On the Expressive Power of a Language for Programmable Coordination Media", Proceedings of the ACM Symposium on Applied Computing, Atlanta (G), 1998.

[12] D. Gelernter, N. Carriero, "Coordination Languages and Their Significance", Communications of the ACM, Vol. 35, No. 2, pp. 96-107, February 1992.

[13] N. R. Jennings, M. Wooldridge, editors, "Agent Technology: Foundations, Applications, and Markets", Springer-Verlag, March 1998.

[14] N. M. Karnik, A. R. Tripathi, "Design Issues in Mobile-Agent Programming Systems", IEEE Concurrency, Vol. 6, No. 3, pp. 52-61, July-September 1998.

[15] P. Noriega, C. Sierra, J. A. Rodriguez, "The Fishmarket Project. Reflections on Agent-mediated institutions for trustworthy E-Commerce", Workshop on Agent Mediated Electronic Commerce (AMEC-98), Seoul, 1998.

[16] T. Sandholm and Q. Huai, "*Nomad*: Mobile Agent System for an Internet-Based Auction House", IEEE Internet Computing, Special issue on Agent Technology and the Internet, 2000, to appear.

[17] P. R. Wurman, M. P. Wellman, W. E. Walsh, "The Michigan Internet AuctionBot: A Configurable Auction Server for Human and Software Agents", 2nd International Conference on Autonomous Agents, May 1998.

Workspace Awareness in Mobile Virtual Teams

Alois Ferscha
Department of Computer Science
University of Vienna
ferscha@ani.univie.ac.at

Abstract

Staying aware of each other in cooperative team work is something we take for granted in the everyday world, even if collaboration is not continuously face-to-face, and team members frequently shift from group to individual activity during work sessions. Maintaining this intuitive fidelity of awareness, e.g. of team members working in the office next door, is on the other hand something that has proven particularly difficult to attain in distributed collaboration systems, where the social interaction protocol is not as established, and the means for becoming aware of the environment are far less common. The work reported in this paper is focussed on workspace awareness, i.e. the "... up-to-the-moment understanding of another person's interaction with a shared workspace" [GuGr 99].

Opposed to the traditional understanding of shared workspaces as being bounded spaces where people can see and manipulate artefacts related to their activities (documents in an office, the whiteboard in a lecture hall or assembly lines in a factory), we consider virtual mobile (team) workspaces as abstract spaces containing objects that constitute the team work.

Keywords: Virtual Spaces, Distributed Cooperative Environments, Multiuser Interaction, VRML, Java.

1 Introduction

The virtualisation of organisational structures is a direct consequence of the availability of new media technologies, global competition, and the advanced mobility of people, devices and services. For team work, improving efficiency, shortening lead times, competence and role based service provision as well as media based remote interactions among co-workers has become crucial. Virtual teams have evolved as a way of working across geographical, time and organisational boundaries. Team members must no longer be co-located, or in the same place, in order to work together. The planning and design of the organisation, the team, and the structuring of business processes is the basis for building a successful virtual team. In addition to these factors, team work must be coordinated through technology, and the team members must interact and keep each other updated.

Virtual spaces based on the metaphor of "shared network places" [FeJo 99] are becoming a well accepted implementation approach for multiuser, multimedia, distributed cooperative work environments to support the work activities and interactions of goal oriented business teams. Similar to real-life physical team rooms, which provide a permanent shared space used by a work group, **TEAMSPACE**, the virtual space presented in this paper, provides a virtual meeting room for (possibly mobile) work teams, i.e. a place to store, retrieve and present multimedia content (documents), to design and construct cooperatively, to brainstorm, to negotiate and make decisions, to run shared applications, to browse enterprise data, or to acquire, formalise and exchange enterprise knowledge. Since physical team rooms rely on the physical proximity of the team members and their easy access to the common work space, this access breaks down when groups are geographically dislocated or moving. For such teams, **TEAMSPACE** provides the electronic equivalent of a physical team room transcending distance, time zones, and organisational boundaries. **TEAMSPACE** is based essentially on open technologies, the virtual reality modelling language (VRML) together with Java. A Java-enabled Web-browser together with a VRML plug-in is thus the only requirement for the execution of **TEAMSPACE** on current consumer hardware.

2 Mobile Virtual Teams

Team work enabled by electronic collaboration technologies has evolved as a potentially effective way to make working across time, space, organisational and cultural boundaries an easy and practical way to achieve superior result need in today's globalised, lean and agile organisations. In the traditional understanding, computer supported cooperative work (CSCW) environments and tools free work teams from the physical limitations of time and place. Technology is the main trigger for team workplace innovations, i.e. with the emergence and availability of new hardware (e.g. PDAs, Multimedia home platforms, SmartCards), software (e.g. new middleware architectures, new CORBA frameworks, new Enterprise Java Beans, etc.) and communication technologies (e.g. xDSL, Bluetooth, Wireless Application Protocol, etc.), new demands are raised and new fields of application emerge.

The traditional classification of cooperation along the time and location dimensions assumes - according to the

This work was supported by the *Oesterreichische Nationalbank*, Vienna, Austria, under grant *Jubiläumsfonds 7022*.

0-7695-0798-9/00 $10.00 © 2000 IEEE

distribution characteristics in time and in place of the participating users - that team members cannot both be in different physical places at the same time as perceiving themselves to be in the same virtual place. We therefore extend the traditional space-time matrix with a "virtual place" category, reflecting the possibility of recent synchronous multi-user environments [FeJo 99] to enable users at different physical places to meet in a virtual place. In addition, for our **TEAMSPACE** design, we have identified the following organisational systems to be crucial for the successful support of effective mobile teams:

- **Information and Knowledge Management System (Team Memory):** this system represents ways that organisations can respond to the information processing and knowledge gathering needs of teams. Team knowledge is time dynamic (i.e. requires on-the-fly acquisition), extends in action/state-change-perception cycles, demands structuring (indexing, annotation) and must be delivered in user customised multi-media formats.
- **Awareness System (Team Awareness):** this system is dedicated to the perceptualisation of the effects of team activity by communicating work context, agenda and workspace information to the user interfaces of involved team members just-in-time, and granting anytime access to team memory.
- **Interaction Systems (Meeting Support):** cooperation among humans is conducted via direct point-to-point or multi-point interaction, or indirectly via the manipulation of commonly accessible, shared artefacts (e.g. documents). Here, an interaction system is understood as space (e.g. virtual meeting space) for human-human cooperation at the confluence of synchronous and asynchronous interaction.
- **Mobility Systems (Mobile Teams):** mobility systems deploy mechanism to enable any-place access to team memory, the capturing of awareness information from and delivery to any place, as well as ubiquitous workplace presence.
- **Organisational Innovation Systems (Team Workplace Innovation):** these systems integrate aspects of *team design*, i.e. the organisational structure, team composition, team location, and team resources, *team leadership*, i.e. goal, priority, role and responsibility settings, *team integration*, i.e. coordination and effort sharing facilities, *performance review and reward systems*, i.e. systems defining how performance is assessed and how team members are recognised for their efforts, systems for *team training* (employee development, learning environments, formal training, and informal learning opportunities) and *organisational change systems*.

Once having argued for the role of awareness solutions in team support systems, we shall now focus on awareness issues in mobile teams in particular, and present the respective awareness features of **TEAMSPACE** in detail.

3 Team Awareness

To maintain an intuitive fidelity of staying aware of each other collaboration software user interfaces have to be found that support social interaction to a much higher extent than observed today. Most of the user interfaces for multi-user cooperative software suffer from their single user origin, and thus appear inefficient and clumsy as compared to face-to-face cooperations. User helplessness, frustration and denial are the consequences of the awkwardness of many contemporary real-time distributed groupware systems. Supporting awareness of others, therefore, promises the improving of the usability of multi-user remote cooperation systems by maintaining the fluidity and naturalness of team cooperation.

Existing research on real-time distributed groupware has addressed awareness issues in isolated and localised situations and created application or domain specific solutions (like e.g. in WYSIWIS groupware systems [RoGr 96]), but has not yet created general design principles for awareness support systems [GuGr 99]. More principled information on the awareness oriented design of teamware is demanded, allowing for a systematic consideration of concepts for situated applications and purposes. The focus is on the support of team-work rather than task-work, i.e. on the issue of how well a system supports activities involving communication, coordination and collaboration among team members, rather than the execution of domain tasks (e.g. the management of ToDo lists). In supporting team members to stay aware of each other in a team workspace, the respective teamware systems usability improves, and by that team performance and efficiency.

Adopting the terminology of [GuGr 99], we look at workspace awareness as the "... up-to-the-moment understanding of another person's interaction with a shared workspace", involving knowledge on who is working in the workspace, where individuals are working, what they are doing or going to do, how and when they are executing their work, and what their motivation is for doing it (why). Figure 1, besides those issues, also highlights the awareness information pipeline and awareness system utility and design factors.

Figure 1: Awareness in workteams

This information is apparently useful in cooperation for the coordinated execution of activities, for finding opportunities for direct interaction or to assist one another, for anticipating others actions, for signalling readiness to physically meet, for notifying the completion of pending and the triggering of new tasks, etc. Opposed to the traditional understanding of shared workspaces as being bounded spaces where people can see and manipulate artefacts related to their activities, we consider virtual (team) workspaces as abstract spaces containing objects that constitute the team work (Figure 2).

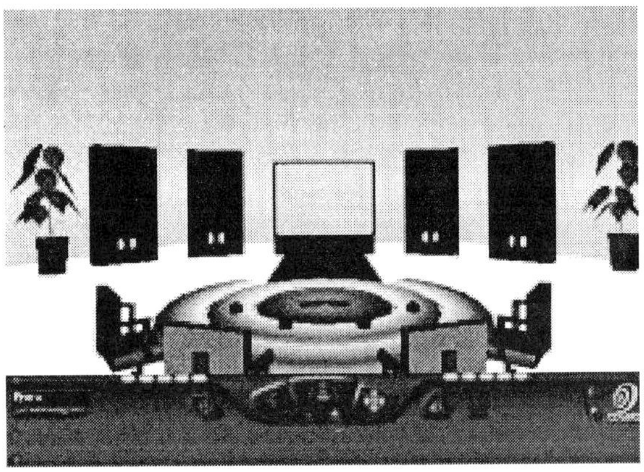
Figure 2: TEAMSPACE – a virtual space for workteams

Unlike real workplaces, not all objects (e.g. documents) need to be visible or co-located with the team member, nor need they do not have a physical representation in the space, nor need they be persistent over time. Activities typically occurring in such spaces are creation (of new objects/artefacts), assembly (combination, aggregation, extraction), manipulation (modification of state like shape, size, colour), organisation (arranging, sorting, reordering), design or exploration (finding certain or new types of artefacts, navigating through e.g. information spaces).

While awareness in face-to-face workspaces is relatively easy to maintain, and the (social and action) protocols of collaboration are intuitive, natural, spontaneous, implicit and unforced, awareness in virtual workspaces is often very difficult to obtain, if not impossible at all. The obvious reasons for this are, that:

- the restrictive communication spectrum of input and output devices allow only for the delivery of a fraction of the perceptual information that is available in face-to-face workspaces. It is essential to preserve (identify, gather and deliver) the media richness of face-to-face interactions for virtual workspaces.
- much of the awareness information in a physical work space (and not represented in virtual spaces) comes from the direct manipulation of shared real world objects (e.g. grasping a folder from the shared book shelf leaves an empty slot in the shelf, while pressing "delete" in a file folder does not), or just changing position in the space (e.g. taking a seat at the conference table). Extending the computational workspace now understood as the influence sphere of the desktop computer display and keyboard, to physical workspaces like the office environment, departments, buildings, cities, regional areas to a global dimension, will improve awareness for virtual team workplaces.
- although a considerable amount of awareness information is available from the physical workspace (like time and frequency of keyboard interaction (team member is busy), the current occupation of a telephone line (team member is not ready for interaction), the GSM terminal is presently located on the highway (team member will be back in office in about 2 hours), etc.), traditional groupware fails to exploit this information to serve virtual teams. We aim to make explicit provision of workspace information readily at hand, and systematically investigate options of gathering awareness information from physical workspaces.

The main challenge for the development of **TEAMSPACE** hence was the provision of team memory and team awareness enabled meeting support systems, in the software instance of media spaces providing virtual teams with **real life meeting fidelity**, a **large scale availability** and **universal access**. Particularly access and availability is forcing a radically new approach opposing e.g. multi-user collaborative virtual environments as coming from virtual reality research [WaBa 97] (like e.g. Massive [GrBe 95], DIVE [Hags 97], COVEN [COVE] or CAVERN [CAVE], which by nature of the highly specialised hardware and software components involved prohibit user access on a broad scale. To this end, the employment of standard and open internet technology appears mandatory, hence we committed to the realisation of **IP based Media (Meeting) Spaces** –or in other words– **Internet Collaboratories**.

Quite a few research projects have attempted inter-connecting (e.g. special interest) teams out of geographical dispersion needs: The Spectro-Microscopy Collaboratory [SMC] is an ad-hoc solution providing remote access to analytical tools at Lawrence Berkeley Laboratory's ALS to spatial visualisations of chemical structure information; DOE2000 is a new initiative to fundamentally change the way scientists work together and how they address the major challenges of scientific computation. To accomplish this change, DOE2000 explores new computational tools and libraries that advance the concept of "national collaboratories"; In the Materials Microcharacterisation Collaboratory [MMC], Centers of Excellence join into a single on-line interactive virtual laboratory - scientists, educators, and students have access to a shared environment also offering control of remote instruments and electronic notebooks; Collaborative Computing Framework [CCF] is a suite of software systems, communications protocols, and tools that enable collaborative, computer-based cooperative work in a virtual work environment on multiple computer systems connected over the Internet; The InterMed Collaboratory Project [IMC] aims to transform the health care information system to a collaborative environment and to develop a robust framework for collaboration over the internet; Finally, dedicated to teams, TeamWave [TeWa] is a set of cooperative tools like e.g. a shared whiteboard and chat options to enable some of the synchronous as well as asynchronous communication demands.

4 Implementation

TEAMSPACE is conceptually developed as shared network places to support distributed cooperative work activities and virtual teams. The TEAMSPACE is an arrangement of one ore more virtual rooms (VIRTUALROOM), which can be used for different work tasks by different team members at different times and for varying purpose. Each of these rooms can have different characteristics tuned on the special needs of the work done therein (Figure 3).

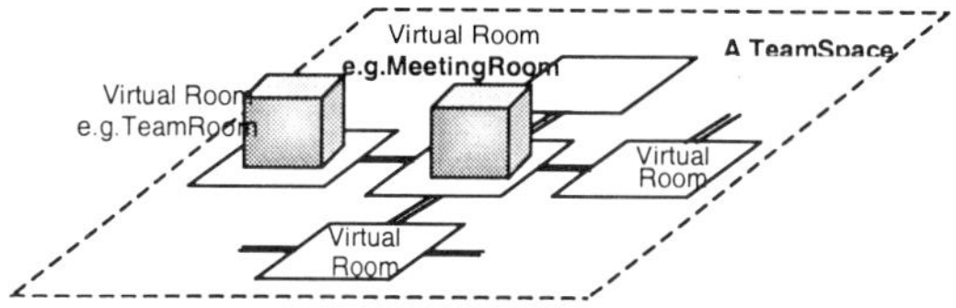

Figure 3: A TEAMSPACE and Virtual Rooms

TEAMSPACE is is based essentially on open technologies, Java together with the virtual reality modelling language VRML. In its software architecture, TEAMSPACE follows a centralized server approach. (A detailed presentation of the software architecture of TEAMSPACE is presented in the companion technical report [Fers 00].) First, the VRML world and its current state must reside (or be stored) somewhere on the Internet when no users are currently in the world. This is most conveniently achieved through the use of a dedicated server. When the server is running, the current state of the world resides in the memory of the server. When new participants join, the server simply has to send descriptions of all active objects (VRML files) and their current state to the new participant. New "rooms" can be added to TEAMSPACE dynamically on demand. Like in other client/server architectures, scaling to a large number of users is limited, since the server soon becomes the communication bottleneck due to the overwhelming amount of messages which must be forwarded [Bla] [AWS]. In typical cases, the number of simultaneous users in client/server DVEs has a practical limit in the range of tens of users, with loss in performance increasing as the number of users grows [Bro 98] – those observations also hold for TEAMSPACE.

5 TEAMSPACE Showcase

As a demonstration showcase we have constructed a virtual meeting space for workgroups, MEETINGROOM – which is just one instance of a "room" on top of the TEAMSPACE software architecture, following an office metaphor for environment visualization (Figure 2). When a user connects to the TEAMSPACE server invoking the log in procedure (ID and password), it is up to him to decide where to get seated in the MEETINGROOM. The log in procedure as handled by the client applet requests user profile data like a UserCard or an image for the users preferred avatar representation. All user information is provided in a location independent way by entering respective Web URLs. The user data (and/or URLs) are transferred to the server, and (in our example) the MEETINGROOM is reloaded to display the virtual room with the contained objects for the participating users. A birds view of the MEETINGROOM is given in Figure 4 (the side-table lists the functionality of objects in this room).

Figure 4: Birds view to MeetingRoom

Every connected user is assigned a seat and cupboard, like outlined in Figure 4, bottom. Given now a user wants to deposit some media content into his cupboard (red arrows indicate the seat to cupboard mapping) to make it available also to other users joining a virtual meeting (let the type of media be a slide based presentation) then upon clicking his cupboard he first chooses "Slideshow" in the Media Dialog box:

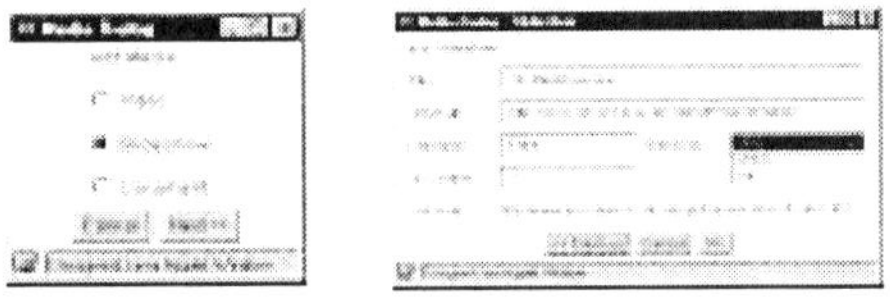

The „Next" button induces a dialog where related data, like title of the presentation, URL path, filename, number of slides and the file extension are to be entered. A variety of other content types could be added to the cupboard, like e.g. video or (text-) documents. Media objects integrated into the scene dynamically (upon user request) are being displayed consistently adhering the real life metaphor: Figure 5 shows the representation of the deposited media items in the cupboard, i.e. a tape like object for a video media object, and a slide drawer for the slide show.

Element:	Description:	interaktiv:
1. Avatar	Users are displayed in the MeetingRoom via multi-functional avatars. Upon a mouse click the UserCard of the user is displayed.	yes (Avatar)
2. Table	The table is the central element of this room, and holds interaction contol mechanisms (indicator).	no
3. Chair	At the start of a session every user is assigned a seat which he keeps until he leaves (logout) the MeetingRoom.	no
4. Indicator	Placed in front of every user is a round button indicating the access right to scen objects, e.g. the monitor to present a slide show.	yes (Indicator)
5. Cupboard	Every user has his own cupboard where he can deposit his documents or media material.	yes (Container)
6. Monitor	The monitor is used to show the media content to every user, e.g. video streams, slide shows.	no
7. Decoration	These elements are for decoration.	no
8. Computer	The computer is used to log in and out of the MeetingRoom.	yes (Entryway)
9. Control panel	The VRML browser control panel.	
10 Phone	This item is used to allow the user to change his/her transfer properties	yes (Property)

Figure 5: Video/Slideshow objects deposited in board

Figure 6: members aware of each others presence

Connecting users upon their "arrival" can already "see" their cooperation partners (their avatar representations) in the MEETINGROOM, and clicking on each others avatar allows them to inspect their UserCards (Figure 6). It is important to stress here, that both the physical position of an avatar in the scene as well as its orientation is glued to the actual browser (viewer) position and orientation of the respective client representing that user. In this way, it is possible for meeting participants to watch both movements (navigation) of other participants in real time. Both the awareness concepts of focus (spatial area of environment perception) as well as nimbus (presentation to surrounding environment) are realized with this kind or user abstractions.

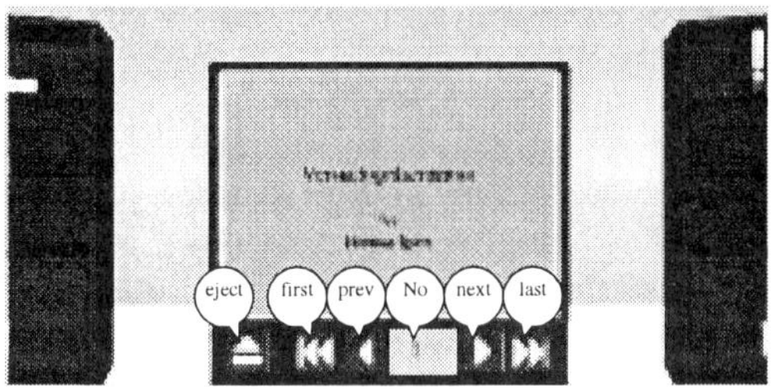

Figure 7: Presentation screen controls

Being in the shared space, the meeting partners can now start collaborating, i.e. exchanging and investigating their documents. To present a slideshow loaded onto the presentation screen for example, a user can use the control buttons to scroll through and jump within the sequence of slides in an intuitive way (Figure 7). Other traditional office oriented documents like text documents or spreadsheets can as well be deposited into the cupboard by simply providing their URL for reference over the WWW, and be opened upon download with local software (wordprocessors, spreadsheetprocessors, etc).

6 Conclusions

Multiuser distributed cooperation environments are one of the fastest growing industrial fields of application of the Internet [WAS 97], particularly its most popular service, the WWW. It is becoming an indispensable vehicle for the interconnection of humans in the interactive execution of their cooperative work agenda. This paper has exemplified the organisation of mobile virtual teams interacting "on the move" and across geographical boundaries, and has developed a workspace awareness solution for a distributed cooperation environment, exclusively based on standard Internet technologies. The commitment to open standards was the consequence after systematically pointing out the misconception of proprietary, platform and application dependent cooperation software. Hence, an integrated software architecture for a distributed cooperative work environment has been developed – the TEAMSPACE – and key features of such an environment have been implemented as a proof of concept. As a showcase, a virtual team room, the MEETINGROOM, has been used to demonstrate selected awareness features.

7 References

[AWS] Active Worlds Servers. www.activeworlds.com

[Bla] Community Server. Blaxxun Interactive. www.blaxxun.com

[Bro 98] W. Broll, DWTP – An Internet Protocol For Shared Virtual Environments, Proceedings of the International Symposium on the Virtual Reality Modeling Language 1998, ACM, pages 49-56, 1998.

[CAVE] CAVERN. www.evl.uic.edu/spiff/covr/

[CCF] Collaborative Comp. Frameworks. emily.mathcs.emory.edu

[COVE] COVEN. chinon.thomson-csf.fr/projects/coven/

[Fers 00] A. Ferscha: Virtual Enterprises. Final Report, Jubiläumsfondsprojekt 7022, Univ of Vienna, 2000.

[FeJo 99] A. Ferscha, J. Johnson: Distributed Interaction in Virtual Spaces. Proc. of the 3rd International WS on Distributed Interactive Simulation and Real Time Applications. IEEE CS-Press, 1999.

[GrBe 95] C.M. Greenhalgh, S.D. Benford: MASSIVE: A Virtual Reality System for Tele-conferencing. ACM Transactions on Computer Human Interfaces (TOCHI), 2 (3), ISSN 1073-0516, ACM Press, September 1995, pp. 239-261.

[GuGr 99] C. Gutwin, S. Greensberg: A Framework of Awareness for Small Groups in Shared-Workspace Groupware. TR 99-1, Dept. of Comp. Scie., Univ. of Saskatchewan, Canada.

[Hags 97] O. Hagsand: Interactive Multiuser Ves in the DIVE System, IEEE Multimedia, Vol. 3, No. 1 , 1997, pp. 30-39.

[IMC] InterMed Collaboratory Project. dsg.harvard.edu/public/intermed/InterMed_Collab.html/

[MCC] Materials MicroCharacterization Collaboratory. tpm.amc.anl.gov/MMC

[RoGr 96] M. Roseman, S. Greenberg: Building Real-Time Groupware with GroupKit, a Groupware Toolkit. In: Transactions on Computer-Human-Interaction, 3(1), 1996, pp.66-106.

[SMC] The Spectro-Microscopy Collaboratory. www-itg.lbl.gov/Collaboratories/ALS.html

[TeWa] TeamWave. www.teamwave.com

[WaBa 97] R.C. Waters, J.W. Barrus: The Rise of Shared Virtual Environments. IEEE Spectrum, Vol. 34, No. 3, 1997, pp. 20-25.

[WAS 97] R.C. Waters, D.B. Anderson, D.L. Schwenke, Design of the Interactive Sharing Protocol. WETICE 97, IEEE Sixth Workshops on Enabling Technologies: Infrastructure for Collaborative Enterprises, MIT, June 1997, IEEE CS Press, Los Alamitos CA, www.meitca.com/opencom/istp.html

Commitment-Based Enhancement of E-Commerce Protocols

Pınar Yolum and Munindar P. Singh*
Department of Computer Science
North Carolina State University
Raleigh, NC 27695-7534, USA

{pyolum, mpsingh}@eos.ncsu.edu

Abstract

Protocols represent the allowed interactions among communicating components. Protocols are essential in electronic commerce to constrain the behaviors of autonomous entities. Traditional representations of protocols include the actions, but not their content, which limits their applicability in settings where autonomous entities must flexibly interact to handle exceptions and exploit opportunities. We develop a commitment-based representation, which provides a content to the protocols, enabling flexible execution. We show how an existing protocol can be systematically enhanced to yield a protocol that allows the given actions as well as other legal moves.

1 Introduction

Although many e-commerce protocols have been developed in recent years, limitations caused by their rigid specification have remained. Traditionally, protocols have been specified directly in terms of legal sequences of actions without considering the fundamental meaning behind the actions.

However, e-commerce protocols should not only constrain the actions of the participating components, but also accommodate the open, dynamic nature of e-commerce interactions:

- *Autonomy*. Components must retain their autonomy and be minimally constrained in their interactions, i.e., only to the extent necessary.

- *Exceptions*. Components must be able to modify their interactions to handle any unexpected conditions.

- *Opportunities*. Components should be able to take advantage of available opportunities to improve their choices or to simplify their interactions.

Traditional approaches are based on the study of network protocols, and lack the key abstractions to handle the above dynamic aspects of e-commerce. By contrast, we develop an agent-based approach that incorporates the key abstraction of *commitments*. *Agents* are persistent computations that can perceive, reason, act, and communicate. Agents can be autonomous and heterogeneous, and can represent different interacting components. The agents' communications affect and are affected by their commitments. The agents' commitments reflect the protocols they are following and the communications they have made.

By stepping through a running example, we first show the different interactions that can take place among the parties and then show how these interactions can be added to the original protocol to yield an enhanced protocol.

Section 2 reviews the keys concepts and challenges dealing with communication. Section 3 describes our proposed approach. Section 4 describes our contributions in relation to the most relevant literature.

2 Semantic Analysis

We now analyze the concepts and challenges underlying communication, especially with regard to the execution of activities. As a running example, we consider the NetBill protocol that has been developed to handle buying and selling of electronic goods, such as software and electronic documents over the Internet [10].

Example 1 As shown in Figure 1, the protocol starts with a customer requesting a quote for a particular good, followed by the merchant sending the quote. If the customer accepts the quote, then the merchant delivers the good and waits for an Electronic Payment Order (EPO). The good delivered at this point is encrypted, i.e., not usable. After receiving the

*This research was supported by the National Science Foundation under grants IIS-9529179 and IIS-9624425 (Career Award).

0-7695-0798-9/00 $10.00 © 2000 IEEE

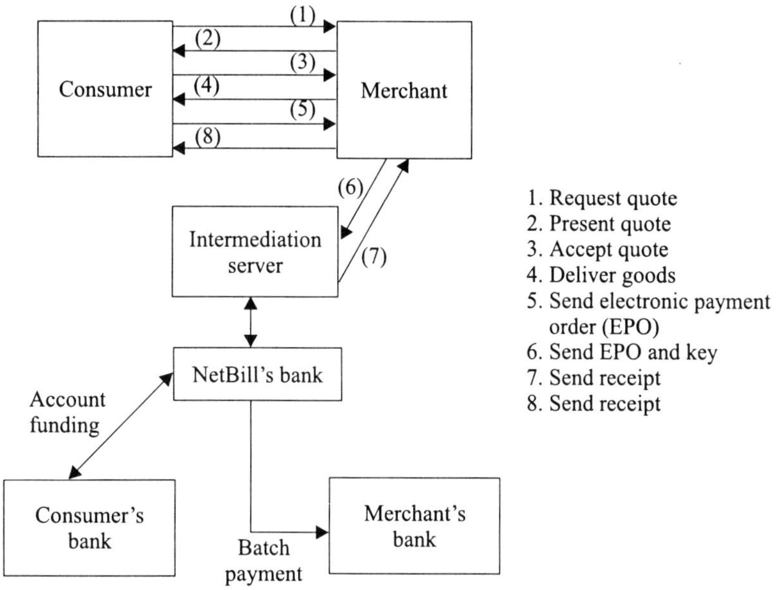

Figure 1. The NetBill payment protocol [10]

EPO, the merchant forwards the EPO and the key to the Intermediation Server, which then contacts the bank to take care of the banking process. Once the debit-credit operations are handled, the intermediation server sends a receipt back to the merchant, which contains the decryption key for the sold good. As the last step, the merchant forwards the receipt to the customer, who can successfully decrypt and use the good. ▮

For our present purposes, we are concerned neither about the details of the actual transactions that take place among the banks nor about the underlying security or encryption mechanisms. Therefore, we simplify the protocol to the point where we assume that once the merchant gets an EPO, he can take care of the banking services successfully. We use this simplified version of the protocol as our main example throughout this paper.

Example 2 Figure 2 shows the simplified version of the NetBill payment protocol as a finite state machine (FSM) labeled with the actions of merchant agent M and customer agent C. ▮

The participating parties in an e-commerce protocol are self-interested and eager to practice a variety of interactions to increase their personal benefit. Thus, in an e-commerce setting, parties should have several choices of actions and be able to practice the action that benefits them the most.

Example 3 The rigid specification in Figure 2 cannot handle some of the natural situations that arise in e-commerce:

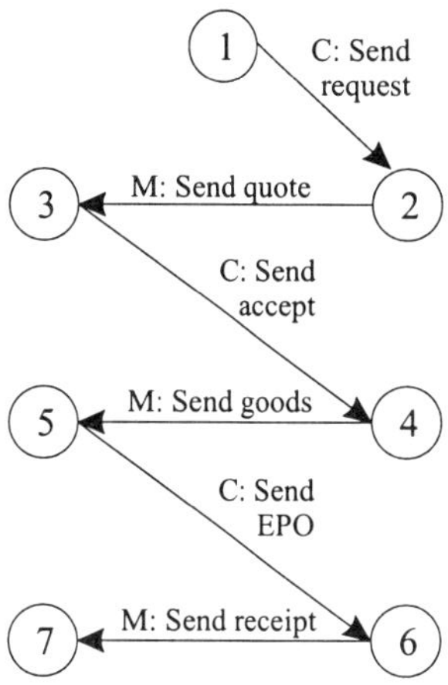

Figure 2. FSM representation of NetBill

- Instead of waiting for the customers to ask for quotes, the merchant may start the protocol by sending a quote, mimicking the idea of advertising.

- The customer may send an accept message without first exchanging explicit messages about the quote. This could very well reflect the level of trust between the parties. That is, the customer who trusts the merchant to give him the best quote may accept the quote without a prior announcement. Alternatively, this action could result from the customer's lack of interest in the quote, emergency of the transaction, insignificance of money, and so on.

- The merchant may send the goods without an explicit price quote. This could represent the trial versions in the software industry where after a certain period of time the customer is expected to pay to continue using the software.

∎

3 Proposed Approach

Our proposed approach is as follows. We begin with the concept of *social commitments* from multiagent systems [2] and reasoning and dialogue [12]. Informally, a commitment is like an obligation from one party to another. A metacommitment is a commitment that refers to other commitments in a conditional form. Additional properties of commitments are discussed in [9, 11]; we lack the space to review those details here.

We propose a new formalism, *commitment-based finite state machine (CFSM)*, to be used in specification of protocols. Instead of specifying protocols merely in terms of legal sequences of actions, we define them with valid meanings based on commitments. This has the effect of enhancing a protocol to allow a broader range of interaction. As long as each state has a well-defined meaning, a variety of interactions can take place without violating the protocol. Thus, using this formalism, we show how the protocols can be enhanced to allow flexible execution.

3.1 CFSM

We define a CFSM conceptually as an FSM whose states and alphabet are given a semantic content, defined in terms of commitments. A CFSM can be specified by a three-tuple $M = \langle \mathbf{M}, \Sigma, \mathbf{F} \rangle$ where M is a set of meanings, Σ is a set of actions defined in terms of commitments, and $\mathbf{F} \subseteq \mathbf{M}$ is the set of valid final meanings.

Example 4 We define the semantic content of each state in Figure 2 based on the participants' commitments.

- By sending a quote to a customer in state 3, the merchant commits to delivering goods and sending a receipt afterwards, if the customer promises to pay.
- By sending an accept to a merchant in state 4, the customer agrees to pay, only if the merchant promises to send a receipt afterwards.
- In state 5, the merchant fulfills first part of his promise by sending the goods.
- In state 6, the customer discharges his commitment of sending the goods.
- In state 7, the merchant discharges his commitment of sending the receipt.

These commitments arise from communications in conjunction with the metacommitments that are in force among the participants. ∎

These informally defined meanings constitute the core meaning set, $\mathbf{M}$, of the protocol. The action set, Σ, includes the actions used in Figure 2, defined in terms of commitments. The set of final meanings, $\mathbf{F}$, contains all the states where no commitments are in force. In our example, this set contains two states. The first one is in effect when both parties make mutual commitments and fulfill their commitments. The second one arises, when one of the parties make a commitment that is not acknowledged by the other party. For instance, if the merchant makes an offer but the customer does not accept the offer, the protocol can end. The customer can either explicitly reject the offer, or remain silent. The latter case can be interpreted as rejecting after a certain time period. The formal definitions for $\mathbf{M}$, Σ, and $\mathbf{F}$ are given in Section 3.2.

Unlike an FSM, the representation of a CFSM does not specify a starting state. The participants may start the protocol from a state where there are no commitments made or by accepting the commitments that are in force in that state. Again, unlike FSMs, the transitions between the states are not specified. The meanings of states are logically represented. Based on the intrinsic meaning of actions, the new state that is reached by performing an action at a particular state can be logically deduced. Thus, instead of specifying the sequences of actions that can be performed, we specify meanings that can be reached.

By specifying a protocol using a CFSM, we emphasize that the aim of executing a protocol is not to perform sequences of actions but to reach a state that represents the meaning of performing these sequences of actions. Once this fact is captured then we can come up with different paths that result in accomplishing the same goal as the original path. Thus, a protocol can be enhanced by finding alternative paths between states.

3.2 Formalization

Our formal language, $\mathcal{P}$ is based on the language $\mathcal{L}$ of propositional logic with the addition of a commitment operator to represent the commitments. Propositional logic is obviously too weak. However, the extension to temporal logic is straightforward [11].

The following Backus-Naur Form (BNF) grammar with a distinguished start symbol L gives the syntax of $\mathcal{L}$. $\mathcal{L}$ is based on a set of atomic propositions. Below, *slant* typeface indicates nonterminals; $\longrightarrow$ is a metasymbol of BNF specification; $\ll$ and $\gg$ delimit comments; and the remaining symbols are terminals.

- $L \longrightarrow$ *Prop* $\ll$atomic propositions$\gg$
- $L \longrightarrow \neg L$ $\ll$negation$\gg$
- $L \longrightarrow L \wedge L$ $\ll$conjunction$\gg$

We now define the syntax of the specification language, $\mathcal{P}$, through the following grammar whose start symbol is *Protocol*. The braces { and } indicate that the enclosed item is repeated 0 or more times.

- *Protocol* $\longrightarrow$ {*Action*}
- *Action* $\longrightarrow$ *Token: L*
- *Commitment* $\longrightarrow$ C_x (*L*)
- $L \longrightarrow$ *Commitment*

Example 5 Following Example 4, the messages can be given a content based on the following definitions:

- *request*: an atomic proposition meaning that the customer has requested a quote.
- *goods*: an atomic proposition meaning that the merchant has delivered the goods.
- *pay*: an atomic proposition meaning that the customer has paid the agreed amount.
- *receipt*: an atomic proposition meaning that the merchant has delivered the receipt.
- *promiseGoods*: an abbreviation for C_m[accept $\rightarrow$ goods] meaning that the merchant is willing to send the goods if the customer promises to pay.
- *accept*: an abbreviation for C_c[goods $\rightarrow$ pay] meaning that the customer is willing to pay if he gets the goods.
- *promiseReceipt*: an abbreviation for C_m[pay $\rightarrow$ receipt] meaning that the merchant is willing to send the receipt if the customer pays.
- *offer*: an abbreviation for (promiseGoods $\wedge$ promiseReceipt)

Based on these definitions, we can now formally define the protocol as a CFSM. For simplicity we place the content of an action in the state that results from it and since each action can be performed by only one party, we do not specify the performers explicitly.

- The set of meanings, **M**, contains the following:
  - State 1: true
  - State 2: request
  - State 3: offer
  - State 4: accept $\wedge$ offer
  - State 5: goods $\wedge$ $\mathsf{C}_c$pay $\wedge$ promiseReceipt
  - State 6: goods $\wedge$ pay $\wedge$ $\mathsf{C}_m$receipt
  - State 7: goods $\wedge$ pay $\wedge$ receipt
- The set of actions, Σ, contains the following:
  - t: request $\ll$Sending a request for quote$\gg$
  - q: offer $\ll$Sending a quote$\gg$
  - a: accept $\ll$Sending an accept$\gg$
  - g: goods $\wedge$ promiseReceipt $\ll$Delivering the good$\gg$
  - e: pay $\ll$Sending an EPO$\gg$
  - r: receipt $\ll$Sending the receipt$\gg$
- The set of final meanings, **F**, contains the states 1, 2, 3, and 7.

∎

3.3 Application of CFSMs

The CFSM specification of a protocol can be used to execute the protocol at run time. Alternatively, using an automated tool, the CFSM specification of a protocol can be converted into a FSM specification at compile time. An agent can then use this FSM representation to execute the protocol at run time.

Run time In a CFSM specification, the states and the effects of performing actions are specified. Given a CFSM description of a protocol, an agent that can process logical formulae can compute the transitions between states. In this respect, the choice of actions is a planning problem for each agent. That is, from the possible end states, the agent first decides on the desired end state, and then logically infers a path that will take him from the current state to the desired end state.

Compile time To reduce the computations at run time, a CFSM can be converted into an FSM representation at compile time. This conversion can be done in several ways, one of which would be based on systematically producing paths and states to reach one of the final states. The meanings that have been already defined and each additional meaning captured in production of the path would map to a state in the FSM. The transitions between the states will follow from the valid paths. The set of final states would be all the states, including the newly produced states, that satisfy the

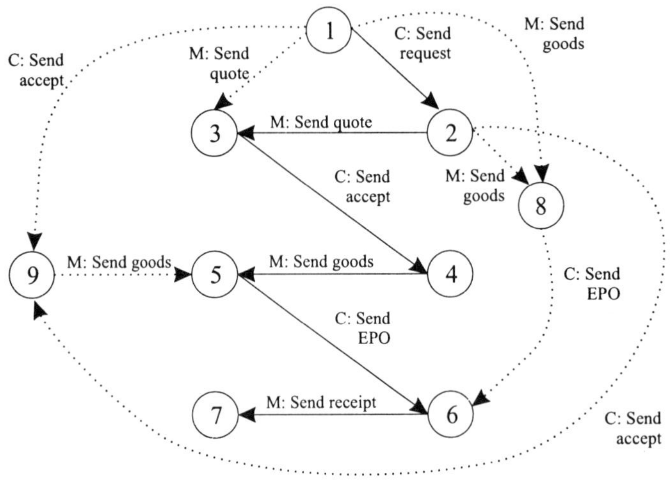

Figure 3. Enhanced FSM

ending constraints of CFSMs: any state where no commitments are in force, or any state where the metacommitment of a party has not been honored. The set of actions will remain the same. In general, we have the following development:

Let $X = \langle \mathbf{M}, \mathbf{\Sigma}, \mathbf{F} \rangle$ be a CFSM. Let $Y = \langle \mathbf{S}, \mathbf{\Sigma}, \mathbf{SInitial}, \mathbf{SFinal}, \delta \rangle$ be an FSM that is correct with respect to X.

Then Y may be constructed as follows:

- **S** = M
- **Σ** = Σ
- **SInitial** = $\{m_1 : (m_1 \in \text{M}) \wedge (m_1 = \text{true})\}$
- **SFinal** = F
- $\delta = \{\langle m_i, s, m_j \rangle : m_i, m_j \in \mathbf{M}, s \in \Sigma \wedge (m_i \not\models m_j \wedge m_i \models_s m_j \wedge (\forall\, m_k \in \mathbf{M}{:}\ m_i \models_s m_k \wedge m_k \models m_j \rightarrow m_j{=}m_k))\}$

If FSM Y allows a computation, then CFSM X allows the same computation.

Example 6 Figure 3 shows the enhanced FSM that can be driven from the CFSM specification of our protocol. We now reconsider the shortcomings described in Example 3.

- The merchant can now start the protocol by sending a quote to a customer. As was the case, by performing this action he creates a metacommitment in state 3, namely that he is willing to send the goods and the receipt if the customer agrees to pay.
- By sending an accept message without prior conversation about the quote, the customer commits to paying if the merchant makes an offer. Thus, we move from a state where no commitments are made (state 1), to a state where the customer is making an offer (state 9). If the merchant does not make an offer, then the protocol ends at this point. On the other hand, if the merchant makes an offer by sending the goods, then both parties have to carry out their commitments; so the protocol moves to state 5.
- By sending the goods without an explicit accept message, the merchant makes an offer to send the receipt if the customer agrees to pay. Thus, we move from a state where no commitments are made (state 1), to a state where the merchant is making an offer (state 8). If the customer does not accept the offer, then the protocol ends at this point. Conversely, if the customer actually sends an accept message, then both parties need to fulfill their commitments: so the protocol moves to state 5.

Compared to the original version of the protocol in Figure 2, we have introduced two new states, state 8 and state 9. Using the definitions in Example 5, these states can be defined as follows:

- State 8: goods ∧ promiseReceipt
- State 9: accept

In addition to these states, we have added distinct links from state 1 to state 8, and 9; from state 2 to state 8 and 9; from state 8 to state 6 and from state 9 to state 5. The new transitions are shown with dashed lines. ∎

As we have demonstrated, specifying protocols using a CFSM enables the protocols to be executed flexibly, and thus improves the performance of the protocol drastically. At this point, it is important to restate what we mean by flexibility. Although we want the agents to practice a flexible protocol, we still want to preserve an ordering that will allow only meaningful conversations. For example, a merchant should not send a quote after sending the goods, or the customer should not start the conversation by sending an EPO. More importantly, flexibility can be introduced to the point where the intended meanings of the actions are preserved. When we allow more flexible interactions, we need to ensure that the original commitments are in force or they are altered by mutual agreement. Thus, if the applicable metacommitments are captured, the execution of a protocol is minimally constrained only to satisfy those metacommitments. This is a major advantage over low-level representations, which require specific execution sequences and provide no basis for deciding on the correct state independent of the execution sequence.

4 Discussion

We motivated a commitment-based treatment of protocol specification, analysis and execution. We developed a new way to specify protocols, CFSM, that is based on the meaning of actions rather than their sequences. The associated meanings are captured in terms of commitments. By walking through an example, we showed how we can define a CFSM specification, and how we can reason about the protocols and enhance them to achieve a flexible execution. We also pointed out how this specification can be realized at run time or compile time.

There is a substantial body of literature on ACLs and their semantics. The Foundation for Intelligent Physical Agents (FIPA) has been standardizing an ACL along with a formal semantics. FIPA also includes interaction protocols, which are characterized purely operationally. Labrou & Finin describe a grammar for constructing conversations or protocols [8].

Traditionally, communication protocols are specified by defining the allowed orders in which communicative acts may take place, but no more. This holds for protocol formalisms such as FSMs, push-down automata, formal grammars, Petri Nets, and temporal logic. Some of these formalisms can be quite powerful, but they are used only to specify allowed actions. The actions are just labels and the states, if explicit, do not capture the conceptual state of a protocol as we have attempted. By contrast, we use commitments to specify the communication protocols and thus analyze them through their intrinsic meaning. Commitments have been studied before [1, 3], but not used for protocol specification as here.

Most traditional deontic logics have had a single-agent focus and are therefore not suited for interoperation. Directed obligations, i.e., from one party to another, are more promising. Hohfeld's approach is an influential one in studies of law [6]. We previously showed that the sixteen main legal relations identified by Hohfeld can be captured using commitments [9]. Herrestad & Krogh propose a formalization of directed obligations that reduces them to preferences of the concerned parties [5]. By contrast, we treat commitments as first-class concepts and leave the preferences to additional inferences that can be made in some cases. Other formal research on interactions among agents includes Haddadi [4], who develops a formal semantics based on beliefs and intentions, but does not give an operational characterization as we do here.

References

[1] C. Castelfranchi. Commitments: From individual intentions to groups and organizations. In *Proceedings of the International Conference on Multiagent Systems*, pages 41–48, 1995.

[2] R. Conte and C. Castelfranchi. *Cognitive and Social Action*. UCL Press, London, 1995.

[3] L. Gasser. Social conceptions of knowledge and action: DAI foundations and open systems semantics. In *[7]*, pages 389–404. 1998. (Reprinted from *Artificial Intelligence, 1991*).

[4] A. Haddadi. Towards a pragmatic theory of interactions. In *[7]*, pages 443–449. 1998. (Reprinted from *Proceedings of the International Conference on Multiagent Systems, 1995*).

[5] H. Herrestad and C. Krogh. Obligations directed from bearers to counterparties. In *Proceedings of the 5th International Conference on Artificial Intelligence and Law*, pages 210–218, 1995.

[6] W. N. Hohfeld. *Fundamental Legal Conceptions as Applied in Judicial Reasoning and other Legal Essays*. Yale University Press, New Haven, CT, 1919. A 1919 printing of articles from 1913.

[7] M. N. Huhns and M. P. Singh, editors. *Readings in Agents*. Morgan Kaufmann, San Francisco, 1998.

[8] Y. Labrou and T. Finin. Semantics and conversations for an agent communication language. In *[7]*, pages 235–242. 1998. (Reprinted from *Proceedings of the International Joint Conference on Artificial Intelligence, 1997*).

[9] M. P. Singh. An ontology for commitments in multiagent systems: Toward a unification of normative concepts. *Artificial Intelligence and Law*, 7:97–113, 1999.

[10] M. A. Sirbu. Credits and debits on the internet. In *[7]*, pages 299–305. 1998. (Reprinted from *IEEE Spectrum, 1997*).

[11] M. Venkatraman and M. P. Singh. Verifying compliance with commitment protocols: Enabling open web-based multiagent systems. *Autonomous Agents and Multi-Agent Systems*, 2(3):217–236, Sept. 1999.

[12] D. N. Walton and E. C. W. Krabbe. *Commitment in Dialogue: Basic Concepts of Interpersonal Reasoning*. State University of New York Press, Albany, 1995.

[13] P. Yolum. Flexible execution of e-commerce protocols: A commitment-based approach. Master's thesis, Department of Computer Science, North Carolina State University, Raleigh, June 2000.

A secure XML/Java-based Implementation of Auction Services for Complex Resource Allocation Problems

Wolfram Conen
Xonar Gmbh,Velbert, Germany
Conen@gmx.de

Fredj Dridi, Eckhart Köppen
Information Systems and Software Techniques
University of Essen, Universitätsstraße 9, D-45141 Essen, Germany
{Fredj.Dridi,Eckhart.Koeppen}@uni-essen.de

Abstract

This paper describes a novel resource allocation service that can be used in cooperations of enterprises to comprehensively and efficiently coordinate resource-related goals and activities. It can also be used to establish "classic" markets for interdependent goods or services. The approach is based on bundled-goods auctions and allows to achieve a high degree of analysability, economic efficiency and usability. The resource allocation service is implemented in Java based on the exchange of XML messages. The utilized schemata are expressed using XML DTDs as a lowest common denominator.

For development and implementation of the allocation service, utilizing (secure) agents seemed to be a natural choice regarding the fact that the cooperating partners are economically autonomous and thus want (1) to keep some of their data/preferences private, (2) want to deploy a secure platform for the exchange of information and the computation of allocation and prices, and should have the freedom to code their needs and strategies into their coordination agents as required. The impact of infrastructure security and application specific trust considerations are briefly discussed, and finally, the key features of the presented resource allocation service are summarized.

1 Motivation: Complex Auctions

> "Cooperation in the economic tradition is mutual assistance between egoists.", Hervé Moulin [13]

The acceleration and automation of procurement processes seems to promise a huge potential to reduce costs and to allow for faster and more flexible exploitation of new market opportunities. It requires some form of standardization of document formats and means of data exchange. In addition, the integration with legacy ERP systems is required to streamline the procurement process and to utilize the benefits of format standardization. With the advent of intermediaries, business-to-business relations will eventually be able to rely on platforms offering open or closed market services along with support for maintaining electronic catalogs, financial transactions via corporate procurement cards, integration with shipping services or, for example, tax services.

This diversity of services may ultimately allow suppliers to "plug-in" their extended ERP system into the infrastructure provided by intermediaries and to exploit the opportunities following from having direct access to a (potentially huge) market of buyers with its largely standardized exchange formats, coordination processes, and additional services. Here, we denote with coordination processes, or, more precisely, a *coordination mechanism*, the means by which actual resource allocation decisions are made. For example, this may refer to the bidding, the final assignment of a price to a good and the allocation of the good to a certain customer in an open-cry English auction.

While simple coordination mechanisms such as standard (English, Dutch, sealed first-bid or Vickrey) auction or reverse auction procedures for one or for many uncoupled goods are easy to implement and to analyze with respect to the quality of the allocation decisions, allocation problems that exhibit complementarities are difficult to assess and to solve. However, such problems present an even greater potential for intermediaries to position them self in the B2B-infrastructure market:

- A huge number of practically relevant problems in logistics and manufacturing (and, consequently, the resulting procurement problems) exhibits complementarities (see below).
- Solving such problems efficiently requires significant expertise with respect to both economic efficiency

0-7695-0798-9/00 $10.00

("find the optimal solution") and computational efficiency ("which algorithm, which data and which infrastructure shall be used to compute the allocation and the prices of goods and services"). This expertise can not easily be "re-implemented" by competitors – *intelligently* solving NP-hard problems needs massive experience (what heuristics to use if optimal solving is intractable, judging the consequences of the use of heuristics, recognizing problem "types" and adapting solution strategies to the requirements of the customer etc.)

We will describe a two-stage sealed-bid auction mechanism to deal with problems exhibiting complementarities below. But first, we will discuss the relevance of complementarities and outline a few application scenarios' calling for the utilization of such a (little more complex) coordination mechanisms.

Complementarities are present whenever the valuation of a good, a service, or an "opportunity" depends upon the availability of another good, service, or "opportunity". A well-known example is the allocation of start and landing slots to airlines – acquiring a start slot at 9:00 am in Singapore for a flight to Bangkok does not make much sense if there is no slot available for a landing in Bangkok between 11:00 and 12:00 am.[1] Interdependent preferences for goods and services can be found nearly everywhere in logistics and production: JIT delivery requires the availability of products *and* of handling and shipping (and other) resources, manufacturing of components requires input from a variety of suppliers, customer care services consists of various stages (request handling, information generation, maintenance services, handling of returned goods etc.) – and each potential buyer of such complex goods/services wants to buy an optimal combination of the required partial services or goods. A platform for the flexible selling and buying of bundles/sub-bundles of goods and services would enable the participants to fully exploit the economic potential of complex services while preserving an extended possibility for competition (on both sides of the market). If a market for "components" exists, buyers may freely and easily exploit the possibility to combine components from a number of suppliers to their best benefit – instead of being forced to wait for the one "big" supplier offering just the optimal component configuration. Additionally, the suppliers can offer their goods and services in a way allowing them to exploit the effects of scales of economics or of efficiently combinable products/services.

Unfortunately (as have been mentioned already in the footnote to the slot example), traditional one-good auctions or even parallel, but otherwise independent multi-good auctions fail to deliver high-quality solutions to the economic allocation problem. A simple 2-agents, 2 goods example will demonstrate one of the key issues behind this observation (from [12], the numbers giving the valuations of the agents):

	Good A	Good B	Both Goods
Agent 1	0	0	3
Agent 2	2	2	2

Table 1. No equilibrium prices for the individual goods exist

The optimal solution is to assign both goods to agent 1. However, the price of each individual goods must exceed 2 currency units to exclude agent 2 from the allocation–which in turn would prevent agent 1 from buying both goods because his valuation is below 4. The solution here: both goods must be sold as a bundle to enable an efficient (i.e. surplus maximizing) solution of the allocation problem. This basic idea, with a lot of non-trivial consequences[2], is the base for what follows.

Our prototype implements a two-stage, sealed-bid auction mechanism. In the first stage, each potential buyer and supplier will submit there bids resp. their reserve prices for each combination of goods or services they want to acquire The system will compute an optimal allocation of bundles of goods/services (and, hence, their suppliers) to buyers. The system will compute a price vector for all the bundles that will actually be exchanged between agents and will publish this vector. The vector will be a self-enforcing equilibrium price vector, i.e. each rational agent that solves his own revenue maximization problem will perform the trade that is part of the set of optimal trades – this is a very important fact if the participants are autonomous and can not be forced to accept allocation decisions, as is the case for the markets described here[3]. In general, the way the overall surplus is distributed among buyers and sellers should

[1] Another reason for the surprising complexity of problems with complementarities in logistics/manufacturing becomes already clear in this simple example: mostly. there is a huge number of possible *alternatives* – every start slot can be combined with a number of technically feasible landing slots. Every combination has its consequences (timing of re-fuel, catering services, availability of terminal facilities etc.) and is thus differently valued. For an optimal solution of the problem, the airline must be able to announce its different alternative preference resp. to use this information in the buying decisions for both slots. Ultimately, it can be shown that auctioning off the slots in two separated auctions (even if they are performed simultaneously) *can not* lead to an efficient allocation.

[2] Three recent papers provide some foundations for the economics underlying bundled-goods auctions, see [2, 9, 15]. In [5], a number of examples for problematic situations and suggestions for their solution are presented. A complete assessment of the theoretic complexities and practical implications of bundled-goods auctions is not yet available.

[3] This setting can easily be accommodated to reverse auctions.

be agreed upon by the participants prior to running a market. There is room to minimize or maximize the buyer (or, resp., maximize or minimize the supplier) surplus within the boundaries set by the required equilibrium property. This, in turn, has a key influence on the incentives to (not) behave strategically for the different parties in the auction process. We assume that either the auctioneer announces the distribution quota (e.g. 50/50) or the participants unanimously instruct the auctioneer to distribute the surplus in a specified way. Now, trade will take place and the efficient solution, i.e. the solution maximizing the sum of individual utilities will be implemented.

A simplified picture of the coordination mechanisms is shown in Figure 1. It looks as follows: Supplier and Buyer (Java agents in our implementation to be plugged into the individual ERP systems) contact a market place that trades goods they are interested to buy or sell based upon an XML description of the market. The buyers submit their valuation for every bundle of goods/services they are interested in. The supplier submit their reservation values for every bundle they are able to supply. All submitted data is transferred as XML documents. After a specific time or after a specific number of bids is received, the coordinator instantiates a market, producing a complete XML description document. This document is passed to the auctioneer. The auctioneer computes (complex tasks - mostly NP-hard!) the efficient (i.e. maximizing the sum of individual revenues) allocation and prices for the bundles to be exchanged and sends the information about bundling and prices to the buyers/suppliers. Each agent decides which trades he wants to perform and submits this information to the autioneer. The auctioneer informs the trade partners (after a feasibility check) accordingly.

During the auctioning process, the updated market data (bundling and pricing information) can be made available to third parties such as a supervisor to warrant fairness of the auction and neutrality of the auctioneer. These are security issues which are of special importance in an auctioning system. They are discussed below. The market data is published as an XML document, making changes of the supervisor implementation easier. Here, we propose an external supervisor that acts as a trusted third party, possibly offering the service of supervision of several auction sites to customers of these sites. All information is passed over HTTP, implying a client/server architecture for the system.

2 Implementation

We will now discuss the reasons that lead us to an XML-, HTTP- and Java-based implementation.

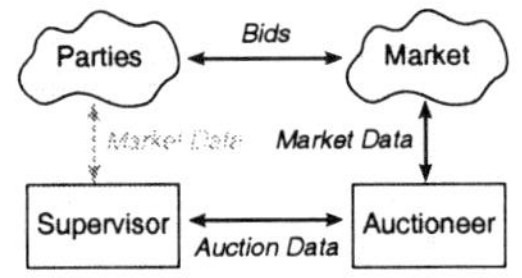

Figure 1. Simplified Architecture

2.1 Interoperability

The market setup phase makes heavy use of XML to facilitate the communication between buyer, seller and the market. XML has proven to be a powerful tool for defining information structures and creating conforming documents. This ability is especially important in the scenario presented in this paper. Here, different parties with different needs, vocabularies and information need to communicate. We use XML and XML DTDs to provide a common ground for information exchange. In this context, a number of efforts have been made to create common vocabularies for electronic commerce, most important the *Common Business Language* (CBL) [6] and *Commerce XML* (cXML) [1], both XML-based. It is important to note that the usage of one vocabulary or schema for information exchange does not prohibit communication to partners using different schemata. Standards and tools associated with XML address this problem of interoperability, namely XML namespaces [3]. Architectural forms [10] and transformation mechanisms such as XSLT [4] can be used as a bridge between different information sources. Because of the availability of these mechanisms, we chose to implement our own vocabulary based on the characteristics of the presented auction scenario. It will be possible to transform incoming information structured using CBL, cXML or other formats to the structures used by the coordination and auctioning mechanisms.

The second mechanism to assure interoperability is the choice of HTTP as the underlying communication protocol. The different components and parties in the given scenario communicate strictly over HTTP, using GET and PUT requests to forward and request information and POST requests for remote method invocations. This reduces the need for special communication methods since HTTP has become a widely available protocol in many information systems, not at last due to its simplicity.

2.2 Transparency

Going even further than just enabling parties with different information sets to communicate and trade, we open the actual market and auction process to external entities via

XML. A first step in this direction has already been mentioned. The instantiated market is made available as an XML document, and the auctioneer relies on XML as an import format for the initial market data. Thus, the presented market setup and auction process implementations can be exchanged with other XML-enabled implementations.

The next step is the representation of the stages of the auction process itself as an XML document. As seen in Figure 1, this could be used to report the progress of the auction to external instances to supervise the fairness of the process or even back to the original parties for adjustments of bids during the auction. Furthermore, a representation of the process could lead to a customization or parameterization of the process by providing a sort of process template document describing characteristics of the underlying auctioning algorithm. This template document would be filled with actual data during the auction. A market place (for different markets) could thus be initialized using such a process description. However, a truly platform independent description of auction algorithms using XML does not seem feasible for complexity reasons. It seems more reasonable to provide building blocks for auctioning algorithms which can be combined and parameterized using process templates.

2.3 Activity, XML and Java Objects

The actual implementation of the auction algorithms is done in Java which, designed to be a portable programming language, complements the role of XML as a portable data exchange format. Interfacing between the XML data on the one hand and the corresponding Java objects on the other hand can be achieved in a number of ways. It is possible to define XML DTDs that model the structure of Java objects closely, i.e. containing elements for class definitions, instance variables or even methods. Other ways make use of intermediate representations such as IDL to map between objects and transferred information. In contrast to this, we chose a different approach to improve transparency and interoperability. For us, not the Java objects but the information which is passed around is the foremost important component of the system. This requires modeling Java classes after XML DTDs, a task that can be automatized to a certain extent. To generate Java classes from DTDs, we implemented a simple tool called DTD2Java that converts elements declared in a DTD to Java classes with instance variables derived from the content model. Furthermore, serialization code for writing out and reading in XML representations is generated. It is obvious that such a tool can only cover a subset of the expressibility of DTDs, e.g. mixed content models containing sequences, alternations and character data cannot be mapped easily to a class definition. We think that this is only a problem when the used DTDs cannot be modified. But even in this case, introducing intermediate DTDs and transformation between documents conforming to these different DTDs is possible using the mentioned techniques.

The second important part of the implementation besides the interfacing between external and internal representation of the used data is the communications layer. Since we chose HTTP as the communication protocol, several implications for the system architecture arise. A model that provides the needed mechanisms (along with an implementation) is the *Active Hypertext Document Model* ([11]) which defines a peer-to-peer HTTP-based communications architecture where a combined client/server network node contains active (scripted) XML documents.

2.4 Security Issues

Typically, an auction application involves a large number of users, who want to share and grant access to documents (data) in a controlled way. Some of those documents may contain sensitive information and consequently must not be disclosed to every user. In addition, because the auction application uses the Internet as its transport mechanism, it inherits all of the security vulnerabilities of the Internet. As a result, the demand for security services (like authentication, access control, non-repudiation, etc.) has grown rapidly. See [7] for more details.

Security Requirements and Potential Attacks

Confidentiality. Information must be only disclosed or revealed for authorized users. Therefore, sensitive information needs to be protected when it is stored or when it is transmitted over the network. This objective is concerned about both, the content of data and its existence (e.g. an existence of a critical bid).

Integrity. Information must not be modified by unauthorized users. This means, that information must be protected from malicious or accidental alteration, including insertion of false data, contamination or destruction of data.

Legitimate Use. Data must be only used by authorized users and in authorized ways. Data with different security requirements is made available to users with different privileges.

Availability. Information must be available to authorized users in a timely fashion. Authorized users must get access the information when they need it.

In general, if an application uses a network (e.g. Internet) as a communication infrastructure without appropriate attention paid to security, several network based security attacks may take place. These security attacks can be divided into two categories [14]: Passive attacks and Active attacks.

Passive attacks may threaten the confidentiality and can take place by intercepting the communication stream between the client and the server. The transmitted data can be eavesdropped (e.g. Bids data may be released) or monitored (e.g. market transactions may be analyzed).

Active attacks can take place by interrupting or modifying the communication stream between the communicating parties. An active attack threatens the availability and integrity of data being transmitted. An active attack may also threaten the confidentiality of identity (masquerading).

Security Services

Figure 2 describes an architecture built up by the means of security services to shield against security threats and to achieve information security for networked systems like a Web based auction application.

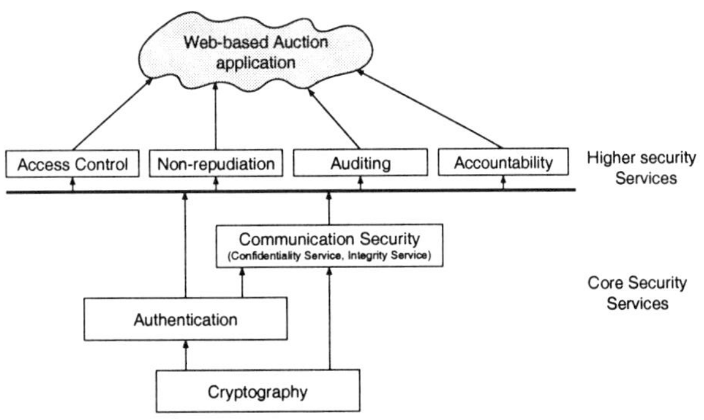

Figure 2. Needed Security Services [7]

The discussion of the implementation of the required, application-independent security services is well-known nowadays, below, we will briefly discuss the application context specific issues that had to be solved:

- The authentication service is a means of identifying (remote) users in a Web based market place, that is to verify that the users are who or what they claim to be. The most important techniques used for authentication are based on user-name/password schemes or use digital signatures or certificates.
- The communication security service should provide market data confidentiality and integrity. The currently most widespread mechanism to ensure communication security is the secure socket layer (SSL) protocol [8]. One common use of SSL is to secure HTTP communication between a Web client and a Web server.
- The Auditing service is responsible to log all security relevant markt place actions and keep them in a safe place (audit trail, logging files). The log data may be used to link an individual to their interactivity with the auction application (accountability).
- The non-repudiation service is often required in an auction application, since the evidence of actions is strongly required. It prevents either the sender or receiver from denying a transmitted message (e.g. a bid). The non-repudiation service can be achieved by utilization of a digital signature, where a trusted third party (e.g. the Supervisor) acting as an arbitrator must be involved.

Security in a Mixed Environment

As mentioned above the market data is published as an XML document and will be deserialized into Java objects upon entering a Java running environment. Java objects will be also serialized to XML if they should be communicated. Due to this mapping between Java and XML some individual document security information (e.g. digital signature, access control information, etc.) could be unconsidered. Therefore, a special mechanism, which (de)serializes such security information, must be implemented in the next version of our prototype auction application.

3 Discussion

The auction-based resource allocation service presented in this paper has a number of key features. It allows to compute allocations and (equilibrium) price vectors in the presence of complementarities. Interdependent and exclusive preferences can be expressed and will be used to compute an economically efficient solution. This is in contrast to standard auction or reverse auction approaches which can only deal to a limited extent with complementarities in multi-good settings.

Furthermore, the core service agents (the auctioneer and the supervisor) are implemented in Java. To increase interoperability, the implementation centers around the information in the system and not around the Java objects. Interfacing with other systems (such as the supervisor, monitoring systems or market setup systems) is based on structures defined in XML DTDs. Differint document structures (e.g. cXML or CBL) can be used by transforming the documents with techniques such as XSLT. Furthermore, XML namespaces make it possible to merge third party information into the original documents.

With the supervisor, an "institution" was introduced that is able to control the auctioneer. The auctioneer has a number of possibilities to manipulate the outcome of the allocation process. Due to the fact that, in some settings, anonymity of the bidders (or, at least, of the bids) is mandatory, the auctioneer may change bids or introduce "fake" bids. The auctioneer is also able to manipulate the result of the bundling and/or the price vector and thus, the subsequent allocation decision. This is not merely a technically solvable security problem but a problem of trust. While it might be viable to force any allocation service to construct its computation device from signed and verified components and to keep the data streams (XML) free from possibilities for manipulations, we didn't investigate this further - mainly because (1) it pushes the problem of trusting the auctioneer to the problem of trusting the component provider and (2) it still seems to be difficult to provide completely not-manipulable computation devices. Due to the fact that the auctioneer has to guarantee certain properties of the resulting allocation (economic efficiency, allocated goods maximize individual utility under the computed price vector for the bundled goods, the surplus is distributed among buyers and sellers due to a certain distribution rule), a supervisor will be able to control the quality of the solution solely based on the input to and the output of the auctioneer. The supervisor might be seen as an example for an institution the will be useful as an authority certifying available auction/allocation services. Clearly, the issue of trust is present again.

We plan to practically deploy the implemented services and open them for public use. Since all communication is based on XML and it is easy to extend the developed DTDs to allow integration of e.g., catalogue data (in the bids) or order processing information (to execute the computed allocation) that are declared in emerging standards such as CBL, the adoption of such services in common business practice will be possible without too much friction.

References

[1] Ariba, Inc.: *cXML/1.0*. http://www.cxml.org/files/cxml.pdf, August 1999.

[2] S. Bikhchandani and J. M. Ostroy: *The Package Assigment Model*, UCLA, Theory Workshop, mimeo (1997)

[3] T. Bray, D. Hollander, A. Layman: *Namespaces in XML*, W3C Recommendation, http://www.w3.org/TR/REC-xml-names/, January 1999.

[4] J. Clark (ed.): *XSL Transformations (XSLT)*, Version 1.0, W3C Recommendation, http://www.w3.org/TR/xslt, November 1999.

[5] W. Conen: *Economic Coordination, Bundled Goods, and the Impact of Complementarities*. In: Parsons, Wooldridge (eds.): Proceedings of the Workshop on Decision theoretic and Game theoretic Agents, London, July 1999

[6] Commerce One, Inc.: *XML Common Business Language*, http://www.commerceone.com/xml/cbl/docs/, July 1999.

[7] F. Dridi and G. Neumann: *Managing security in the world wide web: Architecture, services, and techniques*, In L. Janczewski, editor, *Internet and Intranet Security Management: Risks and Solutions*, chapter, pages 106–139. Hershey PA: Idea Group Publishing, 2000. ISBN 1-878289-71-3.

[8] A. Freier, P. Karlton, and P. Kocher: *The SSL protocol version 3.0*, Netscape, http://netscape.com/eng/ssl3/, 1996.

[9] F. Gul and E. Stacchetti: *Walrasian Equilibrium with Gross Substitutes*, Journal of Economic Theory, 87, 9-124 (1999)

[10] International Organisation for Standardization: *ISO/IEC 10470 Information Processing – Hypermedia/Time-based Structuring Language (HyTime)*, ISO Standard, 1992.

[11] E. Köppen and G. Neumann: *A Practical Aproach towards Active Hyperlinked Documents*, Proc. of the 7th Int'l World Wide Web Conference, (1998)

[12] J. McMillan: *Selling Spectrum Rights*. Journal of Economic Perspectives, 8(3): 145-162, 1994.

[13] Hervé Moulin, *Cooperative Microeconomics.* i Princeton University Press, 1995.

[14] W. Stallings: *Network and Internetwork Security Principles and Practice*. Prentice-Hall, 1995.

[15] P. R. Wurman and M. P. Wellman: *Equilibrium Prices in Bundle Auctions*, Santa Fe Institute Working Paper (1999)

Author Index

Notes

IEEE COMPUTER SOCIETY

IEEE Computer Society Publications

The world-renowned IEEE Computer Society publishes, promotes, and distributes a wide variety of authoritative computer science and engineering texts. These books are available from most retail outlets. Visit the Online Catalog, *http://computer.org*, for a list of products.

IEEE Computer Society Proceedings

The IEEE Computer Society also produces and actively promotes the proceedings of more than 141 acclaimed international conferences each year in multimedia formats that include hard and softcover books, CD-ROMs, videos, and on-line publications.

For information on the IEEE Computer Society proceedings, send e-mail to *cs.books@computer.org* or write to Proceedings, IEEE Computer Society, P.O. Box 3014, 10662 Los Vaqueros Circle, Los Alamitos, CA 90720-1314. Telephone +1 714-821-8380. FAX +1 714-761-1784.

Additional information regarding the Computer Society, conferences and proceedings, CD-ROMs, videos, and books can also be accessed from our web site at *http://computer.org/cspress*

Revised 9 November 1999